A Companion to Hobbes

Blackwell Companions to Philosophy

This outstanding student reference series offers a comprehensive and authoritative survey of philosophy as a whole. Written by today's leading philosophers, each volume provides lucid and engaging coverage of the key figures, terms, topics, and problems of the field. Taken together, the volumes provide the ideal basis for course use, representing an unparalleled work of reference for students and specialists alike.

1. The Blackwell Companion to Philosophy, Second Edition
Edited by Nicholas Bunnin and Eric Tsui-James
2. A Companion to Ethics
Edited by Peter Singer
3. A Companion to Aesthetics, Second Edition
Edited by Stephen Davies, Kathleen Marie Higgins, Robert Hopkins, Robert Stecker, and David E. Cooper
4. A Companion to Epistemology, Second Edition
Edited by Jonathan Dancy, Ernest Sosa and Matthias Steup
5. A Companion to Contemporary Political Philosophy (two-volume set), Second Edition
Edited by Robert E. Goodin and Philip Pettit
6. A Companion to Philosophy of Mind
Edited by Samuel Guttenplan
7. A Companion to Metaphysics, Second Edition
Edited by Jaegwon Kim, Ernest Sosa and Gary S. Rosenkrantz
8. A Companion to Philosophy of Law and Legal Theory, Second Edition
Edited by Dennis Patterson
9. A Companion to Philosophy of Religion, Second Edition
Edited by Charles Taliaferro, Paul Draper, and Philip L. Quinn
10. A Companion to the Philosophy of Language, Second Edition (two-volume set)
Edited by Bob Hale and Crispin Wright
11. A Companion to World Philosophies
Edited by Eliot Deutsch and Ron Bontekoe
12. A Companion to Continental Philosophy
Edited by Simon Critchley and William Schroeder
13. A Companion to Feminist Philosophy
Edited by Alison M. Jaggar and Iris Marion Young
14. A Companion to Cognitive Science
Edited by William Bechtel and George Graham
15. A Companion to Bioethics, Second Edition
Edited by Helga Kuhse and Peter Singer
16. A Companion to the Philosophers
Edited by Robert L. Arrington
17. A Companion to Business Ethics
Edited by Robert E. Frederick
18. A Companion to the Philosophy of Science
Edited by W. H. Newton-Smith
19. A Companion to Environmental Philosophy
Edited by Dale Jamieson
20. A Companion to Analytic Philosophy
Edited by A. P. Martinich and David Sosa
21. A Companion to Genethics
Edited by Justine Burley and John Harris
22. A Companion to Philosophical Logic
Edited by Dale Jacquette
23. A Companion to Early Modern Philosophy
Edited by Steven Nadler
24. A Companion to Philosophy in the Middle Ages
Edited by Jorge J. E. Gracia and Timothy B. Noone
25. A Companion to African-American Philosophy
Edited by Tommy L. Lott and John P. Pittman
26. A Companion to Applied Ethics
Edited by R. G. Frey and Christopher Heath Wellman
27. A Companion to the Philosophy of Education
Edited by Randall Curren
28. A Companion to African Philosophy
Edited by Kwasi Wiredu
29. A Companion to Heidegger
Edited by Hubert L. Dreyfus and Mark A. Wrathall
30. A Companion to Rationalism
Edited by Alan Nelson
31. A Companion to Pragmatism
Edited by John R. Shook and Joseph Margolis
32. A Companion to Ancient Philosophy
Edited by Mary Louise Gill and Pierre Pellegrin
33. A Companion to Nietzsche
Edited by Keith Ansell Pearson
34. A Companion to Socrates
Edited by Sara Ahbel-Rappe and Rachana Kamtekar
35. A Companion to Phenomenology and Existentialism
Edited by Hubert L. Dreyfus and Mark A. Wrathall
36. A Companion to Kant
Edited by Graham Bird
37. A Companion to Plato
Edited by Hugh H. Benson
38. A Companion to Descartes
Edited by Janet Broughton and John Carriero
39. A Companion to the Philosophy of Biology
Edited by Sahotra Sarkar and Anya Plutynski
40. A Companion to Hume
Edited by Elizabeth S. Radcliffe
41. A Companion to the Philosophy of History and Historiography
Edited by Aviezer Tucker
42. A Companion to Aristotle
Edited by Georgios Anagnostopoulos
43. A Companion to the Philosophy of Technology
Edited by Jan-Kyrre Berg Olsen, Stig Andur Pedersen, and Vincent F. Hendricks
44. A Companion to Latin American Philosophy
Edited by Susana Nuccetelli, Ofelia Schutte, and Otávio Bueno
45. A Companion to the Philosophy of Literature
Edited by Garry L. Hagberg and Walter Jost
46. A Companion to the Philosophy of Action
Edited by Timothy O'Connor and Constantine Sandis
47. A Companion to Relativism
Edited by Steven D. Hales
48. A Companion to Hegel
Edited by Stephen Houlgate and Michael Baur
49. A Companion to Schopenhauer
Edited by Bart Vandenabeele
50. A Companion to Buddhist Philosophy
Edited by Steven M. Emmanuel
51. A Companion to Foucault
Edited by Christopher Falzon, Timothy O'Leary, and Jana Sawicki
52. A Companion to the Philosophy of Time
Edited by Heather Dyke and Adrian Bardon
53. A Companion to Donald Davidson
Edited by Ernest Lepore and Kirk Ludwig
54. A Companion to Rawls
Edited by Jon Mandle and David Reidy
55. A Companion to W.V.O Quine
Edited by Gilbert Harman and Ernest Lepore
56. A Companion to Derrida
Edited by Zeynep Direk and Leonard Lawlor
57. A Companion to David Lewis
Edited by Barry Loewer and Jonathan Schaffer
58. A Companion to Kierkegaard
Edited by Jon Stewart
59. A Companion to Locke
Edited by Matthew Stuart
60. The Blackwell Companion to Hermeneutics
Edited by Niall Keane and Chris Lawn
61. A Companion to Ayn Rand
Edited by Allan Gotthelf and Gregory Salmieri
62. The Blackwell Companion to Naturalism
Edited by Kelly James Clark
63. A Companion to Mill
Edited by Christopher Macleod and Dale E. Miller
64. A Companion to Experimental Philosophy
Edited by Justin Sytsma and Wesley Buckwalter
65. A Companion to Applied Philosophy
Edited by Kasper Lippert-Rasmussen, Kimberley Brownlee, and David Coady
66. A Companion to Wittgenstein
Edited by Hans-Johann Glock and John Hyman
67. A Companion to Simone de Beauvoir
Edited by Laura Hengehold and Nancy Bauer
68. A Concise Companion to Confucius
Edited by Paul R. Goldin
69. The Blackwell Companion to Substance Dualism
Edited by Jonathan J. Loose, Angus J. L. Menuge, and J. P. Moreland (Editor)
70. A Companion to Nineteenth-Century Philosophy
Edited by John Shand
71. A Companion Atheism and Philosophy
Edited by Graham Oppy
72. A Companion to Adorno
Edited by Peter E Gordon and Espen Hammer and Max Pensky
73. A Companion to Rorty
Edited by Alan Malachowski
74. A Companion to Chomsky
Edited by Nicholas Allott, Terje Lohndal and Georges Rey
75. A Companion to Spinoza
Edited by Yitzhak Melamed
76. A Companion to Hobbes
Edited by Marcus P. Adams

A Companion to Hobbes

Edited by
Marcus P. Adams

WILEY Blackwell

This edition first published 2021

Registered Office
John Wiley & Sons, Inc., 111 River Street, Hoboken, NJ 07030, USA

Editorial Office
111 River Street, Hoboken, NJ 07030, USA

For details of our global editorial offices, customer services, and more information about Wiley products visit us at www.wiley.com.

Wiley also publishes its books in a variety of electronic formats and by print-on-demand. Some content that appears in standard print versions of this book may not be available in other formats.

Library of Congress Cataloging-in-Publication Data
A catalogue record for this book is available from the Library of Congress

Hardback ISBN: 9781119634997; ePDF ISBN: 9781119634980; epub ISBN: 9781119635031; oBook ISBN: 9781119635079.

Cover image: © Thomas Hobbes, artist John Michael Wright, National Portrait Gallery, public domain, Wikimedia Commons
Cover design by Wiley

Set in 10/12.5pt Photina by Integra Software Services, Pondicherry, India

10 9 8 7 6 5 4 3 2 1

MIX
Paper from responsible sources
FSC® C013604

Contents

Notes on Contributors

Arash Abizadeh, Professor, Department of Political Science and an Associate Member of the Department of Philosophy at McGill University. His research focusses on democratic theory; power; identity, nationalism, and cosmopolitanism; immigration and border control; and seventeenth- and eighteenth-century philosophy, particularly Hobbes and Rousseau. His monograph *Hobbes and the Two Faces of Ethics* (Cambridge) won the 2019 Canadian Philosophical Association Biennial Book Prize (English).

Marcus P. Adams, Associate Professor of Philosophy at the State University of New York at Albany and former Associate Editor of the journal *Hobbes Studies*. His research focuses on perception and natural philosophy in Early Modern Philosophy, in particular on Thomas Hobbes and Margaret Cavendish. His recent papers have appeared in journals such as *British Journal for the History of Philosophy, History of Philosophy Quarterly, Philosophers' Imprint*, and *Philosophical Studies*.

Mónica Brito Vieira, Professor, University of York. Her work in political theory focuses on the languages and concepts through which we make sense of and shape our political world, most notably the concept of political representation. She is the author of *The Elements of Representation in Hobbes* (Brill, 2009), the coauthor of *Representation* (Polity, 2008), and editor of *Reclaiming Representation* (Routledge, 2017). Her work has also appeared in the *American Political Science Review, Journal of the History of Ideas, History of Political Thought, Thesis Eleven, Constellations, Critical Review of International Social and Political Philosophy*, and other journals.

Jacqueline Broad, Associate Professor of Philosophy, School of Philosophical, Historical, and International Studies at Monash University, Melbourne. Her main area of research is early modern women's philosophy. She is the author of *The Philosophy of Mary Astell: An Early Modern Theory of Virtue* (Oxford University Press, 2015), *A History of Women's Political Thought in Europe, 1400–1700* (with Karen Green, Cambridge University Press, 2009), and *Women Philosophers of the Seventeenth Century* (Cambridge University Press, 2002). She is currently the Series Editor for Cambridge University Press's new Elements series on Women in the History of Philosophy.

Michael Byron, Professor and Chair of Philosophy, Kent State University in Kent, Ohio, where he has held an appointment since 1997. He is the author of *Submission and Subjection in Leviathan* (Palgrave Macmillan, 2015), and the editor of *Satisficing and*

Maximizing: Moral Theorists on Practical Reason (Cambridge University Press, 2004). He has published journal articles on ethical theory and theory of rationality. During 2004–5, he was Visiting Fulbright Scholar in Philosophy at Lingnan University in Hong Kong.

Alexandra Chadwick, postdoctoral researcher, University of Jyväskylä and a lecturer at Leiden University College. She is Associate Editor of the journal *Hobbes Studies*. Her chapter in this collection was written while she was a postdoctoral researcher at the University of Groningen. Her research has focused on Hobbes's materialist psychology and its implications for his practical philosophy, and she is currently working on the psychology of sociability in the period between Hobbes and Hume. She received her doctorate in 2017 from Queen Mary, University of London, and from 2016-17 was a Max Weber Fellow at the European University Institute.

Jeffrey Collins, Associate Professor of History, Queen's University, Ontario. A historian of Anglophone political and religious thought, he has authored many articles and chapters on the political, religious, and intellectual history of Britain during the era of the Civil Wars and Restoration. He has written two books: *The Allegiance of Thomas Hobbes* (Oxford, 2005), and *In the Shadow of Leviathan: John Locke and the Politics of Conscience* (Cambridge, 2020). He is currently an editor of the *Journal of British Studies* and is a regular book reviewer in the *Wall Street Journal* and the *Times Literary Supplement*.

Eleanor Curran, Senior Lecturer in Legal Philosophy, Kent Law School, University of Kent at Canterbury. Publications include *Reclaiming the Rights of the Hobbesian Subject* (Palgrave Macmillan, 2007), "Hobbesian Sovereignty and the Rights of Subjects: Absolutism Undermined?," *Hobbes Studies* 32 (2019), "An Immodest Proposal: Hobbes Rather than Locke Provides a Forerunner for Modern Rights Theory," *Law and Philosophy* (2012), "Hobbes on Equality: Context, Rhetoric, Argument" *Hobbes Studies* 25 (2012), and "Blinded by the Light of Hohfeld: Hobbes's Notion of Liberty" *Jurisprudence* (2010).

Stewart Duncan, Associate Professor of Philosophy, University of Florida. He is the author of several articles on Hobbes, Leibniz, and other seventeenth-century philosophers, and is currently working on a book on the history of materialism from Hobbes to Locke.

Sandra Leonie Field, Assistant Professor of Humanities (Philosophy), Yale-NUS College, Singapore. She is the author of *Potentia: Hobbes and Spinoza on Power and Popular Politics* (Oxford University Press, 2020). Her research investigates conceptions of political power and their implications for democratic theory; she approaches these themes through engagement with texts in the history of philosophy. She has also written on non-Western political philosophy.

Luc Foisneau, Director of Research, French National Center for Scientific Research (CNRS). He also teaches political philosophy at the École des Hautes Études en Sciences Sociales in Paris. He is the author of *Hobbes et la toute-puissance de Dieu* (2000) and *Hobbes: La vie inquiète* (2016). He is the editor of *Leviathan after 350 Years* (2004, with T.

Sorell), of *New Critical Perspectives on Hobbes's Leviathan* (2004, with G. Wright), and *Dictionnaire des philosophes français du 17e siècle: acteurs et réseaux du savoir* (2015).

Geoffrey Gorham, Professor and Chair of Philosophy, Macalester College and Resident Fellow, Minnesota Center for Philosophy of Science. He is coeditor of *The Language of Nature: Reassessing the Mathematization of Natural Philosophy* (University of Minnesota, 2016), and author of *Philosophy of Science* (One World, 2009). Other recent publications include "Locke on Space, Time and God: The Van Limborch Correspondence" (*Ergo* 2020); "American Immaterialism: Samuel Johnson's Emendations of George Berkeley" (*Transactions of the Charles S. Peirce Society* 2018); and "Descartes on the Infinity of Space vs. Time" (In *Infinity in Early Modern Philosophy*, Brill, 2018).

Karen Green, Professorial Fellow at the University of Melbourne. She is the author of *A History of Women's Political Thought in Europe, 1700–1800* (Cambridge University Press, 2014), *A History of Women's Political Thought in Europe, 1400–1700*, with Jacqueline Broad (Cambridge University Press 2009), she recently edited *The Correspondence of Catharine Macaulay* (Oxford University Press, 2019). Her most recent book is *Catharine Macaulay's Republican Enlightenment* (Routledge, 2020).

Michael J. Green, Associate Professor of Philosophy, Pomona College. He has published articles on Hobbes's theories of punishment, authorization, and justice in *Pacific Philosophical Quarterly*, the *Journal of the History of Philosophy*, and *Oxford Studies in Early Modern Philosophy*.

Helen Hattab, Professor of Philosophy, University of Houston, specializing in the history of Western philosophy and science from the late sixteenth to late seventeenth centuries. She is the author of *Descartes on Forms and Mechanisms* (Cambridge, 2009) and numerous papers tracing the connections between late Scholastic Aristotelian and seventeenth-century debates about causation, form, matter, substance, laws of nature, and scientific demonstration. Her current research focuses on arguments about the metaphysics of universals from late sixteenth-century philosophers to Spinoza, and the methods of analysis and synthesis from Zabarella and Burgersdijk to Hobbes and Spinoza.

John Henry, Professor Emeritus in History of Science, University of Edinburgh, Scotland. He has published widely in the history of science from the sixteenth to the nineteenth century and from atomism to paleontology. He has a particular interest in the major thinkers who contributed to the new mechanical philosophies of the seventeenth century, from Galileo and Descartes, through Hobbes and Robert Boyle, to Isaac Newton. A selection of his articles can be found in his *Religion, Magic, and the Origins of Science in Early Modern England* (Ashgate, 2012).

Douglas Jesseph, Professor of Philosophy, University of South Florida. His research specializes in the history and philosophy of mathematics in the Early Modern period. He is the author of *Berkeley's Philosophy of Mathematics* and *Squaring the Circle: The War between Hobbes and Wallis*, as well as papers on seventeenth-century mathematics and methodology.

Marcy P. Lascano, Professor of Philosophy, University of Kansas. Her research focus is metaphysics in the works of women philosophers, including Margaret Cavendish, Anne Conway, Damaris Masham, Mary Astell, and Emilie du Châtelet. She is coeditor with Eileen O'Neill of *Feminist History of Philosophy: The Recovery and Evaluation of Women's Philosophical Thought*, and coeditor with Lisa Shapiro of *Early Modern Philosophy: An Anthology of Primary Sources* (Broadview, forthcoming). She has recently edited an online edition of Cavendish's 1663 *Philosophical and Physical Opinions* and is finishing a book on Margaret Cavendish and Anne Conway.

Franck Lessay, Emeritus Professor, Sorbonne Nouvelle-Paris 3 University. He has published *Souveraineté et légitimité chez Hobbes* (1988), *Le débat Locke-Filmer* (1998), and *Les fondements philosophiques de la tolérance* (2002, as coeditor). He is the author of about 100 articles and 30 reviews on various subjects of political theory published in French, English, and Italian journals. He has translated and edited several short treatises of Hobbes.

S. A. Lloyd, Professor of Philosophy and Law, University of Southern California. She writes in the history of political philosophy and contemporary liberal feminism. She is author of *Morality in the Philosophy of Thomas Hobbes: Cases in the Law of Nature* (Cambridge University Press, 2009) and *Ideals as Interests in Hobbes's Leviathan: The Power of Mind over Matter* (Cambridge University Press, 1992); and editor of *Interpreting Hobbes's Political Philosophy* (Cambridge University Press, 2019), *The Bloomsbury Companion to Hobbes*, (Bloomsbury, 2013), and *Hobbes Today: Hobbesian Insights for the 21st Century* (Cambridge University Press, 2012).

Robert W. McIntyre, Assistant Professor of Philosophy, American University in Cairo. His article "Concerning 'men's *affections* to *Godward*': Hobbes on the First and Eternal Cause of All Things" was published in *Journal of the History of Philosophy* (2016). He is the cofounder of the Middle East Society for Analytic Philosophy.

Johan Olsthoorn, Assistant Professor in Political Theory, University of Amsterdam and a senior postdoctoral fellow of the Research Foundation (FWO)-Flanders at KU Leuven (2018–21). His research on Thomas Hobbes has appeared in the *British Journal for the History of Philosophy*, *European Journal of Political Theory*, *History of Political Thought*, and *Journal of Ethics*, among other venues. Oxford University Press is set to publish his first monograph *Hobbes on Justice*.

Rosamond Rhodes, Professor of Medical Education and Director of Bioethics Education, Icahn School of Medicine at Mount Sinai; Professor of Philosophy, The Graduate Center, CUNY; and Professor of Bioethics and Associate Director of the Clarkson-Mount Sinai Bioethics Program. She writes on a broad array of issues, primarily in bioethics. Her new book is *The Trusted Doctor: Medical Ethics and Professionalism* (Oxford University Press, April 2020). In it, she draws on her view of *Leviathan* as Hobbes's construction of ethics for sovereigns, and uses a similar approach in her construction of a distinctive ethics for medicine.

Gabriella Slomp, Reader, University of St. Andrews, Scotland. Former editor of *Hobbes Studies*, she has published *Hobbes and the Political Philosophy of Glory* (2000); edited *Thomas Hobbes* (2007), coedited *International Political Theory After Hobbes* (2016), and has published numerous articles on Hobbes in international journals.

Edward Slowik, Professor of Philosophy, Winona State University in Winona, Minnesota, and Resident Fellow, Minnesota Center for Philosophy of Science, University of Minnesota. His primary area of research is the history and philosophy of science and Early Modern philosophy, with special emphasis on the philosophy of space and spacetime.

Johann Sommerville, Emeritus Professor of History, University of Wisconsin, Madison. He is the author of *Royalists and Patriots: Politics and Ideology in England, 1603–1640* (Longman, 1999), and *Thomas Hobbes: Political Ideas in Historical Context* (Macmillan/St. Martin's, 1992). He is a contributor to *The Cambridge Companion to Hobbes* (1996), *The Cambridge Companion to Hobbes's* Leviathan (2007), *The Oxford Handbook of Hobbes* (2016), and other books on Hobbes. Currently, he is working on an edition of Hobbes's *Elements of Law* for the Clarendon series of Hobbes's works.

Tom Sorell, Professor of Politics and Philosophy, Warwick University. He is the author of *Hobbes* (Arguments of the Philosophers, Routledge, 1986); *Emergencies and Politics: A Sober Hobbesian Approach* (Cambridge University Press, 2013). He has edited *The Cambridge Companion to Hobbes*; *Hobbes and History* (with G. A. J. Rogers); *Leviathan After 350 Years* (with Luc Foisneau); *Leviathan Between the Wars* (with Luc Foisneau and J-C. Merle). He has written dozens of articles on Hobbes in edited volumes and peer-reviewed journals, including *Philosophical Quarterly, The Monist, Philosophy and Rhetoric,* and *History of Philosophy Quarterly*.

Patricia Springborg, Guest Professor, Centre for British Studies of the Humboldt University in Berlin (since 2013), held a Chair in Political Theory at the University of Sydney (1995–2005), and was Professor Ordinario at the Free University of Bolzano in Italy (2007–13). Her research fields include: 1) Thomas Hobbes: Metaphysics, Ecclesiology; 2) The Concept of Needs in Marxist Thought; 3) Early History of the State East and West; 4) Orientalism; 5) Mary Astell (1666–1731) political writings; and currently, 6) Greek into Arabic and Antiquity Transformation, producing 4 books, 4 edited books, and 80 publications in refereed journals and collections.

Justin Steinberg, Professor of Philosophy, Brooklyn College and the CUNY Graduate Center. He is author of *Spinoza's Political Psychology: The Taming of Fortune and Fear* (Cambridge, 2018), coauthor (with Valtteri Viljanen) of *Spinoza* (Polity, 2020), and coeditor (with Karolina Hübner) of the forthcoming *Cambridge Spinoza Lexicon* (Cambridge).

Howard Williams, Honorary Distinguished Professor in the School of Law and Politics, Cardiff University and Emeritus Professor of Political Theory, Department of International Politics, Aberystwyth. He is author of *Marx*; *Kant's Political Philosophy*;

Concepts of Ideology; Hegel, Heraclitus and Marx's Dialectic; International Relations in Political Theory; International Relations and the Limits of Political Theory; Kant's Critique of Hobbes; and *Kant and the End of War*. He is the coauthor of *Francis Fukuyama and the End of History* with David Sullivan and G. Matthews. He is a founding editor of the journal *Kantian Review* and editor of the *Philosophy of Immanuel Kant* in the Cambridge University Press series *Elements*.

Introduction: The Presentation and Structure of Thomas Hobbes's Philosophy

MARCUS P. ADAMS

The shadow of Thomas Hobbes's ideas stretches across the seventeenth century and continues to present day. His oeuvre ranges from translations of texts by figures such as Homer and Thucydides to the interpretation of Biblical texts, and from works devoted to geometry and optics to civil philosophy and religion. His impact in these and other areas was significant, even if in some cases his views functioned primarily as a foil. In Hobbes's own time he was reviled as the "monster of Malmesbury" who threatened the Christian religion and failed to appreciate the rise of experimental philosophy. Regarding religion, Abraham Cowley put it succinctly in *The True effigies of the monster of Malmesbury, or, Thomas Hobbes in his proper colours* (1680) when asserting that "He that will *Hobbes* Applaud must first *Blaspheme*." Similarly, Hobbes received no invitation to join the Royal Society, and he harshly criticized the experimental philosophy as lacking a method when saying "ingenuity is one thing and method [*ars*] is another. Here method is needed" (Hobbes 1985, 347).[1] Given such vitriol, it should be no surprise that the term 'Hobbist' was often used pejoratively to identify all that was seen as wrong with and dangerous in Hobbes's thought.

Many of Hobbes's contemporaries recognized that these points of pressure on Hobbes's ideas, as well as others, were not isolated cases; indeed, many saw these problems as symptoms resulting from the overall system of materialist philosophy that Hobbes was advancing. For example, although Hobbes's extended disputes with John Wallis focused largely on issues in mathematics, Wallis also attacked Hobbes's metaphysics because of its theological implications.[2] Likewise, the wide range of topics in Hobbes's exchanges with Bishop Bramhall shows the extent to which the worries of Hobbes's critics were often founded upon Hobbes's system and not upon what the twentieth-first century reader may, at first glance, see as distinct areas of Hobbes's thought.[3] Hobbes saw himself as offering a system of philosophy with interconnected parts, and his critics frequently attacked it as such.

A Companion to Hobbes, First Edition. Edited by Marcus P. Adams.

Given the wide range of Hobbes's writings, as well as the period of time over which Hobbes was actively writing, revising, and translating his own works, there are many entry points into his thought. For example, one could examine Hobbes by beginning with his early works and tracing the trajectory of his ideas as they developed through differing rhetorical contexts. Such an approach to understanding Hobbes has been greatly aided by some of the excellent resources recently made available to scholars, such as Noel Malcolm's Clarendon edition of *Leviathan* (Hobbes 2012), which provides English (1651) and Latin (1668) facing pages of that work, and Deborah Baumgold's *Three-Text Edition of Thomas Hobbes's Political Theory* (Baumgold 2017), which offers side-by-side comparison of passages in *Elements of Law*, *De cive*, and *Leviathan*. Alongside close attention to textual details, this approach might also examine Hobbes's preceding context and influences as well as his immediate context, such as his correspondence (Hobbes 1994b) or the notes on his works as they were in the process of being written, such as Robert Payne's on *De corpore* held in the Chatsworth House Hobbes papers (Chatsworth A10).

Another approach to Hobbes's ideas could excise key arguments, or parts of those arguments, from his corpus and examine them on their own philosophical merits with less attention to textual minutiae. Such a method would seek to offer something like a rational reconstruction, holding Hobbes subject to requirements such as logical consistency and deductive validity, and in doing so seek to provide the best possible picture of what Hobbes sought to demonstrate. Rather than accusing Hobbes of being misguided, or at times even sloppy in his argumentation, this way of engaging Hobbes might attempt to explain away interpretational difficulties here and there with the aim of constructing a philosophically palatable system. Even if it might depart at times from Hobbes's own explicit statements, taking such an approach may help bring Hobbes's philosophy to bear upon pressing present-day issues and potentially offer guidance about moral quandaries.[4]

The present volume has been organized under the assumption that these two approaches to studying Hobbes, i.e., the textual/philological approach and the philosophical approach, are not mutually exclusive.[5] Our attempts at understanding a figure like Hobbes are aided by close textual and philological engagement with the aim of trying to understanding what Hobbes might have been saying. But these efforts can also be helped by stepping back from the text, as it were, and probing his viewpoints philosophically with the aim of trying to understand what Hobbes *should* have been saying, what he was *committed* to in one area given his claims in another, and what import his ideas might have for us today.

Why feature Hobbes in a series like the *Blackwell Companions to Philosophy*, especially since the range of Hobbes's works is so diverse? Would Hobbes have viewed himself primarily as a *philosopher* and not, say, as a humanist or mathematician?[6] Hobbes did much beyond what today we call by the name 'philosophy', such as his labors, mentioned already, in translating works from Antiquity. However, the scope of Hobbes's own definition of 'philosophy' in *De corpore* I.2 was incredibly broad insofar as it included *any* phenomenon where causes could be conceived, whether from actual causes to effects or from effects to possible causes (Hobbes 1981, 175; OL I.2). Given this definition of 'philosophy,' it is no surprise that Hobbes appealed to causes in contexts such as his geometry, with generative definitions like "a line is made from the motion of a point" (Hobbes 1981, 297; OL I.63), and to possible causes throughout his natural philosophy in *De corpore* Part IV. The appeal to causes is likewise prominent in his famous account in civil philosophy "Of the Causes, Generation, and Definition of a Common-wealth" (Hobbes 2012, 254; 1651, 85).

Given this definition that delineates philosophy from all else, it seems that Hobbes himself might have excluded some of his own works from philosophy since they failed to treat of causes. Indeed, he says in *De corpore* I.8 that "where there is no generation or no properties, then no philosophy can be known" (Hobbes 1981, 189; OL I.9). There Hobbes declares that natural history and political history are not part of philosophy because "such knowledge [*cognitio*] is either experience or authority, not reasoning" (Hobbes 1981, 189; OL I.9). Thus, at first glance it would seem that Hobbes's definition of 'philosophy' excludes some of his own works, such as *Behemoth; Or an Epitome of the Civil Wars of England, From 1640, to 1660* (2010) since it is *prima facie* a work of history.

Perhaps we might see such work as done in the *service* of philosophy rather than as a part of philosophy proper. After all, Hobbes himself admits that natural and civil histories are "very useful (no, indeed necessary) for philosophy" (Hobbes 1981, 189; OL I.9). However, his interests in the civil war of his own time, as well as historical work on prior times, were hardly mere preparatory work for some later philosophical project. Indeed, *Behemoth* was presented in dialogue form, something it has in common with polemical philosophical works such as *Dialogus Physicus*, with interlocutor A of *Behemoth* sometimes seeming to recount Hobbes's view and others times B (see Hobbes 2010, 20ff). Concerning how the civil war came about, Hobbes tells Henry Bennet, Lord Arlington, that the first dialogue "contains the seed" of it and the second shows the "growth" (2010, 106), and at the outset of that dialogue, we find interlocutor B imploring to be enlightened with A's vantage point of the civil war: "...I pray you set me (that could not then see so well) vpon the same mountaine by the relation of the actions you then saw, and of their causes, pretensions, iustice, order, artifice, and euent" (Hobbes 2010, 107). Hobbes's other historical works likewise serve different polemical and rhetorical ends than mere preparatory work for philosophy and often interweave causal claims as he attempts to show not just *that* some event had happened but also tries to explain *why* it did.[7]

A clear reason to treat Hobbes as a philosopher relates to his choice to name his trilogy the *Elements of Philosophy*, which he published in three sections: *De corpore* (1655), *De homine* (1658), and *De cive* (1642). Although the *Leviathan* (1651; 1668) has received significantly more attention, scholarly and otherwise, than these works, Hobbes devoted a great deal of time and attention to the *Elements* trilogy over the course of his writing career. We can infer, for example, that he was composing material related to the early chapters of *De corpore* in the 1630s and 1640s because there are extant notes on related topics from Payne and Cavendish.[8] Indeed, Hobbes recounts for the reader of *De cive* that events beyond his control caused him to publish that work before publishing *De corpore*, his work concerning topics in method, first philosophy, geometry, and natural philosophy: "it happened that my country, some years before the civil war broke out, was already seething with questions of the right of Government and of the due obedience of citizens, forerunners of the approaching war" (Hobbes 1998, 13). Due to this civil unrest, Hobbes notes that he "put the rest aside and hurried on the completion" of *De cive*.

Another reason for examining Hobbes as a philosopher relates to the way in which he claims the parts of his thought depend upon one another. Although many philosophers today often specialize in one area or another of philosophy, Hobbes attempts, like others in his period and in the period preceding him, to offer a philosophical system with connecting points between metaphysics (first philosophy), epistemology, mathematics, natural philosophy, morality, and civil philosophy, among other areas. As has already been mentioned, this interconnectedness often led his critics to attempt to undermine central areas of his philosophy, such as his materialist metaphysics and natural philosophy, because they saw the consequences of his views in other areas as unacceptable. The remainder of this introductory chapter will consider how Hobbes presented his philosophy through his major works. Next it will discuss how *A Companion to Hobbes* has been organized in light of that presentation. Finally, the chapter will briefly outline strategies that try to make sense of how the parts of Hobbes's philosophy depend upon one another.

1 The Presentation of Hobbes's Major Writings

Broadly speaking, Hobbes's major works follow roughly the same manner of presentation, from his early work *Elements of Law* (1640)[9] through the two editions of *Leviathan* (1651 and 1668) and to the works in the trilogy *Elements of Philosophy* that were published between 1642 and 1658. There are *many* differences among these works, as some of the chapters in the present volume expose, but an overarching division in common in these writings is between what Hobbes calls natural bodies ("Bodies Naturall") and political bodies ("Politique Bodies") in the well-known Table provided in the English edition of *Leviathan* chapter 9 (2012, 130; the Table is between 1651, 40–1).[10]

The Table of *Leviathan* chapter 9 traces the consequences from the accidents of natural bodies and political bodies. Following Hobbes's display of the consequences following from the accidents of natural bodies, at the right-hand side of the Table the reader finds the disciplines that study them, such as first philosophy (*philosophia prima*), geometry, architecture, astrology, optics, ethics, and "The *Science* of JUST and UNIUST" (2012, 131). The terminating points of the consequences from accidents of political bodies are just the following:

1. Of Consequences from the *Institution* of COMMON-WEALTHS, to the *Rights*, and the *Duties* of the *Body Politique*, or *Soveraign*.
2. Of Consequences from the same, to the *Duty*, and *Right* of the *Subjects*. (2012, 130)

At first glance, this Table might appear like a schematic overview of the *structure* of Hobbes's philosophy, i.e., it may look like Hobbes is showing the reader how the different parts of his philosophy relate to one another in terms of dependence relationships. However, there are difficulties with understanding the Table in this way. For example, since disciplines such as optics and geometry are both at the furthest right-hand side of the Table, the Table provides the reader without any explanation for why it is legitimate to use geometry in optics, as Hobbes does, for example, in *De homine* 2. Using geometry within optics, or in other investigations such as astronomy, music, or geography, would require one to cross from one terminating point of the Table into another, but the reason why such a move would be legitimate, as Hobbes's practice implies, is not at all evident from the Table.

Similar difficulties arise in taking the Table to show the *structural* dependence relationships of civil philosophy to other parts of philosophy. Indeed, the "*Science* of JUST and UNIUST" follows from "physiques" and not civil philosophy on the Table, showing that the line between natural bodies and political bodies may not be as precise as the Table seems to indicate. Given these difficulties in thinking of the Table as indicative of the structure of Hobbes's philosophy, I suggest the Table is only an outline of subjects to be treated. In other words, the right-most side of the Table shows the order of subjects to be presented and not the dependence relationships among the parts of philosophy.[11]

Even if Hobbes did not intend the Table to display how the parts of his philosophy fit together with one another, the Table does cohere with the overall manner of presentation in his major works. The two parts of *Elements of Law* (1640) fit this general structure, being divided into "Humane Nature" and "De Corpore Politico," and the *Leviathan*'s first two parts, Part I ("Of Man") and Part II ("Of Common-wealth"), likewise mirror that same general structure. However, in the *Elements of Philosophy* trilogy, Hobbes covers much more ground than he does in *Elements of Law* or *Leviathan*. As a result, we can view the right-hand-side terminating points of the Table in *Leviathan* 9 as a guide to many of the additional subjects that one finds in *Elements of Philosophy*, and they appear in roughly the same order as they are presented on the Table. In Figure I.1, the parenthetical additions show where the right-hand-side terminating points of the Table from *Leviathan* 9 correspond to parts within the three sections of *Elements of Philosophy*, i.e., *De corpore*, *De homine*, and *De cive*.

This alignment of the right-hand side of the Table of *Leviathan* 9 with parts of the three sections of *Elements of Philosophy* leaves out some of the disciplines mentioned in the Table, such as "*Science* of ENGINEERS" and "ARCHITECTURE" (2012, 131), but the present aim has been to show the broad overlap in the manner of presentation among Hobbes's major works. The next section discusses the organization of this *Companion*.

2 The Organization of *A Companion to Hobbes*

The ordering of chapters in the present volume has been modeled after the manner in which Hobbes presents his philosophy in his major works, and so it has four sections devoted to Hobbes's thought itself: Part I (First Philosophy, Mathematics, and Natural Philosophy), Part II (Human Nature and Morality), Part III (Civil Philosophy), and Part IV (Religion). The chapters in Part V (Controversies and Reception) consider the reception of Hobbes's ideas by his contemporaries and by later figures. The diversity of the topics discussed by the chapters of Part V reflects the engagement of critics with the different parts of his philosophy, as well as the fact that many of his interlocutors saw those parts as deeply interconnected with one another.

Considering Hobbes's presentation of topics exposes a key fault-line present in his thought: the line between natural bodies and political bodies. If readers attend just to the Table of *Leviathan* chapter 9, discussed already, and to the distinctions between the

- Consequences from the Accidents of natural bodies
  - PHILOSOPHIA PRIMA (*De corpore*, Part II)
  - GEOMETRY(*De corpore*, Part III)
  - ASTRONOMY and SCIOGRAPHY (*De corpore*, Part IV)
  - OPTIQUES and ETHIQUES (*De homine*)
  - LOGIQUE (*De homine* Chapter X; also *De corpore*, Part I)
  - The *Science* of JUST and UNIUST (*De cive*, Part I *Libertas*)
- Consequences from the Accidents of political bodies
  - Of Consequences from the *Institution* of COMMON-WEALTHS, to the *Rights*, and the *Duties* of the *Body Politique*, or *Soveraign* (*De cive*, Part II)
  - Of Consequences from the same, to the *Duty*, and *Right* of the *Subjects* (*De cive*, Part II)

Figure I.1 The order of presentation in Hobbes's Philosophy: The Table of *Leviathan* 9 compared to the *Elements of Philosophy* trilogy.

parts of Hobbes's works, this line between the natural and the political may seem clear and unproblematic. But the line between these two kinds of bodies is not precise, for even if the "*Science* of JUST and UNIUST" is part of the consequences from natural bodies, justice and injustice themselves do not result from human bodies considered on their own, unlike sensation or digestion. Indeed, Hobbes declares that "Justice, and Injustice are none of the Faculties neither of the Body nor the Mind" but are instead "Qualities, that related to men in Society, not in Solitude" (Hobbes 2012, 296; 1651, 63). This fault line in Hobbes's thought figures in the discussions of a number of the chapters of the volume: Abizadeh (Chapter 6), Slomp (Chapter 7), Field (Chapter 8), Lloyd (Chapter 9), Green (Chapter 10), Brito Vieira (Chapter 11), and Rhodes (Chapter 12).

2.1 *First Philosophy, Mathematics, and Natural Philosophy*

Helen Hattab's chapter "Hobbes's Unified Method for *Scientia*" contrasts Hobbes's goal of a unified method for theoretical and practical science with his Scholastic predecessors. Hattab shows that Hobbes uses 'demonstration' equivocally and argues that this has led scholars to think Hobbes had a single form of method in mind. Hattab argues that in fact, for Hobbes and others, there are two types of method at play: first, a universal method concerned with the ordering of concepts and definitions before one begins the work of discovery or teaching in a subject; and second, a particular method used to demonstrate conclusions. The former method provides principles that are drawn upon in applications of the particular method. However, unlike the differences that Hobbes claimed existed between him and Scholastic Aristotelians, Hattab locates this distinction within Zaberella and shows that it was continued by Keckermann and Burgersdijk, Scholastic Protestant philosophers influential in England during Hobbes's time.

There has been interest in the Stoic influences upon Hobbes's political philosophy, but less attention has been devoted to the relationship of Stoic ideas to Hobbes's first philosophy and natural philosophy. Geoffrey Gorham's chapter "The Stoic Roots of Hobbes's Natural Philosophy and First Philosophy" shows how Hobbes's first philosophy was influenced by Stoic thought and how that influence impacted his natural philosophy, focusing in particular on Hobbes's views of space, time, causality, and God. These areas of Hobbes's philosophy were especially pressing for his materialism since they seem to be concerned with incorporeal entities. Indeed, as a result some have attempted to understand Hobbes as an idealist, a subjectivist, or an atheist. Gorham shows that Hobbes's solution, in line with Hobbes's goal of providing a materialism that cohered with mechanical philosophy, was to understand the conceptions that grounded first philosophy as having two aspects: realist and subjectivist.

Hobbes's exalted view of himself as a mathematician did not align with the opinions of his contemporaries. Douglas Jesseph's chapter "Hobbesian Mathematics and the Dispute with Wallis" examines Hobbes's philosophy of mathematics and Hobbes's continual disagreements with John Wallis. Jesseph focuses on Hobbes's attempts to understand geometrical objects and geometrical definitions in accordance with his materialism and furthermore on Hobbes's disdain for analytic geometry. Their exchanges relating to mathematics can be seen as originating in 1655 with the publication of *De corpore* and continuing until Hobbes's death, and beyond issues in mathematics they also concerned broader issues in theology and politics.

Continuing the focus on the unity of Hobbes's philosophy begun in Helen Hattab's chapter, Marcus Adams's chapter "Explanations in Hobbes's Optics and Natural Philosophy" examines how Hobbes's optics and natural philosophy depend upon his geometry. Adams considers Hobbes's descriptions about how the parts of his philosophy fit together with one another and provides case studies to show Hobbes's practice of explanation in optics and natural philosophy. Adams suggests that Hobbes held that explanations in natural philosophy should ideally be like those in optics, showing how Hobbes's explanations in both employ claims from experience and from *a priori* geometry.

2.2 Human Nature and Morality

R.W. McIntyre's chapter "'A Most Useful Economy': Hobbes on Linguistic Meaning and Understanding" directs attention to the human/non-human animal divide to make sense of the role of names in language. McIntyre argues that for non-human animals, like dogs and cats, names play the role of natural signs of the passions and the will. A dog, for example, will take an instance of the name 'walk' as a sign that their owner is about to get the leash and take them outside. However, for humans who are competent at using language names function as symbols that aid in helping bring to mind conceptions that will guide inferences and ultimately human behavior. Beyond aiding in the increase of prudence, this ability to understand words as words that Hobbes posits allows humans to acquire universal knowledge, e.g., of all triangles, while maintaining his commitment to nominalism.

In "Hobbes's Theory of the Good: Felicity by Anticipatory Pleasure," Arash Abizadeh shows how Hobbes's account of felicity was influenced by and modified ideas from Ancient Greek ethics. Abizadeh argues that Hobbes posits an ultimate, overarching good for a human life, which Hobbes conceives not as a final end or state to be realized but as an ongoing process of experiencing greater pleasures relative to pains. Contrasting Hobbes's understanding of felicity with that of the Epicureans and the Cyrenaics, Abizadeh depicts a Hobbes who holds that felicity consists primarily in the mental pleasures arising from anticipating the satisfaction of one's desires.

The role fear plays in humans' escape from their natural state, as well as within the commonwealth after it has been established, has always been a point of focus among interpreters of Hobbes. Gabriella Slomp, in the chapter "In Search of 'A Constant Civill Amity': Hobbes on Friendship and Sociability," compares Hobbes's views with Aristotle's and shows how Hobbes's account differs in terms of the origin, nature, and conditions of "civill amity" within political states. On Slomp's account, what emerges is a picture of Hobbesian amity that results not from reciprocity of love or care but rather from a shared understanding of the function of the Leviathan and the effort among its citizens to support it.

In the chapter "Hobbes on Power and Gender Relations," Sandra Leonie Field considers what Hobbes's philosophy offers to help make sense of gender relations. Field distinguishes between two models of interpersonal power relations: the dominion model and the deference model. The dominion model, which represents power as a vertical relationship of the subjection of one person to another, has been frequently associated with Hobbes by feminist scholars. While this model is reflected in Hobbes's writings, Field suggests that this model has difficulty making sense of gender relations in a post-coverture world. In its place, Field draws attention to the deference model, which understands the complex and often non-vertical ways in which power can be expressed in gender relations. Not only does this model better aid in understanding contemporary power relations, but Field shows that this model can be found within Hobbes's thought.

The natural state of humans – the state of nature – is one of the most evocative parts of Hobbes's philosophy. Against understanding the state of nature as diametrically opposed to the state of civil society, S.A. Lloyd's chapter "The State of Nature as a Continuum Concept" argues that the state of nature differs from civil society in degrees. In other words, there are *states* of nature rather than a simple line that is crossed upon the formation of a commonwealth. Lloyd articulates this spectrum as ranging from a condition of mere nature, characterized by a universal right of private judgment, to a perfectly totalitarian state. This approach to Hobbes's state of nature offers an understanding of humans' natural state that can make sense of how imperfect political systems are more or less like the mere state of nature. Lloyd argues that the continuum view is more theoretically and empirically plausible than alternative views that claim that Hobbes saw civil society as always at risk of falling back, at any moment, into the mere state of nature.

Michael Green's chapter "Hobbes's Minimalist Moral Theory" challenges conceptions of Hobbes's moral theory that have taken it to follow from broader aspects of Hobbes's philosophy, such as an aim to harmonize morality with one's self-interest, as a type of divine-command theory, or following from an account of rationality. In place these accounts, which Green identifies as maximalist theories, Green offers a minimal theory relying upon two theses drawn from Hobbes's discussions of the Laws of Nature: the value thesis, which holds that the laws are valued because of their role in preserving peace, and the conditional thesis, which holds that what the laws require depends upon what others do. In contrast to more maximal moral theories, Green shows that with only this minimal theory Hobbes can accomplish his goals of arguing for the benefits of the state and constructing an alternative to Aristotle's theory of justice.

2.3 *Civil Philosophy*

The break between natural bodies and political bodies occurs with the creation of the commonwealth, but the ability to represent, e.g., one person representing another person, is something possible within humans' natural state, and it is part of what enables commonwealth to be generated. Mónica Brito Vieira's chapter "Hobbesian Persons and Representation" traces Hobbes understanding of "person" and its linkage with a capacity for agency. Persons can be natural (when someone's words and actions are considered their own) or artificial (when someone's words and actions are considered as *representing* those of someone or something else), and whoever owns the words spoken or actions done is considered the author. Hobbes furthermore differentiates between true representation, which is when the represented party authorizes its representation, and representation by fiction, which is when the represented party cannot authorize its representation, but the actions of the representative are nonetheless held (by fiction) to be its own (Hobbes 2012, 244; 1651, 80). However, Hobbes does not explicitly say what sort of person the state itself is, and there has been disagreement among scholars. Connecting Hobbes's discussion of entities such as churches, hospitals, and bridges to the issue of the state, Vieira argues that the state is a person by fiction.

Rosamond Rhodes's chapter "Hobbes's Account of Authorizing a Sovereign" challenges a widely held interpretation of Hobbes's understanding of how humans leave their natural state and authorize the sovereign: that the sovereign is a third-party beneficiary of a covenant between individuals. Against this view of Hobbesian authorization, Rhodes offers a nuanced understanding that relies upon distinguishing two steps: the establishment of the commonwealth and the subsequent authorization of the sovereign. In the time between these two steps, the commonwealth (formed in step 1) selects its form of sovereignty, whether it will be a monarchy, aristocracy, or democracy. The view of Hobbes's sovereign that arises from Rhodes's interpretation is of a sovereign who can be held accountable for their actions since they are party to the covenant.

Moving from focus on the sovereign to the subjects of the commonwealth, Eleanor Curran examines subjects' rights in the chapter "The Strength and Significance of Subjects' Rights in *Leviathan*." Curran argues that subjects do not give up all their rights to a sovereign and that not all Hobbesian rights are simple Hohfeldian liberty rights, i.e., rights without correlative duties. On Curran's account, the theory of rights found in

Hobbes's *Leviathan* is uniquely modern and secular, with no theological premises and no attachment to traditional notions of natural law.

Against the view that Hobbes's account of sovereignty in *Leviathan* is one of an immortal, all-powerful artificial being, Tom Sorell argues in the chapter "Hobbes on Sovereignty and Its Strains" that the Hobbesian model of sovereignty, even when it is functioning as it ideally should, is fragile. While Sorell notes that, according to Hobbes, those who form a commonwealth do so with the *aim* of it continuing indefinitely, there many ways in which that continuity can be broken. Sorell suggests that Hobbes's theory of the rights of sovereigns is crafted in such a way as to correspond to the list that Hobbes provides of the causes of the dissolution of commonwealths, but alongside the rights of sovereigns Hobbes outlines their duties. The recognition of the fragility inherent in this setup makes an ideal Hobbesian commonwealth a balance between the exercise of the rights of sovereigns and the durability of subjects' transfer of the right of nature.

What, if anything, constrains Hobbesian sovereigns or their commonwealths from interacting with one another on the international scene has been a frequent topic of debate among interpreters of Hobbes. Johan Olsthoorn's chapter "Hobbes on International Ethics" draws attention to a change in Hobbes's works on this issue. Olsthoorn argues that a common view among Hobbes's scholars – the claim that in the international state of nature *commonwealths* occupy a normative position analogous to individuals in the interpersonal one (what Olsthoorn calls the "assimilation argument") – has textual support in *De cive*, but that a change Hobbes makes in the *Leviathan* suggests an alternative account. Drawing upon the *Leviathan*, Olsthoorn argues that the norms of international ethics are directly applied to *sovereigns* rather than to commonwealths. The resulting account portrays Hobbesian international ethics as informed by sovereign duties of care to national subjects.

2.4 Religion

Hobbes identifies language as a double-edged sword: linguistic ability is a prerequisite for science and other forms of cooperative activity, but used improperly it may lead users to hold beliefs that lead them astray. Language plays a central role in Hobbes's criticisms of Scholastic metaphysics, and Hobbes's alternative approach to language was meant to reform its usage. Luc Foisneau's chapter "Against Philosophical Darkness: A Political Conception of Enlightenment" shows how this critique, in particular Hobbes's assault on the notion of separated essences, concerns not only claims in metaphysics but also has a broader political end: to show that the language used by the Catholic Church promotes control of citizens' minds. Tracing these criticisms through Hobbes's account of schools in Greek and Jewish antiquity, Foisneau demonstrates that Hobbesian enlightenment is accomplished through state institutions and only by using vernacular language, not the language of Scholastic darkness. Such enlightenment for Hobbes is possible only within the state.

Michael Byron's chapter "Hobbes on Submission to God" addresses the nature of what it means for a human to submit to God. To do this, Byron examines Hobbes's discussion of the "Kingdom of God by Nature" in *Leviathan* 31, understanding Hobbes as committed to a primary state of nature, which is inhabited by atheists, and a secondary state of nature, which is inhabited by subjects of God's natural kingdom. To refine these notions, Byron differentiates subjects of this kingdom not only from atheists but also from non-human animals and deists. Reconstructing Hobbes's account, Byron argues that humans are members of the natural kingdom of God if and only if they acknowledge God's providential involvement in the world. Atheists are excluded because they deny God's existence and deists because, while they believe that God exists, they deny God's providence. Byron furthermore argues that according to Hobbes the act of acknowledgement, unlike that of belief, is voluntary.

Hobbes's extended treatments of topics related to ecclesiology and theology in *Leviathan* Parts III and IV set that work apart from Hobbes's prior works in civil philosophy. Indeed, it is striking that the third part of *Leviathan* ("On the Christian Commonwealth") is the longest part of that work. Jeffrey Collins's chapter "Hobbes and the Christian Commonwealth" examines Hobbes's usage of the phrase "Christian Commonwealth" by first looking to occurrences of that phrase and related phrases by authors preceding Hobbes and then by showing the different purposes for which Hobbes used the phrase, from his ecumenical use in *Elements of Law* to uses in *Leviathan* that are informed by worries about the power of clerics. In the latter, Collins shows how Hobbes first openly rejects Catholic notions of a single Christian commonwealth under Rome and insists, against the views of Bellarmine, that sovereignty lies only in a state and that a sovereign need only endorse minimal theological claims.

The extent to which Hobbes's sovereign could countenance religious toleration is the focus of Johann Sommerville's chapter "Hobbes and Toleration." Sommerville discusses the context in which Hobbes's concerns related to religious belief and practice emerged and shows that Hobbes viewed toleration of non-Christians as compatible with natural law. Hobbes held that the sovereign should have absolute power and could prohibit religious activities that the sovereign viewed as a threat to the security of the state. Although no religious group would receive a permanent right to toleration according to Hobbes's model of the state, since circumstances may change and warrant different laws concerning public behavior, nevertheless a range of religious actions and organizations that posed no threat and did not break the law would be permitted.

The amount of space Hobbes devotes to the topic "Of Power Ecclesiastical" in *Leviathan* 42, as well as his detailed focus upon Cardinal Bellarmine's arguments, may seem initially puzzling. Franck Lessay's chapter "Hobbes, Rome's Enemy" traces this in-depth attack on Bellarmine to broader concerns of Hobbes's with Roman theology and to his views related to political power. In particular, Lessay highlights Hobbes's attack on the notion of the "indirect power," which Bellarmine claimed Rome possessed, showing that for Hobbes this notion was merely a cover for what was in fact *direct* power. In other words, although advocates of the notion of "indirect power" relied upon a distinction between temporal and spiritual power, Hobbes argues that ultimately it reduced to Rome asserting direct power when it claimed doing so was necessary; it amounted to Rome having the ability to "depose Princes and States" if deemed necessary "for the Salvation of Soules" (Hobbes 2012; 1651, 910). Lessay shows how Hobbes's renouncement of this notion, along with the location of power within civil sovereigns alone, led to the rejection of his views by Anglican contemporaries and later Catholic thinkers alike.

In the chapter "Hobbes and the Papal Monarchy," Patricia Springborg argues that the papal monarchy served as the model for the Leviathan in Hobbes's *Leviathan* but also was the subject of Part IV of the *Leviathan* ("Of the Kingdome of Darknesse"). Springborg's chapter links Hobbes's *Leviathan* with his later works, in particular the Latin poem *Historia Ecclesiastica*, and details Hobbes's criticisms of the papacy by showing his analysis focused on three papal strategies: first, papal claims to imperial power by means of a transmission of power from Rome; second, co-opting of Roman law as canon law; and third, the creation of an ecclesiastical system of offices paralleling the administrative offices of the old Roman Empire. Tracing the decline of the papal monarchy not only to its overreach but also to the limits of its philosophy of mind, Springborg shows Hobbes's indebtedness to the canon law tradition alongside his criticisms, in particular related to Hobbes's understanding of the artificial person of the state.

2.5 *Controversies and Reception*

The final section of this *Companion* considers the criticism and reception of Hobbes's philosophy. Hobbes's impact was significant, and the range of figures reflected in this section testifies to that fact.[12] Although Hobbes's impact ranged beyond those engaged in philosophy, the focus of the figures considered in these chapters emphasizes engagement with Hobbes's philosophical ideas.

Descartes's influence upon seventeenth century physics, and upon mechanical philosophy more generally, is well recognized, with Hobbes's work in physics receiving comparatively less attention. Edward Slowik argues in "Body and Space in Hobbes and Descartes" that, although there were similarities in each figure's views, Hobbes's hypotheses concerning body and space show his differences from Cartesian physics. In particular, Slowik draws attention to differences that stem from Hobbes's understanding of imaginary space, which follows from his understanding of phantasms, and his account of the material constitution of bodies.

Hobbes never received an invitation to join the Royal Society, as mentioned already, and he and Robert Boyle criticized each other's work extensively. John Henry's chapter "Hobbes's Mechanical Philosophy and Its English Critics" focuses on Hobbes's natural philosophy by considering how it was attacked by two English critics: Robert Boyle and Henry More. Boyle's aim was to develop an acausal experimental method against Hobbes's speculative philosophy. Doing so, Henry shows, aided Boyle's goal of showing that God must play an active role in the world. More sought to dismiss Hobbes's monistic materialism in favor of a dualism of body and immaterial spirit. Henry suggests that although these critics, and others, wanted to distance themselves from Hobbist ideas, there are similarities between Hobbes's corporeal God and Henry More's concept of an immaterial, three-dimensionally extended God.

Stewart Duncan's chapter "Cudworth as a Critic of Hobbes" looks to Ralph Cudworth's criticisms of Hobbes that relate to atheism and to whether morality is eternal and immutable. Cudworth worries about atheism in his work *The True Intellectual System of the Universe* (1678), and he attacks various versions, singling out Hobbes as a point of focus. Duncan examines Cudworth's criticisms of the claim that finite beings possess no idea of God, and Cudworth's accusation that from that claim it would follow that God does not exist. Cudworth responds to this claim that humans possess no idea of God and to what he understands as the arguments in favor of that view. Duncan also discusses Cudworth's critique of Hobbes in *Treatise on Eternal and Immutable Morality* (1996) and shows Cudworth's claim, against his understanding of Hobbes, that which is good is not made so by human decision.

Margaret Cavendish's natural philosophy offers an interesting contrast to Hobbes's since she understands all of nature to be matter but suggests that all motion happens by *self*-motion. In "Cavendish and Hobbes on Causation," Marcy P. Lascano discusses Cavendish's account of causation and contrasts it with Hobbes's view of causation by means of an "entire cause." Lascano focuses on perception, a key component of Cavendish's natural philosophy, and shows that perceivers are not the entire cause of their perceptions. Against understanding Cavendish as advocating for a libertarian view of causation and of the parts of nature, Lascano links Cavendish to the Hobbesian account of liberty.

Spinoza's debt to Hobbes is well known, in particular the appeal that both figures make to the concept of *conatus* (endeavor). Justin Steinberg's chapter "Striving, Happiness, and the Good: Spinoza as Follower and Critic of Hobbes" shows how both Hobbes and Spinoza reject key features of Scholastic accounts of motivation. Both figures are determinists who dismiss free will and furthermore deny appeals to final causes, offering instead reductive accounts of ends by appealing only to efficient causes. However, after exposing these similarities, Steinberg argues that Spinoza's naturalistic eudaimonism leads him to have views different from Hobbes concerning goodness, happiness, liberty, and the function of the state.

Scholars of Mary Astell have noted how in some of her well-known works, such as *A Serious Proposal to the Ladies, Parts I and II*, she criticizes Hobbesian ideas, in particular those related to the natural state of humans and the social contract needed for leaving that state. Jacqueline Broad's chapter "Hobbes and Astell on War and Peace" shows that in three political pamphlets of Astell's from 1704 she also engages with Hobbesian ideas related to war and peace. Although Astell seeks to distance herself from Hobbes's philosophy, Broad shows how Astell adopts aspects of his view and even extends his ideas to claim that sexist opinions about female sovereigns and about women's susceptibility to seditious opinion represent a threat to social order.

David Hume's account of selfishness and human nature has been contrasted with Hobbes's, with the latter sometimes viewed as an egoist. Alexandra Chadwick's chapter "Hobbes and Hume on Human Nature: 'Much of a Dispute of Words'?" challenges this conception of Hobbes, showing that the differences between Hobbes and Hume on selfishness become less clear when examining their philosophical psychology. Chadwick argues that instead the difference lies in Hobbes's rhetorical aim: Hobbes believes it dangerous to think too highly of human nature. When Hobbes presents individuals who claim to have the interests of the people in mind as driven by self-serving desires, he seeks to discourage citizens from listening to them.

In the chapter "He Shows 'Genius' and Is 'More Useful than Pufendorf': Kant's Reception of Hobbes," Howard Williams examines Kant's reaction to Hobbes's view that open public inquiry can endanger society. Whereas Kant held that such debate among scholars was an essential feature of healthy society, Kant saw Hobbes as wrongly vesting all power in the sovereign to decide what viewpoints may be heard. Alongside this disagreement with Hobbes, Williams shows that Kant agreed with Hobbes on the sovereign's authority being unchallengeable; Kant's claim that open debate was necessary did not allow resistance to the sovereign but implied only a right to communicate. Williams concludes by considering Kant's rejection both of Hobbes's methodology and Hobbes's reliance upon philosophical psychology to understand human nature.

Karen Green's chapter "Catharine Macaulay and the Reception of Hobbes during the Eighteenth Century" shows that although critics of liberal democracy have represented it as grounded in Hobbes's philosophy, the role Hobbes played was not so direct. Green shows that instead Macaulay's view looked forward to a democratic commonwealth, in which the common good would be the common care, and she based her advocacy of democratic institutions in natural law, rational religion, Christian *eudaimonism*, and rational altruism. Green suggests that subsequent philosophical developments help explain why Hobbes came take on the central philosophical position that he currently occupies.

3 Strategies for Unity among the Parts of Hobbes's Philosophy

The earlier discussion of the Table in *Leviathan* 9 suggested that it does not show the *structure* of Hobbes's philosophy. If the Table does not display this, what are strategies for understanding how the parts of Hobbes's philosophy fit together? For example, how does Hobbes's civil philosophy relate to his claims about human nature? Or how is Hobbes's natural philosophy dependent upon geometry or first philosophy? Although Hobbes provides some clues at several points in his writings, there is no largely agreed-upon strategy among Hobbes scholars of accounting for how the different parts of his philosophy depend upon one another.

In terms of the number of its adherents, perhaps the best-represented account of how the parts of Hobbes's philosophy fit together is what might be called the "deductivist" interpretation of Hobbes's philosophy. Those holding the deductivist interpretation often appeal to *De corpore* VI.6[13] and broadly see Hobbes as holding something like the following viewpoint: claims in civil philosophy would be deduced from "morals" (the term Hobbes uses to describe the part of philosophy that considers desire and aversion, as well as the passions generally); claims in "morals" would be deduced from claims in natural philosophy; and claims in natural philosophy would be deduced from geometry and, ultimately, from first philosophy (Hobbes's preferred term for his metaphysics).

Scholars who understand Hobbes in this way have focused both on the shape of his philosophy overall as well as on the relationships among parts of it. For example, in their account of the debate between Hobbes and Robert Boyle concerning the air-pump experiments, Steven Shapin and Simon Schaffer describe Boyle as "protecting the proper procedures of experimental philosophy against the beast of deductivism" (Shapin and Schaffer 1985, 176). On the move from philosophical psychology to civil philosophy (this is the fault line in Hobbes's thought, described already), and how this relates to deduction, there has been significant disagreement among commentators. In particular, if one holds that Hobbes's claims in civil philosophy are grounded in *moral* claims then, if one simultaneously holds the deductivist interpretation, the question of the ground of those moral claims is pressing, since it appears that Hobbes would be guilty of deriving ought-statements from is-statements. In other words, Hobbes would appear to be committing a version of the so-called naturalistic fallacy. R.S. Peters argues that such a deduction was Hobbes's intent and that Hobbes falls prey to this fallacy, asserting that "Hobbes seems to have thought that the basic prescription 'men ought to endeavour peace' can be deduced from psychology and physics. This seems to be a logical mistake" (1956, 171). J.W.N. Watkins agrees that Hobbes's aim was to deduce civil philosophy from philosophical psychology, but Watkins attempts to remove the worry by arguing that Hobbes avoided the fallacy by having "prescriptions [that] are not *moral* prescriptions—they are more like 'doctor's orders' of a peculiarly compelling kind" (1965, 76; emphasis original).

The framing of this debate, focusing on the transition from Hobbes's philosophical psychology to his civil philosophy, is reflective of controversy surrounding an influential paper by A.E. Taylor that advanced what Hobbes scholars have come to refer to as "the Taylor thesis."[14] Taylor argued that "Hobbes's ethical doctrine proper, *disengaged from an egoistic psychology with which it has no logically necessary connection*, is a very strict deontology, curiously suggestive, though with interesting differences, of some of the characteristic theses of Kant" (1938, 408; emphasis added). Despite Taylor's worries, Howard Warrender saw a role for Hobbes's philosophical psychology insofar as it could serve as one of the "validating conditions" of Hobbes's account of obligation to obey the law since, given Warrender's view that Hobbes was committed to the principle that ought implies can, it was necessary to show humans "capable of having an adequate motive to obey it" (1957, 87).[15]

Taylor's thesis, which understood Hobbes's civil philosophy as logically separate from the other parts of his philosophy, weighed against seeing Hobbes as offering a system; or if Hobbes did offer a system, it was an incoherent one.[16] Thus, against Taylor's thesis, defenders of the view that the parts of Hobbes's philosophy were deductively dependent upon one another either embraced that Hobbes's system was guilty of the naturalistic fallacy (Peters) or attempted to show that Hobbes never really meant to offer moral claims but instead gave something less than this, akin to a prescription from a physician (Watkins). More recently, A.P. Martinich (2005) argues against views that hold that there is *no* deductive relationship between the parts of Hobbes's philosophy by focusing on how Hobbes's understanding of human beings must relate to *De corpore*: "men are bodies, and thus what Hobbes says about men in *De homine* has to follow from what he says about bodies in *De corpore*" (2005, 172).

Another understanding of Hobbes's system with affinities to the deductivist account understands him as a type of reductionist. For example, Marjorie Grene argues that according to Hobbes "the only meaningful hypotheses are such as reduce all phenomena to material or, in modern language, to physico-chemical terms" and the reduction happens by reducing "wholes to parts" (1969, 9–10). On Grene's account, there are natural and artificial wholes needing to be reduced, and the role of philosophy is to do just that. The commonwealth or the system of civil laws in a commonwealth would be an example of an artificial whole needing to be reduced:

> They are language systems which constitute sciences when applied to sense, or legal systems invented to assuage our fears and satisfy our needs: needs and fears which, in turn, reduce to a sum of "endeavors" or least motions of our bodies to and from other bodies which have in turn caused such minute internal movements. (Grene 1969, 10)

Such a system, Grene argues, dismisses the "oughts" of morality and offers in the laws of nature (agreeing with Watkins) prescriptions that will aid humans in satisfying their appetite for peace. Although differing on the details of Hobbes's moral and political philosophy, Jean Hampton likewise understands Hobbes as a type of reductionist. Hampton claims that according to Hobbes "[a] materialist explanation of an event will always be in terms of the operation of fundamental physical objects in accordance with laws" and furthermore that Hobbes held that "it is possible to reduce both ethical and psychological language to talk of matter, motion, and the laws of nature" (1986, 12).

There are problems with the deductivist and reductionist interpretations. I will mention the most significant for the deductivist interpretation here. The difficulty is a logical one related to how Hobbes understands deduction and the nature of truth. Hobbes understands deduction as a process of showing containment relationships among categories. According to Hobbes's account in *De corpore* III.7, truth is a property of propositions, and a true proposition is one in which the "predicate contains the subject within itself" (Hobbes 1981, 233; OL I.31). So "All men are mortals" is true just in case 'men' is contained within 'mortals.' Truth is carried through the premises of a syllogism when the proper containment relationships are maintained in each premise.

This account of truth exposes a difficulty for deductivist attempts to make sense of how the parts of Hobbes's philosophy fit together, but to see this we will need to consider how he describes some parts of philosophy as more "abstract" than others. Hobbes differentiates disciplines like geometry and natural philosophy by stating that the former is abstract and the latter concerns real bodies as they exist in the world.[17] Hobbes allows abstraction wherein one considers a body in the imagination as if it had a feature removed, such as considering 'thinking' alone by abstracting away 'human body.' However, he criticizes those who claim that in doing so they have demonstrated that a feature like 'thinking' can exist independently from a body:

> The gross errors of certain metaphysicians take their origin from this; for from the fact that it is possible to consider thinking without considering body, they want to infer that there is no need for a thinking body.... (Hobbes 1981, 231; OL I.30)

Expanding this picture, we could view Hobbes's system of philosophy as organized from more abstract (first philosophy) to less abstract (civil philosophy), and now the problem for any deductivist account should be clearer: if the alleged deduction is supposed to be from the more abstract discipline, then where does the information about the less abstract discipline enter? For example, a principle in geometry is something "abstract" insofar as it does not relate *directly* to bodies in the actual world; bodies that interact with one another are not composed of geometric 'points' or 'lines' but rather have different densities, weights, and apparent colors, and also inhabit media of different densities. If a deduction is to be offered, where in the "abstract" will we find these features of actual bodies *contained*?[18]

Certainly, what Hobbes claims about bodies in general will hold about humans when humans are considered simply as *bodies*, but these claims will not explain actions of human bodies considered as *human* bodies (*pace* Martinich 2005, 172). In other words, the information relating to human bodies will not be contained within true propositions related to bodies in general (i.e., bodies as bodies). For example, if I want to understand why some human body plummets rather than floats when leaving the top of a tall building, I could consider it as a body and explain the falling rather than floating by appealing to physical causes (just like I would if I were explaining an inanimate body falling from that building). However, if I want to understand why that human body climbed the stairs to the top of the building and jumped with a bungee cord attached (also initially plummeting), I must also consider that human body as a *human* body and then uniquely human features become relevant (such as appetites and aversions).[19]

This significant difficulty notwithstanding, the deductivist and reductionist interpretations offer a familiar picture, at least to twenty-first century readers, of how of we might understand a materialist worldview. Twenty-first century readers are used to asking questions like "Does the mind reduce to the brain?" or "Does biology reduce to physics?" Since Hobbes holds that all that exists is matter, modern readers may feel tempted to ascribe a reductionist view to Hobbes, looking backward with contemporary concerns and thrusting them upon his philosophy. But seventeenth-century materialism, like today's materialism, was not monolithic, and there was disagreement among materialists concerning the nature of matter and how that matter behaved, like between Hobbes and vitalist-materialist Margaret Cavendish. Rather than risking "casting out the baby with the bath water," as Taylor seems to do when asserting that Hobbes's civil philosophy has no logical connection to his philosophical psychology or other parts, such as natural philosophy, perhaps it is still possible to salvage the idea that Hobbes's philosophy is systematic. The remains of this section will briefly mention alternative models of the structure of Hobbes's philosophy. These prospective ways of unifying Hobbes's philosophy ascribe less unity than the deductivist or reductionist accounts, but they avoid discarding unity altogether.

Two chapters in this volume directly discuss ways of understanding the unity of Hobbes's philosophy without committing him to deductivist or reductionist views. Hattab (Chapter 1) argues that for Hobbes there are two types of method at play in his philosophy: first, a universal method concerned with the ordering of concepts and definitions before one begins the work of discovery or teaching in a subject; and second, a particular method used to demonstrate conclusions. The first method, Hattab shows, provides the philosopher with principles that can be drawn upon in applications of the particular method within specific disciplines. Adams (Chapter 4) argues that although there is no deductive or reductive relationship between geometry and optics or geometry and natural philosophy, Hobbes held that there was a type of unity nonetheless. Adams argues that in explanations in optics and natural philosophy, one considers natural bodies as if they were mathematical and can then borrow causal principles from geometry. Hobbes identifies this type of explanation as "mixed mathematics" and calls it "true physics."

Another strategy to achieve unity among the parts of Hobbes's philosophy, without committing him to deductive or reductive unity, might examine a foundational concept in Hobbes's thought and see how it plays varying roles within different parts of his philosophy. Given the centrality of the concept "endeavor" to Hobbes's philosophy, it seems as good a candidate as any for bridging between the different parts of his thought. Indeed, endeavor is part of Hobbes's natural philosophy as well as a central concept he uses to understand human passions and thus human action.[20] Although not focused on the issue of the unity of Hobbes's philosophy, Edward Slowik's chapter (Chapter 22) shows how endeavor, understood in terms of actual motion, figures in Hobbes's understanding of sensation and in his criticisms of "heaviness." Further reason 'endeavor' may be promising as a unifying concept is that Hobbes's critics were inspired by and criticized Hobbes's use of this concept. Justin Steinberg's chapter in this volume (Chapter 26) discusses how Spinoza's understanding of striving differed from Hobbes's view of endeavor. Similarly, Howard Williams's chapter (Chapter 29) treats Kant's rejection of Hobbesian endeavor, showing how Kant viewed Hobbesian endeavor as characterizing mere animal choice.

4 Conclusion

This introduction has examined the manner in which Hobbes presents his philosophy in his major works and has considered ways in which scholars have tried to understand the unity and diversity of the parts of that philosophy. The aim of this introduction has been to do just that – introduce the reader to the parts of Hobbes's philosophy generally, using broad brushstrokes, and to introduce the chapters in this *Companion*. Rather than attempting to solve worries related the structure of Hobbes's philosophy, which would not be possible in such a context, this introduction has sought to show different ways of understanding Hobbes as a systematic philosopher.

References

Adams, Marcus P. 2019a. "Hobbes' Philosophy of Science." In *The Stanford Encyclopedia of Philosophy*, edited by Edward N. Zalta. https://plato.stanford.edu/entries/hobbes-science

Adams, Marcus P. 2019b. "Hobbes's Laws of Nature in Leviathan as a Synthetic Demonstration: Thought Experiments and Knowing the Causes." *Philosophers' Imprint* 19 (5): 1–23.

Baumgold, Deborah, ed. 2017. *Three-Text Edition of Thomas Hobbes's Political Theory: The Elements of Law, De Cive, and Leviathan*. Cambridge: Cambridge University Press.

Blau, Adrian. 2019. "Methodologies of Interpreting Hobbes: Historical and Philosophical." In *Interpreting Hobbes's Political Philosophy*, edited by Sharon A. Lloyd, 10–28. Cambridge: Cambridge University Press.

Byron, Michael. 2015. *Submission and Subjection in Leviathan: Good Subjects in the Hobbesian Commonwealth*. New York: Palgrave Macmillan.

Courtland, Shane, ed. 2018. *Hobbesian Applied Ethics and Public Policy*. New York: Routledge.

Cowley, Abraham. 1680. *The True Effigies of the Monster of Malmesbury, Or, Thomas Hobbes in His Proper Colours*. London.

Cudworth, Ralph. 1678. *The True Intellectual System of the Universe*London.

Cudworth, Ralph. 1996. *A Treatise Concerning Eternal and Immutable Morality*, edited by Sarah Hutton. Cambridge: Cambridge University Press.

Duncan, Stewart, 2017. "Thomas Hobbes." In *The Stanford Encyclopedia of Philosophy*, edited by Edward N. Zalta. https://plato.stanford.edu/entries/hobbes

Grene, Marjorie. 1969. "Hobbes and the Modern Mind." In *The Anatomy of Knowledge: Papers Presented to the Study Group on Foundations of Cultural Unity*, edited by Marjorie Grene and Sudy Group on Foundations of Cultural Unity, 1–28. London: Routledge & Kegan Paul.

Hampton, Jean. 1986. *Hobbes and the Social Contract Tradition*. Cambridge: Cambridge University Press.

Hobbes, Thomas. 1839–1845a. *The English Works of Thomas Hobbes*, 11 vols., edited by Sir William Molesworth. London: John Bohn

Hobbes, Thomas. 1839–1845b. *Thomæ Hobbes malmesburiensis opera philosophica*, 5 vols., edited by Gulielmi Molesworth. London: John Bohn. Cited as OL.

Hobbes, Thomas. 1981. *Computatio Sive Logica: Logic*, translation and commentary by Aloysius P. Martinich, edited by Isabel C. Hungerland and George R. Vick. New York: Abaris Books.

Hobbes, Thomas. 1985. *Dialogus Physicus*. Translated by Simon Schaffer in Steven Shapin and Simon Schaffer, *The Leviathan and the Air-Pump*. Princeton: Princeton University Press.

Hobbes, Thomas. 1994a. *Leviathan*, edited by Edwin Curley. Indianapolis: Hackett Publishing Company.

Hobbes, Thomas. 1994b. *The Correspondence*, 2 vols, edited by Noel Malcolm. Oxford: Clarendon Press.

Hobbes, Thomas. 1998. *On the Citizen*, edited by Richard Tuck and Michael Silverthorne. Cambridge: Cambridge University Press.

Hobbes, Thomas. 2010. *Behemoth*, edited by Paul Seaward. Oxford: Clarendon Press.

Hobbes, Thomas. 2012. *Leviathan*, 3 vols., edited by Noel Malcolm. Oxford: Clarendon Press. [First published 1651].

Jesseph, Douglas. 1999. *Squaring the Circle: The War between Hobbes and Wallis*. Chicago: University of Chicago Press.

Jesseph, Douglas. 2016. "Hobbes on 'Conatus': A Study in the Foundations of Hobbesian Philosophy." *Hobbes Studies* 29 (1): 66–85. doi:10.1163/18750257-02901004.

Jesseph, Douglas. 2018. "Geometry Religion, and Politics: Context and Consequences of the Hobbes-Wallis Dispute." *Notes and Records of the Royal Society* 72: 469–86.

Kavka, Gregory. 1986. *Hobbesian Moral and Political Theory*. Princeton, NJ: Princeton University Press.

Lloyd, Sharon A. and Susanne Sreedhar. 2018. "Hobbes's Moral and Political Philosophy." In *The Stanford Encyclopedia of Philosophy*, edited by Edward N. Zalta. https://plato.stanford.edu/entries/hobbes-moral

Malcolm, Noel. 2002. *Aspects of Hobbes*. Oxford: Clarendon.

Martinich, Aloysius P. 1992. *Two Gods of Leviathan: Thomas Hobbes on Religion and Politics*. Cambridge: Cambridge University Press.

Martinich, Aloysius P. 1999. *Hobbes: A Biography*. Cambridge: Cambridge University Press.

Martinich, Aloysius P. 2005. *Hobbes*. New York: Routledge.

Mintz, Samuel I. 1962. *The Hunting of the Leviathan: Seventeenth-Century Reactions to the Materialism and Moral Philosophy of Thomas Hobbes*. Cambridge: Cambridge University Press.

Parkin, Jon. 2007. *Taming the Leviathan: The Reception of the Political and Religious Ideas of Thomas Hobbes in England 1640–1700*. Cambridge: Cambridge University Press.

Peters, Richard S. 1956. *Hobbes*. Baltimore, MD: Penguin Books.

Raylor, Timothy. 2018. *Philosophy, Rhetoric, and Thomas Hobbes*. Oxford: Oxford University Press.

Rogers, Graham A.J. and Tom Sorell. 2000. *Hobbes and History*. New York: Routledge.

Shapin, Steven and Simon Schaffer. 1985. *The Leviathan and the Air-Pump*. Princeton, NJ: Princeton University Press.

Skinner, Quentin. 1996. *Reason and Rhetoric in the Philosophy of Hobbes*. Cambridge: Cambridge University Press.

Skinner, Quentin. 2018. *From Humanism to Hobbes: Studies in Rhetoric and Politics*. Cambridge: Cambridge University Press.

Tarlton, Charles D. 1998. "Rehabilitating Hobbes: Obligation, Anti-Fascism, and the Myth of a 'Taylor Thesis'." *History of Political Thought* 19 (3): 407–38.
Taylor, Alfred E. 1938. "The Ethical Doctrine of Hobbes." *Philosophy* 13 (52): 406–24.
Warrender, Howard 1957. *The Political Philosophy of Hobbes: His Theory of Obligation*. Oxford: Clarendon Press.
Watkins, John W.N. 1965. *Hobbes's System of Ideas*. London: Hutchinson University Libraries.

Abbreviations for Citations to Hobbes's Works

Citations to *Leviathan*

Chapters in this volume cite Hobbes's *Leviathan*, published in English (1651) and Latin (1668), with reference to pagination in the 2012 Clarendon Edition and the 1651 edition. This convention enables readers to locate citations using either the Clarendon edition or one of many modern editions that provide the 1651 pagination.

Each citation to the *Leviathan* occurs within a set of parentheses, such as in the following example: "To know the cause of naturall Sense, is not very necessary to the business now in hand; and I have written else-where of the same at large. Nevertheless, to fill each part of my present method, I will deliver the same in this place" (Hobbes 2012, 22; 1651, 3).

Citations to Hobbes's *English Works* and *Latin Works*

Chapters in this volume cite the nineteenth-century editions edited by Molesworth of Hobbes's works using the following conventions:

- Citations to Hobbes's *English Works* note the volume and page number as follows: EW I.20
- Citations to Hobbes's *Latin Works* note the volume and page number as follows: OL I.31

Each citation to these works occurs within a set of parentheses, such as in the following example: "Later in *De Corpore* I.8, Hobbes demarcates the "subject of philosophy, or the matter upon which it reflects, [as] every body of which any generation can be conceived" (EW I.10; OL I.9).

Notes

1 This introductory chapter will not consider Hobbes's life. For an excellent biography of Hobbes, see Martinich (1999). The *Stanford Encyclopedia of Philosophy* has three articles devoted to Hobbes's philosophy: Adams (2019a), Duncan (2017), and Lloyd and Sreedhar (2018).

2 See Jesseph (2018) for discussion of this interrelation, and see Jesseph (Chapter 3, this volume) for discussion of the criticisms of Hobbes's mathematics.

3 See Gorham (Chapter 2, this volume) on Bramhall's accusation that Hobbes is indebted to Stoic thought; McIntyre (Chapter 5, this volume) on Bramhall and Hobbes concerning the possibility of non-human animal deliberation; Curran (Chapter 13, this volume) for discussion of Bramhall's criticisms of Hobbes's notion of subjects' liberties; Foisneau (Chapter 16, this volume) regarding the dispute between Hobbes and Bramhall on Scholastic distinctions.

4 For example, essays in Courtland (2018) consider Hobbes's ideas as they relate to contemporary issues in applied ethics and political philosophy.

5 For a similar claim, see Blau (2019).

6 Although the present chapter will primarily consider Hobbes as a philosopher, humanism exerted influence upon his thinking and this has been the focus of much scholarly work. For discussion of humanist rhetoric's place in Hobbes's development, see, e.g., Skinner (1996, 2018). Also, see Raylor (2018). The rise and fall of Hobbes's renown in mathematics is documented in Jesseph (1999).

7 Indeed, Hobbes's relationship to history is complex. Concerning Hobbes's history of the genesis of Scholastic philosophy, see Foisneau (Chapter 16, this volume); for discussion of Hobbes's ecclesiastical history, in particular the history of the papal monarchy, see Springborg (Chapter 21, this volume). For discussion of the nature of history according to Hobbes as well as Hobbes's own historical works, the reader is encouraged to consult the volume edited by Rogers and Sorell (2000) and papers in a special issue of *Filozofski vestnik* volume 24, issue 2 (2003).

8 Chatsworth A.10 and Harleian ms. 6083. Also relevant is Ms. 5297 (National Library of Wales).

9 For discussion of the history of the composition of *Elements of Law*, see Baumgold (2017, xi–xv).

10 Hobbes changes the material of chapter 9 between the English and Latin editions. Discussing the differences between these two chapters would go beyond the present confines of this introductory chapter, but the account that he provides in the latter coheres with his discussion in *De corpore* VI.

11 Edwin Curley suggests that the placement of the science of the just and unjust under natural philosophy reflects the order of presentation of *Leviathan* where chapters 14–15 on the laws of nature precede the generation of the commonwealth in chapter 17 (see Hobbes 1994a, 49 fn. 4). Such a reading, i.e., that the table reflects the presentation order of the *Leviathan*, also seems supported by a 17/27 May 1657 letter from François du Verdus to Hobbes where he takes the Table as a reason to encourage Hobbes to publish more in the various subjects listed on it and not as providing insight into the structure of Hobbes's philosophy: "I was recently reading your 'Table of the several subjects of knowledge' in your *Leviathan*: wouldn't you like to give us this entire body of philosophy? If you gave us an outline plan of treatises on architecture, navigation, optics" (Hobbes 1994b, 471–2).

12 Parkin (2007) treats the reception of Hobbes's civil philosophy and views on religion in England from 1640–1700. See also Mintz (1962).

13 Hobbes's claims in *De corpore* VI are discussed in Hattab (Chapter 1, this volume) and Adams (Chapter 4, this volume).

14 Though see Tarlton (1998) for criticism of Taylor, arguing that there is no single coherent "Taylor thesis," and of the reception of Taylor's thesis by scholars.

15 This introduction primarily concerns strategies for how the parts of Hobbes's philosophy fit together, not as much the content within those parts. There has been *significant* disagreement concerning the Taylor–Warrender debate, and to discuss it more would go beyond what is possible in this space. More recently, Martinich (1992, 71ff) argues for a divine

command approach, but Martinich also incorporates conduciveness to self-preservation as necessary to determining whether an action is moral. See also Byron (2015). Green (Chapter 10, this volume) argues that Hobbes does need to incorporate claims about divine command to undergird the moral claims he seeks to provide.

16 Although for different reasons, Kavka (1986) also views Hobbes's civil philosophy as independent from other parts of his philosophy. Kavka argues that Hobbes *claimed* to have provided a deductive system but failed to do so, stating that "[i]t was only by conflating logical deduction and causal reasoning that Hobbes could have dreamed of a purely deductive politics derived solely from definitions and the principle of motion" (1986, 8). Beyond issues of method, Kavka furthermore asserts that "Hobbesian political theory need not be committed to materialism, mechanism, or even determinism; it can remain neutral with respect to these ontological and metaphysical positions" (1986, 11).

17 For example, see *De corpore* XXIV.9 (EW I.386) for the difference between geometry (*De corpore* Part III) and natural philosophy (*De corpore* Part IV).

18 For a similar point, see Malcolm (2002, 147). This is related to, but is more general than, Peters's (1956, 171) objection that premises in psychology or natural philosophy contain only descriptions and therefore no prescriptions can be derived from them.

19 Hobbes countenances this ability to "consider as" in many contexts throughout his philosophy. He famously describes the laws of nature by saying that "if we consider the same Theoremes, as delivered in the word of God, that by right commandeth all things; then they are properly called Lawes" (Hobbes 2012, 242; 1651, 80), and he likewise defines 'person' using "consider as": "A PERSON, is he, whose words and actions are considered, either as his own, or as representing the words or actions of an other man, or of any other thing to whom they are attributed, whether Truly or by Fiction. When they are considered as his owne, then is he called a Naturall Person: And when they are considered as representing the words and action of another, then is he a Feigned or Artificiall Person" (Hobbes 2012, 244; 1651, 80). He also uses this device in mathematics, e.g., a line is a "body considered without its breadth" (EW VII.20), and in natural philosophy. In the latter, for example, if interested only in the annual path of the Earth, we "consider" it as if it were a single point (OL I.98–9), but if interested in the Earth's diurnal motion, we consider it as a body moving with a "simple circular motion" such that all its points describe the circle that the body makes (OL IV.252). I link "consider as" to Hobbes's account of humans' natural state in Adams (2019b, 12–13).

20 Jesseph (2016) explores the roles played by endeavor in different parts of Hobbes's philosophy.

Part I

First Philosophy, Mathematics, and Natural Philosophy

1

Hobbes's Unified Method for *Scientia*

HELEN HATTAB

Hobbes locates the study of humans within the natural world. Not just our physical actions, but our passions, our desires, our willings and to a certain extent, our thoughts and deliberations, are determined by the same natural laws as everything else. To the degree that there is human freedom, it cannot involve actions that lie outside the deterministic course of nature. Hobbes was decried as a radical thinker in his day and is still considered a materialist atheist. A major source of resistance to his philosophy stemmed from the implications of his theory of human nature for the foundations of ethics and politics. How can we be held to moral laws without a personal divinity to hand these down, punish, and reward us, and without free will to overcome the animal drives nature determines in us? How can we secure political authority and stability if the right to govern does not derive from a providential God? Hobbes has an ingenious solution to this problem which is well-studied. If you know anything about Hobbes, you probably know that he was an early proponent of the social contract theory of government. On this theory, political authority derives from the voluntary transfer of the power each person has, by natural law, to preserve and protect his or her life to a commonly recognized sovereign. Hobbes's political theory influenced Benedict de Spinoza, John Locke, and beyond, and his contribution to politics is well researched. Less well-studied is the relationship between Hobbes's view of natural science and his political theory. A major source of confusion lies in his formal presentation of his philosophical and scientific method. Though Hobbes claims that it generates both types of knowledge, his works on physics and politics seem to employ different methods. This chapter examines the role and nature of Hobbes's method for science in its historical context to clarify how his theoretical and practical philosophy are unified.

A Companion to Hobbes, First Edition. Edited by Marcus P. Adams.

1.1 Method, Science, and Hobbes's Project

Hobbes's politics is commonly studied independently of his method and science. This is odd because, despite writing political works that can be read independently, Hobbes claims in the preface to his comprehensive work, *Elements of Philosophy* (EW I.viii–xi) to be the first to develop a *scientia civilis* (civil science), boasting that by securing true foundations, he has done the same for moral and political philosophy as Galileo Galilei did for physics and William Harvey for medicine. In the previously published preface to *De cive* (EW II.x–xi), Hobbes traces the source of all contention and bloodshed to the absence of a scientific foundation for morals among predecessors, a point he repeats in *De corpore*, Part I of his *Elements*: "therefore, from the not knowing of civil duties, that is from the want of moral science, proceed civil wars, and the greatest calamities of mankind" (EW I.10). To illustrate the source of prior philosophers' failure to provide this foundation, Hobbes likens the traditional justification of political authority by appeal to the divine to the ancient fable in which Ixion, a mortal, embraces the goddess Juno (EW II.xiii). His point is that past philosophical attempts to marry human judgments and apprehensions about justice to the divine are illusory. This approach can only beget empty, inconsistent opinions that produce political instability and bloodshed.

In his Dedication of *De corpore* to the Earl of Devonshire, Hobbes employs another analogy to make a similar point about Scholastic Aristotelian philosophy, characterizing it as the Empusa of the Athenian comic poet: "there entered a thing called *school divinity*, walking on one foot firmly, which is Holy Scripture, but halted on the other rotten foot, which the Apostle Paul called *vain*, and might have called *pernicious philosophy*" (EW I.xi). Hobbes proposes to exorcise this monster by distinguishing

> between the rules of religion, that is, the rules of honoring God, which we have from the laws, and the rules of philosophy, that is, the opinions of private men; and to yield what is due to religion to the Holy Scripture, and what is due to philosophy to natural reason. And this I shall do, if I but handle the Elements of Philosophy truly and clearly, as I endeavor to do. (EW I.x–xi)

He then announces the aim of this work:

> I intend now, by putting into a clear method the true foundations of natural philosophy, to fright and drive away this metaphysical *Empusa*; not by skirmish, but by letting in the light upon her. (EW I.xi)

To build a political structure that will prove stable and lasting, one first requires true foundations of natural philosophy. These are to be treated methodically, unadulterated by the mixing in of myths, fables, and religious writings. From the start, Hobbes presents his new moral and civil science as dependent on the true foundations his method provides for natural philosophy. Method is crucial to Hobbes's project.

Hobbes's purging of the non-natural from philosophy in order to base practical philosophy on the scientific foundations of natural philosophy does not imply that he rejects all religion and theology – note that the rotten foot is the philosophical one! Rather his colorful analogies trace the lack of progress in practical philosophy to the *intermingling* of philosophy and religion. A methodical treatment of the true foundations of natural philosophy required for a moral science thus necessitates that one first cordon off the domain of philosophical activity, which *De corpore*'s Epistle to the Reader describes as "the natural reason of man, busily flying up and down among the creatures, and bringing back a true report of their order, causes and effects" (EW I.xiii). Fencing in natural reason prevents it from encroaching on and contaminating neighboring territories. The goal is not to obliterate religion, but to confine philosophy to what Hobbes regards as its proper domain, and thus to contain and purify both. He even suggests that philosophy (which, like René Descartes, he takes to reside confusedly within us) requires a method that keeps the contemplative order separate but parallel to the order of creation.[1]

Hobbes's characterizations of his project, reveal that his formal definition is designed to put Philosophy, and its practitioners, in their place. Philosophy is,

> such knowledge of effects or appearances, as we acquire by true ratiocination from the knowledge we have first of their causes or generation: And again of such causes and generations as may be from knowing their first effects. (EW I.2)

As Hobbes acknowledges afterward, this is a narrower definition than was typical of contemporaneous philosophers. It also equates natural reasoning with ratiocination, which Hobbes characterizes narrowly as computation, a mental composition and resolution of conceptual units which I discuss in the final section. Armed with his definition Hobbes deduces from it that the subject of philosophy is delimited to,

> every body of which we can conceive any generation, and which we may, by any consideration thereof, compare with other bodies, or which is capable of composition and resolution; that is to say, every body of whose generation or properties we can have any knowledge. (EW I.10)

Philosophy, and its activity of ratiocination, is thus confined to the domain of material things. Angels, being immaterial, are excluded, as is Theology, since God is unchanging and eternal. The narrowing of natural reasoning to computation also excludes subjects that rely on other forms of knowing from the domain of Philosophy. Hobbes thus rules history, revealed knowledge, doubtful doctrines like astrology, as well as the doctrine of God's worship out of bounds (EW I.10–11).

In sum, Hobbes places two constraints on philosophers that shape their method. First, he limits them to reasoning, which, equated with computation, brings in the second constraint. Such computation applies only to body, of which there are only two kinds: natural bodies, which are works of nature and the subject of natural philosophy, and the Commonwealth, an artificial body, made by the wills and agreement of humans, which is the subject of civil philosophy. To understand Hobbes's method for attaining a civil science that rests on true foundations, one must recognize that his natural philosophy encompasses both less and more than Scholastic natural philosophy and absorbs what we call STEM today. Chapter IX of the English edition of the *Leviathan* divides natural philosophy into knowledge of the consequences of the common accidents of bodies, and of the consequences of their qualities. The former is subdivided into First Philosophy,

Geometry, Arithmetic, Astronomy, Geography, Engineering, Architecture, and Navigation. The consequences of bodily qualities are studied by Physics, which is further subdivided into Sciography, Meteorology, Optics, Music, and Logic.[2] Unlike *De corpore*, the *Leviathan* places Ethics, and Astrology, Poetry, Rhetoric (all three of which *De corpore* excludes from Philosophy) plus what Hobbes calls "the science of the just and unjust" under Physics (2012, 130–1; 1651, 40–1). The *Leviathan* limits civil philosophy to knowledge of the consequences of "politic bodies" (2012, 130–1; 1651, 40–1) whereas *De corpore* further subdivides it into ethics, which treats of human dispositions and manners, and politics, "which takes cognizance of their civil duties" (EW I.11).

Regardless of which classification one follows, for Hobbes, natural philosophy consists in 1) knowledge of first principles, i.e., foundational definitions that provide the starting points for scientific demonstration (First Philosophy), 2) pure and applied mathematics, and 3) a varying collection of crafts useful to human life. Most Scholastics placed First Philosophy under metaphysics, and the rest either under pure and mixed mathematical sciences or under the arts.[3] Civil philosophy, for Hobbes, primarily concerns the commonwealth and the duties plus rights of its subjects. Ethics straddles natural and civil philosophy; insofar as it studies human manners and dispositions as qualities of human bodies it belongs to physics, insofar as it draws from them the rights and duties of subjects, it belongs to the new civil science. Contrary to our natural/normative divide, Hobbes places theoretical and practical philosophy on a continuum, with ethics in mid-range. Scholastic metaphysics, as the science of being *qua* being, and parts of Aristotelian natural philosophy that challenge theology, like the study of the first cause of motion, biology, and the soul (*qua* principle of life) have been purged.[4]

With the Empusa exorcised, philosophy confined to the study of body and traditional metaphysics firmly under religious control, Hobbes then broadens natural philosophy to include mathematical sciences. Thus the reach of philosophical ratiocination is extended to crafts, like mechanics and engineering, that renaissance philosophers had elevated to *scientiae*.[5] Like his contemporaries, Hobbes defines *scientia* as knowledge consisting in deductive proofs known as syllogisms. In the ideal type of scientific syllogism, which takes the form of *propter quid* demonstrations discussed in Aristotle's *Posterior Analytics*, one reasons deductively from a premise that identifies the cause or explanatory factor (typically a definition), to its effect or consequence. Aristotle developed rules for constructing logically valid syllogisms, which the beginning of *De corpore* like most contemporaneous textbooks, covers summarily. Hobbes follows textbooks that combine Aristotelian and Ramist logic, adding a chapter on Method to his Logic. There he makes the standard claim that the deduction of causes through valid syllogistic reasoning is what scientific knowledge aims at:

> The end of science [*scientia*] is the demonstration of the causes and generations of things; which if they be not in the definitions, they cannot be found in the conclusion of the first syllogism, that is made from those definitions; and if they be not in the first conclusion, they will not be found in any further conclusion deduced from that. (EW I.82)

In *Leviathan* Hobbes spells out how a methodical process of connecting names into propositions, and propositions into deductive proofs known as syllogisms, results in *scientia*. Reason, he says, is:

> attayned by Industry; first in apt imposing of Names; and secondly by getting a good and orderly Method in proceeding from the Elements, which are Names, to assertions made by Connexions of one of them to another; and so to Syllogisms, which are the Connexions of one Assertion to another, til we come to a knowledge of all the Consequences of names appertaining to the subject in hand; and that is it, men call SCIENCE. (2012, 72; 1651, 21)

When Hobbes claims to have inaugurated a *scientia civilis*, he means a body of conclusions about the commonwealth that can be deduced syllogistically from methodically attained premises that ultimately derive from definitions. Hence, though I will follow convention and translate "*scientia*" and the corresponding verb, "*scire*," as "scientific knowledge" and "to know scientifically," I do not thereby speak of experimental science in our sense. For other forms of knowing, which Hobbes labels *cognitio*, I employ the broader term "cognition."

1.2 Hobbes's Method for Scientific Knowing

With the domain of philosophical ratiocination clearly delimited, Hobbes in Chapter 6 of *De corpore* derives what every method has in common from his definition of Philosophy. This generic definition of method superficially echoes Scholastic views of scientific demonstration.

> Therefore, the *Method* of philosophizing is *the shortest investigation of the effect through causes having been cognized, or of the causes through the effect having been cognized.* We are then said to *know* a certain effect *scientifically* [*scire*] *when we both cognize its causes* [*and*] *that they are; and in which subject they inhere, and in which subject they introduce the effect, and in what manner they make it.* Thus, scientific knowledge is τοῦ διότι or of causes; every other cognition which is called τοῦ ὅτι is sense, or imagination or memory remaining from sense. (Hobbes 1999, 57–8; OL I.58–9, translations of this edition are mine)[6]

τοῦ διότι is Aristotle's term for *propter quid* demonstrations whereby effects/consequences are syllogistically deduced from causes/reasons. Methodical philosophizing thus produces *scientia*, i.e., valid causal syllogisms, in the shortest way possible. Hobbes signals that though the final demonstration will be *propter quid*, the methodical process of arriving at such proofs can take its starting point either from the cognition of causes and deduce their effects, or from the cognition of an effect, and deduce its (possible) causes.[7] The mere non-deductive cognition of something lies outside the domain of scientific knowledge although, as Hobbes highlights, ratiocination or computation must begin from the cognition we acquire by sensation that there is an object. Knowing the nature of its causes, that the causes exist, where they reside, and where/how they generate the effect, however, cannot be attained by experience alone. It requires syllogistic demonstration, which Hobbes regards as computation. Hobbes broadens *scientia* by applying scientific reasoning to the commonwealth, as well as natural bodies, thus yielding conclusions in practical philosophy that have the same status as knowledge of the natural world. But his *scientia* is narrower than our science since experiential forms of cognition, though they provide starting points for syllogisms, are not themselves part of scientific knowledge. The latter affirms prior Aristotelian views, the former breaks with it.[8]

Hobbes also replaces the starting points of syllogistic deductions typical of Scholastic scientific knowledge. Scholastic principles are universal claims about existing things known by means other than proof and consist in fundamental truths about the most general kinds of being. These include definitions of corporeal versus incorporeal substance that are further qualified to yield definitions of animate versus inanimate corporeal substances, and eternal versus finite incorporeal substances, and so on down the line. At each level, one can, taking the appropriate definition as one's first premise, then demonstrate *propter quid* the properties that are implied by the essence captured by the definition of that species of being. Accordingly, from the definition of a human being as a rational animal, one can infer that humans are both mortal and capable of understanding. From such properties contained in the essence of a human being one then deduces further effects. There were, naturally, many obstacles to doing this in practice as well as doubts raised about the accurate capturing of essences by definitions. However, in principle, one could, by syllogizing, eventually deduce a comprehensive, consistent structure of true conclusions about the natural world, all ultimately derived from the same first principles. Hobbes's characterizations of scientific knowledge and method signal that he retains this structure but rejects the existing foundation as untrue. Removing Scholastic metaphysics, and incorporeal substance from the domain of philosophy allows Hobbes to replace Scholastic definitions based on genera and species of substance with a "true foundation," consisting in definitions of geometrical objects.[9]

Hobbes further rejects Euclid's definitions of the simplest geometrical entities, like point and line, instead embracing genetic, or generative definitions given by Hero of Alexandria.[10] So, Hobbes not only proposes a different foundation from which syllogistic reasoning begins, but his foundational definitions or first principles are not standard Euclidean definitions, like the definition of a line as a breadthless length. Hobbes could be averting the criticism that the most basic Euclidean definitions do not capture the essential properties of geometrical entities. If Hobbes's foundational geometrical definitions correspond to essential features of bodies, as did the first principles of the Scholastic structure of scientific knowledge, then his move is to recast essences as procedures or recipes for the production of an object.[11] Following Hero, the proper definition of a geometrical object spells out how it is constructed: "a line is made by the motion of a point, superficies by the motion of a line, and one motion by another motion, & c" (EW I. 70–1). Based on such generative definitions, the passages quoted suggest that Hobbes regards scientific knowledge as a unified structure of conclusions ultimately deducible from generative definitions of geometry. As he outlines, one begins with lines or lengths generated from points in motion, and surfaces generated from long bodies – which once demonstrated, then allow one to construct definitions of the more complex phenomena of the science of motion, itself produced by the effects of one body's motion on other bodies. Next, the science of motion provides the starting points for demonstrating the phenomena of physics, which are produced by the motions of the parts of bodies, including our sense organs. Likewise, *De corpore* suggests that having arrived at definitions of human passions, we can progress all the way up to civil science. Hence demonstrative knowledge of all sciences, including politics, will necessarily be generated from geometrical foundations and form a unified whole.

Interpreting Hobbes's method as this kind of a generative construction fits one sense of "demonstration." When discussing the proper method of demonstration in teaching, which he holds to be the same as the method of discovery, Hobbes invokes the original sense that "demonstration" had in ancient geometry:

> that which the Greeks called ἀποδέιξις, and the Latins *demonstratio*, was understood by them for that sort only of ratiocination, in which, by the describing of certain lines and figures, they placed the thing they were to prove, as it were before men's eyes, which is properly ἀποδεικνύειν, or to *shew* by the figure; (EW I.86)

If scientific knowledge consists in demonstrations that prove effects from definitions specifying generative causes, in this geometrical sense of making objects visible (concretely or in the imagination) through construction, then Hobbes's hierarchical structure of knowledge appears as a successive placing before our eyes of ever more complex objects that are built up from previously shown objects, just as a square is constructed from four lines, and the lines, in turn, are drawn by moving a point.[12] The Commonwealth would sit at the pinnacle of this hierarchy, as the most complex object, built up of human bodies (themselves complex bodies generated by motions) whose passions and desire for peace make a social contract necessary. Two mechanical analogies suggest that Hobbes employs demonstration in this sense to methodically arrive at civil science. But since only artificial bodies of geometry and politics can be thus constructed this would imply that either physics lies outside of science, or Hobbes has distinct methods for theoretical and practical science.[13] I argue, instead, that Hobbes has one method, but not a constructive method in this sense.

Hobbes's use of mechanical analogies give the impression that civil science employs a method of mechanical construction at odds with method in physics. In *De cive*, Hobbes claims to have started from the matter of civil government "and thence proceeded to its generation and form, and the first beginning of justice. For everything is best understood by its constitutive causes" (EW II.xiv). Immediately thereafter he makes an analogy to a watch, which one must take apart to understand the matter, shape, and motion of the wheels. Similarly,

> so to make a more curious search into the rights of states and duties of subjects, it is necessary, I say, not to take them insunder, but yet that they be so considered as if they were dissolved; that is, that we rightly understand what the quality of human nature is, in what matters it is, in what not, fit to make up a civil government, and how men must be agreed amongst themselves that intend to grow up into a well-grounded state. (EW II.xiv)

In *Leviathan*, the Commonwealth or State is likened to an artificial person, which one can dissect into its component parts by analogy to the parts of an automaton. This analogy likewise suggests a kind of reverse-engineering methodology not possible with natural phenomena. Here too Hobbes employs Aristotelian notions of a form that is generated, and the matter, or constitutive causes, which once extracted through resolution, can then be recomposed in the correct way. A common interpretation equates Hobbes's reference to resolution in this passage with his method of analysis in *De corpore* and aligns the re-composition with synthesis. Next I show that analysis and synthesis in *De corpore* are not a material resolution and re-composition. Here I argue that these analogies are rhetorical.

The automaton analogy precedes Hobbes's description of the structure of his work, the *Leviathan*. He frames it in terms of the four causes familiar to his Aristotelian-schooled readers. First he treats of human beings, the matter, i.e., material cause, of this artificial body. Next, Hobbes invokes how the commonwealth is made by covenants, which to his readers would evoke its efficient cause. The last two sections of the book explain what a Christian commonwealth is and what the kingdom of darkness is, i.e., the final and formal causes (2012, 18; 1651, 2). Hobbes's automaton analogy is a rhetorical visualization for the organic structure of his work, informing readers that he will present his theory starting from material and efficient causes and concluding with final and formal causes of the Commonwealth. Just as he does not thereby commit himself to a method that employs Aristotelian causes, his mechanical analogies do not commit him to a method of geometrical construction. Indeed, Hobbes's *De corpore* clarifies that knowing scientifically is to syllogize from cause to effect.

The section that follows Hobbes's etymological tracing of "demonstration" back to the ancient Greek geometrical term reveals a different sense of "demonstration":

> It is proper to methodical demonstration, First, that there be a true succession of one reason to another, according to the rules of syllogizing delivered above.
>
> Secondly, that the premises of all syllogisms be demonstrated from the first definitions. (EW I.87)

The formal definition of "demonstration" Hobbes gives just before he invokes its ancient origins confirms that it is "a syllogism, or series of syllogisms, derived and continued, from the definitions of names, to the last conclusion" (EW I.86). Hobbes's recounting of the ancient geometrical sense of "demonstration" is thus a historical side bar to motivate putting geometry at the foundation of scientific knowledge by appeal to the ancients. Once geometry makes visible its foundational definitions, scientific reasoning proceeds syllogistically.

The rhetorical purposes of the watch and automaton analogies, combined with Hobbes's formal definitions of scientific knowledge and "demonstration" caution against taking mechanistic resolution and re-composition as Hobbes's method for civil science.[14] Nonetheless, *De corpore's* analogy between all definitions and geometrical ones reinforces the impression that Hobbes's method of demonstration is one of construction:

> But definitions of things, which may be understood to have some cause, must consist of such names as express the cause or manner of their generation, as when we define a circle to be a figure made by the circumduction of a straight line in a plane, & c. (EW I.81–2)

But Hobbes also affirms the Scholastic view that principles are indemonstrable, adding that there are no principles aside from definitions (EW I.80, 82). Properly speaking, definitions are *not* demonstrated; hence their generation is *not* scientific ratiocination or computation. So, though one might make visible the definitions of natural and civil philosophy in a way that parallels geometrical construction of a figure, this is only a demonstration in a loose, analogous sense. Hobbes's analogies thus do not support the bifurcation into a demonstrative method of construction in civil science *versus* the physicist's method.

With this confusion removed, can we now articulate a unified method that would legitimize Hobbes's claim to inaugurate a moral *science* based on the true foundations of natural philosophy? Even having restricted scientific knowledge derived from the primary geometrical definitions to Hobbes's narrow sense of *propter quid* demonstrations, this remains challenging. If the success of Hobbes's project rests on the capacity of his method to provide a true foundation of definitions or principles about universal causes from which, through a unified chain of syllogisms, ever more specific and complex effects are deduced, then it seems to fail. Notwithstanding that all scientific knowledge is knowledge of bodies, there are key differences between the aspects of body that each individual science takes as its object.

Natural philosophy scientifically knows what follows from the accidents of natural bodies whereas civil philosophy scientifically knows what follows from the accidents of the artificial body that is the commonwealth. Within natural philosophy, geometry, which lies at the base of the hierarchy in *De corpore*, takes as its object the accidents common to all bodies whereas physics takes as its object qualities, i.e., accidents of bodies as sensed by humans. This implies that the application of Hobbes's generic method varies with object. As scholars have long realized, Hobbes's actual procedure in physics differs from that of geometry and civil science since we are not privy to the underlying causes of the bodily qualities we sense.[15] In physics one cannot define a quality by mentally constructing it, as one does with the generative definition of a square or when one imagines a commonwealth coming into being. Rather one must begin from observed effects, like the reddish hue of the setting sun or the passion of joy we feel when we watch it, and reason hypothetically to their possible causes. Since physics lies in the middle of the hierarchy of scientific knowledge providing the bridge between geometry and practical philosophy, *if* one assumes that unity means the sciences present a unified content, via an axiomatic-deductive method whereby all their conclusions trace back through a seamless chain of deduction to the same foundational definitions, then the divergent methodical procedure necessitated by the objects of physics appears to disrupt the unity of the whole.

In the face of these problems, one can 1) deny that Hobbes maintains a unity of theoretical and practical philosophy or 2) affirm a looser unity by denying that it is conditioned upon an axiomatic-deductive method. Advocates of 2) present evidence of Hobbes's commitment to a non-deductivist unity. I draw on two recent views of this unity to propose a third. 2a) reads Hobbes's sciences as unified not by a systematic content ultimately deduced from first principles, but by a common "demonstrative" method analogous to the geometrical method of construction.[16] This strikes me as the correct strategy; however, though one finds procedures resembling constructions throughout Hobbes's works, they cannot, as per his formal definitions constitute *scientific* demonstrations. Hence though they loosely connect practical philosophy with geometrical procedures, they cannot account for a moral *science* in Hobbes's sense. 2a) also excludes physics from science. 2b) holds that Hobbes maintains the possibility of scientifically deducing a consistent body of theoretical and practical knowledge from first principles but includes alternative starting points and methods for non-philosophers to gain knowledge of practical philosophy.[17] This too is promising, but to the extent that there is one method, it is an ideal that does no work. In practice, Hobbes proceeds as though physics and politics are independent domains with their own methods.

Despite these problems, 2) is better supported than 1). Hobbes's view of scientific knowledge and generic definition of method point to one type of cognitive activity that constitutes scientific knowledge of all philosophical subjects. Regardless of whether one studies natural or artificial bodies, starts from cognitions of causes or effects, formal definitions or true cognitions attained by introspection, the process of methodical computation that charts the shortest route between causes and effects should be identical. This fits Hobbes's aim of inaugurating a civil *science* to exorcise the Scholastic philosophy Empusa. Absent a unity of method for science, the boundaries between practical philosophy and religion will blur as non-scientific forms of cognition can then be invoked to confuse the rights and duties of subjects. Hobbes's approach to identifying and removing the source of civil strife then falls apart. Hence overall 2) is the correct approach. I now draw on Hobbes's context to propose a third variation, 2c).

Key is recognizing that Hobbes's generic definition of method is just that. He next distinguishes method into what his contemporaries call universal method versus a method of proof for solving particular problems, known as particular method. Universal method was typically a preliminary hierarchical ordering of the concepts and definitions required for the discovery or teaching of knowledge of a subject, or both. It is distinct from method as a set of rules for scientific proofs, as found in Aristotle's *Posterior Analytics*.[18] Nonetheless, the two methods go hand in hand since universal method provides the systematic framework within which one generates different kinds of proofs by the particular method. This provides a third kind of unity for *all* scientific knowledge, rooted in method, with universal method providing a hierarchically ordered set of principles and definitions one requires as starting points for the deductive arguments one then makes in different domains to answer particular questions. Interpretation, 2c), allows for one computational activity that unifies all the sciences: namely, the rules of syllogistic reasoning for making valid *propter quid* demonstrations once one has the true principles, and applies the relevant definitions to the problem at hand. But to avoid willy-nilly attempts at deduction from any definitions, Hobbes's method includes a preliminary methodical resolution of ideas and orderly composition into definitions, starting from the simplest concepts of geometry. This ensures unity at the level of first principles and the definitions one is permitted to take as starting points for scientific demonstrations at each level of inquiry. 2c) has been overlooked because just as Hobbes uses "demonstration" equivocally, he characterizes both activities as "computation" and labels methodical procedures that make up both the ordering computation and the syllogizing computation as analysis and synthesis.[19] The two branches of method have thus been confused for one. I now disentangle them.

1.3 Analyses and Syntheses Reinterpreted in Context

The bifurcation of philosophical method into a universal ordering of subject matter and a particular method of demonstration was commonplace in the logic textbooks of Hobbes's intellectual context (Hattab 2014). Hobbes makes a similar distinction: "Philosophers either seek scientific knowledge [*Scientia*] simpliciter or indefinitely, that is, having posed no certain question, they [seek to] scientifically know as much as they can ..." (Hobbes 1999, 59; OL I.60) in which case they employ a method that is strictly resolutive and analytical to arrive at universal notions compoundable by synthesis into definitions; or they seek to scientifically know

> the cause of some certain phenomena, or to at least discover something certain, such as whatever would be the cause of *light, heat, heaviness, a proposed shape*, and similar things; or in which subject a certain proposed accident would inhere, or for the purpose of a certain effect which is proposed to be generated from many accidents, which [ones] would conduce most powerfully towards it; or in which manner for the producing of a certain effect, the proposed particular causes ought to be conjoined. On account of this variety of things sought, sometimes the Analytic method, sometimes the Synthetic, and sometimes both is to be summoned. (Hobbes 1999, 59; OL I.60–1)

Method aimed at unqualified knowledge uses resolution/analysis and composition/synthesis in the Scholastic sense to holistically know as much as possible about body. Here computation is conceptual ordering, which Scholastic contemporaries distinguish into "analysis" and "synthesis." Hobbes next turns to the method for answering specific questions about the causes and inherence of particular accidents of body, which may be analytic, synthetic or both, depending on the inquiry. But here he uses the Scholastic terms pertaining to the ordering method for another set of operations, including syllogistic deductions. The second branch of his method gives Hobbes the flexibility to tailor the procedure for the shortest route between causes/explanations and effects/consequences to the context of inquiry. But Hobbes misleadingly uses "analysis" versus "synthesis" plus their derivatives to label procedures that take distinct forms in the particular method. I will thus refer to its operations as analysis2 and synthesis2.[20]

At root, analysis and synthesis, the basic operations of philosophical reckoning, are for Hobbes akin to mathematical subtraction and addition, respectively. Recall that he separates scientific knowledge from experience. Experience consists in sensing or remembering that there is something but cannot yield a causal explanation of it. Hobbes's example is that I see something approaching me and as it gets closer my senses detect a certain shape and motion. All I know by experiential cognition is that this thing exists; I don't know what it is and what its causes are. For that I require computation, which begins with something like subtraction, the mental operation of resolution or analysis. As when we subtract one number from another, analysis in the universal method separates out distinct features from the individual nature that encompasses them to arrive at the simple components of things – the elements. This happens in stages. As a person approaches me, I first separate out body from my perception of the individual, then the property of being animated, and finally rational, in the order of most universal to least[21] (EW I.4). For Hobbes these elements are not physical parts of a thing – resolution is not the mechanistic reduction of a watch or automaton into its component parts (EW I.67). Nor need the elements be linguistic entities, since we can ratiocinate without words (EW I.14). Analysis is a step by step conceptual separating out of general features, contained in an individual concept, from the concept as a whole (EW I.4–5).[22]

Hobbes later gives two examples to illustrate the strictly analytical method that yields the universal notions we need to attain unqualified knowledge of things. Both begin with an idea, from experience, as when we see something approaching, but now resolved from less general to more:

1) My idea of this square is resolved or analyzed into "plain, terminated with a certain number of equal and straight lines and right angles." I can then resolve or analyze these concepts further into the properties common to all material objects: "line," "plane," "angle," "straightness."
2) My conception of gold is resolved into ideas of "solid," "visible," "heavy," I can then further resolve or analyze these ideas into successively more general ones, like "extension" and "corporeity" until I arrive at the most general one: motion.

Once you have analyzed down to the most general, also the simplest, conceptual elements of your ideas you will have the causes of individual concepts of a square and gold. Hobbes's use of the term "cause" suggests that the resolution of gold is a mechanistic reduction into the physical parts of gold. For how can concepts *cause* our ideas? However, Hobbes uses "cause" in the Aristotelian sense of one or more explanatory factors, since he also claims that the causes of concrete names like "body" are abstract names like "extension."

The explanatory factors attained by resolution are common accidents of natural and artificial bodies. Recall that such accidents are the object of scientific knowledge for Hobbes. He explains:

> but we seek this itself, *what is an accident?* in which we seek that which we understand and not that which we should seek. For who does not always and in the same manner understand him who says any thing is extended, or moved, or not moved? But most men will have it be said that *an accident is something*, namely some part of natural things, when, indeed, it is no part of them. To satisfy these men, as well as may be, they answer best that define an *accident* to be *the manner by which any body is conceived;* which is all one and the same as if they should say, *an accident is that faculty of any body, by which it works in us a conception of itself.* (Hobbes 1999, 83; OL I.91)

An accident is not a real thing in the broad Scholastic sense of a *res*, which differs from substance in that it can only naturally exist by inhering in a substance. Rather accidents are the ways in which we conceive of bodies, as well as the faculties bodies possess to cause us to conceive of them in certain ways, e.g., our conception of a moving body plus the power of a body to cause us to sense motion. Basic accidents, like motion, need not be defined since everyone understands them. Hobbes refers to these self-evident ways of conceiving of bodies as "universals," "universal notions," and "simples," despite denying that universals have any existence beyond the names we apply to groups of individuals. Through definitions we acquire "an universal notion of the thing defined, representing a certain universal picture thereof, not to the eye, but to the mind"[23] (EW I.84). Definitions are thus key to the universal claims of science.

According to Hobbes, based on similarities among individual ideas, we signify common accidents with abstract names or universals, e.g., "extension" for similar sensations of bodies being extended, and "corporeity" for similar ideas of existing corporeal things. As long as we do not consider abstractions like extension and corporeity as existing apart from bodies, abstract names are used correctly and are the only means by which we can reason philosophically. Hence, just as we can analyze our concept of an individual square, piece of gold, and person into their conceptual parts, we can analyze the concrete name "body" into abstract names corresponding to the conceptual elements of the idea for which the name is a sign. For example, being extended is an accident we can subtract from our idea of an individual body. The corresponding abstract name "extension" is through resolution identified as a cause/explanation of the concrete name "body." That does not mean abstract extension is thereby reified; it is not something over and above the idea of particular bodies being extended. Nor is extension the cause of the bodies themselves. The abstract name "extension" is an explanatory factor that is revealed when we resolve the idea signified by the concrete name "body." Concrete names resolved into abstract names give us definitions. When a word stands for a compounded conception, like a person, a square or gold, rather than a simple conception, like motion,

> the definition is nothing but a resolution of that name into its most universal parts. As when we define man, saying *man is a body animated, sentient, rational*, those names, *body animated, & c.* are parts of that whole name *man*; (EW I.83)

But how does such an analysis into abstract terms, which combine to form definitional propositions, explain persons in the world, as experienced by us?

Since accidents are both the manner in which we conceive bodies, and the faculties by which bodies produce these conceptions in us, explanations of names obtained by resolution map on to bodily powers via the conceptual parts of ideas to which abstract names attach.[24] The strictly analytical method gives us the definitions of things by separating out the conceptual parts, or explanatory factors that make up our complex ideas of individuals. That is, the abstract name "humanity" is a sign for a conception of an individual body that can be resolved into accidents of being animated and being rational. Via similarity to past ideas of such bodies the abstract names of "animality" and "rationality" attach to these conceptual parts. This allows us to compound these names into propositions, including universal ones like "Every human is a rational animal." Hobbes claims that, without words, specifically, abstract names that stand as markers to remind us of past ideas of similar individuals, "our inventions perish, nor will it be possible for us to go on from principles beyond a syllogism or two, by reason of the weakness of the memory" (EW I.79). Employing the universal method, one combines abstract names into propositions by synthesis.

The particular method is instead a method of demonstration in which one employs synthesis2 to connect propositions by the rules for a valid syllogism. For example, from one's definition of humanity one can deduce a consequence of rationality that is fundamental to civil science:

> All human beings are rational animals.
> Rationality includes the capacity to make compacts.
> Therefore, human beings have the capacity to make compacts.

Hobbes ambiguously uses the terms "computation" and "synthesis" for both the process of methodically compounding the results of strict analysis into definitions, as well as the deductions by which we later connect propositions into syllogisms to answer particular questions. However, properly speaking, scientific knowledge involves syllogistic computation. The analysis and synthesis by which one arrives at definitions is preparatory to natural and moral science. The main feature of universal method for unqualified scientific knowledge is that the analysis of ideas/concrete names and combination of conceptual elements into definitions must proceed in the correct order, so that we resolve step by step from the most complex and particular, to the simplest and most universal ones until we arrive at the most universal explanatory factor signified by the abstract term "motion." We then synthesize definitions following the reverse order. Provided we know where on this hierarchy the definitions relevant to a particular inquiry are located, we can take short cuts when applying particular method.[25] The hierarchically ordered definitions attained by Hobbes's method for unqualified scientific knowledge supply the principles one deduces from in particular method. The latter can be analytic2, synthetic2 or a combination of both. In the methodical pursuit of particular scientific inquiries, computation is not the generation of ordered definitions that follows analysis into universal notions but fits Hobbes's identification of scientific knowledge with deductive reasoning.

This is clear from Hobbes's example of using analysis2 and synthesis2 to inquire after the subject of an accident.[26] The question is: In what subject is the splendor and apparent magnitude of the sun? The methodical steps are:

1) Analysis2: matter in general [*materia universa*] is divided into parts, e.g., object, medium and sentient or "by some other division which seems most suitable to the proposed matter [*rem*]" (EW I.76).
2) Synthesis2: "Next, the individual parts are to be examined according to the definition of the subject; and those which are not capable of those accidents are to be rejected" (EW I.76).
   i) For example, we rule out the body of the sun as the subject by discovering that the sun is greater than its apparent magnitude and hence that magnitude is not in the sun; we discover this through knowledge of optics:
   ii) "if the sun be in one determined straight line, and one determined distance, and the magnitude and splendor be seen in more lines and distances than one, as it is in reflection and refraction, then neither that splendour nor apparent magnitude are in the sun itself, and, therefore, the body of the sun cannot be the subject of that splendour and magnitude" (EW I.76).
   iii) We rule out the air and other parts by the same reasons until we are left with the sentient as the subject of the splendor of the sun.

Synthesis2 is not an aggregation of concepts/names into definitions but a methodical use of prior definitions that universal method orders as more basic (like principles of optics) and other bits of prior knowledge to narrow down possibilities and deduce the correct conclusion.[27] Physicists may require observations to exclude some possibilities whereas geometers or civil scientists may employ constructions and thought experiments before making deductions. These are differences in application, not in the essence of the particular method.

1.4 Conclusion

In this chapter, I have argued that Hobbes's philosophical method is integral to his project of separating philosophy and religion so as to put morals on a true scientific foundation. I have clarified what Hobbes means by "science," "method," and "demonstration," showing that the common attribution of a mechanistic method of resolution to Hobbes is incorrect. Building on recent views regarding whether Hobbes has a unified method for theoretical and practical philosophy I add to available interpretations by drawing on Hobbes's context. Like contemporaneous methods, Hobbes's method comprises a universal and a particular method. This distinction sheds light on how analysis and synthesis function in each branch of Hobbes's method in a way that serves to unify and place both theoretical and practical philosophy on a scientific basis.

Notes

1 Hobbes exhorts those with a sincere desire to be philosophers to "let your reason move upon the deep of your own cogitations and experience; those things that lie in confusion must be set asunder, distinguished, and every one stamped with its own name set in order; that is to say your method must resemble that of the creation. The order of the creation was, *light, distinction of day and night*, the *firmament*, the *luminaries, sensible creatures, man*; and after the creation, the *commandment*. Therefore, the order of contemplation will be, *reason, definition, space, the stars, sensible quality, man;* and after man is grown up, *subjection to command*" (EW I. xiii).
Hobbes echoes the appeal to two parallel, but separate, sources of insight into truth prevalent in seventeenth-century Calvinist Scholastic textbooks and Francis Bacon's work: the book of nature and Holy Scripture. Schmidt-Biggemann explains that for seventeenth-century Calvinist Scholastics, "Knowledge was understood as an inventory of the Revelation made available to humankind, as knowledge found in the Bible, History, and Nature. These three 'books' were the field of experience which according to God's creation plan is inventoried in knowledge" (Schmidt-Biggemann 2001, 394; translation mine).

2 Meteorology, Optics, and Music were all mixed mathematical sciences in the Scholastic tradition; logic was considered the instrument of philosophy, not part of natural philosophy proper.

3 See Hattab (2009, 93–8).

4 Hobbes's division most resembles that of early seventeenth-century Calvinist Scholastic textbooks in which "The framework of metaphysics was theological, not the other way around. Hence one counted metaphysical concepts within natural theology and in this way, natural philosophy and metaphysics were made broadly coextensive" (Schmidt-Biggemann 2001, 394, translation mine). For Hobbes, likewise, topics of traditional Aristotelian metaphysics, like the first cause, its eternity, and the immortality of the soul are relegated to Theology. Remaining metaphysical topics, like the nature of substance, its accidents and causation are absorbed into natural philosophy under Hobbes's First Philosophy.

5 Alessandro Piccolomini and subsequent Aristotelian mathematicians reclassified mechanics, the art of machines, which was traditionally considered a craft, as a mixed mathematical science (Hattab 2009, 93–8). Marcus Adams discusses Hobbes's treatment of physics as a mixed mathematical science, which following the Aristotelian tradition of such sciences, borrows its principles from the more fundamental science of geometry, and applies them to nature to deduce physical effects (Adams 2017, 84–6). This is also the sense in which Descartes considers his natural philosophy mathematical and mechanical and appears to be a common thread in the so-called early modern "mechanists" (Hattab 2009, 120–35, 2019).

6 The English edition misleads since it mistranslates *cognitio* with "science" in the last sentence, falsely implying that Hobbes counts experience as scientific knowledge: "But we are

then said to know any Effect, when we know, *that there be Causes of the same, and in what Subiect those Causes are, and in what Subiect they produce that Effect, and in what Manner they work the same*. And this is the Science of Causes, or as they call it of the διότι. All other science, which is called the ὅτι, is either Perception by Sense, or the Imagination, or Memory remaining after such Perception" (EW I.48–9).

7 This aspect of the generic method generates a persistent misreading of Hobbes's specific method of analysis as akin to the first phase of Jacopo Zabarella's *regressus*, which further gets conflated with a different sense of method in which Zabarella appeals to analysis. For example, see Hanson (1990, 587–626), MacPherson (1968, 25–9), Röd (1970, 10–15), Hungerland and Vick (1981, 25–7), Watkins (1973, 63–5), and Duncan (2003). J. Prins demonstrates how differences between Hobbes's and Zabarella's views on logic affect their views on method and scientific knowledge (Prins 1990, 26–46). Jesseph revised his view noting that any number of extant views on analysis and synthesis could have influenced Hobbes's (Jesseph 2004, 191–211). I show that the *regressus*, a proof enabling one to deduce a possible natural cause from observed effects, and then in turn, deduce that the possible cause is the actual cause of the natural effect, does not map onto Hobbes's method. Linking the two stems from substantive confusions between the *regressus* and what Zabarella calls "method as order." Zabarella only discusses "analysis" in the context of method as order. Wherever Hobbes gets this label, his sense of "analysis" is unrelated to the *regressus* and closer to later Scholastics uses than Zabarella's (Hattab 2014).

8 Most Scholastic Aristotelians accept Aristotle's claim at the start of *Nicomachean Ethics* that practical matters do not allow for the same precision as theoretical matters and hence require a distinct method (Aristotle 1984, 1730).

9 Zabarella notes, when we define mathematical entities, our definitions are advanced as principles "since they are heard and understood at the same time, and are known *per se*" (Zabarella 1597, 159). This is because things like "line" and "surface" are simple accidents, so the declaration of merely the word suffices to signify the essence. In other words, in mathematics, nominal and essential definitions of the object coincide; thus, in mathematics, one has a perfect definition once one obtains a nominal definition. This view was shared by seventeenth-century mathematicians, like the Jesuit Josephus Blancanus, who claims that most mathematical definitions bear the advantage of being both nominal and essential definitions: "when it is said that an equilateral triangle is one having three equal sides, at once you see the cause for both the name and the thing" (Blancanus 1996,181). Blancanus's work is cited in Marin Mersenne's early publications, making it likely that Hobbes was exposed to Blancanus's mathematical theory, via the Mersenne Circle. On this theory, definitions of mathematical objects carry the distinct advantage that their names concurrently tell you how the object is caused.

10 As Karl Schuhmann points out, both Hobbes and Spinoza appear to adopt Hero of Alexandria's generative approach to defining geometrical objects (Schuhmann 1987, 72).

11 Marcus Adams, following Pérez-Ramos, calls this "maker's knowledge" and argues that it constitutes the causal knowledge of *scientia* for Hobbes. On his interpretation, Hobbes's commitment to maker's knowledge accounts for why geometry and civil science are the only instances of science for Hobbes (Adams 2019, 2). Since both the geometer and the political philosopher construct their actual object, the same procedure can be applied in these domains, a procedure not available to the physicist who studies objects generated by natural processes.

12 Oddly, Hobbes's example to reveal the parts into which we resolve our conception of the individual nature of a square does not indicate that these parts would combine to generate the square in the same manner. "Plane" and "line" do not generate a square in the way a

point in motion generates a line. The same can be said of the definition of a triangle that Hobbes introduces in *De corpore*, I, vi.11 and again in *Leviathan* chapter 4 (2012, 54; 1651, 14). Adams (2014, 55–8) proposes a possible explanation for these two different kinds of definitions.

13 Adams gives the strongest defense of the first implied possibility, arguing that the simple conceptions at the foundation of both natural and political philosophy enable an ensuing construction in both that can be thought of as a demonstration, in the sense that Hobbes regards the construction of a geometrical figure, like a square, from its elements as a "demonstration." Adams concludes, "The structure, in civil philosophy and geometry, of thought experiment, definition by explication, and generative definitions allows Hobbes to see himself as providing a demonstration by synthesis in both cases" (Adams 2019, 19). Physics, which does not admit of this kind of geometrical demonstration, lies outside *scientia*. However, Adams also defends the view that physics counts as a science for Hobbes in the Aristotelian sense of a mixed mathematical science (Adams 2017, 84–6). Others embrace the second possibility pointing to inconsistencies in Hobbes's texts (see Sorell 1999).

14 Moreover, seventeenth-century works were rife with analogies between the natural world and machines. As I show in Hattab (2011), they often did not signal a commitment to what we mean by mechanistic explanations. For different seventeenth century senses of "mechanics" and "mechanical demonstration," see also Gabbey (1993) and Hattab (2019).

15 Sorell sums up the apparent tensions within Hobbes's texts (1999, 5–7, 14–15), and Adams (2014, 4–6) gives a good overview of the two previous main lines of interpretation, which he calls the "deductivist" and the "disjoint" accounts – neither resolves the tensions. Sorell's solution is to argue that civil science can be autonomous, resting solely on experiential foundations: "There is a philosophical or scientific understanding of the motions of the mind, arrived at from a prior acquaintance with principles given in physics. There is also a pre-scientific understanding, available to anyone who bothers to introspect and observe within himself the passions that move him" (Sorell 1999, 7). Adams is more sensitive to the fact that merely arriving at the same insights through alternative means does not qualify the result as *scientia* since a certain methodical procedure is integral to Hobbes's view of scientific knowledge. Adams argues that natural and civil philosophy are unified, on the one hand, by a common method, borrowed from geometry, for constructing their definitions, and on the other, in that each science borrows its principles from more fundamental science in the way that Aristotelian mixed mathematical sciences relied on the principles of pure mathematics (Adams 2014, 6–7).

16 Adams advances 2a) in combination with a looser structural unity than strict deductivism.

17 Sorell advocates 2b) arguing for "the autonomy thesis" (Sorell 1999, 7–13). Adams agrees that Hobbes is not committed to the idea that, for every context of inquiry, the same foundational principles constitute the absolute starting points for a hierarchically ordered series of deductions in each branch of philosophy: "if we understand Hobbes as holding that the simples for a science are determined by our explanatory needs – a materialism that does not privilege a single level for explanations – then we can understand why Hobbes grounds civil relations in human bodies apart from civil relations" (Adams 2019, 20). However, Adams also advocates 2a) arguing that the simple conceptions at the foundation of first philosophy and civil science are attained by a common method of thought experiments following fixed steps (Adams 2019, 19).

18 For example, Zabarella's seminal writings on logic divide method, taken broadly, into order and method properly speaking. The task of method in the proper sense is to lead us from a known thing to knowledge of another, unknown thing, as when we are led from substantial change to knowledge of prime matter or, from eternal motion to knowledge of an eternal

unmoved mover. By contrast, method as order does not cause us to infer one thing from another, but rather arranges (*disponere*) the things to be treated, as when the order of teaching demands that we first discuss the heavens and then the elements. It arranges the parts of a discipline. Order takes precedence because one must divide a discipline into parts, before one can articulate the method that will lead us from the known to the unknown that is sought within each part (Zabarella 1597, Vol. I, 139). Scholastic Protestant philosophers, known as systematics, took up Zabarella's teachings to develop a middle path between Aristotelian and Ramist systems of logic. Bartholomaeus Keckermann and Franco Burgersdijk wrote logic texts in this tradition that were influential in England at the time Hobbes wrote the first part of *De corpore*. They make the same distinction between universal and particular method as Zabarella (Burgersdijk 1626, 380; Keckermann 1613, 578–9). Burgersdijk, like Hobbes, claims that the order of discovery is the same as the order of teaching (Burgersdijk 1626, 380–1).

19 Sorell notes of analysis and synthesis "Neither method trades on specialized knowledge" and describes what Hobbes does in *Elements of Law* and *Leviathan* as follows: "One way in which the doctrine is supposed to improve on what we know already, is by imposing an order on it. From a mass of moral lore, common sense psychology, rudimentary information about law and the average citizen's knowledge of which people in the state hold offices of authority, Hobbes purports to sift out what is basic and what is not, what has to be known before other things are known ... Relations of dependence are thus revealed between truths that might otherwise seem on the level" (Sorell 1999, 11). He then adds: "But deductive or demonstrative order is not the whole story" (Sorell 1999, 12). Sorell recognizes that the purpose of analysis and synthesis is to order knowledge but reconstructs the rest of the story differently than I do. Adams likewise identifies two different levels at which Hobbes unifies sciences but takes as central a method of construction that enables the explanations one finds in the mixed mathematical sciences (Adams 2014, 7).

20 A third sense of analysis and synthesis found in logistica, Hobbes's geometrical method, lies outside the scope of philosophical method. William Sacksteder and Richard Talaska concur that, for Hobbes, analysis and synthesis do not function, in philosophy, as they do in geometry. Philosophical propositions arrived at, through analysis, are not, as in geometry, convertible in the corresponding synthesis (Sacksteder 1980, 131–46; 1988, 643–7; Talaska 1988, 207–37).

21 Keckermann and Burgersdijk likewise take the natural order to be one where what is most universal is both prior by nature and prior to us (Burgersdijk 1626, 380; Keckermann 1613, 582–3).

22 As Adams (2019) shows, one may have to employ thought experiments to get at the most universal features of all.

23 It is odd that Hobbes speaks of "universal notions" and "pictures" since universals appear to be neither real things nor abstract general ideas. He writes, "when a *living creature, a stone, a spirit*, or any other thing is said to be *universal*, it is not to be understood that any man, stone, & c. ever was or can be universal, but only that these words, *living creature, stone, & c.* are *universal names*, that is, names common to many things; and the conceptions answering them in our mind, are the images and phantasms of several living creatures or other things" (EW I.20). Such universal notions or pictures could consist in several particular ideas that we link to each other and to an abstract name.

24 Hobbes seems to assume that our universal notions mirror the underlying faculties of real things. He shares this assumption with the Portuguese Jesuit philosopher, Pedro da Fonseca, and early seventeenth-century German Scholastics influenced by Fonseca's metaphysics. Walter Sparn observes of the latter, "Their approach assumes ontologically that *subtilitas*

[acuteness/mental penetration] is suited to experienced things, i.e., there is kinship and internal reference to God, both among things and in relation to the human intellect, by virtue of which they [things] exist in it [the human intellect] as especially representable and abstractable into general concepts. In this manner, the first principles of their knowledge can be drawn from the proportional being of things" (Sparn 2001, 481, translation mine).

25 Notably, Hobbes claims that in moral science, instead of proceeding from the definitions of human will and passions obtained in physics, we can directly resolve our conception of an unjust action into "*fact against law*" and the notion of law into "the *command* of him or them that have *coercive power*" (EW I.74). Power will be further resolvable into the wills and passions of humans constituting the power, but these can be cognized by experience rather than demonstrated from the principles of physics. Hobbes also uses thought experiments to get clear on basic concepts, like space, possibly because simples are not resolvable. Adams draws an interesting parallel between the annihilation thought experiment in *De corpore* and the state of nature device to reveal the concept of equality (Adams 2019, 9–11).

26 It is, admittedly, less clear how one would deduce natural laws using this particular method. This requires more research.

27 Nor is analysis2 a resolution into universal notions since a medium and sentient body are both more specific than matter in general. However, it loosely resembles strict analysis in that it distinguishes something complex into parts.

References

Adams, Marcus P. 2014. *Mechanical Epistemology and Mixed Mathematics: Descartes's Problems and Hobbes's Unity*. PhD diss., University of Pittsburgh.

Adams, Marcus P. 2017. "Natural Philosophy, Deduction, and Geometry in the Hobbes-Boyle Debate." *Hobbes Studies* 30: 83–107.

Adams, Marcus P. 2019. "Hobbes's Laws of Nature in *Leviathan* as a Synthetic Demonstration: Thought Experiments and Knowing the Causes." *Philosopher's Imprint* 19 (5): 1–23.

Aristotle. 1984. "Nicomachean Ethics." In *The Complete Works of Aristotle*, Vol. II, edited by Jonathan Barnes. Princeton: Princeton University Press.

Blancanus, Josephus. 1996. "*De Mathematicarum Natura Dissertatio*, Appendix to *Aristotelis Loca Mathematica*. Translated by Gyula Klima." In *Philosophy of Mathematics and Mathematical in the Seventeenth Century*, edited by Paolo Mancosu, 178–212. New York: Oxford University Press.

Burgersdijk, Franco. 1626. *Institutionum Logicarum Libri Duo*. Leiden: Apud Abrahamum Commelinum.

Duncan, Stewart. 2003. *Hobbes: Metaphysics and Method*. PhD diss., Rutgers University.

Gabbey, Alan. 1993. "Descartes's Physics and Descartes's Mechanics: Chicken and Egg?" In *Essays on the Philosophy and Science of Descartes*, edited by Stephen Voss, 311–23. Oxford: Oxford University Press.

Hanson, Donald W. 1990. "The Meaning of 'Demonstration' in Hobbes's Science." *History of Political Thought* 11: 587–626.

Hattab, Helen. 2009. *Descartes on Forms and Mechanisms*. Cambridge: Cambridge University Press.

Hattab, Helen. 2011. "The Mechanical Philosophy." In *The Oxford Handbook of Philosophy in Early Modern Europe*, edited by Desmond Clarke and Catherine Wilson, 124–64. Oxford: Oxford University Press.

Hattab, Helen. 2014. "Hobbes' and Zabarella's Methods: A Missing Link." *Journal of the History of Philosophy* 52 (3): 461–85.

Hattab, Helen. 2019. "Descartes' Mechanical but Not Mechanistic Physics." In *The Oxford Handbook of Descartes and Cartesianism*, edited by Delphine Antoine-Mahut, Steve Nadler, and Tad Schmaltz, 124–37. Oxford: Oxford University Press.

Hobbes, Thomas. 1999. *De Corpore Elementorum Philosophiae Sectio Prima*, edited by Karl Schuhmann and Martine Pécharman. Paris: Librairie Philosophique J. Vrin.

Hobbes, Thomas. 2012. *Leviathan*. 3 vols., edited by Noel Malcolm. Oxford: Clarendon Press. [First published 1651].

Hungerland, Isabel C. and George R. Vick. 1981. "Misinterpretations of Hobbes: The Correct View." In *Thomas Hobbes Computatio Sive Logica*, edited by Aloysuis P. Martinich, Isabel C. Hungerland, and George R. Vick, 15–148. New York: Abaris Books.

Jesseph, Douglas. 2004. "Galileo, Hobbes, and the Book of Nature." *Perspectives on Science* 12 (2): 191–211.

Keckermann, Bartholomaeus. 1613. *Systema Logicae*. Hanover: Apud Haeredes Guilielmi Antonii.

MacPherson, C.B. 1968. "Introduction." In *Leviathan*, edited by C.B. MacPherson, 25–9. Hammondsworth: Penguin.

Prins, Johan 1990. "Hobbes and the School of Padua: Two Incompatible Approaches to Science." *Archiv für Geschichte de Philosophie* 72: 26–46.

Röd, Wolfgang. 1970. *Geometrischer Geist und Naturrecht, Methodengeschichtliche Untersuchungen zur Staatsphilosophie im 17. Und 18. Jahrhundert*. Munich: Verlag der Bayerischen Akademie der Wissenschaften.

Sacksteder, William. 1980. "Hobbes: The Art of the Geometricians." *Journal of the History of Philosophy* 18 (2): 131–46.

Sacksteder, William. 1988. "Notes and Discussions: Hobbes and Talaska on the Order of the Sciences." *Journal of the History of Philosophy* 26 (4): 643–7.

Schmidt-Biggemann, Wilhelm. 2001. "Die Schulphilosophie in den reformierten Territorien." In *Die Philosophie des 17.Jahrhunderts, Vol.4: Das Heilige Römische Reich Deutscher Nation Nord- und Mittelosteuropa*, edited by Helmut Holzehey and Wilhelm Schmidt-Biggemann, 390–474. Basel: Schwabe & Co AG Verlag.

Schuhmann, Karl. 1987. "Methodenfragen bei Spinoza und Hobbes: Zum Problem des Einflusses." *Studia Spinoziana* 3: 47–86.

Sorell, Tom. 1999. *Hobbes*. London: Routledge and Kegan Paul.

Sparn, Walter. 2001. "Die Schulphilosophie in den luthersichen Territorien." In *Die Philosophie des 17.Jahrhunderts, Vol.4: Das Heilige Römische Reich Deutscher Nation Nord- und Mittelosteuropa*, edited by Helmut Holzehey and Wilhelm Schmidt-Biggemann, 475–587. Basel: Schwabe & Co AG Verlag.

Talaska, Richard A. 1988. "Analytic and Synthetic Method according to Hobbes." *Journal of the History of Philosophy* 26 (2): 207–37.

Watkins, John N. 1973. *Hobbes's System of Ideas*. London: Hutchinson University Library.

Zabarella, Jacobus. 1597. *Opera Logica*. Cologne: Sumptibus Lazari Zetzneri.

2

The Stoic Roots of Hobbes's Natural Philosophy and First Philosophy

GEOFFREY GORHAM

While Hobbes's Natural Philosophy and First Philosophy are indebted to many sources, including fellow travelers (like Bacon and Galileo), late Aristotelians (like Zabarella and the Coimbra Commentators), and the Greeks themselves (like Aristotle and the Epicureans), the Stoic influence is not yet fully clear. To be sure, the impact of Classical and Renaissance Stoicism and Epicureanism upon Hobbes's political philosophy has been well documented (Springborg 2010; Tuck 1983). But the Stoic roots of his science and metaphysics have not been so thoroughly investigated. This imbalance is especially worth correcting since the Stoics and Hobbes both aimed to unify all the branches of knowledge. And as thoroughgoing materialists, they both endeavored to find a place for the apparent "incorporeals", space, time, causality, and God. One option was simply to deny the reality of these beings, and indeed Hobbes has often been characterized as an idealist about space and time, a subjectivist about the causal connection, and an atheist about God. But such characterizations are problematic insomuch as space, time, causality, and God all play important roles in Hobbes's decidedly realist program in natural philosophy. We can better appreciate the subtlety of Hobbes's metaphysics and science by tracing its Stoic pedigree.

The brief first part of this chapter identifies three main sources of the Stoic elements in Hobbes's philosophy: the early Christian-Stoic Tertullian, the modern "Neo-Stoic" school of Justus Lipsius, and the natural philosophers of the Cavendish Circle he frequented. The longer second part explores in detail the Stoic character of Hobbesian space, time, causality, and God, especially as these notions are employed in his natural philosophy. We shall see that Hobbes's metaphysical views, though quite unorthodox in his day, served to buttress his overall materialist, empiricist, and mechanist program in natural philosophy.

A Companion to Hobbes, First Edition. Edited by Marcus P. Adams.

2.1 Stoic Sources

A scholar of classical Greek language and literature throughout his life, Hobbes made translations of Thucydides in his thirties and Homer in his eighties (EW VIII; EW X). He mentions the "Stoa" as a major school of Athens in *Leviathan* XLVI (2012, 1056; 1651, 521) and endorses various insights of Cicero in *Leviathan* V (2012, 68; 1651, 31)[1] though he demurs from the Stoic thesis that all crimes are equal in *Leviathan* XXVII (2012, 466; 1651, 231). The famous Stoic doctrine of fate (*heimarmene*) is referenced in the Latin edition of Leviathan (*Leviathan*, Appendix I; 2012, 1152; OL III. 517). Of course, Stoicism was widely popular in the intellectual culture of sixteenth and seventeenth century Europe (see Barker and Goldstein 1984; Brooke 2012; Lagrée 1994; Long 2003).[2] So whence the particular influence on Hobbes's natural philosophy?

2.1.1 *Tertullian*

Perhaps the most direct Stoical impact on Hobbes was the second/third century Church Father Tertullian. A Roman Christian-Stoic, Tertullian insisted, like Hobbes, on the philosophical and Scriptural truth of materialism about God and finite souls. He endorsed the "probable opinion of the Stoics," which he explicitly adapted from Zeno, Cleanthes, and Chrysippus, that the soul is a corporeal "breath" or "spirit" that permeates the body. This is Hobbes's understanding of Scripture as well in *Leviathan* XLIV (2012, 612, 974; 1651, 303, 481). Like modern materialists, Tertullian argues that dualism makes soul–body interaction problematic since "there is nothing in common between things corporeal and things incorporeal."[3] Hobbes repeatedly invokes the authority of Tertullian in works that develop and defend the corporeal God doctrine (to be discussed later) in the 1660s. The first instance is the 1662 *Considerations Upon the Reputation of Thomas Hobbes*, a late volley in the long battle with Oxford mathematician John Wallis. Against the charge that his materialism is "atheism by consequence," Hobbes quotes verbatim from Tertullian's *De carne Christi*: "whatever is anything is a body of its kind. Nothing is incorporeal but that which has no being" (EW IV.429; Tertullian, *De carne Christi* xi; 1885, 531). Hobbes cites the same passage in two 1660's works that announce the corporeal God doctrine – the Latin *Leviathan* and the *Answer to Bramhall* – as well as in the 1680 *Historical Narration Concerning Heresy* (2012, 1228; OL III.561; EW IV.307, 383; EW IV.398). Although *De carne Christi* is thoroughly materialist, it does not pronounce directly on the corporeity of God. However, in the Latin *Leviathan*'s affirmation of that doctrine, Hobbes cites an additional Tertullian text, against the heretic Praxeas: "every substance is a body of its own kind" (2012, 1228; OL III.561). Hobbes slightly misquotes Tertullian, but he clearly has in mind the following passage, which explicitly asserts the corporeity of God: "Who will deny that God is body (*deum corpus esse*) although God is a spirit?" (*Ad Praxeas* vii, 1885, 602).[4] There are other texts Hobbes might have encountered in his careful reading of Tertullian that reflect even more closely his own formulation of corporeal theism.[5]

2.1.2 *Neo-Stoicism*

The "Neo-Stoical" school, founded by the sixteenth-century Flemish scholar Justus Lipsius, was immensely influential in Hobbes's day. Lipsius' many expositions of Stoic ethics and politics, especially *De constantia* (1584), were widely read and discussed.[6] He also composed several more rigorous summaries of Stoic metaphysics and natural philosophy such as *Physiologiae Stoicorum* (1604). Hobbes himself must have read Lipsius from a relatively young age since he quotes approvingly Lipsius' "true and proper commendation" from *De doctrina civili* (1604) in the biographical introduction to Hobbes's 1629 translation of Thucydides (EW VIII.32). It is possible that Hobbes also read the *Physiologiae*, whose first book comprises a detailed discussion of God's relation to the world according to Stoic doctrine. Like Hobbes, Lipsius rejects the pantheistic tendencies in Stoicism: "The Stoics say that God is the world itself, when strictly speaking he is its soul" (1604 I, 8, 16; see also 1604 II, 4, 78). And he also rejects the full corporeality of God (1604 I, 9, 20; see also 1604 II, 4, 75–8). Nevertheless, Lipsius' thorough scholarship would have provided abundant classical material to inspire and ground a modern materialist theology like Hobbes's.

Another Stoic doctrine discussed in detail in Lipsius' *De constantia*, namely fate, emerges early in one of Hobbes's most famous controversies, the protracted argument about liberty with Bishop Bramhall. Bramhall draws on distinctions made by Lipsius in his critique of Hobbes's views as Stoic or hyper-Stoic.[7] As usual, Hobbes protests that he has not derived his position "from the authority of any sect, but from the nature of things themselves" (EW IV.260–1; see also EW V.244–5). Bramhall's final word in the dispute, his 1658 "*Castigations*" of Hobbes, went unanswered. But the *Castigations* were published together with Bramhall's "Catching of Leviathan." He there again disparagingly saddles Hobbes with the epithet "Stoic": "If he had not been a professed Christian, but a plain Stoic ..." (1842–1844, IV.426).

2.1.3 *The Cavendish Circle*

Finally, there was fertile Stoic soil in Hobbes's closest intellectual community, the so-called Cavendish Circle, which comprised the prominent Cavendish brothers, William and Charles, Margaret (wife of William), Walter Charleton, Kenelm Digby, and others. Lipsius' thought was a major inspiration for the Circle. But the philosophy of Margaret Cavendish is especially pertinent in relation to Hobbes. Although she was explicitly opposed to Hobbes's mechanistic version of materialism, Cavendish's own thought was distinctly Stoic in ways similar to Hobbes's. In order to account for the immense diversity and activity in nature she found it necessary to demarcate self-moving "animate" from inert "inanimate" matter.[8] Like Hobbes's corporeal God, (as we will see below) her animate matter was thoroughly intermixed with inanimate matter and like Hobbes she tries to explain "how so fine, subtle and pure a part as the animate matter is can work upon so gross a part as the inanimate" (2001, 158).

She declined to deify animate matter, though she does say it is "a kind of God or Gods to the dull part of matter" (Cavendish 2001, xxi).[9] Hobbes and Cavendish are at bottom kindred Stoic spirits, though their systems diverge on the precise nature of material activity.

2.2 Stoic Roots

2.2.1 *Space and Body*

Hobbes and the Stoics agree that space and time are infinitely divided and extended, that space has the same dimensions as body, and that time has the successive being of motion. But these structural features are accepted by many philosophers, ancient and modern. I would like to focus on two more controversial ontological questions in Hobbes's philosophy of space and time: the reality of space independently of body and the reality of time independently of mind. The similar way that Hobbes and the Stoics struggled to meet these philosophical challenges is testimony to the affinity of their systems and Hobbes's deep Stoic debt.

For Hobbes, our concept of pure space is causally and perceptually derived from body. A person left alone after a "universal annihilation," remembering the former locations of bodies, would form a "conception of that we call space; an imaginary space indeed, because a mere phantasm, yet that very thing which men call so" (EW I.93). Hobbes is emphatic that whereas the magnitude of body is real, imaginary space is not: "For imaginary space is the effect and magnitude is the cause; this an accident of the mind, that of body existing out of the mind" (OL I.93; EW I.105). Place or *locus* is likewise merely an abstraction from magnitude: "place is nothing out of the mind, nor magnitude anything within it ... place is feigned extension, but magnitude true extension" (OL I.93; EW I.105). So it is not surprising that Hobbes is antagonistic toward ancient (e.g., Lucretian) and modern (e.g., Torricellian) demonstrations of local vacuums (EW I.411–26) and dismissive of void space beyond the world: "there is no real space outside it; but there is no imaginary space either" (*Anti-White* III.2; 1976, 41).

Hobbes also heaps abuse on Cartesian *a priori* arguments against the vacuum: "to argue that that there can be no vacuum 'because vacuum is nothing' is as cogent as maintaining that 'no man can fast because to fast is to eat nothing' ... and nothing cannot be eaten" (EW I.109; Cf. *Anti-White* III.3; 1976, 42). Furthermore, Hobbes affirms that merely imaginary space is sufficient to separate one body from another: "if there intercede any imagined space, which may receive another body, then those bodies are not contiguous" (EW 1.108). He even holds there is real distance in imaginary space: "The 'distance' between two bodies, or even between two vacant spaces, is the shortest space lying between them. So if some intermediate part is removed from a continuous body the distance between its extreme parts is not thereby removed" (*Anti-White* III.3; 1976, 42).

Hobbes's quasi-realism about imaginary space is highly reminiscent of the Stoics' conception of pure space as one of the problematic "incorporeals." As materialists they officially insist that the void is strictly non-existent or "nothing" (Stobaeus; SVF 2.503/LS 49A; 1987, 294). Accordingly, like Hobbes, they make place corporeal: "place is what is occupied by an existent and made equal to what occupies it (by 'existent' they mean body)" (Sextus Empiricus; SVF 2.505/LS 49B; 1987, 294). And, like Hobbes, although the Stoics deny the actual existence of local vacua, they do not rule them out *a priori*. As Galen puts it: "they leave void in the nature of existing things even if they deny its presence within the world" (Galen, SVF 2.503/LS 49E; 1987, 295). There is good reason to think the void extends infinitely beyond the world since it is there capable of receiving body: "it is incorporeal and without contact, neither has shape nor takes on shape, neither is acted upon in any respects nor acts, but is simply capable of receiving body" (Cleomedes, SVF 2 542; LS 49C; 1987, 294). So this "incorporeal" non-existent "subsists" as the possible places of bodies: "void is what can be occupied by an existent but is not occupied, or an interval empty of body, or an interval unoccupied by a body" (Sextus Empiricus; SVF 2.505/LS 49B; 1987, 29). This is just how Hobbes characterized imaginary space: "no man calls it space for being already filled but because it may be filled" (EW I.93).

2.2.2 *Time and Mind*

For Hobbes, just as our conception of space is derived from the image of body, our notion of time is derived from perceived motion: "a moved body leaves a phantasm of motion, namely an idea of that body passing out of one space and into another by continual succession. And this idea or phantasm ... is that which I call TIME" (OL I.83; EW I.94).[10] He insists that his own definition of time – "the phantasm of before and after in motion" – is in conformity with Aristotle's canonical definition – "*the number of motion with respect to before and after*" (OL I.84; EW I.94; see also *Anti-White* XXVII, 1976, 339–40; Aristotle, *Physics*, Bk. IV, Ch. 11; 220a25-6; Aristotle 1971, Vol. 1, 373) – since "numbering is an act of the mind" (OL I.84; EW I.95).

But there is another, more radical, sense in which Hobbesian time is imaginary or subjective: "when people speak of the times of their predecessors, they do not think that after their predecessors are gone their times can be anywhere else other than in the memory of those that remember them" (OL I. 84; EW I.94).[11] Likewise, in the other temporal direction, "this word *future* is a name but no future thing has yet any being ... nevertheless, since our thought is used to conjoin [*subnectere*] things past with things present the name *future* serves to signify such conjoining" (EW I.17; OL I.15). Despite this apparent *presentism*, Hobbes seems to grant mind-independent reality to time. For "*it is inconceivable that anything can be moved without time*" (OL I.97 EW I. 110)[12] and he clearly regards motion as mind-independent. Motion, after all, is the real cause of the image of time just as magnitude or "real space" is the cause of imaginary space: "time is the image of motion and has the same relation to real motion as a reflection in a mirror to the true face and a mirrored shape to a true shape" (*Anti-White* XXVIII.2; 1976, 339). Furthermore, Hobbes frequently treats the successive duration of motion as mind-independent. Sense, for example, is "some internal motion in the sentient generated by some internal motion of the parts of the object" (*Anti-White* XXVIII.2; 1976, 339). Indeed, the internal motions in the brain themselves "remain there for some time" (OL I.320; EW I.393).[13] This persistence of sensory motions, which enables memory, is precisely what separates us from mindless objects. So rather than reduce motion and time to the mind, mental processes are themselves explained by motion and time.[14]

The Stoics are ambivalent about time for similar reasons. For one thing, it is not a body: "in their view time is one of the incorporeals, which they disparage as inactive and non-existent and subsisting merely in thought" (Proclus, SVF 2.521/LS 51F; 1987, 305). Furthermore, they are presentists. Thus, according to Stobaeus, Chrysippus held "only the present belongs; the past and the future subsist but belong in no way" (Stobaeus, SVF 2.509/LS 51B; 1987, 304; see also Plutarch, SVF LS 51C; 1987, 305). And yet, like Hobbes, they recognize that time is essential to motion: "time is the dimension of motion according to which the measure of speed and slowness is spoken of, or the dimensions accompanying the world's motion" (Stobaeus, SVF 2.509/LS 51B; 1987, 304; see also Sextus Empiricus, LS 50F; 1987, 299). And there is no indication in Stoic physics that the motion of the universe, or its parts, require imagination. So they classify time, like the void, as an "incorporeal": something subsisting, which we can speak about and quantify in science and in ordinary life, but lacking independent existence (Sextus Empiricus SVF 2331/LS 27D; 1987, 162).[15]

Some scholars have perceived in Hobbes's philosophy of space and time an anticipation of Kant (Herbert 1977); others (more plausibly) have detected the influence of late scholastic Aristotelianism and nominalism.[16] But the guiding principles of Hobbesian metaphysics, materialism, and (what Brandt calls) "motionalism" (Brandt 1917, 379), are what most inform and complicate his treatments of space and time. Without resorting to a "subsistent" incorporeal kind of being, Hobbes nevertheless followed the Stoics in giving time and space a sufficient reality to employ them as independent parameters of mechanistic physics.

2.2.3 *Causality*

For Hobbes, the knowledge of effects from their causes, and *vice versa*, is the defining feature of philosophy (EW I.3). His own analysis of the causal relation, presented mostly in chapter IX "Of Cause and Effect" in *De corpore*, is rich and somewhat neglected.[17] Here, I will explore one important aspect of this analysis, which is strongly reminiscent of the Stoics'. Together with Spinoza, Hobbes is perhaps the strictest early modern "necessitarian" about the causal connections among bodies. A cause "simply" or "entirely" is a collection of accidents such that "when they are all thought to be present it cannot be understood but that the effect is produced at that same instant. And if any of them be wanting it cannot be supposed but that the effect is not produced" (EW I.122). Men call things "contingent, whereof they do not perceive the necessary cause" (EW I.130). Hobbes argues the conceptual inter-dependence of simple causes and their effects is crucial for several principles at the foundation of his physics, including "no action at a distance" (EW I.125), "same cause/same effect" (EW I.125-6), and the inertia of both motion and rest (EW I.125).

The Stoics are committed to very similar causal principles. Alexander attributes to the Stoics that "from everything that happens, something else follows, with a necessary causal dependence on it, and everything that happens has something prior to it with which it causally coheres" (LS 1987, 337; see also LS 1987, 333; 389–90). Like Hobbes, the Stoics emphasize that the necessary connection applies to what they call "complete" or "sustaining" causes, i.e., "one during whose presence the effect remains and on whose removal the effect is effect is removed" (LS 1987, 336). As Hobbes later does, they derive from this conception of complete causality the principle that "where all the same circumstances obtain it is impossible that a result that does not ensue on one occasion should ensue on another" (LS 1987, 338). We call things "accidental" or "spontaneous" only because "there are causes hidden from our sight" (Plutarch, *On Stoic Self Contradictions*; In Sambursky 2014, 56). And they hold that all causal connections are by direct contact or through the medium of *pneuma* (Sambursky 2014, 54). As Hobbes later would, albeit from a more sophisticated and quantitative perspective, the Stoics perceived their necessitarian causal principles as required by their overall materialist cosmology: "the world would be wrenched apart and divided and no longer form a unity, forever governed by a single ordering and management, if an uncaused motion were introduced" (LS 1987, 337–8; see also Sambursky 2014, 130).[18]

2.2.4 God

Since Hobbes was avowedly both a theist and a materialist, his God must be some sort of body. As noted above, he says so much in a brief dialogue appended to the Latin edition of *Leviathan* (1668), where Hobbes's mouthpiece "B" brashly "affirms, of course, that God is body."[19] Concurrently, his longtime intellectual frenemy, Anglican Bishop John Bramhall, pressed Hobbes on the same question: since Hobbes considers "incorporeal substance" contradictory, Bramhall asks, what then does he "leave God himself to be?" (1842–1844, IV.525). Hobbes pulls no punches: "I leave him to be a most pure, simple, invisible spirit corporeal" (EW IV.313).[20] In recent scholarship, this late confession of corporeal theism has generally been dismissed as either atheistic dissimulation or a clumsy statement of sincere of Calvinist minimalism.[21] This is understandable. After all, taken on its face, where could Hobbes have obtained such an idea?[22] The answer is: from classical Stoicism.

Consider two passages. The first is Diogenes Laertius' gloss of the role of God in Stoic physics:

> They believe there are two principles of the universe, the active and the passive. The passive is unqualified substance, i.e., matter, the active is the rational principle (logos) in it. i.e., God ... In the beginning he was by himself and turned all substances into water via air and just as the seed is contained in the seminal fluid so this being the spermatic principle of the cosmos remains like this in the cosmos and makes the matter easy for itself to work with in the generation of subsequent things. (Diogenes Laertius *Lives of the Philosophers* Bk. 7, 134; LS 1987, 268–9, 275)[23]

The second is Hobbes's (1662) account of his corporeal God's operation in the world:

> I have seen, and so have many others, two waters, one of the river and the other mineral water, so that no man could discern one from the other from his sight; yet when they are both put together the whole substance could not be distinguished from milk. How then could the change be made in every part, but only by the activity of the mineral water, changing it everywhere to the sense and yet not being everywhere and in every part of the water. If such gross bodies have such great activity what then can we think of spirits, whose kinds be as many as there are kinds of liquor, and activity greater? Can it then be doubted that God, who is infinitely fine spirit, and withal intelligence, can make and change all species and kinds of bodies as he pleaseth? (EW IV.310)

The parallels between these passages are striking: (i) each makes God a special kind of corporeal substance that produces the diversity among familiar bodies by acting on passive and homogenous matter; (ii) each says the divine body operates by thoroughly pervading ordinary matter (though Hobbes denies this involves complete mixing); (iii) each conceives of the divine body as intelligent. I maintain this similarity is no accident: Hobbes adapted his corporeal God from Stoic sources.

Two aspects of the parallel are worth emphasizing. First, consistent with tradition, Hobbes and the Stoics both trace the source of change and diversity to the continuous and ubiquitous activity of God on something like prime matter (OL I.105; EW I.118).[24] However, departing radically from tradition, they both hold that God acts on matter by direct contact and local motion. On the Stoics' biological metaphor, God acts like the seed in seminal fluid; on Hobbes's chemical metaphor, God is the catalyst in a cosmic cocktail. But in order to avoid a regress, the Stoics and Hobbes both insist that the corporeal God must be in some sense inherently active: a sort of fiery air (*pneuma*) for the Stoics, an infinitely subtle fluid or spirit for Hobbes (Alexander, *on Mixture* III, 216, 14–20, T 115, LS 1987, 290; OL I.340; EW I.417). Hobbes signals to Bramhall his debt to the Stoic tradition, on this point, noting that "spirit" in Latin signifies "breadth, air, wind" and "in Greek πνεῦμα (*pneuma*)" (EW IV.309; see also 2012, 612; 1651, 303).[25]

A second important parallel is the common fixation on mixing. Hobbes emphasizes that God pervades ordinary matter though it is impossible they fully mix "unless two bodies can be in the same place" (EW IV.309–10). In Stoic physics the admixture of distinct bodies, particularly God and matter, is hotly debated but generally admitted.[26] Hobbes embraces the Stoic theology but follows more orthodox thinkers like Aristotle in opposing strict co-location. His opposition to full mixing is based on his austere geometrical or Cartesian view of extension, which makes the co-extension of distinct bodies impossible. What is most noteworthy for us is that Hobbes even bothers to engage this esoteric and antiquated debate about mixing. This betrays his sympathy for the Stoic materialist program, inside and out.[27]

2.3 Conclusion

A recent commentator has astutely observed that Hobbes's expansive philosophy of "accidents" like space, time, and causality, always seem to involve "a curious twofold description of our ideas" (Leijenhorst 2002, 107). In the case of causality, for example, Hobbes indicates he is concerned primarily with the accidents of bodies considered subjectively, i.e., "that faculty of any body by which it works in us a conception of itself" (EW VIII.103; see Leijenhorst 2002, 157). But he is also concerned with real causal connections. A similar and parallel dual-aspect is evident in the case of both space and time. But, as we have seen above, wholesale subjectivism about space and time cannot support Hobbes's – or the Stoics' – cherished and ambitious program in mechanistic science. God, of course, is not an accident; but like the "incorporeals," space, time, and causality, it is difficult to find a place for the traditional attributes of a transcendent God within a thoroughly materialist and mechanist cosmology. My suggestion is that we can better understand Hobbes's curious "twofold" metaphysics if we align his project with the overarching worldview originating at the Stoa of Athens.

Notes

1 See also *Leviathan* XVI (2012, 244; 1651, 155), *Leviathan* XXIV (2012, 388; 1651, 190).

2 Thomas Stanley's influential *History of Philosophy*, devoted many chapters to Stoicism, including chapters on the corporeal God, the void and time (see Stanley 1655–1660, Vol. II, Part 8, 115–19, 123–4).

3 *De anima* v (1885, 185): "The soul certainly sympathizes with the body, and shares in its pain, whenever it is injured by bruises, and wounds, and sores: the body, too, suffers with the soul, and is united with it (whenever it is afflicted with anxiety, distress, or love)." See also *De anima* vii (1885, 187).

4 As with finite souls, Tertullian emphasizes the Stoic objection to dualism that an incorporeal substance cannot act on body. See Evans (1948, 234–7) for discussion of the Stoic background to these texts. On Hobbes's appeal to these texts in support of materialism, see Riverso (1991, 92).

5 For example, in the tract against yet another heretic, Hermogenes, Tertullian invokes with sympathy the Stoic model of God's mixture with matter: "The Stoics maintained that God pervaded matter, just as honey the honeycomb" (*Ad Hermogenes* xliv; 1885, 501). Hobbes hints at a closer reading of Tertullian in the *Answer to Bramhall*, mentioning that *De carne Christi* is "now extant among his other works" (EW IV.307).

6 See Saunders (1955). While in exile, the Cavendishes occupied the former residence of Peter Paul Rubens, who was sympathetic to Stoicism and whose brother, Philip, was a follower of Lipsius. See O'Neill's Introduction to Cavendish (2001, xiv). On the Rubens' involvement in the Neo-Stoic circle at Antwerp, see Morford (1991).

7 "Discourse of Liberty and Necessity", section xviii (Bramhall 1842–1844, IV, 116). See also "Defence of True Liberty" (Bramhall 1842–1844, IV, 119). In his Introduction to the defence or "vindication," Bramhall labels Hobbes's position "sublimated stoicism" (EW IV.20).

8 It is not surprising that the vitalist Cavendish objected to Hobbes's principle in *Leviathan* II that "when a thing lies still, unless somewhat else stirs it, will lie still forever" (2012, 26; 1651, 13. cf. *De corpore*; EW I.115; OL I.102) because it seems to make self-motion impossible (Cavendish 1664, 21). Hobbes's corporeal God doctrine was not yet formulated.

9 On Cavendish's concerns viz. the foundations of natural philosophy, see Clucas (1994), James (1999), Detlefson (2006), and Sarasohn (2010).

10 "In any part of space in which motion is made three times may be considered: past, present and future" (OL I.176; EW 204; see also OL I.98; EW I.110–11).

11 For an illuminating discussion of Hobbes's presentism, which emphasizes different issues than the present discussion, see Medina (1997).

12 See also *De corpore* XV (OL I.176; EW I.204).

13 See also *De corpore* XXV (OL I.318; EW I.391). Memory allows animate beings to compare fleeting successive sensations: "sense ... has necessarily some memory adhering to it, by which former and later phantasms may be compared together and distinguished from one another" (OL I.321; EW I.393).

14 For more on the reality of Hobbesian time, see Gorham (2014b).

15 For a detailed, recent discussion of the Stoic incorporeals, especially void and time, see Tzamalikos (1991).

16 Leijenhorst (2002, ch.3); Slowik (2014).

17 Though see Brandt (1917), Spragens (1973), and Leijenhorst (1996).

18 Leijenhorst (1996, 430) notes some Aristotelian features of Hobbes' conception of causality in early works like the *Short Tract*, but acknowledges that in his mature natural philosophy Hobbes affects a "radical breach" with Aristotle.

19 "*Affirmat quidem Deus esse Corpus*" (2012, 1228; OL III.561).

20 Hobbes seems to embrace corporeal God in at least two other places: *An Historical Narration Concerning Heresy* (EW IV.398) and *Considerations Upon the Reputation, Loyalty, Manners and Religion of Thomas Hobbes* (EW IV.427). Also in the much earlier (1641) letter to Mersenne, Descartes dismisses Hobbes's mention (in a lost letter to Descartes) of "the corporeal soul and God" (*anima & Deo corporeis*) (AT 3.287).

21 Curley (1992), Jesseph (2002), and Martinich (1992).

22 Fortunately, a number of authors have very recently presented detailed discussions of the corporeal God doctrine; but they do not investigate in much detail its likely sources. See Lupoli (1999), Leijenhorst (2004), Weber (2009), and Springborg (2012).

23 See also Alexander of Aphrodisias' similar complaint against the Stoics for "claiming the existence of two universal principles, matter and God," which are mixed yet unequal (*On Mixture* XI, 224–5, T 1976, 139; LS 1987, 273, 275).

24 See also Diogenes Laertius, *Lives of the Philosophers* 7, 150; 1997, 137; Sextus Empiricus, *Against the Professors* 9, 75–6, LS 1987, 269; Plutarch, *On Stoic Self-Contradictions*, 1053f; LS 1987, 284.

25 See also *Leviathan* XXXIV (2012, 612; 1651, 303). The editor of this volume has rightly observed that in passages of *Leviathan* in which Hobbes equates spirit and breath or *pneuma*, he is mainly dealing with the Christian (not necessarily Stoic) sources of this doctrine. Hobbes's appeal to the doctrine in the *Answer to Bramhall*, however, is revealing since it comes just before his detailed defense of the corporeal god. So it is ironic that the Cambridge Platonist Ralph Cudworth, in his vehemently anti-Hobbesian tome, *The True Intellectual System of the Universe* (1678), diagnoses atheists as suffering from "pneumatophobia": "an irrational but desperate abhorrence from spirits or incorporeal substances" (1845, Vol. I, 200).

26 For discussion see Sambursky (2014, ch. 3), Todd (1978), and especially Sorabji (1988, chs. 5–7).

27 For further discussion of the parallels between the Stoic and Hobbesian physico-theologies, see Gorham (2014a). See Gorham (2013) for more on the role of corporeal God in Hobbesian physics.

References

Aristotle. 1971. *Complete Works of Aristotle*, 2 vols., edited by Jonathan Barnes. Princeton: Princeton University Press.

Barker, Peter and Bernard R. Goldstein. 1984. "Is Seventeenth Century Physics Indebted to the Stoics?" *Centaurus* 27: 148–64.

Bramhall, John. 1842–1844. *Works of John Bramhall*, 4 vols. Oxford: John Henry Parker.

Brandt, Frithiof. 1917. *Thomas Hobbes' Mechanical Conception of Nature*. Copenhagen: Levin & Munksgaard.

Brooke, Christopher. 2012. *Philosophic Pride: Stoicism and Political Thought from Lipsius to Rousseau*. Princeton: Princeton University Press.

Cavendish, Margaret Lucas, Lady. 1664. *Philosophical Letters*. London: n.p.

Cavendish, Margaret Lucas, Lady. 2001. *Observations upon Experimental Philosophy*, edited by Eileen O'Neill. Cambridge: Cambridge University Press.

Clucas, Stephen. 1994. "Atomism of the Cavendish Circle: A Reappraisal." *The Seventeenth Century* 9: 247–73.

Cudworth, Ralph. 1845. *True Intellectual System of the Universe*, 3 vols. London: Thomas Tegg.

Curley, Edwin. 1992. "'I Durst Not Write So Boldly' or How to Read Hobbes' Theological-Political Treatise." In *Hobbes e Spinoza*, edited by Daniela Bostrengi, 497–593. Naples: Bibliopolis.

Detlefson, Karen. 2006. "Atomism, Monism, and Causation in the Natural Philosophy of Margaret Cavendish." In *Oxford Studies in Early Modern Philosophy*, Vol. 3, edited by Daniel Garber and Steven Nadler, 199–240. Oxford: Oxford University Press.

Evans, Ernest 1948. *Adversus Praxean Liber*. London: S.P.C.K.

Gorham, Geoffrey. 2013. "The Theological Foundations of Hobbesian Physics: A Defense of Corporeal God." *British Journal for the History of Philosophy* 21: 240–61.

Gorham, Geoffrey. 2014a. "Mixing Bodily Fluids: Hobbes's Stoic God." *Sophia: International Journal for the Philosophy of Religion* 53: 33–49.

Gorham, Geoffrey. 2014b. "Hobbes on the Reality of Time." *Hobbes Studies* 27: 80–103.

Herbert, Gary B. 1977. "Hobbes's Phenomenology of Space." *Journal of the History of Ideas* 48: 709–17.

Hobbes, Thomas. 1839–1845a. *The English Works of Thomas Hobbes*, 11 vols., edited by Sir William Molesworth. London: John Bohn. Cited as EW.

Hobbes, Thomas. 1839–1845b. *Thomæ Hobbes malmesburiensis opera philosophica*, 5 vols., edited by Gulielmi Molesworth. London: John Bohn. Cited as OL.

Hobbes, Thomas. 1976. *Thomas White's De Mundo Examined*, edited by Harold W. Jones. London: Bradford University Press.

Hobbes, Thomas. 2012. *Leviathan*, 3 vols., edited by Noel Malcolm. Oxford: Clarendon Press. [First published 1651].

James, Susan. 1999. "The Innovations of Margaret Cavendish." *British Journal for the History of Philosophy* 7: 219–44.

Jesseph, Douglas. 2002. "Hobbes's Atheism." *Midwest Studies in Philosophy* edited by P. A. French and H. K. Weinstein, 26: 140–66.

Laertius, Diogenes. 1997. In *Hellenistic Philosophy: Introductory Readings*, 2nd ed., edited by Brad Inwood and Lloyd P. Gerson. Indianapolis: Hackett Publishing.

Lagrée, Jacqueline. 1994. *Juste Lipse et La Restauration to Stoïcisme*. Paris: Vrin.

Leijenhorst, Cees. 1996. "Hobbes Theory of Causality and It's Aristotelian Background." *The Monist* 79 (1996): 426–47.

Leijenhorst, Cees. 2002. *The Mechanisation of Aristotelianism: The Late Aristotelian Setting of Thomas Hobbes' Natural Philosophy*. Leiden: Brill.

Leijenhorst, Cees. 2004. "Hobbes's Corporeal Deity." *Revista di storia della filosofia* 59 (1): 73–95.

Lipsius, Justus. 1604. *Physiologiae Stoicurm libre tres*. Antwerp: J. Moretus.

Long, Anthony A. 2003. "Stoicism in the Philosophical Tradition: Spinoza, Lipsius, Butler." In *The Cambridge Companion to the Stoics*, edited by Brad Inwood, 365–92. Cambridge: Cambridge University Press.

Long, Anthony A. and David N. Sedley, eds. 1987. *The Hellenistic Philosophers, Vol. 1: Translation of the Principles Sources with Philosophical Commentary*. Cambridge: Cambridge University Press. Cited by LS and page number.

Lupoli, Agostino. 1999. "Fluidismo e Corporeal Deity nella filosofia naturale di Thomas Hobbes." *Revista di storia della filosofia* 54 (4): 573–609.

Martinich, Aloysius P. 1992. *The Two Gods of Leviathan: Thomas Hobbes on Religion and Politics*. Cambridge: Cambridge University Press.

Medina, José. 1997. "Les Temps Chez Hobbes." *Études Philosophiques* 2: 171–90.

Morford, Mark. 1991. *Stoics and Neostoics: Rubens and the Circle of Lipsius*. Princeton: Princeton University Press.

Riverso, Emanuele. 1991. "Denotation and Corporeity in Leviathan." *Metalogicon* IV: 78–92.

Sambursky, Samuel. 2014. *Physics of the Stoics*. Princeton: Princeton Legacy Library.

Sarasohn, Lisa T. 2010. *The Natural Philosophy of Margaret Cavendish*. Baltimore: Johns Hopkins University Press.

Saunders, Jason. 1955. *Justus Lipsius: The Philosophy of Renaissance Stoicism*. New York: Liberal Arts Press.

Slowik, Edward. 2014. "Hobbes and the Phantasm of Space." *Hobbes Studies* 14 (2014): 61–79.

Sorabji, Richard. 1988. *Matter, Space & Motion: Theories in Antiquity and Their Sequel*. Ithaca: Cornell University Press.

Spragens, Thomas A. 1973. *The Politics of Nature: The World of Thomas Hobbes*. Lexington: University Press of Kentucky.

Springborg, Patricia. 2010. "Hobbes's Fool the *Stultus*, Grotius, and the Epicurean Tradition." *Hobbes Studies* 23: 29–53.

Springborg, Patricia. 2012. "Hobbes's Challenge to Descartes, Bramhall and Boyle: A Corporeal God." *British Journal for the History of Philosophy* 20: 903–34.

Stanley, Thomas. 1655–1660. *History of Philosophy*, 3 vols. London: Humphrey Mosley and Thomas Dring.

Tertullian. 1885. *The Ante-Nicene Fathers, Vol. III: Tertullian*, edited by Alexander Roberts and James Donaldson. Buffalo: The Christian Library.

Todd, Robert. 1978. "Monism and Immanence: The Foundations of Stoic Physics." In *The Stoics*, edited by John M. Rist, 136–70. Berkeley: University of California Press.

Todd, Robert C. 1976. *Alexander of Aphrodisias on Stoic Physics: A Study of the De Mixtione with Preliminary Essays, Text, Translation and Commentary*. Leiden: Brill. Cited as T with page number.

Tuck, Richard. 1983. "Grotius, Carneades and Hobbes." *Grotiana* 4: 43–62.

Tzamalikos, Panayiotis 1991. "Origen and the Stoic View of Time." *Journal of the History of Ideas* 52: 535–61.

Weber, Dominique. 2009. *Hobbes et le Corps de Dieu*. Paris: J. Vrin.

3

Hobbesian Mathematics and the Dispute with Wallis

DOUGLAS JESSEPH

Mathematics plays a prominent role in Hobbes's grand intellectual project. In the course of more than two decades he published over a dozen mathematical works, ranging from brief pamphlets to synoptic treatments of the subject.[1] Quantity of output is no guarantee of its quality, however, and Hobbes's mathematics is remembered primarily for his many failed attempts to square the circle and solve other famous mathematical problems. His long and humiliating controversy with John Wallis, Oxford's Savilian Professor of Geometry, annihilated Hobbes's mathematical reputation and has left the widely shared impression that there is nothing of value to be found in his many mathematical writings.[2] My purpose here is not to defend Hobbes's attempts to solve what we now know to be unsolvable problems, but rather to examine the philosophical and methodological basis upon which his mathematics was founded and the broader context in which it developed. Toward that end, this chapter is divided in two sections. The first is an overview of Hobbes's materialistic philosophy of mathematics. The second investigates his controversy with Wallis.

3.1 The Hobbesian Philosophy of Mathematics

The significance that Hobbes attached to mathematics (and, more particularly, to geometry) is attested by a famous anecdote recorded by his friend John Aubrey. He reports that Hobbes was initiated into the study of mathematics by happening to come across Euclid's proof of the Pythagorean Theorem (Euclid 1925):

> He was ... 40 yeares old before he looked upon geometry; which happened accidentally. Being in a gentleman's library in ___, Euclid's Elements lay open, and'twas the 47 El. libri. I. He read the proposition. "By G___," sayd he, "this is impossible!" So he reads the demonstration of it, which referred him back to such a proposition; which proposition he read.

A Companion to Hobbes, First Edition. Edited by Marcus P. Adams.

> That referred him back to another, which he also read. *Et sic deinceps*, that at last he was convinced of that trueth. This made him in love with geometry. (Aubrey 1898, 1: 332)

There can be little doubt that this account is embellished,[3] but it does comport with some things Hobbes wrote. His Latin *Vita* reports that in a 1629 journey to the Continent in the company of Sir Gervase Clifton "he began to read Euclid's *Elements*; and, well-pleased by its method, not because of the theorems, but rather because of its art of reasoning, he read through it most carefully" (OL I.14). Likewise, the first edition of his *Examinatio et emendatio mathematicæ hodiernæ* (hereafter *Examinatio*) contains a passage that closely resembles Aubrey's account.[4] Thus, even if it is unlikely that a chance encounter with Euclid's statement of the Pythagorean Theorem was literally Hobbes's first introduction to geometry, there is no doubt that he held the mathematical sciences in high esteem.

What attracted Hobbes to the mathematical "art of reasoning" is the notion that simple and indisputable first principles can lead, by way of rigorous deductions, to important and non-obvious results that are thereby established with demonstrative certainty. He took this as a model for all proper sciences, including the "science of politics," which he claimed to have founded. There is nothing unique in Hobbes assessment that mathematics provides a model of scientific and philosophical method, but he proposed a philosophy of mathematics that was quite distinctive. In particular, his mathematical ontology rejects the seventeenth century's received view of the subject and his proposed first principles departed quite significantly from the tradition.

3.1.1 Hobbes's Mathematical Ontology

A central tenet in Hobbes's first philosophy is the denial of immaterial substances. As he famously declared in *Leviathan* chapter 4, "puzzled philosophers" will often "make a name of two names, whose significations are contradictory and inconsistent; as this name, an *incorporeall body*, or (which is all one) an *incorporeall substance*" (Hobbes 2012, 60; 1651, 17). This amounts to a declaration that the terms 'substance' and 'body' are convertible, which entails that any doctrine purporting to deal with a realm of non-physical objects is either arrant nonsense to be dismissed or a confusion standing in need of a fundamental reinterpretation.

In point of fact, mathematics was traditionally understood to be a science whose proper objects are immaterial. The fifth-century CE neo-Platonist Proclus Diadochus summed up the traditional view when he complained that the consideration of matter "muddies" the intellectual apprehension of geometric objects (Proclus 1970, 87). Aristotelians rejected the Platonic concept of a realm of ideal geometric forms, but they nevertheless held that the objects of mathematical investigation must be radically distinguished from the contents of the material world. Christopher Clavius, professor of mathematics at the Jesuit *Collegio Romano*, summed up the sixteenth-century Aristotelians' doctrine that mathematics deals with a particular kind of abstract objects that are "considered apart from all matter" or abstracted from any underlying material substrate (Clavius 1612, 1:5). Wallis followed a broadly Aristotelian understanding in his 1657 *Mathesis Universalis*, proclaiming magnitude to be the object of geometry, adding that "By *magnitude* I understand lines, surfaces, and bodies taken mathematically, that is, abstracted from matter, whose various affections and properties geometry demonstrates" (Wallis 1693–1699, 1:21).

Where the tradition sought to develop an account of mathematics that makes it independent of the structure or contents of the material world, Hobbes pursued a radically materialistic treatment of the subject. The basis of this program is developed in chapter 8 of *De corpore*, which bears the title "Of Body and Accident." In *De corpore* VIII.4 Hobbes offers a definition of the term 'magnitude' with the remark that "The Extension of a Body, is the same thing with the MAGNITUDE of it, or that which some call *Real Space*" (EW I.105). Having identified magnitude with the extension of body, Hobbes proceeds in *De corpore* VIII.12 to define the geometric terms 'point' and 'line' in terms of the central concept of body:

> Though there be no Body which has not some Magnitude, yet if when any Body is moved, the Magnitude of it be not at all considered, the way it makes is called a LINE, or one single Dimension; & the Space through which it passeth, is called LENGTH; and the Body it self, a POINT; in which sense the Earth is called a *Point*, and the Way of its yearly Revolution, the *Ecliptick Line*. (EW I.111)

Surfaces and solids are then definable in the same manner. This account of magnitude has an obvious connection to Hobbes's materialistic ontology. Because he takes only bodies to be real, and because he maintains that it is only through the motion of bodies that anything can be brought about, Hobbes must base all of mathematics on the principles of matter and motion. Mathematical objects must therefore be interpreted as bodies or things produced by the motion of bodies. In particular, the geometric point is a body, which requires that the point be divisible and have magnitude (even if that magnitude is disregarded), while lines, surfaces, and solids arise from the motions of points, lines, and surfaces, respectively.

At first sight, it might seem that there is no place for arithmetic in this scheme. Taking space, motion, and body as fundamental concepts might make tolerable sense of geometry, but it is unclear how this can work for arithmetic. Classical authors drew a firm distinction between the continuous magnitudes of geometry and the discrete "multitudes" of arithmetic. Geometric magnitudes such as lines, angles, surfaces or solids are divisible into lesser magnitudes of the same kind (lines divide into lines, angles into angles, etc.). In contrast, the discrete multitudes of arithmetic were taken to be only finitely divisible and to be ultimately composed from indivisible units. Viewed in this way, geometry and arithmetic are fundamentally different sciences with essentially different objects. Hobbes, however, held that arithmetic could be based on the uniform division of continuous magnitudes into equal parts. As he put the matter, "because any given continuous magnitude can be divided into any number of equal parts, with its ratio to any other magnitude remaining unchanged, it is manifest that arithmetic is contained in geometry" (OL IV.28).

3.1.2 *Hobbes on Geometric First Principles*

Hobbes's understanding of geometry as a generalized science of material bodies puts him at odds with the traditional notion that the objects of geometrical investigation are radically distinct from the realm of material things. The difference becomes clearer when we examine the Hobbesian treatment of first principles, and more specifically the definitions upon which the science of geometry is based. True to his materialistic principles, Hobbes demands not only that all geometric objects be defined as bodies, but also that proper definitions must identify the causes by which such objects are produced, with the further requirement that the only such causes can be motions. The result is a conception of geometry that diverges significantly from the tradition.

Euclid defines the point as "that which has no part," while a line is defined as "breadthless length" (*Elements*, Book I, Defs. 1, 2). Hobbes argues in *De Principiis et Ratiocinatione Geometrarum* (hereafter *PRG*) that these definitions are ambiguous:

> these words "which has no part", can be understood in two ways, either for *undivided* (a part indeed not being understood except where a division has gone before) or for *indivisible*, because it is by its nature incapable of division. In the former sense a point is rightly called a quantity, in the latter not; as all quantity is always divisible into divisibles. And thus if a point is indivisible, every line will lack breadth, and because there is nothing long that does not have breadth, the line would clearly be nothing. Although length is indeed not broad, nevertheless everything long is broad. It seems that Euclid himself was also of this opinion, that although a point has no parts actually, it is nevertheless divisible potentially and is a quantity, otherwise he would not have postulated that a straight line can be drawn from a point to a point.[5] Which is impossible unless the line has some breadth. (OL IV.391)

Elaborating this doctrine in reply to some of Wallis's criticisms, Hobbes insisted in *Six Lessons to the Professors of the Mathematiques* (hereafter *SL*)

> That which is indivisible is no Quantity; and if a point be not Quantity, seeing it is neither substance nor Quality, it is nothing. And if Euclide had meant it so in his definition, (as you pretend he did) he might have defined it more briefly, (but ridiculously) thus, *a Point is nothing*. (EW VII.201)

Hobbes held that the Euclidean definitions of point, line, and surface can be remedied by resolving the ambiguity. He asserted in Dialogue 1 of *Examination* that understanding the point as a divisible body whose magnitude disregarded implies that "the quantity of a point is not nothing, but rather not computed. Nor is the point itself nothing, or indivisible, but undivided" (OL IV:33).

The flaws in other Euclidean definitions cannot be so easily mended. In particular, Euclid's definition of 'ratio' is entirely uninformative, reading; "A ratio is a sort of relation in respect of size between two magnitudes of the same kind" (*Elements*, Book V, Def. 3). Hobbes dismisses this in *SL* Lesson 2 as "insignificant" and amounting to no more than saying a ratio "is a *whatshicalt habitude of two Quantities*" (EW VII.229). In its place he offers a definition that takes a ratio to be the comparison of the relative magnitude of two bodies. He claims in *De corpore* XI.3 that a ratio is the "Excess or Defect" of one body when compared with another (EW I.133). The ratio between two bodies therefore expresses the amount by which they differ in some quantity. As it happens, there are various kinds of quantities associated with bodies: volume, mass, velocity, temperature, density etc. Moreover, the difference in these magnitudes can be expressed in alternative ways. Consider two bodies, one with a weight of 5 kg, the other weighing 3 kg This difference could be expressed as the *arithmetical ratio* of 2 kg, corresponding to 5 – 3, or it could be expressed as the *geometric ratio* 5:3, arising from the division of five by three. In general, it is the geometric ratio that is of interest when volumes, arc lengths or areas are compared. Although many kinds of quantities can stand in geometric ratios, Hobbes holds that any ratio can be "exposed" or "exhibited" by displaying two straight lines whose lengths stand in the desired ratio.

Where Hobbes dismissed the Euclidean definition of 'ratio' as uninformative, he took the definition of 'same ratio' to be both overly complex and capable of definition from more basic principles. In Euclid's presentation, the definition reads

> Magnitudes are said to *be in the same ratio*, the first to the second and the third to the fourth, when, if any equimultiples whatever be taken of the first and third, and any equimultiples whatever of the second and fourth, the former equimultiples alike exceed, are alike equal to, or alike fall short of the latter equimultiples respectively taken in corresponding order. (*Elements*, Book V, Def. 5)

This definition attracted a great deal of commentary over the centuries,[6] and Hobbes was not alone in thinking that it was too intricate and obscure to be numbered among the first principles of geometry.

In Hobbes's view, sameness of ratio can be properly defined only in terms of the motion of bodies. Thus, rather than following Euclid and explicating this concept in terms of order preservation under arbitrary equimultiples, he seeks to find a more general principle from which the Euclidean definition can be derived. As he puts the matter in *PRG* chapter 12: "I define "the same ratios" to be "those which uniform motion exposes in two straight lines in equal times"; or more universally, "those things are in the same ratio which are determined by some cause producing equal effects in equal times" (OL IV.420). Hobbes's "more universal" definition cited here comes from *De corpore* (2.13.6), and he bragged that Euclid's definition of 'same ratio' could be demonstrated from it. Speaking of himself in the third person in the second dialogue of *Examinatio*, he insists that the Euclidean definition "is true, I say, but not a principle, because it is demonstrable and demonstrated by Hobbes in article 12 of chapter 13 of the book *De corpore*, but demonstrated from a definition of *the same ratio* by generation that is different from this of Euclid" (OL IV.76–7).[7]

Hobbes also critiques the Euclidean definition of the circle, which defines it as "a plane figure contained by one line such that all the straight lines falling upon it from one point among those lying within the figure are equal to one another" (*Elements*, Book I, Def. 15). In Hobbes's estimation, this has the virtue of stating something true about the circle, but it fails to be a proper definition because it does not identify its causal generation, as he claims in *SL* Lesson 1:

> But if a man had never seen the generation of a Circle by the motion of a Compass or other æquivalent means, it would have been hard to perswade him, that there was any such Figure possible. It had been therefore not amiss first to have let him see that such a Figure might be described. Therefore so much of Geometry is no part of Philosophy, which seeketh the proper passions of all things in the generation of the things themselves. (EW VII.205)

In the Hobbesian scheme of things, the correct definition of the circle – found in *De corpore* XIV.4 – is in terms of the rotational motion of a straight line about one of its termini (EW I.180–1). Such a definition not only identifies the cause of the circle, but also enables the geometer to investigate its properties.

Hobbes's methodology holds that demonstrative knowledge must be based on definitions that identify the causes of things. This is summarized in the Dedicatory Epistle to the *SL*, where he insisted that "where there is place for Demonstration, if the first Principles, that is to say, the Definitions contain not the Generation of the Subject; there can be nothing demonstrated as it ought to be" (*SL* Epistle). As he explains a greater length in *PRG* 12:

> "But", you will ask, "what need is there for demonstrations of purely geometric theorems to appeal to motion?" I respond: first, all demonstrations are flawed, unless they are scientific, and unless they proceed from causes they are not scientific. Second, demonstrations are flawed unless their conclusions are demonstrated by construction, that is, by the description of figures, that is, by the drawing of lines. For every drawing of a line is motion: and so every demonstration is flawed, whose first principles are not contained in the definitions of motions by which figures are described. (OL IV.421)

In Hobbes's view, once proper causal definitions are in place, the development of a science is a matter of relative routine. The guiding thought here is that knowledge of causes should provide easy access to knowledge of effects. In particular, since geometric objects are brought into being by motions through which the geometer literally constructs the object of investigation, so that "in his demonstration [the geometer] does no more but deduce the Consequences of his own operation" (EW VII.183–4). This approach to demonstration led Hobbes to believe that, once proper geometric definitions were in place, the solution of any geometric problem should follow with ease. Thus, the failure of previous generations of geometers to solve such problems as the quadrature of the circle did not arise from intractability of the problems, but from flawed first principles. Once the Euclidean definitions have been replaced by Hobbes's causal definitions, the royal road to the solution of geometric problems was open. Or so Hobbes believed. As we will see, this confidence in the efficacy of his geometric first principles ultimately led Hobbes to serious error.

3.1.3 *The Status of Algebraic and Infinitesimal Methods*

Hobbes's approach to geometry clearly set him against the traditional view of the subject, but he also opposed some of the innovations that were the most important advances in seventeenth-century mathematics. In particular, he was quite hostile to the algebraic methods characteristic of Descartes's analytic geometry, and he found fault with some presentations of the "method of indivisibles" that is an important precursor to the calculus. A brief summary of these issues can bring our investigation into the Hobbesian philosophy of mathematics to a close.

The 1637 publication of Descartes's *Géométrie* as one of the three *Essais* that accompanied the *Discours de la méthode* is generally taken to be the advent of analytic geometry. The details of this approach are widely enough understood that they need not detain us.[8] The fundamental idea is that geometric curves can be represented algebraically, first by taking algebraic operations (addition, subtraction, multiplication, division, and the extraction of roots) as geometric constructions, and then identifying curves with indeterminate equations in two unknowns that correspond to the familiar co-ordinate axes in the Cartesian plane. Curves that are truly geometrical and susceptible to analysis can be given a "precise and exact" formulation expressed as a single equation showing the relation between the curve and the points on one axis (AT 6:392).

The 'analytic' aspect of Cartesian geometry stems from its use of a so-called analytic method that begins with the assumption that a problem has been solved, and then proceeds to investigate the conditions under which such a solution can be achieved. As he put the matter

> If, then, we wish to solve any problem, we first suppose the solution already to have been effected, and give names to all the lines that seem needful for its construction – to those that are unknown as well as to those that are known. Then, making no distinction between known and unknown lines, we must unravel the difficulty in any way that shows most naturally the relations between these lines, until we find it possible to express a single quantity in two ways. This will constitute an equation, since the terms of one of these equations are together equal to the terms of the other. And we must find as many such equations as we have supposed lines which are unknown. (AT 6: 372–3)

The use of algebraic techniques to investigate the solution conditions for geometric problems was not an entirely Cartesian innovation. The procedure often went under the name of the "analytic art" and was widely regarded as a universal method for the solution of geometric problems. François Viète's 1591 *In Artem analyticem Isagoge* famously employed algebra to seek solutions to geometric problems and concluded that the "analytic art … claims for itself the greatest problem of all, which is: To Solve Every Problem" (Viète 1591, 9). In England, Thomas Harriot's *Artis Analyticæ Praxis* and William Oughtred's *Clavis Mathematicae* were important developments in the application of algebra to geometry.[9]

A critical difference between the Cartesian approach to geometry and its classical counterpart involves the issue of the homogeneity of magnitudes under multiplication. In the Cartesian scheme, multiplication of two lines yields another line, and likewise the multiplication of any number of lines produces yet another line. Thus, Cartesian geometry sees lines as homogeneous when subject to multiplication. In contrast, classical geometry takes the product of two lines to be a surface, so that multiplication yields a magnitude heterogeneous to that of the multiplicands. Similarly, classical geometry takes the product of three lines to be a solid, with the consequence that multiplication beyond the third ("cubic") power has no geometric interpretation. Such powers were termed "biquadrate" (fourth power) or "quadrato-cube" (fifth power), etc., but they were not taken to have specific geometric meaning.

Hobbes's disdain for analytic geometry was boundless. In part, his objections amount to little more than "aesthetic" complaints to the effect that algebraic symbols deface geometric demonstrations, as when he complains in *SL* Lesson 3 that "Symboles are poor unhandsome (though necessary) scaffolds of Demonstration; and ought no more to appear in publique, then the most deformed necessary business which you do in your Chambers" (EW VII.48). A more substantive complaint is that the employment of algebra in geometry is either methodologically suspect or (at best) irrelevant. If the application of algebra to geometry is warranted by underlying principles, these principles must ultimately be vindicated by appeal to geometric constructions, thereby making algebra superfluous. Yet if algebraic techniques are not grounded geometrically, there is no guarantee that an algebraic transformation corresponds to a legitimate geometric operation. Hobbes poses the dilemma this way in Dialogue 1 of *Examinatio*:

> What else do the great masters of the current symbolics, Oughtred and Descartes, teach, but that for a sought quantity we should take some letter from the alphabet, and then by *right* reasoning we should proceed to the consequence? But if this be an art, it would need to have been shown what this *right* reasoning is. Because they do not do this, the algebraists are known to begin sometimes with one supposition, sometimes with another, and to follow sometimes one path, and sometimes another .... Moreover, what proposition discovered by algebra does not depend upon Euclid (Book VI, Prop. 16) and (Book I, Prop. 47), and other famous propositions, which one must first know before he can use the rules of algebra? Certainly, algebra needs geometry, but geometry does not need algebra. (OL IV.9–10)

This sort of objection highlights a difficulty in the analytic approach, which is that it is not always clear how a problem is to be "unraveled" (in Descartes's phrase), and it is occasionally problematic to discern whether the manipulation of symbols by algebraic rules reflects an acceptable geometric construction.

Hobbes further complains that the "intrusion" of algebra into geometry fails to recognize the fundamental difference between algebraic multiplication and the "drawing of lines into lines" that generates geometric objects. Among the "Manifest Principles" at the outset of his treatise *Lux Mathematica*, he numbers:

> A square figure is made by the drawing of a straight line into a line equal to it and placed at right angles to it. This drawing of a line therefore describes a surface, that is a new species of quantity, and this surface drawn into another straight line equal to the first two and orthogonal to them, will describe a solid, that is the third and last species of quantity.
>
> For geometry recognizes no quantity beyond the solid. For the sur-solids, quadrato-quadrates, the quadrato-cubes, and cubi-cubes are mere numbers, but not figures. Thus there is a great difference between what is made by the drawing of two lines into one another and what is made by the multiplication of two numbers into one another, truly as much as there is between a line and a surface or between a surface and a solid. These differ in kind, so much that one of them could by no multiplication exceed the other; and thus (as Euclid says) they can have no ratio to one another, nor could they be compared according to quantity. There is likewise a great difference between the root of a square number and the side of a square figure. For the root is a number, and an aliquot part of its square; but the side is not a part of a square figure. (*Lux*, Introduction 8; OL V.96)

This amounts to a wholesale rejection of Descartes's thesis on the homogeneity of geometric lines under multiplication, and it set the stage for Hobbes's bizarre claim that algebraic calculation could never refute a supposed geometric deduction.

Hobbes's resolute rejection of analytic geometry contrasts with his ambivalent attitude toward another important innovation in seventeenth-century mathematics – the "method of indivisibles" pioneered by Bonaventura Cavalieri. The method is based on the notion that we can reason about the areas of plane figures by comparing "all the lines" contained within them, which Cavalieri called "the indivisibles" of the figures.[10] The method first appeared in Cavalieri's 1635 *Geometria indivisibilibus continuourm nova quadam ratione promota*, and its fundamental concept is illustrated in Figure 4.1. Take the circle ACEG and the ellipse JLNP, of equal height and both based on the line RS (which Cavalieri terms the *regula*). If the *regula* is understood to move parallel to itself upward until it reaches the position TU, its intersection with the two figures will produce "all the lines" in each. Cavalieri then proceeds to argue that "all the lines" in a figure can be treated as magnitudes and are subject to ordering relations. So, in Figure 3.1, the fact that "all the lines" of the circle exceed "all the lines" of the ellipse means that the area of the circle must be greater than that of the ellipse.

Cavalieri used the method to investigate the areas of figures and volumes of solids, and specifically to establish ratios between pairs of such magnitudes. In the two-dimensional case, he first shows that a specific ratio holds between the indivisibles of two figures, and then concludes the areas stand in the same ratios as the indivisibles. As he put it

> When we want to find what ratio two plane figures or two solids have to one another, it is sufficient for us to find what ratio all of the lines of the figure stand in (and in the case of solids, what ratio holds between all of the planes), relative to a given *regula*, which I lay as the great foundation of my new geometry. (1635, 115)

This procedure leads to the theorem now known as "Cavalieri's Principle": if two figures have equal altitudes and sections made by lines parallel to the bases at equal distances are always in a given ratio, then the areas of the figures stand in the same ratio.

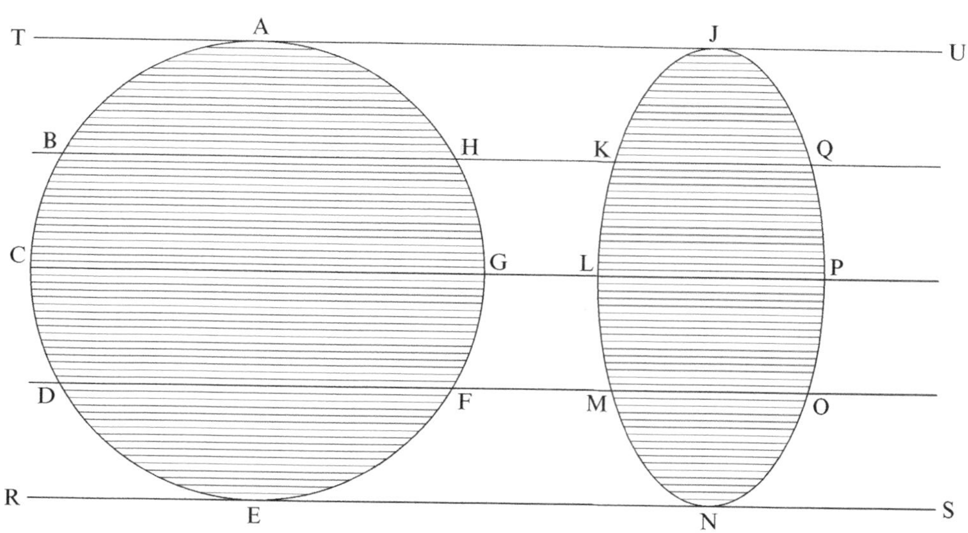

Figure 3.1 Cavalieri's indivisibles.

At first sight it may seem that Cavalieri takes continuous magnitudes (figures) to be composed of infinite collections of indivisibles (lines). He steadfastly denied this, however, and insisted that his method did not run afoul of traditional strictures against the use of infinitely small magnitudes. Other mathematicians who followed Cavalieri were not so cautious. Most notable for our purposes is Wallis's pronouncement that "I suppose, to begin with (according to the Geometry of Indivisibles of Bonaventura Cavalieri) any plane to be made up (so to speak) out of an infinity of parallel lines; or (which I prefer) from an infinity of parallelograms of the same altitude. Let the altitude of any one of them be $1/\infty$ of the whole ... and the altitude of all together being equal to the altitude of the figure" (1693–1699, 1:297). Wallis was hardly alone in this interpretation of Cavalieri: Evangelista Torricelli and Gilles Personne de Roberval were similarly inclined to take the method of indivisibles as based on the notion that continuous magnitudes are composed of infinite collections of infinitesimal parts.[11]

For his part, Hobbes approved of Cavalieri's method while dismissing Wallis's approach as incoherent. In particular, he interpreted Cavalier's notion of "all the lines" in a figure as consistent with his own principle that lines are not breadthless, but rather have a (negligible) breadth that is disregarded in a demonstration. On this interpretation, surfaces are literally composed of finite collections of lines, and Cavalieri's method is fully consistent with the Hobbesian approach to geometry. It is in this sense that Hobbes could insist in *Examinatio* Dialogue 2 that:

> Those things which can exceed one another when multiplied are homogeneous, and these are measurable by a measure of the same kind, as lengths are measurable by lengths, surfaces by surfaces, and solids by solids. However, things heterogeneous are measured by different kinds of measures. Nevertheless, if lines are considered as the most minute parallelograms, as they are considered by those who use the method of demonstration Bonaventura Cavalieri uses in the doctrine of indivisibles, then there will be a ratio between a right line and a plane surface. And indeed such lines, when multiplied, can exceed any given finite plane surface. (OL IV.75)

Hobbes insisted that Wallis had failed to understand Cavalieri's method, and by taking it to require infinite sums of infinitesimal elements he had rendered it incoherent. According to Hobbes in *Lux* chapter 3, Wallis

> supposes two principles; the first is one that (so he says) comes from Cavalieri, namely this: "that any continuous quantity consists of an infinite number of indivisibles", or of an infinity of infinitely small parts. Although I, having read Cavalieri's book, remember nothing of this opinion in it, neither as an axiom, nor a definition, nor a proposition. For it is false. A continuous quantity is always by its nature divisible into parts: nor can there be anything infinitely small, unless there were given a division into nothing. (OL V.109)

In fact, a significant portion of Hobbes's mathematical efforts are modeled on his understanding of the method of indivisibles, and involve taking "least parts" of lines and surfaces in order to determine areas, volumes, or angles.

3.2 The Dispute with Wallis

Any discussion of Hobbes's mathematics takes place against the background of his controversy with Wallis. Indeed, the majority of Hobbes's mathematical writings aim either at countering Wallis's objections or mounting a case against Wallis's own mathematics. The quarrel was ignited in 1655 with the publication of Hobbes's *De corpore*, whose third part (entitled "On the Ratios of Motions and Magnitudes") contains a wide variety of mathematical material, including an attempted circle quadrature in chapter XX. Wallis responded in the same year with *Elenchus geometriæ Hobbianæ*, and the two traded polemics on and off for decades until Hobbes's 1679 death put an end to the matter.[12]

Although the exchange of polemics centered on mathematics, it would be a mistake to think that other factors were absent, as questions of politics and religion (along with fine points of grammar and philology) were raised and debated in the course of the dispute. I propose to recount its origins briefly, and then examine the "method of motion" that Hobbes thought would solve all geometric problems.

3.2.1 *Origins of the Dispute*

Although the 1655 publication of *De corpore* can be taken as the controversy's precipitating event, Hobbes had earned Wallis's enmity years earlier. The appearance of *Leviathan* in 1651 made Hobbes a notorious figure in the English "republic of letters," and Wallis was one of many who was outraged by its materialism, anticlericalism, unorthodoxy, and political theory (Parkin 2010, chapters 2–3). Of particular concern to Wallis (and his Oxford colleague Seth Ward) was Hobbes's hostility to the universities, which *Leviathan* portrayed as intellectual backwaters thoroughly beholden to the authority of Aristotle and home to ambitious churchmen and lawyers who sought to undermine sovereign power (Serjeanston 2006). Matters came to a head in 1653 when several Puritan radicals published tracts attacking the English universities and Parliament entertained a bill to disband them.

Ward took up the cause of defending the universities and in 1654 published *Vindiciæ Academiarum*. Although Hobbes was not Ward's primary target,[13] an Appendix to the work took issue with the status of the universities in *Leviathan* and challenged Hobbes to make good on his claims to have made great contributions to the sciences, and particularly to geometry. Ward wrote "I have heard that M. *Hobbs* hath given out, that he hath found the solution of some Problemes, amounting to no lesse than the Quadrature of the Circle" (1654, 57). Clearly aware of the inadequacies in Hobbes's geometric argumentation he cautioned that

> Geometry hath now so much place in the Universities, that when Mr. *Hobbs* shall have published his Philosophicall and Geometricall Pieces, I assure my selfe, I am able to find a great number in the University, who will understand as much or more of them then he desires they should, indeed too much to keep up in them that Admiration of him which only will content him. (1654, 58)

In the course of events these taunts proved effective and moved Hobbes to include a circle quadrature in chapter XX of *De corpore*. The haste with which Hobbes produced this quadrature resulted in his having to revise it at least twice even as *De corpore* was being printed. In the end, what he had announced as an exact solution to the ancient problem was mournfully downgraded to no more than an approximation that was stated "problematically" rather than demonstratively (Jesseph 1999, 120–5).

Wallis's *Elenchus Geometriæ Hobbianæ* appeared only a few months after *De corpore* and took issue with the entirety of Hobbes's geometrical enterprise. The evisceration of Hobbes's circle quadrature was particularly harsh. Having procured an unbound copy of the first impression of *De corpore*, Wallis traced the sorry history of Hobbes's hastily revised efforts in a way that portrayed the philosopher from Malmesbury as a mathematical incompetent whose failed demonstrations were the product of incurable ignorance and boundless arrogance. Hobbes was quick to respond, publishing a reply to both Wallis and Ward as *Six Lessons to the Professors of the Mathematiques* as an appendix to the 1656 *Of Body*, the English translation of *De corpore*. The resulting controversy dragged on for the remainder of Hobbes's life, and it is fair to say that all of his mathematical publications after 1655 are directed against Wallis and written in the shadow of his *Elenchus*. As he summed up the case in the Preface to *Lux*:

> A certain book of Hobbes's, *De corpore*, published early in 1655, provided the occasion for this dispute. The book contains among other things certain geometrical principles differing from the principles accepted today, and also a demonstration (as he termed it) of the equality of a certain right line and the fourth part of the circumference of the circle. This confidence of Hobbes displeased many mathematicians, especially in the famous universities, some of whom had perhaps thought that all the most difficult problems in geometry had been reserved for only them to solve. And so, in order to overturn this demonstration and the whole geometry of Hobbes, John Wallis, public professor of geometry at the university of Oxford published a book entitled *Elenchus Geometriae Hobbianae*. Εκ τοῦδε ἄρχεται ὁ πόλεμος [From thence arises the war] And this perpetual geometric war has been waged between them without pause. For almost nothing is written by one which is not publicly opposed by the other. (OL V.93)

There is little to be gained from a close examination of each disputant's contributions. Indeed, Hobbes himself dismissed Wallis's works as "puerile, unsophisticated, unlearned, and boorish," adding "Nor do I judge the replies I have made to your works to be worthy to be read by posterity" (OL IV.522). We can, however, gain some insight into Hobbes's approach to geometry by examining some details of his method.

3.2.2 The Method of Motion and Hobbes's Geometric Ambitions

Part III of *De corpore* bears the title "On the Proportions of Motions and Magnitudes" and contains the core geometric chapters of the treatise (namely chapters XV–XXIV). Hobbes intended these to establish his reputation as the foremost geometer in Europe. This outsized ambition is on display at the beginning of chapter XV, where he advises the attentive reader to "take into his hands the works of *Euclide, Archimedes, Apollonius*, and others as well Antient as Modern Writers" in order to appreciate the wealth of new results that will follow (EW I.204). He then lists 11 principles that outline the fundamental properties of motion, which are the basis for what he termed the "method of motion" that would yield straightforward solutions to all manner of geometric problems.

Hobbes's approach is closely connected with Roberval's method of "composition of motions," which he employed in the solution of a wide variety of geometric problems (Julien 2015). The fundamental idea in the method can be illustrated through the comparison of the arc length of the Archimedean spiral and the semiparabola. The spiral *abcdefn* in Figure 3.2 arises from the uniform revolution of a point through the radius *an* in the same time that *an* completes a full revolution about the point *a*. The parabola GT is traced by the combination of a uniform motion through the horizontal axis GA and a uniformly accelerated motion downward to arrive at T. However, the spiral also arises from the combination of a uniform motion and a uniformly accelerated motion: as the point tracing the spiral moves through *an*, the revolution of the radius will make it describe portions of ever greater circular arcs and the lengths described will be as the square of the time. As a consequence, if GA is equal to the radius *an* and AT is equal to half the circumference of the circle with radius *an*, the motion producing the spiral will cover a distance equal to the length of the parabola GT.

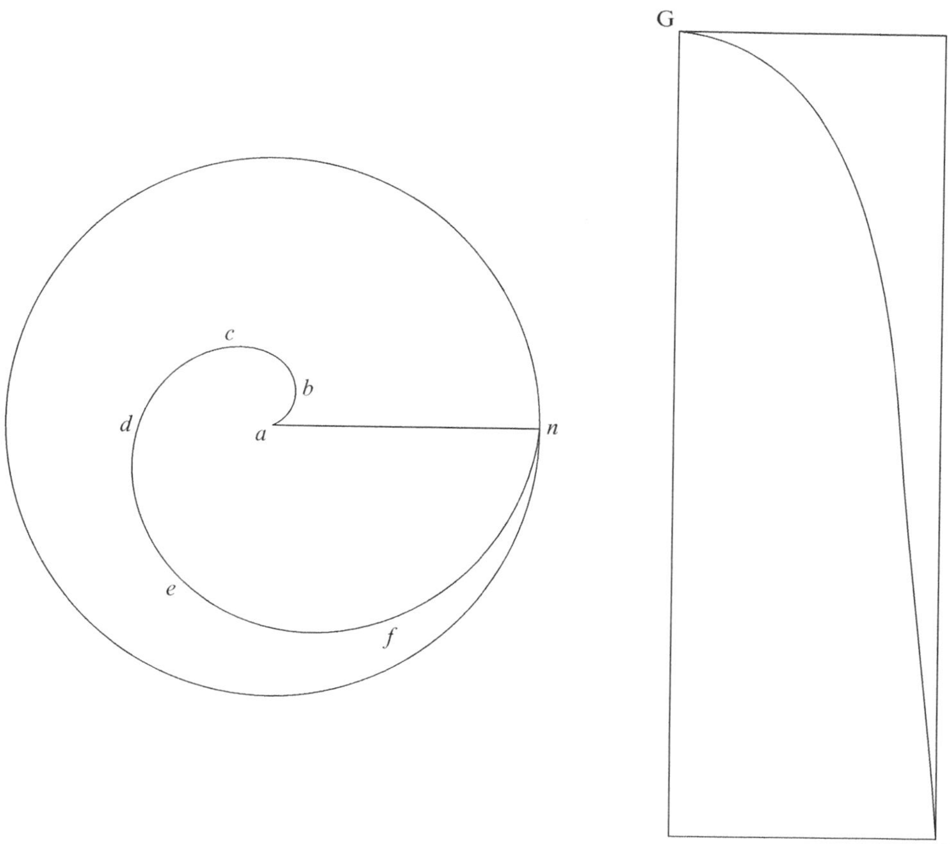

Figure 3.2 Spiral parabola.

This result was first published in the *Hydraulica* of Marin Mersenne, which was part of his 1644 collection *Cogitata Physico-Mathematica*. Mersenne reported the discovery of the result: "when I was concerned with this result, a learned man proposed a certain straight line that he though equal to the first revolution of the spiral *abcdefn*, but the revolution of the spiral was greater than this proposed line, and our geometer showed that the spiral was equal to the parabola *GT*" (Mersenne 1644, 129). The "learned man" is Hobbes, and "our geometer" is Roberval. It is therefore clear that Hobbes was well acquainted with the method of motion in the 1640s through his contact with Roberval by way of Mersenne (Malcolm 2002).

The method of motion dominates the geometrical sections of *De corpore* and it is the source of the putative results with which Hobbes hoped to assert his claim to preeminence in geometry. The catalog of these mathematical contributions includes an analysis of parabolic arcs in the style of Galileo (chapter XVI), the quadrature of parabolic segments that builds on Cavalieri's approach (chapter XVII), a supposed rectification of parabolic arcs (chapter XVIII) and a putative quadrature of the circle (chapter XX). Throughout these chapters Hobbes examines the motions by which geometric magnitudes are generated or transformed – comparing the uniform motion of a point in one direction with its accelerated motion orthogonal to that motion, or examining the "flexion" by which a curved arc can be straightened and compared to a given line (Dunlop 2016; Jesseph 2017).

Hobbes portrays his method of motion as a technique of analysis that went beyond what could be attained with the method of indivisibles in the style of Cavalieri or the algebraic procedures of Viète and Descartes. In *De corpore* XX.6, he appends an interesting account of three styles of analysis to the circle quadrature, contrasting their fitness for determining the equality or inequality of two geometrical quantities. The first method is analysis by motion, because "if to a certain quantity given, it be required to construct another quantity equal, there may be some that will enquire whether this may not be done by means of some motion" (EW I.312). This is Hobbes's preferred style of analysis, which holds out the prospect of solving any geometric problem because it proceeds by analyzing the causes that produce magnitudes. A second method of analysis arises when "equality and inequality are found out often by the division of the two quantities into parts which are considered as undivisible; as *Cavallerius Bonaventura* has done in our time" (EW I.313). This is analysis by indivisibles, which Hobbes clearly took to be an acceptable approach, although inferior to the method of motion. The final sort of analysis involves "the consideration of the *Powers* of lines, or the roots of those *Powers*, and by the multiplication, division, addition, and subtraction, as also by the extraction of the roots of those *Powers*" (EW I.313). This is the style of analysis pursued by Viète and other proponents of algebraic techniques. Hobbes held that this style of analysis "though it be esteemed by some Geometricians (not the chiefest) to be the best way of solving all Problemes, yet it is a thing of no great extent" (EW I.314). Hobbes takes the method to be limited because the algebraic manipulation of squares, cubes, roots, and other powers is confined to the consideration of rectangular areas and rectangular solids. From this, he concluded that "in the quantities of angles, and of the arches of Circles, there is no use at all for the *Analyticks* which proceed by *Powers*" (EW I.315). Consequently, the analysis by powers can offer no insight into such problems as angular section, arc length determination, or the quadrature of curved surfaces.

3.3 Conclusion

Hobbes's mathematical program reached its apogee with the publication of *De corpore*. Wallis's *Elenchus* was such a devastating rebuttal that it moved Christiaan Huygens to wonder why he had bothered to expose Hobbes's mathematical shortcomings in such detail and at such great length.[14] Hobbes never admitted substantive or conceptual errors in his mathematics, and as he continued to publish a stream of works in defense of his claims to mathematical glory he became a laughing stock. By 1662 Huygens could report that "through his frequent mistakes, he has so diminished his credit with everyone, that almost as soon as they see a new problem propounded by Hobbes, they declare that a new ψευδογράθημα has appeared" (Huygens 1888–1950, 2:537). An examination of the record shows the justice of Huygens's judgment: Hobbes's mathematical errors were so fundamental that they generally could not be glossed over with a reinterpretation or mended by modification (Jesseph 1999, Appendix).

The desperate state of Hobbes's mathematical program becomes clear when we note that his quadratures and other putative results are refuted by elementary trigonometric calculation. Thus, the original quadrature in chapter XX of *De corpore* gives a value for π in excess of 3.1419, which exceeds the bounds established by Archimedes. Although Hobbes initially accepted the validity of such trigonometric refutations,[15] he eventually decided that mere "algebraic" calculation could have no bearing on the validity of a purely geometric result because the algebraic multiplication of numbers is fundamentally distinct from the geometric drawing of lines into lines. By 1666 Hobbes was moved to complain in *PRG* chapter 21 that his quadrature in *De corpore* was demonstrated "as manifestly as any proposition in Euclid," but "as soon as it first appeared our professors of mathematics (moved by great anger, while others who shared their opinion heaped praises upon them) attacked this [result], which has been sought with such industry by the greatest geometers of every era" (OL 4.449). In defense of his efforts Hobbes announced:

> This was opposed by the said professors, in part from the tables of sines, tangents, and secants, and in part from the authority of Archimedes. Yet because those tables were constructed by the multiplication of lines by numbers (whose product they falsely computed as a number of squares), and by the extraction of roots from those squares (which roots they falsely computed as a number of lines), the argument taken from those tables has no refutative force. And since Archimedes himself demonstrates his dimension of the circle by the extraction of roots, his authority need not prevail in this matter. (OL IV.450–1)

Doggedly following this line of thought, Hobbes concluded in *PRG* chapter 23 that "the greater part of the propositions that depend on Proposition 47 of Book I of Euclid (and there are many) are not yet demonstrated. Second, the tables of sines, tangents, and secants are entirely false" (OL IV.462–3). Proposition 47 of Book I is the Pythagorean Theorem, whose chance discovery supposedly inspired Hobbes's love of geometry. But to defend his claims to geometric glory, he found himself forced to abandon it. This, more than anything else, shows just how poorly Hobbes fared in his mathematical exploits.

Notes

1 See Scott (1938, chapter 10) and Jesseph (1999, 10–16) for an overview of the many published pieces in the dispute.

2 This is not to say that Hobbes's mathematics has been altogether ignored. See Dunlop (2016), Grant (1996), Jesseph (1999) for treatments of Hobbes's mathematics. Richard Peters summed up the general scholarly embarrassment at Hobbes's mathematical work in claiming that "[e]ven when allowance has been made for the fact that squaring the circle did not then seem quite such a preposterous project as it does now, it remains evident that Hobbes' sublime confidence in his own ability led him to make rather a pathetic exhibition of himself" (1956, 40).

3 In particular, the anecdote requires us to suppose that Hobbes was utterly ignorant of geometry even though he was educated at Oxford, where geometry was a required part of the curriculum. Moreover, Aubrey's story relates the remarkable coincidence that the copy of Euclid that Hobbes came across happened to be open to the Pythagorean Theorem (*Elements*, Bk I, Prop. 47). Further, even allowing for this coincidence, the Euclidean proof is sufficiently complex that it is essentially unintelligible to a complete geometric novice (as Hobbes allegedly was).

4 The passage from the *Examinatio* (Hobbes 1660, 154) is remarkably close to Aubrey's account. Bernhardt (1986) examines it in some detail.

5 Euclid, Elements, Book I, Postulate 1: "Let the following be postulated: to draw a straight line from any point to any point".

6 See Palmieri (2001) for an account of the definition and the discussions it engendered.

7 The actual proof in *De corpore* 2.13.12 (EW I.156–7) is convoluted enough that it need not detain us; Hobbes in fact shows that his definition of sameness of ratio can be used to derive the Euclidean definition as a consequence.

8 See Bos (2001), Jesseph (2016), Mancosu (2008), and Serfati (2005) on the Cartesian program for geometry.

9 For an overview of Viète's approach see Bos (2001, chapter 11). Shirley (1983), and Cajori (1916) give accounts of the contributions of Harriot and Oughtred, respectively.

10 See Andersen (1985) and Jesseph (2020) on Cavalieri's approach.

11 See Bascelli (2015) on Torricelli and Julien (2016) on Roberval.

12 See Jesseph (2018) for an overview of the dispute.

13 Ward was principally concerned with publications by the Puritan radicals John Webster and William Dell. See Debus (1970) for details.

14 "I was amazed that you judged [Hobbes] worthy of such a lengthy refutation, although I read your learned and rather sharp *Elenchus* with some pleasure" (Huygens 1888–1950, 1:392).

15 Hobbes writes: "Having full confidence in his demonstrations, he did not doubt that Archimedes thought the same as he. But after having realized that his geometric methods disagreed with the arithmetical methods of Archimedes, which themselves were properly worked out, he undertook (as far as he could) to alter his so as to agree with the calculations of Archimedes. Yet when he could not succeed in this, he struck the whole chapter; and upon taking the matter up again he did not discern that it reduced to the very same numbers before he handed the book over to the printer. And so he at last reduced his demonstration to a mere approximation, out of respect for Archimedes. So far was he from thinking (as his adversaries claim) that learned men of previous centuries have achieved little, that he abandoned truth itself because of their reputation, even as he was on the point of making it public" (Hobbes 1660, 149–50).

References

Andersen, Kirsti. 1985. "Cavalieri's Method of Indivisibles." *Archive for History of the Exact Sciences* 24: 292–367.

Aubrey, John. 1898. *Brief Lives, Chiefly of Contemporaries*, edited by Andrew Clark, 2 vols. Oxford: Clarendon Press.

Bascelli, Tiziana. 2015. "Torricelli's Indivisibles." In *Seventeenth-Century Indivisibles Revisited*, edited by Vincent Julien, 105–36. Heidelberg, New York, Dordrecht, and London: Springer.

Bernhardt, Jean. 1986. "Témoinage direct de Hobbes sur son 'Illumination Euclidienne'." *Revue Philosophique* 2: 281–2.

Bos, Henk J. M. 2001. *Redefining Geometrical Exactness: Descartes' Transformation of the Early Modern Concept of Construction*. Berlin and New York: Springer.

Cajori, Florian. 1916. *William Oughtred: A Great Seventeenth-Century Teacher of Mathematics*. London and Chicago: Open Court.

Cavalieri, Bonaventura. 1635. *Geometria Indivisibilibus Continuorum Nova Quadam Ratione Promota*. Bologna: J. Monti.

Clavius, Christopher. 1612. *Christophori Clavii Bamburgensis E Societate Jesu Opera Mathematica*, 5 vols. Mainz: R. Eltz.

Debus, Allen G. 1970. *Science and Education in Seventeenth-Century England: The Webster-Ward Debate*. London: Macdonald.

Descartes, René. 1964–1996. *Œuvres de Descartes*, edited by Charles Adam and Paul Tannery. Revised edn. 11 vols. Paris: Vrin. [cited as AT]

Dunlop, Katherine. 2016. "Hobbes's Mathematical Thought." In *The Oxford Handbook of Hobbes*, edited by Aloysius P. Martinich and Kinch Hoekstra, 76–104. Oxford: Oxford University Press.

Euclid. [1925] 1956. *The Thirteen Books of Euclid's "Elements" Translated from the Text of Heiberg*. edited and translated by Thomas L. Heath, 3 vols. Cambridge: Cambridge University Press. Reprint New York: Dover.

Grant, Hardy. 1996. "Hobbes and Mathematics." In *The Cambridge Companion to Hobbes*, edited by Tom Sorell, 108–29. Cambridge: Cambridge University Press.

Hobbes, Thomas. 1660. *Examinatio et emendation mathematicæ hodiernæ*. London: J. Crooke.

Hobbes, Thomas. 1839–1845a. *The English Works of Thomas Hobbes*, 11 vols., edited by Sir William Molesworth. London: John Bohn. Cited as EW.

Hobbes, Thomas. 1839–1845b. *Thomæ Hobbes malmesburiensis opera philosophica*, 5 vols., edited by Gulielmi Molesworth. London: John Bohn. Cited as OL.

Hobbes, Thomas. 2012. *Leviathan*, 2 vols., edited by Noel Malcolm. Oxford: Clarendon Press. [First published 1651].

Huygens, Christiaan. 1888–1950. *Les œuvres completes de Christiaan Huygens*, edited by La Société Hollandaise des Sciences, 22 vols. The Hague: Nijhoff.

Jesseph, Douglas. 1999. *Squaring the Circle: The War between Hobbes and Wallis*. Chicago: University of Chicago Press.

Jesseph, Douglas. 2016. "Geometry." In *The Cambridge Descartes Lexicon*, edited by Lawrence Nolan, 321–9. Cambridge: Cambridge University Press.

Jesseph, Douglas. 2017. "Hobbes on the Ratios of Motions and Magnitudes: The Central Task of De Corpore, Part III." *Hobbes Studies* 30: 59–82.

Jesseph, Douglas. 2018. "Geometry, Religion, and Politics: Context and Consequences of the Hobbes-Wallis Dispute." *Notes and Records of the Royal Society* 72: 469–86.

Jesseph, Douglas. 2020. "The Indivisibles of the Continuum: Seventeenth-Century Adventures in Infinitesimal Mathematics." In *The History of Continua: Philosophical and Mathematical*

Perspectives, edited by Stewart Shapiro and Geoffrey Hellman, 104–22. Oxford: Oxford University Press.

Julien, Vincent. 2016. "Roberval's Indivisibles." In *Seventeenth-Century Indivisibles Revisited*, edited by Vincent Julien, 177–210. Heidelberg, New York, Dordrecht, and London: Springer.

Malcolm, Noel. 2002. "Hobbes and Roberval." In *Aspects of Hobbes*, edited by Noel Malcolm, 156–99. Oxford: Oxford University Press.

Mancosu, Paolo. 2008. "Descartes and Mathematics." In *A Companion to Descartes*, edited by Janet Broughton and John Carriero, 103–23. Oxford: Blackwell.

Mersenne, Marin. 1644. *Cogitata Physico-Mathematica*. Paris: Bertier.

Palmieri, Paolo. 2001. "The Obscurity of the Equimultiples: Clavius' and Galileo's Foundational Studies of Euclid's Theory of Proportions." *Archive for History of Exact Sciences* 55: 555–97.

Parkin, Jon. 2010. *Taming the Leviathan: The Reception of the Political and Religious Ideas of Thomas Hobbes in England (1640–1700)*. Cambridge: Cambridge University Press.

Peters, Richard. 1956. *Hobbes*. Harmondsworth: Penguin.

Proclus. 1970. *A Commentary on the First Book of Euclid's "Elements"*, edited by Glen R. Morrow. Princeton, NJ: Princeton University Press.

Scott, Joseph F. 1938. *The Mathematical Work of John Wallis*. London: Taylor and Francis.

Serfati, Michel. 2005. "René Descartes' *Géométrie*." In *Landmark Writings in Western Mathematics, 1640–1940*, edited by Ivor Grattan-Guinness, 1–22. Amsterdam: Elsevier.

Serjeanston, Richard. 2006. "Hobbes, the Universities, and the History of Philosophy." In *The Philosopher in Early Modern Europe*, edited by Conal Condren, Stephen Gaukroger, and Ian Hunter, 113–39. Cambridge: Cambridge University Press.

Shirley, John W. 1983. *Thomas Harriot*. Oxford: Oxford University Press.

Viète, François. 1591. *In Artem Analyticem Isagoge*. Tours: Mettayer.

Wallis, John. 1655. *Elenchus Geometriæ Hobbianæ*. Oxford: J. Crooke.

Wallis, John. 1693–1699. *Johannis Wallis S. T. D. ... Opera Mathematica*, 3 vols. Oxford: At the Sheldonian Theater.

Ward, Seth. 1654. *Vindiciæ Academiarum*. Oxford: L. Litchfield.

4

Explanations in Hobbes's Optics and Natural Philosophy

MARCUS P. ADAMS

In the Epistle Dedicatory of *De corpore*, Thomas Hobbes claimed that in his time natural philosophy was only in its infancy, having been born with work of Copernicus, Galileo, Harvey, Kepler, Gassendi, and Mersenne (EW I.ix). Although he portrayed himself as the progenitor of civil philosophy, Hobbes also saw himself as contributing to the (in his opinion) juvenile disciplines of optics and natural philosophy. For example, he claimed in 1646 in *A Minute or First Draught of the Optiques* (hereafter *Minute*) that he would "deserve the Reputation of having beene the first to lay the ground of two Sciences, this of Opticques, the most curious, and that other of naturall Justice, which I have done in my book *De cive*, the most profitable of all other" (Hobbes 1983 [1646], 622; cf. EW VII.471).

Hobbes's bombastic appraisals of himself aside, his contemporaries took his work in optics seriously and Mersenne included an optical treatise of Hobbes's in *Ballistica* (1644).[1] Hobbes's 1641 correspondence with Descartes ended with Descartes saying that he "to have nothing more to do with [Hobbes]" because he thought that Hobbes was trying to gain reputation at Descartes' expense (AT III.320, CSMK 173), but their correspondence shows disagreements between them concerning, for example, refraction in media and the nature of light (see Letters 29–30 and 32–4 in Hobbes 1994a).

Hobbes's interests in optics should make sense to anyone familiar with the opening chapters of *Leviathan*. If one seeks to ground all ideas, and thus all knowledge, in sensation, as Hobbes declares in *Leviathan* chapter 1 (2012, 22; 1651, 3), then developing an optical theory is paramount. Hobbes's aim in optics, and in natural philosophy generally, was to explain various phenomena in a way that cohered with mechanical philosophy, so, for example, no appeal to *species* would be permitted. However, rather than looking to Hobbes's optics and natural philosophy in themselves, the present chapter explores these areas of Hobbes's thought from another angle: to show that Hobbes's explanations in optics take the same form as how he understood ideal explanations in natural philosophy. When providing an explanation in both of these disciplines Hobbes

A Companion to Hobbes, First Edition. Edited by Marcus P. Adams.

appeals both to everyday, unaided sense experience and to geometry. Hobbes explicitly identifies this form of explanation with "mixed-mathematics," and he goes so far as to say that "true physics" depends upon geometry in this way (Hobbes 1994b [1658], 42; OL II.93).

First, I discuss Hobbes's *statements about* the structure of philosophy and suggest that a focus on these reflections – rather than on Hobbes's explanatory practice – has led some scholars to understand Hobbes as an armchair speculative philosopher, both in his own natural-philosophy endeavors and his well-known criticisms of Robert Boyle and other experimental philosophers. Beyond Hobbes's *statements about* natural philosophy, I argue that a more complete understanding of his natural philosophy must also consider his *practice of* explaining in natural philosophy and optics. Next, I show that explanations in optics and natural philosophy are, according to Hobbes, ideally a mixture of appeals to everyday sense experience and Hobbes's own *a priori* geometry by providing two case studies: a case study from Hobbes's optics in *De homine* II and a case study of Hobbes's explanation of sense in *De corpore* XXV. Rather being an armchair speculative philosopher who devalued experience, in Hobbes's practice of explanation everyday experience, not experiments like those of the Royal Society, played an integral role insofar as it provided what was to be explained (the "that") while geometry provided the probable cause (the "why").

4.1 Statements about the Relationships among the Parts of Philosophy

Hobbes reflects on the relationships among the areas of his philosophy in several places in the corpus, but his most extensive reflection upon these relationships is in *De corpore* VI.6. At first glance, it may seem that Hobbes is advancing a reductionist program along the following lines: all natural phenomena are reducible to minute bodies in motion. If this reductionist picture is correct, then it looks as though the parts of philosophy can be organized from first philosophy to physics, and from "morals" to civil philosophy, with first philosophy serving as the foundational discipline for all philosophy, as displayed in Figure 4.1.

Indeed, in *De corpore* VI.6, Hobbes details how one should begin from the knowledge of the "universals" of first philosophy, such as the knowledge of what "place," "body," and "motion" are, and then use that knowledge to develop geometrical definitions. For example, using the knowledge of such universals as these one can form the definition of "line" as that which is "made by the motion of a point" (OL I.63; Hobbes 1981, 297). After working in geometry, which he says studies motion *simpliciter*, Hobbes suggests that there should be a general study of "those things which occur from the motion of the parts" (OL I.64; Hobbes 1981, 299). This will lead to considering "sensible qualities" such as light, color, sound, odor, and flavor, but before these can be explained the human senses that perceive these qualities must be understood. These third and fourth parts of philosophy together constitute physics (*physica*).

Finally, Hobbes notes that "[a]fter physics we come to morals" in which desire and aversion, and passions generally, are examined as "motions of the mind" (OL I.64; Hobbes 1981, 299). He explains that the reason why the study of the passions follows physics is

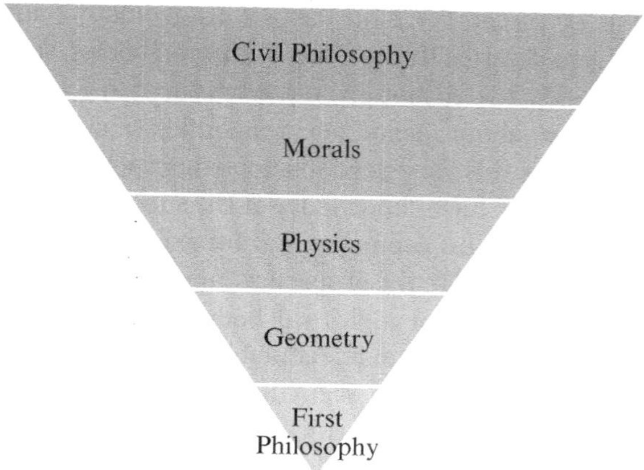

Figure 4.1 Hierarchy of the parts of philosophy.

that the passions have their "causes in physics" (OL I.64; Hobbes 1981, 299). Hobbes concludes this reflection on the relationships among the parts of philosophy by claiming that anyone who attempts to engage in natural philosophy without taking principles from geometry will be making vain attempts. Furthermore, he declares that anyone who engages in such useless activity will "abuse their listeners" (OL I.65; Hobbes 1981, 301).

This reflection Hobbes offers *about* natural philosophy and its relationship to the other parts of philosophy suggests a deductive relationship, and many Hobbes scholars have argued that such a view was Hobbes's (Martinich 2005; Peters 1967; Shapin and Schaffer 1985; Watkins 1965). An even stronger view sees Hobbes as a type of reductionist (for example, Hampton 1986; Ryan 1970). For example, Alan Ryan offers a version of this reductionist interpretation of Hobbes as follows:

> Hobbes believed as firmly as one could that all behaviour, whether of animate or inanimate matter, was ultimately to be explained in terms of particulate motion: the laws governing the motions of discrete material particles were the ultimate laws of the universe, and in this sense psychology must be rooted in physiology and physiology in physics, while the social sciences, especially the technology of statecraft, must be rooted in psychology. (1970, 102–3)

As is clear from the *De corpore* VI.6 passage discussed already, there is some textual support for this understanding of Hobbes's philosophy. If this view that ultimately all behavior of matter is explained in terms of the most basic physical laws is correct, then we might expect that in Hobbes's actual practice he would provide explanations that appeal to more "basic" particles and laws about how those particles behave. Furthermore, we would expect him to provide bridge principles stating how statements about macroscopic entities, like human bodies or commonwealth (artificial) bodies, reduce to statements about microscopic entities.

A significant difficulty faces the deductivist and reductionist interpretations: How would a deduction or reduction actually work between, say, a statement in "morals" and statements in geometry or physics? Consider the concept of "endeavor," which

Hobbes introduces in *De corpore* XV.2 (in Part III on geometry) and then uses again within civil philosophy to describe the motions of human bodies, since the passions are endeavor (2012, 78; 1651, 23). Although endeavor is used in geometry, moral philosophy must add information about *human* passions understood as endeavor. As will be discussed, Hobbes describes this very need to supplement with additional information in *De homine* X.5 as needing to have "knowledge of the subject" (in Hobbes's description of the relationship between pure geometry and mixed mathematics; Hobbes 1994b [1658], 42; OL II.93). In particular, the properties "appetite" and "aversion" are added, but these properties obviously do not apply to all bodies in general. As a result, endeavor in human bodies (the passions) will not be reducible to endeavor in geometry (for similar discussion, see Malcolm 2002, 147). Were this reduction what Hobbes had in mind, we would expect him to provide bridge principles to show how "endeavor" in human bodies can be reduced to "endeavor" in bodies in general.

Two additional statements that Hobbes makes in the surrounding context of *De corpore* VI.6 further complicate things for the deductivist or reductionist interpretations. First, after making the link between physics and morals, he advises that what he has described is the order of investigation:

> That all these things ought to be investigated in the order I have said [*Haec autem eo ordine quem dixi investiganda esse*] consists in the fact that physics cannot be understood unless the motion which is in the minutest parts of bodies is known and such motion of the parts unless what it is that effects motions in another thing is known, and this unless what simple motion effects is known. (OL I.64–5; Hobbes 1981, 299–301)

Labeling this as about the order of investigation suggests that one should engage in preparatory work in First Philosophy and geometry *before* attempting to provide explanations in natural philosophy or about the human passions. As will be discussed, understanding these comments as about the order of *investigation*, and not as advocating for a deductivist or reductionist mode of explanation, makes sense of Hobbes's actual practice of natural philosophy where one borrows (already known, and thus first in order) causal principles from geometry for use within an explanation.

Second, Hobbes's discussion in *De corpore* VI.7 further confounds claims that he held a deductivist or reductionist view. There Hobbes states that although civil philosophy is connected to "morals," the latter of which is connected to the other parts of philosophy, civil philosophy can be "detached" from it because the "causes of the motions of the mind are not only known by reasoning but also by the experience of each and every person observing those motions proper to him only" (OL I.65; Hobbes 1981, 301).

How is this flexibility for learning the "principles of politics" possible according to Hobbes? Elsewhere, Hobbes distinguishes between two paths that one can take in philosophizing – synthesis and analysis – and he incorporates these two paths in definitions of "philosophy" in *De corpore* (for example, in *De corpore* I.2; OL I.2; Hobbes 1981, 175). Hobbes uses synthesis and analysis simplistically, sometimes calling them compounding or composing and resolving and other times calling them adding and subtracting (for example, *De corpore* VI.1; OL I.59; Hobbes 1981, 289). For example, he describes how the conception "square" is resolved in analysis into "plane," "bounded by a certain of lines equal to one another," and "right angles," which parts of "square" are further resolved into the "universals or components of every material thing: *line, plane* (in which a surface is contained), *being bounded, angle, rectitude,* and *equality*" (OL I.61; Hobbes 1981, 293). Then, those component parts are put back together (in synthesis), and by doing so learns that these parts are the "cause of square."[2]

Applying these two paths of synthesis and analysis to the issue at hand, Hobbes says that one can proceed (in the order of one's investigation) synthetically by beginning in First Philosophy with (already known) conceptions such as "space" and "motion *simpliciter*" and working through geometry, physics, and morals, adding the relevant concepts proper to each discipline along the way, until coming to the principles of politics (OL I.63–5; Hobbes 1981, 297–301). Alternatively, Hobbes claims that "those who have not learned the earlier part of philosophy ... can nevertheless come to the principles of civil philosophy by the analytic method" (OL I.65; Hobbes 1981, 301). How does this analysis work for such individuals? Hobbes suggests that whenever the everyday person without prior philosophical training is presented with a question (such as "whether such and such an action is just or unjust"), they are capable of resolving or analyzing the conceptions in that question into component parts. This analysis will break apart "unjust" into "fact" and "against the laws" and by continuing to resolve these conceptions will arrive at "the fact that the appetites men and the motions of their minds are such that they will wage war against each other unless controlled by some power" (OL I.66; Hobbes 1981, 303).

Hobbes optimistically claims that once the everyday person arrives at this knowledge of humans in their natural state simply by analysis from a question like "is X just or unjust" that they will be able to determine whether *any* possible action is just or unjust "by composition" (OL I.66; Hobbes 1981, 303). Thus, the everyday person will engage in *both* analysis and synthesis. The picture that emerges is that by either means one may arrive at the principles of civil philosophy, and that either path (in Figure 4.2) is a legitimate means of doing so.

Against the portrayal of Hobbes as a reductionist or deductivist, Hobbes's claims about these two orders of knowing eschews reduction or an attempted strict derivation from one "level" to another. On the first path of synthesis (the left inverted

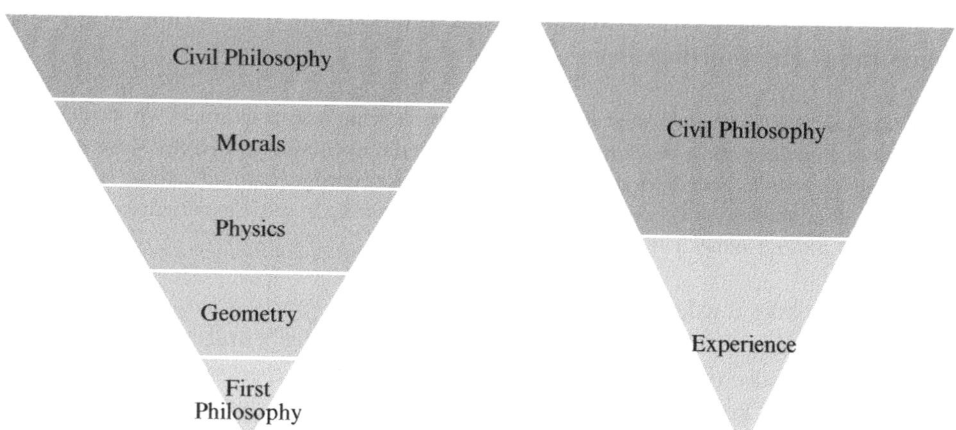

Figure 4.2 Orders of knowing to arrive at civil philosophy.

pyramid in Figure 4.2), one begins in First Philosophy and clarifies conceptions like "space," "place," and "motion *simpliciter*." These conceptions are then used within geometry when making figures such as lines and squares. Those geometrical figures incorporate the conceptions from First Philosophy but are in no way reducible to them; indeed, geometry *adds to* these earlier conceptions as it makes figures and determines their natures. Continuing upward, as it were, geometry will be used within physics but physics must add to geometry when it treats features of actual bodies in nature, such as "the action of shining [bodies]" (Hobbes 1973 [1642–1643], 106; 1976 [1642–1643], 24–5). This "adding to" activity, as has been discussed already, constitutes synthesis for Hobbes.

However, Hobbes held that an alternative order of knowing from the everyday experience of one's own mind to the principles of civil philosophy was an equally legitimate way to arrive at the principles of civil philosophy. In this case (the right inverted pyramid in Figure 4.2), one subtracts or resolves the questions made salient in one's personal experience, such as "is X just or unjust?" by considering one's conception of "just" and examining its component parts. This subtracting or resolving will continue until reaching a claim about humans in their natural state. Then moving from that claim – in synthesis – one can determine whether *any* action would be just or unjust.[3] Hobbes does not assume that those moving from everyday experience to the state of nature have stopped in an inferior place compared to the starting point for those beginning in First Philosophy. In other words, he does not claim that ideally there should be a further reduction; these two orders are simply different means for reaching the same result.

The following section and the next turn away from Hobbes's *statements about* how the parts of his philosophy fit together and focus instead on Hobbes's *actual practice* of providing explanations. Scholarly attention has mostly been directed toward the former, but in actual practice we find Hobbes weaving together principles from geometry into explanations that simultaneously rely upon everyday experience and geometry. What could allow him to do this, assuming his statements and practice are consistent with one another? Before turning toward Hobbes's practice, I will first discuss briefly what Hobbes describes in *De homine* as "true physics" (Hobbes 1994b [1658], 42; OL II.93).

The starting point for considering what Hobbes calls "true physics" is a division that he makes in *De corpore* VI.1 between knowing with certainty (*scientia*) and more mundane forms of knowing (*cognitio*):

> We are said to know [*scire*] some effect when we know what its causes are, in what subject they are, in what subject they introduce the effect and how they do it. Therefore, this is the knowledge [*scientia*] τοῦ διότι or of causes. All other knowledge [*cognitio*], which is called τοῦ ὅτι, is either sense experience or imagination remaining in sense experience or memory. (OL I.58–9; Hobbes 1981, 287–9)

Essentially, Hobbes divides all human knowledge into two parts: *scientia*, for which we possess knowledge of the causes (i.e., knowledge of the "why"), and *cognitio*, for which we have mere sense experience or the remnants of sense experiences in the form of imaginations (i.e., knowledge of the "that"). These two parts provide different levels of certainty to knowers. Since *scientia* is knowledge of the *actual* causes of some effect, knowers possess certainty concerning how that effect came to be.[4]

How could Hobbes, with his reliance upon sense as the source for all ideas (e.g., 2012, 22; 1651, 3), hope to lay claim to epistemic certainty? The move he makes is that humans possess *scientia* only in cases where they act as the maker of some effect, and so geometry and civil philosophy are the only contexts in which this is possible, a claim Hobbes makes in *Six Lessons* (EW VII.184) and in *De homine* (OL II.93–4; Hobbes 1994b [1658], 41). In both geometry and civil philosophy, human knowers begin from abstract objects, such as bodies in imagination *considered as* geometrical points or human bodies in imagination *considered as* being in their natural state. There are no such entities in the natural world, as Hobbes's criticisms of Euclid make clear (e.g., EW VII.202), but humans can create them by considering their imaginations in certain ways. Human knowers next move around those abstract objects in their imagination and consider the effects of combinations of those bodies and the motions of those bodies. In doing this, they create some effect, such as "lines and figures" in geometry (EW VII.184) or "the principles – that is, the causes of justice (namely laws and covenants) ..." in civil philosophy (OL II.94; Hobbes 1994b [1658], 42). They possess *scientia* of those effects because they, as makers, brought them about as they actively constructed them.

The second part of Hobbesian human knowledge – *cognitio* – provides the basis for nearly all human decisions. When I hear a sound outside at night, suspect that sound is a coyote, and decide to check the security of the chicken coop, this results in a *conjecture*. The conjecture I make is only as good as my prior experiences: those of nocturnal animal noises, my comparison between the current sound and those in the past, and the linkages related to what happened to the coop following my hearing of past sounds from coyotes (stored as "Transitions from one imagination to another ..." from past sense experiences; see *Leviathan* 3; 2012, 38; 1651, 8). The likelihood that my conjecture "The hens are about to be eaten!" will be accurate will thus depend upon the quantity and quality of those past experiences, what Hobbes describes in *Leviathan* 3 as "*Foresight*, and *Prudence*, or *Providence*; and sometimes *Wisdome*" (2012, 42; 1651, 10).

Hobbes recognizes that conjectures of this sort can be "very fallacious" because of the "difficulty of observing all circumstances" (2012, 42; 1651, 10). His example of such a conjecture is when someone "foresees what wil become of a Criminal," and he seems to mean that if someone saw all of the linkages between *every* criminal and the punishment each of those criminals received for each crime (an induction by simple enumeration), then that person would have certainty about statements like the following: "This criminal will be sent to the gallows." Were human knowers able to observe "all circumstances" in this way, then the distinction between *scientia* and *cognitio* would dissolve. However, since humans have different experiences from one another, both in terms of quantity and quality, Hobbes states that prudence comes in degrees: "by how much one man has more experiences of things past, than another; by so much also he is more Prudent" (2012, 42; 1651, 10).

A *prima facie* worry concerning Hobbes's bifurcation of all human knowledge into *scientia* and *cognitio* is that, so far, it appears that natural philosophy may merely be the result of prudence. Indeed, Hobbes is explicit in *Six Lessons* that unlike in geometry and civil philosophy human knowers fail to possess knowledge of the causes of natural phenomena, since they are not the Creator: "But because of natural bodies we know not the construction but seek it from the effects there lies no demonstration of what the causes be we seek for but only of what they may be" (EW VII.184). Likewise, in *De corpore* XXV.1 he emphasizes that he will not offer explanations of how natural phenomena *are* generated by rather how they *may be* generated (OL I.316; EW I.388). In that same context, he identifies the *explananda* of natural philosophy as the phenomena, or effects of nature, which are "known through sense [*per sensum cognitis*]" (OL I.316; EW I.388), harkening back to his bifurcation of knowledge by using a cognate of *cognitio*.

What sets apart an explanation in natural philosophy, say, of the possible cause of some phenomenon like the sun warming a rock, from my conjecture, relying upon prudence, that the hens are about to be devoured by a coyote? The difference, Hobbes holds, lies in the source of the inference that we make. Rather than merely relying upon past associations from experiences stored as trains of imaginations, when I provide a possible cause for some phenomena in natural philosophy I *borrow the cause from geometry*.[5] Since human knowers can possess *scientia* in geometry, when I use a geometrical principle within a natural-philosophical explanation what I provide is transformed from being a potentially "very fallacious" conjecture to what we may call suppositional certainty (Adams 2016, 47; 2017, 104). I cannot be certain that the cause borrowed from geometry is the *actual* way that nature brings about a given appearance, but I can be certain that *if* nature behaved according to the geometrical principle borrowed *then* the phenomenon would follow necessarily. The two case studies below will give examples of this borrowing that provides suppositional certainty.

Thus far, we have seen how natural philosophy is distinct from and lies epistemically between *scientia* and *cognitio*; indeed, explanation in natural philosophy involves *mixing* something from both. In an ideal natural-philosophical explanation, one will rely upon sense experience to show *that* some phenomenon occurs and then borrow a causal principle from geometry to provide a plausible reason for *why* it occurs. This understanding of natural philosophy as mixing places value on both the "that" and the "why," and Hobbes admits in *De homine* XI.10 that "histories are particularly useful, for they supply the experiences/experiments [*experimenta*] on which the sciences of the causes [*scientiae causarum*] rest" (OL II.100; see also OL I.9). Hobbes thinks about this mixing in light of discussions preceding him of the relationship between mathematics and natural philosophy, and his use of Greek terminology suggests that he had Aristotle's view in mind, though he did not apply it strictly (Adams 2016; see also discussion of Hobbes and mixed mathematics in Biener 2016).

Hobbes explicitly identifies explanations in natural philosophy as a mixing these two types of knowledge in *De homine* X.5, where he argues that

> since one cannot proceed in reasoning about natural things that are brought about by motion from the effects to the causes without a knowledge of those things that follow from that kind of motion; and since one cannot proceed to the consequences of motions without a knowledge of quantity, which is geometry; nothing can be demonstrated by physics without something also being demonstrated a priori. Therefore physics (I mean true physics) [*vera physica*], that depends on geometry, is usually numbered among the mixed mathematics [*mathematicas mixtas*].

> Therefore those mathematics are pure which (like geometry and arithmetic) revolve around quantities in the abstract [*in abstracto*] so that work [in them] requires no knowledge of the subject; those mathematics are mixed, in truth, which in their reasoning some quality of the subject is also considered, as is the case with astronomy, music, physics, and the parts of physics that can vary on account of the variety of species and the parts of the universe.[6] (Hobbes 1994b [1658], 42; OL II.93)

Hobbes is clear: ideally physics of the proper sort – what he calls "true physics" – should be classified as part of "mixed mathematics." According to Hobbes, the difference between pure mathematics and mixed mathematics is that for the latter in addition to quantity "some quality of the subject is also considered." For example, rather than treating refraction and reflection of bodies in general – "in the abstract" (EW I.386) – like Hobbes does in *De corpore* XXIV, in optics one must also include reference to the behavior of light and light-producing bodies as well as to the properties of the parts of the eye, such as the crystalline humor, *processus ciliares*, and retina. In *Anti-White* I.1, Hobbes makes this point by describing mixed mathematics as treating "quantity and number, not in the abstract [*non abstracte*], but in the motion of the stars, or in the motion of heavy [bodies], or in the action of shining [bodies], and of those which make sounds" (Hobbes 1973 [1642–1643], 106; 1976 [1642–1643], 24–5).

This move Hobbes makes drastically expands the purview of mixed mathematics, or what Aristotle the subalternate sciences, beyond domains such as optics, harmonics, and mechanics. Indeed, in *Posterior Analytics* Aristotle holds that one should ideally *not* attempt to "prove by any other science the theorems of a different one, except such as are so related to one another that the one is under the other – e.g. optics to geometry and harmonics to arithmetic" (*Posterior Analytics* I.7, 75b14–17; Aristotle 1984, 122).[7]

4.2 Hobbesian Optics: The Visual Line and the Optic Axis in *De Homine* II

Hobbes's chapters on optics in chapters II–IX of *De homine* (OL II.7–87) are oddly placed within his three-volume *Elementa Philosophiae*, which comprised three sections: *De corpore*, *De homine*, and *De cive*. Since these optical writings are purported to be about vision for *all* animals and not just vision for humans, it is strange to find them placed within that work, especially since discussion of uniquely human features does begin in chapter X (*De sermone*) of that work.[8] This odd placement may result from the circumstantial manner in which *De cive* (1642) was published first, long before Hobbes was satisfied with *De corpore* (1655). Hobbes waited even longer to publish *De homine* (1658), and its publication was a topic of conversation for Hobbes's correspondents.[9]

Such delay in publishing his optical work, which had already been sketched out in his unpublished *Minute* (1983), as part of the *Elementa* trilogy may just be haphazard editing work on Hobbes's part. However, another possibility is that Hobbes developed his view of how tightly linked the methodology of optics, which was part of mixed mathematics, or subalternate science by his predecessors, was to natural philosophy only after *De corpore* had already been published. Indeed, we only find him making the claim, mentioned above, that "physics (I mean true physics), that depends on geometry, is usually numbered among the mixed mathematics" (Hobbes 1994b [1658], 42; OL II.93) three years *after* publishing his most significant work in physics (Part IV of *De corpore*). In *Anti-White* I.1 (1642/43) Hobbes had boldly asserted that "all the sciences would have been mathematical had not their authors asserted more than they were able to prove; indeed, it is because of the temerity and the ignorance of writers on physics and morals that geometry and arithmetic are the only mathematical ones" (Hobbes

1973 [1642–1643], 106; 1976 [1642–1643], 24). Indeed, in *Anti-White* Hobbes does not identify natural philosophy as mixed mathematics, including only astronomy, mechanics, optics, and music in a list (Hobbes 1973 [1642–1643], 106; 1976 [1642–1643], 24). It is not until 15 years later in *De homine*, reflecting backward upon his own work in *De corpore*, that Hobbes declares that "true physics" is mixed mathematics. This is speculative, but had Hobbes arrived at this connection earlier, it would have made more sense to include the *De homine* II–IX within *De corpore* Part IV rather than within the second section of the *Elementa*. For the present discussion, Hobbes's optics is of interest because of what it shows about Hobbes's understanding of the relationship between geometry and explanations of natural phenomena.

Hobbes based his optics upon what he called the "visual line" and a claim that distinct vision occurs through the optic axis, i.e., the line through which rays from an external object strike the eye perpendicularly and then, after hitting the retina, reflect back outward from the eye by following the same line on which they entered. This line moving back outward is the visual line, which Hobbes defines in *Minute* as "the line wherein any point in the object shall appeare" (1983 [1646], 336). Only rays traveling through the optic axis will generate distinct vision, and he declares that vision outside the optic axis will be "confused and feeble" (OL II.14). This is why it is necessary when perceiving an object in motion, or even a very large object, for human perceivers to move their eyes or turn their head. In moving their eyes or their head, perceivers' tracking movements keep the parts of an external object within their optic axis, making distinct vision possible.

These two foundational components to Hobbes's optics – the visual line and the optic axis – are present in Hobbes's *Minute* of 1646 (1983), which pre-dates *De homine*. However, in the *De homine* rendition of these ideas Hobbes now has available his own geometry from *De corpore* Part III, and he provides citations to geometrical principles from it. He uses these geometrical principles in *De homine* II to explain the apparent location of external objects with reference to the optic axis. Hobbes saw his account of the apparent location of objects as what differentiated his optics from others; indeed, he claimed in *Minute* that others working in optics had failed sufficiently to focus on apparent locations of objects and had instead focused on the "place of the Image" (1983 [1646], 335). An additional foundational component to Hobbes's optics (discussed later) is that sensation generally, of which vision is one kind, is caused by pressure propagated through media and that when a human perceiver's body is affected by pressure from external objects their body will resist that pressure. This resistance from the perceiver's body will reflect that pressure outward, similar to how light reflects after shining on a mirror. That outward reflection generates distinct vision when the pressure inward occurs in the optic axis and results in "confused and feeble" vision when not.

Hobbes argues that objects perceived through the optic axis will have an apparent location that corresponds to their actual location. To show this, in *De homine* Hobbes explicitly cites a geometrical principle from *De corpore* XXIV.2 related to refraction: "[i]f a body pass, or there be generation of motion from one medium to another of different density, in a line perpendicular to the separating superficies, there will be no refraction" (EW I.376). Within a demonstration that distinct vision happens through the optic axis, Hobbes cites this *general* geometrical principle to derive that when a ray, understood as motion (pressure), passes from one medium to another medium of different density (such as from the air to the eye and through the crystalline humor before striking the retina) it will not refract if it strikes the new medium perpendicularly. Since there is no refraction, after striking the retina the motion will be continued outward from the perceiver's body along a line perpendicular to the surface of the eye. This will result, Hobbes claims, in an object's apparent location (subjective to a perceiver) matching that object's actual location.

In terms of Figure 4.3, object F will appear in the same location as its actual location because the ray from F, strikes B perpendicularly and returns along the same line after striking D. Hobbes makes this move with a direct citation "(*per* De corpore *cap. XXIV. art. 2*)" (OL II.8), signaling that the "abstract" geometrical principle has now been used directly within this explanation. A simple analogy may help explain what Hobbes has in mind. Imagine shining a flashlight at a mirror so that the light from the flashlight strikes the surface of the mirror perpendicularly. In that case, the line the light follows from the mirror in reflection will match its initial path from the flashlight to the mirror; the light will end where it started. Likewise, when a ray from an external object strikes the eye perpendicularly, Hobbes claims that the rebounding ray from the eye will make it so that the apparent location of the object matches the object's actual location.

Hobbes appeals to a second geometrical principle in *De homine* II, this time to explain why vision that occurs by means of a ray striking the eye obliquely, i.e., outside the optic axis, will result in an object's apparent location not matching its actual location. This time he borrows and cites a geometrical principle from *De corpore* XXII.6 that establishes that when some body A presses against body B, without penetrating the body B, body A will "recede in a straight line perpendicular to its superficies in that point in which it was pressed" (EW I.336). Although Hobbes holds that rays entering the eye obliquely will be refracted through the humors inside the eye toward the center of that organ, they will ultimately strike the retina in a different place compared to rays

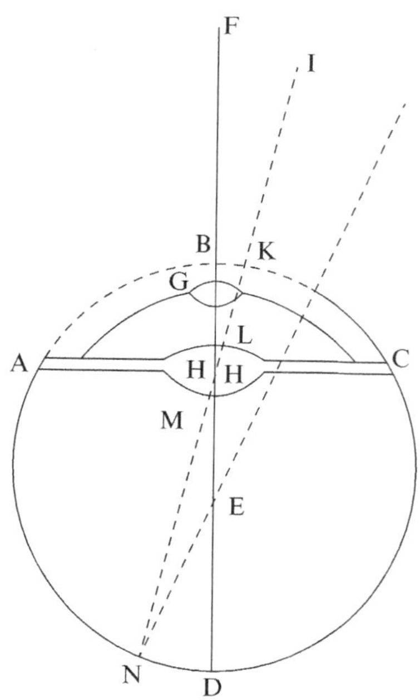

Figure 4.3 Diagram from *De homine* II.

entering through the optic axis. As a result, he claims that when reflecting from the retina and continuing out of the eye, the visual line for such an object will present its apparent location as different from its actual location. In terms of Figure 4.3, the ray from object I strikes the eye obliquely and ultimately hits the retina at N. Given the principle from *De corpore* XXII.6, the ray reflects from the surface of the retina perpendicularly, which results in the apparent location of object I being along the line from N to E.

These two appeals to, and explicit citations of, geometrical principles are clear (these both provide the "why"), but if this is supposed to be a *mixed* mathematics explanation where are the appeals to experience (the "that")? Foundational to the discussion of the visual line and the optic axis are two claims to which anyone with everyday visual experiences would agree: first, sometimes an object's apparent location is different from its actual location; and second, to view objects that are moving or are very large, human perceivers must move their eyes and, sometimes, their head, to perceive well. These two claims, which arise from everyday experience, are the "that," and the two principles from geometry provide the "why."[10]

4.3 Hobbesian Natural Philosophy: Sense in *De Corpore* XXV

Hobbes had a keen interest in understanding human sensation, especially since he held that all ideas began in whole or in part in sense. His discussion of sense in *Leviathan* 1 is well known, but Hobbes himself states that what he offers there is not so much an explanation on its own but rather has been provided to prevent there being a gap in the account offered in *Leviathan*:

> To know the cause of naturall Sense, is not very necessary to the business now in hand; and I have written else-where of the same at large. Nevertheless, to fill each part of my present method, I will deliver the same in this place. (2012, 22; 1651, 3)

Hobbes may have had *Elements of Law* in mind with this reference to what had been "written else-where," or perhaps he had the explanation offered in *De corpore* XXV that would be published later (as Malcolm notes; see 2012, 23 fn. a). Regardless, the explanation that Hobbes provides in *De corpore* XXV will be the focus of this section because, just as in the case from *De homine* examined above, in that chapter Hobbes provides an explicit citation to a principle from geometry as well as to two principles from first philosophy, the latter of which underwrite exchanging equivalent terms. The importance of this explanation in *De corpore* chapter XXV is clear since Hobbes opens Part IV of that work ("Of Physics, or the Phenomena of Nature") with it, and Hobbes emphasizes the significance of understanding the nature of "appearing itself" before one can understand nature's appearances (OL I.316).

Hobbes's explanation of sense in *De corpore* XXV is in a series of steps, beginning as follows:[11]

(1) All sensation is a mutation of a sentient body;
(2) All mutation is *either* motion or endeavor, but endeavor is also motion;
(3) Therefore, all sensation is motion of a sentient body (derived from 1 and 2).

(4) The motion of any body A occurs only by means of some other body B, which is contiguous to A and presses upon A; and
(5) Therefore, all sensation occurs by contiguous bodies pressing upon a sentient body, i.e., the organs of sense, which motion continues in the sentient body (derived from 3 and 4).

The first step of this explanation, I suggest, is known from the everyday experiences of human perceivers (the "that" of the explanation). Hobbes describes this as something that we can "observe" as we consider the character of our own experiences, claiming that we "observe that our phantasms are not always the same, but new ones are constantly being created and old ones are disappearing, just as the organs of sense are turned now to one, now to another object. Therefore, they are produced and pass away, *from which it is understood that they are some mutation of the sentient body*" (OL I.317; emphasis added). As objects enter and depart our visual field, we have different phantasms, or conceptions, that result from those objects and from this any human perceiver will recognize that throughout the process of any act of sensation their body changes in response to stimuli, i.e., as their body senses it undergoes mutation.

Next, Hobbes provides a citation to his first philosophy from earlier in *De corpore*, which allows him to exchange the term "mutation" with "motion": "But that all mutation is something having been moved or endeavoured, (which endeavour is also motion) in the internal parts of the thing changed has been shown ([in *De corpore*] cap. 9., art. 9.)" (OL I.317). This definitional linkage provides Hobbes with the ability to move to the third step above, namely, that all sensation will be motion in the sentient body, or, as Hobbes puts it: "sensation in the sentient can be nothing other than motion of some of the parts inside the sentient, which moved parts are parts of the organs by which we sense" (OL I.317).

Step four likewise incorporates a borrowed principle from first philosophy in *De corpore* IX.7: "it has been shown ([in *De corpore*] cap. 9., art 7.) that motion cannot be generated except by [some body] moved and contiguous. From which the immediate cause of sensation is understood to be in this, that it both touches and presses the first organ of sense" (OL I.318). This principle requiring body–body contiguity rules out the possibility of sensation by action at a distance. However, so far Hobbes has explained only motion from objects that *enters* the eye; recall the discussion above of Hobbes's optics regarding the motion from the retina *outward*. In earlier works and in *De corpore* XXV, Hobbes recognized a need to explain why human perceivers see objects *as* outside them rather than seeing them as inside them, since internal motions partly constitute sensation. The reason why humans perceive bodies as outside them, Hobbes posited, is due to an outward endeavor that results from bodily resistance to the pressure from outside.

This outward resistance, which explains us taking objects of perception to be outside of us and not mere fancy, was part of Hobbes's early optics. For example, he notes in *Minute* that "this fancie, though it bee butt a motion within Yet *because the motion tendeth outward by reaction* it appeareth to us to bee without and not a motion, but that thing which wee call light" (1983, 334). In *De corpore*, Hobbes similarly claims, after noting that he has "almost defined what sense may be" (OL I.318), that perception of external objects *as external to us* is due to an outward endeavor: "Likewise, it has been shown ([in *De corpore*] cap. 15., art. 2.) that all resistance is the endeavor contrary to [another] endeavor, that is, reaction" (OL I.318). Although the *explanans* (resistance tending outward) is the same between *Minute* of 1646 and *De corpore* of 1655, in the latter work Hobbes gains the ability to appeal directly to his geometry from *De corpore*, and this is exactly what he does. With this last step of the explanation in place (this last step is the "why" of the explanation), Hobbes can define "sense" as "a phantasm made by means of a reaction from an endeavor to [the] outside, which is generated by an internal endeavor from the object, and there remains for some time" (OL I.319).

This borrowing of the causal principle related to endeavor and reaction outward does not constitute a claim by Hobbes of how bodies *actually* act. As he emphasizes at several points in *De corpore*, the aim of natural philosophy is to provide possible causes. Instead, this borrowing of a principle from geometry provides a *possible* cause to explain why bodies appear to perceivers as outside them. This provides the natural philosopher with the ability to say that *if* this causal principle describes how the parts of the bodies of human perceivers behave, *then* the consequence (sensation) would necessarily follow.

4.4 Conclusion

This chapter has contrasted Hobbes's statements about natural philosophy, and the structure of his philosophy, generally, with two cases from his practice of explaining in optics and natural philosophy. These cases show that rather than providing deductions from first philosophy or geometry, within particular explanations Hobbes blended everyday experience (the "that") with appeals to causal principles from geometry (the "why"). In doing so, Hobbes treats physical bodies as if they are mathematical objects. Furthermore, Hobbes provides no bridge principles that would expose a reduction of these phenomena to minute particles. This "mixing" of two areas (geometry with everyday experience), places natural philosophy in the middle of his bifurcation of knowledge into *scientia* and *cognitio*. On the one hand, humans lack certain knowledge since they are not the creators of natural phenomena, but on the other hand natural philosophy strives to be more than mere prudence and, when mixed with causal principles from geometry, can offer suppositional certainty.

Notes

1 My goal is not to establish the reception or broad influence of Hobbes's optics. Shapiro (1973) has done so by tracing the influence of Hobbes's account of refraction and theory of light upon Emmanuel Maignon, Isaac Barrow, and Robert Hooke, among others. See also Malet (2001, 315–17) for discussion of Hobbes's criticisms of the optics of Claude Mydorge and Walter Warner. On accusations by Seth Ward that Hobbes plagiarized others' work in his optics, see Prins (1993).

2 See Adams (2019) for discussion of this example of "square" and connection to Hobbes's assertion that humans "make the principles" of civil philosophy. Helen Hattab (this volume, Chapter 1) connects this example to Hobbes's universal method.

3 Adams (2019, 12–13) connects these two routes to Hobbes's discussion of the individual, "not trusting this Inference, made from the Passions," who might want to have it "confirmed by Experience" (Hobbes 2012, 194; 1651, 62).

4 For discussion of how Hobbes's view of causality relates to Aristotle's and to Scholastic Aristotelians, see Leijenhorst (1996).

5 Hobbes requires that geometrical definitions be generative, and he rejects Euclidean definitions because they are not (EW VII.184).

6 I have modified Gert's (1994b [1658]) translation to reflect the wording in OL.

7 See also *Posterior Analytics* I.9 (76a4-13; Aristotle 1984, 123) and *Metaphysics* M.3 1078a14-16 For discussion of Aristotle's view of subalternate sciences and Galileo, see Lennox (1986).

8 Indeed, in *Minute* Hobbes describes vision "in general" as "that fancie which is caused in *any living creature*" (1983 [1646], 334). Médina (2016, 42) suggests that the placement of optics within *De homine*, rather than in *De corpore*, relates to Hobbes's division in *Minute* between illumination (Part I) and vision (Part II) and suggests that this division is similarly reflected in Hobbes's separation of *sciography* from *optiques* in the Table in *Leviathan* 9 (2012, 131). The former studies consequences "from the Qualities of the Starres" and the latter consequences from the "Qualities of Bodies Terrestriall." However, were this strict division Hobbes's intention behind placing optics within *De homine* (and not within *De corpore*), it would not explain why *De corpore* Part IV (chapter XXV) opens with the discussion of "sense".

9 du Verdus to Hobbes (August 17/27, 1656; Hobbes 1994a, 298, 299); Sorbière to Hobbes (December 13/23, 1656; Hobbes 1994a, 388, 391); du Verdus to Hobbes (May 17/27, 1657; Hobbes 1994a, 468, 471); Fermat to Hobbes (June 5/15, 1657; Hobbes 1994a, 474, 475); de Martel to Hobbes (July29/ August 8, 1657; Hobbes 1994a, 480, 482); and de Martel to Hobbes (August 7/17, 1657; Hobbes 1994a, 483, 484).

10 Although geometry plays this role in the account of the optic axis and the visual line in *De homine*, and elsewhere in Hobbes's optics, geometry does not serve as the "why" in all explanations, such as in *Minute* where Hobbes's account of the nature of light plays an explanatory role in understanding the production of heat (see Malet 2001, 320).

11 I develop this explanation in more detail in Adams (2016, 47–8). I discuss Hobbes's borrowing (and citing) of geometrical principles in his criticisms of Robert Boyle in *Dialogus Physicus* in Adams (2017).

References

Adams, Marcus P. 2016. "Hobbes on Natural Philosophy as 'True Physics' and Mixed Mathematics." *Studies in History and Philosophy of Science* 56: 43–51.

Adams, Marcus P. 2017. "Natural Philosophy, Deduction, and Geometry in the Hobbes-Boyle Debate." *Hobbes Studies* 30: 83–107.

Adams, Marcus P. 2019. "Hobbes's Laws of Nature in *Leviathan* as a Synthetic Demonstration: Thought Experiments and Knowing the Causes." *Philosophers' Imprint* 19 (5): 1–23.

Aristotle. 1984. *The Complete Works of Aristotle*, Vol. I, edited by Jonathan Barnes. Princeton, NJ: Princeton University Press.

Biener, Zvi. 2016. "Hobbes on the Order of Sciences: A Partial Defense of the Mathematization Thesis." *The Southern Journal of Philosophy* 54 (3): 312–32.

Hampton, Jean. 1986. *Hobbes and the Social Contract Tradition*. Cambridge: Cambridge University Press.

Hobbes, Thomas. 1839–1845a. *The English Works of Thomas Hobbes*, 11 vols., edited by Sir William Molesworth. London: John Bohn. Cited as EW.

Hobbes, Thomas. 1839–1845b. *Thomæ Hobbes malmesburiensis opera philosophica*, 5 vols., edited by Gulielmi Molesworth. London: John Bohn. Cited as OL.

Hobbes, Thomas. 1973 [1642–1643]. *Critique du De Mundo de Thomas White*, edited by Jean Jacquot and Harold Whitmore Jones. Paris: Vrin.

Hobbes, Thomas. 1976 [1642–1643]. *Thomas White's De Mundo Examined*, translated by Harold Whitmore Jones. London: Bradford University Press.

Hobbes, Thomas. 1981. *Computatio sive Logica: Logic*. Translation and Commentary by Aloysius P. Martinich, edited by Isabel C. Hungerland and George R. Vick. New York: Abaris Books.

Hobbes, Thomas. 1983 [1646]. *Thomas Hobbes's a Minute or First Draught of the Optiques: A Critical Edition*, edited by Elaine C. Stroud. PhD Dissertation. Madison, WI: University of Wisconsin-Madison.

Hobbes, Thomas. 1994a. *The Correspondence of Thomas Hobbes*, 2 vols., edited by Noel Malcolm. Oxford: Clarendon Press.

Hobbes, Thomas. 1994b [1658]. *Man and Citizen: De homine and De cive*, edited and translated by Bernard Gert. Indianapolis, IN: Hackett.

Hobbes, Thomas. 2012 [1651]. *Leviathan*, 3 vols., edited by Noel Malcolm. Oxford: Clarendon Press.

Leijenhorst, Cees. 1996. "Hobbes's Theory of Causality and Its Aristotelian Background." *The Monist* 79 (3): 426–47.

Lennox, James. 1986. "Aristotle, Galileo, and the 'Mixed Sciences'." In *Reinterpreting Galileo*, edited by William A. Wallace, 29–51.Washington, DC: Catholic University Press.

Malcolm, Noel. 2002. *Aspects of Hobbes*. Oxford: Clarendon Press.

Malet, Antoni. 2001. "The Power of Images: Mathematics and Metaphysics in Hobbes's Optics." *Studies in History and Philosophy of Science* 32 (2): 303–33.

Martinich, Aloysius P. 2005. *Hobbes*. New York, London: Routledge.

Médina, José. 2016. "Hobbes's Geometrical Optics." *Hobbes Studies* 27 (1): 39–65.

Peters, Richard. 1967. *Hobbes*. Baltimore, MD: Penguin Books.

Prins, Jan. 1993. "Ward's Polemic with Hobbes on the Sources of His Optical Theories." *Revue d'histoire des sciences* 46: 195–224.

Ryan, Alan. 1970. *The Philosophy of the Social Sciences*. London: Macmillan.

Shapin, Steven and Simon Schaffer. 1985. *Leviathan and the Air-Pump: Hobbes, Boyle, and the Experimental Life*. Princeton, NJ: Princeton University Press.

Shapiro, Alan. 1973. "Kinematic Optics: A Study of the Wave Theory of Light in the Seventeenth Century." *Archive for the History of the Exact Sciences* 11: 134–266.

Watkins, John W.N. 1965. *Hobbes's System of Ideas: A Study in the Political Significance of Philosophical Theories*. London: Hutchinson.

Part II

Human Nature and Morality

5

"A Most Useful Economy": Hobbes on Linguistic Meaning and Understanding

R.W. MCINTYRE

Hobbes holds that there is an intimate connection between linguistic meaning and thought. In *Leviathan* Hobbes defines linguistic understanding in the following way:

> When a man upon the hearing of any Speech, hath those thoughts which the words of that Speech, and their connexion, were ordained and constituted to signifie; Then he is said to understand it: *Understanding* being nothing else, but a conception caused by Speech. And therefore if Speech be peculiar to man (as for ought I know it is,) then is Understanding peculiar to him also. (Hobbes 2012, 62; 1651, 17)

From passages such as this, it is easy to conclude that *signification* – the relationship between a linguistic expression and that thought the expression signifies – is Hobbes's primary semantic notion. Yet, this conclusion does not square well with Hobbes's definition of a sign:

> A *Signe*, is the Event Antecedent, of the Consequent; and contrarily, the Consequent of the Antecedent, when the like Consequences have been observed before. (Hobbes 2012, 44; 1651, 10)

As Ian Hacking observes, given this definition of "sign," it is "very difficult to foist any theory of meaning on to Hobbes" (1975, 20; cf. Abizadeh 2015 and Ott 2003, 13–21). Indeed, since understanding is "conception caused by speech," it seems that Hobbes is confusing *natural meaning* and *non-natural meaning* in Grice's sense (Grice 1957). Moreover, given that names in speech register thoughts, signify thoughts in communicative acts, and that one understands speech when one "hath those thoughts" names in speech signify by their "connexion," it sounds as though Hobbes is suggesting a distinctly unattractive "encoding" theory of meaning and "decoding" theory of communication – as if by a kind of mental transduction.

A Companion to Hobbes, First Edition. Edited by Marcus P. Adams.

The purpose of this chapter is twofold. First, to provide a general overview of Hobbes's views on language; second, to argue that Hobbes holds an inchoate, but recognizable, version of an inferential role or functional role semantics. On Hobbes's theory of language use and linguistic meaning, the meaning of an expression is the functional role of that expression in cognition. Linguistic competency – manifested in the capacity to understand names in speech as signs of thought – is a matter of knowing how to deploy names to recall thoughts, make judgments, and syllogistic inferences.

In the first section, I provide a broad overview of Hobbes's views on the mind's natural cognitive powers. In that section, I analyze signification and signs, arguing that signification is a causal relation and not a semantic one, so that the signification of a linguistic expression *is not* that expression's linguistic meaning. In the third and fourth sections, I describe Hobbes's account of the use of names in cognition – names are marks, applied to objects, for the sake of recalling thoughts of those objects. I argue that this use of names is the fundamental one; the communicative use of names in speech to signify thoughts is derivative of this latter, principal use. Finally, I turn back to Hobbes's account of linguistic understanding. I argue that the understanding of linguistic expressions characteristic of mature, fully language-competent humans is determined by the ability of language-competent humans to deploy names in reasoning. To understand words in speech – to take them as signs of thought – presupposes a grasp of linguistic meaning and this is a matter of knowing how to reason and calculate with names: "For words are wise mens counters, who do but reckon by them" (Hobbes 2012, 58; 1651, 15).

5.1 Cognition and the Signification of Signs

According to Hobbes, the mind – unconditioned by the use of language – is, to adopt an expression from Sellars, a "Humean representation system" (Sellars 1981). "Singly," Hobbes writes, conceptions, ideas, or thoughts – terms he uses interchangeably – "are every one a *Representation* or *Appearance*, of some quality, or other Accident of a body without us" (2012, 22; 1651, 3) and the "Originall of them all, is that which we call Sense" (2012, 22; 1651, 3). Sensory experiences are states of an animal's brain – motion caused by the activity of physical bodies in that animal's environment (Hobbes 2012, 22–4; 1651, 3–4; EW I. 391–4; EW IV.2–9; see also Barnouw 1980). These informational states are retained in the brain after sensory stimulation has ceased. Over time they "decay," becoming informationally impoverished. Hobbes compares the effect of time on ideas to the effect of distance on a visual image: coarse-grained information can be recovered, but the "details" are lost (EW IV.12–13; 2012, 28; 1651, 5). Hence, Hobbes defines "imagination" as "decaying sense" (think "force and vivacity"). Further, since all conceptions are "totally, or by parts ... begotten upon the organs of Sense" (2012, 22; 1651, 3) he holds that conceptions are also memories, in the sense that they are derived from sensory stimulation (2012, 28; 1651, 5; see also EW I.396–7).

Conceptions are not concepts, for they are mental particulars, representing the accidents and qualities of the individual bodies that caused them in sensory experience (see e.g., EW V.197). However, in virtue of the role played by conceptions in their overall behavioral and psychological economy, animals are capable of possessing some concepts. Hence, while Hobbes holds that organisms lacking linguistic competency are not capable of the full range of cognitive powers enjoyed by adults humans – they are unable to form concepts, such as *justice* or *number*, the possession of which constitutively depends on language mastery – non-human animals and humans without linguistic competency (such as very young children) do have the ability to think and deliberate, contrary to that which is sometimes asserted (Hull 2006, 2013; Pettit 2008).[1] Hobbes holds that a wide variety of cognitive activity is explicable in terms of transitions between conceptions, which Hobbes calls "the discourse of the mind" (EW I.399) and "the Tryane of thought" (2012, 38; 1651, 8). Hobbes allows that an animal can abstract features of a conception by a Berkeleyan mechanism of selective attention (e.g., EW I.34 and EW I.394; cf. Berkeley 2008, 72).[2] In its most basic form, thinking is a matter of attending to and comparing features of "the phantasms that pass" through the imagination; an animal is thinking when it "taketh notice of their likeness or unlikeness to one another" (EW I.399). The connections between the ideas in the train of thought – their "consequence," one to another – are determined by their association in sensory experience (EW IV.2; 2012, 38; 1651, 8). Hence, the natural cognitive powers are sufficient to enable an animal to form concepts, in the sense that they can develop an ability to make discriminations that regulate expectations and behavior.

For example, Archibald J. Dog's cognitive system does not contain any general representations of *red* or *tomato*, but he is capable of attending to the color of a tomato, he can distinguish between red and green tomatoes and, with repeated experience, he forms a preference for the red tomatoes, and will pluck them from the vine when he finds them. Archie learns to associate visual sensations of red tomatoes and gustatory sensations of ripe tomatoes. This association, in the form of a train of thought, guides his behavior and, from the sight of the red color, he expects a tasty ripeness in a tomato, as he "compareth the phantasms that pass" (EW I.399). He comes to learn that tomatoes similar to one another in respect of their redness are likely to be similar to one another in respect of ripeness. Hobbes calls Archie's ability to make perceptual discriminations and to project regularities on the basis of associative learning natural "prudence" – an ability to make conjectural inferences on the basis of signs "taken by experience" (EW IV.17; 2012, 44; 1651, 10).

Regularly connected events are signs of one another, "when the like Consequences have been observed before" (2012, 44; 1651, 10). Only those who have learned from experience to associate "antecedents" with their regular "consequents" are "trained to see" them *as* signs, indicating what they signify (Hobbes 1976, 371). The repeated experience of the sign followed by its significate conditions an organism, forming in it a disposition to expect the significate of the sign. *Signification*, then, is a species of causal relation – the signification of signs is constituted by the functional role played by signs in the cognition and behavior of animals.

This account of signification applies equally well to conventional signs. Hobbes only ever provides one definition of "sign" – the definition (in its different expressions) quoted above. A sign makes an interpreting animal think about its significate, in the sense that the sign determines a train of thought that terminates in an idea and expectation of the significate. There is no alternative definition for the signification of specifically artificial signs and, so, we are invited to conclude that the signification of artificial signs is a causal relation after the manner of natural signification – a conventional sign makes you think about the thing it signifies, when you have had the appropriate conditioning (indeed, this is exactly what the definition of "understanding" would indicate, as we will see). This is supported by the fact that immediately after the definition of "sign" in *De corpore*, Hobbes provides examples of *both* natural and artificial signs. He gives the example of dark clouds signifying rain (as he usually does), but then he comments:

> And of signs, some are *natural* ..., others are *arbitrary*, namely, those we make choice of at our own pleasure, as a bush hung up, signifies that wine is to be sold there; a stone set in the ground signifies the bound of a field; and words so and so connected, signify the cogitations and motions of our minds. (EW I.15)

Given that the definition of "sign" supplied in that paragraph is the one according to which a sign is that which is commonly observed and remembered to be the antecedent of the significate, such that the observation of the sign provokes thoughts of the significate, the signification of conventional signs must also be a relationship of this kind. The difference between natural signs and conventional signs is that the regularity grounding the associative connection between the sign and the significate is a regularity established, in the case of the latter, by human institution. In the case of conventional signs, to see the sign as significant and to have the right disposition, you must be trained in the convention; that is, you must know how the sign is used.

This is also true of the signification of names in speech. One might think that although signification is a causal relation, nevertheless the linguistic meaning of a term is that which is signified – that of which the expression makes you think, qua sign. But this is not Hobbes's position. Names in speech signify a speaker's conceptions. As Hobbes puts it in *De corpore*:

> But seeing names ordered in speech ... are signs of our conceptions, it is manifest that they are not signs of the things themselves; for that the sound of this word *stone* should be the sign of a stone, cannot be understood in any sense but this, that he that hears it collects that he that pronounces it thinks of a stone. (EW I.17)

Given Hobbes's account of signification and given that names in speech are "a sign of what thought the speaker had, or had not before his mind," he is exactly right that the only sense in which the word "stone" can be a sign of stones is that someone hearing the word uttered in a sentence "collects" that the speaker thought of a stone.[3] If the *only* sense in which "stone" signifies anything is that it is a sign that the speaker *thought about stones*, then the signification of a linguistic expression cannot be the linguistic meaning of the expression.

Linguistic meaning determines, however, the signification of thoughts in speech. In addition to the definition of "understanding" cited in the introduction of this chapter, Hobbes also gives the following, general definition in *Leviathan*, in which he notes two different senses in which an animal can be said to understand speech or "other voluntary signs":

> The Imagination that is raysed in man (or any other creature indued with the faculty of imagining) by words, or other voluntary signes, is that we generally call *Understanding*: and is common to Man and Beast. For a dogge by custome will understand the call, or the rating

> of his Master; and so will many other Beasts. That Understanding which is peculiar to man, is the Understanding not onely his will; but his conceptions and thoughts, by the sequell and contexture of names of things into Affirmations, Negations, and other formes of Speech. (2012, 36; 1651, 8)

Human and non-human animal understanding of speech are established by distinct routes. The non-human animals "can be taught to grasp what we wish and command in words, [but] they do not do so *through words as words*, but as signs only" (Hobbes 1991, 37; OL II.88, emphasis added). Though language-competent humans and non-human animals can both understand linguistic expressions as signs, human understanding is a manifestation of linguistic competency. Language-competent humans understand "words as words" – as *symbols* – whereas the non-human animals can only understand them as (natural) signs, "forced out" by fear, desire, joy, or other passions (Hobbes 1991, 37; OL II.88). It is in virtue of a prior mastery of linguistic expressions that language-competent humans are in a position to interpret human speech as significative of conceptions. But what is it to grasp "words as words" according to Hobbes?

5.2 The Uses of Names

In each of his major discussions concerning the function of language, Hobbes remarks that names are words that serve as marks, "imposed on" objects for the sake of recollecting thoughts or conceptions of those objects. Let us examine these, starting with *Anti-White*, where Hobbes writes that "a name or appellation is a human sound [*vox*]. Say a person has something in mind, of which he retains from mind-picture [*imagio*]. He applies to, or imposes on, the thing the human vocal sound as a "note" enabling him to conjure up a similar mind picture" (Hobbes 1976, 373–4). In the *Elements of Law* Hobbes writes:

> In the number of these marks, are those human voices (which we call the names or appellations of things) sensible to the ear, by which we recall into our mind some conception of the things to which we give those names or appellations. As the appellation *white* bringeth to remembrance the quality of such objects as produce that colour or conception in us. A *name* or appellation ... is the *voice* of a man *arbitrary*, imposed for a *mark* to bring to his mind some conception concerning the thing on which it is imposed. (EW IV.20)

In *Leviathan*:

> The generall use of Speech, is to transferre our Mentall Discourse, into Verbal; or the Trayne of our Thoughts, into a Trayne of Words; and that for two commodities; whereof the one is, the Registering of the Consequences of our Thoughts; which being apt to slip out of our memory, and put us to a new labour, may again be recalled, by such words as they were marked by. So that the first use of names, is to serve for *Markes*, or *Notes* of remembrance. Another is when many use the same words to signifie (by their connexion and order,) one to another, what they conceive, or think of each matter ... for this use they are called *Signes*. (Hobbes 2012, 50; 1651, 12–13)

And, finally, Hobbes writes in *De corpore*: "A NAME *is a word* [*vox*] *taken at pleasure to serve for a mark, which may raise in our mind a thought we had before, and which, being pronounced to others, may be to them a sign of what the speaker had, or had not, before is mind*" (EW I.16).

These definitions characterize names by their function. As Biletzki (1997) and Hungerland and Vick (1981) emphasize, Hobbes's nominalism and materialism effectively preclude him from adopting any view about the metaphysics of meaning according to which there are entities answering to the "meanings" of sentences. Hence, although names in speech signify thoughts, *thoughts* must be taken as psychological episodes and not abstract objects (i.e., Russellian propositions or Fregean *Sinne*), since Hobbes denies such things exist. Furthermore, the signification of a name is not anything denoted by the name. Hobbes very clearly distinguishes that which a name signifies from that which a name denotes, or is "imposed" on (about which I shall say more below).[4]

These definitions confirm that the pragmatic "use" theory of meaning reading is the correct one. The essence of a name consists in the use to which that name is put. It is a mark, for the sake of recalling thoughts of the objects on which it is imposed; it is an interpersonal communicative sign, when "pronounced to others," in the context of a sentence, to express thoughts. Although Hobbes has a lot to say about communicative speech acts and the non-cognitive, expressive uses of language (e.g., Hobbes 2012, 94; 1651, 29), and although these feature prominently in his political and ethical theory (Biletzki 1997; Holden 2016; Pettit 2008), it is clear from the foregoing definitions that the *cognitive* use – registering the consequences of thoughts in declarative sentences – is the primary one.

Both *Leviathan* and *De corpore* are straightforward regarding the relative priority of the two uses of names in speech. In *Leviathan*, the cognitive use is called, explicitly, the *first* use of names. In both *Leviathan* and *De corpore*, Hobbes gives brief arguments justifying the definition of names and both of these imply that the communicative function of names in overt speech as signs of thought derives from the use of names as notes for the sake of remembrance. In *Leviathan*, Hobbes argues that it is *because* the general use of speech is to "register thoughts" that the "first use of names" is to serve as notes of remembrance. What speech *generally is useful for* is registering thoughts; so, then, an individual name primarily is a token for thought. In *De corpore*, Hobbes argues that, since an individual person – working alone – can construct names for the things he observes and register his thoughts about them, a name is a mark for thought. But, given that he is a social being and dependent upon others for the preservation and enlargement of his knowledge, he must teach his marks to other people, making them into signs of his thought (EW I.14–15). Hence, although names are both marks for private cognition and also signs for communication, "they serve for marks before they be used as signs" (EW I.15) and cannot be signs "otherwise than by being disposed and ordered in speech" (EW I.15). "*So that*," Hobbes says, "the nature of a name consists *principally* in this, that it is a mark taken for memory's sake; but it serves also *by accident* to signify and make known to others what we remember *to ourselves*" (EW I.15; emphasis added). Therefore, he concludes, names are accurately defined in the manner expressed at *De corpore* 2.4 (EW I.16) – marks as instruments for thinking and, also, when expressed to others, signs for the communication of thought (EW I.15).

5.3 Truth and Propositional Judgments

Without the use of language an animal's ability to make inferences, to navigate, know about, and manipulate the world, is exhausted by its power to make successful conjectures by signs. Though good enough for an animal's daily needs, natural prudence is limited in two important respects, both of which Hobbes characterizes as problems with the memory (e.g., EW I.13–14; EW IV.20). First, as I have already pointed out, since conceptions are not general concepts, the mind cannot naturally form general representations – concept possession, without language, consists in an organism's ability to project regularities, remembered and recalled as signs. In *Leviathan* (Hobbes 2012, 52; 1651, 13) and *De corpore* (EW I.80), Hobbes gives the example of a person doing geometry without using language to make the point. By observing figures in sensory experience – by drawing a diagram and visually inspecting it, perhaps – a person can come to recognize that the sum of the interior angles of a triangle equal two right angles. However, without a general representation of *triangularity*, "if another triangle be shewn him different in shape from the former, he cannot know without a new labour, whether the three angles of that also be equall to the same" (Hobbes 2012, 52; 1651, 4). Using only his natural cognitive powers his possession of the concept of *triangle* is limited to his ability to reliably conjecture, from his memories of particular triangles, that the next triangle he encounters will also have interior angles equivalent to two right angles; without the capacity to deploy general representations in cognition, he cannot permanently store the inferential sequence that led him to discover that the interior angles of a three-sided figure are equal to two right angles.

The second problem is that the decay of conceptions introduces errors into the natural process of inference. Since natural cognitive processes involve a "comparison" of ideas, as ideas lose their informational capacity, so they become less and less reliable when deployed in inferences. "Tacit errors, or errors of sense and cogitation" arise, therefore, in the transition from one mental representation to another in inferential processes (EW I.56–7). Hence, for example, without a "sensible measure" by which to preserve the fact that a given figure was so many units wide, it will not be possible for a person to reliably infer that some new figure she encounters has a width of the same number of units (EW I.13).

To overcome these limitations, human beings invent marks: "sensible things taken at pleasure, that, by the sense of them, such thoughts may be recalled to our mind as are like those thought for which we took them" (EW I.14; also EW IV.20). Marks are genuine *symbols*, in the sense that they are physical tokens, the meaning of which is fixed by conventions governing their use. The point of marks is not so much to help forgetful people remember things they would not otherwise have remembered (although marks *can* do this); rather, more generally marks help the mark-user raise conceptions in her mind to make inferences and to guide her behavior. The symbolic import of a mark is constituted by its function in cognition. The example Hobbes gives in *Elements of Law* of sailors who float a buoy to mark a submerged rock to "remember their former danger, and avoid it" (EW IV.20) illustrates the point. The sailors in Hobbes's example recall *that* there is a potentially dangerous rock below the water's surface; they just cannot see the rock from their boat, as they approach it. The buoy, as a mark, causes the sailor to think about the rock (i.e., to raise conceptions of the rock) and they can take appropriate action; that is the sense in which the buoy helps the sailors' memory. The sailors introduce the device to help themselves recall the rock so that they can then make deliberations, take action, etc. The buoy thereby "points to" the submerged rock, because it causes a sequence of conceptions involving conceptions (memories) of the rock. What makes the buoy a mark is the functional role played by the buoy in cognition. By a standing convention – a rule governing its use – the causal role of the buoy is fixed and, as a mark, it is able to reliably convey information from one time to the next. To grasp the symbolic import of the buoy as a mark is to know the role of the buoy in cognition.

Hobbes does not say much about the relationship between marks and conventional signs beyond the comment in *De corpore* that "[t]he difference, therefore, betwixt marks and signs is this, that those we make for our own use, but these for the use of others" (EW I.15). I will return to this point below, when I discuss the relationship between names in their role as marks and names as signs of thought, but here I point out the following. First, although Hobbes does not explicitly walk his readers through the process, I think it is reasonably easy to see how a mark, invented for the sake of private cognition, can become a sign to other people of what it marks. Take one of Hobbes's examples of an artificial sign – stones set in a field to mark the boundary of the field. One can imagine a case in which a farmer, having trouble recalling the exact extent of his field (without "present and sensible measures"), hits upon the idea of putting stones in the ground to mark the boundary. A stone's function as a mark is to cause the farmer to think about the boundary of his field; once his neighbor knows that this is how the farmer uses these stones, the stones become a sign to his neighbor of the same, causing *him* to think about the boundary of the field. It is not hard to imagine the community adopting this method – setting stones into the ground – to mark the boundaries of their fields and, also, to signify to their neighbors what they take to be that boundary. It is also easy to imagine this mark-to-sign process happening without explicit teaching. By observing the sailors' behavior, for example, it would become clear what they are using the buoy for. In both cases, experience could "train someone to see" the mark as a sign, that is, to develop the right cognitive disposition.

Second, a "sensible moniment" is a mark when it is used in private cognition, but a sign where there is common knowledge of its function as a mark; this common knowledge, however, is not essential to the symbolic import of a mark. *That* is constituted by its role in individual cognition (EW I.14–15).

Names are distinguished from other "human voices" and from other sorts of marks by their specific role in cognition. Names are *constituted* by the role they play in the act of reasoning. They are *imposed on objects, for the sake of recalling conceptions of those objects*. Strung together into grammatical sentences, names "register" and "record" the consequences of thoughts *through* their imposition and their concatenation in the act of reasoning.

"Imposition" is a technical term, which, like "signification," is borrowed from Scholastic semiotic theory. Hobbesian names function as *categorematic terms* and not *singular terms*. To "impose" a name is to establish a convention that fixes the extension of the name. Names "appellate" what they are "imposed on" or that of which they are truly predicable.[5] A common name, "as *Man, Horse, Tree*, [is] the name of divers particular things; in respect of all which together, it is called an *Universall*" (Hobbes 2012, 52; 1651, 13). Proper names, "singular to one onely thing," (Hobbes 2012, 52; 1651,

13) are a limiting case. They are also categorematic terms, imposed upon objects for the sake of recalling conceptions of those object, but which apply to exactly one thing as "*he that writ the Illiad*" (EW I.19) is imposed upon Homer to register the thought that he authored the *Illiad* or "Appius" and "Lentulus" apply to Appius and Lentulus for "(as Cicero has it) *Appiety* and *Lentulity*" (EW I.32). Imposition marks out a class – the class of objects, unified by the fact that each individual member of the class causes a similar suite of sensory appearances in the human organism. As I pointed out above, Hobbes is clear that, prior to the use of language, animals are capable of making perceptual discriminations, selectively attending to features of individual objects, recognizing similarities between individual objects, and remembering these, albeit imperfectly. A name is imposed upon many distinct individuals that resemble one another with respect to some feature. There are no universal properties *ex parte rem* nor universal mental representations, according to Hobbes's austere nominalism. Class membership is analyzed in terms of the brute resemblance each individual member of the class bears to the others – the feature in virtue of which the name was chosen as a mark.[6]

A name allows its user to think about an *entire* class of objects, without having to think about each one of them individually. Names go proxy in the act of reasoning for the individuals in the name's extension. Again borrowing from Sellars, we might call the imposition of the name the establishment of "language-entry" rules for the name (Sellars 1954). Imposition fixes the empirical conditions governing the appropriate use of the name. Knowing how to use a universal name is knowing the perceptual stimulus conditions governing its correct application – the conditions an object must meet to count as having the name predicable of it. In this way, although there is no general mental representation of, say, *luminosity*, only many memories and sensory experiences of lucid bodies, we grasp the universal name "luminous" because we know it applies to things that appear similar to us in a certain, visual way. The name "luminous" is a symbol that goes proxy for the individual luminous things in the act of reasoning.

Reason, "when wee reckon it amongst the Faculties of the mind," is nothing other than "*Reckoning* (that is, Adding and Subtracting) of the Consequences of generall names agreed upon for the *marking* and *signifying* of our thoughts" (Hobbes 2012, 64; 1651, 18). As several authors have argued (e.g., Abizadeh 2017; Hull 2006; Pettit 2008; Soles 1996), the imposition of names – categorematic terms – introduces universal representations into the cognitive system. The use of names transforms the human mind from a mere Humean representational system into an "Aristotelian" representational system, in Sellars' sense (Sellars 1981). "By this imposition of Names," Hobbes writes, "some of larger, some of stricter signification, we turn the reckoning of the consequences of things imagined in the mind, into a reckoning of the consequences of Appellations" (2012, 52; 1651, 14). In imposing names on things to mark our conceptions and then appending names together into sentences, the discourse of ideas – which consists in "the innumerable acts of thinking about individual things" – is registered in language, "and is reduced to fewer but universal theorems ... and this is a most useful economy" (Hobbes 1976, 375).

Hobbes's example of the geometer recording his discovery about the properties of triangles is a nice illustration. Without the use of names in speech, the geometer can construct a triangle and determine that the interior angles are equivalent to two right angles, but he has to put himself to "new labor" and make a new conjecture every time he wants to know whether any new triangle has this property. This necessarily involves "innumerable acts of thinking" about particular triangles, comparing them and noting their similarities. But with the use of words:

> [W]hen he observes that the equality was consequent, not to the length of sides, nor to any particular thing in his triangle [i.e. the one he has constructed]; but onely to this, that the sides were straight, and the angles three; and that that was all, for which he named it Triangle; and will boldly conclude Universally, that such equality of angles is in all triangles whatsoever; and register his invention in these generall terms, *Every triangle hath its three angles equall to two right angles.* And thus the consequence found in one particular, comes to be registered and remembered, as an Universall rule. (Hobbes 2012, 54; 1651, 14)

Each mental representation is still a conception – and so particularistic and imagistic – but via the symbolic medium of language, thoughts are "registered and remembered." However, this "registering" is not a simple one-to-one mapping of a name to a conception. The consequences of thoughts – each of which is just a train of mental particulars – are registered as a universal rule, expressed in the structure of a sentence.

As Hobbes defines truth, it is a semantic property – a property of sentences (or "propositions" as Hobbes calls them):

> A *true* proposition is that, whose predicate contains, or comprehends its subject, or whose predicate is the name of everything, of which the subject is the name; as *man is a living creature* is therefore a true proposition, because whatsoever is called *man*, the same is also called *living creature*; and *some man is sick*, is true, because *sick* is the name of *some man* ... these words *true, truth*, and *true proposition*, are equivalent to one another; for truth consists in speech, and not the things spoken of. (EW I.35)

"True" is a metalinguistic predicate (a "name of a name" [Hobbes 2012, 1078; 1651, 372]) and applies to those sentences such that, by the imposition rules governing the names composing the sentence, the extension of the subject term is subsumed or contained within the extension of the predicate term (EW IV.23–4). The truth conditions of a sentence are given by the imposition of the component names – the application conditions that fixed the extensions of the names. Thus, the truth conditions of a sentence can be expressed as a rule of inference concerning the names involved in the sentence, capturing their proper use in cognition: The sentence "man is a living creature" is true if and only if all of the objects in the extension of "man" fall within the extension of "living creature" or, "If *x* is in the extension of 'man', then *x* is in the extension of 'living creature'."

According to Hobbes, a propositional attitude is a relation between a language-using animal and a sentence (2012, 98–100; 1651, 30–1; EW IV.2–8). To judge that a sentence of the form "S is P" is true is to accept that "If *x* is in the extension 'S,' then *x* is in the extension of 'P'." That is, propositional judgments involve grasping the truth conditions of sentences. But this implicitly involves semantic ascent, recognizing metalinguistic information expressed in the structure of the sentence; it is tantamount to acceptance of a rule for linking names to one another in reasoning. In order to grasp the truth conditions of a sentence, one must have an understanding of the imposition rules governing the use of the component names deployed in the sentence. To grasp the truth conditions of "S is P," one must know how to use "S" and "P" as marks for thought. This, to anticipate the argument of the next section, is just what it is to "understand a name": "to remember, by means of a name, those things which have to be considered in some matter, and for which the name has been imposed ... the name 'man' is understood when this word brings to mind not only a human shape, but also its reasoning-capacity" (Hobbes 1976, 52).

The relationship between a language user and the sentences she judges to be true is a kind of causal relation, insofar as names play a functional role in the thought patterns of a language user. A name is a mark and, as a mark, it plays a role in the cognitive activity of the user. It causes the user, who has internalized the rule governing its application, to recall those ideas for which it was set up (Abizadeh 2015). As the buoy causes the sailors to think about the submerged rock when they see the buoy, so a name causes the person who grasps the "imposition" of the name to recall conceptions of the objects on which the name is imposed. A sentence read or heard or "tacitly thought" (EW V.197), causes a person to recall a chain of conceptions, corresponding to the impositions of the names concatenated together into the sentence. This is what Hobbes refers to as "remembering the use of names." Conceptions are raised upon the hearing or reading of a sentence insofar as there is an associative habit to use a name as a mark for the sake of recalling conceptions. So, when I read the sentence, "red tomatoes are ripe," the name "red tomato" causes me to think about some tomato and to selectively attend to its color. Then, there is a train of thought that takes me to various memories of ripe tomatoes, with that color. I recall that "ripe tomato" is applied to tomatoes for the sake of this gustatory appearance and judge that the sentence "red tomatoes are ripe tomatoes" is true (cf. EW I.23–4). So, while Archie and I can expect to experience the sensation ripeness from *this* red tomato on the basis of memory and the associative connections between conceptions, and thereby evince possession of the general concepts of *tomatoes* and *ripeness*, only I am able to grasp these concepts through a universal representation, preserved in the sentence I judge to be true. Returning to the case of the geometer, while he can see that two figures are triangles because they resemble one another in respect of having three sides (because he can selectively attend to their shape), with the use of the name "triangle" he is able to make and retain a universal judgment about *all* triangles, that is, everything within the extension of "triangle".[7]

5.4 Understanding Linguistic Signs

With the foregoing in mind, let us return to Hobbes's account of understanding linguistic signs. Language-competent humans understand "words as words" because they know how to use names in sentences to register thoughts. In the first part of *Elements of Law*, there is another brief comment on the distinction between human and non-human animal understanding of language that helps illuminate Hobbes's views on linguistic meaning. Knowledge necessarily involves both truth and evidence, which Hobbes defines as "the concomitance of a man's *conception* with the *words* that signify such conception in the act of ratiocination" (EW IV. 28). Hence, someone who merely speaks the words of the propositions composing a valid syllogism – perhaps by rote, "as it is with beggars, when they say their *paternoster*" (EW IV.25) – will "make always true conclusions" so long as he begins with true propositions, but he will not have knowledge of the conclusion of his syllogism, as "his conclusions [are not] *evident* to him, for want of the *concomitance of conception* with his words" (EW IV.28). Evidence, in Hobbes's sense, is necessary for the possession of knowledge for,

> [I]f the words alone were sufficient, a *parrot* might be taught as well to know truth, as to speak it. Evidence is to truth, as the sap to the tree, which, so far as it creepeth along with the body and branches, keepeth them alive; where it forsaketh them, they die: for this evidence, *which is meaning with our words*, is the life of truth. (EW IV.28; emphasis added in second set of italics)

As I understand Hobbes's point, although there would be formal truth-conditions for a sentence uttered by a parrot, the parrot would not be able recognize the truth-conditions of what he utters; hence, he would not understand the meaning of what he says. To understand the meaning of a sentence is to grasp the conditions under which it would be true. To know the truth-conditions of a sentence he utters, the parrot would need to know the empirical conditions for which the impositions of the component names were fixed – as Hobbes puts it in *De cive*, "to *know a truth* is the same as to *remember* that it was made by ourselves by the very use of names" (Hobbes 1991, 374; OL II.419).[8] Hence, although Hobbes distinguishes the truth-conditions of a sentence from its verification conditions, the latter constitutes "meaning with our words" and grasping meaning is matter of knowing the application conditions of the names out of which a sentence is composed.[9]

Sentences are signs of thought because they express propositional judgments. "Is" is a sign of judgment, used to "shew the Consequence, or Repugnance of one name to another; as when one saith, *A Man is a Body*, hee intendeth that the name of *Body* is necessarily consequent to the name of *Man*; as being but severall names of the same thing, *Man*" (2012, 1078; 1651, 372; also, 2012, 1080; 1651, 372). By *displaying* how she uses names in the syntax of her affirmation, a speaker who asserts "S is P" conveys her judgment *that S is P* by expressing her assent to the linguistic rule that "If *x* is 'S', then *x* is 'P'." A language-competent human interprets another person's utterance as a sign of thought "by the sequel and contexture of names" into sentences. In other words, the syntax of a sentence carries significance for humans who understand speech, but carries no special significance for those non-human animals who do not. The placement and "contexture" of the word "biscuit" in the sentence, "These biscuits are dry and flavorless," and the sentence, "Don't eat the dog's biscuits," is of no consequence to Archibald. To him an utterance of "biscuit," whatever the sentential context, is a sign that someone will get up and give him a treat – everything else is just another noise humans make. But to members of the English linguistic community, it is easy to see that these sentences can be used to express different things and perform different speech acts. There is, of course, a sense in which Archie understands the linguistic meaning of "biscuit," since, when he hears that word, he expects to be fed a biscuit and not to be given a bath; however, Archie clearly cannot see that the name has a semantic value, which, in part because of its placement within a sentence, it contributes to the meaning of the sentence as a whole. That contribution has to do with the use of "biscuit" as name, a placeholder in the sentence, standing for *biscuits*. Hence, the linguistic meaning of names – their use in individual cognition, to register thoughts – determines the signification of names in speech. An utterance of "biscuit" as a sign that the speaker thought of biscuits only when the hearer is in a position to interpret the sentence in which the name is deployed *as* a sign of thought.

Communication between members of a language community succeeds when, as Hobbes says, "the same marks or notes be common to many" (EW I.14).[10] Given that each conception is a mental particular and, indeed, a discrete physical event, no two speakers can literally share the same conceptions. The sense in which speakers "share notes" in common must not be that the same names raise precisely the same conceptions in the minds of each member of the community, but rather that the names they use as marks play the same role in the cognitive activity of the speakers in the linguistic community. Sharing a common linguistic habit – using the same names as marks for the sake of thought – the speech of members of the community causes them to recall the thoughts for which the names are deployed as marks. The name "stone" in the sentence "no man is a stone," signifies that the speaker conceived of a stone because that is function of the name "stone" in the cognitive activity of the members of English language community. The communication of the *content* of the propositional judgment *that no man is a stone* succeeds via the common recognition of the manner in which the names "man" and "stone" (and so on) are deployed in thought. This is a matter of knowing the rules of imposition demarcating the extensions of the names concatenated together into a sentence. Hobbes's comparison between the use of "man" as a term with universal signification and a painter, asked to paint a picture of a man – any man – illustrates the point. Just as a painter who is asked to a paint a picture of "man in general," paints some particular person they feel like painting, whom it is understood will stand as representative of all humankind for being relevantly similar to the rest, so the name "man" signifies "man in general" because, when it is used to express a judgment, "we limit [the extent of the name] not ourselves, but leave them to be applied by the hearer" (EW IV.22). Hobbes's point is that two people who understand the English term "man" as a universal term recognize that it applies to John, Paul, Ringo, etc., and it does not matter *which* of the members of the extension an idea is raised, so long as the speaker and hearer raise ideas of members of the same set of objects meeting the same suite of conditions. Another way to put the point is that Hobbes can respond to Descartes's (1984) objection that (monolingual) French and German speakers will not be able to grasp the same conceptual content when they judge, respectively, that "la neige est blanche" and "Schnee ist weiss" (AT VII:179/CSM II:126). Hobbes's answer, if the foregoing interpretation is correct, would be that so long as "neige" and "Schnee," "blanche" and "weiss," play the same role in the cognitive activity of the French speaker and the German (*viz.* applied to snow, to recall thoughts of snow; applied to white things to recall that color), then these two words mean the same thing in their respective languages.[11]

5.5 Conclusion

I have argued that although Hobbes holds that the linguistic meaning of a name is determined by the role of that name in the cognitive activity of a language user. Names arranged in sentences are signs of thought because the syntax of the sentence expresses metalinguistic information concerning the role the names in the sentence play in the cognition of the speaker. A name so-disposed in an asserted sentence can be a sign only to an audience disposed to interpret speech *as* significative of thought. But to do this, they must possess prior know-how – the audience must know how to use names as cognitive tools for the sake of recording thoughts into judgments and syllogisms.

Notes

1 Hobbes is self-consciously operating against the backdrop of Scholastic faculty psychology, which he regards as pseudo-explanatory. If there *were* some cognitive power that *could not* be explicated as a function of sensation and imagination, this would undercut his argument against the Scholastics, the whole point of which is to establish that it is unnecessary to posit purpose-specific mental faculties to explain different cognitive powers. This comes out clearly in his debate with John Bramhall. For example, Bramhall contends that the non-human animals cannot deliberate because they lack the requisite intellectual faculty; Hobbes retorts that since "it is manifest by continual experience that beasts do deliberate" (EW V.365), deliberation must not be a power of a special intellectual faculty, but an operation of a faculty common to all animals – humans included – namely, sensation and imagination (see also EW IV.242–5; EW V.92–5; EW V.195–7; EW V.363–5; EW V.401).

2 For example, in *Anti-White*, Hobbes claims that an image of running water represents "not that particular water, but any water, or air, or body of the same size and shape" (Hobbes 1976, 53), for it is possible to selectively attend to the surface of the running water and to note the similarity between this and other surfaces.

3 This passage indicates an elliptical sense in which words signify things – names in speech signify thoughts and thoughts are mental representations of things.

4 See Duncan (2011) for a contrary view.

5 *Pace* Abizadeh (2015), Hobbes does not reject a word-world connection. Since a Hobbesian name does not function as a singular term, there is no threat to Hobbes's nominalism in allowing that general terms truly apply to objects. A Hobbesian name is a general term. It has an *extension* and purports to *apply to* every individual in its extension. Its generality arises from this function; it does not thereby refer to some general thing.

6 Some have argued that grounding imposition in similarity vitiates Hobbes's nominalism (e.g., Pettit 2008, 33–4; Watkins 1973, 104–9). That could be, but Hobbes's position is just a version of "resemblance nominalism" (Armstrong 1989); if this is a problem, it is a problem for resemblance-based nominalism generally, not Hobbes specifically.

7 The geometrical truth would be regarded by Hobbes as necessary and *a priori*; the claim about tomatoes is contingent. Hobbes discusses his views on the truth conditions of necessary and contingent sentences at *De corpore* III.10 (EW I.37–8), however, the difference is not relevant to the present argument.

8 I have modified the Molesworth English translation.

9 See De Jong (1990) for an argument that Hobbes holds a "warranted assertability" theory of truth.

10 I have modified the English translation to reflect OL I.12.

11 I have not discussed the reason why, on my interpretation, insignificant speech is insignificant. The account should be clear: insignificant speech cannot signify thoughts because it cannot be used to register thoughts, for the names used in insignificant speech lack clear empirical conditions of application (see, e.g., Hobbes 2012, 46; 1651, 11, 2012, 60–2; 1651, 17, 2012, 122; 1651, 39–40; also EW I.29–30).

References

Abizadeh, Arash. 2015. "The Absence of Reference in Hobbes' Philosophy of Language." *Philosophers' Imprint* 15: 1–17.

Abizadeh, Arash. 2017. "Hobbes on Mind: Practical Deliberation, Reasoning, and Language." *Journal of the History of Philosophy* 55: 1–34.

Armstrong, David M. 1989. *Universals: An Opinionated Introduction*. Boulder, CO: Westview

Barnouw, Jeffery. 1980. "Hobbes's Causal Account of Sensation." *Journal of the History of Philosophy* 8: 115–30.

Berkeley, George. 2008. "A Treatise Concerning the Principles of Human Knowledge." In *Philosophical Writings*, edited by Desmond Clarke, 67–150. Cambridge: Cambridge University Press.

Biletzki, Anat. 1997. *Talking Wolves: Hobbes on the Language of Politics and the Politics of Language*. Dordrecht: Springer.

De Jong, Willem. 1990. "Did Hobbes Have a Semantic Theory of Truth?" *Journal of the History of Philosophy* 28: 63–88.

Descartes, René. 1984. *The Philosophical Writings of Descartes*, vol. 2, translated and edited by John Cottingham, Robert Stoothoff, and Dugald Murdoch. Cambridge: Cambridge University Press. [CSM II].

Duncan, Stewart. 2011. "Hobbes, Signification, and Insignificant Names." *Hobbes Studies* 24: 158–78.

Grice, H. Paul 1957. "Meaning." *Philosophical Review* 66: 377–88.

Hacking, Ian. 1975. *Why Does Language Matter to Philosophy?* Cambridge: Cambridge University Press.

Hobbes, Thomas. 1839–1845a. *The English Works of Thomas Hobbes*, 11 vols., edited by Sir William Molesworth. London: John Bohn. Cited as EW.

Hobbes, Thomas. 1839–1845b. *Thomæ Hobbes malmesburiensis opera philosophica*, 5 vols., edited by Gulielmi Molesworth. London: John Bohn. Cited as OL.

Hobbes, Thomas. 1976. *Thomas White's, De Mundo, Examined*, translated by Harold Whitmore Jones. London: Bradford University Press. [*Anti-White*].

Hobbes, Thomas. 1991. In *Man and Citizen (De Homine and De Cive)*, edited by Bernard Gert. Indianapolis, IA: Hackett. [*De Homine/De Cive*].

Hobbes, Thomas. 2012. *Leviathan: The English and Latin Texts*, edited by Noel Malcolm. Oxford: Clarendon Press. [First published 1651.]

Holden, Thomas. 2016. "Hobbes on the Function of Evaluative Speech." *The Canadian Journal of Philosophy* 46: 123–44.

Hull, Gordon. 2006. "Hobbes's Radical Nominalism." *Epoché* 11: 201–23.

Hull, Gordon. 2009. *Hobbes and the Making of Modern Political Thought*. New York: Continuum.

Hull, Gordon. 2013. "Meaning." In *The Bloomsbury Companion to Hobbes*, edited by Sharon A. Lloyd, 99–103. London: Bloomsbury Academic.

Hungerland, Isabel C. and George R. Vick. 1973. "Hobbes's Theory of Signification." *Journal of the History of Philosophy* 11: 459–82.

Hungerland, Isabel C. and George R. Vick. 1981. "Hobbes's Theory of Language, Speech, and Reasoning." In *Introductory Essay to Thomas Hobbes: Computatio, Sive, Logica*, edited by Isabel C. Hungerland and George R. Vick, translated by Aloysius. P. Martinich. New York: Abaris Books.

Leijenhorst, Cees. 2002. In *The Mechanisation of Aristotelianism: The Late Aristotelian Setting of Thomas Hobbes' Natural Philosophy*, Medieval and Early Modern Science, edited by Johannes M.M.H. Thijssen and Cristoph Lüthy, vol. 3. Leiden: Brill.

Malcolm, Noel. 2002. *Aspects of Hobbes*. Oxford: Clarendon Press.

Ott, Walter. 2003. *Locke's Philosophy of Language*. Cambridge: Cambridge University Press.
Pettit, Philip. 2008. *Made with Words: Hobbes on Language, Mind, and Politics*. Princeton, NJ: Princeton University Press.
Ross, George MacDonald. 1987. "Hobbes's Two Theories of Meaning." In *The Figural and the Literal: Problems of Language in the History of Science and Philosophy, 1630–1800*, edited by Andrew E. Benjamin, Geoffrey N. Cantor, and John R.R. Christie, 31–57. Manchester: Manchester University Press.
Sellars, Wilfrid. 1954. "Some Reflections on Language Games." *Philosophy of Science* 21: 204–28.
Sellars, Wilfrid. 1981. "Mental Events." *Philosophical Studies* 39: 325–45.
Soles, Deborah Hansen. 1996. *Strong Wits and Spiders Webs: A Study in Hobbes's Philosophy of Language*. Aldershot, UK and Brookfield, VT: Avebury.
Watkins, John W.N. 1973. *Hobbes's System of Ideas: A Study in the Political Significance of Philosophical Theories*. 2nd edn. London: Hutchinson.

6

Hobbes's Theory of the Good: Felicity by Anticipatory Pleasure

ARASH ABIZADEH

One of the central assumptions of ancient Greek ethics is that human beings have a single supreme and ultimate good – *eudaimonia* or "well-being" – which includes and integrates all other final goods into an account of the good life (Annas 1993). As Cicero understood it, eudaimonist ethical theories also assume that the supreme good serves as the final end of every valuable action. This is why he began his survey of Greek ethics, *De Finibus Bonorum et Malorum* (Cicero n.d.), by asking:

> what is the end [*finis*], which is final [*extremum*] and ultimate [*ultimum*], to which all our deliberations on living well and acting rightly should be directed? What does nature pursue as the supreme [*summum*] good to be sought, and what does she shun as the utmost evil [*extremum malorum*]? (DF I.11)[1]

Cicero then proceeded to consider three rival eudaimonist theories of the good life: the Epicurean view, according to which *felicitas* – as *eudaimonia* was rendered into Latin – consists in a life of pleasure and freedom from pain; the Stoic view, according to which it consists in a life of virtue; and the Peripatetic view, according to which it consists in a life of virtue combined with bodily and external goods.

Hobbes agreed with the Epicureans that *felicitas* consists in a life of pleasure and freedom from pain,[2] but departed from Epicurean hedonism in two significant ways. First, he rejected a key aspect of Epicurean eudaimonism: the assumption that felicity must be the ultimate *aim* of all valuable action, in the sense that it must be the intentional object of the mental state giving rise to action. This assumption had also been rejected by the Cyrenaic hedonists, who alone amongst the ancient philosophers had departed from eudaimonism, and who took the aim of all valuable action to be *particular* episodes of pleasure rather than felicity as a whole. But Hobbes was no Cyrenaic either. He rejected the assumption that all actions are or should be aimed at any single final good – whether felicity *or* pleasure. For Hobbes, pleasure and felicity are typically the by-products of desiring and pursuing other aims. The Cyrenaics' wholesale

A Companion to Hobbes, First Edition. Edited by Marcus P. Adams.

rejection of eudaimonism entailed denying that felicity – which they understood to consist in no more than the aggregation of individual episodes of pleasure (discounted by episodes of pain) – gives any coherent ordering of pleasures.[3] Hobbes, by contrast, was a eudaimonist who held that felicity is an overarching good giving coherence to a valuable life; he therefore agreed with the Epicureans that it is good to forgo lesser pleasures for greater future ones. He also rejected the Cyrenaic assumption that felicity simply measures the aggregate amount of pleasure (minus pain) over the course of one's life: felicity concerns not just the *aggregate* amount of net pleasure, but also its relative *distribution* or continuity over time. As he put it in *Leviathan* 11.1, the proper "object of mans desire, is not to enjoy once onely, and for one instant of time; but to assure for ever, the way of his future desire" (2012, 150; 1651, 47). Hobbes defined the felicitous life as a life of *ongoing* or – to quote *Elements of Law* – "continual delight" (1640, 9.7).

Second, Hobbes also rejected the assumption that felicity is a final end in the sense that attaining it would mark the *termination* of desire. Like the Stoics, the Epicureans held that felicity comprises an attainable and ongoing state of repose or tranquility (*ataraxia*) which, according to the Epicureans, consists in the pleasure of being free from the pain of unsatisfied desires (Annas 1993; Mitsis 1988). For Hobbes, by contrast, unsatisfied desires are not intrinsically painful, the absence of pain does not itself constitute a type of pleasure, and felicity is not a state of rest but is an ongoing motion or progression from pleasure to pleasure. It is not characterized by absence of desire. Hobbes was here echoing the Cyrenaics, even repeating the Cyrenaic criticism – which he would have encountered in Diogenes Laertius's *Lives of Eminent Philosophers* (Laertius n.d.) – that tranquility is the state of a corpse, not a life (*Lives* I.2.8.89; cf. Plato's *Gorgias* 492e [Plato n.d.]).[4] As he put it in *Leviathan* 6.58, "there is no such thing as perpetuall Tranquility of mind, while we live here; because Life it selfe is but Motion, and can never be without Desire, nor without Feare, no more than without Sense" (2012, 96; 1651, 29–30).

But Hobbes did not reject, as he has often been taken to have done (Hampton 1992, 333; Schneewind 1998), the notion of a *summum bonum* or felicity as such. The relevant passages express instead his two key departures from Epicureanism: his denial that felicity is the utmost *aim* of every valuable action, and his denial that it is composed of *ataraxia* or the pain-free state of having no unsatisfied desires, i.e., the termination of desire. Hobbes was committed to the intrinsic value of pleasure and, in line with his eudaimonism about the good, to felicity as the overarching and ultimate value of a human life. Unlike the Cyrenaics, who held that the aim of every action is some individual episode of pleasure, and that one ought not to be concerned with one's overall felicity, Hobbes's prudentialism committed him to treating felicity as the ultimate ground for the value of one's actions and, indeed, as *a* proper "object of mans desire" in its own right (2012, 150; 1651, 47).

Hobbes posited an ultimate and overarching good for a human life, which he conceived not as a final end or state to be realized, but as an ongoing process of experiencing greater pleasures relative to pains. Felicity for Hobbes consists not primarily in the *fulfilment* of one's desires, but in ongoing anticipatory pleasure engendered by the experience of repeated past success in satisfying one's desires. Whereas the Epicureans held that felicity consists in the tranquil state of *having satisfied* one's desires, and the Cyrenaics held that it consists in the somatic pleasures that arise while *satisfying* one's desires, Hobbes held that felicity consists primarily in the mental pleasures that arise from *anticipating* the satisfaction of one's desires.

6.1 Four Distinct Questions about Goodness and "Good"

To get a handle on Hobbes's theory of the good, we must carefully keep apart four questions: (1) In what does the property of goodness *consist*? (2) What *makes* something good (i.e., in virtue of what features does something have or acquire the property of goodness)? (3) What *causes* agents to see something as good and/or to call it "good"? And (4) what does the term "good" *mean*? The first two questions are metaphysical and concern a substantive theory of the good, the third question is psychological, and the fourth semantic. Because Hobbes considered "good" to be one of the fundamental terms of his science of ethics, understanding his answer to the fourth, semantic question requires carefully distinguishing the term's customary, pre-scientific meaning as Hobbes understood it from the "apt" or *reforming* definition he proposed in light of his substantive, scientific account of goodness.[5] How Hobbes understood the term's customary meaning depends on his answers to the psychological question, but the reforming, scientific definition he proposed depends on his answers to the two metaphysical questions.

We should begin with a preliminary observation about the first question. Aristotle had noted that things are customarily called "good" in two senses: good unconditionally (*haplos*) or good for somebody (NE 7.12).[6] Hobbes rejected the first usage as unscientific. Although he recognized that by custom people often use "good" to mean what is good *simpliciter*, he insisted that the property of goodness is a *relational* property: a good thing is always good *for* someone in particular. In *Elements*, he flatly denied that there is "any such thinge as ἄγαθον ἀπλῶζ [*agathon haplos*] that is to say simply good," a point he illustrated with the dramatic example that "even the goodness which we attribute to God Almighty, is his goodnesse to us" (1640, 7.3). He reiterated in *Leviathan* that there is "nothing simply and absolutely" good (2012, 80; 1651, 24), and in *Questions* we find that even to speak of a good horse, in a scientifically informed way, is to speak of its goodness for some individual(s) (EW V.192). *De homine* clarifies that "since whatsoever is Good, is Good for someone or other," nothing is *simpliciter Bonum*; nevertheless, there can be things that are a common good for many (*communiter Bonum*) or, indeed, a universal good for everyone (*omnibus Bonum*) (DH 11.4; OL II.96; see AW 30.26).

In denying that anything is "absolutely" good Hobbes was not claiming that nothing has *ultimate* value for agents; he was claiming that nothing has value apart from its value *for* agents. This assertion that goodness is relational does not furnish a full answer to our first question, about the nature of goodness, but it does yield enough to shed light on our second question, about what makes something good. The relational nature of goodness suggests that something is good in virtue of contributing to an *agent*'s ultimate good.

6.2 The Meaning of "Good": The Customary vs. Reforming Sense

The discussion of the word "good" in chapter 7 of *Elements* proceeds in terms of pleasure: "Every man for his owne part calleth that which pleaseth and is delightful to himselfe Good, and that Evill which displeaseth him" (1640, 7.3). By contrast, the better-known, corresponding formulation in chapter 6.7 of *Leviathan* is in terms of desire: "whatsoever is the object of any mans Appetite or Desire; that is it, which he for his part calleth *Good*: And the object of his Hate, and Aversion, *Evill*" (2012, 80; 1651, 24).

Some commentators have suggested this difference reveals a shift in Hobbes's substantive theory of value, from a hedonist theory in 1640 to a desire-fulfilment theory by 1651.[7] In fact, Hobbes was committed to a hedonist theory, and the references to appetite can be explained in its terms. We can see this in light of the fact that these passages do not answer to our second question, about what makes something good, but to our third question, about what causes individuals to *call* something good. Thus Hobbes wrote in *Elements* that "Every man for his owne part calleth that which pleaseth and is delightful to himselfe Good," and in *Leviathan* that "whatsoever is the object of any mans Appetite or Desire; that is it, which he for his part calleth *Good.*" Once we realize Hobbes was engaged in psychological explanation here, his alternation between the language of pleasure and desire becomes perfectly understandable: it does not indicate any equivocation or shift, but rather the substantive equivalence of the alternative formulations. For on Hobbes's account, desire and pleasure are two aspects of a single passion: desire is the conative aspect, i.e., the motion or *conatus* toward an intentional object that propels the agent to act, while pleasure is the cognitive or representational aspect, i.e., the "appearance" of the intentional object in which the object is represented as good. Desire is always accompanied by pleasure – both correspond to the same internal bodily motions – which is why Hobbes could write in *Elements* that terms such as "pleasure" or "delight" and "desire" or "appetite" are but "diverse names for diverse Considerations of the same thinge." Desire is "the Indeavour, or internall beginning of animall motion" toward some intentional object, and it is always desire for an object insofar as "the object delighteth" (1640, 7.2).

In other words, Hobbes was a psychological egoist and hedonist of sorts, according to whom (a) all action is prompted by desire, (b) all desire is accompanied by pleasure, and (c) whenever we desire anything, we desire it only if we represent it as something pleasant to ourselves. As he put it in *De cive*, "whatsoever a man would [*voluerit*], it therefore seems good to him because he wills it," and "whatsoever seemes Good, is pleasant [*iucundum*], and pertains either to the senses, or the mind" (1.10, 1.2; 1983, 95, 91). Hobbes's language might even seem to commit him, as many of his readers have thought, to a stronger form of psychological egoism and hedonism – the kind advanced by the Cyrenaics – according to which the *object* of every desire, and hence the aim of every action, is one's own pleasure (Nagel 1959). This statement in *Leviathan* 25.2 is representative: "the proper object of every mans Will, is some Good to himselfe" (2012, 398; 1651, 132). But Hobbes in fact asserted that we can and do desire things other than our own pleasure: writing at *Leviathan* 6.22 and 6.35, for example, that benevolence is "*Desire* of good to another" (which rules out strong psychological egoism), and curiosity is a "*Desire* to know why, and how," not a desire for pleasure (which rules out strong psychological hedonism). Despite the occasionally strong formulation, Hobbes did not intend to endorse psychological egoism and hedonism in the strong sense. The point Hobbes was making in his apparently stronger formulations is that insofar as we desire things such as the good of another or knowledge, we do so only as a result of the fact that we see these objects as pleasurable, because we take, for example, "delight in the ... generation of Knowledge" (2012, 84, 86; 1651, 26). Although our own pleasure is not the *object* of every desire, on Hobbes's mechanistic psychology the fact that an intentional object appears pleasurable to us is a necessary part of the *causal* process by which our desire for it arises. We do not necessarily desire the *pleasantness* of acquiring knowledge, but its pleasing aspect plays a causal role in explaining our desire for it.[8]

The result is that people are disposed to *call* the objects of their desire good, because in desiring them they not only experience pleasure but also conceive them as pleasurable and hence as good for themselves. This is why Hobbes could alternate between the language of pleasure and desire. The passages in question about "good" articulate Hobbes's constant view about the *customary meaning* of the term, not a substantive, allegedly shifting, *theory* of the good: part of what it means to call something good in common discourse is to signify one's desire for it or, concomitantly, to signify one's conception of it as pleasant.

Hobbes's distinction between the customary and scientific senses of the term "good" is grounded in a further distinction, namely, between two types of pleasure that can cause people to call things good: pleasures of satisfaction or *fruition*, which arise from perceiving something *presently* satisfying one's desire, and pleasures of imagination or *anticipation*, which arise from imagining one's desire being satisfied – paradigmatically in the future. If merely *having* a desire involves anticipatory pleasure, then presently perceiving the object of one's desire being satisfied yields a pleasure of fruition: if "the beginning of animall motion toward something which pleaseth us" is "Appetite" and hence involves anticipatory pleasure, then "the END of that motion" is "the attayning thereof," and "when wee attaine that end the delight we have thereby is called FRUITION" (1640, 7.5). It is true that when Hobbes came explicitly to distinguish between types of pleasure, his classification was in terms of pleasures of *sense* and *mind*, rather than pleasures of fruition and anticipation. When in *Elements* he declared "There are two sorts of pleasures," he contrasted the "SENSUAL" kind, such as the pleasure of sex or eating, which "seemeth to affect the Corporiall organ of sense," to "the Delight of the minde" or "JOY," which "sort of delight is not particular to any part of the body" (1640, 7.9). But from early on Hobbes *equated pleasures of sense with those of satisfaction, and pleasures of mind with those of anticipation*. Pleasures of sense involve "Conception of the present," while pleasures of the mind "consist in Conception of the Future, that is to say in Conception of power past, and the Acte to come" (1640, 8.2–3). Similarly, in *Leviathan* 6.12 Hobbes defined "*Pleasures of Sense*" as those arising "from the sense of an object Present" to one's sensory organs, while he defined "JOY" or the "*Pleasures of the mind*" as those arising from the "Expectation, that proceeds from foresight of the End, or Consequence of things" (2012, 84; 1651, 25).

Hobbes's distinction between sensory pleasures and mental pleasures is rooted in ancient Greek ethics, and we can best appreciate the significance of his having collapsed it into the distinction between pleasures of satisfaction and anticipation by highlighting what differentiates Hobbes's account from his hedonist predecessors. Epicurus made two, cross-cutting distinctions between pleasures: he contrasted sensual or *somatic* pleasures to mental or *psychic* pleasures on the one hand, and *kinetic* pleasures to *katastematic* ones on the other. Kinetic pleasures are pleasures of motion and consist in presently *satisfying* one's desire. Epicurus held that some kinetic pleasures are somatic (*euphronysê*), as when some object is presently titillating the relevant sensory organ, while other kinetic pleasures are psychic (*chara*), as when one reflects on kinetic pleasures of the body. Katastematic pleasures, by contrast, consist in the freedom from pain that comes either from *already having satisfied* or having *relinquished* one's desires or aversions. This type of pleasure can either be somatic (*aponia*), as when one has satisfied one's thirst, or it can be psychic (*ataraxia*), as when one has relinquished the fear of death. Epicurus taught that felicity is composed of katastematic, not kinetic, pleasure (*Lives* II.10.136; Wolfsdorf 2013, 147–9).

Cicero translated "katastematic" into Latin as "static" (*stante*) because he took such pleasures to consist in the absence of motion; he also interpreted Epicurus in such a way as to equate kinetic with sensual pleasures, and static with mental pleasures. As a result, on the Ciceronian interpretation of Epicureanism – which Hobbes took for granted – felicity wholly consists in a static condition of repose or tranquility of the mind (DF II.10; Annas 1993, 336). Hobbes opposed this Epicurean view in part because, like the Cyrenaics and Cicero, he rejected the notion of static pleasures: he took pleasure to arise from motion, such that pleasure consists neither in having satisfied or relinquished a desire nor in the absence of pain. He understood all sensory pleasures to be "kinetic" pleasures that persist only so long as one is presently *satisfying* one's desire. This is what a pleasure of fruition is for Hobbes. A Hobbesian pleasure of mind, by contrast, does not wholly map onto either katastematic or kinetic pleasure: it is like kinetic pleasure in that it arises from motion, but it is unlike kinetic pleasure in that it arises not from presently satisfying one's desire, but from *imagining* one's desire being satisfied. Just as imaginations are parasitic on sensory perceptions, pleasures of mind are parasitic on pleasures of sense: whether "foresight of the End, or Consequence of things" yields a mental pleasure or mental pain depends on "whether those things in the Sense Please or Displease" (*Leviathan* 6.12; 2012, 84; 1651, 25). Because Hobbes took the process of *satisfying* one's desire to be constituted by the titillation of senses, pleasures of mind ultimately arise from imagining a satisfying process that yields sensory pleasures.

Hobbes did acknowledge a somewhat hybrid case between pleasures of sense and pleasures of imagination – *somewhat* hybrid because it is ultimately a pleasure of imagination, but caused by present sensory perception. The hybrid case touches on a potential ambiguity behind describing a pleasing object as "present" or presently pleasing. On the one hand, a pleasing object may be "present" either in the temporal sense that it is presently satisfying one's desire, or in the spatial sense that it is present to the senses. These two senses can come apart: a parched desert traveler who had given up hope may suddenly *see* an oasis nearby, without yet *drinking* the water and quenching her thirst. In such a case, the water she desires is an object of sensory perception, but her desire for it is not yet being satisfied since it is present to her *visual* rather than gustatory sensory organ. Although Hobbes characterized the intentional objects of desire as bodies, in reality the objects of desire are for him always bodies *under some particular description* – such as the traveler's desire for water *as* being drunk by her. Thus, while the *water* is an object of sensory perception and hence is present to the traveler in the spatial sense, the desire for water-as-being-drunk-by-her is presently not yet being satisfied.

On the other hand, something may be presently pleasing either in the sense that one's desire is being presently satisfied (yielding a pleasure of sense) or in the sense that one presently anticipates its future satisfaction (yielding a pleasure of mind). But the case in which the traveler sees the water she desires to drink is a case in which she experiences an anticipatory pleasure of mind in part *thanks to* her sensory perception of the water: seeing the water both nourishes the hope of satisfying her desire and intensifies her desire for water by making her representation of it more vivid. (Sensory perception is more vivid because imagination "is nothing but *decaying sense*" [*Leviathan* 2.2; 2012, 26; 1651, 5].) Seeing a physical object may even give birth to entirely new desires: the wayfarer wandering through a Persian orchard initially desires only to take in its sights, but in stumbling upon the pomegranate tree is overtaken by the desire to taste its unfamiliar scarlet fruit. Strictly speaking, the pleasure involved in such cases is a mental pleasure, but it is distinct from other cases of anticipatory pleasure in that it is partly grounded in sensory perception. One takes pleasure from simultaneously perceiving an object and imagining it in some as-yet unrealized state or event. As Hobbes put it in *Anti-White*, "delight and pain consist sometimes in sense, sometimes in imagination," but also "sometimes in sense and imagination simultaneously" (Hobbes 1973 (hereafter AW) 30.23). This hybrid type of anticipatory pleasure is significant for Hobbes because he took the desires associated with it – desires in part grounded in present sensory perception – to be more powerful motivators in general than desires associated with pure mental pleasure. This is precisely why, as he put it in *De cive*, "men cannot put off this same irrationall appetite, whereby they greedily prefer the present good [*bona præsentia*] before the future" (3.32; 1983, 120); *præsentia* either in the sense of presently satisfying one's desire or of being present to the senses.

It is this complex set of distinctions – (1) between (a) sensory pleasures arising from present satisfaction and (b) mental pleasures concerning future satisfaction, and (2) between (a) hybrid pleasures of anticipation and (b) pure mental pleasures of anticipation – that undergirds Hobbes's distinction between the customary and scientific senses of "good." We find the latter distinction in *De cive* in a political context, for example. Because whenever people desire something they conceive it as good and pleasant (1.10, 1.2; 1983, 95, 91), it is customary for them to call the objects of their desires "good": "Such is the nature of man, that every one calls that *good* which he desires, and *evill* which he eschewes," so that in practice "*Good* and *Evill* are names imposed upon things to signifie appetite for, or aversion to what are thus named" (14.17, 3.31; 1983, 213, 119). The problem with this customary use of "good" – the genesis of which Hobbes's psychological account is meant to explain – is that it cannot be the basis for any stable *agreement* about what to call good. Because "the appetites of men are diverse," people are prompted to disagree about what to call good, so that "what this man *commends* [Laudat], (that is to say, calls *Good*) the other *undervalues* [vituperat], as being *Evil*; Nay, very often the same man at diverse times, *praises*, and *dispraises* [laudat & culpat] the same thing." The customary sense of "good" therefore cannot serve either as the basis for a *science* of the good, or as the basis for peace. So long as individuals use "good" and "evil" in this customary way – to signify whatever appetites and aversions they happen to have at the time – they will face "discord, and strife" and hence find themselves in "the state of War" (3.31; 1983, 119).

There is, however, a rational basis for a solution to the problem of war and for establishing a reformed, scientific meaning for "good." That basis lies once again in distinguishing the two types of pleasure that might prompt people to call something good: "we all measure *Good* & *evill* by our own delight & pain (which is either present, or expected)"

(14.17; 1983, 213). Those trapped in a state of nature are unable to agree on any common object of *present* sensory pleasure or, indeed, of hybrid anticipatory pleasure from objects they can presently *perceive* via the senses, because, as long as they are in that state, "by reason of the diversity of the present appetites, they mete *good & evill* by diverse measures." But it is possible to agree on an imagined common future object of *anticipatory* pleasure, since "All men easily acknowledge this state [which is a state of war], as long as they are in it, to be evill; & by consequence that *peace* is *good*." The anticipatory pleasure raised in everyone's mind by the prospect of peace and its pleasures is a potential basis for agreeing about what to call good. Calling peace and its relevant means "good" is therefore not only itself a potential basis for actually securing peace, it also corresponds to the term's scientific meaning: "They therefore who could not agree concerning a present, doe agree concerning a future good; which indeed is a work of reason; for *things present* are perceived by the senses, *things future* by nothing except Reason." Reason both engenders anticipatory pleasure concerning a future peace and itself declares "peace" and all the relevant "means to peace [to] be good." Calling peace good therefore aligns with the reforming definition proposed by Hobbes's philosophy. In this respect, Hobbes sharply contrasted his own philosophy to those of his predecessors, who had failed to "observe the goodnesse of actions to consist in this, that it was in order to Peace," and who had consequently "built a *morall Philosophy* wholly estranged from the *morall law*, and unconstant to it self" (3.31–2; 1983, 119–21).

In *Leviathan* 15.40, Hobbes reiterated his argument that, on the one hand, "Morall Philosophy is nothing else but the Science of what is *Good*, and *Evill*" and that, on the other hand, speakers customarily use the terms "good" and "evil" to signify whatever appetites and aversions they happen to have at the moment, which leads to semantic inconstancy, disagreement, and consequently war (2012, 242; 1651, 79–80). But in *Leviathan* 4.23–4 he also laid out with perfect clarity the implications for any scientific undertaking of these "kinds of Speeches," which "signifie the Appetites, Aversions, and Passions of mans mind": "The names of such things as affect us, that is, which please, and displease us, because all men be not alike affected with the same thing, nor the same man at all times, are in the common discourses of men, of *inconstant* signification" and, as such, "can never be true grounds of any ratiocination." Because words that, "besides the signification of what we imagine of their nature, have a signification also of the nature, disposition, and interest of the speaker" are disposed to inconstant signification, "therefore in reasoning, a man must take heed of [such] words" and begin by first firmly *settling* their scientific meaning (2012, 62; 1651, 17).[9] Hence the need for reforming, scientific definitions.

Hobbes was proposing to settle or fix the meaning of "good" such that it names not whatever people happen to desire or find pleasant at any given point in time – as the ancient Greek philosophers had supposedly done, whose "Morall Philosophy is but a description of their own Passions" and who "make the Rules of *Good*, and *Bad*, by their own *Liking*, and *Disliking*" (*Leviathan* 46.11; 2012, 1058–60; 1651, 369; cf. 1640, 27.13) – but what is good for them in reason, their true, long-term good. Hobbes was proposing a reforming definition for "good" firmly grounded in his substantive theory of what goodness consists in and of what makes it the case that something has that property.

6.3 What Makes a Life Good: Anticipatory Pleasure

Hobbes explicitly contrasted agents' apparent good to their true good for the first time in *Anti-White*, noting that whether an action contemplated in deliberation is good for them overall depends on whether its total, long-run consequences involve a greater amount of pleasure relative to pain:

> the things that please are connected with those that pain in a series so long that we are not able to foresee at one glance all the way to the end of the chain, & the connection between those that delight and pain, i.e., the good & evil, is so tight that they are taken up or relinquished together. If in this series there is more good than evil, the whole is good, so it is *better* to take up the whole, and worse to relinquish; if by contrast there is more evil than good, the whole is evil & it is worse to take up, better to relinquish. (AW 30.25)

Hobbes followed up this evaluative point – which echoes Epicurus[10] – with the observation that as a matter of fact individuals will be disposed to undertake actions that merely *seem* to them to promise greater net pleasure. Because of limited foresight, the apparent goodness of actions will not always coincide with individuals' true good, i.e., with the action that will actually produce greater net pleasure for them in the long run:

> We take up & relinquish according to the distance we foresee along some delimited [*determinatam*] expanse, in which there may be more good than evil, but in the part not foreseen there may be so much evil that in the whole there is more evil than good, because it is necessary to take up the whole, on account of the connection we take up not what is truly good, but what has appeared good, and this is what is called *apparent good*, which is sometimes evil and displeasing [i.e., overall]. (AW 30.25)

This distinction between *bonum verum* and *bonum apparens* appears again in *Leviathan* 6.57 (2012, 94; 1651, 29) and *De homine* (11.5, 12.1; OL II.97–8, 104), but *Anti-White* remains the text in which Hobbes provided his clearest and most detailed exposition on the true good and on felicity. If Hobbes's discussion of *bonum verum* concerns the instrumental value of the actions contemplated in deliberation, felicity is what is ultimately valuable in a human life. There are two intrinsic constituents of felicity on Hobbes's account. The first reflects Hobbes's *hedonism*: the value of a life is intrinsically constituted by pleasure (and absence of pain): "felicity consists in living a life with pleasure, i.e., maximum delight [*jucunditate maxima*]" (AW 38.8). Like the Cyrenaics, Hobbes took every experience of pleasure to be intrinsically good for agents – a constituent of their felicity – and whatever promotes their pleasure to be instrumentally good for them. The second intrinsic feature of felicity reflects Hobbes's *eudaimonism*. Hobbes's eudaimonism does not merely involve his agreement with the Epicureans that future pleasures count as much as present pleasures. More significantly, Hobbes conceived felicity as an overarching good that integrates the value of discrete experiences of pleasure into a coherent whole. This is why he rejected the Cyrenaic assumption that felicity is a mere aggregation of pleasures. Hobbes assumed that the relative distribution of pleasures over time is an independent and second intrinsically valuable feature of a felicitous life: a life in which all pleasures are experienced in a single moment is less felicitous and therefore less valuable than one in which an equal amount of aggregate pleasure is distributed more evenly and hence continuously experienced throughout one's life. To be sure, Hobbes did not have a metric for adjudicating trade-offs between the aggregative versus temporally distributive dimensions of felicity. But he posited the ongoing or "continual" experience of pleasure as an intrinsic dimension of felicity in its own right. Felicity consists in pleasure "that is not brief" and, indeed, "lies not in the goal but in the path itself" (AW 30.8, 9). Felicity is an integrative value: it consists in (a) pleasure (and absence of pain) (b) experienced on an ongoing basis continually over time.

This second, integrative dimension of felicity frames the whole of Hobbes's inquiry in *Anti-White* and motivates his focus on anticipatory pleasures. Even if one grants that "felicity consists in living a life with pleasure, i.e., maximum delight," nevertheless "the question remains as to where such delight lies" (AW 30.8). In other words: What *kinds* of pleasures primarily constitute a felicitous life and by what *means* do we experience them? Hobbes's answer starkly diverges from his ancient hedonist predecessors. The Epicureans took felicity to consist in the "static" pleasures of being pain-free in virtue of having satisfied or relinquished one's desires. They also placed greater emphasis on psychic pleasures than somatic pleasures; indeed, on the Ciceronian interpretation, static pleasures just are mental pleasures. The Cyrenaics, by contrast, located felicity in the somatic pleasures of satisfying one's desires. Hobbes rejected both accounts.

The first point Hobbes made in response to his question is that felicity primarily consists in the anticipatory pleasures of mind that accompany desire, rather than in the pleasures of fruition that accompany sensory perception: "as nothing can be desired unless desired with regard to the future [*sub ratione future*], it is necessary to place felicity in the appetite for future good." Why is felicity not, as the Cyrenaics taught, composed of sensory pleasures of fruition concerning the present? Hobbes answered by echoing the Epicurean view that such pleasures are too fleeting to contribute intrinsically to an agent's *ongoing* experience: they last only so long as one's senses are being titillated and one's desire is *being satisfied.*

> It might be asked whether the present does not please while one enjoys [*fruimur*] it. Certainly it pleases, moreover it may seem that felicity consists in present enjoyment [*fruition*], rather than in appetite for the future; it is therefore necessary to consider that the delight which is aroused by present things is brief, in fact we are said to be enjoying them only so long as we sense [*sentimus*] them, i.e., so long as the delightful object [*objectum jucundum*] acts on our sensory organs in the very action that delights, which time in every variety of pleasure is short. (AW 38.5)[11]

Moreover, like the Epicureans, Hobbes added that, beyond being fleeting, pleasures of sense also tend to give way to pain: "those pleasures are usually called sensual in which the object's action, which was at first delightful [*jucunda*], on account of its lingering and of the feeling of alteration presently becomes painful [*molesta*]" (AW 38.5). Hobbes proceeded to argue that even if a pleasure begins as a sensory pleasure of fruition, it can persist only as a pleasure of mind; any subsequent pleasures of fruition arise from perceiving the object of sense while we satisfy consecutive appetites:

> if we consider the present to be not time, but an instance, we shall confess that a pleasure of sense, if it persists, is no longer in the sense, but in the memory. What is in the memory, does not please as something past, except insofar as the past events are signs of similar

> pleasures expected in the future. But the future does not exist, except in the imagination of we who suppose that the past is connected to the present as what follows [the past]; but what follows the present, we call the future. Hence fruition [*fruitio*] itself is nothing, in the very object we enjoy [*fruimur*], other than the latest appetite arising from the contemplation of the object's parts [*orta à partium eius contemplatione appetitio ulterior*]; hence it remains true that the basis of good [*rationem boni*], and hence of felicity, consists in appetite. (AW 38.5)

If felicity requires a greater amount of ongoing mental pleasures relative to pains, then Hobbes's second point was that the amount of ongoing joy relative to grief is maximized when *desires* combine with the *hope* of satisfying them, rather than with the fear of frustrating them. For such fear would offset anticipatory pleasure by inflicting anticipatory pain. This amounts to rejecting the Epicurean dictum that unfulfilled desire is intrinsically painful: whether the presence of desire is more painful than pleasant overall depends on how confident or fearful one is about its potential satisfaction. His third point was that desire combines with hope when one has experienced the repeated satisfaction of one's desires via a constant *accumulation* of desired goods. Felicity

> consists in the progress of appetite from an acquired good to another good to be acquired ... [but] There is no felicity in the appetite or acquisition of goods, if a greater or equal fear of losing them perpetually accompanies the appetite and hope of acquisition. For the delight [*Iucunditas*] that lies in hope is offset by the anxiety that lies in fear. It is therefore necessary for felicity to combine the hope of acquiring with the hope of conserving; and so consequently felicity consists in the progress of acquiring, such that the new acquisitions seem to protect the old. (AW 38.6)

Thus Hobbes shared the Epicurean concern with the elimination of mental anxiety, but in rejecting the view that desire is inherently ridden with anxiety, he offered a solution sharply contrasting with the Epicurean one. In the famous opening of book 2 of *De Rerum Natura* (Lucretius n.d.) – to which Hobbes explicitly referred in *Anti-White* – Lucretius, like his master Epicurus, had portrayed the pursuit of power as noxious to felicity (DRN II, ll 1–61; AW 38.16).[12] Hobbes, by contrast, made felicity depend on it. His fourth point was that awareness of continual success in having satisfied one's desires spawns hope only because it makes one aware of one's *power* to satisfy desires:

> consider that passion which we call joy, or delight of the mind, which differs from those stimulations of the body and organs that constitute sensual pleasures. Whatever is troublesome [*molestum*] for the mind, is troublesome because it lowers one's high sense of one's own power. And since power [*potentia*] concerns the future, to determine one's judgement of that power, by which all goods are acquired by us, is to determine hope. (AW 38.7)

Felicity originates in awareness of one's power to satisfy desires in the future: "since not only acquiring, but also protecting one's gains, are a power, felicity will be the perpetual progress of appetite and hope from lesser to greater power" (AW 38.6).

The upshot is that, although the subjective satisfaction of desires and the accompanying pleasures of fruition do not intrinsically contribute much to ongoing felicity – their contribution is too fleeting – they do play a significant *instrumental* role, by fostering anticipatory pleasures: "felicity consists not in sensory enjoyment [*fruitione sensibili*], but in delight of imagination [*jucunda imaginatione*] of progressing from the enjoyment [*fruitione*] of one good thing to the enjoyment [*fruitionem*] of another. This however is to be understood such that the progression pleases not as a progression [of fruitions], but as a proof of one's own virtue, & excellence, which are the progression's cause" (AW 38.8). The point of the cautionary second sentence is that, whereas felicity primarily *consists* in ongoing delight of the imagination, a succession of pleasures of fruition plays a primarily instrumental role in promoting felicity, by fostering hope and hence net anticipatory pleasure.

Hobbes rounded out this hedonist account by advancing the even starker thesis that *all* pleasures of mind ultimately reduce to a form of "glory," which was Hobbes's name for the anticipatory joy that accompanies contemplating one's own power:

> if in fact every mental grief [*dolor animi*] lies in recollecting or feigning [*fictione*] one's own weakness, then every mental delight [*animi jucunditas*] consists in the recollection, or at least feigned imagination [*fictâ imaginatione*], of one's own power, or excellence. Therefore joy, or delight of the mind [*delectatio animi*], is nothing but a kind of triumph of the mind, whether internal glory, or glorying over one's own power & excellence with respect to another to whom one compares oneself. (AW 38.8)

This was a recurring theme of Hobbes's psychology: the assertion that all mental pleasures are reducible to glory appears in all three political treatises.[13] It is also firmly grounded in the basic assumption behind Hobbes's classification of pleasures: that mental pleasures are parasitic on sensual pleasures. Mental pleasure ultimately consists in anticipating the satisfaction of desire, which anticipation depends on contemplating one's power to satisfy it.

It is therefore no surprise that Hobbes tightly linked felicity to glory: if pleasures of mind amount to the joy of glorying, then felicity consists in the maximum ongoing experience of glory (relative to dejection of mind). Yet because felicity requires ongoing, and not just fleeting pleasures, Hobbes insisted that it requires *true* glory grounded in a true record of success:

> Now if glory be such that it springs from assessing one's power on the basis of previous deeds, they bring about hope, because he who has done, seems to have the power to do again. Therefore such a self-assessment gives rise to diligence [*industria*], & frequent success, through a true and just assessment of power; moreover one success causes another, thanks to the new power secured with each success; and this continuous manner of successes, together with a reason for hope if they persist, is called felicity. (AW 38.8)

Hobbes contrasted this true glory with two forms of vainglory, not grounded in true successes, and neither of which ordinarily conduces to felicity. One kind of vainglory arises from the fictional imagination of one's power, which, because it does not engender any hope of future success, produces a merely fleeting pleasure.[14] The other kind arises from being falsely persuaded of one's power on the basis of flattery from others, which ordinarily produces a merely fleeting pleasure because, although it initially fosters hope, the hope is short lived: hope is immediately dashed by failures that expose one's feebleness (AW 38.8; cf. 1640, 9.1; *Leviathan* 6.39 and 11.11–12; 2012, 88, 154–6; 1651, 26–7, 49).

In short, felicity consists primarily in pleasures of mind, not sense; pleasures of mind are anticipatory pleasures, not fruition; pleasures of mind thrive relative to grief when desires combine with hope of satisfying them; hope depends on awareness of repeated success in having satisfied one's desires; and repeated success spawns hope and confidence or true glory because it generates awareness of one's power to satisfy desires.

6.4 Conclusion

It is sometimes thought that, rather than a *summum bonum*, Hobbes posited only a *summum malum*, namely death, such that survival, rather than contentment or felicity as a whole, is the proper object of desire. But this is mistaken: Hobbes had a positive conception of the *summum bonum*, that is, of *felicitas*. Hobbes conceived of felicity as the ultimate good grounding the value of all other goods; it is not, however, the proper *aim* of all valuable action. To live a felicitous life one must desire and pursue other objects as well. Indeed, it was a fundamental tenet of his political philosophy that, given the human condition, felicity can be realized only by directly desiring and pursuing the conditions of *survival*. Although the criteria of a felicitous life in Hobbes's theory of *value* are maximum and ongoing net pleasure, individuals' affective and practical reasons are not necessarily, in Hobbes's theory of normative *reasons*, directly to aim for maximum, ongoing pleasure or felicity. Under conditions of uncertainty, the most reasonable course of action may involve a disaster-avoidance rather than distributed-utility-maximizing strategy (although the normativity of disaster-avoidance would still be conditional on and derived from its ability to serve expected-distributed-utility-maximization) (Kavka 1986, 202–7). This is why in his published works he rhetorically subordinated the language of "contentment" to the language of "self-preservation," even as he periodically reminded his readers that self-preservation encompasses not just survival but also "contentment" or "commodious living."

Hobbes emphasized the hedonist and processual character of felicity as early as *Elements*: by felicity "we mean continual delight"; it "consisteth not in having prospered, but in prospering" (1640, 9.7), i.e., not in fruition or a *state*, but in an ongoing process of repeated success spawning hopeful anticipation. Hobbes sharply contrasted his own anticipatory theory of felicity, as a progression from one appetite and anticipatory pleasure to another, to the ancient doctrine according to which felicity lies in the *end* or complete *satisfaction* of desire: "But for an utmost ende in which the Ancient Philosophers have placed Felicity ... there is noe such thing in this world, nor way to it ... for while we live we have desires, and desire presupposeth a farther Ende" (1640, 7.6). In *De cive*, Hobbes's more political focus was restricted to individuals' "civil felicity" (*fælicitatem civilem*)" (13.6; 1983, 197; cf. *De cive* 3.22, 1983, 116). But in *Leviathan* 11.1 he returned to characterizing felicity in general terms. Again rejecting the view that felicity consists in the tranquility of mind that was supposed to come with the end of desire, he reiterated that:

> the Felicity of this life, consisteth not in the repose of a mind satisfied. For there is no such *Finis ultimus*, (utmost ayme,) nor *Summum Bonum*, (greatest Good,) as is spoken of in the Books of the old Morall Philosophers. Nor can a man any more live, whose Desires are at an end, than he, whose Senses and Imaginations are at a stand. Felicity is a continuall progresse of the desire, from one object to another; the attaining of the former, being still

> but the way to the later. The cause whereof is, That the object of mans desire, is not to enjoy [LL: *fruatur*] once onely, and for one instant of time; but to assure for ever, the way of his future desire [LL: *sed ut fruitionem suam securam in futuram reddat* (but to render his enjoyment secure in the future)]. (2012, 150–1; 1651, 47)

Neither the passage from *Elements*, nor this one from *Leviathan*, nor the equivalent one in *De homine* 11.15 (OL II.103) says, as Hobbes has often been taken to say, that there is no *summum bonum*. It is true that, because individuals take pleasure in different objects, Hobbes denied any shared content beyond ongoing pleasure to the *summum bonum*; but he nevertheless insisted that the *summum bonum* just is ongoing pleasure. These passages say that the supreme and ultimate good for all humans consists not in the fruition or realization of some end – not in some state – but in a continual *process* of having one hopeful desire and hence anticipatory pleasure after another.[15] They reiterate the fundamentally hedonist, processual, and anticipatory character of felicity, which Hobbes again explicitly linked to leading "a contented life" (2012, 150; 1651, 47).

Earlier, in chapter 6.58 of *Leviathan*, Hobbes had characterized felicity as "*Continual Successe* in obtaining those things which a man from time to time desireth, that is to say, continuall prospering" (2012, 96; 1651, 29). The apparent contrast with *Elements*' formulation, which is in terms of "continual delight" rather than success and desire, has led some to read *Leviathan*'s chapter 6 passage, unlike the chapter 11 passage, as reflecting a desire-fulfilment theory of well-being (McNeilly 1968, 129–36). We can now see why it does no such thing. Desire satisfaction *does* play a role in Hobbes's hedonist account, but only when one is subjectively aware of it, and even here subjective desire satisfaction plays a primarily instrumental role, by giving rise to self-confidence or true glory and hence to the hopeful anticipation of ongoing *future* satisfaction.

Acknowledgment

This chapter is reproduced with permission from Abizadeh, Arash. 2018. *Hobbes and the Two Faces of Ethics*. Cambridge: Cambridge University Press.

Notes

1 Classic texts are available with English translation at the Perseus Digital Collection, accessed October 28, 2020: http://www.perseus.tufts.edu/hopper/text?doc=urn:cts:latinLit:phi0474.phi048.perseus-lat1:praef.

2 For the sources of Epicurean influence on Hobbes, see Friedle (2012).

3 *Lives* (I.2.8.87-88), accessed October 28, 2020: http://data.perseus.org/citations/urn:cts:greekLit:tlg0004.tlg001.perseus-eng1:1.prologue. See also Mitsis (1988, 55) and Annas (1993, 227–35).

4 Plato's *Gorgias*, accessed October 28, 2020: http://data.perseus.org/citations/urn:cts:greekLit:tlg0059.tlg023.perseus-eng1:447a.

5 On the philosopher's need for "apt" reforming definitions, see *Leviathan* 4.13 (2012, 56; 1651, 15), 5.17 (2012, 72; 1651, 21), 34.1 (2012, 610; 1651, 207). On the notion of reforming definitions, see Brandt (1979) and Railton (1989).

6 Aristotle (n.d.), *Nicomachean Ethics*, accessed October 28, 2020: http://data.perseus.org/citations/urn:cts:greekLit:tlg0086.tlg010.perseus-eng1:1094a.

7 McNeilly (1968, 120–1; 129–36; cf. 139, 145) argues that Hobbes's characterization of felicity in *Leviathan* chapter 6 reflects a shift to the desire-fulfilment theory, but that his characterization in *Leviathan* chapter 11 harks back to the older, hedonist (and egoist) account. The desire-fulfilment theory is attributed to Hobbes by Gauthier (1979), Hampton (1986, 27–42, 53), Ripstein (1987), and Meyers (2013).

8 See Gert (1965, 1967), Hampton (1986, 17–24), and Boonin-Vail (1994, 42–7). Unlike Gert's "tautological" egoism, the weak egoism/hedonism combination has substantive behavioral consequences: we do not desire things we cannot see as pleasant. For criticism of Gert, see Olsthoorn (2014).

9 Philosophers must begin "their Ratiocination from Definitions; that is, from settled significations of their words" *Leviathan* 5.8 (2012, 70; 1651, 20; cf. *Leviathan* 5.4, 2012, 66; 1651, 19).

10 Hobbes would have encountered Epicurus's so-called "hedonistic calculus" passage in *Lives* (II.10.129; Cf. Epicurus 1926, 87–9). Some scholars deny the passage commits Epicurus to a pleasure-maximizing calculus, on the grounds that katastematic pleasures are neither quantifiable nor ordinally rankable (Annas 1993, 85–7, 334–5).

11 See also AW 38.8.

12 *De Rerum Natura*, accessed October 28, 2020: http://data.perseus.org/citations/urn:cts:latinLit:phi0550.phi001.perseus-lat1:1.1-1.49.

13 EL 27.3; 8.8, 8.6; DCv 1.2, 1.5, 15.13, 1983, 90–4, 225; *Leviathan* 17.8, 2012, 258, 1651, 86. *Leviathan* 17.8 speaks against Slomp's (2007, 184–5) thesis that Hobbes changed his mind in *Leviathan*. Slomp's reading is facilitated by the mistaken claim that Hobbes earlier held that "*all* human passions derive from the pleasure or displeasure" of glory. But Hobbes's thesis concerned only *mental* pleasures. Cf. Slomp (1998).

14 "But if someone assesses his power on the basis of his own fiction (for anyone can attribute to himself, by means of a fiction of fancy [*per fictionem phantasticam*], whatever actions contrived [*fictas*] by the poets), no hope for future success arises, but a passing & vain delight [*delectatio*] only, on account of which it is called vain glory, which in no way conduces to felicity" (AW 38.8).

15 The ancients arguably did not understand felicity as an "end" in this sense either (Annas 1993, 34–6), and it may be that Hobbes was responding more to ancient ethics in translation.

References

Annas, Julia. 1993. *The Morality of Happiness*. Oxford: Oxford University Press.

Aristotle. n.d. *Nicomachean Ethics*. Available at: http://data.perseus.org/citations/urn:cts:greekLit:tlg0086.tlg010.perseus-eng1:1094a

Boonin-Vail, David. 1994. *Thomas Hobbes and the Science of Moral Virtue*. Cambridge: Cambridge University Press.

Brandt, Richard B. 1979. *A Theory of the Good and the Right*. Oxford: Clarendon Press.

Cicero. n.d. *De Finibus Bonorum et Malorum*. Available at: http://data.perseus.org/citations/urn:cts:latinLit:phi0474.phi048.perseus-lat1:praef

Diogenes Laertius. n.d. *Lives of Eminent Philosophers*. Available at: http://data.perseus.org/citations/urn:cts:greekLit:tlg0004.tlg001.perseus-eng1:1.prologue

Epicurus. 1926. *Epicurus: The Extant Remains*, edited by Cyril Bailey. Oxford: Clarendon Press.

Friedle, Simon. 2012. Thomas Hobbes and the Reception of Early-Modern Epicureanism. PhD Thesis, Faculty of History, University of Cambridge.

Gauthier, David. 1979. "Thomas Hobbes: Moral Theorist." *The Journal of Philosophy* 76 (10): 547–59.

Gert, Bernard. 1965. "Hobbes, Mechanism, and Egoism." *The Philosophical Quarterly* 15 (61): 341–9.

Gert, Bernard. 1967. "Hobbes and Psychological Egoism." *Journal of the History of Ideas* 28 (4): 503–20.

Hampton, Jean. 1986. *Hobbes and the Social Contract Tradition*. Cambridge: Cambridge University Press.

Hampton, Jean. 1992. "Hobbes and Ethical Naturalism." *Philosophical Perspectives* 6: 333–53.

Hobbes, Thomas. 1640. *The Elements of Law*. Harley MS 4235 (British Library, London) [chapters renumbered consecutively].

Hobbes, Thomas. 1839–1845a. *The English works of Thomas Hobbes*, 11 vols., edited by Sir William Molesworth. London: John Bohn. Cited as EW.

Hobbes, Thomas. 1839–1845b. *Thomæ Hobbes malmesburiensis opera philosophica*, 5 vols., edited by Gulielmi Molesworth. London: John Bohn. Cited as OL.

Hobbes, Thomas. 1973. *Critique du De Mundo de Thomas White*, edited by Jean Jacquot and Harold W. Jones. Paris: Vrin-CNRS. [1642/43] [cited as AW, chapter, article].

Hobbes, Thomas. 1983. *De cive: The Latin Version*, edited by Howard Warrender. Oxford: Clarendon Press. [1642, 2nd ed. 1647].

Hobbes, Thomas. 2012. *Leviathan*, 3 vols., edited by Noel Malcolm. Oxford: Clarendon Press. [First published 1651.]

Kavka, Gregory S. 1986. *Hobbesian Moral and Political Theory*. Princeton, NJ: Princeton University Press.

Lucretius. n.d. *De Rerum Natura*. Available at: http://data.perseus.org/citations/urn:cts:latinLit:phi0550.phi001.perseus-lat1:1.1-1.49

McNeilly, F.S. 1968. *The Anatomy of Leviathan*. New York: St. Martin's Press.

Meyers, Chris D. 2013. "Hobbes and the Rationality of Self-Preservation: Grounding Morality on the Desires We Should Have." *The European Legacy* 18 (3): 269–86.

Mitsis, Phillip. 1988. *Epicurus' Ethical Theory: The Pleasures of Invulnerability*. Ithaca, NY: Cornell University Press.

Nagel, Thomas. 1959. "Hobbes's Concept of Obligation." *The Philosophical Review* 68 (1): 68–83.

Olsthoorn, Johan. 2014. "Worse than Death." *Hobbes Studies* 27 (2): 148–70.

Plato. n.d. *Gorgias*. Available at: http://data.perseus.org/citations/urn:cts:greekLit:tlg0059.tlg023.perseus-eng1:447a

Railton, Peter. 1989. "Naturalism and Prescriptivity." *Social Philosophy and Policy* 7 (1): 151–74.

Ripstein, Arthur. 1987. "Foundationalism in Political Theory." *Philosophy & Public Affairs* 16 (2): 115–37.

Schneewind, Jerome B. 1998. *The Invention of Autonomy: A History of Modern Moral Philosophy*. Cambridge: Cambridge University Press.

Slomp, Gabriella. 1998. "From *Genus* to *Species*: The Unravelling of Hobbesian Glory." *History of Political Thought* 19 (4): 552–69.

Slomp, Gabriella. 2007. "Hobbes on Glory and Civil Strife." In *The Cambridge Companion to Hobbes's Leviathan*, edited by Patricia Springborg, 181–98. Cambridge: Cambridge University Press.

Wolfsdorf, David. 2013. *Pleasure in Ancient Greek Philosophy*. Cambridge: Cambridge University Press.

7

In Search of "A Constant Civill Amity": Hobbes on Friendship and Sociability

GABRIELLA SLOMP

Does anything, other than fear, bind the citizens of the Hobbesian commonwealth together?[1] From Hobbes's times to our own, many readers have pondered this question. The answer is rarely a resounding "yes." In "A Review, and Conclusion" to *Leviathan*, Hobbes acknowledges such concerns:

> And to consider the contrariety of mens Opinions, and Manners in generall, *It is, they say, impossible to entertain a constant Civill Amity* with all those, with whom the Businesse of the world constrains us to converse: Which Businesse, consisteth almost in nothing else but a perpetuall contention for Honor, Riches, and Authority. (Hobbes 2012, 1132; 1651, 389; emphasis added)[2]

Hobbes comments that these "are indeed great difficulties, but not Impossibilities" (Hobbes 2012, 1132; 1651, 389); however, he does not elaborate on this claim. This chapter seeks to shed light on the origins, nature and scope of Hobbesian amity. It explores Hobbes's stance on two concepts – sociability and friendship – that a long tradition of writers, inspired by Aristotle, have employed to explain why and how people form bonds and live peacefully in political associations.

From ancient to early modern times, "sociability" was conventionally presented as a natural disposition that led people to seek each other's company; "friendship" indicated the relationship that people naturally form with each other, but also represented an ideal or model of citizenship (Hutter 1978; King 2000). To justify the need for the mighty Leviathan, it was important for Hobbes to undermine the idea that man is by nature sociable; he did so in well-known passages of his political writings that have attracted considerable attention from interpreters. Regarding friendship, however, Hobbes made only scattered remarks, and the secondary literature is correspondingly very limited.[3]

A Companion to Hobbes, First Edition. Edited by Marcus P. Adams.

In this chapter, I contend that Hobbes's neglect of friendship is as relevant as his vocal rejection of natural sociability; it shows Hobbes altered the usual interpretation of both concepts, thereby offering a new take on the origin, nature, and conditions of "civill amity" within political states. In the chapter I argue that the "constancy" of amity among Hobbesian citizens does not derive from reciprocity of love or care but from a shared understanding of the Leviathan's function and the joint endeavor to support its accomplishment.

The argument proceeds in steps.[4] First, I examine Hobbes's understanding of friendship vis-à-vis Aristotle's; second, I explore Hobbes's refutation of the explanatory value traditionally attributed to friendship; third, I investigate his dismissal of friendship as virtue; fourth, I consider Hobbes's rejection of sociability as a descriptive term and his endorsement of this disposition as a norm that summarizes the natural laws; and finally, I argue that constant civil amity is the result of education and discipline.

7.1 Hobbesian Friendship: Power and Contract

> Friendship seems too to hold states together ... For unanimity [concord] seems to be something like friendship, and this they aim at most of all, and expel faction as their worst enemy. (Aristotle 1984, 1825; NE VIII 1155a 21–5)

> It [friendship] exists least in the worst form; in tyranny there is little or no friendship. (Aristotle 1984, 1835; NE VIII 1161a 33–5)

Friendship was a cornerstone of Aristotle's ethics and played a major role in his politics insofar as it captured the essence of civic concord and provided the criterion for distinguishing between good and bad regimes. Aristotle's concept of friendship is multifaceted and constitutes one of the most challenging and controversial aspects of his theory (Mulgan 2000, 15); even so, there is some consensus among scholars (Pangle 2003; Price 1989) that Aristotelian friendship is a voluntary bond between individuals, entailing reciprocity of good will and driven by three possible sources: pleasure, utility, and virtue.

Aristotle, as well as a long tradition of writers inspired by him, assigned to friendship descriptive and prescriptive functions. On the one hand, they employed friendship – especially of the utility-based variety – to describe and illuminate the nature of citizenship; on the other, they adopted virtue-based friendship as an ideal, leading individuals and communities toward the flourishing of man and the attainment of "the good life."

Hobbes was no stranger to Aristotle's notion of friendship. In addition to being well-acquainted with the *Nicomachean Ethics*,[5] Hobbes summarized the meaning of Aristotelian friendship (EW VI. 454–6) in his abridgement of the *Art of Rhetoric* (EW VI.419–510).[6]

Hobbes did not provide us with his own understanding of friendship in a neat package, but nevertheless he made the key components of the concept clear. He wrote that "[t]o have friends, is Power" (Hobbes 2012, 132; 1651, 41) but suggested that the power derived from friendship is less reliable than the power connected with riches and places of authority;[7] he believed that "[b]y nature ... we are not looking for friends but for honour and advantage (*commodum*) from them" (Hobbes 1998, 22), and that friendship is a sort of "contract" (Hobbes 1969, 44), entailing provision of assistance in exchange of honor among unequals[8] or trade of favors among equals.[9]

The association that Hobbes postulated between friendship, power, and contract filled some readers with indignation (e.g., Sir Leslie Stephen 1904). On one level, such indignation is unwarranted. Although Hobbes stresses in *De homine* XI.6 that "friendships are good, certainly useful" (Hobbes 1972, 49), he does not exclude that man is capable of genuine love and affection for family and friends.[10] Indeed, evidence from Hobbes's own life[11] and his correspondence[12] points against the conclusion that Hobbes understood friendship to be based on crude calculations of self-interest. His reference to Sidney Goldolphin in *Leviathan* (Hobbes 2012, 1133; 1651, 390) shows that for Hobbes it is not beyond human nature to love one's friends for their character and virtue.

It could be argued, therefore, that by explaining friendship in terms of power and contract, Hobbes was simply translating the ancient understanding of friendship into the more scientific parlance of his times (Pagden 1987). If man is a form of "motion" generated by, and generating, "power," then the claim that "friends are power" amounts – in the language of Hobbes's physics – to the statement that friends contribute to the formation of an individual's identity.[13] Similarly, the likening of friendship to a "contract" can be understood – in the context of Hobbes's mercantilist times – as a contemporary rephrasing of the ancient notion that a core ingredient of friendship is reciprocity of goodwill and trust.[14]

On another level, however, Hobbes's position on friendship does represent a sharp break with the tradition before him, as I aim to show in the subsequent sections.

7.2 Friendship: Glue or Solvent?

The ancients employed the concepts of φιλία (*philia*) or *amicitia* to explain the formation of bonds between men unrelated by blood and to shed light on how citizenship and concord can be built. Hobbes rejected such explanations of the origin and nature of political relationships; in his theory, the notions of friendship-as-contract and friendship-as-power are unsuitable to support the bond-forming and citizenship-building weight that the ancients would have φιλία (*philia*) or *amicitia* carry.

First, because of its contractual nature, Hobbesian friendship is unreliable in natural conditions that are characterized by a lack of both common values and trust. Indeed, Hobbes maintains in *Elements of Law* I.19.4 that contracts do not hold in the state of nature; all leagues and alliances eventually collapse because

> by the diversity of judgements and passions in so many men contending naturally for honour and advantage one above another: it is impossible, not only that their consent to aid each other against an enemy, but also that the peace should last between themselves without some mutual and common fear to rule them. (Hobbes 1969, 101–2)

In other words, although alliances can, in principle, develop in natural conditions, they cannot deliver man from his miserable plight. Fear undermines the possibility of coherence and size; individual glory-seeking frustrates a league's pretensions to co-ordination and permanence. For Hobbes only the creation of the mighty Leviathan (and the sword) can bring peace and order:

> [s]omething more is needed, an element of fear to prevent an accord on peace and mutual assistance for a common good from collapsing in discord when a private good subsequently comes into conflict with the common good. (Hobbes 1998, 71)

Although Hobbes refers to the body politic as "a league of all Subjects together" (Hobbes 2012, 370; 1651, 121), he maintains that the state-league is not a natural development of alliances of friends. In the Aristotelian tradition, the concept of friendship helped explain the transition from the family to the village and finally to the polis. For Hobbes, the inverse is true: the state is the precondition for the occurrence of friendship. In this way, one can see that Hobbes's friendship-as-contract does not just describe a relationship of "self" and "other"; rather, the concept depends on and is inextricably linked to an environment – including mutual trust, shared signification of language, and commonality of values – that is only made possible by the creation of the Leviathan.

Second, Hobbesian friendship, as it is a form of "power," may generate discord instead of concord within the state. Pride – that characteristic that differentiates Hobbesian man from bees and ants, and that prevents him from seeing that his private interest concurs with the common interest[15] – induces citizens to create societies, clubs, and affiliations that are not only selective, but also exclusionary, thereby generating enmity; it can also tempt officials and governments to give special treatment to their friends, thereby undermining justice and fomenting discontent and civil unrest.[16]

In chapter 22 of *Leviathan*, Hobbes discusses partial societies within the state[17] and stresses that such affiliations can have ambivalent effects on the commonwealth: they can resemble the "Muscles of a Body naturall" (Hobbes 2012, 348; 1651, 115) or harbor the disease that will bring sickness and death:

> Systemes, and Assemblyes of People, which may be compared (as I said,) to the Similar parts of mans Body: such as be Lawfull, to the Muscles; such as are Unlawfull, to Wens, Biles, and Apostemes, engendred by the unnatural conflux of evill humours. (Hobbes 2012, 374; 1651, 123)

In Hobbes's view, it is for the Leviathan to decide which systems are lawful "muscles," or unlawful "wens." He claims in *Elements of Law* II.9. 1 that it makes its arbitration using the criterion of *salus populi*, "by which must be understood, not the mere preservation of [men's] lives but generally their benefit and good" (Hobbes 1969, 179). Thus, duly monitored by the Leviathan, affiliations and systems in all their forms can improve the quality of life, wealth, and security within a society. But here, once again, Hobbes shows us that the Leviathan is the necessary condition for friendship to be a source of benefit. As, without the Leviathan to police and protect its citizens, social associations may develop that are divisive, corrupt, or otherwise detrimental to the common good.

In sum, Hobbes inverted the relationship between friendship and the state that he inherited from his Aristotelian forebears. Rather than friendship being a precondition for the development of the state, the state becomes the precondition for the occurrence of friendship. Before the creation of the political state, friendship, being a contract, cannot but fail. After the creation of the state, being a form of power, friendship can create divisions rather than unity and needs careful monitoring by the state. The acknowledgment of the ambivalence of friendship is according to many the distinctive trait of modernity.[18] Therefore, for Hobbes, authority is the stable glue that holds people together in political associations; friendship is at best a weak adhesive, and at worst a solvent – this is a major change with the Aristotelian tradition.

Having said this, friendship plays a role in Hobbes's discussion of "commodious living" especially in *Leviathan*,[19] where systems, partial societies, affiliations, and friendships transform the "thin" legal peace created by the social contract into "thick" social peace. Even though *forensis quaedam amicitia* among Hobbesian citizens is not the result of love and benevolence, but the outcome of their desire of profit and glory (Hobbes 1983, 90),[20] it nevertheless provides the framework that allows individuals to improve the quality of their life; it reinforces solidarity in war efforts against an external enemy; it is a fundamental tool for enriching the country and increase its security vis-à-vis other states.

7.3 True Friendship: Virtue or Vice?

Aristotle used utility-based friendship as a way to understand political life; he maintained that

> [I]t is for the sake of advantage that the political community too seems both to have come together originally and to endure. (Aristotle 1984, 1833; NE VIII. 1160a.11–12)

> Civic friendship ... is based on utility. (Aristotle 1984, 1969; EEVII.10.1242b22)

But utility-friendship was for Aristotle an imperfect relationship, its perfect counterpart being a friendship driven by love of virtue. There was consensus in the Greco-Roman world that perfect or virtue-friendship was accessible only to a minority of excellent men, capable of loving their friends selflessly (Schollmeier 1994), instead of using them as means to achieve selfish ends:

> Perfect friendship is the friendship of men who are good, and alike in excellence; for these wish well alike to each other *qua* good, and they are good in themselves. Now those who wish well to their friends for their sake are most truly friends. (Aristotle 1984, 1827; NE VIII 1156b 7–10)

Virtue-friendship was anchored to an external truth – "the good life," "summum bonum" (Mulgan 2000; Schall 1996) – that philosophers had not invented but discovered.

In the early modern period, nominalism and skepticism put the existence of this "external truth" that grounded ancient virtue-friendship in doubt. A new, individualistic model of friendship emerged whereby the friends decide the foundations and content of their own truth, as exemplified by Montaigne's famous essay[21] (Lewis 1960; Lochman, Lopez, and Hutson 2011; Schall 1996).

Hobbes was arguably among the first to pick up a shovel in the demolition of the foundations of ancient virtue-friendship: he mounted an attack against Aristotelian teleology, against the idea that there is only one conception of the good life,[22] and against the notion of a *summum bonum* (Rutherford 2003).

For sure, against the widespread agreement among the ancients that

> Friendship exists only between good men, whereas the bad man never achieves true friendship with either a good or a bad man. (Plato 1987, 147; *Lysis* 214 d)

> Friendship can exist only between good men. (Cicero 1991, 86; *De Amicitia* V.18)

Hobbes denounced as "patently false" the claim that "it is not the evil but the good that have friends"; in his work on Thomas White, he asked, suggestively:

> And depraved though they are, do not conspirators aid and comfort one another, and share common designs? (Hobbes 1976, 479)

For Hobbes, conspirators bent on destruction are no less able than obedient citizens to have friends and stand by them; being "depraved" citizens does not prevent them from being caring friends. In all three his political works, Hobbes criticized Aristotle and "the writers of moral philosophy" for placing virtue "in a mediocrity of passions" (Hobbes 1998, III.32.56, 1969, I.17.14.94, 2012, 242; 1651, 80) rather than evaluating actions and attitudes on the ground of their consequences.

From a Hobbesian perspective, it is not the quantity of egoism or selflessness in the relationship that renders friendship a virtue or a vice, rather it is the effect of friendship on peace.[23] For instance, the groups of friends that commenced enterprises such as mathematics and the performing arts may have been more selfish than the groups of friends that founded religious sects and political factions; yet the latter have caused more wars and troubles to mankind than the former, and therefore are far less virtuous in Hobbesian terms.

In other words, from a Hobbesian point of view, the difference between self-interested and selfless friendship is largely irrelevant, as the important distinction about human behavior is between ignorance and knowledge of Hobbes's science of political obligation. There is reason to believe that ignorance of "the Elements of moral virtue and civil duties" (Hobbes 1969, Epistle dedicatory, 6) is spread evenly among the selfish and the selfless.

Though Hobbes was keen to dismantle ancient virtue-friendship, the emerging individualistic model of friendship, whereby friends decide their own truth and become "laws unto each other" (Schall 1996, 134), was no more appealing. For Hobbes, when individuals are free to decide what is true and good, chaos ensues. It is therefore unsurprising that in Hobbes's theory we find an alternative model whereby the terms of friendship are neither anchored to an eternal truth as in antiquity, nor chosen by the friends themselves as in modernity, but decided by an artificial entity created by man – the Leviathan. It is one of the charges of the Hobbesian sovereign to identify and eradicate affiliations and societies that can endanger the health of the commonwealth while encouraging any enterprise that strengthens peace.

Pace the ancients, for Hobbes friendship is not a school of virtue; the duties of friendship do not prepare one to the duties of citizenship; being a good friend does not make one a good citizen. Being a good citizen derives only from a correct understanding of political obligation – an understanding that is accessible "even to the meanest capacity" (Hobbes 2012, 240; 1651, 79), though attained only by the few willing to invest time and effort. As Hobbes argues in *De cive* XIII.9, it is the responsibility of the Leviathan to provide and promote this civic education – an important constituent of its overall endeavor to secure lasting peace:

> I hold therefore that it is a duty of sovereigns to have the true Elements of civil doctrine written and to order that it be taught in all the Universities in the commonwealth. (Hobbes 1998, 147)

7.4 Sociability: Natural Remedy or Prescription Drug?

In western political thought, the concepts of friendship and sociability often go hand in hand, the former signifying a relationship facilitated by the disposition denoted by the latter:

> Sociability, Aristotle notes, has no name of its own ... it resembles *philia* but differs from it in that the sociable person lacks feeling and affection for those with whom he mingles. (Konstan 1997, 102)

While Hobbes's position on friendship was mainly one of disregard, he argued forcibly against the supposedly natural sociability of man.

Hobbes tells us in *Elements of Law* I.14.4 that men are, by nature, "divers ways largely offensive one to another" (Hobbes 1969, 71) and that they "have no pleasure, (but on the contrary a great deale of griefe) in keeping company" (Hobbes 2012, 190; 1651, 61). This does not imply that individuals are misanthropes or loners; on the contrary, Hobbes notes that "perpetual solitude is hard for a man to bear by nature or as a man" (Hobbes 1998, 24) and that being cast out of society is an intolerable punishment. Hobbes acknowledges "the love men bear to one another, or the pleasure they take in one another's company" (Hobbes 1969, 43) and describes men as attracted to parties, gatherings, assemblies, public speeches, and parliaments. The reason, however, that people seek the company of others "is not for friendship" but for "honour and profit" (Hobbes 1998, 22).[24]

While Hobbes rejects sociability as a descriptive concept, he endorses it as a prescription. In fact, he goes as far as to suggest in *Elements of Law* I.18.15 that the recommendation to be sociable summarizes the laws of nature:

> The sum of virtue is to be sociable with them that will be sociable ... And the same is the sum of the law of nature; for in being sociable, the law of nature taketh place by the way of peace and society ... (Hobbes 1969, 95)

In so far as it includes the long list of virtues recommended by the natural laws, Hobbesian sociability is a thicker concept than medieval courtesy or early modern civility (Bryson 1998; Thomas 2018); to be sociable, for a Hobbesian individual, means to be modest, grateful, forgiving, accommodating, fair, and so forth:

> Reason teaches that peace is good; it follows by the same reason that all necessary means to peace are good, and hence that modesty, fairness, good faith, kindness and mercy (which we have proved above are necessary to peace) are good manners [mores], or habits, i.e. virtues. (Hobbes 1998, 55)

While many Hobbesian men are instinctively proud, partial, and self-centered, through (Hobbes's) reason they understand the importance of not harming others with actions or words, of being sensitive to others' needs, of forgiving their shortcomings, of adapting to their idiosyncrasies, and of showing gratitude and generosity when the occasion requires it. In other words, sociability as recommended by the laws of nature, is the reasoned, conscious, constant, and rational endeavor to show respect to others and cultivate universal good will.

Tellingly, the laws of nature do not recommend pursuing friendship, the overarching virtue of Aristotelian ethics. This is because friendship – unlike the many virtues listed by Hobbes, such as modesty, gratitude, mercy, and so on – is, as argued in previous sections, a double-edged sword that can have a negative impact on peace.

Not only is friendship absent from the list of natural laws, but in Hobbes's argument it represents a potential threat to the natural law of equity or fairness.[25] In his writings, Hobbes often observes that a person's partiality and pride leads them to give preferential treatment to their friends, thereby generating enmity.[26] Referring to the recent civil war, Hobbes reminds his readers that the "greatest Complaint by them made against the unthriftiness of their Kings was for the enriching now and then a favourite" (Hobbes 2005, 15; see also Hobbes 1969, II.5.5 and 6, 142, 1998, 119). The unfairness of rulers is damaging to peace, according to Hobbes, and "sovereigns are obliged by natural law to impose the burdens of the commonwealth upon the citizens equally" (Hobbes 1998, XIII. 10. 147).[27] Indeed, for Hobbes, peace requires fairness and impartiality in the application of all laws (May 2013); for instance, we read in *De cive* III.15:

> Natural law commands: in awarding rights to others, you should be fair [aequalis] to both sides ... This law forbids us from giving more or less to one person as a *favour*. For if you do not keep to natural equality but give more or less to one than to another, you are *insulting* the person who is not favoured. (Hobbes 1998, 50)[28]

In a nutshell, sociability for Hobbes does not describe how people are but how they can and ought to be. Hobbes replaces the ancient norm of virtue-friendship with the natural law of universal sociability, which gives a key role to fairness and impartiality. The natural law of sociability is inoperative in the state of nature but must be captured by civic legislation.[29] Rulers must also obey the law of sociability: they should treat the commonwealth as their friend, and every private friend as anyone.

In Hobbes's construct, the ancient notion of *alter ipse amicus*, which is regarded as one of the cornerstones of classical theory on friendship (Pakaluk 1991), acquires a novel and unexpected meaning. We may recall that in his essay on friendship, Francis Bacon mentions the dictum that "a friend is another himself" and gives it a strikingly utilitarian slant (1985, 144). He takes the expression to mean that, in public life, our friends are our helpers: we may not be able to blow our own trumpets, but our friends can. And in so doing, they become "other selves," facilitating our success and augmenting our popularity. Hobbes cannot but have smiled in agreement with Bacon's understanding of *alter ipse amicus*. However, it can be argued that in his theory there is, in fact, someone who is "one soul in bodies twain" in a deeper sense, and he is the Leviathan.

By entering the political state, Hobbesian men create the trustworthy friend that they could not find in the state of nature. The Leviathan exhibits qualities that one associates with the ancient notion of friendship. First, the Hobbesian man can entrust the Leviathan with his life, and can be sure that the Leviathan will regard his well-being as its own. Second, the Hobbesian citizen has no private property vis-à-vis the Leviathan, thereby reminding us of the ancient saying that "friends ... have all things in common" (Plato 1987, 135; Lysis 207c).[30] Thirdly, Leviathan and citizen share the same truths and values, as ancient friends did (Lewis 1960, 80).

However, the Leviathan is an artificial friend, an ersatz one, and thus lacks some of the characteristics of the ancient friend. For in the bond between Hobbesian man and his Leviathan, there is not the traditional mutual openness between friends or the love. Instead of openness, both Leviathan and citizen have their private, impenetrable spheres: the *arcana imperii* of the Leviathan and the private conscience, the interior forum, of the citizen. Instead of the deep love that bound ancient friends together, the Hobbesian citizens fear the Leviathan; their fear, however, is mixed with love. Indeed, when the king is hated by the people as an enemy, rather than loved as a friend, rebellion follows, as the execution of Charles demonstrated.

Ultimately, the common concern for self-preservation and commodious living, the sharing of truths, values, and resources, make for a lasting and reliable relationship between Leviathan and citizens: the artificial friend is in principle indestructible.

7.5 Conclusion: A Constant Civil Amity

In search of the origin, nature and scope of "a Constant Civill Amity" within the Hobbesian state, this chapter has explored Hobbes's stance on friendship and sociability. First, this chapter has shown how friendship was pushed by Hobbes, from the central stage the concept occupied in the Aristotelian tradition, to the background of political discourse. Hobbes's understanding of friendship-as-power-and-contract enabled him to undermine the traditional function attributed to the concept, namely that of explaining how unrelated individuals may create bonds among one another and live in concord. Being a contract, Hobbesian friendship is unreliable in the state of nature and incapable of providing a stepping-stone toward the establishment of the political state. The Leviathan provides the conditions of mutual trust and positive disposition that make friendship possible, and not *vice versa*. Moreover, being a form of power, Hobbesian friendship may create exclusions, divisions, and enmity. This risk can only be mitigated if associations are appropriately policed and, if necessary, purged by the Leviathan. Again, it is authority, and not friendship, that ensures union, inclusion, and concord.

Second, the chapter explored Hobbes's views on sociability. On the one hand, throughout his works, Hobbes rejected the notion that sociability describes man's natural inclinations or dispositions. On the other, Hobbes presented sociability as a prescription that summarizes natural law and ensures peace. Although the decision how to interpret sociability and embody it in civil law ultimately rests with the Leviathan, which is accountable only to God, the chapter suggested that the existence, wellbeing, and longevity of the Leviathan depends on the people's decision of trusting it as an artificial friend.

So, neither natural friendship nor sociability is the origin of civil amity. Civil amity arises through the establishment of Authority. As to its character or nature, Hobbesian amity does not consist in reciprocity of love or care among citizens – even if these characteristics were to become more prominent, peace would not be necessarily strengthened as a result. The chapter disagreed with Gert's well-known view that: "[Hobbes's] point is simply that love of others is limited and cannot be used as a foundation upon which to build a state" (Gert 1972, 9). For Hobbes, people disrupt peace not because love is rare but because ignorance is spread universally; for Hobbes ignorance is not the prerogative of egoists; well-meaning people can be ignorant too. For Hobbes, only a full understanding of the foundations of political obligation can secure lasting peace. In "A Review, and Conclusion," addressing the concerns about the possibility of a constant civil amity among men, Hobbes points to "Education and Discipline" as the way forward and stresses that "There is therefore no such Inconsistence of Humane Nature, with Civill Duties, as some think" (Hobbes 2012, 1133; 1651, 390).

In a nutshell, constant civil amity is the result of "Education and Discipline," a shared understanding of the function of authority (rulers may be ignorant too, according to Hobbes) and a steadfast endeavor to support the Leviathan in the accomplishment of that function.

For his part, Hobbes offers his work to the authorities for the education of all:

> I think [this whole Discourse] may be profitably printed, and more profitably taught in the Universities, in case they also think so, to whom the judgement of the same belongeth. (Hobbes 2012, 1140; 1651, 395)

Notes

1 I wish to thank very much Marcus Adams for very helpful feedback on an earlier draft. All remaining mistakes are my own.

2 For details about the literature Hobbes is referring to, see Skinner (1972).

3 Among the exceptions, Stanlick (2002) and Smith (2008).

4 The second and third steps draw on ideas I have discussed in Slomp (2019a, 2019b).

5 Strauss notes that "[A]mong the Hobbes papers at Chatsworth there is a free digest from the *Nicomachean Ethics*" (1963, 42).

6 Even though Hobbes "may not have been the author" of the digest of the *Art of Rhetoric* in the Molesworth edition of his English works, scholars are certain that he provided the Latin basis for that version "truncating, reshaping and supplementing Aristotle's text" (Skinner 2002, 53).

7 Hobbes argues that we participate in the dishonor of our friends as much as in their honor (Hobbes 1969, I.9.13, 42). Thus, if we support and help friends who fall into disgrace, the

result will be public shame also for us. So, we help friends who are dishonored or outlawed at our own peril (Hobbes 2005, 104). It follows that wealth is a more reliable source of power.

8 In chapter 10 of *Leviathan* Hobbes describes this form of friendship between unequals, explaining that, in return for the gifts and favors of the superior, the subordinate offers honor, respect, and recognition. Thus, Hobbes suggests, both parties gain from the relationship: the more powerful man benefits insofar as he reinforces his dominance over other party; his less powerful friend receives the assistance he needs to attain his goals.

9 Exchange of favors among equal friends is exemplified by Hobbes's correspondent Du Verdus thus: "What is human life if not a succession of favours which one does for one's friends and from time to time not without inconvenience to oneself" (Malcolm 1994, vol II, 358).

10 "[N]othing in Hobbes's theory requires that men not have friends for whom they are willing to make some sacrifice" (Gert 1972, 8). Several distinguished interpreters have agreed with this view (among them, Lloyd 2009; Rawls 2007; Sorell 1986).

11 "When he [Hobbes] was at Florence he contracted a friendship with the famous Galileo Galilei, whom he extremely venerated and magnified; and not only as he was a prodigious wit, but for his sweetness of nature and manners" (Aubrey 1982, 161).

12 The correspondence shows that Hobbes was fond of his friends (see Malcolm 1994, for example, letters 62, 56); his friends often acknowledge Hobbes's "trust, esteem and affection" (letter 75); Hobbes exchanged gifts and favors with his friends (see letters 69, 72, 73).

13 "In *De corpore* X.I Hobbes indicates that power/act are different names for cause and effect. So, since motion is the only cause, and thus all causes are motion, it must follow that all powers are motions" (Marcus Adams, private correspondence, August 2020).

14 Aristotle emphasized that a friend is someone who loves us back: "So a man becomes a friend when he is loved and returns that love, and this is recognized by the two men in question" (Aristotle 1984, 1958; EE. VII.2.15–16).

15 For a comparison of the three passages on bees and ants see Baumgold (2017, 200–1).

16 In *Elements of Law* II. 9. 6, Hobbes warns about the "disturbance of the common peace" that can occur when people take upon themselves to punish magistrates "corrupted by gifts, or intercession of friends" (Hobbes 1969, 182).

17 In chapter 22 of *Leviathan* Hobbes uses the term "Systeme" to refer to institutions as diverse as colonies, churches, and universities. Examples of systems are also casual encounters such as "conflux of People to markets, or shews" either driven by design or proceeding only from a similitude of wills and inclinations (Hobbes 2012 348; 1651, 115). Hobbes emphasizes that there is "an unspeakable diversitie" of systems in a political association: in fact "the variety of Bodies Politique, is almost infinite" (Hobbes 2012, 358; 1651, 117–18). Although Hobbes does not use the word "friendship" in these cases, many systems deploy the characteristics of Hobbes's definition of friendship as an empowering contractual relationship.

18 "Friendship (as the ancients saw) can be a school of virtue; but also (as they did not see) a school of vice. It is ambivalent" (Lewis 1960, 97).

19 The topic of systems, which earns a dedicated chapter in *Leviathan*, receives only brief mentions in *Elements of Law* (for the discussion of subordinate unions and corporations created "for counsel, trade and the like" see Hobbes 1969, 104); also in *De cive* Hobbes refers only briefly to the case when "many citizens, by the permission of their commonwealth, unite as one person, for the purpose of transacting certain business" (Hobbes 1998, 73). A possible and even probable explanation for this development is that while in *Elements of Law* and *De cive* Hobbes's main concern was to discuss the origin and nature of law and government, in *Leviathan* he extends the scope of his investigation: he tries to establish what binds people together, what can produce concord and agreement, and explores governance. It is with respect to this last element that the notion of a "system" is particularly useful to Hobbes's project.

20 The whole passage is thus: "Non socios igitur, sed ab illis honore vel commodo affici natura quaerimus; haec primario, illos secundario appetimus. Quo autem consilio homines congregantur, ex iis cognoscitur quae faciunt congregati. Si coeant enim commercij causa, unusquisque non socium, sed rem suam colit; si officij causa, nascitur forensis quaedam amicitia, plus habens mutui metus quam amoris; unde factio aliquando nascitur, sed benevolentia nunquam" (Hobbes 1983, 90).

21 Montaigne explains that he became friend with Estienne de la Boetie not because the latter was virtuous or truthful or excellent but "Because it was he, because it was I" (Montaigne 1991, 192); according to Schall (1996), this statement captures the spirit of the new individualistic model of friendship.

22 As Gert puts it, "unlike Aristotle ... [Hobbes] not only does not put forward the life of the philosopher as the best life, he does not put forward any view of the best life" (Gert 2010, 65).

23 "[Moral philosophers] have not observed that the goodness of actions lies in their tendency to peace, their evil in their tendency to discord" (Hobbes 1998, 56).

24 "I am not denying that we seek each other's company at the prompting of nature ... [but] man is made fit for Society not by nature, but by training" (Hobbes 1998, I. 2. 24–5).

25 The Hobbesian laws of nature address multiple audiences: natural men, governments, citizens, states (Slomp 2015); to every agent they recommend the pursuit of peace, which in turn seems to entail mainly adaptability for the common people, and fairness for governments.

26 According to Hobbes, an "inconvenience of monarchy is this: that the monarch, besides the riches necessary for defence of the commonwealth, may take so much more from the subjects, as may enrich his children, kindred and favourites, to what degree he pleaseth" (Hobbes 1969, II. 5, 5, 142). Even so, according to Hobbes, a monarchy is preferable to an aristocracy, and *a fortiori* preferable to a democracy, because there is a limit to the number of friends and favorites that a single man can have, while the number of friends of an assembly of men can be significantly large.

27 In *Elements of Law* I.16.12: "It is also a law of nature, *That men allow commerce and traffic indifferently to one another*" (Hobbes 1969, 87).

28 Divine law reinforces natural law and recommends that: "[man] should esteem his neighbour worthy all rights and privileges that he himself enjoyeth; and attribute unto him, whatsoever he looketh should be attributed unto himself; which is no more but that he should be humble, meek, and contented with equality" (Hobbes 1969, I.18. 6. 97).

29 The natural laws are supposed to inspire the Leviathan's civil laws: "the Civill Laws; in which also are contained all the Laws of Nature, that is, all the Laws of God" (Hobbes 2012, 952; 1651, 330).

30 *Amicorum communia omnia* remained the first proverb in the editions of Erasmus Adages from 1508 onwards (Erasmus 2001, 28).

References

Aristotle. 1984. *The Complete Works of Aristotle*. The Revised Oxford Translation, edited by Jonathan Barnes, vol. II. Princeton, NJ: Princeton University Press.

Aubrey, John. 1982. *Brief Lives*, edited by Richard Barber. Woodbridge: The Boydell Press.

Bacon, Francis. 1985. *The Essays*. Harmondsworth: Penguin Books.

Baumgold, Deborah. 2017. *Three-Text Edition of Thomas Hobbes's Political Theory*. Cambridge: Cambridge University Press.

Bryson, Anna 1998. *From Courtesy to Civility: Changing Codes of Conduct in Early Modern England.* Oxford: Clarendon Press.

Cicero. 1991. "De Amicitia." In *Other Selves. Philosophers on Friendship*, edited by Michael Pakaluk, 77–116. Indianapolis and Cambridge: Hackett Publishing Company.

Erasmus. 2001. *The Adages*, edited by William Barker. Toronto, ON: University of Toronto Press.

Gert, Bernard. 1972. *"Introduction" to Man and Citizen. Thomas Hobbes's De homine and De cive Also Known as Philosophical Rudiments Concerning Governments and Society*, 2–32. New York: Anchor Books.

Gert, Bernard. 2010. *Hobbes: Prince of Peace*. Cambridge: Polity.

Hobbes, Thomas. 1839–1845. *The English works of Thomas Hobbes*, 11 vols., edited by Sir William Molesworth. London: John Bohn. Cited as EW.

Hobbes, Thomas. 1969. *The Elements of Law Natural and Politic*, edited by Ferdinand Tönnies. London: Frank Cass.

Hobbes, Thomas. 1972. *Man and Citizen. Thomas Hobbes's De homine and De cive Also Known as Philosophical Rudiments Concerning Governments and Society*, edited by Bernard Gert. New York: Anchor Books.

Hobbes, Thomas. 1976. *Thomas White's De Mundo Examined*, translated by Harold W. Jones. London: Bradford University Press.

Hobbes, Thomas. 1983. *De cive: The Latin Version, Entitled in the First Edition Elementorum Philosophiae Sectio Tertia De Cive and in Later Editions Elementa Philosophica De Cive a Critical Edition by Howard Warrender*. Oxford: Clarendon Press.

Hobbes, Thomas. 1998. *On the Citizen*, edited by Richard Tuck and Michael Silverthorne. Cambridge: Cambridge University Press.

Hobbes, Thomas. 2005. *Writings on Common Law and Hereditary Right*, edited by Alan Cromartie and Quentin Skinner. Oxford: Clarendon Press.

Hobbes, Thomas. 2012. *Leviathan*, 3 vols. edited by Noel Malcolm. Oxford: Clarendon Press.

Hutter, Horst. 1978. *Politics as Friendship*. Waterloo, ON: Wilfrid Laurier University Press.

King, Preston. 2000. *"Introduction" to the Challenge to Friendship in Modernity*, edited by Preston King and Heather Devere, 1–14. London: Frank Cass.

Konstan, David. 1997. *Friendship in the Classical World.* Cambridge: Cambridge University Press.

Lewis, C.S. 1960. *The Four Loves*. London: Harper Collins.

Lloyd, S.A. 2009. *Morality in the Philosophy of Thomas Hobbes. Cases in the Law of Nature.* Cambridge: Cambridge University Press.

Lochman, Daniel T., Maritere Lopez, and Lorna Hutson, eds. 2011. *Discourses and Representations of Friendship in Early Modern Europe, 1500–1700*. Farnham: Ashgate.

Malcolm, Noel, ed. 1994. *The Correspondence of Thomas Hobbes*. Oxford: Clarendon Press.

May, Larry. 2013. *Limiting Leviathan: Hobbes on Law and International Affairs*. Oxford: Oxford University Press.

Montaigne, Michel de. 1991. "Of Friendship." In *Other Selves. Philosophers on Friendship*, edited by Michael Pakaluk, 185–99. Indianapolis and Cambridge: Hackett Publishing Company.

Mulgan, Richard. 2000. "The Role of Friendship in Aristotle's Political Theory." In *The Challenge to Friendship in Modernity*, edited by Preston King and Heather Devere, 15–32. London: Frank Cass.

Pagden, Anthony, ed. 1987. *The Languages of Political Theory in Early Modern Europe*. Cambridge: Cambridge University Press.

Pakaluk, Michael. 1991. *Other Selves: Philosophers on Friendship*. Indianapolis, IN: Hackett Publishing.

Pangle, Lorraine S. 2003. *Aristotle and the Philosophy of Friendship*. New York and Cambridge: Cambridge University Press.

Plato. 1987. "Lysis." In *Early Socratic Dialogues*, edited by Trevor Saunders, 119–61. London: Penguin Books.

Price, Anthony W. 1989. *Love and Friendship in Plato and Aristotle*. Oxford: Clarendon Press.

Rawls, John. 2007. *Lectures on the History of Political Philosophy*, edited by Samuel Freeman. Cambridge, MA and London: Harvard University Press.

Rutherford, Donald. 2003. "In Pursuit of Happiness: Hobbes's New Science of Ethics." *Philosophical Topics* 31 (1/2): 369–93.

Schall, James V. 1996. "Friendship and Political Philosophy." *The Review of Metaphysics* 50: 121–41.

Schollmeier, Paul. 1994. *Other Selves*. New York: State University of New York Press.

Skinner, Quentin. 1972. *"Conquest and Consent: Thomas Hobbes and the Engagement Controversy" in the Interregnum: The Quest for Settlement 1646–1660*, edited by Gerald E. Aylmer. London: Macmillan.

Skinner, Quentin. 2002. *Visions of Politics, Volume III: "Hobbes and Civil Science"*. Cambridge: Cambridge University Press.

Slomp, Gabriella. 2015. "Limiting Leviathan: An Advice Book for Rulers?" *Social Theory and Practice* 41 (1): 149–63.

Slomp, Gabriella. 2019a. "On Benevolence and Love of Others." In *Interpreting Hobbes's Political Philosophy*, edited by S.A. Lloyd, 106–21. Cambridge: Cambridge University Press.

Slomp, Gabriella. 2019b. "As Thick as Thieves: Exploring Thomas Hobbes' Critique of Ancient Friendship and Its Contemporary Relevance." *Political Studies* 67 (I): 191–206.

Smith, Travis. 2008. "Hobbes on Getting by with Little Help From." In *Friendship and Politics: Essays in Political Thought*, edited by John Heyking and Richard Avramenko, 221–47. Notre Dame, IN: University of Notre Dame Press.

Sorell, Tom. 1986. *Hobbes*. London: Routledge & Kegan Paul.

Stanlick, Nancy. 2002. "Hobbesian Friendship: Valuing Others for Oneself." *Journal of Social Philosophy* 33 (3): 345–59.

Stephen, Leslie. 1904. *Hobbes*. London: Macmillan.

Strauss, Leo. 1963. *The Political Philosophy of Hobbes: Its Basis and Its Genesis*, translated by Elsa M. Sinclair. Chicago: University of Chicago Press.

Thomas, Keith. 2018. *In Pursuit of Civility: Manners and Civilization in Early Modern England*. New Haven, CT and London: Yale University Press.

8

Hobbes on Power and Gender Relations

SANDRA LEONIE FIELD

In this chapter, I articulate two Hobbesian models of interpersonal power relations that can be used to understand gender relations: what I will call the dominion model and the deference model. The dominion model discerns vertical subjection to another's will, whereas by contrast the deference model places individuals in complex and shifting webs of favor and disfavor.

Hobbes himself analyses the relation between men and women through the dominion model. Indeed, more broadly this is the most prominent model of interpersonal power relations throughout his texts. It is this model that is also reflected in the very rich existing feminist literature on Hobbes. However, the deference model, emerging only later in Hobbes's oeuvre, offers a superior general rubric for understanding interpersonal power relations. In particular, in light of its ability to grasp informal and diffuse relations of power, I argue that it offers useful insights for thinking about gender relations in our post-coverture era.

I will proceed as follows. First, I lay out Hobbes's model of interpersonal power relations as dominion, including his application of the model to the case of gender relations. Second, I indicate some shortcomings of the dominion model for grasping contemporary social life. Third, I establish Hobbes's alternative model of power as deference. Finally, I apply the alternative model to gender relations.

8.1 Dominion and Gender Relations

Power may be a central term in Hobbes's political theory, but the bulk of the scholarship has not considered his theory of interpersonal power, instead limiting its interest to his account of state power. The major exception to this rule is feminist studies of Hobbes. When Pateman seeks to understand power relations between men and women in her seminal feminist text *The Sexual Contract* (1991 [1988]), she defends an explicitly

A Companion to Hobbes, First Edition. Edited by Marcus P. Adams.

Hobbesian analysis, centered on his notion of dominion, or – in Pateman's preferred language – the contract of domination. In the present section, I set out Hobbes's conception of interpersonal power relations as dominion, and explain how it applies to gender relations.

The centerpiece of Hobbes's method is his "state of nature" thought experiment. Hobbes imagines the state of nature as a domain of wary and isolated human beings without any political power ruling them (Hobbes 1983a, 41–50; 2012, 188–96; 1651, 60–3). While the thought experiment is most famous for its bleak picture of natural human isolation and for its conclusions regarding state power, the thought experiment also lays out Hobbes's basic model of interpersonal power relations. In broad preliminary terms, when I speak of an interpersonal power relation, I am indicating a relation in which one individual is subject to the will of another; if the individual is subject only to their own will, then there is no power relation.

In Hobbes's state of nature, each individual is endowed with their own capacity-power – their *potentia*[1] – including such components as their physical strength and their wit. Between such individuals, there are precisely three possible configurations of interpersonal relations: solitude/dissociation (*solitudo*), association (*consensio* or *societas*), and dominion (*dominium*; Hobbes 1983b, 91–2, 137, 171). Of these, only the last is a power relation. Which of the three configurations manifests in a given case will depend on a comparison of the various individual capacity-powers. In Hobbes's initial discussion, he proposes that there are not generally great differences of capacity-power between humans (Hobbes 1983a, 45; 2012, 188–90; 1651, 60–1). Presuming individual A and B's respective capacity-powers are more or less equal, the two parties face two options. Either they could "dissociate" (stay separate), as they each pursue their particular ends on their own. Or the two parties could enter into a horizontal relationship of "association," laterally agreeing to work together for specific shared ends (Hobbes 1983a, 50, 86–8; 2012, 256–8; 1651, 86–7). Neither of these options amounts to a power relation. In the dissociation case, to be sure, the parties may find themselves in competition as they pursue their own ends, and whichever individual's capacity-power is even a little inferior will likely find less success in achieving those ends (EW IV.38). But losing out in a competition is not the same as having one's will subordinated to another. In the dissociation case, just as much as in the association case, each individual remains their own master.

Despite his initial proposal that humans are more or less equal in individual capacity-power, Hobbes goes on to consider the case where they are not. If it does happen that individual A's capacity-power is so much inferior to individual B's that A's life is in B's hands, Hobbes says that A ought to trade, or covenant,[2] their submission to B in return for B sparing their life (EW IV.85; 1983a, 50). In this way, for instance, a sick person in the state of nature may find themself subjected to a strong and healthy person. The covenant of submission establishes what Hobbes calls dominion or lordship. Dominion's structure is vertical: the submitting individual (A) becomes subject to the will of the lord or master (B), no longer their own will. As such, it is a relation of power between the parties. The relation of dominion rests on identifying what covenant would be rationally appropriate or can rationally be inferred, rather than on the actual existence of such a covenant. Hobbes does presume that there must be a deliberate desire on the side of the lord or master to assert dominion (Hobbes 1983a, 90). But there need not be any explicit consent from the submitting individual: instead, "every man is supposed to promise obedience, to him, in whose power it is to save, or destroy him" (Hobbes 2012, 310; 1651, 103).[3]

Hobbes scales this taxonomy of relations up to the entire population in order to think about the civil state. The civil state or commonwealth comes about either "by institution" – where equals, fearful of one another and finding association insufficiently durable, mutually covenant to establish an absolute sovereign over them (EW IV.199; Hobbes 1983a, 86–9; 2012, 256–62; 1651, 86–8) – or "by acquisition" – where the weak fear a conqueror and submit to the conqueror as their absolute sovereign (EW IV.149; Hobbes 1983a, 66, 117; 2012, 256, 306, 314; 1651, 86, 101, 104). Nonetheless, the states established by these alternative pathways share a final political structure: Hobbes conceives the absolute sovereignty of any commonwealth as dominion writ large. The commonwealth's subjects submit to the sovereign's will in just the same way that a subordinate within an interpersonal relation of dominion submits to their lord or master's will.

For Hobbes, the relation between a commonwealth's sovereign and its subjects is necessarily one of dominion, but the quality of the interpersonal relations between subjects of the commonwealth is not so constrained. At the sovereign's pleasure and subject to the sovereign's law, associations may be permitted within state (Hobbes 2012, 370; 1651, 121). Similarly, the sovereign can choose, as an exercise of its own power, to tolerate or establish little dominions. Although subjects can only obey one master, there is no conflict between sovereign A and lord B both claiming the submission of subject C, because lord B only remains lord at sovereign A's pleasure (Hobbes 1983a, 119; 2012, 310, 314, 350; 1651, 103–4, 115–16).

I have presented the machinery of interpersonal relationships in the abstract, but in Hobbes's own presentation, it finds its sharpest illustration in the conjugal (male/female) and parental (parent/child) relationships comprising the family in the state of nature. Hobbes's analysis is radical insofar as he understands familial relations according to the general model of interpersonal relations just outlined, without any reference to *sui generis* principles.[4]

On Hobbes's account, there is a power relation of dominion of parent over child, simply in virtue of the stark difference of strength and wit between them, such that the child is dependent on the parent to preserve their life. Just as any denizen of the state of nature comes under the dominion of a greater power in return for sparing their life, the child comes under the dominion of the parent. But a subject can only obey one master. So which parent? If the father held dominion over the mother, then the child would also fall under the father's dominion, because of the transitivity of dominion. But in state of nature, "the inequality of their naturall forces is not so great, that the *man* could get the Dominion over the *woman* without warre" (Hobbes 1983a, 122; see also Hobbes 2012, 308; 1651, 102). With no dominion between them, men and women may either come together in horizontal voluntary association for shared ends, or just as likely they may only have transient contact, remaining isolated and wary of one another. The answer to who holds dominion over the child cannot be found from the relation between the parents but instead must be deduced from the different respective situations of the parents with regard to the child. Hobbes observes it is the mother who nurses the infant and cares for the child, even though she could abandon them. The obedience and allegiance the child owes for the preserving of their life is owed to their mother (EW IV.154–6; Hobbes 1983a, 121–3; 2012, 308–10, 102–3). The state of nature is thus a matriarchy of little maternal dominions over children.

Against this backdrop, the reader might be surprised to find the Hobbesian civil state organized around the traditional patriarchal family. Hobbes envisages a sovereign ruling over a polity of male political subjects, each of whom is simultaneously the lord over his own household, including the wife, children, and servants within it (EW IV.157; Hobbes 1983a, 124; 2012, 402, 528; 1651, 133, 178). Hobbes himself does not make explicit how specifically the patriarchal society emerges from the matriarchal state of nature, and this has sparked considerable discussion in the literature. Two main alternative reconstructions have been proposed. Pateman argues that matriarchy is displaced by patriarchy already prior to the establishment of the civil state. Still in the state of nature, Hobbes mentions the existence of male-headed family units, which he analyzes as little commonwealths (Hobbes 1983a, 123, 126; 2012, 254–5, 368; 1651, 85, 121). Pateman speculates that such family units come about through women's weakness due to pregnancy, bearing, and feeding infants, rendering otherwise robust women vulnerable to male domination.[5] The social contract to establish the commonwealth occurs between male heads of households, subjecting the little family dominions to an overarching sovereign without interrupting their internal structure (Pateman 1991, 45–50; see also Hobbes 1983a, 124; 2012, 308; 1651, 102–3; Schochet 2012). Others commentators disagree, finding the origin of patriarchy after the establishment of the civil state. On this alternative view, the social contract is truly universal, simultaneously conveying all adults – male and female – out of the state of nature as equals. But the sovereign then uses its absolute prerogative to establish male domestic dominion over the women of the commonwealth, whether in recognition of characteristic differences of capacity-power between the sexes (Lloyd 2012; 2020), or whether as a pure decision to empower men over women in spite of the absence of any deep underlying differences (Hirschmann 2012; Slomp 1994).

For the purposes of this chapter's argument, nothing hangs on which reconstruction is favored. The key point is that Hobbesian feminists, despite their other disagreements, carry over Hobbes's framework for analyzing interpersonal power relations. Whether commentators celebrate women's equal status in the state of nature or regret their subordination in the commonwealth, they draw on a Hobbesian division between (on the one hand) vertical power relations of dominion/domination and (on the other hand) equality in lateral mutual associations.[6]

8.2 Sexual Stratification Without Domination

In this section, I argue that Hobbes's model of power relations as dominion is analytically impoverished. While it is useful for understanding coverture and its long shadow over law and society, it fails to grapple with some prominent elements of contemporary sexual hierarchy.

Let me start by outlining why Pateman thinks Hobbes's model of power relations as dominion is a good model – indeed, the model – of contemporary patriarchy. *The Sexual Contract* is driven by a suspicion of an orthodoxy concerning political progress. According to this orthodoxy, politics was once was concerned with naturalized relationships and status, emblematically patriarchal politics, where the political authority of kings was both founded on and modelled on the natural authority of father over son. According to this orthodoxy, through the early modern period the politics of status and hierarchy gave way to a politics of freedom and equality, whereby authority can only be founded on contract and consent. Pateman's book challenges the simple association between contract and freedom. For there is such a thing as a contract of domination, canonically the slave contract. And Pateman's central claim is that "contract is the means through which modern patriarchy is constituted" (Pateman 1991, 2). The much-celebrated social contract between equal male citizens is quietly underpinned by the sexual contract, a contract of domination between men and women (Pateman 1991, 1–12). Hobbes's work takes a central place in Pateman's argument. First, Hobbes's theory explicitly recognizes what Pateman calls contracts of domination (Hobbes's dominion). Second, Hobbes's unsentimental willingness to apply his analysis of contract and domination to familial relations unmasks a stark power relation otherwise often concealed by ideas of natural roles or bonds of love (Pateman 1991, 39–50).

Consider now how Pateman's Hobbesian model of sexual domination fares in grasping real-world arrangements of sexual difference. To defend its applicability, Pateman marshals considerable evidence from "Western" (primarily US and UK) legal codes and social histories. On her account, the core institution of sexual domination has been the marriage contract under the legal doctrine of coverture. By this doctrine, the husband's legal identity "covers" for that of the wife. But Pateman argues that the marriage contract under coverture brings about the wife's civil death, like a slave (Pateman 1991, 119).[7] Under coverture, although women "consented" through marriage to their place in the male-headed household, women had no real option not to marry, and the standard terms to which they had to consent gave them over to their husbands as slaves to masters. She points to a long history of wife-selling in England as one of the starkest illustrations of the slave-like status of wives (Pateman 1991, 121). But the slave-like status of wives found more quotidian expression in the unlimited right of husbands to their wives' unremunerated labor and husbands' unlimited sexual access to their wives' bodies. For labor, this was manifested in laws excluding women from employment on marrying, or requiring the husband's permission for a woman to work outside the home, and assigning damages if a woman is prevented from working at home (Pateman 1991, 126–40). For sexual access, entering into marriage was taken to constitute permanent consent to sexual contact, making rape within marriage a legal impossibility (the so-called marital rape immunity; Klarfeld 2011; Pateman 1991, 7, 123–4).

Even as the legal doctrine of coverture has been incrementally dismantled, Pateman sees its long shadow well into her (1980s) present (Pateman 1991, 222–7), and that shadow still lingers today. In law: marital rape has only been criminalized in all US states since 1993, and in some states it is only a criminal offense if there is aggravated force or violence (Klarfeld 2011, 1819, 1834). In broader social structure: the domestic division of labor has persisted,[8] and has been laid bare particularly sharply during the current (2020) COVID-19 pandemic insofar as the normal public helps to domestic functioning (notably, schools and daycares) are not available.

Nonetheless, I propose that Pateman's model of domination cannot usefully serve as a general rubric for understanding power relations between men and women. I now consider two current issues in the feminist literature and in public debate. The first issue is sexual harassment outside the home. The #metoo social media movement has brought to light the previously hidden prevalence of sexual harassment and assault, mostly of women, by people in gatekeeping positions, mostly men (MacKinnon 2019). *The Sexual Contract* offers a brief discussion of sexual harassment. Workplace sexual harassment is analyzed as "help[ing] maintain men's patriarchal right in the public world" (Pateman 1991, 142). Men harass women to punish them for being "trespassers" into the male public world, rather than staying in their proper domestic servitude where they belong (Pateman 1991, 141).

The second issue is the reckless and harmful treatment of women's medical conditions. A key current example is the vaginal mesh tape scandal. In recent decades, mesh tape came to be aggressively promoted as a treatment for some common complications of childbirth, but the normal best practices establishing use and tracking safety of medical devices were not followed. While successful for many recipients, the mesh tape caused excruciating pain and permanent incapacitation for a significant proportion of cases. A recent UK inquiry determined that the widespread harm was a systematic result of the medical and scientific community downplaying and ignoring the women's testimony and complaints (Cumberlege 2020, 17–18, 153). *The Sexual Contract* emphasizes the submersion of the wife into the husband's civil personality. As a corollary, men's voices are authoritative, and women's voices need to find male mediation to be acknowledged. This feature of gender relations is reflected in the once-common practice of addressing a woman by her husband's name (Mrs. John Doe), and in the extreme hostility directed toward wives of famous intellectuals who do not simply cheer on their husbands but who have an independent intellectual life of their own (Pateman 1991, 160). From this point of view, it is no surprise that complaints regarding procedures performed only on women are poorly heard.

My suggestions for how Pateman's (1980s) framework would analyze these current cases necessarily remain speculative, but I have held to the core of her understanding of gender relations throughout her book: when there are power relations between men and women, they either approximate or attempt to reinstitute the sexual contract. The man is to be master over the woman, the woman is to be removed from the public domain and is to access it only through the man. This analysis reflects a Hobbesian understanding of the possible configurations of interpersonal relations: either voluntary horizontal association or deliberate vertical dominion.

The difficulty is that these two contemporary cases do not convincingly fit the terms of Hobbes's analysis. I will suggest that the hierarchy in these two cases is frequently much more informal, diffuse, and unintentional, neither approximating nor aspiring to approximate vertical domination. For sexual harassment, I grant there are surely cases where the perpetrator of the sexual harassment or assault either wishes to achieve total dominion over a woman, or to force her back into the domestic domain. But equally, surely there are cases where the perpetrator lacks aspiration to either of these things.

Some perpetrators may harass because it is pleasurable or funny to them, and because they face no serious repercussions or negative blowback for their behavior. They may harass to build rapport, prestige, or authority with onlooking coworkers. Putting aside perpetrator intent, the concrete outcome of the behavior also in many cases may neither approach nor approximate dominion. Some women may find themselves totally dominated, their will in full thrall of their harasser. But other times, the woman does not lose full control of her will, instead she strategically accommodates the various male wills around her in order to achieve her other goals. In particular, she may put up with sexual harassment from various men because she judges that the prospects of addressing it are poor, and because putting up with it might put her in better stead for the other priorities she wishes to pursue.

Now consider the reckless treatment of women's health and the failure to listen to complaints. In this day and age, in the jurisdictions that are Pateman's foci, most would vehemently oppose the idea that women lack the standing to speak on their own account. The issue to be explained is how these explicit egalitarian commitments coexist with differential modes of behavior, such as taking women's testimony less seriously, paying less attention, and extending less respect to women's ideas and needs. Even those combatting this differential respect for women's testimony can fall into habits of privileging men: Cumberlege herself gives early and disproportionate prominence to the testimony of the *husband* of one of the sufferers of pelvic mesh complications (Cumberlege 2020, 19). But the dominion model is implausible as an account of the motivation and outcome of these behaviors. As to motivation, the dominion model would understand the lesser credence accorded to women's testimony, by both men and women, as a manifestation of patriarchal crypto-desire to silence women and only allow husbands to speak on their wives' behalf. Is this really the best explanation of the behavior? As to outcome, it is not generally the case that women are required to mediate their voices through male spokespeople (although sometimes that does occur). The general phenomenon is that they are allowed to speak, but are just taken less seriously, which hardly amounts to the clean vertical subordination that is the core of the model of dominion.

Pateman's purpose in introducing the concept of a contract of domination is to awaken readers to "systematic social injustice" (Mills 2007, 93). But to take dominion/domination as the general rubric for understanding interpersonal power is to risk distorting our understanding of contemporary cases. If a Hobbesian feminist like Pateman is convinced that men and women are not cooperating as free and equal associates, then they need instead to locate a relation of dominion. That is, they need to argue that the man is making (or is attempting to make) the woman fully subject to his will, or is attempting to remove the woman from the public domain as an actor with an independent will. A skeptic might quite reasonably view this analysis or imputation of motives as exorbitant, and deny that domination occurs. Without the conceptual vocabulary to grasp any middle ground between association and dominion, our Hobbesian feminist and skeptic are locked in a polemical debate. What would be needed is some way to talk about power relations short of dominion. The core phenomenon for this kind of relation will be a partial asymmetrical influencing of wills, a partial shaping of behavior, that I will call deference.

8.3 The Alternative Model: Deference

A power relation is one in which one party finds their action mediated by the will of the other, rather than each simply doing what they what they want to do to the extent that they can. To this point, I have followed Hobbes's early work in presuming that being subject to another's will must amount to dominion/domination, or in other words, vertical total subjection to the will of a single master. But dominion is not Hobbes's only way of thinking about power relations. In this section, I reconstruct an alternative concept of what I call power as deference, whereby individuals routinely mediate their desires via others' wills, but without being totally subjected.[9] The relation of deference is a relatively durable asymmetrical relationship of wills that falls short of dominion, but which is irreducible to lateral associations for shared ends.[10]

The relationship of deference emerges in Hobbes's *Leviathan* chapter 10, in the course of Hobbes's discussion of honor. The key terms are (Hobbes 2012, 132–6; 1651, 41–2):

> In *Leviathan* 10.1, a person's capacity-power: their "present means, to obtain some future apparent Good."
> In *Leviathan* 10.16, a person's value: "his Price; that is to say, so much as would be given for the use of his Power."
> In *Leviathan* 10.17, honor/dishonor: "the manifestation of the Value we set on one another ... To Value a man at a a high rate, is to *Honour* him; at a low rate, is to *Dishonour* him."

Honor is thus the rubric under which we can group all action manifesting desire for the use of another's capacity-power. This desire turns out to be a central driver of human action. Indeed, Hobbes's understanding of honor in *Leviathan* 10.20 can account neatly for the functioning of interpersonal dominion.

> To obey, is to Honour; because no man obeyes them, whom they think have no power to help, or hurt them. And consequently to disobey, is to *Dishonour*. (Hobbes 2012, 136; 1651, 41)

The person submitting to a lord's dominion, which centrally involves obedience to the lord, does so to secure their life in the face of the lord's threats. The analysis in terms of honor gives a characterization of the motivation of the submitting party: their obedience is a manifestation of their hope to channel the lord's power in a useful rather than hostile way.

Is dominion's complete pledged submission the only way to try to get use of another's capacity-power? Hobbes spends some time exploring other behaviors that might contribute to shaping the actions of those around us. We have the very obvious strategy of directly requesting help:

> To pray to another, for ayde of any kind, is *to* HONOUR; because a sign we have an opinion he has power to help; and the more difficult the ayde is, the more is the Honour. (Hobbes 2012, 136; 1651, 41)

But Hobbes extends beyond obvious examples to the full gamut of interpersonal conduct: for him, a huge array of everyday behaviors has a valence either as honor or as dishonor (Hobbes 2012, 136–48; 1651, 42–7). It is honor:

> *Leviathan* 10.22: "To be sedulous in promoting anothers good"
> *Leviathan* 10.23: "To give way, or place to another, in any Commodity"
> *Leviathan* 10.24: "To shew any signe of love, or feare of another"
> *Leviathan* 10.26: "To speak to another with consideration, to appear before him with decency, and humility"
> *Leviathan* 10.27: "To believe, to trust, to rely on another"
> *Leviathan* 10.28: "To hearken to a mans counsell"
> *Leviathan* 10.30: "To agree with in opinion"
> *Leviathan* 10.32: "To honour those another honours."

How do all these examples count as honor, that is, as expressing a desire to make use of the capacity-power of the honoree? In Hobbes's discussion of these behaviors, a certain model of social life emerges. By this model, we constantly encounter others whose actions may assist or inhibit our own, to greater or lesser degree. But every little thing we do may influence to the propensity of those others to assist us and not inhibit us, depending on how our actions impinge upon their desires and preferences. For instance, being slovenly rather than decent might cause offense and irritation, and diminish the inclination of the offended party to help out (Hobbes 2012, 136; 1651, 43). As we negotiate the social field, we take care to draw the favor and/or avoid the hostility of those around us, in particular by taking care not needlessly to hinder their desires and preferences. I propose calling all these behaviors forms of "deference." For the common point between all honors is that they serve to placate and propitiate those identified as powerful, or in other words, they "defer" to the desires of the powerful. Social life is constituted as complex and constantly recalibrating webs of deference.

There are a number of striking features to this model of social relations as deference. First, an individual's behavior has a valence as honor or dishonor, and an impact on others, regardless of that individual's intentions (Hobbes 2012, 136–8; 1651, 42–3). Suppose A is oblivious to the subtleties of interpersonal power. A does not positively desire to garner B's assistance, nor does A fear offending B. A just does as they please, not taking care to ensure their actions respect B's needs and concerns (Hobbes 2012, 136; 1651, 42–3). A's obliviousness does not allow A to opt out of the web of deference. If in fact A is less powerful than B, then A's failure to render the expected honor to B is likely to be read as dishonor, and may incur B's irritation or retribution. If in fact A is more powerful than B, then A's conduct unwittingly incites B's deference. For A's potentially harmful indifference to B's interests gives B all the more reason to seek to placate and propitiate them.

The second feature is the tendency to inequality. An egalitarian social domain, in which all give and receive deference in more or less equal measure, is not impossible. But the Hobbesian analysis reveals a tendency away from such equality. We cannot agree with everyone's opinion, even if we try; we cannot be sedulous with everyone's good. Instead, we tend to distribute our energies according to the risk and benefit in question. In other words, we take special care with those who hold more power, leaving lesser energy available for care for those who appear less positioned to help or to harm. An insignificant person is likely to find no one deferring to them, instead facing dismissive and inconsiderate treatment from the rest of society. Worse, they may find that even their own deference to the powerful is hardly rewarded (Hobbes 2012, 136; 1651, 42), reflecting the limited help or harm they are capable of inflicting on the powerful. These inequality-generating dynamics can come in play even if the parties have no desire to increase inequality.

The third striking feature is the low salience of specific individual capacity-powers. Deference is given to the powerful, but who are they? In Hobbes's discussion of the state of nature, the key examples of capacity-power are wit and strength (EW IV.81–2; Hobbes 1983a, 45; 2012, 188; 1651, 60–1; see also EW IV.38–9). But in *Leviathan*'s core analysis of power and deference, these erstwhile key examples are displaced, and patterns of deference become potentially disconnected from any particular independently specifiable personal attribute or faculty (Field 2014). Capacity-power's definition as "means to future goods" is open: in principle, personal attributes or faculties could constitute capacity-power. But candidate capacity-powers that are not socially upheld are practically useless as means to future goods. For instance, by Hobbes's own account, science – knowledge of causality and of consequences – is the way to achieve the "Benefit of man-kind" (Hobbes 2012, 72–4; 1651, 21–2). Yet Hobbes insists that science is "small power," because most people do not recognize its benefits and so do not render assistance and service to its bearers (Hobbes 2012, 134; 1651, 42). Someone who has attained great knowledge still may find their everyday actions thwarted and impeded by the people around them. Because personal attributes count as powers primarily in virtue of the assistance or forbearance they generate, they recede from the center of Hobbes's analysis, leaving in their place remarkable looping formulations (Hobbes 2012, 132–4; 1651, 41):

> *Leviathan* 10.7: "what quality soever maketh a man beloved, or feared of many, or the reputation of such quality, is Power; because it is a means to have the assistance, and service of many"
> *Leviathan* 10.5: "Reputation of power, is Power; because it draweth with it the adhaerence of those that need protection"
> *Leviathan* 10.2: "the nature of Power, is [...] like to Fame, increasing as it proceeds."

Deference to power is action within the existing uneven social web, guided by the judgement of social support for or hostility to various courses of action. For instance, if I believe that someone has many supporters, I should take care not to draw their displeasure. In other words, deference is action guided by judgements about others' likely patterns of deference and non-deference; deference both recognizes and constitutes power. The patterns of deference congeal not primarily around individual capacities, but instead around networks of allegiance, shaped by frameworks of law and political status (Hobbes 2012, 136–40; 1651, 42–4).

I claim that deference represents a new form of social relations not recognized in the previous three-way taxonomy of dissociation, association, and dominion that structures Hobbes's discussion of the state of nature.[11] According to the model of lateral association, equal individuals decide to pursue a particular shared goal or end, but all the while, each remains master of their own will (Hobbes 1983a, 87). By contrast, in the relation of deference there need not be shared ends. The deferring individual (the honorer) advances their own goals only indirectly, by trying to bring the powerful to have a general disposition to help and not hinder their projects. To do this, the honorer often works directly for the powerful person's goals, being "sedulous in promoting [the powerful person's] good" and "giv[ing] way" to their priorities (Hobbes 2012, 136; 1651, 42). I propose that, unlike the parties in an association for shared ends, the deferring individual is not fully master of their own will. Granted, the deferring individual is working in the best way they can to advance own ends. But for Hobbes, everyone, whether slave or master, seeks to advance their own ends as best they can. The deferring individual is not fully their own master because the particular way that they advance their own ends is through deferring to the ends of another, in hope that this may yield some future recompense. As a result, the bond between the collaborators is stronger and more asymmetrical than association. In the case of association for shared ends, equal collaborators on a shared project can simply go their separate ways when they disagree (Hobbes 2012, 256; 1651, 86). By contrast, in a relationship of deference, a client may continue to cooperate on their patron's projects, despite skepticism regarding the project's goals or the patron's chosen means to achieve them, in order to keep the patronage relationship alive. In this sense, there is a hierarchical relation between wills, with the deferring individual partially submitting to the honoree's will. Consequently, I propose that the relationship of deference merits being classed as a relation of power.

At the same time, even though deference is a power relation involving a hierarchical positioning of wills, it does not in general amount to the vertical mastery/subjection of dominion. On the dominion model, the lord has the intent to rule over their subordinate, and the lord is the master of subordinate's will. Correspondingly, the subordinate submits fully to the lord's will, recognizing only a single master. By contrast, in the model of deference, the subordinate (the deferring individual, the honorer) is likely to be simultaneously honoring multiple actors. They undertake a partial and contextual bending of their conduct to various others' wills in order to gain the social support they need, and they are not entirely beholden to any particular honoree if the desired support can be achieved elsewhere. Furthermore, the power relation of deference does not rely on any intent of powerful honoree to control the honorer. A powerful person may act deliberately to influence the action of their subordinate, but equally they may remain oblivious to the efforts made by the honorers to attract their favor or avoid their malice. On the model of deference, there is a power relation without the powerful being masters of the subordinates.

The relation of deference is neither association nor dominion, but it should not be classed as a fourth variety for a social relationship to our previous taxonomy of three. Rather, I suggest that the relation of deference can be conceived as the fundamental form of social relationship, pervasive throughout human social life; association and dominion can be conceived as special cases of deference. For relations of deference can be more or less asymmetrical. The situation where the parties' reciprocal estimate of each other's power is symmetrical stands as one extreme possibility or limit case, corresponding to horizontal association on mutual ends. Vertical dominion stands as the other extreme, where the deferring individual's hope of help and the fear of harm focused entirely onto a single master. Thus, we have a continuum of power relations, running from the small reciprocal deferences that may occur every day even between friends, encompassing the unfortunate need to bow and scrape to those who hold the keys to money or public opinion, right through to near-vertical deference to a single overpowering master, which may better be termed dominion or domination.

What explains Hobbes's early insistence on dominion as the rubric of power relations, and the absence of a conception of power relations as degrees of deference? I speculate that many of the real-world phenomena commanding Hobbes's attention were *prima facie* plausibly interpreted through the rubric of a stark choice between vertical dominion and horizontal association. In the context of a breakdown of authority like the English civil war, a critical question of power is the juridical one, who has the right to make decisions and issue commands? Such a question naturally receives a binary answer: either a certain person has the right to command, or they do not. Indeed, for Hobbes, any ambiguity regarding the right to command is fatal to peace (Hobbes 1983a, chapter 6). The same binary approach is also natural at the more interpersonal level: in Hobbes's time, various individuals (women, children, servants) fell formally under the domestic authority of others. The roles and the relationships are well defined; the question is simply the justification for this arrangement. Thus, in some times and places, the relations between members of society may well take the form of dominion. But the idea of deference opens up the conceptual possibility that a social order can be pervaded by power relations even in the absence of dominion.

8.4 Deference and Gender Relations

Hobbes himself does not apply the model of deference to power relations between the sexes. Indeed, this is not particularly surprising. For first, the central phenomenon of sexual hierarchy in Hobbes's time – coverture – remained more or less adequately accommodated by the dominion model, whereas by contrast its deficiencies as a model for understanding the commonwealth were laid bare by the protracted turmoil of the English civil war (Field 2020, chapters 2–4). Second, it is not clear that Hobbes has any particular interest in gender relations himself, except insofar as their analysis can serve as a polemical tool against his theoretical opponents who model politics on the family (Schochet 2012; Wright 2002). In this final section, I will do what Hobbes did not, and apply the model of deference to the question of gender relations. The model of deference can accommodate coverture's relations of domination, but it also provides a theoretical frame for understanding a broader range of gendered power relations.

According to the model of deference, people defer to those who are positioned to help or harm them; dominion counts as the extreme case of total deference to a single overpowering master. Under the law of coverture, each woman's husband was uniquely[12] well positioned to advance or thwart her desires and needs, for she was under his sway with respect to her body (his free and exclusive sexual access) and her labor (both inside and outside the home). In consequence, the woman's deference was tightly focused on her husband, with the deference so vertical as to count as dominion. In the present day, the full law of coverture is no longer in place, although we live with some of its legal, political, and cultural remnants. Indeed, these remnants go a long way to constituting the difference between men and women's average respective capacity-powers. But I have suggested that contemporary interpersonal relations between men and women are not overall usefully conceived as dominion, by pointing out two contemporary cases that are too diffuse and thoughtless to fit dominion's requirements. I don't deny that there are still many cases of actual or attempted domination. Some of the more lurid cases of sexual assault and domestic abuse take the form of an assertion of male mastery over women; some people may willfully hark back to the old gender configuration of the male dominion and female subordination (Hill 2019; Manne 2017). But focusing on those cases can lead us to miss or mischaracterize more quotidian contemporary phenomena.

Let us see how the deference model neatly accounts for the #metoo phenomenon of pervasive sexual harassment. Recall my objection, that the dominion model implausibly imputes to all harassers the aspiration to dominate and control. On the deference model by contrast, harassment can be explained without this imputation. On this model, we can expect the powerful not to pay attention to the needs and desires of those judged less powerful; or even if they are aware of those needs and desires, they may be insufficiently motivated to rein in their own behaviors that negatively impinge upon others. Core behaviors of harassment – being obscene, neglecting a person's good (Hobbes 2012, 136; 1651, 42 [10.22–3]) – readily arise when that person is viewed as low in power. Thus, if #metoo harassers find pleasure or satisfaction in harassing, they may persist in their conduct because women do not have significant enough power and status to demand that they desist.

Recall my further objection, that the dominion model implausibly models women's compliance and silence in the face of harassment as evidence of deep subjection. But on the deference model, compliance can also be a more ambivalent phenomenon: alongside cases of deep subjection, there will be cases closer to appeasement or propitiation. On the deference model, one key motivator of behavior is seeking to shape the conduct of the powerful in one's favor, seeking to secure their support and avoid their hostility. This is done by taking care not to annoy powerful people, instead ingratiating oneself with them and accommodating their desires: don't annoy your boss, smile for the guy in the street, don't complain about handsiness. In this way, women may weigh up their priorities and end up reluctantly accommodating the sexual advances of men who are in a position to affect their fate.

Finally, there was one further feature of the #metoo cases left poorly explained by the dominion model. In many cases, bystanders do not call out the poor behavior of harassers. Instead, they often circle the wagons around the perpetrator. Even other women, whom one might have thought would feel common cause and sympathy with the victims of harassment, may fail to display any meaningful solidarity. This phenomenon is readily explained by the deference model: "To honour [a powerful individual's] Enemies, is to Dishonour him" (Hobbes 2012, 138; 1651, 43 [10.32]). Third parties to a problematic incident don't want to draw the ire of the powerful by criticizing or displeasing them in any way. They may even take extra pains to affirm and support their patron, recognizing the dangers of standing up to bullies, and the rewards for turning a blind eye.

Let us now turn to the case of reckless treatment of women's medical issues. Recall Cumberlege's diagnosis: the recklessness is a consequence of women's testimonies not being taken seriously. I objected to viewing this phenomenon through the dominion model, because it implausibly accounts for self-proclaimed egalitarians not taking women's ideas seriously as a matter of a subterranean crypto-desire to silence women or to deny women's right to speak on their own behalf. A superior approach for theorizing the phenomenon is provided by Fricker's concept of "testimonial injustice." In this approach, women's ideas are not taken less seriously than men's because of the listeners' desire to silence women, but rather because listeners (both men and women) have internalized stereotypes that assess women's testimony as less credible than that of men (Fricker 2007, 9–30). But Fricker's account raises questions of its own. She notes that in fact less-powerful groups are stereotyped as less authoritative, but why is this so? and where do these stereotypes come from? The Hobbesian model of deference can offer an answer. In this model, people fail to take less-powerful individuals seriously precisely *because* they are less powerful.

For Hobbes, various positive listening practices – believing, trusting, listening, paying attention, agreeing, respecting judgement – all count as honor, and their contraries count as dishonor (Hobbes 2012, 136; 1651, 43). But there are two ways in which this might be the case. First and more obviously, these honors might manifest an opinion of the specific powers of wisdom, wit, or good judgement of the person honored; in Fricker's testimonial injustice, honor is withheld because the listener (mistakenly) has a low opinion of the speaker's possession of these specific powers. For Hobbes, however, there is also a second way. As I have shown, people may be powerful in terms of having considerable social support, even though they lack specific capacity-powers such as wisdom. According to the deference model, such powerful persons are likely to be honored by others who seek to draw their assistance and avoid their hostility. But to honor someone, you must do those things "which he takes for signes of Honour" (Hobbes 2012, 138; 1651, 43 [10.29]) – as for instance the positive listening practices outlined above. We may listen and pay attention to the powerful even if we do not judge them to be wise, because otherwise we risk incurring their wrath or missing out on their favors. An employee will not generally yawn or roll their eyes to their boss's face. Conversely, there is no sanction for ignoring unimportant or uninfluential people. The social consequence is that there are mechanisms generating differential attention and credence in ways that map social power rather than any strong opinion of the good judgement or trustworthiness of the persons so honored. This process may well give rise to stereotypes: it would be easy to misunderstand a pervasive social practice dishonoring certain people's wisdom and trustworthiness by failing to listen respectfully to them as constituting good evidence of an actual underlying lack of wisdom and trustworthiness in those people. But the salient point here is that one can genuinely reject a stereotype of a group's epistemic unreliability yet still behave in negative differential ways toward that group. It was easier for doctors and scientists to downplay women's reports of intense pain as their mesh implants cut through their viscera, than to entertain seriously challenging the established understanding of the medical profession and the enthusiastic representations of the medical device manufacturers, just as it was useful for Cumberlege to foreground a husband's testimony in order to underscore the trustworthiness of her claims to her readership.

Conclusion

The Hobbesian model of dominion provided a striking analytical frame for grasping – and in the hands of later feminists, critiquing – the power relations between men and women in the shadow of coverture. Nonetheless, in this chapter I have argued that it struggles to account for the diffuse and informal sexual hierarchization that we often see in contemporary societies. Happily, I locate an alternative and superior model of power relations within Hobbes's later work: power relations as deference. On this model, women's subjection to male desires, projects, and understanding can be characterized without the need either for overstating the degree and character of women's disempowerment, or for positing a general society-wide crypto-desire to control women, silence them, or put them back in the home.

Notes

1 Hobbes's Latin terms *potentia* and *potestas* correspond to his single English term power. I disambiguate by referring to *potentia* as capacity-power.

2 A covenant is a variety of contract. A contract is a mutual exchange of right; if the right to a thing is exchanged but the thing itself is only delivered in the future, then the contract is a covenant (Hobbes, 2014, 204; 1651, 66).

3 Hobbes does make the point that bound slaves are not in the master's dominion. But the failure of dominion is due to the binding, not the lack of explicit covenant. Unbound slaves, even without explicit covenant, are taken to have consented to dominion (Hobbes 1983a, 118; 2012, 312; 1651, 104).

4 There is an ample and excellent literature discussing the remarkable extent of Hobbes's defiance of contemporary wisdom and pieties about women. Notably Sreedhar (2020) and Wright (2002).

5 Pateman herself doesn't think it quite works (1991, 49): who would rationally want children, if the predictable consequence is slave-like subjection to men?.

6 Lloyd furnishes a partial exception, see note 9.

7 Slavery is not merely a rhetorical point of reference. While *The Sexual Contract* focuses on sex, it also already flags a racial underbelly to the social contract (Pateman 1991, 62–76, 220–1, & *passim*), a suggestion fleshed out in greater detail in Pateman's later collaborations with Charles Mills (Pateman and Mills 2007).

8 Hochschild's classic 1989 sociological investigation remained sufficiently relevant to be reissued 23 years after its original publication (Hochschild 2012).

9 Generally, feminist Hobbes scholars have limited themselves to the question of dominion. However, in her reconstruction of the origins of Hobbesian sexual dominion, S.A. Lloyd (2012; 2020) has given a central role to socially generated relational power (power as deference in my terms). I want to dwell on what this power might amount to taken in itself, even when it does not intensify to the point of supporting dominion.

10 Related themes are developed in more detail in Field (2014; 2020, chapters 2–4).

11 *Leviathan*'s initial sketch in chapter 10.3 appears to reassert the division between lateral association of independent wills and vertical dominion with one will master over the others (Hobbes 2012, 132; 1651, 41). However, as I argue, the new vision of association that is developed through the chapter involves partial dependence of wills.

12 This characterization might only be sustainable for women in dominant social groups: for women in subjected classes or racialized groups, there may also be other power figures apart from their husbands to contend with.

References

Cumberlege, Julia. 2020. "First Do No Harm: The Report of the Independent Medicines and Medical Devices Safety Review." UK Government Report. Accessed November 3, 2020. https://www.immdsreview.org.uk/Report.html

Field, Sandra. 2014. "Hobbes and the Question of Power." *Journal of the History of Philosophy* 52 (1): 61–86.

Field, Sandra Leonie. 2020. *Potentia: Hobbes and Spinoza on Power and Popular Politics*. New York: Oxford University Press.

Fricker, Miranda. 2007. *Epistemic Injustice: Power and the Ethics of Knowing*. Oxford: Oxford University Press.

Hill, Jess. 2019. *See What You Made Me Do: Power, Control, and Domestic Abuse*. Melbourne: Black Inc.

Hirschmann, Nancy J. 2012. "Gordon Schochet on Hobbes, Women, and Gratitude." In *Feminist Interpretations of Thomas Hobbes*, edited by Nancy J. Hirschman and Joanne H. Wright, 125–45. University Park: Penn State University Press.

Hobbes, Thomas. 1839–1845a. *The English Works of Thomas Hobbes*, 11 vols., edited by Sir William Molesworth. London: John Bohn. Cited as EW.

Hobbes, Thomas. 1839–1845b. *Thomæ Hobbes malmesburiensis opera philosophica*, 5 vols., edited by Gulielmi Molesworth. London: John Bohn. Cited as OL.

Hobbes, Thomas. 1983a. *De cive: The English Version Entitled, in the First Edition, Philosophicall Rudiments Concerning Government and Society*, edited by Howard Warrender. Oxford: Clarendon Press.

Hobbes, Thomas. 1983b. *De cive: The Latin Version Entitled in the First Edition Elementorum Philosophiae sectio tertia de cive and in Later Editions Elementa philosophica de cive*, edited by Howard Warrender. Oxford: Clarendon Press.

Hobbes, Thomas. 2012. *Leviathan*, 3 vols edited by Noel Malcolm. Oxford: Clarendon Press.

Hochschild, Arlie Russell. 2012. *The Second Shift*, Revised edn. New York: Penguin. First published 1989.

Klarfeld, Jessica. 2011. "A Striking Disconnect: Marital Rape Law's Failure to Keep up with Domestic Violence Law." *American Criminal Law Review* 48 (4): 1819–42.

Lloyd, S.A. 2012. "Power and Sexual Subordination in Hobbes's Political Theory." In *Feminist Interpretations of Thomas Hobbes*, edited by Nancy J. Hirschman and Joanne H. Wright, 47–62. University Park: Penn State University Press.

Lloyd, S.A. 2020. "By Force or Wiles: Women in the Hobbesian Hunt for Allies and Authority." *Hobbes Studies* 33: 5–28.

MacKinnon, Catherine. 2019. "Where #Metoo Came From, And Where It's Going." The Atlantic, March 2019. Accessed November 3, 2020. https://www.theatlantic.com/ideas/archive/2019/03/catharine-mackinnon-what-metoo-has-changed/585313

Manne, Kate. 2017. *Down, Girl: The Logic of Misogyny*. New York: Oxford University Press.

Mills, Charles. 2007. "The Domination Contract." In *Contract and Domination*, edited by Carole Pateman and Charles Mills, 79–105. Cambridge: Polity.

Pateman, Carole. 1991. *The Sexual Contract*. Cambridge: Polity.

Pateman, Carole and Charles Mills, eds. 2007. *Contract and Domination*. Cambridge: Polity.

Schochet, Gordon J. 2012. "Thomas Hobbes on the Family and the State of Nature." In *Feminist Interpretations of Thomas Hobbes*, edited by Nancy J. Hirschman and Joanne H. Wright, 105–24. University Park: Penn State University Press.

Slomp, Gabriella. 1994. "Hobbes and the Equality of Women." *Political Studies* 1994 (XLII): 441–52.

Sreedhar, Susanne. 2020. "Hobbes on Sexual Morality." *Hobbes Studies* 33: 54–83.

Wright, Joanne H. 2002. "Going against the Grain: Hobbes's Case for Original Maternal Dominion." *Journal of Women's History* 14 (1): 123–55.

9

The State of Nature as a Continuum Concept

S.A. LLOYD

It is tempting to conceptualize the state of nature and the state of civil society as diametrically opposed, mutually exclusive, conditions. Any condition other than the civil condition of a commonwealth is the state of nature, with all its attendant horrors. Hobbes's own language sometimes suggests as much. In *De cive* X.1 Hobbes writes:

> Outside the commonwealth every man has a right to all things, but on the terms that he may enjoy nothing. In a commonwealth every man enjoys a limited right in security. Outside the commonwealth, we are protected only by our own strength; within by the strength of all. Outside the commonwealth, no one is certain of the fruits of his industry; within the commonwealth all men are. To sum up: outside the commonwealth is the empire of the passions, war, fear, poverty, nastiness, solitude, barbarity, ignorance, savagery; within the commonwealth is the empire of reason, peace, security, wealth, splendour, society, good taste, the sciences and good-will. (Hobbes 1998, 116)

This passage suggests that any individual is either a member of a commonwealth, or a solitary army of one within a war of every man against every man; that the state of nature/civil society distinction is a kind of toggle switch.[1]

There are several interpretations of what a state of nature *is* that fit comfortably with an "all or nothing" conception of the state of nature, including the state of nature as a lawless condition and the state of nature as an empirically impossible condition of entirely asocial human beings.[2] Nevertheless, I shall argue that on the most plausible interpretation of Hobbes's conception of what a state of nature is – namely a condition of the *morally permissible exercise of private judgment* and action on it – the state of nature is actually a continuum concept that allows not only for conditions that are "more or less" states of nature *outside* commonwealths, but also for incomplete removals from the state of nature *within* established commonwealths. I shall argue that there is a spectrum of degrees of permissible exercise of private judgment varying across dimensions

A Companion to Hobbes, First Edition. Edited by Marcus P. Adams.

of how many people may exercise private judgment and over which matters, allowing for states of nature ranging all the way from the condition of mere nature with its universal right of private judgment, to commonwealths in which the essential rights of sovereignty are divided or their exercise constrained by rules.

9.1 What Is the State of Nature?

9.1.1 *The Condition of Atomistic Asocial Individuals*

Jean Hampton saw Hobbes's state of nature as a "presocietal" condition of "isolated asocial individuals," "stripped of their social connections." She attributed to Hobbes the view that "humans are not in any fundamental way products of their social environment" (Hampton 1986, 7–11). I suspect that her interpretation of the state of nature rested in part on a misunderstanding of the meaning of the term "engagement" in Hobbes's famous characterization of persons in the state of nature in the *Philosophical Rudiments* translation of *De cive* VIII.1 "as if but even now sprung out of the earth, and suddenly, like mushrooms, come to full maturity, without all kind of engagement to each other" (EW II.108–9).[3] In ordinary language, the term "engagement" often denotes a formal agreement, or an undertaking with another that involves obligations, rather than simply any interaction at all; and Hobbes's use of "*obligatio*" in *De cive* suggests this ordinary language use was what he had in mind. *Pace* Hampton, who writes "Gauthier is right to find in Hobbes's theory a very strong brand of individualism, one that regards individual human beings as conceptually prior ... to *all* social interactions" (1986, 6), Hobbes is speaking of the absence of any *obligations to obey* others, or any rights to others' obedience. Hobbes makes his meaning clearer at *De Corpore Politico* 2.III.2, where he invites the reader to consider "men therefore again in the state of nature, without *covenants or subjection one to another*, as if they were but even now all at once created male and female" (EW IV.149; emphasis added).

Although Hobbes does not in *De cive* XIII.1 speak specifically of covenants of *political* subjection, as opposed to other sorts of agreements, we have strong evidence that political subjection is what the "pure," or "mere," state of nature lacks altogether. Hobbes concedes in his note to *De cive* I.10 that such a state is empirically impossible because "a son cannot be understood to be at any time in the state of nature, as being under the power and command of them to whom he owes his protection as soon as ever he is born" (EW II.10). He insists in *Leviathan* XX.5 that every child "oweth its life to the mother; and is therefore obliged to obey her rather than any other; and by consequence the dominion over it is hers ... for ... every man is supposed to promise obedience to him in whose power it is to save or destroy him" (2012, 310; 1651, 103). If all who are born are never in a state of nature precisely *because* they are under an obligation to obey those who have preserved them, it follows that the mere state of nature is a condition in which political relations of obligation to obey and the corresponding right to be obeyed are absent.

A further striking piece of evidence that what the pure state of nature altogether lacks are relations of political subjection appears in *De cive* XI.3, where, speaking again of the "natural state" Hobbes writes "everyone is an enemy to everyone whom he neither obeys nor commands" (1998, 108) Hobbes consistently describes the pure state of nature as a condition of universal enmity and war, "and not simply war, but a war of every man against every man" (1998, 29).[4] If, as Hobbes states at *Leviathan* XIII.9, in a time of a war of every man against every man "every man is enemy to every man" (2012, 192; 1651, 62); and if not standing in a political relation (of obedience or command) is sufficient to make men enemies; and if in a pure state of nature each man is an enemy to every other; then in a pure state of nature no man stands in a political relation to any other. It may well be that people there have many other sorts of relationships – as friends, lovers, co-religionists, cooperators, or competitors, and even perhaps as parties to other sorts of contracts for example. What they lack are obligations to obey, or claim-rights to demand obedience, from anyone else. And, as I shall argue shortly, absent political relations, all are at moral liberty to act on their own private judgments.

In Hampton's view, "the last thing Hobbes would want to do is attribute to human beings a passion that is based on a desire to be socially interrelated in a particular way to other human beings. Doing so would destroy ... Hobbes's radical individualism" (1986, 74). Thus Hobbes would not want to attribute to anyone a desire to rule others, or not to be ruled by others, or to be respected by others, or to outdo others. There is plentiful evidence against Hampton's interpretation of the state of nature as an "asocial" condition in Hobbes's insistence across all his political writings that men care deeply about their relative social standing and reputations, and that this is a major source of conflict *in a state of nature*. At *Leviathan* XIII.5, he asserts that "every man looketh that his companion should value him at the same rate he sets upon himself" and will attempt to extract such recognition from those who treat him with contempt (2012, 190; 1651, 61); at *De cive* I.5 Hobbes makes the more extreme claim that "all the heart's joy and pleasure lies in being able to compare oneself favourably with others and form a high opinion of oneself" (1998, 26).[5] In Hampton's view, it is *because* Hobbes was a radical individualist that Hobbesian men cannot desire to stand in any social relations with each other. To this we may recall that one person's *modus ponens* is another person's *modus tollens*: it is because Hobbesian men all *do* desire the esteem, recognition, or deference of others (as Hobbes's texts confirm) that we can infer that Hobbes was *not* the radical individualist imagined by Gauthier and Hampton, and the state of nature not a condition of "isolated, asocial individuals."

9.1.2 A Condition Absent Law

A potentially more promising way of understanding the state of nature is as a *lawless* condition. A. P. Martinich (2015, 1967) characterizes the state of nature as "that condition in which human beings are not constrained by any laws." On Hobbes's conception of law as the command of one whom we are formerly obligated to obey, a condition in which no one has any obligation to obey anyone else will indeed lack laws. His characterization of the natural condition as one in which nothing can be unjust, and his explanation in *Leviathan* XIII.13 that "where there is ... no law, no injustice" (2012, 196; 1651, 63), would seem to support Martinich's conception of the state of nature as lawless.

To the obvious objection that the *laws of nature*, which Hobbes describes as eternal, immutable, and always binding in conscience, exist in the state of nature, most commentators have replied that the laws of nature are not really laws, but merely rational conclusions pertaining to self-interest. Martinich proposes that we should think of the state of nature as containing two conceptual "moments." Considered in isolation from the laws of nature – in what he terms the "primary" state of nature – "not even the existence of God is considered" (1992, 76). Before we undertake or discover ourselves to have an obligation to obey God as our sovereign, the laws of nature are not actually laws. Once we consider our obligation to obey God – the "secondary" state of nature – natural law becomes literally law for us, albeit often binding only *in foro interno*. What Hobbes calls the pure natural condition, or condition of mere nature, would then correspond to Martinich's "primary" state of nature; and that would be a condition in which we are not constrained by any laws of any sort.

I believe Martinich sees it as the advantage of his primary/secondary state of nature distinction that it reconciles Hobbes's apparently conflicting positions on whether there can or cannot be valid covenants in "the" state of nature. Covenants are invalidated upon reasonable suspicion of non-compliance; and where there is no coercive guarantor of performance, suspicion is often reasonable. Martinich thinks Hobbes needs the possibility of valid state of nature covenants in order to make sense of the social contract creating the commonwealth (1992, 83), for if there were no valid covenants there, how could the social contract obligate us? The secondary state of nature allows for the making and keeping of valid covenants, hence of justice, which presupposes law, in a state of nature, because a sovereign God can both issue natural laws and enforce them by punishment (in an afterlife).

On this account, the laws of nature are binding laws only in the secondary state of nature, and only in virtue of God's sovereignty over us in his natural kingdom. This sort of account (endorsed in Byron 2015), faces the central question how we can be obligated to obey God and so his natural laws. One possibility is that people are obligated in virtue of having entered into a covenant with God to have God as their civil sovereign. Every rational adult would need to be understood as having so covenanted, because Hobbes insists that natural law binds *everyone* in possession of natural reason (thereby excepting only children and madmen from its demands).

However, atheists do not covenant to obey the entity whose existence they deny, Hobbes holding in *Leviathan* XXVI.41 that "unbelief is not a breach of any of [God's] laws, but a rejection of them all, *except the law natural*" (2012, 444; 1651, 149; emphasis added). Had atheists covenanted, their disobedience to any of God's laws would count as injustice (the not keeping of covenant); yet Hobbes writes (*De cive* XIV.19 note) "I am so much an enemy to atheists, that I have both diligently sought for, and vehemently desired to find some law whereby I might condemn them of injustice. But ... I found none" (EW II.198). If the claim of natural law on atheists depended on their having undertaken such a covenant, and they did not, then the fact upon which Hobbes insists, namely that they *are* bound by the natural laws, entails that the binding force of natural law *cannot depend on any covenant* to obey God. A further difficulty with the idea that natural law becomes obligatory for us in virtue of our covenanting to obey God, is Hobbes's insistence that it is impossible for anyone who is not in direct, supernatural, communication with God to enter into any covenant with Him. So very few, if indeed any, individuals have had the requisite direct contact, that the universality of our subjection to the natural law would be inexplicable on the covenant account of God's sovereignty.

Alternatively, Byron (2015, 89–92) has argued that mere *belief* in the existence of a providential God who propounds the laws of nature and punishes violations of them in an afterlife suffices to make the laws of nature literal laws to those holding that belief: "we become God's subject in some doxastic way, simply by belief ... in a providential God."[6] One worry about such a view is that, generally speaking, agreeing that something is true does not entail endorsing it, let alone obligating oneself to act to preserve its continued truth. Even if it were plausible to equate agreeing *that* the laws of nature are God's instructions with consenting *to* abide by those, in *Rudiments* XVII.13 Hobbes explicitly *denies* that we can have natural knowledge of an afterlife, including among "those points of faith which cannot be understood by natural reason, but only by revelation" "*that there are rewards and punishments after this life*" (EW II.270). Similarly, in his reply to the Foole in *Leviathan* XV.8 Hobbes insists that "there is no natural knowledge of man's estate after death" (2012, 226; 1651, 74). So unaided natural reason cannot arrive at belief in a penal god who legislates and punishes violations of the laws of nature, severely limiting the number of people who could have any obligation to obey natural laws on Byron's suggested doxastic account of obligation.

A third suggestion for grounding the laws of nature as literal laws issued by a God whom all are formerly obligated to obey, proposed by Martinich, is by appeal to God's irresistible power. Whereas ordinary might does not make right, irresistible might somehow does: "the only way for something to become obligatory is for it to be commanded by an irresistible force. Only God is such a force" (Martinich 1992, 122). Martinich acknowledges that the natural laws are "promulgated" through individuals' exercises of their natural reason; such exercises may produce the *content* of natural law, but cannot verify its *authority*, because natural reason cannot verify the existence of an irresistibly powerful lawgiver and enforcer promulgating those laws *via* our natural reasoning (which is fallible, and its causes non-transparent to us). It would seem to follow that even if we were obligated to obey God's laws in virtue of God's irresistible force – a puzzling notion – we could have no way of knowing we were obligated.

These obstacles to understanding the laws of nature as literal laws may seem to speak in favor of viewing the state of nature as a lawless condition. Although Martinich saw the validity of the social contract conferring right or authority on a human sovereign as in need of underwriting by God's third law of nature making covenant-keeping mandatory, the alleged political obligation to obey God's natural laws may do more harm than good. If individuals already have a political sovereign in God, it would seem that they are not at moral liberty to undertake a new covenant of subjection to a human sovereign. Their prior obligation would seem to preclude entering into a valid covenant of subjection with the latter.

Even those inclined to accept these interpreters' arguments that the laws of nature are literal laws in a (secondary) state of nature may nevertheless agree that the state of nature remains, in one sense, a lawless condition. Martinich himself does, I believe, view the state of nature as a condition lacking *effective* law *enforcement*, and such a condition is, at least for practical purposes, lawless. God's punishments for violations of natural law are seldom evident in this life, Hobbes acknowledging that the wicked do in fact prosper; and threatened punishments in an afterlife are too remote or uncertain to compel compliance with natural law much of the time. So regardless of whether the laws of nature are or are not literal laws,[7] the state of nature may be in practice a lawless condition. But, I suggest, the *reason* a state of nature lacks effective law enforcement, when it does, is that individuals may permissibly rely on their own private judgments concerning the interpretation of natural law's requirements and whether theirs or others' actions have violated natural law.

Gathering these considerations, we have a simple three-pronged argument against taking lawlessness to be the *defining* feature of a state of nature. First, if the precepts of natural law, which always bind *in foro interno*, including in a state of nature, are literal laws, then the state of nature is *not* a lawless condition. Second, if a state of nature is lawless only in the practical sense that there is no effective enforcement of natural laws, its lawlessness is the *effect* of the differing private judgments of individuals exercising their moral liberty to decide how those laws are to be interpreted, when or whether they have been violated, and what if anything to do about it. Individuals have the moral liberty that undermines effective enforcement of the natural laws *only because* they are under no political obligation to defer to the judgment of one who, in virtue of that deference could coordinate interpretation, adjudication, and enforcement of natural law. Third, for a precept to be a law, there must be someone whom we are already obligated to obey who has commanded that precept. So if a state of nature is an entirely lawless condition, despite the fact that the precepts of natural law pertain there, it is so *because* we stand in no political relation of obligation to obey the author of those precepts. It is thus the absence of political relations, and not the absence of precepts, that accounts for the lack of law there. Lawlessness is a symptom, not the disease; an effect, not the cause of a state of nature.

9.1.3 A Condition of the Rightful Exercise of Private Judgment

A third possible conception of the state of nature, and the one I find most supported, is as a condition in which each individual may permissibly exercise and act on her own private judgment in every matter. Such universal moral liberty would not obtain were anyone obligated to obey another. If some had obligations to defer their private judgment to the judgments of a political master, they would act impermissibly in following their own private judgments. Thus, the absence in the condition of mere nature of any political obligations, documented earlier in the section on atomistic asocial individuals, allows for a condition wherein a universal right to exercise and act on one's own private judgment in all matters obtains. Because "all matters" includes interpretation of the requirements of natural law, and judgment of whether one's own or others' actions do or don't conform to natural laws, the natural condition will also be practically, if not technically, lawless. On this conception, a pure state of nature – which would have to abstract away the political obligations of children to those who preserved their lives – is empirically unrealizable. Yet there is no difficulty in concluding with Hobbes that, considering the vast diversity in individuals' private judgments – which he explains as the effect of differences in their bodily constitutions, appetites, circumstances, upbringings, and educations, as well as similarity in in their tendencies to judge themselves superior to others – individual governance by private judgment could be expected to yield disputes, mutual frustration, and enmity.

What it means to be without any obligation of obedience to another, without obligation to defer to the judgment of any other as to how one is to act, is to be in the position that one may *rightfully* act on one's own (good-faith) private judgment, on every question – of right and wrong, good and bad, mine and thine. In *Elements* I.xiv.8 Hobbes both stresses the permissibility of individual private judgment and explains his reasoning in attributing that right universally in a state of nature. He writes:

> every man by right of nature is judge himself .... For if it be against reason that I be judge ... myself, then it is reason, that another man be judge .... But the same reason that maketh another man judge of those things that concern me, maketh me also judge of that that concerneth him. And therefore I have reason to judge of his sentence.... (1969, 72)

This argument assumes that reason requires that *someone* must have the right to make a terminal judgment as to how to act. If, for *any* individual judge(r), *only* someone *else* had the right to judge the correctness of their judgments, a vicious regress would ensue, with no one having the right to make a terminal judgment. But if it is not the case that only someone else has the right to judge, it must be the case that the individual judge(r) has the right to judge, as Hobbes concludes comports with reason.

A person thinks good what she desires, or has an appetite for; and according to Hobbes at *Leviathan* XV.40, "so long a man is in the condition of mere nature, which is a state of war, as private appetite is the measure of good and evil" (2012, 242; 1651, 80). That is, a man is in a condition of mere nature as long as everyone uses their own private appetite, or private judgment of good and evil, as the measure of all things. So long as individuals judge what ought and ought not to be done by their own standard, they are in a condition of mere nature, (which Hobbes has argued is a condition of continual fear and danger of violent death). He explains at *Elements* II.5.2 that subjects of commonwealths experience some frustration at loss of such a complete liberty as they might have enjoyed in a condition of mere nature, seeing that "a subject may no more govern his own actions according to his own discretion and judgment, or, (which is all one) conscience, as the present occasions from time to time shall dictate to him; but must be tied to do according to [his sovereign's will]" (1969, 139). Nevertheless, preserving that universal permission to act on private judgment is self-defeating, for, as he puts the point in *De cive* 10.8:

> [I]f every man would grant *the same liberty to another, which he desires for himself*, as is commanded by the law of nature; *that same natural state would return again*, in which all men may by right do all things; which if they knew, they would abhor, as being worse than all kinds of civil subjection whatsoever. (EW II.135; emphases added)

These passages make clear that what is distinctive about a pure state of nature is that all individuals are permitted to act on their own private judgments in each and every matter (including those concerning the correctness of other people's judgments). As Hobbes puts the point simply in *Leviathan* XIV.4, in the condition of mere nature "everyone is governed by his own reason" (2012, 198; 1651, 64), having a right so to govern himself.[8] Departures from that pure natural condition must then involve some narrowing of the scope of permissible exercise of private judgment. This narrowing can be achieved by limiting either the number of persons who may permissibly exercise private judgment, or the range of issues over which they may exercise it, or both.

9.2 The State of Nature as a Continuum Concept

One of the smallest units of political association is comprised of a caretaking adult and a child, who is presumed to have promised obedience to its protector. Another small unit of political association is the "married" family wherein one adult, and possibly dependent children, submit in all matters to the rule of another adult. Marital associations can be established through warfare or by covenant. When these sorts of political associations grow large enough, through acquisition of servants and/or breeding of children, that they can deter aggressors, they become "patrimonial kingdoms." A condition containing many such ordered households, each with no obligation to defer to the judgment of any other household, is a state of nature, with potential for an enormous amount of conflict, albeit slightly less fraught than the pure state of nature, imagined as absent any political obligations at all.

Larger units of political association may be formed when, through agreement or conquest, groups with commonalities form themselves into tribes, or, say, feudal fiefdoms comprised of peasants, vassals, and knights bound to obey a lord.[9] As more individuals are incorporated in these sorts of political associations, the number of individuals who may permissibly act on their own private judgments diminishes; yet there remains room for significant conflict among leaders of those associations. They are in a state of nature with respect to each other. They provide their members with some measure of an orderly social environment within which members can hope to achieve their ends; but the fact that so many other associations may also rightfully pursue competing ends continues to leave their members vulnerable.

Perhaps surprisingly, certain forms of government within commonwealths will achieve *incomplete removals* from a state of nature, just to the degree that those forms permit the use of private judgment by multiple parties. Systems that divide the essential rights of sovereignty among multiple parties allow for permissible exercises of private judgment by those rights-holders that may create practical conflicts among themselves. Systems that limit sovereignty, must, if those limits are to be meaningful, afford other parties the right to exercise private judgment as to whether the limits have been overstepped, raising the specter of conflict with those exercising sovereign rights. These systems, because they permit multiple parties to exercise and act on their own judgments are types of state of nature. They are, of course, usually much preferable to the condition of mere nature, because in them there are significantly fewer agents entitled to exercise private judgment that may interfere with the agency of the rest. But once we understand the argument from the state of nature for restricting the scope of private judgment, we will see that a system of undivided, unlimited sovereignty, *properly exercised*, provides subjects with maximum prospects for achieving their ends. Governments exercise sovereignty properly when they secure subjects' safety, prosperity, and the largest range of personal liberty compatible with those goods.[10]

The present suggestion is that the state of nature is a continuum notion that lies in a segment along a larger continuum of the scope of private judgment, as does the continuum notion of civil authority. There are many states of nature, and many forms of political society, that differ not starkly in kind, but only in degree of the scope of permissible private judgment exercised in them. Imagine a conceptual line, depicted in Figure 9.1, the leftmost point of which represents the condition of rightful universal private judgment over all issues (the condition of mere nature) in which each individual may exercise their private judgment over every matter, and the rightmost point of which represents the condition of entirely singular public judgment, in which a single natural person permissibly exercises their private judgment to settle every issue for all subjects (call this the perfectly totalitarian sovereign).

As we move from left to right we diminish the scope of permissible private judgment, either by constricting the number of individuals who may exercise it, or the range of issues over which it is exercised, or both. From its origin we move to government by small families, to patrimonial kingdoms, to savage or tribal government, to feudal systems, to civil wars between contenders to sovereignty, to political systems of divided and/or limited government, until we arrive at the Archimedean point of Hobbes's absolute but properly governing sovereign, which allows the maximum scope for subjects' liberty compatible with their security. We then continue rightward to reduce the sphere of private judgment left to individuals in matters that pose no danger to others – the sphere of harmless liberty – to invasive regimes, extremely oppressive regimes, and finally to the perfectly totalitarian regime in which a single governmental body (in extremis a single natural person) decides every issue for every subject.

As a state increasingly encroaches upon subjects' "harmless liberty" – the realm within which subjects can pursue their ends without harming others – the advantage of civil society for any individual over the various states of nature correspondingly diminishes. Figure 9.2 maps the scope for effective exercise of personal agency on to the

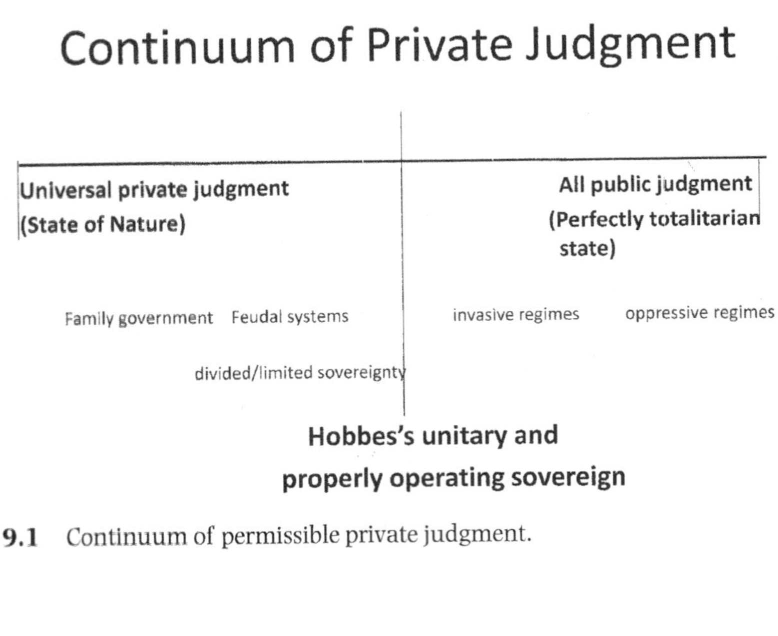

Figure 9.1 Continuum of permissible private judgment.

continuum of private judgment represented in Figure 9.1. Should the state's interference with subjects' pursuit of their ends become so pervasive that it rivaled the degree of interference posed by fellow individuals in the condition of mere nature, we would expect Hobbesian rational agents not only to be increasingly indifferent as between those two conditions, but increasingly motivated to risk rebellion (to "reshuffle the deck," as Hobbes says) in hopes of getting a better deal that would increase their prospects for effective agency by establishing a less restrictive government.

It is not that subjects would have any moral justification for rebellion; it is merely that as a matter of psychological fact, subjects would be increasingly motivated to risk rebellion. One of what Hobbes identified as the three necessary conditions for sedition – namely discontent – would increase dramatically, as subjects find that the regime hinders their well-being, and their prospects for improving their well-being. This introduces a different kind of instability into absolutist regimes than that caused in non-absolute regimes by the presence of multiple centers for the permissible exercise of private judgment.

At the beginning of this chapter, I quoted a passage from *De cive* X.1 that seemed to present commonwealth/state of nature as a stark distinction akin to a toggle switch. Hobbes's *Leviathan* chapter XVII.13 official *definition* of a commonwealth as "one person, of whose acts a great multitude, by mutual covenants one with another, have made themselves every one the author, to the end he may use the strength and means of them

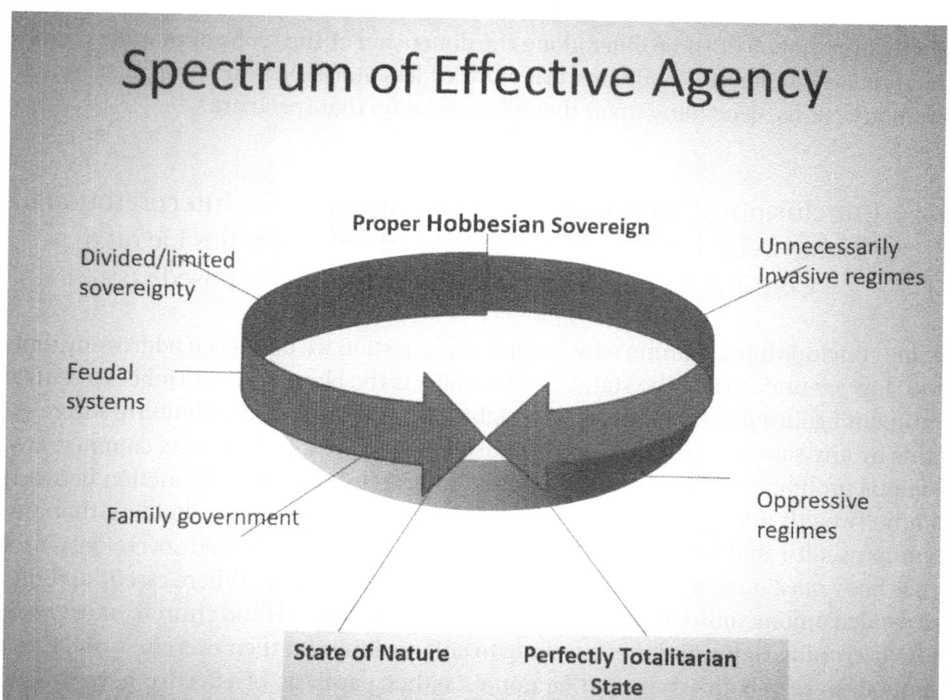

Figure 9.2 Scope for effective personal agency mapped onto the continuum of permissible private judgment.

all, as he shall think expedient, for their peace and common defense" seems also to exclude every kind of state of nature (2012, 260–2; 1651, 88). Whether we understand "one person" as a single natural person or an artificial person such as a properly ordered assembly, so long as a commonwealth is *defined* as a single, unified public judgment constituted by the authorization of every one of its members to substitute its judgment for theirs, any individual will be either inside a commonwealth, having no right to exercise private judgment without leave of the sovereign, or outside it, retaining that right. As a philosopher, Hobbes may have been attracted to the conceptual clarity provided by such a dichotomy, even though it does not carve reality at the joints, as Hobbes himself appreciated. On the interpretation I have offered, it is true that any political system satisfying Hobbes's *definition* of a commonwealth will not count as any type of state of nature. Yet considering that most systems of political authority throughout history have failed to satisfy Hobbes's strict definition of a commonwealth, it remains fair to say that most established states (including pre-civil war England) occupy a point on the state of nature continuum, according to the degree to which they morally permit multiple parties to exercise and act on their private judgment. Both Hobbes's aspiration to effect practical change by means of his political philosophy, and the preponderance of textual evidence, give us reason to understand Hobbes's state of nature as a continuum concept extending from the universal permissibility of action on private judgment all the way through the divided or limited systems of government he was so keen to criticize.

What I have argued is that there are many states of nature beyond the condition of mere nature; many commonwealths that fall short of Hobbes's definition of a commonwealth; and that all of these differ along the dimension of the scope of morally permissible private judgment. Conditions are more or less states of nature, or more or less commonwealths, depending upon their placement on that spectrum.

9.3 Conclusion: What Difference Does It Make to the Interpretation of Hobbes Whether States of Nature and Civil Societies Lie on a Continuum or Are Instead Diametrically Opposed?

Let me conclude by explaining why I believe the question we have been addressing matters. How we understand the state of nature affects the plausibility of Hobbes's central argument against dividing the essential rights of sovereignty and/or limiting sovereign rights by any sort of constraint (e.g., a constitution, traditional practice, common law, religious prohibitions). On the toggle-switch interpretation of the distinction between commonwealth and state of nature, it is natural to view Hobbes as holding that any commonwealth that falls short of establishing undivided, unlimited sovereignty in a single body *must inevitably collapse* into the pure state of nature. Where essential rights are divided among multiple bodies such as crown, parliament, and church, or between those exercising rights and those seeking to enforce limits on their exercise – and these agents disagree about what is to be done – either paralysis of effective government ensues (returning everyone to a state of nature), or civil war ensues (again returning all to a state of nature as each individual must decide which side to take or how else to respond). This position however, that the only possibilities are absolutism or the mere state of nature, is both theoretically implausible and belied by experience. Plenty of political systems, both pre-dating Hobbes's writings and since then, have remained stable over considerable stretches of time despite not being absolute sovereignties.[11] It would be both irresponsible and uncharitable to saddle Hobbes with such a position, if his theory provides resources to avoid doing so.

What the toggle-switch interpretation obscures, and the continuum interpretation highlights, is that whether division or limitation of sovereignty will or will not become problematic depends on the private judgments of the various agents under consideration in particular historical circumstances. Should their private judgments *converge* on the right course of action, there is no threat of paralysis nor cause for war. Because there is no reason to *assume* that the private judgments of various rights-holders *must necessarily* diverge, there is no justification for concluding that divided or limited sovereignties *inevitably* and of necessity collapse into a state of nature. Such systems do indeed increase the *risk* of stalemate and subsequent war to resolve it, because they institutionalize avenues for rightful action on possibly diverging private judgments. That is a perfectly plausible conclusion of Hobbes's science of politics. The wider these avenues, the greater the risk, which is presumably why Hobbes recommends foreclosing them by uniting sovereignty. Attention to the *scope* of permissible exercise of private judgment on the continuum conception of state/state of nature both explains the degree of risk inherent in various political systems, and allows us to see the importance for political stability of efforts to *condition consensus* in private judgments, through educational and other processes. Societies exhibiting a high degree of consensus among private judgments may be able to tolerate incomplete removal from the mere state of nature, without threat to their stability.

One consequence of the view under discussion is that whereas states of nature are always risky to some degree, they are not always, nor equally, horrible. That too comports with common sense. In imperfectly designed political systems, although it sometimes happens that there is sufficient disagreement among a large enough number of the possessors of different sets, or overlapping sets, of essential rights of sovereignty that they resort to war to resolve their dispute, it is much rarer for such disagreement to return *every individual* to anything close to the "pure" state of nature. Even in civil wars, troops for both sides continue to view themselves as under orders from political superiors; families retain their internal authority structures; church hierarchies and corporate structures and local governance and police may continue to receive deference. As terrifying as the prospect of a pure state of nature is, the probability of any ongoing political society's lapsing into that particular state is miniscule. If Hobbes's practical program for civil obedience depended on sustaining a lively dread of that pure prospect in society's members, that program would be very weak.

A second implication of our interpretation is that falling into or remaining in *some* or another state of nature is a real and ever-present possibility. On the continuum conception, unless Hobbes's recommendations for the design of commonwealth and the socialization of subjects are followed, the odds of finding oneself in *a* state of nature, with potentially bad consequences, is quite high. True, a pure state of nature promises to undermine our ability to achieve *any* of our ends, making it a condition any rational agent must be concerned to avoid. But a civil war is apt also to interfere with our agency, as is a paralysis of government with its corresponding diminution of effective adjudication of disputes or law enforcement. These are quite bad enough, and much more realistic possibilities than the pure state of nature.

For these reasons, while I agree with Evrigenis that interpreters err in seeing a simple antithesis between civil society and state of nature, and agree that Hobbes wanted his readers to understand that a state of nature is always a live threat to themselves, I do not see reason to attribute to Hobbes the implausible view that any state of nature is to be avoided at *any* cost. Evrigenis explains

> Hobbes knew well that no amount of supervision, coercion, and civic education was sufficient to persuade everyone to submit and obey. Necessary though they were, these measures would always have to be supplemented by the threat of a relapse into the state of nature, *a condition so undesirable as to be avoided at any cost*. It is not uncommon to present the state of nature as the antithesis of civil society, but this simple opposition misses an important aspect of the state of nature, which is that it is never too far away. As Hobbes reminded his readers in *Leviathan*, even in the best run commonwealths, one locks one's doors at night. (2014, 178; emphasis added)

Does the admitted fact that we in civil societies lock our doors at night for fear of possible criminal encroachments provide evidence that "a condition so undesirable as to be avoided at any cost" is nearly upon us? That is hard to believe. As I see it, because it is so wildly implausible that civilized commonwealths could collapse on a hair-trigger into a condition of atomic individuals so extreme that Hobbes himself conceded that condition's empirical impossibility, showing citizens that a state of nature is "never too far away" will require counting as states of nature conditions far less extreme than the "pure" natural condition. Doing so has the advantage that it avoids undermining Hobbes's stated aspiration to produce a *science*[12] of politics, as would be done by rendering his argument dependent at its core on myth, ideology, or rhetorical fiction. Understanding the condition of mere nature instead as a logical *reductio* of permissible private judgment, and a state of nature as a condition in which multiple persons may permissibly exercise their private judgment, allows for a continuum of empirically realizable or realized states of nature presenting various degrees of threat to achieving our desired ends. The wider the scope of private judgment, the greater the threat; the narrower the scope, the smaller the threat. Such an interpretation comports with Hobbes's description of systems of family government, of the "savages" of America, of Germanic factions in earlier ages, and of the international condition all as states of nature, and makes sense of his emphasis on the perils of private judgment. Importantly, it enhances the plausibility of the central argument of Hobbes's political philosophy, his argument establishing the desirability of absolute sovereignty.

Notes

1 Hobbes's insistence that nations remain in a state of nature with respect to one another need not be incompatible with a conceptualization of the state of nature as "all or nothing" for any individual, because Hobbes defines commonwealths as unions of sufficient size and

strength that they can deter attacks on their members, making the existence of an international state of nature irrelevant for their members.

2 Other possible interpretations, which I shall not discuss, include the state of nature as a condition lacking science and philosophy, or the condition of vicious humans fallen from grace.

3 Hampton had access to this volume. Tuck and Silverthorne's translation – "in the pure natural state (*), or before men bound themselves by any agreements with each other" (Hobbes 1998, 28) – post-dates Hampton's book. There is no evidence of Hampton having consulted Hobbes's Latin works.

4 See also *Leviathan* XIII.8 (2012, 192; 1651, 62).

5 All men, including those in the condition of mere nature "compete for honour and dignity" and "for man virtually nothing is thought to be good which does not give its possessor some superiority and eminence above that enjoyed by other men" (*De cive* V.5; 1998,71).

6 To be precise, Byron takes mere belief to be a form of tacit covenant. "Merely acknowledging [God's] right [to rule], typically by believing in a providential God, is sufficient for submission" and so for the obligation to obey the laws of nature. "Submission to God creates the obligation to obey the proper laws [of nature] because it is a voluntary act, namely believing in God" (2015, 91). I doubt this because, whereas it is true that Hobbes insists in *Leviathan* XL.2 that undertaking an obligation requires some voluntary act, he explicitly denies that belief is voluntary, writing, "as for the inward *thought* and *belief* of men ... they are not voluntary" (2012, 738; 1651, 249). For critical discussion of Byron's doxastic view and the suggestion addressed below that God's power makes the laws of nature literal law, see Lloyd (2017, 215–18).

7 I have argued elsewhere that for purposes of grasping their operation in Hobbes's political theory, the laws of nature are best understood as *natural duties*, rather than as contractual obligations, legal obligations, or mere precepts of prudence (Lloyd 2017). I agree with Martinich that Hobbes *also* viewed them as divine laws and rational precepts; however, I do not see that their status as divine law plays any role in Hobbes's argument for the duty to submit to government.

8 It makes sense that Hobbes would characterize a pure state of nature as a condition of universally permissible private judgment, because his aim is to justify a unitary public judgment (a sovereign) by making vivid the perils of its absence, and unitary judgment is most absent when every individual enjoys moral liberty to judge every matter.

9 Gangs formed as protective organizations or for plunder may also emerge as political associations. For discussion of the possible emergence of ordered alliances in a state of nature see Lloyd (2020).

10 Hobbes discusses the art of good government in *De cive* XIII.

11 The United States is obviously not among these, but then it is *exceptionally* non-absolutist, having not only a limiting constitution, and separation of legislative, executive, and judicial powers at the federal level, but also duplication of the essential rights of sovereignty at the level of the states (as well as a culture of radical individualism, and a citizenry armed with military-grade weapons precisely in order to resist any perceived government encroachment).

12 The continuum conception of a state of nature for which I have argued here is of a piece with non-atomistic and non-reductionist conceptions of Hobbes's metaphysics and natural philosophy. Marcus Adams has shown Hobbes to hold that there are no physical minima (2017), and that we can flexibly consider or understand bodies in various ways (2016); these imply a spectrum account of physical reality not dissimilar to the spectrum account of political reality I have attributed to Hobbes. I regard the consistency of the present account of Hobbes's political philosophy with Hobbes's scientific practice in other domains of his philosophy to count in its favor.

Bibliography

Adams, Marcus. 2016. "Hobbes on Natural Philosophy as 'True Physics' and Mixed Mathematics." *Studies in History & Philosophy of Science* 56: 41–53.

Adams, Marcus. 2017. "Natural Philosophy, Deduction, and Geometry in the Hobbes-Boyle Debate." *Hobbes Studies* 30: 83–107.

Byron, Michael. 2015. *Submission and Subjection in Leviathan*. New York: Palgrave Macmillan.

Evrigenis, Ioannis D. 2014. *Images of Anarchy: The Rhetoric and Science in Hobbes's State of Nature*. Cambridge: Cambridge University Press.

Hampton, Jean. 1986. *Hobbes and the Social Contract Tradition*. Cambridge: Cambridge University Press.

Hobbes, Thomas. 1839–1845a. *The English Works of Thomas Hobbes*, 11 vols., edited by Sir William Molesworth. London: John Bohn. Cited as EW.

Hobbes, Thomas. 1969. *The Elements of Law; Natural and Politic*, edited by Ferdinand Tonnies. London: Frank Cass & Co. Ltd.

Hobbes, Thomas. 1998. *On The Citizen*, edited by Richard Tuck and Michael Silverthorne. Cambridge: Cambridge University Press.

Hobbes, Thomas. 2012. *Leviathan*, 3 vols., edited by Noel Malcolm. Oxford: Clarendon Press. [First published 1651].

Lloyd, S.A. 2017. "Duty Without Obligation." *Hobbes Studies* 30: 202–21.

Lloyd, S.A. 2020. "By Force or Wiles: Women in the Hobbesian Hunt for Allies and Authority." *Hobbes Studies* 33 (1): 5–28.

Martinich, Aloysius P. 1992. *The Two Gods of Leviathan*. Cambridge: Cambridge University Press.

Martinich, Aloysius P. 2015. "Review of Ioannis D. Evrigenis. Images of Anarchy." *American Historical Review* 120 (5): 1967–8.

10

Hobbes's Minimalist Moral Theory

MICHAEL J. GREEN

A law of nature, according to Thomas Hobbes, "is a Precept, or generall Rule, found out by Reason, by which a man is forbidden to do, that, which is destructive of his life, or taketh away the means of preserving the same; and to omit, that, by which he thinketh it may be best preserved" (Hobbes 2012, 198; 1651, 64). Hobbes's theory of the laws of nature covers only a subset of these rules, namely, those that "concern the doctrine of Civill Society" (Hobbes 2012, 238; 1651, 78). I will defend a minimalist interpretation of this theory. This holds that Hobbes's theory consists in two theses. According to what I will call the *value thesis*, the laws of nature are valued because of their role in preserving peace. According to what I will call the *conditional thesis*, what the laws of nature require an individual to do depends on what others do.

There are many interpretations that attribute more ambitious aims to Hobbes, such as reconciling the claims of morality and interest (Darwall 1995, chap. 3; Hampton 1986, 46–51; Kavka 1986, chap. 9), defending a version of divine command theory (Byron 2015; Martinich 1992; Taylor 1938; Warrender 1957), showing that some aims are supremely rational (Gert 2010), or using a theory of reciprocity to unite reason and morality (Lloyd 2009). While I will compare the minimalist theory with two of these more ambitious interpretations, my chief argument will be that that Hobbes can accomplish his most important goals with the minimalist theory. In particular, I will show that it aids his case for the state and that it enables him to present an alternative to Aristotle's theory of justice.

10.1 Textual Arguments for the Minimalist Theory

Hobbes introduces the laws of nature as "Articles of Peace" and ends his discussion of them by declaring that he is the first philosopher to have shown that they are "praised, as the meanes of peaceable, sociable, and comfortable living" (Hobbes 2012, 196 and

A Companion to Hobbes, First Edition. Edited by Marcus P. Adams.

242; 1651, 63 and 80). This is a direct assertion of the value thesis. Nonetheless, it is worth retracing the steps Hobbes takes to arrive at it. These begin with what he regards as the three fundamental causes of war: people fight over scarce resources, they attack others for defensive reasons, and they use violence to defend their honor. Hobbes famously argues that these features of human nature lead to perpetual conflict among those who live without government in the state of nature. Given this analysis, there is an obvious path to peace. If those living in the state of nature can establish property rights, enter into nonaggression pacts, and accept limits on violent behavior, they can counteract the causes of war. The laws of nature are rules for accomplishing these things. The most important of these rules defines a covenant, a kind of contract in which at least one party is trusted to do its part in the future. For example, a nonaggression pact is a kind of covenant in which each side agrees not to attack the other, provided the other does the same, into the indefinite future. An agreement to establish property rights has the same form in that the parties agree not to interfere with one another's property rights for the indefinite future. If all the parties to the agreement follow the third law of nature by complying with these covenants, they will blunt the causes of conflict in the state of nature.

The other laws of nature are rules for maintaining the stability of the system established by these covenants. Some of these concern the content of the covenants. For example, the tenth law of nature holds that the covenants must leave everyone with rights to what they need to live well (Hobbes 2012, 234; 1651, 77). The other laws of nature address three problems that a covenanted peace would face: provocation, enforcement, and disagreement (Hobbes 2012, 230–8; 1651, 75–8). Provocation is a problem because covenants cannot rule out all socially destructive behavior. For example, failing to express gratitude for gifts undermines trust even if it does not violate an explicit agreement; the fourth law of nature addresses this by forbidding ingratitude. Similarly, the needy will be hard-pressed to respect property rights when others hoard goods, and those who are treated with contempt will sate their anger rather than respect the rules governing violence. These strains on the commitment to keep the rules are addressed by the fifth and eighth laws of nature. The former requires accommodating the needs of others while the latter forbids declarations of contempt. Enforcement is a problem when punishments lead to more antisocial behavior than they prevent. This problem is addressed by the sixth law of nature, which requires pardoning the repentant so they can rejoin society, and the seventh law of nature, which forbids punishments that are more harsh than necessary for correcting the offender or deterring others. Finally, even people who sincerely try to keep the rules will disagree about particular cases and will resort to violence if there is no other way of resolving their controversies. The laws of nature concerning arbitration address this problem. The sixteenth law of nature requires people to use arbitrators to settle their disputes. Other laws of nature are addressed to the arbitrators themselves; their purpose is to ensure that arbitration is seen to be fair so that it can serve its function in preserving the peace. Hobbes concludes that the laws of nature are valued as the means to peace, then, because they tell people how to use covenants to counteract the natural causes of war and how to maintain peace once it is established.

The conditional thesis follows straightforwardly from the value thesis. If the laws of nature are valued because they preserve peace, complying with them makes sense only when others do so. If a critical portion of the population does not comply with the laws of nature, there will be no peace to be kept and so there will be little point to anyone's following them. Since this is so, it is not surprising that Hobbes asserts the conditional thesis several times. What he calls the fundamental law of nature holds "*That every man, ought to endeavour Peace, as farre as he has hope of obtaining it; and when he cannot obtain it, that he may seek, and use, all helps, and advantages of Warre*" (Hobbes 2012, 200; 1651, 64; italics in original). He argues that "if other men will not lay down their Right, as well as he; then there is no Reason for any one, to devest himselfe of his: For that were to expose himselfe to Prey ... rather than to dispose himselfe to Peace" (Hobbes 2012, 200; 1651, 65). If covenants are made, they will be rendered invalid "upon any reasonable suspicion" that one party will not do its part; this is so because "he which performeth first, does but betray himselfe to his enemy; contrary to the Right ... of defending his life" (Hobbes 2012, 210; 1651, 68). Finally, Hobbes claims that there is no unconditional obligation to act on any of the laws of nature. The laws of nature, he says, "oblige *in foro interno*; that is to say, they bind to a desire they should take place: but *in foro externo*, that is, to the putting them in act, not alwayes." He reasons that, "he that should be modest, and tractable, and performe all he promises ... where no man els should do so, should but make himselfe a prey to others, and procure his own certain ruine, contrary to the ground of all Lawes of Nature" (Hobbes 2012, 240; 1651, 79).

While these passages all assert the conditional thesis, they do not settle exactly what Hobbes means. This is because there is gap between Hobbes's description of the conditions that waive the obligation to act on the laws of nature and the arguments he gives for treating the laws of nature as conditional. Hobbes says that individuals are not obliged to comply with the laws of nature if others do not do so or, in some cases, even if they simply doubt that others will comply. His arguments in support of this claim all assert that unreciprocated compliance would put one's life at risk. The gap is evident. For example, in many cases, one party can safely do its part in a covenant even if the other party does not. These covenants would be invalid according to the conditional thesis and valid if Hobbes's point is that performance is excused only if it would pose a threat to one's life. Scholars disagree about how to understand Hobbes here. A. E. Taylor (1938, 411) and Gregory Kavka (1986, 344–349) support the conditional thesis, while Howard Warrender (1957, 74–75) and S. A. Lloyd (2009, 31) maintain that only danger excuses noncompliance.

There are two reasons for favoring the conditional thesis. First, it is hard to see why Hobbes would think that someone is required to perform their side of a covenant when the other party does not, even if performance is not dangerous. That would be an unusually strict understanding of promissory obligations by anyone's lights. Second, there is no purpose to compliance with many of the laws of nature when others do not reciprocate. What is gained if only one party submits a disagreement to arbitration? Why would mediators worry about maintaining their neutrality if no one follows their decisions? Doing these things would be pointless but not perilous. It is true that Hobbes's arguments all invoke the hazards of unilateral compliance. However, there is a plausible explanation of why he does so that is compatible with the conditional thesis. Hobbes is primarily concerned with the specific case of agreements to end the war in the state of nature. The first thing that would have to be agreed to is a nonaggression pact, as peace will be impossible without that. Given his analysis of the dynamics of the state of nature, misplaced confidence that others will keep these pacts could be genuinely fatal. The prominence of this particular case might explain why he emphasizes the risks of complying with the laws of nature when defending the conditional thesis even though the conditional thesis also covers cases in which compliance is not especially dangerous.

10.2 Problem Cases: Cruelty and Covenants

According to the historian Barbara Donagan, it was widely believed in the seventeenth century that, "in the context of war" the law of nature "required that faith be kept, and that soldiers abstain from gratuitous acts of cruelty" such as "blood lust, pleasure in killing, private vengeance, and unnecessary bloodshed" (Donagan 2008, 137). On the face of it, Hobbes should have disagreed, because during war there is no peace to preserve, and the laws of nature are not generally followed. Hobbes, however, did not do this. Instead, he tried to make his theory conform to the standard practice of his time on both counts.

The seventh law of nature holds that punishment may be inflicted only for forward-looking reasons, such as correcting the offender or deterring others. It forbids what Hobbes calls cruelty, which he characterizes as "glorying in the hurt of another, tending to no end" and "to hurt without reason" (Hobbes 2012, 232; 1651, 76). According to the conditional thesis, cruelty is wrong only if others comply with the laws of nature. Hobbes's explanation for why cruelty is wrong is that it "tendeth to the introduction of Warre" (Hobbes 2012, 232; 1651, 76). If that were all there is to say about why cruelty is wrong, then there would be no point in prohibiting it during war. However, Hobbes is unwilling draw that conclusion. He writes in *De cive* that the observance of the natural law against cruelty "does not cease even in war" because "I cannot see what drunkenness or cruelty (which is vengeance without regard to future good) contribute to any man's peace or preservation" (Hobbes [1647] 1998, 54). Hobbes is evidently uncomfortable with the conditional thesis here, and for good reason, as it is wrong to inflict pointless suffering no matter what others do.

While Hobbes does not directly confront the problem in *Leviathan*, two passages suggest ways of avoiding it while retaining the conditional thesis. First, in his theory of the passions, Hobbes claims that cruelty, as it is defined in the seventh law of nature, never occurs. "I do not conceive it possible," he writes, "that any man should take pleasure in other mens great harmes, without other end of his own" (Hobbes 2012, 90; 1651, 28).[1] This rare moment of innocence might have been motivated by the knowledge that cruelty raises a problem for the moral theory, as the problem dissipates if no one genuinely pursues cruelty for its own sake. The second way of avoiding the problem involves a gesture to a system of values outside the laws of nature. Hobbes describes the behavior of societies in the state of nature whose members support themselves by raiding other cities. While they do not live by the laws of nature, and they consider it honorable to "robbe and spoyle one another," their code of honor leads them to "abstain from cruelty, leaving to men their lives, and instruments of husbandry" (Hobbes 2012, 254–6;

1651, 85). The thought here is that the revulsion toward pure cruelty stems from considerations of honor apart from concerns about the conditions of peace.

As for the requirement to keep faith even in war, Hobbes is inconsistent. On the one hand, he employs sweeping formulations to the effect that no covenants are valid in war. For instance, he argues that, because covenants are invalid when one party fears the other will not perform, "the Validity of Covenants begins not but with the Constitution of a Civill Power, sufficient to compell men to keep them" (Hobbes 2012, 220; 1651, 72). On the other hand, when describing specific cases, Hobbes treats at least some covenants made during war as valid. For example, he claims that prisoners of war who are freed on the condition that they pay a ransom "are obliged to pay it" and that princes are "bound to keep" disadvantageous treaties made with stronger powers (Hobbes 2012, 212; 1651, 69). In addition, in the reply to the Foole, Hobbes imagines that the Foole lives in a condition of war and belongs to a confederacy whose members agree to defend one another. While the other members of the confederacy have "performed already," presumably by fighting on behalf of the confederacy, the Foole proposes to break the covenant for his own benefit. Hobbes takes it for granted that the covenant among the members of the confederacy would be valid, despite the fact that they are in a "condition of Warre, wherein every man to every man ... is an Enemy," and argues that the Foole would be irrational to break the convenant and risk being expelled to fend for himself (Hobbes 2012, 224; 1651, 73).

The conditional thesis is not the source of Hobbes's problem with covenants. As Donagan's history of the civil war shows, the practice of keeping faith was sustained by expectations of reciprocity. In Hobbes's case of the Foole, all of the other members of the defensive confederacy have done their part. If they had no expectation that covenants would be kept, after all, the Foole would not be expelled for his duplicity. Here the problem concerns the relationship between the value thesis and the conditional thesis. Hobbes's basic strategy is to move from the thesis that the laws of nature are valuable because they produce peace to the conclusion that there is no point to complying with them when peace cannot be had. But Hobbes's own examples show that there is a point to following the laws of nature governing covenants during war. Doing so makes possible a variety of mutually beneficial exchanges: prisoners can buy their freedom and defensive confederacies can be formed. This does not threaten Hobbes's larger project, as he can plausibly maintain that covenants are not reliable enough to end war in the state of nature even if they can sometimes function during war. But it does suggest that the connection between the two theses is not as tight as he makes it out to be.

10.3 Analytical Arguments for the Minimalist Theory

This section argues that Hobbes accomplishes two important goals with the minimalist theory. He uses it to explain the value of the state, and he presents it as an alternative to Aristotle's theory of justice.

The first argument begins with the observation that Hobbes is principally concerned with political philosophy. Why does he have a moral theory at all? The answer is that Hobbes uses the minimalist moral theory to show that the moral rules we take for granted do not accomplish their purpose outside the state. The laws of nature are mostly commonplace rules, and Hobbes's claim that they play an important role in keeping the peace is, while not obvious, not surprising. What is original about Hobbes's moral theory is its contention that many familiar moral rules would not play their accustomed role in social life if they were not backed by the state's power. He argues that people will not keep the covenants establishing property rules and nonaggression pacts when there is little assurance that the others will do their part. If these covenants are ineffective, the causes of war will remain unchecked, and there will be little point in the other laws of nature, whose purpose is to preserve the peace.

The need for the state to create an environment in which the laws of nature can function is explained in a celebrated passage:

> For the Lawes of Nature ... of themselves, without the terrour of some Power, to cause them to be observed, are contrary to our naturall Passions .... And Covenants, without the Sword, are but Words, and of no strength to secure a man at all. Therefore notwithstanding the Lawes of Nature, (which every one hath then kept, when he has the will to keep them, when he can do it safely,) if there be no Power erected, or not great enough for our security; every man will, and may lawfully rely on his own strength and art, for caution against all other men. (Hobbes 2012, 254; 1651, 85)

Hobbes implicitly identifies two classes of people: those who are unwilling to obey the laws of nature and those who are willing to abide by them if they can do so safely. Some people will not be content with peace and order. Those who are needy, audacious, or ambitious for military command will find conflict to their advantage even in a peaceful society (Hobbes 2012, 152; 1651, 48). However, most people living in a peaceful society will find it in their interests to comply with the laws of nature. They will take up the arts of peace, such as farming, commerce, navigation, and building, and so will have neither the skills nor the desire to devote their lives to war. They will keep the laws of nature if they can do so safely because doing so is more convenient for them. When they are tempted to cut corners, the threat of punishment will deter them from doing so. Hobbes's idea is that the state forces those in the first class to comply with the laws and convinces those in the second class that compliance will be safe. With deterrence and assurance in place, social life can be governed by the laws of nature. Without the state, the laws of nature will not play a significant role in social life, and there will be no peace.[2]

Hobbes's moral theory makes the case for the state because it holds that social life governed by the laws of nature is available only within the state. His political theory, in turn, fills a gap in the moral theory by explaining why people would be motivated to comply with the laws of nature. This gap exists because neither of the theses in the minimalist moral theory gives a satisfying answer to that question. The value thesis says that the laws of nature are valued as the means to peace. However, an individual's behavior will rarely make a noticeable difference between peace or war. From the individual's perspective, it is good if everyone else follows the laws of nature to produce peace, but it does not follow that it is necessarily good to follow the laws of nature oneself. If others do not follow the laws of nature, then there is no point in doing so oneself. The conditional thesis does not speak to the question either, as it only proposes a necessary condition, namely, that compliance with the laws of nature makes sense only when others comply. Hobbes does assert that individuals are required to comply with the laws of nature when others do (see Hobbes 2012, 240; 1651, 79). However, neither thesis in the minimalist moral theory explains why that would make sense from the individual's perspective. Hobbes uses his political theory to answer this question rather than his moral theory when he contends that the combination of deterrence and reassurance provided by the state fills the motivational gap left by the minimalist moral theory.

In addition to supporting Hobbes's political theory, the minimalist theory presents an alternative to Aristotle's theory of justice. Specifically, it enables Hobbes to distinguish his views from Aristotle's on two points: Aristotle's individualism and his claim that justice is a mean state. This would be another significant accomplishment from Hobbes's perspective.

Aristotle's theory concerns justice as a quality of an individual person. He takes it as evident that "all men mean by justice that kind of state which makes people disposed to do what is just and makes them act justly and wish for what is just; and similarly by injustice that state which makes them act unjustly and wish for what is unjust" (Aristotle 1984a, 1129a9–11). Specifically, Aristotle theorizes that injustice is motivated by "that pleasure that arises from gain" with respect to three kinds of goods: honor, money, and safety (Aristotle 1984a, 1130b1). Justice, on the other hand, consists in the disposition to distribute good and bad things according to a complex scheme of equality. Aristotle distinguishes between what he calls distributive justice, rectificatory justice, and reciprocity; he argues that each species of justice aims at achieving distinct kinds of equality. Distributive justice, for Aristotle, concerns the distribution of what he calls common goods such as honors and money. The just person distributes these goods in proportion to the recipients' merit, so that the ratio of goods to merit is equal for everyone (Aristotle 1984a, V.3). Rectificatory justice addresses private injustices. For example, a theft creates an imbalance between the thief, who has too much, and his victim, who has too little. A judge will attempt to restore the two parties to an equal footing by taking away the thief's gain and returning the victim's loss (Aristotle 1984a, V.4). In the case of reciprocity, Aristotle thinks it is important to show that exchanges are equal, such that each side gets as much as it gave up (Aristotle 1984a, V.5). The point of this complex theory of equality is to show that justice conforms to Aristotle's theory that every virtue can be characterized as a mean state between two extremes. In the case of justice, the various kinds of equality are described as intermediate between some having too much and others having too little. The just person's dispositions occupy a mean between extremes, he says, because they aim at producing these intermediate results while avoiding the extremes.

Hobbes uses the conditional thesis to dispute Aristotle's individualism. As noted above, Aristotle thinks that injustice arises from desires for three goods: money, safety, and honor. Hobbes argues that conflict in the state of nature is due to the pursuit of the same three things: gain in the competition for scarce goods, safety, and reputation (Hobbes 2012, 192; 1651, 62). But Hobbes does not think that the desires for these goods can be just or unjust on their own. He writes that "Justice, and Injustice are none of the Faculties neither of the Body, nor Mind," as they are "Qualities, that relate to men in Society, not in Solitude" (Hobbes 2012, 196; 1651, 63). In the state of nature, the desires for gain, safety, and honor are excessive in the sense that they are the source of war. However, Hobbes denies that there is anything faulty about the individuals who have these desires. On the contrary, it is entirely appropriate in these circumstances to want as much of these things as can be acquired. According to the conditional thesis, it makes sense to follow the laws of nature and limit one's acquisitiveness only if others do the same. Given that, the character traits of an individual could be just in some circumstances and unjust in others. Since that is so, Hobbes believes, Aristotle has not identified the fundamental nature of justice.

Hobbes's value thesis is aimed at Aristotle's doctrine of the mean. After beginning his moral theory with Aristotle's three goods, Hobbes's discussion of the laws of nature largely parallels Aristotle's account of justice in the *Nicomachean Ethics*. The topics that both authors cover include: the distinction between being a just or unjust person and doing particular just or unjust actions; whether it is possible to be voluntarily unjust to oneself; the distinction between distributive justice and reciprocity ("commutative justice" for Hobbes); gratitude; retribution; whether some people naturally merit political power more than others; equity; and the use of arbitrators.[3] At the conclusion of this survey, Hobbes declares that he has presented the "true and onely Moral Philosophy" (Hobbes 2012, 242; 1651, 79). He notes that all moral philosophies identify the same virtues and vices. However, he says, others have not seen that these virtues are "praised, as the meanes of peaceable, sociable, and comfortable living"; they instead "place them in a mediocrity of passions" (Hobbes 2012, 242; 1651, 80). While Hobbes is clearly referring to Aristotle's doctrine of the mean, I do not think he is saying that Aristotle maintained that the virtues are valuable because they aim at a mean. His point is rather that his theory identifies something important about the laws of nature while Aristotle's doctrine of the mean does not.

10.4 Comparison with Other Interpretations

The best case for the minimalist interpretation is that it shows how Hobbes can accomplish his most important goals without requiring elaborate analyses of the text or its arguments. Other interpretations hold that Hobbes had different, and usually more ambitious, aims for his moral philosophy. I only contend that the minimalist interpretation captures the central thrust of Hobbes's theory. I do not mean to deny that he might have had aspirations for his moral theory in addition to the ones that I have identified. Nonetheless, in this section I wish to explain why I am reluctant to embrace two less minimal interpretations.

On one common interpretation, Hobbes's aim is to reconcile the demands of morality and self-interest. In his moral theory, according to this interpretation, Hobbes tries to show that compliance with the moral rules is dictated by the rational pursuit of one's own interests (see Darwall 1995, chap. 3 and Kavka 1986, chap. 9). This is so, it is said, because obeying the laws of nature is necessary for peace and everyone's interests are best served by peace. Hobbes certainly thinks that it is important that obeying the laws of nature serves our interests, generally speaking. He says as much in the value thesis. However, there are significant difficulties with a moral theory that tries to show that it is always in everyone's interests to do what the laws of nature require. First, while the laws of nature are generally valued because they produce peace, peace does not serve everyone's interests. As noted earlier, Hobbes identifies several classes of people whose interests are best served by war.[4] Furthermore, those who do value peace know that their actions do not make a significant difference between peace and war. The state is needed to tip the motivational balance towards compliance. Finally, Hobbes's most sustained argument for the conclusion that obeying the moral rules best serves the individual's interests is the reply to the Foole. The Foole's immorality is said to be unwise because his confederates will expel him from their defensive alliance, putting his life at risk (Hobbes 2012, 224; 1651, 73). However, they might also reward him for immoral behavior, such as cheating those outside their confederation. Among other things, a Foole who burns his bridges with outsiders will have to stay on good terms with the insiders, as he will have nowhere else to go. So even this argument will only show that compliance with moral rules can sometimes promote an individual's interests; it does not show that it always does so.

There is also a textual objection concerning Hobbes's aims. As Gregory Kavka reads him, Hobbes's "primary aim is to make the traditional moral virtues—justice, equity, and so on—attractive to his fellows, whom he views as (at best) predominant egoists" (Kavka 1986, 383). However, that is not how Hobbes characterizes his project. He says that his theory is the only one that explains how the virtues "come to be praised," namely, "as the meanes of peaceable, sociable, and comfortable living" (Hobbes 2012, 242; 1651, 80). The question that Hobbes thinks he answers is not, "How can we convince those who do not care about the laws of nature to change their minds?" Rather, the question is, "What best explains why we value the laws of nature as we do?" On the minimalist interpretation, the assumption that the laws of nature are held in high esteem is used to make Hobbes's case for the state. The state is said to be good because the laws of nature are good when they are effective, and the state makes the laws of nature effective. By contrast, showing that egoists benefit from following the laws of nature would not help Hobbes to make a case for the state. A theory addressed to them would try to show that they benefit from complying with the state. Whether this is so presumably depends on how effective any particular state is. Whether egoists benefit from keeping the moral rules would be a separate, and secondary, question.

The other alternative that I will discuss is S. A. Lloyd's reciprocity interpretation. Lloyd reads Hobbes as showing that a specific kind of reciprocity is a requirement of reason and then using this conception of reciprocity as the basis for a theory of the laws of nature. Reciprocity, as Lloyd understands it, involves consistency. If Able judges that Baker is wrong to do acts of type T, then Able must judge that it would be wrong for Able himself to do acts of type T (Lloyd 2009, 4). She contends that this reciprocity requirement forms the core of all of the laws of nature, and she uses it to account for Hobbes's views on a wide variety of topics, including the right of nature, the duty to submit to government, the powers of government, the liberties of subjects, and the duties of sovereigns.

I will look at one part of Lloyd's interpretation, namely, her contention that there is a duty to submit to government. On the minimalist interpretation, the laws of nature would not condemn individuals for failing to pursue peace if the other members of their society do not do so. Thus people in the state of nature do not violate the laws of nature even if they are at war with one another. On Lloyd's reciprocity interpretation, by contrast, Hobbes aims to show that there is a natural-law duty to leave the state of nature and submit to political authority. Life in the state of nature, on her understanding of Hobbes, is not just undesirable but immoral.

Hobbes's argument for the natural duty to submit to the state, as Lloyd understands it, is complex. The part of the argument I will discuss has three steps. The first step maintains that rational agents must desire peace, that is, they must desire that others behave peacefully. The argument for this step holds that rational agents must desire peace. Where war is pervasive, people cannot reliably control the resources they need to achieve their aims and so, according to the argument, they must all "see themselves as lacking the power needed to exercise effective agency *no matter what their particular ends*" (Lloyd 2009, 245). Since one mark of rationality is securing the necessary means to achieve one's ends, a rational agent must value peace. The second step of the argument moves from the value rational agents must put on peace to their evaluations of the behavior of other people. A society will be at peace only if a critical portion of its members act peacefully, and so the rational agent is committed to insisting that others do so. The third step applies the judgments rational agents make about others to their own behavior. Hobbes's theory of the laws of nature, according to Lloyd, is that they spell out the implications of a reciprocity theorem, according to which it is unreasonable to do the kinds of things that one blames others for doing. The agents who find fault in those who do not seek peace are thus required to seek peace themselves as a matter of consistency. Because peace can be secured only under a state, it follows that the law of nature requires people to quit the state of nature and submit to political authority (Lloyd 2009, 249).

It is important for the argument that the evaluations in the second step are moral ones. When rational agents insist that others submit to the state, they mean that this is mandatory and not just something that they would like to happen. The reciprocity theorem holds that we must apply our evaluations of others to ourselves. In order to yield the conclusion that the rational agent has a duty to submit to the state in the third step, the agent's thought in the second step has to be that others have a duty to submit.

The minimalist and reciprocity interpretations agree that the laws of nature require individuals to seek peace if it is available. They also agree that submission is required only when others are willing to submit as well. After all, if the bulk of a society was unwilling to live under a state, it is hard to see how there could be a government to submit to in the first place. The interpretations differ in two ways. First, the minimalist interpretation does not treat the natural-law duty to seek peace as a central part of Hobbes's case for the state. Second, on the minimalist interpretation, Hobbes does not attempt to show that rational agents are committed to acting morally.

Lloyd makes a formidable case for her interpretation by describing a line of argument that appears to run through a wide array of topics in Hobbes's moral and political philosophy. Her interpretation's ability to bring unity to Hobbes's thought is a powerful consideration in its favor. This particular argument, however, is open to question on both textual and analytical grounds.

The textual objection is that Hobbes does not seem to have been interested in showing that the laws of nature require submission to the state. When he summarizes his argument at various points in *Leviathan*, he refers to what people hope to avoid or to gain by leaving the state of nature rather than what reason or duty require. For example, Hobbes describes the motivation to leave the state of nature like this: "The Passions that encline men to Peace, are Feare of Death; Desire of such things as are necessary to commodious living; and a Hope by their Industry to obtain them" (Hobbes 2012, 196; 1651, 63). Bishop Bramhall criticizes Hobbes on this point. According to Bramhall, "Those rays of heavenly light ... which God himself hath imprinted in the heart of man, are more efficacious towards preservation of a society" than Hobbes's social contract. In reply, Hobbes first notes that the heavenly light imprinted in the heart of man means "natural reason." He then tartly asks whether Bramhall hopes "to make any wise man believe, that when this nation very lately was an anarchy, and dissolute multitude of men, doing every one what his own reason or imprinted light suggested, they did again out of the same light call in the king, and peace again, and ask pardon for the faults, which that their illumination had brought them into, rather than out of fear of perpetual danger and hope of preservation?" (EW IV.286–7). Hobbes's tone does not suggest that he put much stock in the project of showing that reason and the laws of nature require submission to the state.

There is also reason to doubt one of the moves in the argument for the conclusion that reason and natural duty require submission to the state. I have added bracketed numbers to identify the three stages of the argument as Lloyd recounts it.

> Supposing Hobbes's substantive argument is sound, it follows that *if* we are *rational agents*, we ought to be willing to join into a scheme of reciprocal universal restriction of the scope of private judgment. [1] Unless others join such a scheme, our agency will be thwarted, [2] thus as agents, we must insist that they join; and [3] reason forbids us to fault them for not joining unless we will join ourselves, thus as rational, we must join. (Lloyd 2009, 249)

The movement from the second point to the third is unobjectionable. Those who insist that others do something cannot consistently refuse to do the same themselves. The move from the first step to the second, however, is open to question. The first step maintains that there are things that people need in order to be effective agents; in this case, what each rational agent needs is everyone else's peaceful submission to the state's authority. The second step involves a moral evaluation: the rational agent *insists* that others submit and blames them if they fail to do so. The move from needing something to insisting on having it is a natural one to make, but it is not one that must be made as a matter of rationality. I do not have to insist that I get what I need or find fault with those whose actions prevent me from getting what I need. For example, I might need a kidney transplant to survive. My being alive is surely necessary for me to be an effective agent, but I would not be irrational if I did not insist that you give me one of yours. We are not rationally required to use moral concepts even in cases like these. If the move from the first step to the second is not rationally required, however, the argument does not show that the duty to submit to the state is one that rational agents must accept.

There is indirect evidence that Hobbes would have agreed with this objection. Earlier in this chapter noted Hobbes's discussion of people who do not live by the laws of nature but nonetheless abstain from cruelty (Hobbes 2012, 254–6; 1651, 85). Hobbes is clearly copying a passage in Thucydides that describes behavior of earlier Greek societies. Thucydides's point is that these people, who lived by raiding others, were regarded positively in their own milieu. Here is the relevant passage in Hobbes's translation:

> For the Grecians in old time ... became thieves and went abroad under the conduct of their most puissant men, both to enrich themselves and to fetch in maintenance for the weak, and falling upon towns unfortified and scatteringly inhabited, rifled them and made this the best means of their living, being a matter at that time nowhere in disgrace but rather carrying with it something of glory. This is manifest by some that dwell on the continent, amongst whom, so it be performed nobly, it is still esteemed as an ornament. The same also is proved by some of the ancient poets, who introduce men questioning of such as sail by... whether they be thieves or not, as a thing neither scorned by such as were asked nor upbraided by those that were desirous to know. (Thucydides [1628] 1989, 3–4)

Those who lived in coastal towns did not blame the thieves or insist that they give up raiding. On the contrary, they regarded thievery as an occupation like farming. In the society Thucydides describes, people do not blame those who violate the laws of nature, even when the violations come at their expense. When Hobbes discusses this passage in *Leviathan*, he draws a parallel with international relations and says that states "justly" seek to subdue their neighbors "and are remembered for it in after ages with honour" (Hobbes 2012, 256; 1651, 85). That strongly suggests he regards Thucydides's observation as accurate.

Hobbes maintains that life under the laws of nature is better than life under the codes of honor that the thieves live by. A society whose members generally follow the laws of nature will enjoy all the fruits of peace: industry, agriculture, trade, building, public projects, knowledge, arts, literature, and freedom from the fear of violent death at the hands of one's neighbor (Hobbes 2012, 192; 1651, 62). Hobbes's theory is that this life is available only within the state. That is a compelling argument for the state even if it is not one that any rational agent would have to accept.

10.5 Conclusion

Hobbes's minimalist moral theory consists of the value and conditional theses. It is a substantial moral theory in its own right as the two theses are plausible without being platitudinous. The most important feature of the minimalist theory is that it supports Hobbes's case for the state. Hobbes argues that the state is desirable because social life governed by the laws of nature is desirable and that this is only possible under the coercive power of the state. More ambitious interpretations set a higher bar for the moral theory to clear in order to succeed. While it would be rash to dismiss them, one advantage of the minimalist theory is that it shows how Hobbes can accomplish some of his most important aims without running the risk of putting more weight on his moral theory than it can bear.

Notes

1 Hobbes proposes an alternative definition of cruelty as "*Contempt*, or little sense of the calamity of others" (Hobbes 2012, 90; 1651, 27). The cruel person, on this definition, is unmoved by the suffering of others rather than taking pleasure in it.
2 There is a third class that cuts across the other two: those who are primarily concerned with following what they take to be God's will. Since threats of earthly punishment have little effect on them, Hobbes believes the state has to have control over the religious institutions that shape their beliefs.
3 Compare the fifteenth chapter of *Leviathan* (Hobbes 2012, 226–38; 1651, 74–8) with the fifth book of the *Nicomachean Ethics* (Aristotle 1984a, V.3–11). For the point about merit and political power, Hobbes refers to Aristotle's *Politics* (1984b, I.5–6).
4 Lloyd has a more extensive discussion of these kinds of cases (2009, 121–8).

References

Aristotle. 1984a. "Nicomachean Ethics." Translated by William D. Ross and James O. Urmson. In *The Complete Works of Aristotle*, Vol. 2, edited by Jonathan Barnes, 1729–1867. Princeton, NJ: Princeton University Press.

Aristotle. 1984b. "Politics." Translated by Benjamin Jowett. In *The Complete Works of Aristotle*, Vol. 2, edited by Jonathan Barnes, 1986–2129. Princeton, NJ: Princeton University Press.

Byron, Michael. 2015. *Submission and Subjection in Leviathan: Good Subjects in the Hobbesian Commonwealth*. New York: Palgrave Macmillan. Doi:10.1057/9781137535290.

Darwall, Stephen L. 1995. *The British Moralists and the Internal 'Ought': 1640–1740*. Cambridge: Cambridge University Press. Doi:10.1017/CBO9780511608957.

Donagan, Barbara. 2008. *War in England 1642–1649*. Oxford: Oxford University Press. Doi:10.1093/acprof:oso/9780199285181.001.0001.

Gert, Bernard. 2010. *Hobbes: Prince of Peace*. Cambridge: Polity Press.

Hampton, Jean. 1986. *Hobbes and the Social Contract Tradition*. Cambridge: Cambridge University Press. Doi:10.1017/CBO9780511625060.

Hobbes, Thomas. 1839–1845. *The English Works of Thomas Hobbes of Malmesbury*, 11 vols., edited by William Molesworth. London: J. Bohn. Cited as EW in the text.

Hobbes, Thomas. [1647] 1998. *On the Citizen*, edited and translated by Richard Tuck and Michael Silverthorne. Cambridge: Cambridge University Press. Doi:10.1017/CBO9780511808173.

Hobbes, Thomas. [1651] 2012. *Leviathan*, 3 vols. edited by Noel Malcolm. Oxford: Clarendon Press.

Kavka, Gregory. 1986. *Hobbesian Moral and Political Theory*. Princeton, NJ: Princeton University Press.

Lloyd, Sharon A. 2009. *Morality in the Philosophy of Thomas Hobbes: Cases in the Law of Nature*. Cambridge: Cambridge University Press. Doi:10.1017/CBO9780511596759.

Martinich, Aloysius P. 1992. *The Two Gods of Leviathan: Thomas Hobbes on Religion and Politics*. Cambridge: Cambridge University Press. Doi:10.1017/CBO9780511624810.

Taylor, Alfred E. 1938. "The Ethical Doctrine of Hobbes." *Philosophy* 13 (52): 406–24. https://www.jstor.org/stable/3746387.

Thucydides. [1629] 1989. *The Peloponnesian War: The Complete Hobbes Translation*, edited by David Grene, translated by Thomas Hobbes. Chicago, IL: University of Chicago Press.

Warrender, Howard. 1957. *The Political Philosophy of Hobbes: His Theory of Obligation*. Oxford: Clarendon Press.

Part III

Civil Philosophy

11

Hobbesian Persons and Representation

MÓNICA BRITO VIEIRA

In *Leviathan* (1651), Hobbes offers a novel conceptualization of the modern representative state as an incorporated person empowered to act on our behalf, but also *in our name*.[1] This made any state's pronouncements or actions ours and ours to bear. Insofar as the sovereign represents us both singularly and collectively, Hobbes combines true representation and representation by fiction in the making of the modern representative state. This chapter examines how this is done and to what effect.

> Of Persons
>
> A PERSON, is he, *whose words and actions are considered, either as his own, or as representing the words or actions of an other man, or of any other thing to whom they are attributed, whether Truly or by Fiction.*
>
> When they are considered as his owne, then is he called a *Naturall Person*: And when they are considered as representing the words and action of an other, then is he a *Feigned or Artificiall Person.* (Hobbes 2012, 244; 1651, 80)

To speak of a "person" is, for Hobbes, to speak of agency, or the capacity to speak and act. We can either speak and act for ourselves, as natural persons, or speak and act for others, as artificial persons. The artifice of artificial persons consists in the fact that they do not address others as themselves (that is, in their own person) but as representing someone or something else (that is, in the person of another). One should be cautious, however, of taking natural persons as devoid of artifice. For Hobbes, a "person" is always already of the order of artefact: their actions are acts of representation, either of themself or another.

Hobbes's adoption, in the English *Leviathan* (1651), of a broad and elastic concept of person as an agent capable of speech and action marks a departure from his earlier works. In both *The Elements of Law* (1640) and *De cive* (1642) Hobbes had worked with a distinctively juristic understanding of "person"; with "person" referring in those

A Companion to Hobbes, First Edition. Edited by Marcus P. Adams.

works to an entity recognized by the law as a subject of rights and obligations, typically a civil person. In *Leviathan*, the natural habitat of the person shifts from law to theater. "Person," we are told, originally referred to the "*outward appearance* of man, counterfeited on the Stage" (Hobbes 2012, 244; 1651, 80). Stage actors, when constructing *dramatis personae*, commodify their verbal and gestural outputs. Words and actions are also the "outward appearances" that make up the Hobbesian person. Similar to commodities, they are amenable to transferral. This makes it possible for one and the same words and actions to have a distinct *causal* and *moral* source. For instance, in some jurisdictions, one can marry by proxy by making oneself represented by another, often a family member. And insofar as words and actions may be correctly attributable to one person (*moral* cause) on the basis of the words and actions of another person (*causal* source), the need arises "to consider" to whom or what responsibility for the observed words and actions is to be assigned.

The root meaning of "to consider," the specific verb employed by Hobbes, is to believe someone or something to be, or think of them or it, as being something. The broader outlook of "person" in the English *Leviathan* becomes, if anything, more apparent once one recognizes that the perspective from which words and actions may be attributed ranges from social conventions, and theatrical conventions, to legal conventions. In patriarchal civil societies, men are understood to represent women and children in the wider society. In the theater, most spectators are familiar with the conventions of drama, such that when they hear the words "To be, or not to be: that is the question" on the stage, they consider them correctly attributable to Hamlet. Legal conventions are especially designed to add certainty to beliefs about action attribution. In Hobbes's time, questions of ownership and responsibility for common performative acts, such as entering contracts, were part and parcel of "an increasingly placeless and timeless market," in which "new and often elusive forms of exchange" depended on forms of surrogate agency and the legal fictions being developed to authorize them (Agnew 1986, x and 58). As such, it is not surprising to find that the technical meaning of "to consider" was "to understand as in the view or sense of the law; to construe, to hold legally."[2]

But law – and in particular the fictions of legal personality it sustained – was only one of the artifices that men used to expand agency. In *Leviathan*, Hobbes's conceptualization of men as artificers capable of fashioning a social and political world that best suits their needs led him to turn instead to the person's theatrical origins and their defining performative powers: "So that a *Person*, is the same that an *Actor* is, both on the Stage and in common Conversation" (Hobbes 2012, 244; 1651, 80). Persons are actors. In acting, they do things either in their own name (or their own person) or in the name (or person) of someone or something else. For to "*Personate*, is to *Act*, or *Represent* himselfe, or an other" (Malcolm 2002, 244). The notion of self-representation might first strike us as odd. And it is indeed unusual: it did not and still does not belong to the primary meaning of "to personate."[3] But it was not unfamiliar to Hobbes, nor frivolously used by him.[4] For it is precisely because we are self-representors that we are able to have ourselves represented (or personated) collectively *in* and *by* multiple corporate persons, or systems constituted by representation, from states (the primary human association, and the only one representing us unconditionally), and trading companies, to families.

The word "person," Hobbes further explains, was derived from the Latin word *persona*, which originally designated the mask worn by an actor on the stage. This definition of the "person" by reference to the mask, the social role, or the *persona*, is Ciceronian, and merits particular attention, since, as I have noted elsewhere, it inscribes a lasting ambiguity into the Hobbesian notion of person (Brito Vieira 2009, 168–9). The ambiguity emerges in the following way. Hobbes's person is literally the mask "counterfeited on the Stage" and by extension "an Actor," that is, "a *Representer*, or *Representative*" (Hobbes 2012, 244; 1651, 81). The chain of equivalences advanced by Hobbes – person/mask/actor/representative – is meant to be seamless, but it invites an immediate question: after all, the theatrical mask is not the actor or representative, but that which the actor represents. To be more specific, the mask is/signifies the *persona*, that is, the impersonated (fictional) role or character adopted by the actor on stage.

Hence, while, in chapter 16 of *Leviathan*, Hobbes explicitly defines the person as "an *Actor*" (or representative), the person's root meaning as the theatrical mask opens up to the possibility that the person might (also) be the represented (that is, the *persona*). In effect, if one takes a closer look at that chapter, one sees that person is already being used to refer *both* to the representative and to that which is being represented (the *persona*). Upon reflection this much seems to be entailed by Hobbes's basic understanding of person as a capacity for agency, and his treatment of representation as a matter of conferring agency *via* personation, or *via* – to use the Ciceronian expression Hobbes himself adopts – "bearing the person of." To personate is for X to represent Y as (if) an agent, or the source of words and actions – that is, as a person – and X is the same person *qua* representer as Y is *qua* representee (Abizadeh 2013, 923). Hence, as chapter 16 draws to a close, and Hobbes expounds the process of incorporation whereby the state is generated, he does not hesitate in using person to designate both the party being represented and the representative: the multitude of men found in nature are "made *One* Person [the person of the commonwealth], when they are by one man, or one Person, Represented [the person of the sovereign]" (Hobbes 2012, 248; 1651, 82). If there are any doubts about Hobbes's interchangeable use of the term "person," then chapter 42 dissuades them. For there, in an explicit cross-reference to chapter 16, "person" comes to be defined as "that which is Represented by another" (Hobbes 2012, 776; 1651, 268). The cross-reference has sometimes been dismissed as a glitch, but as I have argued elsewhere (Brito Vieira 2009, 168), I think Hobbes means exactly what he says: that there is an identification between representer and representee in the register of representation.[5] Peter and John are different natural persons. But if Peter gives John powers of attorney to purchase a house for him, then in negotiating and sealing the real estate contract John is the same person as representative as Peter is as represented. To return to the theater, actor and character are surely different persons (say, Kenneth Branagh and Hamlet, respectively). But the play – its roles and characters – properly exists first and only when they are played, and for the play's duration Kenneth Branagh is the same person as *representer* as Hamlet is as *representee*. It happens similarly with the state: sovereigns are not identical to the one incorporated person they bear. However, while in power the sovereign *qua* representative is the same person as the state *qua representee*.[6]

11.1 Of Authors, Actors and Authorization

The Hobbesian term "person" refers, in its most fundamental sense, to the capacity for agency. A twofold division thus emerges. Natural persons are persons whose words and actions are considered their own. Artificial persons are persons whose words and actions are considered as representing the words and actions of someone or something else, that is, artificial persons are representatives. Having established that artificial persons are representatives, Hobbes explains that the attribution of words and actions to someone/something other than the performing agent can be made either truly or by fiction.[7] True attribution occurs when the entity represented has authorized its representation, which means that that entity is an author meeting the conditions of moral and legal responsibility, and has ownership of the words and actions uttered and undertaken in their name. By contrast, attribution by fiction occurs when the represented party cannot authorize its representation, but the actions of the representative are nonetheless held (by fiction) to be its own.

As the distinction between true representation and representation by fiction shows, at the core of Hobbes's theory of representation lie the notions of authorization and attributed action. Hobbes articulates these notions with reference to the simpler agency relationship, true representation:

> Of Persons Artificiall, some have their words and actions *Owned* by those whom they represent. And then the Person is the *Actor*; and he that owneth his words and actions, is the AUTHOR: In which case the Actor acteth by Authority. For that which in speaking of goods and possessions, is called an *Owner*, and in latine *Dominus*, in Greek Kurios, speaking of Actions, is called an Author. And as the Right of possession, is called Dominion; so the Right of doing any Action, is called AUTHORITY. So that by Authority, is always understood a Right of doing any act: and *done by Authority*, done by Commission, or Licence from him whose right it is. (Hobbes 2012, 244; 1651, 81)

Artificial persons are persons whose actions are attributed to the person being represented. True attribution occurs when the representative has been authorized by the person being represented and therefore the representative's actions are really owned by the represented. In naming the representative and the represented engaging in true representation Hobbes resorts, once again, to a theatrically suggestive language of actors and authors: "And then the [authorized] Person [Artificiall] is the *Actor*; and he that owneth his words and actions, is the AUTHOR" (Hobbes 2012, 244; 1651, 81). In the process, the meaning of authorization is being constructed, through an exploration of the ambiguity between two possible senses of "to own," in the proprietary sense and in the liability sense: the person who authorizes makes themself the *owner* of that which their selected representative does in their name (Green 2015, 27).

There is little doubt that, for Hobbes, to make oneself the owner of another's actions implies to take them upon oneself or accept responsibility for them. This means that authorization allows us to identify who is responsible for the action. This is no minor matter. Certainty about ownership of actions is a necessary condition for the development of trustworthy relationships. This is because it is integral to how contracts are made to work: the state must be known to compel ownership of actions, so that no one may simply disown actions correctly attributable to one on the basis of actions performed by others when consequences following from them are unfavorable. Should disowning be an ever-present possibility, trust sustaining contractual arrangements – and *civility* itself – would be at risk. This is a risk greatly diminished, but never fully eliminated, in the civil condition. For as societies grow more complex, such a risk – which was paramount in nature – re-emerges to the extent that demands for surrogate forms of agency increase. These inevitably raise concerns of "identity, intentionality, accountability, transparency and reciprocity" (Agnew 1986, 202), which must be assuaged by sturdy mechanisms for establishing and externally enforcing the ownership of words and actions: what may be considered an individual's own, and what must be considered another's. Even where these mechanisms are known to exist, however, one must make sure to take responsibility for one's own part in availing oneself of them, by, for instance, inspecting the signs of authority before entering any transactions. For, as Hobbes gloomily warns, if the actor is unauthorized, or acts beyond his authority, there can be no distribution of responsibility to another, so "he that maketh a Covenant with the Actor, or Representer, not knowing the authority he hath, doth it at his own perill" (Hobbes 2012, 246; 1651, 81).

While Hobbes is keen to stress that ownership of an action entails responsibility for that action, in the passage cited he quickly moves back from the understanding of ownership as owning up, or taking responsibility, to possessing *simpliciter*. The shift occurs through an extended analogy between ownership and authorship. An owner is the person who owns "goods and possessions," Hobbes tells us, and "an Author" is the person who owns actions (Hobbes 2012, 244; 1651, 81). Owning things, Hobbes tells us, presupposes having a "Right of possession," just as owning actions implies "the Right of doing any action," also called "AUTHORITY" (Hobbes 2012, 244; 1651, 81).

Goods and freedoms, so the suggestion goes, are "owned" in the same way, so that our "property" in intangibles similarly to our property in tangibles is mediated by a right. The analogy between authorship and ownership sounds somewhat strained, however, since, as Hobbes stresses, "there can be no Propriety, no Dominion, no *Mine* and *Thine* distinct" in nature (Hobbes 2012, 196; 1651, 63), and yet the unlimited "Right of doing any action" (Hobbes 2012, 244; 1651, 81) he refers to in the passage has the unlimited remit of action of the right of nature (see Hobbes 2012, 198; 1651, 64). It is true that the analogy gains some traction in light of the encompassing notion of property Hobbes embraces in chapter 18, extending to goods, words, and actions. But this refers specifically to the civil condition, where exclusion-from-a-thing is framed around exclusive liberties to use that thing or indeed to do that action without being interfered with by others (Hobbes 2012, 274; 1651, 92). Since in the civil condition we have property in actions protected by exclusive rights, we can extend one such right in the sense of a liberty to a representative, and it then makes sense to say that we have property in what the representative does when acting on our extended right. Yet there are no such rights in nature, and if most of the sovereign's rights are exclusive liberties, it is because we take on an obligation not to interfere by laying down our right to the same (Green 2015, 32–3). Returning to chapter 16, however, the fact remains that Hobbes is intent on drawing an isomorphism between the way we relate to possessions and the way in which we relate to actions as "things" we possess or have a claim to grounded on a right. This has a new implication for our understanding of authorization.

Authorizing actions implies not one, but two things: as we have previously seen, it implies taking on responsibility for actions, which presupposes holding the power and capacities necessary for moral/legal responsibility; but as it has now been clarified, it also implies having or possessing a right to that action in the first instance. This much is spelled out by Hobbes in the conclusion he draws from the property analogy: "So that by Authority, is always understood a Right of doing any act; and *done by Authority*, done by Commission, or Licence from him whose right it is"[8] (Hobbes 2012, 244; 1651, 81).

Hobbes's conclusion, that to act by another's authority is to act on a right originally belonging to that other, supports the reading of authorization as an act extending rights to the representative (Brito Vieira 2009, 152; Copp 1980, 586; Gauthier 1969, 124; Skinner 1999, 9). This reading entails that: 1) an actor who has been authorized acts with the relevant right from the author; (2) who must therefore have owned that right in the first instance; and 3) that it is because of this original ownership that the author whose right it is must *own up to* what that other does when acting on his right. Even though Hobbes runs the notions of authorship and ownership close together, to the point of making them virtually indistinct, this reference to an original right is necessary to carry over the distinctive idea of "authorship": that is, of the author as he who is the originator *of* – or he who gives existence *to* – the actions in question.

It is, of course, true that the reading of authorization as extending rights, rather than simply establishing ownership, seems to present insurmountable difficulties, most notably that of how to reconcile the authorization and alienation clauses of the covenant instituting the commonwealth, "*I Authorise and give up my Right of Governing my selfe*" (Hobbes 2012, 260; 1651, 87). After all, it makes no sense to extend a right one has just alienated.[9] In addition to this, the right available for extending on the part of the multitude of natural persons instituting the commonwealth, their natural right of self-government, is not only the right being laid down, but is also a right that the sovereign does not need to acquire *via* extension, as, not being a party to the covenant, it preserves it intact.[10] But there might be a way to, at least partly, address the inconsistency. To act by authority, one must have been authorized, or granted a license or commission, by the person or persons who possessed the right to act themselves. In normal cases of authorization, the receipt of such a commission is *not* equivalent to the acquisition of the transferred right, since it involves no renunciation or transfer, in Hobbes's technical sense. In other words, there is no alienation, but merely a "lease." A caretaker I employed to look after my house, enters it on my right, but I can still enter it too, and will take away the right from my employee once the work is over. But commissioning takes a different form in the social contract. In this case, authorization is necessarily without stint: unlimited in remit and non-revocable. As such, then and only then, "the receipt of such a commission must be equivalent to the *acquisition* of the transferred right of performing the action" (Skinner 1999, 9; emphasis added). Thus, even if the sovereign holds a right of the same extension, it is only now that he can be said to exercise it by the (irrevocable) authority of all the sovereign's subjects.

For those unconvinced by my proposed solution, the difficulties exposed above will lend credence to the contention that authorization is best understood as establishing mere ownership (or responsibility for) the sovereign's actions, without extending rights (Green 2015). But the textual evidence does not support this view. What is more, it is normally argued that the superiority of the authorization as ownership view lies in showing that it is possible to authorize and own (or bear responsibility for) actions that are unlawful or immoral (e.g., Hobbes 2012, 330; 1651, 110), that is, actions that one could not have a right to do. This is important because only then will the sovereign have been rendered unaccountable for a broad range of wrongs he might (have to) do (Green 2015, 39). In other words, in a Hobbesian commonwealth, responsibility must be fully removed from the "shoulders" of state and sovereign, to be placed strictly on the shoulders of citizens. Citizens must own *all* actions of the sovereign, including those they themselves lack the right to do, because they are wrong (or violate the law of nature), such as the punishment of the innocent, or are lawful and done with right but not with a right that citizens could have, such as the arbitrary seizure of property (Van Apeldoorn 2020, 56).[11] Even if the objective is to preserve the unrestrained freedom of the sovereign by releasing the sovereign from the burden of responsibility, as I agree it is, the alleged superiority of the authorization as ownership view in accommodating both types of action is not self-evident, since both would be authorized actions if the extended right by which the sovereign acts has an unlimited remit of action, such as is the case with the right of nature.[12]

What seems to be undeniable is that, in elaborating the notion of authorization in chapter 16 of *Leviathan*, Hobbes specifies that to authorize is to take on ownership *by* extending a right, and that he seems to want to say this specifically about the social contract, given his explicit reference to "the Right of doing any Action" (Hobbes 2012, 244; 1651, 81). Authorization as mere ownership might have been effective in immunizing the sovereign and lower officials from future complains from subjects (Green 2015, 38–46). It would even have sufficed to establish the state as a system of shared liability, distributing responsibility for the sovereign's actions across the members of the commonwealth. But Hobbes seems to have still found it wanting. A few reasons for this can be suggested. Hobbes did not want subjects to simply accept ownership of state's actions, even those that they might not have willed. He wanted them to consider themselves positively invested and actively implicated in a sovereign authority that they believed to exist by their rational acts of will. Hence, he made their continuing presence *in* the state activity manifest by suggesting that the state always acted by their authority, on their one fundamental right, "the Right of doing any Action," for the protection of their one most fundamental end, self-preservation. This was necessary because a right of *self*-government, allowing everyone sovereignty, was as complete as it was self-defeating, unless there were one sovereign representative, a *unitary* center of interpretation and enforcement of rights, shaping freedoms by means of laws and thus effectively protecting those freedoms from arbitrary interference. Their equal right to self-preservation would only be secure where a sovereign exercised it *for* them. The state's activity in the exercise of its members rights could therefore be justly considered to implicate their will at all times. It was as owners of those rights that citizens individually bore and mutually shared responsibility for what their state did on their behalf, and in their name.

11.2 Of the Person of the State

Hobbes never explicitly tells us what kind of person the state is (Runciman 2000, 274). Disagreement over the nature and person of the state has been common amongst interpreters. Although many have come to agree that Hobbes's state is best characterized as a person by fiction (Abizadeh 2013; Brito Vieira 2009; Newey 2014; Runciman 2000; Skinner 2007; Turner 2016), the argument has been recently advanced that this somewhat misconstrues Hobbes's theory (Olsthoorn 2020; Sagar 2018), with some going so far as to question whether the state is a person at all (Pettit 2008, 56; Tuck 2016, 99–105).

The evidence for Hobbes's treatment of the state as one person is compelling and predates the English *Leviathan* (Brito Vieira 2020, 315–16). From the early 1640s onward, Hobbes conceived the state as a type of corporation, body politic, or civil person, preserving its identity over time, enjoying capacity to perform actions, and entitled to hold rights and property. Accordingly, in *The Elements of Law* (1640), he stresses his surprise at the fact that the commonwealth has not been treated as a corporate person: "though in the charters of subordinate corporations, a corporation be declared to be one person in law, yet the same hath not been taken notice of in the body of a commonwealth or city" (Hobbes 1969, 174). Hobbes's surprise is clearly overdrawn, as he must have known he was following in the footsteps of medieval jurists in treating the commonwealth as a corporate person.[13] Medieval corporate law maintained that a community was not a real person but a represented one (*persona non vera sed repraesentata*), and thus a fiction of the juristic mind – a person in law. Commentators such as Bartolus of Sassoferrato (1314–1357) and his disciple, Baldus de Ubaldis (1327–1400), whose theories of corporate personhood stand the closest to Hobbes's, insisted that a corporation was a body "composed of a plurality of human beings and an abstract unitary entity perceptible only by the intellect and thus distinct from its human members" (Canning 1987, 186). In other words, by legal contrivance, an aggregate of individuals could be represented by a single abstract personality with a separate existence and real capacity to act. Variously qualified as "fictive" (*ficta*), "imaginary" (*imaginata*), or "represented" (*representata*), the representational and fictional person of the corporation was readily dismissed by nominalists like William of Ockham (c. 1280–1349): "what is only represented or imaginary is a fantasy," claimed Ockham, "and does not exist in reality outside the mind" (Ockham 2001, 428). For Ockham, fictitious persons existed entirely in the mind, and nowhere outside it. They were pure mental constructions – abstractions deprived of any capacity to be, let alone act. Nominalists were, of course, right if "we speak about reality properly," Bartolus acknowledged; but, he immediately objected, "according to legal fiction they err[ed]."[14] For within legal systems, corporations were indeed persons, which the law invested with reality and with their respective duties and rights (Lind 2015, 87).

Of paramount importance for corporations *qua* single persons at law were their unity, distinctiveness, perpetuity, and identity over time. These are concerns that we find echoed in *Thomas White's "De Mundo" Examined* (1642–1643), where Hobbes maintains that "when any citizen dies the material of the state is not the same, i.e., the state is not the same *ens*" but "the uninterrupted order and motion of government that signal a state ensure that, while they remain as one, the state is the same in number" (Hobbes 1976, 141). Hobbes's indebtedness to the doctrine corporate personality becomes, if anything, clearer in his early political treatises. In *The Elements of Law* (1640), the commonwealth comes to be defined as "a multitude of men, united as one person by a common power" (1969, 104; see also, 1969, 108; EL 19.8; see also EL 20.1). In *De cive* 5.9 (1642), Hobbes reiterates that the person resulting from the incorporation is a civil person: "Union so made is called a *commonwealth* or *civil society* and also a *civil person*; for since there is *one will* of all of them, it is to be taken as *one person*; and is to be distinguished and differentiated by a *unique* name from all particular men, having its own rights and its own property" (1998, 73; see also *De cive* 10.5). A civil person is an incorporated collective of natural persons from which one artificial will can be extracted (through a pre-agreed decision mechanism), and to which a single will can thus be attributed. The commonwealth was one such civil person, resulting from the multitude agreeing "that the will of some one man or the consenting wills of a majority of themselves is to be taken as the will of [them] all" (1998, 76). That is, in agreeing to submit to a common unitary external will (the sovereign's), which they take as the will of all, the multitude incorporates itself into one person. It is the capacity to will and act in matters that are of common concern that make the commonwealth a person. The commonwealth's or the incorporated people's will is the sovereign's will, and, as such, we see Hobbes using civil person interchangeably for the collective artificial person and for the sovereign (1969, 124; EL 21.11). But it would be wrong to conclude from this that the only person here is the sovereign's (Tuck 2016). The multitude of particular men is that matter out of which the commonwealth is made; sovereignty is the form giving it unity (1998, 221; *De cive* 17.21). *De cive* already treats the sovereign as the essence of the commonwealth, but *Leviathan* puts the point across more forcibly by deeming the sovereign to be its "Soul," the principle of its form, that which animates it, that which holds "all together within a single and specific form": a person (Cavarero 2002, 172). Sovereign and commonwealth thus "coincide in life" (Cavarero 2002, 176). But the commonwealth nonetheless constitutes a distinctive person, resulting from a union between form (sovereignty) and matter (subjects; Abizadeh 2013, 133; Olsthoorn 2020, 6).

It is one thing to establish that the commonwealth is one person, and another to argue, as I do, that it is a person by fiction. According to Hobbes, representation by fiction is the only form of representation available to people, things or abstractions who "cannot be Authors, nor therefore give Authority to their Actors" (Hobbes 2012, 246; 1651, 81–2). Some people, things, or abstractions are in no position to authorize a representative because they cannot be held responsible for their actions and the consequences of those actions, including the act of authorizing. The possibility of their representation arises, nonetheless, from the existence of a third-party entitled to authorize a representative on their behalf. This will normally be a third-party with a right of ownership or governorship over the people or thing in question, or indeed the state itself can act as the third-party by directly appointing a representative (Hobbes 2012, 246; 1651, 81–2). The fiction here is that the actions of the selected representative are those of the represented, even though, in reality, the represented cannot normatively stand in an authorial relationship to them. Expressed in a different way, in the case of representation by fiction, unlike that of true representation, the very act of representation is constitutive of the represented thing's, abstraction's, or collective's *persona*, which the representative is thus actively involved in bringing into being. The mediation of a third, authorizing party extends dramatically the range of things capable of being represented and thus of acting in the manner of a person by having an authorized representative's actions attributed to them not truly, but by fiction (as they cannot truly author or own them). Hobbes's list of candidates for representation by fiction includes: things inanimate, "as a Church, an Hospital, a Bridge"; people who have no or limited use of reason, "Children, Fooles, and Mad-men"; purely fictional entities, "[a]n Idol, or meer Figment of the brain"; and finally, the "true God." This list immediately precedes – and builds up to – Hobbes's account of the state as *one* person.

One objection that has been recently raised against applying the "representation by fiction model" to the state is that – as the examples given by Hobbes seem to show – it does not involve a collective or its incorporation (Olsthoorn 2020, 9), which is obviously concerning if we want to use the model to make sense of how one person may be made out of many. But the objection fails to take into account the context of Hobbes's examples. As the literature from which Hobbes must have drawn these examples makes clear, the personation of churches, hospitals, and bridges did presuppose incorporation. Both *universitates personarum* (associations) and *universitates rerum* (foundations) were aggregates – of people and things/assets, respectively – endowed with juristic personality by the prescript of law or a special grant and gaining their capacity for action through the agency of representatives. Civil and canon law had long included cathedral chapters and hospitals as specific instances of *universitates personarum*, that is, as a group of individuals legally considered to be a single *persona* or independent entity, such as a corporation. Hence even though it is true that bridges are "personated, not incorporated, by an overseer" (Olsthoorn 2020, 9), the capacity to "procure their maintenance" (Hobbes 2012, 246; 1651, 81) presupposed incorporation. The bridgebuilding brotherhoods (*fratres pontis*) of Medieval Europe were corporations responsible for building and repairing bridges over rivers, and the hospitals, chapels, and cemeteries associated with them, especially in Southern France (Boyer 1964; Skinner 2018, 21–2). Hobbes's interest in the examples of "a Church, an Hospital, a Bridge" (Hobbes 2012, 246; 1651, 81) seems therefore to betray a deeper interest in the process whereby a collection of individuals or things are incorporated into *one* whole ordered to one purpose: to procure the maintenance of something in their charge, which is thereby recognized to have interests of its own that need protecting over time.

Representation by fiction, we have shown, could be closely related to incorporation. The second, related objection, to treating the state as a case of representation by fiction is that the latter requires a legal framework, and this requires, in turn, an institutional framework, that is, a state. In other words, fictional personation cannot generate a state, because it is the creature of the state: a state is necessary to structure and authorize it. Most notably, representation by fiction requires third-party authorization as grounded on dominion of things or persons, rights of ownership or governorship, which have no place outside the state. As the previous example made clear, representation by fiction may even, in some cases, presuppose the establishment of subordinate systems, namely religious associations, similar to guilds, with authority to procure the maintenance of things incapable of acting themselves, such as bridges. These corporations are legal fictions, which only the state can ultimately authorize.

But while it is true that all of this makes it impossible for non-authors to be "Personated, before there be some state of Civill Government" (Hobbes 2012, 246; 1651, 82), it does not necessarily rule out the possibility of Hobbes conceiving the state as a case of fictional representation. For Hobbes, someone/something is represented by fiction when it could not have authorized the representative to speak and act on its behalf, and in its name, but third-party authorization must intervene to make representation – and thus the attribution of secondary actions to the individual/thing represented – possible. The state could not have authorized its representation by the sovereign since the state does not pre-exist its representation – all there is then is an unincorporated multitude. But the multitude of natural persons who make up the state are also those who make it. They are "many Authors," capable of authoring actions, including that of commissioning the sovereign to act on a right they *possess* to perform actions on their behalf, whose effects they take on themselves – thus sustaining the fiction that such actions are the represented *persona*'s. If the authorizing third-party is here the multitude, the question must be raised of whether the multitude can be said to stand in a relationship of ownership or governorship with the state. This seems an impossibility, since the sovereign is the state's governor (Runciman 2000, 273). But ownership cannot be discarded as easily: for, as we have seen, Hobbes tells us that we *possess* the rights by which the state acts and he requires that we take *ownership* of any actions done by those rights. In conclusion, as owners of both, the rights by which the state acts and any state actions done by those rights, the multitude, severally considered, meet, after all, the conditions to act as the authorizing third-party, commissioning a selected common sovereign representative to "beare their Person; and every one to owne, and acknowledge himselfe to be Author of whatsoever he that so beareth their Person, shall Act, or cause to be Acted, in those things which concerne the Common Peace and Safetie" (Hobbes 2012, 260; 1651, 87). As the singular form used by Hobbes indicates, the person that comes to be borne by the sovereign is a newly created *persona*, a unified corporate person, and it comes to have this unitary person on account of the "*Unity* of the Representer" (Hobbes 2012, 248; 1651, 82). There is no unity without representation, or, as Hobbes puts it, "the Commonwealth is no Person ... but by the Representative" (Hobbes 2012, 416; 1651, 137). Only a unitary sovereign can represent them *as if* they were one, that is, as "*One Person*" (Hobbes 2012, 260; 1651, 88), capable of acting with one will and speaking with one voice.

11.3 Conclusion

As I hope to have shown, the making of the commonwealth constitutes a specific case of representation by fiction. But the fiction of their corporate person is ultimately sustained by the true representation of each and every natural person comprising it (Brito Vieira 2009, 180–2; 2017, 39; 2020, 318–19, 322–3). To explain: in authorizing the sovereign, subjects agree to give the sovereign the right to represent them, bear them, or act in their name. "Them" means here them both severally and jointly considered, which means that two distinct things are packed into granting the sovereign the "right to present" (Green 2015, 37): *first*, that the sovereign shall represent all its prospective subjects; *second*, that the sovereign shall represent the collective person into which they incorporate. This is done by giving themselves in representation to one – and just one and the same – representative, who, being one (person), enacts them as capable of words and actions, and moved by one singular will, that is, as if one person. While their collective person can only be represented by fiction, their individual persons are represented truly: they all agree to grant the sovereign authority to act by their rights and thus to be taken for authors of the sovereign's actions and liable for their effects. In Hobbes's own words, every sovereign's act is "done in the Person, and by the Right of every one of them in particular" (Hobbes 2012, 266; 1651, 89). It is the system of shared liability constituted through a reciprocal agreement to enter relations of true representation with a common representative that underpins – or lays the most solid foundation for – the fiction of the state's personality.[15]

Hence, we see Hobbes speaking of the multitude as granting the sovereign authority "to represent them every one" (Hobbes 2012, 286; 1651, 95) *and* of them as a unitary person. Given that representation by fiction is held together – so to say – by the ties of true representation, Hobbes sometimes runs both processes close together. What is more, given the way Hobbes constructs these processes, there is no possible conflict between them (Brito Vieira 2009, 180–2), for in representing each and every one, the sovereign is not representing them in what differentiates them from one another, but in as much as they are the same as each other (persons desiring self-preservation, but caught up in the dilemma of self-sovereignty) and have a stake in a common purpose (co-ordination for the sake of security and peace), which only a state, acting by their right of sovereignty, can oversee and enforce. In sum, it is only when united in the one person that establishes their political will "from an outside" (Downes 2015, 58) that they can see their freedoms, and indeed any interests and private satisfactions they may aspire to, protected and enabled to a degree that is incomparable with anything they could achieve as self-sovereigns (Brito Vieira 2017, 43).

Should we conclude from this that the "commonwealth is simply all the citizens united" (Olsthoorn 2020, 13)? To borrow Bartolus's words, this would be right if "we speak about reality properly" (1998 [1526–1528]), but dangerously reductive if one follows Hobbes in admitting how real – and necessary – a coordinating fiction, or an intersubjectively shared political imaginary, are (Brito Vieira 2020).[16] In *Leviathan*, Hobbes makes it patently clear that "people must save themselves from themselves" by collectively living by "representations of themselves" that "do not simply and wholly coincide with themselves" (Downes 2015, 58).[17] This implies two distinct senses (Fossen 2019) in which representation works in *Leviathan*, as the action of speaking and acting for others, on which we have been focusing, and as imagining or portraying something *as* something, the meaning to which I want to turn now. Both, I submit, combine in bringing into being a commonwealth. On the one hand, Hobbes tells us that the state is nothing but us acting in union through a common representative. On the other hand, he requires us "to believe in the "person" of the commonwealth as something outside [us] and greater than any of [us]" (Malcolm 2002, 228) and even greater than all of us together. Hobbes was convinced that our individual authorization of the sovereign and the relationship of mutual accountability and shared ability in which this placed us sustained the state but did not sustain itself. Representation was equally necessary, now understood as the representation of the commonwealth itself as a formidable image of unity that transcended the mere sum of its authorizing parts. The latter was, of course, a fiction of the mind, not a true person but a person represented to the collective imagination. But Hobbes believed in the unique power of fictions to make the world in their image and elicit a "passionate obedience" whereby naturally enthroned individuals ("self-sovereigns") would take on the *persona* of the subject and the "logic of authorisation" would effectively "come into play" (Malcolm 2002, 228). The fiction of a *Leviathan* state, with power to (con)form the wills and actions of its subjects, for the sake of the commodious benefits of peace, and to avert any fall back into the wretchedness of nature, could not "have reality for us without us doing the work of imagining it as such, and without us engaging in the practices that keep that imaginary alive" (Ferguson 2012, 74). A failure to hold a simultaneous vision of the state as us *and* as something different and bigger than us (i.e., as ruler), and to perform accordingly, could easily slide into a failure of state. Our best protection is to stick with it.

Notes

1 Hobbes's treatment of persons changes considerably from the English *Leviathan* (1651) to *De homine* (1658) and then from *De homine* to the Latin *Leviathan* (1668). My discussion is in this chapter refers exclusively to the English *Leviathan*.

2 OED, s.v., IV.16.

3 The English verb "to personate" appeared around the turn of the seventeenth century, with the first example of its use registered in the OED dating from 1597–1598. It commonly referred to the action of passing oneself off as someone else for fraudulent purposes.

4 In 1649, Hobbes's friend, the poet John Hall, wrote about personation in terms that put one in mind of Hobbes's formulations in the English *Leviathan*: "Man in business is but a Theatricall person, and in a manner but personates himself" (Hall 1953 [1949], 37).

5 For a similar position, see Abizadeh (2017, 923).

6 The sliding seen in Hobbes was not uncommon. Sir Edward Coke and William Blackstone used person for both representative and representee. Coke wrote "'Parson', Persona. In the legall signification it is taken for the rector of a church parocchiall and is called *persona ecclesiae*, because he assumeth and taketh upon him the parson of the church: he only is said *vicem feu personam ecclesiae gerere*" (Coke 1794, III.9.528: 300b). This is taken up by Blackstone, for whom "A parson, *persona ecclesiae*, is one that has full possession of all the rights of a parochial church. He is called parson, *persona*, because by his person the church, which is an invisible body, is represented; and he is in himself a body corporate, in order to protect and defend the rights of the church (which he personates) by a perpetual succession. He is sometimes called the rector, or governor, of the church: but the appellation of parson, (however it may be depreciated by familiar, clownish, and indiscriminate use) is the most legal, most beneficial, and most honorable title that a parish priest can enjoy; because such a one, (Sir Edward Coke observes) and he only, is said *vicem seu personam ecclesiae gerere* ('to carry out the business of the church in person')" (Blackstone 1862 Comm. I.11.V, p. *372).

7 In equating the artificial person with the representative, rather than the represented, Hobbes is at variance with its common use in law from medieval times onwards. To the legal mind, artificial persons were, and still are, entities represented, namely collectives that are treated as persons in law, such as corporations.

8 And it is, if anything, made clearer in *De homine*, where Hobbes writes: "They are said to have authority who do something by the right of someone else," so that "unless he who is

the author himself possesses the right of acting, the author has not authority to act" (Hobbes 1999 [1839], 15.2, 131).

9 As Hobbes explains in chapter 14, rights can be laid down by being renounced or transferred. Transferred, when one deprives oneself of the freedom of "hindring another of the benefit of his own Right to the same," that is, when one obliges oneself to stand out of his way (Hobbes 2012, 200; 1651, 65). Renounced, when one obliges oneself not to interfere with anyone in the exercise of that right.

10 As Michael Green, citing Hobbes, rightly puts it, "the social contract does not give the sovereign any new liberty of action but rather reduces 'impediments to the use of his own right original'" (Green 2015, 33).

11 It has been argued on the basis of *Leviathan* 18.4 (Lloyd 2016) that the problem of authorized wrong actions could be resolved if the right extended from subjects-to-be to sovereign were the right to bear their persons, or act in their names. However, the right explicitly mentioned by Hobbes, prior to the conclusion that any act "done by Authority" is "done by Commission, or Licence from him whose right it is" is "the Right of doing any Action" (Hobbes 2012, 244; 1651, 81).

12 It should be noted that Hobbes frees the sovereign of two burdens of responsibility: for actions it does and towards the authors of those actions, its subjects. In Hobbes, (sovereign) authority equals perfect unanswerability.

13 Although in *Leviathan* he will avoid defining the state as a corporation – as subordinate systems could be inspired to ask for more autonomy so that they could grow into almost commonwealths – and will instead put corporations in their (subordinate) place by defining them as "lesser Common-wealths" (Hobbes 2012, 516; 1651, 175).

14 Bartolus, *Commentary* on D. 48.19.16.10.

15 On this aspect my position has been unchanging over the years, and I am therefore in agreement with the claim that "personation occurs at two levels" (but not that they are sequential; Olsthoorn 2020, 2). Insofar as I nonetheless hold to a "fictionalist interpretation," and want to hold to the claim that the state does not exist before its representation by the sovereign as if one person (as underpinned by authorisation and thus ownership of this person's actions by subjects), it is worth noting that this position is misunderstood when said to mean that the commonwealth comes into existence *solely* "by being represented by the sovereign" and thus "existing apart from the multitude of individuals who compose it." (Olsthoorn 2020, 2).

16 Bartolus, *Commentary* on D. 48.19.16.10.

17 Downes speaks of the people as "generating" these representations, but Hobbes wants to keep control over the representations by which we live; hence my deliberate alteration of the quote (for which I need to apologize).

References

Abizadeh, Arash. 2013. "The Representation of Hobbesian Sovereignty: Leviathan as Mythology." In *Hobbes Today: Insights for the 21st Century*, edited by Sharon A. Lloyd, 113–52. Cambridge: Cambridge University Press.

Abizadeh, Arash. 2017. "Hobbes's Conventionalist Theology, the Trinity, and God as an Artificial Person by Fiction." *The Historical Journal* 60: 915–41.

Agnew, Jean-Christophe. 1986. *Worlds Apart: The Market and the Theater in Anglo-American Thought, 1550–1750*. Cambridge: Cambridge University Press.

Bartolus di Sassoferrato. 1998 [1526–1528]. *Opera Omnia*, 8 vols. Rome: Il Cigno GG Edizioni.

Blackstone, William. 1862. *Commentaries on the Laws of England*, 4 vols. London: John Murray, Albemarle Street.

Boyer, Marjorie Nice. 1964. "The Bridgebuilding Brotherhoods." *Speculum* 39: 635–50.

Brito Vieira, Mónica. 2009. *The Elements of Representation in Hobbes: Aesthetics, Theatre, Law, and Theology in the Construction of Hobbes's Theory of the State*. Leiden and Boston, MA: Brill.

Brito Vieira, Mónica. 2017. "Performative Imaginaries: Pitkin versus Hobbes on Political Representation." In *Reclaiming Representation: Contemporary Advances in the Theory of Political Representation*, edited by Mónica Brito Vieira, 25–49. New York: Routledge.

Brito Vieira, Mónica. 2020. "Making Up and Making Real." *Global Intellectual History* 5 (3): 310–28.

Canning, Joseph. 1987. *The Political Thought of Baldus de Ubaldis*. Cambridge: Cambridge University Press.

Cavarero, Adriana. 2002. *Stately Bodies: Literature, Philosophy, and the Question of Gender*. Ann Arbor, MI: University of Michigan Press.

Coke, Sir Edward. 1794. *The First Part of the Institutes of the Lawes of England, or a Commentary upon Littleton*. London: E. and R. Brooke.

Copp, David. 1980. "Hobbes on Artificial Persons and Collective Actions." *Philosophical Review* 89: 579–606.

Downes, Paul. 2015. *Hobbes, Sovereignty, and Early American Literature*. Cambridge: Cambridge University Press.

Ferguson, Michaele. 2012. *Sharing Democracy*. Oxford: Oxford University Press.

Fossen, Thomas. 2019. "Constructivism and the Logic of Political Representation." *American Political Science Review* 113: 824–37.

Gauthier, David. 1969. *The Logic of Leviathan*. Oxford: Clarendon Press.

Green, Michael J. 2015. "Authorization and Political Authority in Hobbes." *Journal of the History of Philosophy* 53: 25–47.

Hall, John. 1953 [1949]. *The Advancement of Learning*, edited by A.K. Croston. Liverpool: Liverpool University Press.

Hobbes, Thomas. 1969. *The Elements of Law Natural and Politic*, edited by Ferdinand Tönnies. London: Cass.

Hobbes, Thomas. 1976. *Thomas White's 'De Mundo' Examined*, translated by Harold W. Jones. London: Harper Collins.

Hobbes, Thomas. 1998. *On the Citizen*, edited by Richard Tuck and Michael Silverthorne. Cambridge: Cambridge University Press.

Hobbes, Thomas. 1999 [1839]. *Elementorum Philosophiae Sectio Secunda De Homine. In Opera Philosophica Omnia*, edited by Sir William Molesworth, Vol. II, 1–132. London.

Hobbes, Thomas. 2012. *Leviathan*, 3 vols., edited by Noel Malcolm. Oxford: Clarendon Press. [First published 1651].

Lind, Douglas. 2015. "The Pragmatic Value of Legal Fiction." In *Legal Fictions in Theory and Practice*, edited by Maksymillian Del Mar and William Twining, 83–109. New York, Dordrecht, London: Springer.

Lloyd, Sharon A. 2016. "Authorization and Moral Responsibility in the Philosophy of Hobbes." *Hobbes Studies* 29: 169–88.

Malcolm, Noel. 2002. "The Title Page of Leviathan." In *Aspects of Hobbes*, 200–29. Oxford: Clarendon Press.

Newey, Glen. 2014. *The Routledge Guidebook to Hobbes's Leviathan: Second Edition*. New York: Routledge.

Ockham, William. 2001. *A Translation of William of Ockham's Work of Ninety Days*. Lewiston, NY: Edwin Mellen Press.

Olsthoorn, Johan. 2020. "Leviathan Inc.: Hobbes on the Nature and Person of the State." *History of European Ideas* Doi:10.1080/01916599.2020.1779466.

Pettit, Philip. 2008. *Made with Words: Hobbes on Language, Mind and Politics*. Princeton, NJ: Princeton University Press.

Runciman, David. 2000. "What Kind of Person Is Hobbes's State? A Reply to Skinner." *Journal of Political Philosophy* 8: 268–78.

Sagar, Paul. 2018. "What Is the Leviathan?" *Hobbes Studies* 31: 75–92.

Skinner, Quentin. 1999. "Hobbes and the Purely Artificial Person of the State." *Journal of Political Philosophy* 7: 1–29.

Skinner, Quentin. 2007. "Hobbes on Persons, Authors, and Representatives." In *The Cambridge Companion to Hobbes's Leviathan*, edited by Patricia Springborg, 157–80. Cambridge: Cambridge University Press.

Skinner, Quentin. 2018. *From Humanism to Hobbes: Studies in Rhetoric and Politics*. Cambridge: Cambridge University Press.

Tuck, Richard. 2016. *The Sleeping Sovereign: The Invention of Modern Democracy*. Cambridge: Cambridge University Press.

Turner, Henry S. 2016. *The Corporate Commonwealth: Pluralism and Political Fiction in England, 1516–1651*. Chicago, IL: University of Chicago Press.

Van Apeldoorn, Laurens. 2020. "On the Person and Office of the Sovereign in Hobbes' Leviathan." *British Journal for the History of Philosophy* 28: 49–68.

12

Hobbes's Account of Authorizing a Sovereign

ROSAMOND RHODES

Thomas Hobbes has long been considered a major figure in the development of political philosophy. On the one hand, his genius is revered for his psychological insights and the clarity and persuasiveness of his arguments. On the other hand, criticizing and debunking his masterwork, *Leviathan*, has been the focus of philosophers for hundreds of years (Baumrin 1964). From the perspective of both admirers and critics, however, his account of the authorization of a sovereign has become a model for thinking about the social contract and the relationship of governments to subjects in civil societies.

Unfortunately, many authors have glossed over critical details of his description, and their interpretations have been incorporated into the canonical understanding of Hobbes. Their misreading of how Leviathan and the commonwealth are created is not a small quibble: A great deal turns on it. Is Hobbes the champion of totalitarianism or does he regard sovereignty as a fiduciary responsibility? Is Hobbes the defender of unchecked authoritarianism or the proponent of constraints on rulers' powers and privileges? Because we are living through a period of rising authoritarian regimes, including the unconstrained self-serving maneuvers of the Republican party and the Trump presidency in the United States, this issue is now an especially critical important feature of Hobbesian political thought.

12.1 Hobbes's Account

In sections of chapters 17 and 18 of *Leviathan*, Hobbes presents his account of "The Generation of a Commonwealth" (Hobbes 2012, 260; 1651, 87). The little he says goes by very quickly and, at best, serves as a bare-bones sketch of what would be required to explain the creation of a commonwealth and institution of a sovereign. Neither of the parallel accounts of the generation presented in *De cive* V and *The Elements of Law* I.19 and II.1 contribute more to understanding this keystone of his political theory.

A Companion to Hobbes, First Edition. Edited by Marcus P. Adams.

Standard explications take the establishment of civil society as a simple procedure of creating a sovereign as the third-party beneficiary of a covenant between individuals. Such accounts have been put forward by Bertman (1982), Botwinick (1983), Copp (1980), Gierke (1934), Goldsmith (1966), Grover (1980), Husak (1979), Ladenson (1980), May (1980), and Sorell (1986). The subsequent limited attention to the issue in Hobbes scholarship suggests that the third-party beneficiary account has been incorporated into the party line.[1] These readings lead to the familiar conception of the Hobbist sovereign as a tyrant in an authoritarian Hobbist state.

In what follows, I argue against the commonly accepted reading, which was most fully articulated by Larry May in his article "Hobbes's Contract Theory" (1980). Contrary to that widely accepted interpretation, I show that scholars overlook crucial distinctions that play a critical role in Hobbes's account. Concentrating on one selection of passages from *Leviathan* yields the now commonly accepted reading of the sovereign as a duty-free third-party beneficiary of a contract between the individuals who become his subjects. Considering them together with additional ignored selections suggests a more complex authorization process. Both the simple third-party beneficiary account and my own two-step analysis preserve Hobbes's emphasis on "the individual citizen, not the mass of citizens, as the most basic component in the establishment of political sovereignty" (May 1980, 207). Only the complex reading that I defend establishes and explains the sovereign's and subjects' obligations.[2]

12.2 Contracts and Covenants

Definitions and correct use of terms was a critically important element in Hobbes's philosophy. As Noberto Bobbio explained, for Hobbes, language is a human creation, and as an artifact, its careful and rigorous use allows people to produce demonstrable knowledge of civil philosophy (Bobbio 1989, 35–8). In fact, throughout *Leviathan*, Hobbes systematically offers readers guidance by indicating the terms he defines by printing them in a distinctive way. When he offers his definition of a term, the *definiendum* is shown all in block letters, and the defining statement, the *definiens*, is presented just before or after. Subsequently, when he reuses the *definiendum* in his technical sense, the word is printed with the first letter capitalized.[3] Attending to Hobbes's capitalization provides a tool for understanding his positions.

To understand the process of generating civil society, we must therefore begin with Hobbes's definitions of the key terms, "contract" and "covenant." Hobbes defined them both in chapter 14. There he writes, "The mutual transferring of Right, is that which men call CONTRACT" (Hobbes 2012, 204; 1651, 66). In a contract both parties transfer rights immediately and at once, whether or not "the delivery of the Thing it selfe … be delivered together with the Translation of the Right" (Hobbes 2012, 204; 1651, 66) or at some later time. Under some contracts, Things are exchanged by the parties simultaneously "as in buying and selling with ready money; or exchange of goods, or land" (Hobbes 2012, 204; 1651, 66). In the special kind of contract called a "COVENANT or PACT," however, "one of the Contractors, may deliver the Thing contracted for on his part, and leave the other to perform his part at some determinate time after, and in the mean time be trusted" (Hobbes 2012, 204; 1651, 66).

Significantly, simple contracts are transfers of rights and do not require trust while covenants depend on trust. When contracting involves delivering the "Thing," together with the right to it, each party pretty much can see whether he is getting the "Thing" for which he bargained. Even when rights are transferred before "Things," it is apparent to each party when the other is acting as if he will do his part and each party retains his possession until the exchange occurs. In contrast, when people enter into a covenant, for some period, one party has to act on the faith that the other will keep his promise. Without some security that the trusted other will later perform his part, it would be rash to perform first. Hobbes explained that crucial limitation of covenants:

> If a Covenant be made, wherein neither of the parties performe presently, but trust one another; in the condition of mere Nature, (which is a condition of Warre of every man against every man), upon any reasonable suspition, it is Voyd: But if there be a common Power set over them both, with right and force sufficient to compel performance; it is not Voyd. For he that performeth first, has no assurance the other will performe after; because the bonds of words are too weak to bridle mens ambition, avarice, anger, and other Passions, without the feare of some coercive Power; (Hobbes 2012, 210; 1651, 68)

In "the condition of mere Nature" contracts (i.e., immediate transfers of rights) can be enacted, but no one who followed the dictates of Reason should covenant and perform first (i.e., trust another for future performance) because "a man cannot tell" (Hobbes 2012, 202; 1651, 66) whether the person he has to trust is a trustworthy agent or a short-sighted fool.

While this distinction between covenants and other contracts is straightforward and crisp in its presentation, readers tend to ignore Hobbes's distinction.

12.3 Erecting a Common Power

The account of establishing a sovereign offered in the key paragraphs of chapter 17 contains most of what Hobbes wrote on the subject. There Hobbes explained that reasonable men would appreciate the necessity of creating an artificial power to ensure that covenants would be "constant and lasting" (Hobbes 2012, 260; 1651, 87).

> The only way to erect such a Common Power, ... is to conferre all their power and strength upon one Man, or upon one Assembly of men, that may reduce all their Wills, by a plurality of voices, unto one Will: which is as much as to say, to appoint one Man, or Assembly of men, to beare their Person; and every one to owne, and acknowledge himselfe to be Author of whatsoever he that so beareth their Person, shall Act, or cause to be Acted, in those things which concerne the Common Peace and Safetie; and therein to submit their Wills, every one to his Will, and their Judgements, to his Judgement. This is more than Consent, or Concord; it is a reall Unitie of them all, in one and the same Person, made by Covenant of every man with every man, in such manner, as if every man should say to every man, *I Authorize and give up my Right of Governing my selfe, to this Man, or to this Assembly of men, on the condition, that thou give up thy Right to him, and Authorize all his Actions in like manner.* This done, the Multitude so united in one Person, is called a COMMON-WEALTH, in latine CIVITAS. This is the Generation of that great LEVIATHAN, or rather of that *Mortall God*, to

> which wee owe, our peace and defence *One Person of whose Acts a great Multitude, by mutual Covenants one with another, have made themselves every one the Author, to the end he may use the strength and means of them all, as he shall think expedient, for their Peace and Common Defence.* (Hobbes 2012, 254–8; 1651, 87–8)

Three paragraphs later, in chapter 18, Hobbes goes on to explain that "From this Institution of a Common-wealth are derived all the *Rights*, and *Facultyes* of him, or them, on whom the Soveraigne Power is conferred by the consent of the People assembled" (Hobbes 2012, 264; 1651, 88). After this explanation, however, the specific details remain somewhat vague.

12.4 The Simple Account

Larry May and those with similar interpretations of these hypothetical interactions regard them as an agreement between the individuals who will enter the society. Each party promises every other party that he will give up his right of governing himself to the sovereign and actually transfers his right as he utters the promising words. The sovereign, whom they view as the third-party beneficiary of the contracting individuals' transfer of rights, is "not strictly a contracting party to the contract" (May 1980, 204). The sovereign immediately gains the relinquished rights as the consequence of the performance of all the others, receiving them as a free gift. The individual citizens in their promise to one another accept obligations to obey the sovereign's commands, but, on this account, the sovereign makes no promises and takes on no special obligations. At the moment of institution (T1) individuals give up their right of governing themselves and become obligated to obedience while the sovereign gains the right to govern and be obeyed (See Figure 12.1).

12.5 Problems with the Simple Account

This seemingly plausible explication is unacceptable for at least four reasons. First, although May and others collapse the distinction between contract and covenant by claiming "that Hobbes mixes the notion of covenant and free-gift transfer to form the new notion of third-party beneficiary contract" (May 1980, 205), the foundational

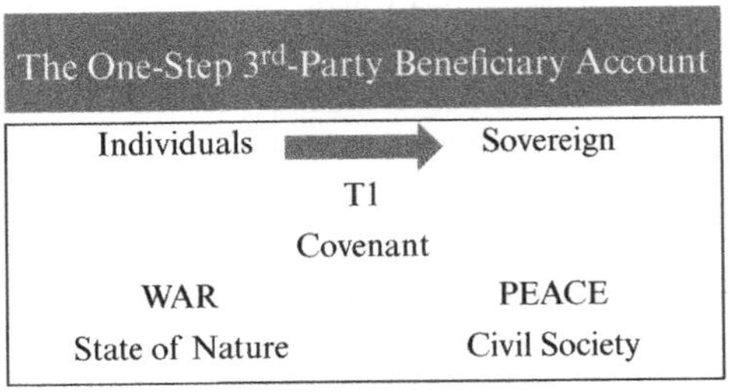

Figure 12.1 The one-step third-party beneficiary account.

agreement must be considered a covenant because Hobbes himself is most consistent in referring to the agreement that binds citizens to obedience as a covenant. If the agreement described above must be acknowledged as a covenant then the simple interpretation is untenable because Hobbes is also unequivocal in maintaining the unreasonableness of entering into covenants while living in the State of Nature. Covenants require trust, so, without grounds for faith there is no justification for confidence that others will perform as promised and acting accordingly. Pursuing peace by forming a commonwealth is a dictate of Reason. As such, it should not rely on rash irrationality. If covenanting from the State of Nature were the necessary route for authorizing a sovereign and instituting a commonwealth, no person who obeyed Reason should participate in the establishment of peace. Reason dictates both the pursuit of peace through commitment to a commonwealth and evading the predictable danger of performing first on a covenant in the State of Nature. If Hobbes's political theory has any legitimacy, it cannot be based on a contradiction (i.e., Reason commanding us to covenant [for Peace] and not covenant [for self-preservation]).

Second, we should remember that Hobbes presents two routes for the attainment of sovereign power. While "Commonwealth by Institution" is the paradigm for comprehending his political theory, he presented his alternative account, "Commonwealth by Acquisition," as a special case of the former rather than an irreconcilable second kind of generation. In chapter 20, "Of Dominion PATERNAL, and DESPOTICALL," which is devoted to the "Commonwealth by Acquisition," he holds that the two kinds of generation "differeth *onely in this*, That men who choose their Soveraign, do it for fear of one another, and not of him whom they Institute" (Hobbes 2012, 306; 1651, 102; emphasis added). In the discussion of situations in which sovereignty is achieved by force, both at the end of chapter 17 and in chapter 20, he described the sovereign gaining authority from the consent of the vanquished. He explained that "[i]t is not therefore the Victory, that giveth the right of Dominion over the Vanquished, but his own Covenant. Nor is he obliged because he is Conquered ... but because he commeth in, and Submitteth to the Victor" (Hobbes 2012, 312; 1651, 104). As in the case of "Commonwealth by Institution" individual "men singly, or many together by plurality of voyces" (Hobbes 2012, 306; 1651, 101) covenant with the sovereign when they consent to his governance. Similarly, when Hobbes compared the sovereign and subject to the parent and child he maintained that parent's "[d]ominion ... is not so derived from the Generation, as if therefore the Parent had Dominion over his Child because he begat him; but from the Childs Consent" (Hobbes 2012, 308; 1651, 102).

In chapter 20, Hobbes blatantly described the sovereign as a party to the covenant.[4] The victor offers conditions for sparing the life of the vanquished, he deliberates on the trustworthiness of the vanquished to uphold his agreement, and he demonstrates his own agreement by releasing him "with his corporall liberty" (Hobbes 2012, 312; 1651, 104). The victor is actively engaged in the covenant, and by performing first, he is the party who is counting on the future performance of the vanquished. This understanding of the relationship of the parties is consistent with Hobbes's discussion in chapter 14 of why there cannot be covenants with beasts. There he wrote, "without mutuall acceptation, there is no Covenant" (Hobbes 2012, 210; 1651, 69). If the "acceptation" must be "mutuall" then the sovereign must be a party to the covenant that creates "Commonwealth by Acquisition"; if he is a party there, then, by symmetry, he must also be a party to the creation of a "Commonwealth by Institution." By taking on the obligation to establish and maintain peace, whoever becomes sovereign accepts obligations and becomes accountable.

Third, Hobbes's example in part 3, chapter 35, of the institution of the KINGDOME OF GOD, which is "a *Kingdome properly so named*" (Hobbes 2012, 634; 1651, 216), shows that the sovereign obliges himself. There he presents God's authority over the People of Israel as deriving from "the Votes of the People ... wherein they chose God for their King by Covenant made with him, upon Gods promising them the possession of the land of Canaan" (Hobbes 2012, 634; 1651, 216; similarly, Hobbes 2012, 636; 1651, 216). In this instance, Hobbes presents God as a proper party to the covenant who committed himself to delivering Canaan to the People of Israel. Because this is Hobbes's example of sovereignty by institution, it is a model of the authorization procedure acknowledging the sovereign as a duty-bound party to the covenant.

Fourth, as Larry May noticed (May 1980, 206), Hobbes requires unanimity for the formation of the commonwealth. This unanimity is a tautological necessity because whoever does not become a party to the original contract does not become a member of the congregation: The commonwealth is only composed of assenters (Rhodes 2002). The selection of the sovereign, however, requires only a majority. The divergence in voting requirements implies that the authorization procedure must be more complex than the third-party beneficiary account allows: The institution of civil society entails at least two distinct votes, the moment of unanimous mutual individual commitment and the moment of institution of the sovereign by majority vote are distinct points in time.

These problems associated with the popular third-party beneficiary view of the generation of civil society justify searching for an alternative account (Goldsmith 1969, xviii–xx). I suggest that instead of seeing the institution as occurring in a single move, it should be analyzed as a two-step procedure (See Figure 12.2). The first step at T1 creates a Commonwealth: the second later step at T2, authorizes a Sovereign.

Two passages from *Leviathan* chapter 18 have particular bearing on understanding the generation as a two-step process. The chapter begins with the statement that,

> A *Common-wealth* is said to be *Instituted*, when a *Multitude* of men do Agree, and *Covenant*, *every one, with every one*, that to whatsoever *Man*, or *Assembly of Men*, shall be given by the major part, the *Right* to *Present* the Person of them all, (that is to say, to be their *Representative*;) every one, as well he that *Voted for it*, as he that *Voted against it*, shall

The Two-Step Account

Individuals → Commonwealth ↔ Sovereign

T1 *interval* T2

Contract Covenant

WAR PEACE

State of Nature Civil Society

Figure 12.2 The two-step account.

> *Authorise* all the Actions and Judgements, of that Man, or Assembly of men, in the same manner, as if they were his own, to the end, to live peaceably amongst themselves, and be protected against other men. (Hobbes 2012, 264; 1651, 89)

This section is shortly followed by Hobbes's discussion of why "*No man can without injustice protest against the Institution of the Soveraigne declared by the major part*" (Hobbes 2012, 268; 1651, 90, margin note). There he argued that,

> because the major part hath by consenting voices declared a Soveraigne; he that dissented must now consent with the rest; that is be contented to avow all the actions he shall do, or else justly be destroyed by the rest. For if he voluntarily entered into the Congregation of them that were assembled, he sufficiently declared thereby his will (and therefore tacitely covenanted) to stand to what the major part should ordayne: (Hobbes 2012, 268; 1651, 90)

In both sections there is the strong suggestion of the temporal sequence of the two separate actions. At the time (T1) when the commonwealth "is" instituted "a *Multitude* of men do Agree" that at a future time (T2) their representative "shall be given ... the *Right* to Present the Person of them all." Then (at T2) whoever may have voted against the elected representative is bound "to avow all the actions he shall do" because each person previously (at T1) "entered into the Congregation ... (and therefore tacitely covenanted [at T1]) to stand to what the major part should ordayne" (at T2). At T1, from what had previously been a mere multitude, the commonwealth is created, "a reall Unitie of them all in one and the same Person" (Hobbes 2012, 260; 1651, 87).

12.6 The First Step

A contract, enacted at T1, is the first step of the process. Contracting creates the largely ignored, morally central artificial person, the commonwealth. In other words, for Hobbes, the commonwealth is a distinct entity that men "Cause" into existence by accepting "restraint" on their liberty in order to achieve "their own preservation, and a more contented life thereby" (Hobbes 2012, 254; 1651, 85). At T1 each person in the group communicates to every other his commitment to participating in a commonwealth and his willingness to elect a sovereign and authorizes the sovereign's actions as his own. At the moment of commitment each cooperating individual relinquishes his own right to disassociate himself and remain at war with the others. In their contracting, everyone (at T1) immediately becomes bound to unite with all of the others who, simultaneously, accept comparable obligations. No one has to rely on faith in another's promise to deliver something because, as yet, nothing is transferred. Each party becomes obliged by his own contract, but he is only committed to cooperate with the others in selecting and then authorizing a sovereign at T2. No one is required to give up his "Right of Governing" himself until T2 when a sovereign is authorized. At that instant, with the authorization of the sovereign, it becomes safe for every individual to relinquish the same rights that each yields to the sovereign.

12.7 Leviathan, the Person

Before moving on to describe the second step in the construction of civil society, it is crucial to understand Hobbes's definitions of the terms "Person," "Actor," "Author," and "Authority" and to raise the question, who is the Leviathan? At the beginning of chapter 16, Hobbes defined these important concepts. A PERSON is

> he, *whose words or actions are considered, either as his own, or as representing the words or actions of any other man, or of any other thing to whom they are attributed, whether Truly or by Fiction.* (Hobbes 2012, 244; 1651, 80)

> When they are considered his owne, then is he called a *Naturall Person*: And when they are considered as representing the words and actions of an other, then is he a *Feigned* or *Artificall person.* (Hobbes 2012, 244; 1651, 80)

He goes on to explain,

> that a *Person*, is the same that an *Actor* is ... and to *Personate*, is to *Act*, or *Represent* himselfe, or an other; and he that acteth another, is said to beare his Person, or act in his name;
>
> Of Persons Artificial, some have their words and actions *Owned* by those whom they represent. And then the Person is the *Actor*; and he that owneth his words and actions, is the AUTHOR: In which case the Actor acteth by Authority so the Right of doing any Action, is called AUTHORITY. So that by Authority, is always understood a Right of doing any act: and *done by Authority* ... from him whose right it is. (Hobbes 2012, 244; 1651, 81–2)

When "[a] Multitude of men, are made *One* Person" (Hobbes 2012, 248; 1651, 82) by their contract with one another, though "the Multitude naturally is not *One*, but *Many*," (Hobbes 2012, 250; 1651, 82) they become the single, mighty, artificial "Person," referred to as "Civitas" (Hobbes 2012, 260; 1651, 87), the "Congregation" (Hobbes 2012, 268; 1651,90), and the "People" (Hobbes 2012, 264, 268, 634; 1651, 88; 1651, 216).[5] As Philip Petit notes, for Hobbes, artful use of language occasions transformations (Petit 2008, 37), in this case their words convert a bunch of individual people into a powerful Leviathan.

From Hobbes's definitions we can understand that the commonwealth itself is "that great LEVIATHAN" (Hobbes 2012, 260; 1651, 87). Contrary to the standard assumption, Leviathan is the commonwealth, not the sovereign. Leviathan is the actor who acts on the authority of each natural person who, by contract, participated in creating the commonwealth. Every natural person is the author of the authorized acts performed by their actor.

In all of Hobbes's English writings there are, in fact, only three uses of the term, "Leviathan" (as distinguished from mentions of the title of the book). Besides the initial explication of the term in chapter 17, the term also appears in the introduction of that book and at the end of chapter 28. In the introduction Hobbes distinguishes "that great LEVIATHAN called a COMMONWEALTH, or STATE, in Latin CIVITAS, which is but an artificial man;" (Hobbes 2012, 16; 1651, 1) from sovereignty which "is an Artificial

Soul, as giving life and motion to the whole body" of Leviathan (Hobbes 2012, 16; 1651, 1; also see similar description of Sovereign at Hobbes 2012, 518; 1651, 174). In this mention, Leviathan is clearly *not* the sovereign: The sovereign personates Leviathan acting as his agent while Leviathan, that is, the State, Civitas, Congregation, People, is comprised of the natural individuals who authorize his actions. Again in the last paragraph of chapter 28 Hobbes compares the might of the governor of men to the biblical *Leviathan* and refers to the next chapters where he will "speak of his Diseases, and the causes of his Mortality; and of what Lawes of Nature he is bound to obey" (Hobbes 2012, 496; 1651, 167). Then, in chapter 29, he immediately makes it clear that the "he" who is "Leviathan" is that artful creation of men, the Congregation (Hobbes 2012, 16; 1651, 1).

In presenting his detailed picture of Leviathan, up front in his very first paragraph, Hobbes is making the point that the People are powerful, more formidable than any sovereign. As the frontispiece of the book illustrates, Leviathan, the People, "which is but an Artificiall Man; though of greater stature and strength than the Naturall" has at its service their combined "*Strength*" from "The *Wealth* and *Riches* of all the particular members" (Hobbes 2012, 16; 1651, 1). In light of Leviathan's awesome power, the introduction's concluding paragraphs warn the sovereign, "He that is to govern a whole Nation," that it is in his interest to attend to the "Passions, which are the same in all men, *desire, feare, hope, &c;*" and use that wisdom to avoid "the barbarous state of men in power, toward their inferiors" (Hobbes 2012, 18; 1651, 2).

All of this is consistent with what Hobbes writes in chapters 14 and 16. Leviathan is the actor who represents the natural person authors and covenants with the sovereign.

> From hence it followeth, that when the Actor maketh a Covenant by Authority, he bindeth the Author, no lesse than if he had made it himselfe; and no lesse subjecteth him to all the consequences of the same. And therefore all that hath been said formerly, (*Chap.* 14.) of the nature of Covenants between man and man in their naturall capacity, is true also when they are made by their Actors ..., that have authority from them, so far-forth as in their Commission, but no farther. (Hobbes 2012, 246; 1651, 81)

12.8 The Second Step

Returning to the explication of the institution of civil society, we can identify the *covenant* as the second step in the generation process. The covenanting parties are (1) the Leviathan, i.e., the People, and (2) the sovereign. The People promise to be governed by the sovereign's laws while the sovereign promises to act for the "*Peace and Common Defence*" (Hobbes 2012, 262; 1651, 88; similarly, 2012, 520; 1651, 175) of his subjects "and to direct their actions to the Common Benefit" (Hobbes 2012, 260; 1651, 87).

When the covenant is made (at T2) each individual member of the congregation transfers his power to the sovereign trusting him to use the combined strength of all "*for their Peace and Common Defence*" (Hobbes 2012, 262; 1651, 88). Because every natural person who participates in the congregation is author of all commissioned acts of the People, the covenant between Leviathan and the sovereign binds each author to obey the Dictates of the sovereign.

The sovereign, who transfers to the People his Right of Nature to act freely "as he will himselfe, for the preservation of his own Nature" (Hobbes 2012, 198; 1651, 64), simultaneously (at T2) accepts the obligation to direct the power of the office toward enabling subjects to "nourish themselves and live contentedly" (Hobbes 2012, 260; 1651, 87; similarly, 2012, 520; 1651, 175). By his promise he creates the People's correlative right to his future protection. In agreeing to limit his own liberty, the sovereign trusts the People not to unleash their considerable confederated Leviathan strength against him.

When a person(s) accepts the "Office of the Sovereign," he assumes the "duty" to act so as to achieve "the end, for which he was trusted with the Soveraign Power, namely the procuration of *the safety of the people*; to which he is obliged" (Hobbes 2012, 520; 1651, 175). Throughout chapter 30 of *Leviathan* Hobbes enumerates the acts that the sovereign is obliged to perform and those that would be "*Against the duty of a Soveraign to*" (Hobbes 2012, 520, margin note; 1651, 175) do. By his repeated use of the language of obligation in this chapter,[6] he demonstrates that the sovereign undertakes special duties when he accepts the office (Rhodes 2002).

While there is no person outside this original covenant who can exercise enforcing power and assure that each party will perform according to his promise, the covenant is rational, nonetheless, because those covenanting are no longer in the State of Nature. Once the commonwealth is created, the contractors have escaped the condition and danger of the State of Nature. The power fused in the People gives the congregation inordinate strength for security against the sovereign; the might of a Leviathan exceeds the power of any solitary sovereign. So, by trusting a sovereign the People are not violating Reason. On his part, the authorized sovereign, who is beneficiary of the power and authority conferred upon him by each of his subjects, also has a tremendous extra measure of strength allowing him sufficient security to covenant without violating the dictates of his own Reason. In effect, the covenant artificially creates a balance of power that allows people to establish peace by overcoming the natural state of war.

12.9 The Interval Between the Steps

During the time intervening between T1 and T2 the commonwealth must select its form of sovereignty between Monarchy, Aristocracy, and Democracy (Hobbes 2012, 324; 1651, 94), settle on a voting procedure, and define what will count as "the major part" (Hobbes 2012, 268; 1651, 90) of the People in declaring a sovereign. Furthermore, the People may decide to reserve some portion of the Right of Nature (beyond the inalienable right of self-preservation) from the sovereign's authority and, if so, which rights will be withheld (e.g., those rights enumerated in the United States "Bill of Rights").[7] Because agreements on these issues must be made before a sovereign can be authorized, and because a congregation must be formed before it can begin working out compromises on these issues, the institution procedure must involve the three distinct stages of contract at T1, the intervening agreements, and covenant at T2. The sovereign cannot therefore be a third-party beneficiary authorized immediately and spontaneously by the original contract. The sovereign instituted in that process acquires his authority only as a party to the authorizing *covenant*, which is distinctly different from the original *contract*.

Further support for this analysis emerges from chapter 16. There it seems that Hobbes was fully aware of the fact that each natural person may fill several distinct roles. He reminds the reader that Cicero had held such a view and that a person "is called in diverse occasions, diversly; as a *Representer*, or *Representative*, ... an *Actor* and the like" (Hobbes 2012, 244; 1651, 80). Though the implications of this position are not drawn out in the text, it follows that in the political context alone, an individual may bear different natural and artificial roles. One natural person is a member of the congregation, a subject, and perhaps even a sovereign or part of a sovereign body. If someone "is called in diverse occasions, diversly;" (Hobbes 2012, 244; 1651, 80) we again have, in those sequentially distinct occasions, the suggestion of the temporal ordering of the several steps in the creation of civil society.

12.10 Counter-Evidence and Hobbes's Defense

By this point, my case for the two-step reading of Hobbes's account of the generation of civil society and the institution of a duty-bound Sovereign may seem worth considering, even though the picture it presents is not the Hobbes you thought you knew. Hobbes's numerous arguments in chapter 18, "Of the RIGHTS of Soveraignes by Institution," may, however, appear to rebut my reading. Most specifically, in the section explaining why "*Soveraigne be forfeited*" (Hobbes 2012, 264; 1651, 89, margin note), Hobbes seems to be arguing against the kind of reading that I have offered. Indeed, Deborah Baumgold asserts that Hobbes was making arguments against the conditionality of sovereign authority and rebutting "parliamentary" claims by Henry Parker and other advocates of parliamentary government (Baumgold 1988, 38), and similar claims are made by Richard Tuck (1989, 66), Philip Petit (2008, 125–9), and Quentin Skinner (2002, 208). There Hobbes writes:

> The opinion that any Monarch receiveth his Power by Covenant, that is to say on Condition, proceedeth from want of understanding this easie truth, the Covenants being but words, and breath, have no force to oblige, contain, constrain, or protect any man, but what it has from the publique Sword; that is from the untyed hands of that Man, or Assembly of men that hath the Soveraignty, and whose actions are avouched by them all and performed by the strength of them all, in him united. (Hobbes 2012, 268; 1651, 89)

In that section, it may seem that Hobbes is arguing against the parliamentarians' preference for legislation by "a Popular Government" rather than a "Monarchy," but his arguments do not cut against their assertion of there being conditions on sovereign power. Hobbes makes three distinct points. First, the covenant that creates civil society is an agreement between the People and the Sovereign. The individuals involved make promises to one another to relinquish their "*right to all things; and be content with so much liberty against other men, as he would allow other men against himself*" (Hobbes 2012, 200; 1651, 65). This is significant because individuals do not covenant with the Sovereign, it is the People, Leviathan, that covenants with the individual who assumes the position of sovereign. Thus, no individual subject is, *per se*, a party to the covenant with the sovereign. Therefore, no individual subject or group of subjects has standing to challenge the sovereign's performance.

Second, as Michael Byron (2015, 74) and Eleanor Curran (2007) note, until the covenant is made, there are no subjects or sovereign, only individuals. Those roles and others are created only with the institution of a sovereign. In that vein, Hobbes remarks, until the sovereign is personated there is "no Judge to decide the controversie" (Hobbes 2012, 200; 1651, 65). Without a judge to determine whether, or not, the covenant was breached, there is no verdict, no way to settle a charge against a sovereign for failing in his obligations.

Third, Hobbes's final argument in that section is that it is irrational for an individual or group to accuse the sovereign of breaching the covenant because doing so, in effect, returns everyone to the state of war. Charging a sovereign with failure to abide by the conditions of the covenant is in effect accusing him of being unfit to hold the position. To the contrary, Hobbes argued that "*Covenants* [are] *not discharged by the Vice of the Person to whom they are made*" (Hobbes 2012, 226; 1651, 74). As he explained, "For if any fault of a man be sufficient to discharge our Covenant made; the same ought in reason to have been sufficient to have hindered the making of it." We know that mortals are capable of vice, and "we cannot tell" (Hobbes 2012, 202; 1651, 66) which men will succumb to which vice. If the only options are either authorizing a vice-prone creature to personate the Commonwealth or remaining in a state of war, it is reasonable to accept the imperfect option. It would be inconsistent with the goal of covenanting and authorizing a sovereign in order to escape the intolerable state of nature to reject his authority for violating the covenant.

12.11 Conditionality

In sum, it is fair to say that Hobbes's account is consistent with the parliamentarians' claim that in accepting his role the sovereign undertakes duties. Clearly, when he declared that "without mutuall acceptation, there is no Covenant" (Hobbes 2012, 210; 1651, 69), he asserted that as a party to the covenant, the sovereign accepts obligations and creates rights in his subjects. And when he defined COVENANTS as contracts in which "one of the Contractors, may deliver the Thing contracted for on his part, and leave the other to perform his part at some determinate time after, and then in the mean time be trusted" (Hobbes 2012, 204; 1651, 66), Hobbes affirmed the position that the sovereign binds himself. He becomes obliged to keep his part of the bargain by accepting the "Right reciprocally transferred to himself" (Hobbes 2012, 202; 1651, 66) and committing himself to promoting the good of those who empowered him by divesting themselves of their former "*right to all things*" (Hobbes 2012, 200; 1651, 65). And he asserted the obligation again when he held that, "He that performeth first in the case of a Contract is said to MERIT that which he is to receive by the performance of the other; and he hath it as Due" (Hobbes 2012, 208; 1651, 67).

Describing the authority of a sovereign, the parliamentarian, Parker, maintained that "His interest in the Crown is not absolute, or by a meere donation of the people, but in part conditionate and fiduciary" (1642, 3–4). Although, as Eleanor Curran (2007, 102) has shown, there are significant differences between Hobbes's positions and the parliamentarians' positions on issues related to the form of government, civil law, and historical precedents, they agreed on there being limits to sovereign authority and the sovereign having fiduciary duties to his subjects.

In chapter 16, Hobbes made the possibility of constraints on sovereign authority explicit. He wrote:

> And because the Multitutde naturally is not *One*, but *Many*; they cannot be understood for one; but many Authors of every thing their Representative saith, or doth in their name; Every man giving their common Representer, Authority from himselfe in particular; and owning all the actions the Representer doth, in case they give him Authority without stint; *Otherwise, when they limit him in what, and how farre he shall represent them, none of them gave him commission to Act*. (Hobbes 2012, 250; 1651, 82; emphasis added)

And he concluded the chapter by legitimizing constraints on sovereign authority once more:

> Of Authors there be two sorts. The first simply so called; which I have before defined to be him, that owneth the Action of another simply. The second is he, that owneth an Action or Covenant of another conditionally; ... And these Authors conditionall, are generally called SURETYES in Latine *Fidujussores* and *Sponsores*. (Hobbes 2012, 252; 1651, 83)

In both of these sections, Hobbes's distinction appears to reflect a difference that could derive from the authorizing covenant, or from the establishment of sovereignty by acquisition (i.e., granting "Authority without stint"), or by a limiting covenant (i.e., granting authority conditionally and creating a fiduciary relationship).

I have claimed that in Hobbes's account of the creation of civil society, the sovereign's authority is vested with the covenant between the sovereign and the People, the unity of them all. Furthermore, Hobbes's rebuttal of the suggestion that there might be covenants between individuals and the sovereign is an abjuration of his own account of "Sovereignty by Acquisition" presented in chapter 20 where he explicitly described how obligations of the victor and the vanquished derive from their covenant with one another. Even though the covenant, from the condition of war, is undertaken out of fear of the victor, it is nevertheless obliging. As Hobbes wrote in chapter 14, "For it is a Contract, wherein one receiveth the benefit of life; the other is to receive mony, or service for it, ... the Covenant is valid" (Hobbes 2012, 212; 1651, 69). For the sake of consistency, either most of chapter 20 and all of the other textual evidence for Hobbes actually holding the view that the sovereign is a party to the covenant should be discounted or the odd words that suggest otherwise must be. The historical analytic choice to save all of the central passages you can, supports my conclusion.

In a footnote to the section just cited above in the French translation of *Leviathan*, Francois Tricaud remarked on several peculiarities in the passage (Hobbes 1971, 181 fn. 5). He noted that in Hobbes's later Latin version of *Leviathan* there is an unexpected use of the concept of "civitas" as something relatively distinct from "the Sovereign."[8] In the Latin version Hobbes adds the following:

> Then, to want to oblige him who holds the supreme power by covenants is to want to oblige the civitas itself. And if we concede that whoever holds the supreme power can make covenants with the civitas, and violate them, who will decide this case, when he who would have violated such a covenant will deny it.[9]

The objection Hobbes raises here has serious implication because one of the justifications for instituting a sovereign is the need for mediating disputes between the individuals who interpret the Laws of Nature to their own advantage (Ewin 1991, 34). The problem of having no mediator for resolving disputes between the sovereign and the civitas does not, however, eliminate the possibility of the sovereign covenanting with the People, as Hobbes apparently concedes in the Latin edition. In fact, Hobbes presents a solution to his problem by putting God forward as the mediator between sovereign and civitas. In *Leviathan* chapter 30 (Hobbes 2012, 520; 1651, 175), the sovereign is held accountable to God, and throughout part 3 God is named as the ultimate judge over the actions of both subjects and sovereigns. Regardless of whether or not the lack of an earthly mediator is crucial, Hobbes's identifying the distinction between "civitas" and "Sovereign" lends further credence to interpreting the text with the assumption of these as two distinct entities.

The lines of text alone may not be fully conclusive in settling the question of whether the sovereign is the third-party beneficiary or an assenting party to a covenant with the People. Hobbes's underlying motivation of teaching citizens to reject revolution as an irrational choice explains why he might have avoided highlighting the conditions on sovereign power. Once the sovereign is acknowledged as an obligated party to the covenant, personal judgments that he failed to meet his commitments could be seen as justifying disobedience or rebellion. Hobbes had reason to avoid emphasizing that implication.

12.12 Conclusion: Implications of the Complex Account

On this reading of the creation of civil society and institution of a sovereign, the previously unacknowledged Leviathan emerges as a distinct entity with a crucial place in the creation of Peace. Identifying the People as the Leviathan and its intermediary position in the series of state-creating commitments allows the community to emerge as the proper focus for the sovereign's actions. The sovereign has obligations to the congregation and his duty is to act and legislate for the peace and security of the People. Understanding the pivotal place of Leviathan, as the axial subject and beneficiary of the sovereign's acts, by right conceded in the covenant between the People and the sovereign, makes the welfare of Leviathan the proper goal of all sovereign acts and gives new meaning and significance to the book's title. The overlooked commonwealth itself, not the individuals who create it, and not the sovereign who is its agent, turns out to be the central conceptual political institution of *Leviathan.*

Seeing the Leviathan People as a powerful potential force eliminates an unsettling seeming contradiction in Hobbes's theory. It would have been incongruous for apprehensive Hobbes, who had taken the fear of each single individual as sufficient motivation for entering civil society, to put all power and rights in the uncheckable hands of an almighty sovereign. Allowing the commonwealth to limit sovereign authority theoretically protects individual subjects from the unbridled whims of over-reaching, selfish, sovereigns who lack empathy.

The one-step third-party beneficiary interpretation regards individuals as only promising each other to obey whoever will be lawmaker and undertaking no direct

260; 1651, 87), rather than individual citizens each acting on personal initiative, chooses to replace the sovereign, the act need not compromise peace. Mechanisms for the recall of a sovereign by the People are, in fact, institutionalized in modern societies (e.g., elections, votes, and impeachment), and the acceptability of such action is even recognized by Hobbes who reminds us of the example of the People of Israel who replace God with Saul as their sovereign (Hobbes 2012, 750; 1651, 253–5).[11]

Adopting the complex account of the creation of civil society and the authorization of its sovereign has important implications for understanding Hobbes's political theory. It offers a fresh perspective on the Leviathan and the source of subjects' and sovereign's obligations. These revisions in reading Hobbes's philosophy make his theory compatible with modern liberal democratic thinking and incompatible with authoritarianism (Coleman 1977). In addition, the complex reading enriches our understanding of concepts such as "We the People" and gives new meaning to the motto "e pluribus unum." Thus, the most dramatic consequence of the complex account may be its implications for our understanding of the history of political philosophy. On this view, Hobbes's construction of civil society prefigures Rousseau's, and it identifies Hobbes as the legitimate forbearer of Rawls's just state.

Notes

1 Many of the more recent books on Hobbes's political theory do not include detailed discussions of the authorization of the sovereign, e.g., Gauthier (1969, 1999), Hampton (1986), Kavka (1986), Kraynak (1990), Lloyd (1992), Martinich (1992), Shelton (1992), Kraus (1993) Gert (2010), Byron (2015).

2 I develop this view in Rhodes (1994).

3 When Hobbes uses a term that he previously defined without the first letter capitalized, he is contrasting his correct usage with colloquial misleading usage. As I have previously argued, attending to his capitalization is particularly useful in understanding his response to the fool (see Rhodes 1992).

4 As a sovereign, the power that he has from his supporting subjects makes it reasonable for him to trust the vanquished individuals who he considers trustworthy.

5 It should be noted that Hobbes treats the terms "Congregation" and "People" as representing an individual artificial person who can authorize another to serve as its representative.

6 In elaborating the particular aspects of the duty to procure "the Good of the People" (Hobbes 2012, 520; 1651, 175, margin note) of which "THE OFFICE of the Soveraign, consisteth" Hobbes uses such phrases as: "his duty" (Hobbes 2012, 520; 1651, 175, margin note), "requireth" (2012, 534; 1651,180), "ought not" (2012, 538; 1651, 181), "the care of the Soveraign" (2012, 540; 1651, 181), "belongeth" (2012, 542; 1651,182), "belongeth to the Office and Duty of the Sovereign" (2012, 544; 1651, 183), "against the Duty of the Soveraign" (2012, 544; 1651, 183), "Business of the Soveraign" (2012, 546; 1651, 183), "dischargeth not his Office as he ought to do" (2012, 546; 1651, 184).

7 Kavka, who sees the actual authorization of the Sovereign as a free gift from the individual members of the society, nevertheless finds the process of creating civil society to be a two-step procedure. He devotes most of his chapter 5 to a discussion of the interval between the two steps. He provides a valuable, insightful, Rawlsian fleshing-out of the party's characteristics and their prisoners-dilemma analyses of the decisions that are made between the steps. See Kavka (1986).

8 In the same footnote Tricaud indicates that the Latin counterpart for this passage (Hobbes 2012, 278; 1651, 92) also includes the distinction between "civitas" and "the Sovereign." One summer day in the mid-1980s, when Professor Tricaud was in New York City for a Hobbes conference, he escorted me to the 42nd Street New York Public Library. There he showed me a portrait of Oliver Cromwell to point out its resemblance to the picture on the frontispiece. Cromwell was in power when *Leviathan* was published. We will never know if the facial resemblance was a prudent choice or Hobbes's acknowledgement of the alignment of some of his views with Cromwell's parliamentarian positions. Tricaud was suggesting that there was some significance to the similarity.

9 My translation from Tricaud's French translation of the Latin.

10 This position is also consistent with what Hobbes maintains in *De homine* X.5: "politics and ethics ... can be demonstrated a priori; because we ourselves make the principles – that is, the causes of justice (namely laws and covenants) – whereby it is known what justice and equity, and their opposites injustice and inequity, are" (OL II.94). See also *Six Lessons*: "civil philosophy is demonstrable because we make the commonwealth ourselves" (EW VII.184).

11 As Hobbes recounts the incident, God consents to being replaced by a mortal King. Hobbes, however, presents no argument for this consent being a required feature of a just substitution.

References

Baumgold, Deborah. 1988. *Hobbes's Political Theory*. New York: Cambridge University Press.

Baumrin, Bernard H.. 1964. *Introduction to the New Edition, British Moralists*, edited by Lewis A. Selby-Bigge. Indianapolis, IA: The Bobbs-Merril Company.

Bertman, Martin. 1982. "Regulative and Constructive Rules in Hobbes." In *Thomas Hobbes: His View of Man*, edited by Johannes G. van der Bend, 9–16. Amsterdam: Rodopi.

Bobbio, Norberto. 1989. *Thomas Hobbes and the Natural Law Tradition*, translated by Daniela Gobetti, 35–8. Chicago, IL: University of Chicago Press.

Botwinick, Aryeh. 1983. "Hobbes's Concept of Law and Representation: Some Reflections on Past and Future." *Journal of Social Philosophy* 14: 34–51.

Byron, Michael. 2015. *Submission and Subjection in Leviathan*, 74. New York: Palgrave Macmillan.

Coleman, Frank M.. 1977. *Hobbes and America: Exploring the Constitutional Foundations*. Toronto, ON: University of Toronto Press.

Copp, David. 1980. "Hobbes on Artificial Persons and Collective Actions." *The Philosophical Review* 89: 579–606.

Curran, Eleanor. 2007. *Reclaiming the Rights of the Hobbesian Subject*. Houndsmills and New York: Palgrave Macmillan.

Ewin, R.E.. 1991. *Virtues and Rights: The Moral Philosophy of Thomas Hobbes*. Boulder, CT: Westview Press.

Gauthier, David. 1999. "Hobbes's Social Contract." In *The Social Contract Theorists: Critical Essays on Hobbes, Locke, and Rousseau*, edited by Christopher W. Morris, 59–71. Lanham, MD: Rowman & Littlefield Publishers, Inc.

Gauthier, David P.. 1969. *The Logic of Leviathan: The Moral and Political Theory of Thomas Hobbes*. Oxford: Clarendon Press.

Gert, Bernard. 2010. *Hobbes*. Cambridge, UK: Polity Press.

Gierke, Otto. 1934. *Natural Law and the Theory of Society: 1500–1800*, translated and with an introduction by Ernest Baker. Cambridge: Cambridge University Press.

Goldsmith, Maurice M. 1966. *Hobbes's Science of Politics*. New York: Columbia University Press.

Goldsmith, Maurice M. 1969. "Introduction to the Second Edition." In *The Elements of Law Natural and Politic*, edited by Ferdinand Tonnies, xviii–xx. London: Frank Cass & Co. Ltd.

Grover, Robinson. 1980. "The Legal Origins of Thomas Hobbes' Doctrine of Contract." *Journal of the History of Philosophy* 18 (April): 177–94.

Hampton, Jean. 1986. *Hobbes and the Social Contract Tradition*. New York: Cambridge University Press.

Hobbes, Thomas. 1839–1845a. *The English works of Thomas Hobbes*, 11 vols., edited by Sir William Molesworth. London: John Bohn. Cited as EW.

Hobbes, Thomas. 1839–1845b. *Thomæ Hobbes malmesburiensis opera philosophica*, 5 vols., edited by Gulielmi Molesworth. London: John Bohn. Cited as OL.

Hobbes, Thomas. 1971. *Leviathan*, translated from the English, annotated and compared with the Latin text by Francois Tricaud. Paris: Editions Sirey.

Hobbes, Thomas. 2012. *Leviathan*, 3 vols., edited by Noel Malcolm. Oxford: Clarendon Press. [First published 1651].

Husak, Douglas N.. 1979. "Sovereigns and Third Party Beneficiaries." *Journal of Value Inquiry* 13 (Summer): 145–53.

Kavka, Gregory S.. 1986. *Hobbesian Moral and Political Theory*. Princeton, NJ: Princeton University Press.

Kraus, Jody S.. 1993. *The Limits of Hobbesian Contractarianism*. Cambridge, UK: Cambridge University Press.

Kraynak, Robert P.. 1990. *History and Modernity in the Thought of Thomas Hobbes*. Ithaca, NY: Cornell University Press.

Ladenson, Robert F.. 1980. "In Defense of a Hobbesian Conception of Law." *Philosophy and Public Affairs* 9 (Winter): 134–59.

Lloyd, S.A. 1992. *Ideals as Interests in Hobbes's Leviathan: The Power of Mind over Matter*. New York: Cambridge University Press.

Martinich, Aloysius P.. 1992. *The Two Gods of Leviathan: Thomas Hobbes on Religion and Politics*. Cambridge, UK: Cambridge University Press.

May, Larry. 1980. "Hobbes's Contract Theory." *Journal of the History of Philosophy* XVIII (2): 195–207.

Parker, Henry. 1642. *Observations upon Some of His Majesties Late Answers and Expresses*. London.

Petit, Philip. 2008. *Made with Words: Hobbes on Language, Mind, and Politics*. Princeton, NJ: Princeton University Press.

Rhodes, Rosamond. 1992. "Hobbes's Unreasonable Fool." *Southern Journal of Philosophy* 30 (2): 93–102.

Rhodes, Rosamond. 1994. "Creating Leviathan, Sovereign, and Civil Society." *History of Philosophy Quarterly* 11 (2): 177–89.

Rhodes, Rosamond. 2002. "Obligation and Assent in Hobbes's Moral Philosophy." *Hobbes Studies* XV: 45–67.

Shelton, George. 1992. *Morality and Sovereignty in the Philosophy of Hobbes*. Houndsmills, UK: Macmillan.

Skinner, Quentin. 2002. *Visions of Politics, Volume III, Hobbes and Civil Science*. Cambridge: Cambridge University Press.

Sorell, Tom. 1986. *Hobbes*, 116. London and New York: Routledge.

Tuck, Richard. 1989. *Hobbes*. Oxford: Oxford University Press.

13

The Strength and Significance of Subjects' Rights in *Leviathan*

ELEANOR CURRAN

Hobbes says a great deal about the rights of subjects, particularly in *Leviathan*, and yet, despite his apparent insistence on the importance of the rights of the subject, the prevailing view amongst modern Hobbes scholars has been that the rights of Hobbesian subjects are weak. For some commentators, the subjects' rights in a Hobbesian commonwealth are non-existent, having been given up to the sovereign (Kymlicka 1990; Macpherson 1968; Ryan 1996; Skinner 2008). For others, the subjects do have so called rights, but they are rights that convey no protections upon the right holders (Finkelstein 2001; Gauthier 1969; Hampton 1986; Kavka 1986; Sreedhar 2010). The arguments that support the view of Hobbesian rights as weak coalesce around two main themes. The first is that the absolutism of the Hobbesian sovereign simply won't allow for any significant subjects' rights and certainly not any rights held directly against the sovereign. The second, following Wesley Hohfeld's analysis of legal rights (Hohfeld 1919), is that all the subjects' rights are Hohfeldian liberty rights, sometimes referred to as "bare freedoms" or "permissions," which have no correlative duties and therefore offer no protections to Hobbesian subjects and no threat to the power and authority of the sovereign. I argue, against both sets of arguments, that in *Leviathan* Hobbes proposes a theory of rights according to which the rights of subjects are both strong and significant.

The dominant view of Hobbesian rights as weak and insignificant is the view of *modern* Hobbes scholarship, which analyses Hobbes's political theory at a great distance from his intellectual milieu and from the dramatic political events of the time. This view also developed during a time in the middle and late twentieth century when the preference in political philosophy, as in philosophy generally, was for analysis of arguments with no reference to the context within which those arguments were developed. In this case, the context of the English Civil War and the associated political arguments of the royalists and parliamentarians. (There are, of course, some very distinguished exceptions to this, most obviously perhaps, in the work of Quentin Skinner.) And so, Hobbes

---

A Companion to Hobbes, First Edition. Edited by Marcus P. Adams.

scholars wrote books on Hobbes's political philosophy without addressing, or in some cases even mentioning, the civil war that raged in England as he wrote *Leviathan*, in exile, in Paris. This was to ignore Hobbes's own comments in the dedication of *Leviathan* to Francis Godolphin:

> I humbly Dedicate unto you this my discourse of Common-wealth. I know not how the world will receive it, nor how it may reflect on those that shall seem to favour it. For in a way beset with those that contend on one side for too great Liberty, and on the other side for too much Authority, "tis hard to passe between the points of both unwounded." (Hobbes 2012, 4; 1651, A2v)

Similarly, in the Review and Conclusion of *Leviathan*, Hobbes notes "I have brought to an end my Discourse of Civill and Ecclesiasticall Government, occasioned by the disorders of the present time, without partiality," (Hobbes 2012, 1141; 1651, 395). Clearly, Hobbes thought that the events and political arguments of the time were relevant to what he had written. And yet, all matters of context, historical, political, or intellectual, were ignored by many commentators, particularly those writing in the middle of the twentieth century. When such writers do enter into any discussion of historical context, this has usually been to declare, often without argument or textual support, that Hobbes was a royalist and absolutist of the most extreme kind and was writing in support of Charles I (Martinich 1995; 1999; Sommerville 1992; Tuck 1993).

Hobbes's contemporaries, on the other hand, were more likely to think that the extensive liberties granted to subjects in *Leviathan*, as well as remarks, for example, on natural equality, brought him dangerously close to arguing in favor of Oliver Cromwell's side in the English Civil War. Bishop Bramhall famously declared that the name *Leviathan*, should be changed to "the *Rebells catechism*." He said that Hobbes's suggestion that it was up to the individual subject to judge whether or not he was being sufficiently protected by the sovereign (and if he judged that he was not then he had a right to disobey him), opened a large window to "sedition and rebellion." To reiterate the point he says,

> [e]ither it must be left to the sovereign determination, whether the subjects security be sufficiently provided for, ... or to the discretion of the subject, (as the words themselves do seem to import,) and then there need be no other bellowes to kindle the fire of a civill war, and put a whole commonwealth into combustion, but this seditious article. (Bramhall 1995, 144–5)

The Earl of Clarendon is similarly scathing in his remarks, when discussing the rights of the sovereign and then the rights of subjects.

> tho he be so cruel as to divest his Subjects of all that liberty, which the best and most peaceable men desire to possess, yet he liberally and bountifully confers upon them such a liberty as no honest man can pretend to, and which is utterly inconsistent with the security of Prince and People. (Clarendon 1995, 234)

Clarendon follows this with an accusation that such an,

> unreasonable Indulgence of his, cannot but be thought to proceed from an unlawful affection for those who he saw had power enough to defend the transcendent wickedness they had committed. (Clarendon 1995, 234)

In other words, that Hobbes could only have argued for such liberties for subjects if he was trying to support the parliamentarian side in the civil war.

We should, I argue, take some notice of the views of people who were immersed in the politics, propaganda, and political theorizing of the day and who knew Hobbes personally. We should not be too quick to dismiss those whose thoughts on *Leviathan* were published when its author was still able to respond in person. If such people as these were convinced that Hobbes's statements on the rights of the subjects and the rights of the king made him vulnerable to accusations of supporting Cromwell against the royalists, then we should conclude that at the very least, Hobbes *appears* to grant strong rights to subjects, even to the point of limiting the absolute power of the sovereign. This gives us sufficient reason to examine very carefully his statements on the rights of subjects and the implications for their duties of obedience to the sovereign.

One of the elements of Hobbes's pronouncements on the rights of subjects that both Bramhall and Clarendon have strong objections to is the proposition that the right to self-preservation (sometimes referred to as the more narrow right to self-defense), cannot be given up to the sovereign and is carried into the commonwealth and held even against the sovereign. If there are rights that cannot be given up, then these are *inalienable* rights. Royalists always opposed the notion that subjects have inalienable rights. Parliamentarians, particularly radicals such as the Levellers, on the other hand, did argue that subjects have inalienable rights. Similarly, if there are rights held against the sovereign then there are rights of resistance. These are both the kinds of rights that were advocated by the parliamentarians (particularly the radicals) and vehemently opposed by royalists of all stripes. In the following section I set out Hobbes's theory of rights as presented in *Leviathan*.

13.1 Hobbes's Theory of Rights

Hobbes starts chapter 14 of *Leviathan* with these words,

> The RIGHT OF NATURE, which Writers commonly call *Jus Naturale*, is the Liberty each man hath to use his own power, as he will himself, for the preservation of his own Nature; that is to say, of his own Life; and consequently, of doing any thing, which in his own Judgement and Reason, hee shall conceive to be the aptest means thereunto. (Hobbes 2012, 189; 1651, 64)

This is the starting point of the political argument that will demonstrate how individuals in a (hypothetical) state of nature can get themselves out of that state of danger and into a commonwealth that will provide for their security and give them the chance of a commodious life. Hobbes goes on to provide definitions, first, of "law of nature" and then, of "right" and "law."

> A LAW OF NATURE, (*Lex Naturalis*,) is a Precept, or generall Rule, found out by Reason, by which a man is forbidden to do, that, which is destructive of his life, or taketh away the means of preserving the same; and to omit, that, by which he thinketh it may be best preserved. (Hobbes 2012, 198; 1651, 64)

So, the foundation of the law of nature, for Hobbes, is not the objective moral order approved by God, and known by individuals through their (God given) reason, of traditional natural law theory, but rather, those rules, discovered by each individual, using their reason, which will enable them to preserve themselves. Self-preservation, is, in other words, at the heart of Hobbes's argument and his political theory. And the right to self-preservation, I argue, is what drives the argument for government.

For Hobbes, all rights are liberties and here he makes it clear that the distinction between obligations and liberties is sharp. Law defines an obligation, something we are bound to follow. A right, on the other hand, defines a freedom and a choice to do or not do something. I should mention Hobbes's infamously restrictive definition of liberty as "the absence of externall Impediments" (Hobbes 2012, 202; 1651, 64), which seems to apply only to physical impediments and therefore to rule out impediments of other kinds such as legal or moral impediments. It is a strangely stark notion of liberty that says that as long as a person is not in chains, they are free to act. I agree with Michael Goldsmith however, that Hobbes also uses the term in a way that is closer to ordinary usage. Goldsmith points out that in chapter 21 of *Leviathan* Hobbes uses the term "liberty" to include freedom from *civil bonds*, (e.g. laws), as well as physical ones.[1]

In the state of nature, which is a state of war and constant danger to each of us, Hobbes says that we have a right to anything that may help us to preserve ourselves: "It followeth, that in such a condition, every man has a right to every thing; even to one anothers body" (Hobbes 2012, 198; 1651, 64). This "right of nature" is an aggregate right to any and every action or inaction that we may perceive as aiding our preservation. It is a completely unrestricted freedom that allows us to do anything, up to and including attacking other people. Commentators have been quick to point out that this untrammeled freedom will not provide security for anyone. On the contrary, it will only exacerbate the insecurity and danger of the state of nature. What commentators have sometimes been less quick to acknowledge is that Hobbes himself also immediately points this out and then proceeds to argue for a system of subjects' rights and a political system that will overcome the problem.

> And therefore, as long as this natural Right of every man to every thing endureth, there can be no security to any man, (how strong or wise soever he be,) of living out the time, which Nature ordinarily alloweth men to live. (Hobbes 2012, 198; 1651, 64)

It is the *second* law of nature that is crucial for the development of Hobbes's theory of rights. He starts to explain the process by which the unrestricted freedom of the state of nature is transformed into a set of rights that will help us to live and to live well and which are given protections in the form of the duties of others. The second law states,

> That a man be willing, when others are so too, as farre-forth, as for Peace, and defense of himself he shall thinketh it necessary, to lay down this right to all things; and be contented

with so much liberty against other men, as he would allow other men against himselfe. (Hobbes 2012, 200; 1651, 64–5)

Hobbes then describes the laying down and transferring of rights between individuals that must take place if they are to succeed in leaving the state of nature. The rights to be laid down or transferred are those, as he says, that we wouldn't want others to hold against us. So, any rights that are invasive or threatening must be given up; the most obvious example being the right "to one anothers body" of the right of nature. Clearly, any rights to attack others must be given up, along with all other rights that threaten others. What Hobbes means by laying down a right is that the right holder gives up the liberty of "hindring another of the benefit of his own Right to the same" (Hobbes 2012, 200; 1651, 65). Not, he points out, that the person laying down or transferring the right, gives to the person any right he did not have before "because there is nothing to which every man had not Right by Nature:" (Hobbes 2012, 200; 1651, 65). But it does commit him to *respect* the right held by the other person and allow him or her to freely exercise it. He will "standeth out of his way, that he may enjoy his own originall Right, without hindrance from him" (Hobbes 2012, 200; 1651, 65).

An example may help to illustrate the process Hobbes is describing. My right to your body is a right I hold under the right of nature. If I transfer that right to you I do not give you a new right to your body as you already had the right, but it means I will *give up my right to your body* and I will now be obliged to allow you to freely exercise your right to your body without any interference from me. The inclusion of obligation is significant. Hobbes scholars have often argued that there are no subjects' rights with correlative duties on the part of others; that there are no *claim rights* (to use the Hohfeldian terminology) for subjects in Hobbes's theory. In *Leviathan* Hobbes does describe what we might call claim rights for subjects, under the process of transferring and laying down of rights. He says that,

> when a man hath ... abandoned or granted away his Right; then is he said to be OBLIGED, or BOUND, not to hinder those, to whom such Right is granted, or abandoned, from the benefit of it: and that he *Ought*, and it is his DUTY, not to make voyd that voluntary act of his own: and that such hindrance is INJUSTICE, and INJURY. (Hobbes 2012, 200/202; 1651, 65)

It could not be clearer that Hobbes is saying that individuals, when they conform to the second law of nature, undertake a process whereby they transfer and give up their dangerous and invasive rights to each other so that no one will any longer have rights that are a threat to others. As part of this process, they take on duties to respect the rights of others, allowing them to freely exercise their rights. The resulting, strengthened rights for individuals seem to fit easily into the definition of claim rights, given by Hohfeld. I do not wish to characterize them as Hohfeldian claim rights, however, for reasons I will explain below, but I am happy to concede that they seem to fit the definition of claim rights.

Hobbes says "the mutuall transferring of Right, is that which men call CONTRACT" (Hobbes 2012, 204; 1651, 66). Much has been made of this by commentators who draw attention to the fact that when Hobbes describes the instituting of the sovereign, he leaves the sovereign out of the contract. The contract to institute the sovereign exists only between the individuals who will become the subjects, leaving the sovereign free of all contractual obligations. This had great significance when Hobbes was writing *Leviathan*, as the parliamentarians and radicals often insisted that the king had broken his contact with the people and that the people under such circumstances had the right to resist. Henry Parker (secretary to the commons from 1645) argued that resistance to the king was justified if he broke pre-existing law and "attacked the people."

> we must not think that it can stand with the intent of any trust, that necessary defence should be barred, and natural preservation denied to any people; as no man will deny, but that the People may use means of defence, where Princes are more conditionate, and have a sovereignty more limited. (Parker 1642, 20)

Hobbes clearly rejects this argument, leaving the sovereign out of the contract and making him unbound by any laws. Commentators have used this as part of an argument that Hobbesian subjects hold no significant rights, as they assume that for such rights to exist, there must be correlative duties on the part of the sovereign held to subjects. If he is outside the contract, the argument goes, he owes no (contractual) duties that would give rise to the rights. I shall argue that despite this Hobbes does provide sovereign protections for subjects' rights in two ways. First, by making the laws of nature actual laws and enforcing them and second, by the general duty of the sovereign to protect the people.

The next step in the theory of rights Hobbes is constructing is the section next to the squib that reads, "Not all Rights are alienable" (Hobbes 2012, 202; 1651, 66). Again, commentators have often denied the existence of inalienable rights for subjects in Hobbes's theory, despite Hobbes's clear statements to the contrary. Hobbes says that all voluntary acts aim at some good to oneself and the renouncing and transferring of rights is an example of where giving up certain rights (those that we wouldn't want held against ourselves) is in our own interests. Equally, he says, "there be some Rights, which no man can be understood by any words, or other signes, to have abandoned or transferred" (Hobbes 2012, 202; 1651, 66). Once again this emphasizes the centrality of the notion that our right to self-preservation, broadly construed,[2] is a right we can never give up. There are strict limits on which rights we should renounce and which we must not give up. Hobbes gives as examples, the right to resist anyone who assaults me and tries to kill me and equally anyone who wounds or imprisons or ties me up. This is partly because there is no good to oneself in not resisting such actions and secondly, because when we are attacked we don't know whether or not our assailant intends to kill us. In concluding this section, Hobbes makes clear again just how extensive the right to self-preservation is.

> And lastly the motive, and end for which this renouncing, and transferring of Right is introduced, is nothing else but the security of a mans person, in his life, and in the means of so preserving life, as not to be weary of it. (Hobbes 2012, 202; 1651, 66)

With these words, Hobbes illustrates the nature of the aggregate right to self-preservation as a right not just to live, but to the means to live well. In chapter 30, he reiterates the point: "As it is necessary for all men that seek peace, to lay down certaine Rights of

Nature; ... so it is necessarie for mans life to retain some; as right to governe their owne bodies; enjoy aire, water, motion, waies to go from place to place; and all things else without which a man cannot live, or not live well" (Hobbes 2012, 234, 1651, 77).

Hobbes spells out some of the specific rights that are inalienable in the infamous chapter 21 of *Leviathan*, "Of the LIBERTY of Subjects." He says,

> to come now to the particulars of the true Liberty of a Subject; that is to say, what are the things, which though commanded by the Soveraign, he may neverthelesse, without Injustice, refuse to do. (Hobbes 2012, 336; 1651, 111)

And the list includes: the right to defend himself against attack, the right to food, air, medicine "or any other thing without which he cannot live" (Hobbes 2012, 336; 1651, 111–12); and if ordered to abstain from any of these "yet hath that man liberty to disobey" (Hobbes 2012, 336; 1651, 112). Interestingly, he adds the right not to incriminate himself, the right not to kill anyone and not to "execute any dangerous or dishonourable office" (Hobbes 2012, 338; 1651, 112), though he adds the proviso that a subject is at liberty to disobey except when doing so "frustrates the End for which the Soveraignty was ordained; then there is no Liberty to refuse: otherwise there is" (Hobbes 2012, 338; 1651, 112). He also adds the right to refuse to fight in the army, if the person is of a timorous nature or if he is able to substitute another soldier, and he infamously says that if a "great many men together, have already resisted the Sovereign Power unjustly" they have the Liberty then "to joyn together, and assist, and defend one another" (Hobbes 2012, 340; 1651, 112). This last right has been said by some to amount to a right to rebellion. And finally, Hobbes says that there are many other liberties where the law is silent. "In cases where the Soveraign has prescribed no rule, there the Subject hath the liberty to do, or to forbeare, according to his own discretion" (Hobbes 2012, 340; 1651, 113).

Now we can start to see the shape of Hobbes's theory of rights. It is a theory that starts, after defining a right as a liberty, by granting individuals in a state of nature the right to anything that may help them to preserve themselves. So, he starts by giving all individuals total freedom, or a complete set of liberties. Then he acknowledges that having the freedom to do anything, rather than making people safer in a state of nature, makes them less safe. To make them safer, Hobbes first introduces a process whereby individuals give up and transfer dangerous and invasive rights and take on duties not to interfere with the original rights of others. This provides subjects with some protected rights against each other where invasive or dangerous rights have been given up and transferred but leaves them with no protections for the all-important aggregate right to self-preservation. (These protections will come with the institution of the sovereign.) He starts to address this by saying that the rights that are required for self-preservation must be held on to by subjects. Hobbes confirms this by saying (as earlier) that these rights are inalienable. They cannot be given up to the sovereign or transferred or given up to each other (as the invasive rights are). He does then provide protections for them but not by directly correlated duties on the part of the sovereign. Instead, they are protected indirectly, once the sovereign is instituted, by both the laws of nature that the sovereign makes into real, enforceable laws and by the sovereign's duty of office, to protect the people.

> The OFFICE of the Soveraign, (be it a Monarch or an Assembly) consisteth in the end for which he was trusted with the Soveraign Power, namely the procuration of *the safety of the people*; to which he is obliged by the Law of Nature. (Hobbes 2012, 520; 1651, 175)

Hobbes demonstrates the inalienability of the right to self-preservation and its connection to the sovereign duty to provide for the safety of the people: "The Obligation of Subjects to the Soveraign, is understood to last as long, and no longer, than the power lasteth, by which he is able to protect them" (Hobbes 2012, 344; 1651, 114). And lest we doubt his intentions, next to this, in the squib, he says "*In what Cases Subjects are absolved of their obedience to their Soveraign*" (Hobbes 2012, 344; 1651, 114). Hobbes is clear that once the sovereign fails to protect the subjects then they are free of their obligations to obey him and may seek protection elsewhere.

> The end of Obedience is Protection; which, wheresoever a man seeth it, either in his own, or in anothers sword, Nature applyeth his obedience to it, and his endeavour to maintaine it. (Hobbes 2012, 344; 1651, 114)

It has been a point of contention whether or not it is for the subjects to judge when they are not being protected.[3] As I mentioned earlier, Hobbes's contemporaries recognized the importance of this point and were heavily critical of him for giving the impression that he thought it was for the subjects to decide, rather than the sovereign. When Hobbes says, "wheresoever a man seeth it," referring to protection, it is hard to understand any meaning other than that it is for the subjects to judge when they are no longer being protected.[4] In the following sections, I shall discuss the two sets of arguments that are used to support the claims of commentators that the rights of Hobbesian subjects are weak and insignificant.

13.2 The Absolutism of the Hobbesian Sovereign Precludes Strong Rights for Subjects

It is "a truth universally acknowledged" that a Hobbesian sovereign must be absolute. This is hardly surprising as there are many good reasons for believing it, not least, Hobbes's many pronouncements to that effect. What is surprising is that he should also put in place apparently strong, retained rights for subjects, which will somehow coexist with an absolute sovereign. Hobbesian absolutism is usually understood to rule out rights of any strength or significance on the part of Hobbesian subjects and particularly, any rights held *against* the sovereign. Indeed, the notion of an absolute sovereign whose subjects hold inalienable rights against him is almost a contradiction in terms.[5] And yet a close reading of *Leviathan* seems to give us exactly that.

Commentators have found ways to explain the apparent inconsistency. The most common way, is simply to insist that Hobbesian subjects give up all their rights, bar the right to a bare physical defense that is said to hold no significance as a right and not to threaten the absolutism of the sovereign. Alan Ryan echoes many others when he says that Hobbes is arguing that we can,

> infer that the way to achieve peace is to give up as much of our natural rights as others will. It appears that we must renounce *all* our rights, save only the right to defend ourselves *in extremis*. (Ryan 1996, 223)

C.B. Macpherson says the following on subjects transferring their rights under the second law of nature,

> So, reasonable men ... would see that that they had not only to give up their right to everything, but had also to transfer to some authority their natural powers to protect themselves ... The person or body of persons to whom these rights were transferred would be the sovereign .... (Macpherson 1968, 44)

Macpherson doesn't even acknowledge a bare right to self-defense. On his view, subjects simply give up all their rights to the sovereign.[6] There are two problems with these ways of characterizing what Hobbes says on the subjects' rights, or lack of rights. The first is that the right to self-preservation has been narrowed down to a right to mere physical self-defense when under attack or, as in Macpherson's case, there is no right at all as this too has been given up to the sovereign. I argue that this is to misread the right to self-preservation, which, as explained previously, is not only inalienable but is a much broader right than has been generally acknowledged, as it includes all those rights required for subjects not just to live but to live well. The second problem is that the *implications* of the inalienable right to self- preservation are ignored. The implications for the sovereign's power and authority are serious and significant. His sovereignty dissolves if he fails in his duty to protect the people and ensure their safety. The sovereign's duties of office protect the right to self-preservation, albeit indirectly.

The idea that subjects might have rights of resistance against the sovereign was a contested and highly controversial subject at the time Hobbes was writing *Leviathan*. To borrow Susanne Sreedhar's characterization of absolutism as rule by "a supreme, unlimited, undivided ruler who is unaccountable to those who are ruled" (Sreedhar 2012, 145), it is easy to see the extent to which it is seemingly incompatible with subjects having any rights that are held against the sovereign. All authority lies with the sovereign and all obligations to obey lie with the subjects.

One of the orthodoxies of Hobbes scholarship has been to treat Hobbes's political theory as one consistent theory expressed three times, first, in *The Elements of Law* (Hobbes 1994), then *De Cive* (Hobbes 1998) and finally, in *Leviathan*. I argue that the theory changes significantly on the question of subjects' rights in *Leviathan*. (It is worth noting that *Leviathan* was written during the latter stages of the civil war, when Charles I was on the losing side, while the other two works were written close to the beginning, when one might have assumed a royalist victory.)

Hobbes changes what he says on the right to resist the sovereign in *Leviathan*. His position in previous works takes the conventional (royalist, absolutist) position against resistance rights. In *De Cive* (Hobbes 1998) he says, when individuals subject themselves to the sovereign, each person "has given up his right to resist" (Hobbes 1998, ch. V, 74). There is some ambiguity, however, as he also says that a subject "is understood to retain the right of defending himself against violence" (Hobbes 1998, ch. V, 72). The ambiguity is compounded when he then says "[e]ach man retains the

Right to defend himself at his own discretion, as long as his security is not provided for" (Hobbes 1998, ch. VI, 75), implying that once the sovereign has been instituted (to provide that security), this right will no longer exist.[7] What we can say with some certainty is that in *De Cive* (Hobbes 1998) the only right that might be retained and held against the sovereign is that of physical self-defense when under attack. In *Leviathan*, however, the situation is markedly different. Hobbes sets out a whole slew of rights that must be retained and cannot be given up. Subjects retain all the rights they need to live and to live well (as earlier). Not only does Hobbes broaden the retained right to self-preservation beyond the mere right to fend off physical attack of *De Cive* (Hobbes 1998) he also changes the very definition of a right. He wrenches the meaning of it away from the ties to notions of traditional natural law that it has in *De Cive* (Hobbes 1998)[8] to the simple, modern, subjective notion in *Leviathan*: "RIGHT consisteth in liberty to do, or to forebeare" (Hobbes 2012, 198; 1651, 64).

13.3 Against the Orthodoxy: Hobbesian Rights Are Not All Hohfeldian Liberty Rights

The final piece of the puzzle in unravelling what Hobbes says and doesn't say about subjects' rights in *Leviathan* is revealed when we examine the orthodoxy that has gripped much of Hobbes scholarship on rights for the past 70 years and more. This is the view, mentioned earlier, that subjects' rights, as described by Hobbes, fit the definition of Hohfeldian "privileges," often termed "liberty rights" (Finkelstein 2001; Green 2013; Hampton 1986; Sreedhar 2010). The significance of defining subjects' rights as Hohfeldian liberty rights is that liberty rights lack any correlative duties on the part of others. And it is those correlative duties that are said to be what is required to protect the rights of the right-holders; in this case, Hobbesian subjects. Again, commentators draw attention to the fact that the sovereign is outside the contract made between individuals and so owes no contractual duties directly to subjects. Therefore, the argument goes, the rights of subjects remain unprotected. Some more detail on the Hohfeldian system will help to clarify the relevance of this for Hobbes's theory of rights and the way it has been categorized and understood.

Wesley Hohfeld's analysis of the ways that the term "right" is used in the legal literature, primarily in legal case law, is justly famous (Hohfeld 1919). It is undoubtedly a brilliant piece of analytical jurisprudence, and his categories of rights are now used ubiquitously. He picks out four types of right or meanings of the term "right," that are referred to in the legal literature and then analyzes their implications in terms of legal correlatives and legal opposites. The four categories of right are: claim or "claim right," privilege (or "liberty right"), powers, and immunities.

For our purposes, the first two are the most important. Claims or "claim rights" are rights that have directly correlated duties on the part of another or others, to respect them or allow their exercise or protect them. So, my claim right not to be assaulted is correlated with everyone else's duty not to assault me. Privileges or "liberty rights" are justified liberties or freedoms to do (or not do) something or have (or not have) something that has *no* correlated duties. So, my liberty right to walk on the common means

I am free to walk there but no one else has any duties to stay off my path or get out of my way to allow me to walk.

Each Hohfeldian category or "incident" has a legal correlative and a legal opposite. A claim right has the legal correlative of a duty and the legal opposite of a "no-right." A "liberty right" (privilege) has the legal correlative of a "no-right" and the legal opposite of a duty. We can see immediately the significance of these categories for an application to political rights. Any right categorized as a liberty right cannot give rise to any duties to protect it. Similarly, any claim right will, by definition, give rise to such duties.

Hohfeld's analysis of legal rights has been widely accepted and used by those writing on political theory and moral theory as well as legal theory. The notion of a "claim right" has been adopted by political philosophers to the extent that it is now more or less synonymous with "political right." As Jeremy Waldron puts it, "Hohfeld's claim-right is generally regarded as coming closest to capturing the concept of individual rights used in political morality" (Waldron 1984, 8). The implication for the way that political rights are now conceived, is that an individual right will count as a *political right*, if and only if, it is directly correlated with a duty or duties on the part of another or others to allow its exercise or respect it or provide it.

Commentary on Hobbes's theory of rights generally takes the view that Hobbes describes only liberty rights for subjects and no claim rights. There are two main reasons for this. The first, is that Hobbes defines all rights as liberties (Hobbes 2012, 198; 1651, 64), and the second, is that he specifically denies the existence of sovereign duties correlative to subjects' rights. This is especially relevant given that political rights have come to be seen (at least since Locke) as correlated specifically with the duties of *the state* toward its citizens. Yet, as I have shown, Hobbes does describe what could be called claim rights, when subjects transfer and lay down some of those rights, held under the right of nature, that might be a threat to others. When x transfers a right to y, he takes on an obligation to stand out of y's way so that the right can be exercised. y now has a claim right in relation to x.

> when a man hath ... abandoned or granted away his Right; then is he said to be OBLIGED, or BOUND, not to hinder those, to whom such Right is granted, or abandoned, from the benefit of it. (Hobbes 2012, 200; 1651, 65)

It might be argued that these rights are less important than the rights held under the aggregate right to self-preservation, which are never transferred or given up and need to be protected. If Hobbes's theory of individual rights is as strong and significant as I claim it is, then I must demonstrate how the right to self-preservation is protected. I argue that to give an accurate reading of Hobbesian rights (in *Leviathan*) we must give up the Hohfeldian interpretation, which hamstrings our analysis of Hobbesian rights by forcing us to conceive the rights as *either* liberties *or* claims. To argue against the Hohfeldian interpretation of Hobbesian rights, I need to argue against the Hohfeldian system itself, or at least, against its wholesale application to political rights.

One of the (presumably unintended) consequences of the use of the Hohfeldian system in political theories of rights has been to *separate* the notion of liberty from that of a political right. This may seem odd when we consider the rich history, within political thought, of the notion of "liberty" and how closely tied it has been to that of a "right," particularly within theories of "natural rights." The Hohfeldian "privilege" or "liberty right" has rendered the older understanding of liberty impotent in political theory. It has relegated "liberties" to the category of "bare freedoms," which have no protections and therefore no real value for right holders. Claims, on the other hand, are so tied to their correlative duties as to exist only as entitlements to those duties.

If we extricate ourselves from the Hohfeldian categories and look simply at what Hobbes says about subjects' rights in *Leviathan*, it becomes clear that he describes rights that are liberties or freedoms. These rights are justified freedoms to act or not act and they are protected in various ways. Some are protected by duties taken on by subjects to each other when they transfer and lay down the dangerous and invasive rights they held under the right of nature. These duties become laws once a sovereign is in place. The aggregate right to self- preservation, that is, all the rights that we need to preserve ourselves in such a way that we can live a good life, are protected (indirectly) by the duties of the sovereign. These are not contractual duties held directly toward individual subjects as Hobbes makes clear. They are the duties of the *office* of sovereign.

> The OFFICE of the Soveraign, ... consisteth in the end, for which he was trusted with the Soveraign Power, namely the procuration of the safety of the people; ... But by Safety here, is not meant a bare Preservation, but also all other Contentments of life, which every man by lawfull Industry, without danger, or hurt to the Commonwealth, shall acquire to himselfe. (Hobbes 2012, 520; 1651, 175)

Despite much being made of the fact that the sovereign is outside the contract and therefore owes no duties directly to subjects, the duties of the *office* of sovereign are significant and failure to perform these duties has serious consequences. The subjects are only obliged to obey the sovereign as long as he is protecting them. They are "absolved of their obedience" (Hobbes 2012, 344; 1651, 114) if he ceases to protect them: "The Obligation of Subjects to the Soveraign, is understood to last as long, and no longer, than the power lasts by which he is able to protect them" (Hobbes 2012, 344; 1651, 114). This demonstrates that there are ways in which rights can be protected other than by directly correlated duties that attach to each right, as in the Hohfeldian system. It also demonstrates the possibility of having rights that are both liberties and also protected.

The (mis)reading of Hobbesian rights as Hohfeldian liberty rights is understandable in terms of the Hohfeldian definitions but fails to take account of the fact that many of the legal rights Hohfeld discusses are complex bundles of liberties and claims. Rights that may seem to have no duties to protect them do gain protection through the claim rights they are attached to. To expand my previous example, my liberty right to walk on the common is not directly protected by anyone's duty to allow me to walk or stand out of my way. But my accompanying claim right to walk on the common without being assaulted, is protected by everyone else's duty not to assault me. Combined together, I have a right to walk freely and safely on the common. Although no one is obliged to stand out of my way, all others are obliged not to assault me as I walk. An example Hohfeld gives himself is of property rights, which are complex bundles of claims and liberties.[9]

These complexities of the Hohfeldian system are overlooked by Hobbes commentators who simply define all subjects' rights as simple liberty rights and infer that there are therefore no protections at all for subjects' rights. This leads them to conclude that Hobbes's theory of rights is weak and of no benefit to subjects.

13.4 Conclusion

The fact that in *Leviathan* Hobbes describes strong rights for subjects, some of which are held against the sovereign, creates a puzzle for our interpretation of Hobbes's political theory. If he is arguing for absolutism – and there is strong evidence that he is – then why does he allow subjects to hold strong rights, including rights of resistance against the sovereign? Also, why does he make the sovereign's right to rule conditional upon judgements by the people, that he is securing their safety? There are no easy answers to these questions in my view and there is not the space here to explore possible explanations.

The second theme, regarding the application of Hohfeldian categories of rights to Hobbes's theory, is more easily resolved. Hobbesian rights should be re-examined without the Hohfeldian categories, so that they can be analyzed in a way that accurately reflects Hobbes's descriptions.

As I have demonstrated, a careful reading of the text of *Leviathan* reveals a theory of rights according to which the rights of subjects are both strong and significant. Subjects have extensive rights that are protected in various ways and that ultimately open the door to justified disobedience if the sovereign fails to protect them. Equally, the sovereign's authority and right to rule are made dependent on his ability and willingness to protect the subjects' aggregate right to self-preservation.

Notes

1 For a discussion of Goldsmith's view as well as my own arguments on Hobbes's extended use of the term 'liberty' see Curran (2010) and for Goldsmith's arguments see Goldsmith (1989).
2 For a full discussion of the breadth of the right to self-preservation see Curran (2006).
3 For example, see Hampton (1986). Hampton thinks that allowing the subjects to judge whether they are being protected, "makes the subjects the judges of whether or not they will obey any of the sovereign's laws" (1986, 201) and uses this as part of her argument that Hobbes's argument for absolute sovereignty fails.
4 For a fuller version of this argument see, Curran (2006).
5 As Lloyd and Sreedhar (2019) put it, "His ascription of apparently inalienable rights – what he calls the 'true liberties of subjects' – seems incompatible with his defense of absolute sovereignty." And Will Kymlicka, says, "as Hobbes puts it, there is a 'power irresistible' on earth, and for Hobbes and his contemporary followers, such power 'justifieth all actions really and properly, in whomsoever it is found.' No one could claim rights of self-ownership against such power" (1990, 130).
6 For a detailed discussion showing why subjects do not give up their rights to the sovereign see, Curran (2019).

7 For a more detailed discussion of the change in retained rights from *De Cive* (Hobbes 1998) to *Leviathan*, see Curran (2019).

8 "...what is not contrary to right reason, all agree is done justly and *of Right*. For precisely what is meant by the term *Right*, is the liberty each man has of using his natural faculties in accordance with right reason. Therefore the first foundation of natural *Right* is that *each man protect his life and limbs as much as he can*" (Hobbes 1998, ch. 1, 27).

9 "In the example last put. Whereas x has a right, or claim that y, the other man, should stay off the land, he himself has the privilege of entering the land" (Hohfeld 1919, 38–9).

References

Bramhall, John. 1995. "The Catching of Leviathan, or the Great Whale." In *Leviathan: Contemporary Responses to the Political Theory of Thomas Hobbes*, edited by Graham A. J. Rogers, 115–79. Bristol: Thoemmes Press.

Clarendon, Edward, Earl of. 1995. "A Survey of Mr Hobbes His Leviathan." In *Leviathan: Contemporary Responses to the Political Theory of Thomas Hobbes*, edited by Graham A. J. Rogers, 180–300. Bristol: Thoemmes Press.

Curran, Eleanor. 2006. "Can Rights Curb the Hobbesian Sovereign? The Full Right to Self-preservation, Duties of Sovereignty and the Limitations of Hohfeld." *Law and Philosophy* 25: 243–65.

Curran, Eleanor. 2010. "Blinded by the Light of Hohfeld: Hobbes's Notion of Liberty." *Jurisprudence* 1 (2010): 85–104.

Curran, Eleanor. 2019. "Hobbesian Sovereignty and the Rights of Subjects: Absolutism Undermined?" *Hobbes Studies* 32: 209–30.

Finkelstein, Claire. 2001. "A Puzzle about Hobbes on Self-defense." *Pacific Philosophical Quarterly* 82 (3–4): 332–61.

Gauthier, David. 1969. *The Logic of Leviathan: The Moral and Political Theory of Thomas Hobbes*. Oxford: Clarendon Press.

Goldsmith, Michael. 1989. "Hobbes on Liberty." *Hobbes Studies* 23: 23–39.

Green, Michael. 2013. "Hobbes and Human Rights." In *Hobbes Today*, edited by Sharon A. Lloyd, 320–34. New York: Cambridge University Press.

Hampton, Jean. 1986. *Hobbes and the Social Contract Tradition*. Cambridge: Cambridge University Press.

Hobbes, Thomas. 1994. *The Elements of Law. Human Nature and De corpore Politico*, edited by John C. A. Gaskin. Oxford: Oxford University Press [First published 1640].

Hobbes, Thomas. 1998. *On the Citizen*, edited by Richard Tuck and Michael Silverthorne. Cambridge: Cambridge University Press [First published 1640].

Hobbes, Thomas. 2012. *Leviathan*, 3 vols., edited by Noel Malcolm. Oxford: Clarendon Press. [First published 1651.]

Hohfeld, Wesley. 1919. *Fundamental Legal Conceptions as Applied in Judicial Reasoning*, edited by Walter Wheeler Cook. New Haven, CT: Yale University Press.

Kavka, Gregory. 1986. *Hobbesian Moral and Political Theory*. Princeton, NJ: Princeton University Press.

Kymlicka, Will. 1990. *Contemporary Political Philosophy*. Oxford: Clarendon Press.

Lloyd, S.A. and Susanne Sreedhar. 2019. "Hobbes's Moral and Political Philosophy." In *The Stanford Encyclopedia of Philosophy*, edited by Edward N. Zalta. Accessed November 5, 2020. https://plato.stanford.edu/archives/spr2019/entries/hobbes-moral

Macpherson, Crawford B. 1968. "Introduction to Leviathan." In *Leviathan*, edited by Crawford B. Macpherson, 9–63. Reprinted 1985. Aylesbury: Penguin Books.

Martinich, Aloysius P. 1995. *A Hobbes Dictionary*. Oxford: Blackwell.

Martinich, Aloysius P. 1999. *Hobbes. A Biography*. Cambridge: Cambridge University Press.

Parker, Henry. 1642. *Observations upon Some of His Majesties Late Answers and Expresses*, Vol. X. London: London Tracts.

Ryan, Alan. 1996. "Hobbes's Political Philosophy." In *The Cambridge Companion to Hobbes*, edited by Tom Sorell, 208–45. Cambridge: Cambridge University Press.

Skinner, Quentin. 2008. *Hobbes and Republican Liberty*. Cambridge: Cambridge University Press.

Sommerville, Johann P. 1992. *Thomas Hobbes: Political Ideas in Historical Context*. New York: St. Martin's Press.

Sreedhar, Susanne. 2010. *Hobbes on Resistance: Defying the Leviathan*. Cambridge: Cambridge University Press.

Sreedhar, Susanne. 2012. "Absolutism." In *Bloomsbury Companion to Hobbes*, edited by Sharon A. Lloyd, 145–7. London: Bloomsbury Publishing Inc.

Tuck, Richard. 1993. *Philosophy and Government 1572–1651*. Cambridge: Cambridge University Press.

Waldron, Jeremy. 1984. "Introduction." In *Theories of Rights*, edited by Jeremy Waldron, 1–20. New York: Oxford University Press.

Wesley, Hohfeld. *Fundamental Legal Conceptions*, [2019], Law Book Exchange 2010, 36.

commitment to the sovereign. In the absence of an obligation immediately tied to the sovereign, the duty to obey civil law seems remote and suspiciously weak. Furthermore, if subjects have no rights against their sovereign and he has no obligations to them, he is free to legislate for his own purposes and in opposition to his subjects' interests. When the sovereign is a tyrant, and an individual subject can expect little or no "*Good to himselfe*" (Hobbes 2012, 202; 1651, 66) from obedience, Hobbes considered the subject's commitment terminated. Clearly, that was not compatible with his aim.

The two-step approach provides a comprehensible and convincing account of how individuals become bound to obey civil law. On the complex account, each individual personally commits himself to being a congregant of the commonwealth. Then, acting as a congregant rather than an egocentric individual, each as part of the Leviathan, whether in the majority or not, covenants with the sovereign to be his lawmaker and yields him the powers that the People chose to relinquish. Thereby, each individual becomes personally committed to obeying the civil law while the sovereign assumes obligations to act in the interest of the commonwealth. With the sovereign morally bound to pursue peace and security for the commonwealth, empowered by individual subjects, and constrained by fear of the Leviathan entity, every subject has a strict duty and reasons to obey the sovereign's laws. *Fear* of the sovereign's punishment or expulsion from society provides powerful motivation for even short-sighted foolish individuals. Furthermore, individuals become committed to obedience by their *consent* to do what each recognizes as serving his interests. Hence, transgressions would also contradict the plan prescribed by each person's own *reason*. And because the sovereign's actions are *authorized* by each individual who, as a member of the commonwealth, covenants with the sovereign and relinquishes his power to rule himself, the sovereign's laws are truly *one's own laws created by each for himself*. The self-made laws are implicitly binding because they carry one's own assent.

Whereas the third-party beneficiary account can present a case for *fear*, one reason to obey civil law, and an arguable case for *reason* and *consent*, only the complex account can adequately defend the additional reason that they are *one's own laws*. This justification is the one Hobbes repeatedly identified as the morally significant ground for the obligation to obey the civil law.[10]

The relationship between obligated subjects and sovereign, which emerges from the complex interpretation, is also more palatable in contemporary society than the alternative. On this view, there are grounds for holding a sovereign accountable for his actions and the mighty Leviathan is the means for opposing his unauthorized actions. The sovereign, as a covenanting party, is committed to acting in pursuit of peace, security, and a good life for his subjects. If the sovereign fails to fulfill those duties to the congregation, the People could replace him as its agent just as one could fire a lawyer and engage another representative. Such voiding of a covenant and disenfranchisement of a sovereign would not be an injustice because once confidence in his performance on the covenant is eroded by failures to fulfill his duty there is no imminent "coercive Power to compell" (Hobbes 2012, 220; 1651, 71) future compliance. Theoretically, the People could affect such a change in leadership without bringing about a bloody revolution (e.g., Bill Clinton replacing George Bush in the United States, Corazone Aquino replacing Ferdinand Marcos in the Philippines). When Leviathan, the commonwealth, "a real Unitie of them all, in one and the same Person" (Hobbes 2012,

14

Hobbes on Sovereignty and Its Strains

TOM SORELL

Hobbes's theory of sovereignty is the centerpiece of his science of politics. That science has two audiences: citizens or subjects on the one hand, and rulers on the other. For citizens the rules of appropriate behavior can be boiled down to one: obey the law. Obey the law or invite civil war with all its misery. For rulers, Hobbes systematically states precepts for avoiding civil war and conquest by foreign powers. These precepts are bound up with the rights and duties of sovereigns.

According to Hobbes, a sovereign's rights are extensive. Indeed, it is easy to read him as saying that the rights of sovereigns are virtually unlimited in practice, if sovereignty is ideally instituted, that is, instituted by the contract among the many that he outlines in his political writings. Nearly anything the sovereign does, short of putting subjects in fear of imminent death, is permitted. Accordingly, one question to be considered in what follows is this: does Hobbes's theory of sovereignty by institution rationalize *over-mighty* government?[1] Again, does it exaggerate the degree to which a government can take control (or take back control) of its people's affairs? I shall suggest that the answer to both questions is "No," despite the presence in Hobbes's writings of many rhetorical flourishes that suggest the contrary. Hobbes is always conscious of the many sources of *fragility* in sovereignty, including the tendency to over-regulate and to give too little weight to the interests of the many.

In *Leviathan*, which contains the most mature and elaborate version of Hobbes's politics, the theory of sovereignty is in three parts. One part is to do with the typical historical causes of the breakdown of states; another is to do with the rights needed to pre-empt that breakdown; and the third is to do with constraints on the exercise of those rights. After expounding the theory, I shall review what can be gathered from Hobbes's writings about the usual *strains* of sovereignty. I shall divide these into internal and external strains, corresponding to the distinction between the domestic affairs of the commonwealth and international relations. Other sources of strain arise from the

A Companion to Hobbes, First Edition. Edited by Marcus P. Adams.

constitutional form of sovereignty, and in particular from differences between its being realized in one-person form, as a monarchy, or in many-person form, as a council.

14.1 What Is a Sovereign?

I begin with something like a near-definition of the role of sovereign, and then pass to Hobbes's normative theory of the exercise of sovereignty. To prepare for the definition we need the idea of the *right of nature*, or "the Liberty each man hath, to use his own power, as he will himself, for the preservation of his own Nature; that is to say, of his own Life; and consequently, of doing any thing, which in his own Judgement and Reason, hee shall conceive to be the aptest means thereunto" (Hobbes 2012, 198; 1651, 64). Or, in other words, each person naturally has the right to be his own judge of the best means of preserving his life, and to implement those means.

Hobbes has a famous argument to the conclusion that people who live together and exercise the right of nature will end up being involved in general violence: a war of all against all. According to him, people who live in groups without government not only *tend* to compete by life-threatening means for the enjoyment of things they want; they cannot be blamed for doing so, if not doing so seems to them to put their life at risk. And not behaving violently with competitors *can* put people's lives at risk, since competitors may well judge that killing is the best means of getting what they want, and may judge that abstaining from violence is a sign of weakness, which invites opportunistic attack. Thus, the distribution of the right of nature among many competitors is an important ingredient of the war of all against all.

Giving up by transferring the right of nature is the one way, according to Hobbes, that the many have of escaping an otherwise chaotic, conflicting, and probably fatal, many-person pursuit of personal safety and prosperity. Submitting to a sovereign brings it about that a single judgment operates in the interests of all who agree to be directed by it. And this is where the idea of sovereignty starts. It is a way of turning many wills into one, of turning a mere "crowd" or "concourse" of people into a *unified* body politic (Hobbes 2012, 268; 1651, 90). In the version of Hobbes's political theory in *Leviathan*, the individual or council who accepts the mass transfer of the right of nature *personifies* a majority who authorize the individual or council to act in their interests.[2]

In the light of the preceding, we may define a sovereign (by institution) as

> the willing recipient of a voluntary transfer of the right of nature from each of a majority of locally interacting people in the state of nature.

If the sovereign is a human *individual*, that person receives the right of nature on the understanding that they will act for the survival and prosperity of the many. If the sovereign is a legislative body, that body too acts for the survival and prosperity of the many.

The first thing to be said about the sovereign is that they are a *third party* to the contract among the many. The many agree among *themselves* to lay down the right of nature as an ingredient of war. They agree to be directed by someone or some group of people, if the sovereign accepts to give them direction. But the many do not contract with the sovereign (Hobbes 2012, 266; 1651, 89). Instead, the sovereign receives a *gift*, in a technical sense (Hobbes 2012, 204; 1651, 66), of the right of nature of each of the others. The sovereign is offered obedience if the sovereign accepts to direct them, not if the sovereign accepts to direct them according to a certain plan that the many have to understand and consent to in advance. The many get no plan, only a sign that the sovereign will decide how to direct the many in the interests of collective peace.

In other words, the sovereign individual or council acts on the joint willingness of the many to be told how to behave for their own protection from one another. Accepting the transfer of the right of nature is what makes someone a sovereign over those who have initiated the transfer. By accepting the transfer an individual or a council is authorized to decide the means by which the many live in peace, and the sovereign declares those means through laws requiring different kinds of behavior of all of the many. The many lend their wills to the law by complying unquestioningly, or, in other words, by *submission*. It is as if each of the many says to the sovereign, "You be the judge of the means of protecting me (the laws that keep us at peace); my will is at your service (I will comply with those laws)."

The most important source in *Leviathan* for Hobbes's normative theory of the role of the sovereign – the theory of what the sovereign is permitted and required to do – is not, as it may seem to be, chapter 18, on the rights of sovereigns. It is chapter 18 read together with chapter 29, on the causes of the dissolution of the commonwealth, and chapter 30, on the duties of the sovereign.[3] The relation between *Leviathan* chapters 18 and 29 can be put by saying that the rights of sovereigns are, among other things, those necessary for *counteracting* the causes of state failure seen in history. As for the duties of sovereigns, these *limit* the exercise of the rights of sovereigns – based on the idea that the over-riding purpose of the sovereign is not merely the elimination of life-threatening violence, but the achievement of something more ambitious, namely "public safety" once the many have submitted to the sovereign. We shall come back to the difference between preserving life and achieving public safety.

14.2 Sovereignty and the Causes of State Collapse

Starting with *Leviathan* chapter 29, then, the causes of the dissolution of commonwealths are (in order of discussion in chapter 29):

- Lack of sufficient power for maintenance of commonwealth
  - For example, because of a concession of powers to the Church

- Seditious doctrines
  - that good and evil to be judged privately
  - that conscience is morally authoritative
  - that faith and sanctity are acquired by inspiration
  - that the sovereign is subject to civil laws
  - that a subject owns goods to the exclusion of the right of the sovereign
  - that sovereign power is divisible

- Imitation of foreign powers
  - Greek and Roman history and policy

- Mixed Government: separation of the powers of taxation, legislation, and command of military
- Lack of money for state purposes
- Concentration of private money in a few
- Popularity of a private subject
- Centers of non-state power able to raise armies
- Appetite for enlarging dominion
- Ease (life without industry)
- Riot (in the sense of lavish display) and vain expense.

Hobbes begins chapter 29 with the point that commonwealths are instituted to last indefinitely, perhaps even eternally. The people who agree among themselves to transfer their respective rights of nature to a would be single directing intelligence do not bargain for government that lasts only as long as the life of a single monarch, or only as long as the lives of members of an original assembly. They bargain for *continuity* of sovereign power (Hobbes 2012, 258; 1651, 86). Conquest by a foreign state can break that continuity, but so, more importantly, can internal weaknesses, weaknesses ascribable to the defective *institution* of the commonwealth (Hobbes 2012, 498; 1651, 167).

First in Hobbes's list of internal weaknesses is a willingness on the part of the sovereign individual or sovereign council to hold back in the exercise of power. Misguided self-restraint of this kind can consist of tolerating centers of power alongside the sovereign power, such as centers of ecclesiastical power, or constitutional power sharing, as in Rome between the Senate and the people. Hobbes thinks that proper sovereign power is always unitary and always total: in a monarchy, the people are personified and made one by a single individual. They are made one by the monarch's willingness to be their lawgiver, by his duty to identify with their interests, and by their agreement to be passively law-abiding (i.e., obedient to the commands of the sovereign). A council is less unitary, as the members each retain some prerogative of judgment and can disagree among themselves. They also need to disregard their own individual interests and competitive instincts. But the more individual interests need to be ignored by a sovereign in order to identify with the interest of the public, the harder it is to identify with the interests of the public. So, a council is not the ideal vehicle of sovereignty.

Many of the other things that tend to the dissolution of the commonwealth, according to chapter 29, are connected with supposed sources of practical decision outside a monarchy or assembly. These extraneous sources of practical decision include calls to action by orators, or subversive teachings in available books that a sovereign has neglected to outlaw or censor. In the first part of *Leviathan* chapter 29, Hobbes dwells on *doctrines* that are sources of subversion. These can be divided into two kinds: doctrines that undermine the agreement of the many in the Commonwealth to abstain from a range of practical judgement; and doctrines that limit or reduce the powers needed by the sovereign for keeping the peace.

To begin with the doctrines of the first kind, he condemns the belief that each person can individually judge what is good and what is evil. This doctrine in effect endorses the presumption of Adam and Eve before the Tree of Knowledge, when, according to the biblical Book of Genesis, they aspired to be judges of the difference between good and evil by eating the fruit of that tree. The belief that each person can individually judge good and evil recalls disobedience to one of the first commands of the God of the Hebrew Bible – that Adam and Eve *not* eat from the Tree of Knowledge. People who give up the right of nature as part of the original contract agree to do what Adam and Eve did not do but should have done: abstain from judgment about right and wrong in matters of the public good.[4] The doctrine that one should follow one's conscience is another invitation to judge good and evil privately, and so to go back on a transfer of the right of nature to the sovereign. Differently, the theological doctrine that people are supernaturally inspired to faith encourages people to think they might be directly affected by God, and that they should listen to (what they take to be) divine inspiration as well as to the sovereign in choosing how to behave. These are the ingredients for divided loyalties and a breach of their mutual agreement to be guided by the sovereign.

A second kind of doctrine that Hobbes associates with sedition is to do with limiting sovereign powers (Hobbes 2012, 504; 1651, 169). This kind of doctrine runs contrary to the force of the original contract among the many – which is to the effect that the sovereign alone has complete discretion to decide for them all what the means of peace are, and to declare those means through laws. The original agreement does not dictate or constrain what the laws should say: that is left to the judgment of the sovereign. Nor does the original contract imply that, once declared by a sovereign, a law cannot be changed, even reversed, by that sovereign. The contract gives the sovereign a virtually free hand. If there is any constraint on the means a sovereign can deploy to secure the peace, it is only that the means should not be life-threatening to subjects. For subjects promise submission only if it is safe to do so, and if their lives are in peril if they obey the sovereign, they regain the right of nature.

Many doctrines that Hobbes considers subversive limit the scope of sovereign power not only unwisely but incoherently. For example, the doctrine that the sovereign himself is subject to the rule of law (incoherently) implies that the law is binding even on an agent who alone rightfully *decides* what the law shall be. The doctrine that a subject's property rights limit a sovereign's property rights implies (incoherently) that a sovereign authorized to decide what all the laws are is not entitled to decide what the laws of property are. The doctrine that sovereign power can be divided – as in a constitutional order that separates executive, legislature, and judiciary – strongly contradicts the idea that *all* the means of keeping the peace are for vested in a unitary recipient of the mass transfer of right. The doctrine that monarchs are tyrants, who should be resisted by the people, is spread by books about the Greeks and Romans (Hobbes 2012, 508; 1651, 171): this in effect glorifies the terrifying anarchy of the state of nature, which is what subjects have agreed to leave behind. According to Hobbes, it is subjects who authorize the sovereign to rule over them: sovereigns do not *impose* their will.

Hobbes traces the weaknesses of weak states not only to bad doctrines but to bad practices, sometimes bad practices that implement bad doctrines. Thus, the practice of mixed government (Hobbes 2012, 514; 1651, 173) and not just the normative claim that government *should* be mixed (*should* exhibit a separation of powers) undermines sovereignty. Similarly, according to Hobbes, the subversive doctrine that people's land and assets are exclusively their own and that sovereigns have no claim on them greatly increases the difficulty of raising finance for public defense (Hobbes 2012, 514; 1651, 173). Again, allowing towns or cities to become centers of wealth of power in their own right creates conditions for disputing the sovereign's powers (Hobbes 2012, 516; 1651, 174).

Other bad practices are tied less to doctrine and more to poor decisions on the part of sovereigns. Granting monopolies can lead to concentrations of money that are diverted from the public treasury. Allowing popular figures to cultivate followings and to act as powers unto themselves is another example. Allowing money to be used by subjects to finance idleness and wasteful luxury is another. A final one is the decision to enlarge sovereign dominion through foreign conquest, which spreads attention and military activity thin, eroding the ability to keep the domestic population safe from one another (Hobbes 2012, 518; 1651, 174).

14.3 The Rights of the Sovereign

If I am right in claiming that Hobbes's theory of the rights of sovereigns corresponds systematically to his list of the causes of the dissolution of Commonwealths, then we should expect the rights of sovereignty to include such things as the control of doctrines available to the public, unconstrained judgment about the property rights that conduce to peace, unseparated powers of legislation, judicature, taxation, and foreign war-making. And this *is* what we find in *Leviathan* chapter 18 on "The Rights of Soveraignes by Institution."

The rights of the sovereign correspond systematically to the causes of the dissolution of the commonwealth. The list of those causes in chapter 29 starts with a sovereign's failing to take or exercise sufficient powers, for example, by ceding or sharing power. Accordingly, in chapter 18 the Rights of Sovereigns are said to be indivisible and non-transferable (Hobbes 2012, 278; 1651, 92). The theory of the rights of sovereigns in *Leviathan* implies that sovereign powers or rights are never genuinely ceded or shared, because anyone or any institution to which they were apparently ceded is subject to the sovereign, who is free to reverse his decision if he thinks it promotes public protection. Anyone who might seem to vie with the sovereign in power on account of personal wealth, for example, is liable to have that wealth confiscated if it is perceived as a source of state insecurity. For the sovereign is "Judge both of the meanes of Peace and Defence; and also of the hindrances and disturbances of the same; and to do *whatsoever* he shall think necessary to be done" (Hobbes 2012, 271; 1651, 91; emphasis added).

Chapter 29 lists many doctrinal sources of sedition. Chapter 18 says that

> It is annexed to the Sovereignty, to be judge of what Opinions and Doctrines are averse, and what conducing to Peace; and consequently, on what occasions, how farre and what, men are to be trusted withal, in speaking to Multitudes of people, and who shall examine the doctrine of all books before they are published. (Hobbes 2012, 271; 1651, 91)

The rights of the sovereign to decide what belongs to whom (Hobbes 2012, 272; 1651, 91), and to impose taxation and to regulate economic exchange (see *Leviathan* chapter 23) have a bearing on the following four causes of dissolution of states previously discussed:

- Lack of money for state purposes;
- Concentration of private money in a few;

- Ease (life without industry); and
- Riot (in the sense of lavish display) and vain expense.

Necessary taxation, together with the power of expropriation, can assemble the necessary resources for emergencies, including conducting wars. They can also remove the resources that fuel waste and sloth.

What about the cause of dissolution of states that consists of sovereigns being too interested in conquest, too interested, as Hobbes puts it, in enlarging dominion? Hobbes's theory acts against this as well. Each sovereign by institution personifies and unifies a *local* population, that is, a population living close together as contractors and with which the person who receives the gift of sovereignty is involved. The sovereign will be someone plucked from this population who is a beneficiary of a transfer of right from the contractors in that population. The contractors, then, not the inhabitants of the whole world, entrust their safekeeping to the sovereign. It is these people, not all people, whom the sovereign is supposed to protect if he is not to disappoint the covenanters who make a gift of their obedience. (The natural law requirement of gratitude obliges people, including sovereigns, not to disappoint those who give them gifts (Hobbes 2012, 230; 1651, 65).)[5] Enlarging dominion means widening the number of people who are under a sovereign's protection. It means straining the never sufficient resources required for the protection of a local population. So there is a sense in which enlarging dominion never fits the purpose the rights of instituted sovereigns promote, namely securing the peace of the population who transfer their right of nature and establish a sovereign.

Hobbes justifies his choice of the rights of sovereigns by reference to what the contractors bargain for when they establish a sovereign. The contractors bargain for freedom from the threat of imminent violence, where the threat of imminent violence partly proceeds from the operation of many wills seeking their own apparent good by any means they choose. The contract has the effect of reducing the number of apparent goods being pursued ruthlessly by large numbers of agents. The contractors say to the person they are making sovereign, "You tell us how we must behave or refrain from behaving to escape violence and secure our lives: we will do that." But the contractors are not thereby paralyzed. They volunteer for active lives channeled by the prohibitions of the sovereign. Within the zones of life where there are no prohibitions subjects retain liberty. And they agree to observe the prohibitions only where it is not life-threatening to do so.

The contractors do not trade obedience for something each conceives as happiness; instead, they trade obedience for the end of war, where the means of preventing war are determined by the sovereign. Contractors cannot justly dispute the sovereign's choice of officials, for they gave him total discretion in legislation and in appointments when they asked the sovereign to direct them. And they agreed among themselves not to second-guess either the legislation or the appointments. In short, they have authorized whatever the sovereign does for the purpose of keeping the peace. Some of what the sovereign does may be irksome or annoying or "inconvenient" to subjects, including in ways that did not occur to them when they joined the original contract. It does not follow that the sovereign is unjust. Injustice is a matter of failing to perform a covenant

(Hobbes 2012, 220; 1651, 72), and, as has been pointed out previously, the sovereign has not entered into any covenant with the many.

Again, the inconvenience of some of the sovereign's measures does not mean they are unconducive to peace. Paying taxes will probably always be inconvenient, but that does not mean that building up financial reserves through taxation for military defense and policing is not a peace-promoting or security-promoting measure. The sovereign's conception of the means to peace, then, is not one the sovereign's subjects have to like; they may dislike it even when the means adopted by the sovereign succeed in eradicating violence. But if violence *is* eradicated, they have got what they bargained for, and so cannot justly go back on their agreement to obey. This is the message of the first part of *Leviathan* chapter 18.

The contractors bargain for the eradication of violence by means the sovereign chooses unilaterally. The only ground for disobedience is the non-eradication of violence. The sovereign's resort to occasionally restrictive laws and even harsher punishments for violations of those laws is not itself a form of violence. The fact that fear is aroused by the laws does not mean that the threshold for disobedience is reached. Only fear of imminent loss of life, the fear experienced constantly in the state of nature, reinstates the right of nature, and, with that, the right to take action against anyone, including the sovereign, if an individual judges that doing so contributes to personal survival.

The beginning of chapter 18 is a reminder that contractors who institute a sovereign power are no longer at liberty unilaterally to withdraw; or to make a new covenant; or to invoke a God with whom they have a prior or overriding covenant (Hobbes 2012, 264; 1651, 88). Again, because the wills of the covenanters invest the sovereign with the authority to declare laws with punishments, there is a sense in which the covenanters are not just liable to suffer the punishments if they disobey: they *endorse* the punishments, as they authorize the sovereign to be the judge of punishments and to execute them (Hobbes 2012, 264; 1651, 88). As for the sovereign, nothing he does can be a breach of the covenant, as he is not a party to it. He can of course make decisions that have the effect of putting everyone's lives in danger, e.g., by starting a war that leads to defeat and conquest by another. But that is not an injustice, since it breaks no agreement, and justice is a matter of keeping agreements (Hobbes 2012, 220; 1651, 72). At most, bad decisions of this kind free subjects from obedience by returning them to a justified fear for their lives and the restoration of the right of nature.

Hobbes often writes as if the agreement of the many to delegate security planning to the sovereign means that they authorize even very severe exercises of power, and that nothing authorized by a person *p* can actually harm *p*. The idea that authorization or voluntariness confers harmlessness has many counter-examples, including willing participation in extreme sports, endorsement of laws that require the death penalty for things one has done, and putting one's signature to an imprudent scheme predictably involving huge financial loss to oneself. But even if a subject is harmed by an action or punishment of the sovereign, that is not strictly an "*injury*" (Hobbes 2012, 270; 1651, 90), if the sovereign sincerely judges it to be necessary for peace: the covenant makes him sole and ultimate judge, and the punished person authorized the prerogative of judgment for the sovereign.

14.4 The Limits of Sovereign Rights

The rights of sovereigns are extensive. Are they *too* extensive – a kind of dictator's charter? An *authorized* dictator, such as Hobbes's sovereign, is still a dictator, and isn't so much power potentially threatening to the lives and well-being of subjects? Here is where Hobbes's theory of the *duties* of sovereigns comes in. According to this theory, there are good and bad ways of exercising the rights of sovereignty, and although the sovereign does nothing wrong whenever he uses his judgment in pursuing public protection and legislates accordingly, *whatever* that scheme of legislation turns out to be, some executions of sovereignty are better than others. Chapter 30 of *Leviathan* outlines the preferred exercise of sovereignty. In a sense this is the chapter of *Leviathan* that has the strongest claim to have rulers as its intended audience. It is also the chapter in which, according to at least some commentators, Hobbes's otherwise authoritarian-looking politics takes a liberal turn. I shall deny that even here Hobbes is genuinely a liberal.[6]

Before looking at what is unusual in chapter 30, and how it constrains chapter 18 on the rights of sovereigns, it is worth noting some of the ways in which it *reinforces* chapter 18. For example, the first on Hobbes's list of duties of sovereigns in chapter 30 is the duty not to relinquish any of the rights of sovereignty (Hobbes 2012, 520; 1651, 175). Next, there is a duty to educate subjects in the grounds of the rights of sovereigns and some of the laws promulgated, the importance of not supporting prominent powerful subjects of the sovereign, the importance of not looking to other jurisdictions for models of government, and of using universities for inculcation of sovereign-supporting doctrines (Hobbes 2012, 525–31; 1651, 175–9).

Coming now to what is unusual in chapter 30, the first thing to note is the redefinition of the purpose of the role of sovereign. In chapter 18, this purpose is associated with the picture of all-out war conjured up in chapter 13. According to chapter 13, people bargain in the state of nature for the eradication of life-threatening violence – the permanent termination of the war of all against all. The war of all against all is to be avoided because it is a total threat to all of the good things in life – the arts, sciences, goods resulting from the division of labor, even survival itself. Accordingly, the invention of sovereignty is for *delivering* people from war, delivering people from lethal fighting or the fear of lethal fighting.

In chapter 30, on the other hand, the purpose of sovereignty is broadened. It is no longer just a matter of delivering people from premature violent death. It is a matter of "the safety of the people," where by "safety" is meant not only survival

> but also all other Contentments of life, which every man by lawfull Industry, without danger, or hurt to the Common-wealth, shall acquire to himself. (Hobbes 2012, 570; 1651, 175)

What is the significance of this change? In earlier chapters, Hobbes has been saying that life, including life in the Commonwealth, cannot be without some major inconveniences, but that these are insignificant when compared to the "miseries, and horrible calamities, that accompany a Civil Warre" (Hobbes 2012, 282; 1651, 94). He has been saying that the inconveniences are hardly complaint-worthy given the alternative. Now he seems to suggest that the threshold for justified complaint is reached when the mere preservation of life is delivered without additional contentments. In other words, he has gestured at a connection between the exercise of sovereignty and securing the happiness of subjects. This connection is, admittedly, hinted at in chapter 13, where Hobbes describes the passions that lead people to make peace. One is fear, but another is a desire for "things necessary to commodious living" (2012, 196; 1651, 63). This is a desire for more than survival, but it is a desire whose satisfaction depends on the fulfilment of a hope "the hope [on the part of peacemakers] by their industry to obtain [things necessary for commodious living]." The conditions for fulfilling this hope are nothing less than the sovereign's success in securing the public safety.

The connection between the permitted contentments of subjects and the duties of sovereigns emerges again in chapter 30, where Hobbes introduces the idea of good law. Not every law that a sovereign declares is a good law, though any law he declares is just (Hobbes 2012, 540; 1651, 181):

> A good Law is that which is Needful, for the *Good of the People*, and withall *Perspicuous*. (Hobbes 2012, 540; 1651, 182)

For a law to be good, it must be clear, and it must be necessary for the good of the people. What does Hobbes mean by "the good of the people"?

The relevant sources for his views on this matter are, in addition to chapter 30 of *Leviathan*, chapter 28 of *The Elements of Law*, and chapter 13 of *De cive*.[7]

In *The Elements of Law*, Hobbes divides the "temporal good of the people" into four elements:

> (1) Multitude (2) Commodity of living (3) Peace amongst ourselves (4) Defence against foreign power. (Hobbes 1994, xxviii, §3)

By "multitude" he means the result of heeding the divine command to go forth and multiply, and he lists many legal prohibitions on unnatural copulation that are required to keep human numbers up. Next on his list is commodity of living:

> The commodity of living consisteth in liberty and wealth. By liberty I mean that there be no prohibition without necessity of any thing to any man, which was lawful to him in the state of nature; that is to say, that there be no restraint of natural liberty, but what is necessary for the good of the commonwealth; and that well-meaning men may not fall into the danger of laws, as into snares, before they be aware ... And for the wealth of the people, it consisteth in three things: the well ordering of trade, procuring of labour, and forbidding the superfluous consuming of food and apparel. (Hobbes 1994, xxviii, § 4)

The commodity of living seems to be at the core of the good of the people, and is largely defined by liberty (permission to act as one wills within the law), in its turn exercised in the pursuit of objects of the appetites (which fill out the pre-philosophical understanding of the good). This liberty is constrained twice over – by what is lawful in the state of nature, i.e., permitted by natural law; and what is consistent with avoiding war once the state of nature has been left behind. As for wealth, it is not a stock of possessions, according to the *Elements of Law*, but the regulation of trade, procurement of labor and consumption.

Four further long sections are required to list the requirements of domestic peace – including the institution of property and a legal system. These sections recapitulate much of the doctrine of the laws of nature. Finally, a single section covers the requirements of defense against foreign attack, including the commandeering of money and shelter, the maintenance of fortifications, and accumulations of arms and ships.

De cive drops multitude from the components of the good life, treats the requirements of domestic peace and protection from foreign attack before wealth and natural liberty, and speaks at much greater length than the *Elements of Law* about liberty. The overall message, however, is the same. Natural liberty is not to be restricted more by civil law than by natural law except for some benefit to the public or commonwealth. In general, the restriction must not be so limited as to lead to the dissipation of the people nor so great as to rob them of all initiative (Hobbes 1998, xiii, §15). Furthermore, keeping the peace requires a kind of ideological hygiene as well as the containment of violence and poverty. Ideological hygiene requires teaching, not threats merely (Hobbes 1998, xiii, §9). Factions, ambition, and other organized divisiveness must be outlawed, (Hobbes 1998, xiii, §13). The burdens in money and effort of keeping the peace and avoiding or prevailing in a foreign war must be borne equally or proportionately (Hobbes 1998, xiii, §§ 10–11).

So *De cive* anticipates *Leviathan*'s doctrine of public instruction, and shows by its reordering of the elements of the good life that restrictions or allowances of liberty are to be understood against the background of the requirements of domestic peace and external defense. *De cive* also reinforces the point that it is the duty of the sovereign to provide for the people a readily recognizable kind of well-being. Not just life but the enjoyment of life is associated with public safety in the three political treatises, and this expansive conception of safety is evidently *not* realized if the predominant perspective on the commonwealth is that afforded by the multiplying glasses that magnify small costs of protection into great grievances. For people to feel safe, and also to provide supply for a defense effort, they must have a sense of well-being simply, not a grudging sense of life being tolerable all things considered.

Chapter 30 of *Leviathan* keeps in play expansively conceived safety, develops *De cive*'s embryonic conception of public instruction and brings together into the concept of the good law the idea that natural liberty is only to be restricted when safety requires it. Because of the central place all three versions of his political theory reserve for liberty in the definition of the public good, and the importance attached to not abridging liberty unnecessarily, Hobbes's text in chapter 30 is uncharacteristically liberal-sounding. But is it genuinely liberal?

The liberty in question is not liberty simply, but liberty-without-hurt-to-the-commonwealth. And what is liberty-without-hurt-to-the-commonwealth? It is liberty that seems permissible, all things considered, to the sovereign. This liberty may turn out to be very limited. It is true that for Hobbes the ideal sovereign identifies very thoroughly with his subjects' interests – so thoroughly that no restriction of liberty that seems reasonable to him should ever be unnecessary. But this is an ideal. At most he is inviting actual sovereigns to do their best to rule in their subjects' interests.

Sovereigns are invited not only to identify with their subjects. They are invited to deal with them consistently and impartially when they seek adjudication of disputes, or remedies for injury and misapplication of law. They are to be treated equally also in taxation and in handing out punishments. Here is where the exercise of sovereignty is subject to the norm of Equity (Hobbes 2012, 534; 1651, 180). This is not the liberal requirement of the rule of law, for Hobbes has already insisted that the sovereign is above or at the source of law. It is rather the indication of an ideal that a sovereign may wish to realize if he pursues the goal of public safety expansively defined.

14.5 The Strains of Sovereignty

I come now to the strains of sovereignty. Many of these are implicitly or explicitly acknowledged by Hobbes. His recognition of the strains – the fragility – of sovereignty shows that he probably did not think that an eternal, all-powerful "mortal god," the man-made counterpart of God himself, was a practical possibility. But acknowledging the fragility of sovereignty is not a roundabout way of endorsing liberalism. When he says that good laws should not encroach on liberty *unnecessarily*, he is not ruling out significant encroachment. On the contrary, Hobbes consistently argues for a regime that curtails or eliminates the separation of powers, free speech, property rights, freedom of association, and freedom to consume and spend. At the same time, he thinks that a modicum of liberty is required for productive work, economic exchange, savings, and activity producing revenue for education, a judicial system, and, above all, a security force. Liberty-sufficient-for-enabling-public safety, not liberty simply, is what Hobbes's politics values.

Two strains of sovereignty seem to me to be central. The first is the strain of acquiring and maintaining a deep identification with the good of the people. It may be true, as Hobbes's insists, that the interests of the sovereign and of the people coincide, on a sufficiently detached view of the consequences of sacrificing the public interest (Hobbes 2012, 540; 1651, 182). But what if the sovereign cannot achieve this detachment? If the sovereign is a human individual, he or she will have strong unsatisfied appetites for personal gratification or acquisition which the power conferred by sovereignty will enable him or her to satisfy very easily. Again, they will be the object of ritual personal praise and even worship or something like it.

Surely it is hard to fill the role of sovereign without letting all of this go to one's head. Perhaps one will start to believe one's own publicity, so that one feels entitled to any material rewards of office that one can get. One may decide one deserves another palace, or another dozen banquets, paid for by public revenues that could have built fortifications or ships for the navy. If so, one is taking one's eye off the ball of public safety. What could motivate a sovereign in Hobbes's theory to use his assets less frivolously? Perhaps simple prudence. For if self-indulgent spending does lead to weakened defenses and actual conquest, so that one's subjects are left as badly off as in the state of nature, then people will be entitled to rise up, freed from submission, and treat the sovereign individual as an enemy, putting his life in danger. Presumably there is a way of avoiding the extremes of individual self-denial for the sake of the public, and individual self-indulgence at the expense of the public, but this is a balancing act that the sovereign cannot avoid having to work at all the time.[8]

The second strain emerges from a right of sovereignty that has not yet been mentioned, namely the right to

> Give titles of Honour; and to appoint what Order of place, and dignity, each man shall hold; and what signs of respect, in publique or private meetings, they shall give to one another. (Hobbes 2012, 276; 1651, 92)

This is a reminder that the sovereign has the right to affect particular subjects by direct intervention, either for good or for ill. The prerogative of personal enrichment or ennoblement not only gives status to people who could become the sovereign's rivals, but it creates obstacles to doing equal justice, if someone who has already been honored or enriched comes into legal conflict with another citizen of lower status. In other words, the right of raising or lowering people in the social pecking order is a standing threat to discharging the natural law duty of Equity. More than that, the right of personalizing the exercise of sovereignty is in tension with the impersonal exercise of sovereignty in the form of legislation that is addressed in the same way to everyone.

A third strain concerns life-threatening duties or punishments. Since no one, not even someone justly convicted of a capital crime, can be obliged to submit to death without that person's regaining the right of nature and having the right to resist,[9] according to Hobbes's theory (Hobbes 2012, 214; 1651, 69), military conscription is problematic, as is capital punishment (Heyd 1991). And because the public safety that the sovereign pursues involves military defense, and other possibly lethal uses of force against outlaws, this problem is not unimportant. More generally, there is a tension in Hobbes's theory between the inalienability of judgments of *imminent* threats to life, and the obligation to obey the sovereign. If many people genuinely believe that they are in danger of losing their lives or suffering major injury if they carry out the sovereign's commands, but that belief is created by local misinformation or paranoia or a lack of confidence that the police or army will cope, then many people can blamelessly revert to being their own judges of how to defend themselves.

Our list of strains is not yet complete. There is a trade-off in Hobbes's politics, between unity of sovereign power and longevity of sovereign power. A legislative council can in principle last as long as there are suitable members: it is not unusual for councils to last centuries. On the other hand, as noted earlier, a council is prone to internal competition and each member of it faces the difficult challenge of genuinely selfless public service. The struggle to forget self-interest is a struggle both against the self and other council members. The struggle not only has a bad outcome when the interests of council members are preferred to the public interest; it also has an unfavorable result when council members disagree and can reach no decision at all. In the form of monarchy sovereignty may be less prone to indecision, but it is also confined to a single adult human lifetime. And yet, as already noted, the original contractors aim at permanent escape from the state of nature.

The ideal of sovereign decisiveness is complicated in practice by division of labor and delegation. Although only the sovereign has the right to make war, the conduct of the war is usually a responsibility delegated to commanders, who have some discretion over the means. A bad military campaign can lead to the dissolution of the state. The sovereign has the right of judicature, but in practice he does not personally decide cases. He delegates the power of decision to authorized judges. A badly decided case can create public discord leading to civil war. Again, the stability of sovereignty depends on the effectiveness of public education in the duties of subjects. This education needs consistency and permanence – two tall orders already – and its effectiveness will vary with public understanding of the sovereign's military and other policies. In times of publicized scarcity or military setback, the burden of inducing reverence for the sovereign may become overwhelming. Moreover, since the sovereign cannot do everything personally, and since even a sovereign who delegates does not live forever, the tension in the ideal of a unitary and permanent center of decision seems to be ineliminable.

Sovereigns have the duty to pre-empt civil war *and* conquest. But how is conquest to be pre-empted? Perhaps by a show of force or military power. But might this not be misinterpreted by potential conquerors as a sign of belligerence that *invites* war? Some of the tensions of international relations can be relaxed through diplomacy and trade (Hobbes 2012, 386; 1651, 127), according to Hobbes, but trade, with its use of monopolies, poses further risks to sovereignty, through its power of generating wealth for potential domestic rivals of the sovereign.

14.6 Conclusion

At the best of times, sovereignty is a matter of maintaining an equilibrium between the exercise of the rights of sovereigns and the durability of the subjects' transfer of the right of nature. Life under the sovereign cannot deprive subjects of the essentials of life, or of conditions for gainful industry. For both the essentials of life – sufficient food, shelter, and protection from attack – as well as the conditions for gainful industry – a system of imports of goods, markets for manufactures, trusted systems of payments – are written into the public safety that sovereigns are charged with securing. If sovereigns fail in providing public safety – if subjects are *un*safe, despite the sovereign's laws and law-enforcement, then subjects revert to the state of nature, and sovereigns are reduced to mortal beings whose lives are at risk.

It is *hard* to maintain the equilibrium between the exercise of sovereignty and rightful subjection. If the sovereign is an individual, he has a duty to rule selflessly by identifying with the good of the people he or she personifies. If the sovereign is a council, it must overcome the self-interest and selfishness of its members, and also overcome honest disagreement to reach decisions. Many things required for public safety will inevitably be disliked by subjects. Taxes and conscription are two examples. In order for these disliked things to be acceptable, people need not only the liberty to pursue personal projects and associations up to a point; they need to be schooled in the connections between taxation and conscription and their own well-being. Such public education is itself not easy to arrange for.

The sovereign may have immense power in relation to his subjects and yet very little power in relation to international counterparts. How does he keep his subjects safe from conquest? With difficulty. By trade arrangements that potential rivals benefit from. By internal policies that discourage undue consumption and dependence on foreign goods.

Hobbes disapproves of campaigns of conquest, on the ground that it stretches the sovereign's attention and military and administrative resources unduly. But how does one refrain from conquest without projecting military weakness that may invite conquest? Both internally and externally sovereignty is always under strain. Not only subjection has inconveniences.

Notes

1 Recent discussions of this question include Shelton (1992), (May 2013), and (Dyzenhaus 2001).

2 In addition to sovereignty by institution, Hobbes recognizes sovereignty by acquisition or conquest (*Leviathan* chapter 20). A subject who submits to a conquering foreign ruler in return for his life acquires obligations to obey a new sovereign's laws. The fact that death is the alternative to submission does not make submission involuntary, according to Hobbes, and so in that sense obedience to a conquering ruler proceeds from a voluntary act and is consensual, as in the case of sovereignty by institution. In both kinds of sovereignty, as Hobbes puts it, submission proceeds from fear, but in sovereignty by acquisition it is fear of the conqueror rather than fear of others in the state of nature. In this sense, the two kinds of sovereignty and obligation are on a level. From the point of view of Hobbes's normative theory of sovereignty, on the other hand, sovereignty by conquest is inferior to sovereignty by institution, since conquest stretches very thin the power of a foreign conqueror to fulfil his duty to protect the people of a home jurisdiction. I come later to Hobbes's disapproval of conquest.

3 The relevant chapters of *The Elements of Law* are chapter XX (corresponding to *Leviathan* chapter 18); Chapter XXVII (corresponding to *Leviathan* chapter 29); and chapter XXVIII (corresponding to *Leviathan* chapter 30). *De cive* chapter VI corresponds to *Leviathan* chapter 18; chapter XII corresponds to *Leviathan* chapter 29; and chapter XIII corresponds to *Leviathan* chapter 30.

4 In Leviathan 20, Adam and Eve not only took it upon themselves to judge that it was all right to eat from the tree, but also, when they realized that they were naked, that it was unattractive to be naked, even though God ordained that they should be unclothed in Eden (2012, 318–20; 1651, 106).

5 How is it that the sovereign is subject to natural law, and in particular the natural law obligation to be grateful for free gifts? In the simplest case – where the sovereign is a human individual – the answer is that the individual never leaves the state of nature, and it is in the state of nature that one has natural law obligations. Like other people in the state of nature, the sovereign is not obliged to *show* gratitude before others for a free gift if the sovereign judges that it is unsafe to do so: natural law obligations oblige absolutely only in the private sphere of thoughts and intentions. This means that a sovereign has at least to *feel* grateful, and could show gratitude in various ways if he judges it is safe to do so.

6 I have argued against the liberal interpretation (Sorell 2016). For a very different approach to a similar conclusion, see Section 5 of van Apeldoorn (2020). For a treatment that does justice to both liberal and illiberal elements in Hobbes's thought as well as to the historical context, see Malcolm (2016).

7 Points in the next three paragraphs are anticipated in Sorell (2016).

8 See Sorell (2004).

9 See Heyd (1991).

References

Dyzenhaus, David. 2001. "Hobbes and the Legitimacy of Law." *Law and Philosophy* 20 (5): 461–98. Doi:10.2307/3505220.

Heyd, David. 1991. "Hobbes on Capital Punishment." *History of Philosophy Quarterly* 8: 119–34.

Hobbes, Thomas. 1994. *The Elements of Law, Natural and Politic*, edited by John C.A. Gaskin. Oxford: Oxford University Press.

Hobbes, Thomas. 1998. *(De cive) on the Citizen*, edited and translated by Richard Tuck and Michael Silverthorne. Cambridge: Cambridge University Press.

Hobbes, Thomas. 2012. *Leviathan*, 3 vols., edited by Noel Malcolm. Oxford: Clarendon Press. [First published 1651].

Malcolm, Noel. 2016. "Thomas Hobbes: Liberal Illiberal." *Journal of the British Academy* 4: 113–36. Doi:10.5871/jba/004.113.

May, Larry. 2013. *Limiting Leviathan*. Oxford: Oxford University Press.

Shelton, George. 1992. *Morality and Sovereignty in the Philosophy of Hobbes*. London: Palgrave Macmillan.

Sorell, Tom. 2004. "The Burdensome Freedom of Sovereigns." In *Leviathan after 350 Years*, edited by Tom Sorell and Luc Foisneau, 183–96. Oxford: Oxford University Press.

Sorell, Tom. 2016. "Law and Equity in Hobbes." *Critical Review of International Social and Political Philosophy* 19: 29–46. Doi:10.1080/13698230.2015.1122353.

van Apeldoorn, Laurens. 2020. "On the Person and Office of the Sovereign in Hobbes' Leviathan." *British Journal for the History of Philosophy* 28: 49–68. Doi:10.1080/09608788.2019.1613632.

15

Hobbes on International Ethics

JOHAN OLSTHOORN

This chapter explores the character and normative foundations of Hobbes's international ethics.[1] By international ethics,[2] I will mean all moral norms applying to international actors, both those authorizing and restraining conduct. In Hobbes's case, international ethics is composed of three distinct sets of norms: natural rights, the laws of nature, and justice. His account of international ethics is reductionist in this respect: Hobbes had no place for a separate law of nations and subsumed all rights of war under natural rights. Hobbes's international ethics is reductionist in a second respect as well: the exact same norms nominally apply to any agent in the state of nature, be they individuals, states, or sovereigns – even if these norms differ in their application and normative grounding. As *De cive* 14.4 states: "the Elements of *natural law* and *natural right* ... may, when transferred to whole *commonwealths* and *nations*, be regarded as the Elements of the *laws* and of the *right of Nations* [*legum* et *juris gentium*]" (Hobbes 1998, 156).

I will offer a novel reconstruction of the arguments behind both reductionist moves. The explanation predominant in the existing literature, I contend, does not hold for *Leviathan*. To buttress the claim that *jus gentium* (the moral principles regulating interactions between states) is identical to the laws of nature (dictating to individuals the socially necessary means for peace and self-preservation), commentators have argued that in the international state of nature commonwealths occupy a normative position analogous to individuals in the interpersonal one. As Boucher (2018, 152) writes, Hobbes's reductionist account of international ethics "requir[ed] the state to be viewed as an artificial person if it was to be subject in a similar way to the law of nations as individuals are to its exact equivalent the law of nature." Call this the Assimilation Argument. The argument has clear textual support in *De cive* 14.4. Yet it is dropped from *Leviathan* onward. Not without reason: natural law, binding in conscience alone (the sole court of natural justice), seems to lose its prescriptive force when applied to

A Companion to Hobbes, First Edition. Edited by Marcus P. Adams.

states. Neither the prospects of this-worldly preservation nor of otherworldly bliss seem capable of explaining why *jus gentium* is normative for states.

In *Leviathan*, the norms of international ethics are directly applied to sovereigns rather than to commonwealths. While in substance the same as those of interpersonal ethics, these principles consequently differ, I maintain, in their normative grounds. The sovereign's duty to seek peace with foreign enemies and the concomitant right to resort to armed force when peace cannot be had are not morally foundational (as individual rights of self-defense are). Rather, rights and duties of international ethics are normatively underpinned by the natural law duty of gratitude, which morally requires the sovereign to duly discharge his role-specific duties, including providing defense against external enemies. In *Leviathan*, Hobbes's international ethics are thus informed by sovereign duties of care to national subjects – not unlike the tacit ethical assumptions of some modern realist theories of international relations.

15.1 States of War

Hobbes's state of nature is, by default, a state of war. This holds true for both the prestatist interpersonal state of nature (inhabited by individuals) and the extra-statist international one (inhabited by commonwealths). "For the state of commonwealths towards each other is a *natural* state, i.e., a state of hostility. Even when the fighting between them stops, it should not be called Peace, but an intermission" in fighting (Hobbes 1998, 144–5).[3] Hobbes's bellicose portrayal of the international arena resembles that of his erstwhile employer Francis Bacon (1561–1626): "there is ever between all Estates a secret Warre" (Bacon 1629, 11).[4] Enduring peace requires a common power capable of providing security and of punishing injustices; such a common power is by definition absent outside the state.

Cruder interpretations have taken the Hobbesian natural condition to be void of morality. Morgenthau (1952, 34), for instance, attributes to Hobbes the "extreme dictum" that "the state creates morality as well as law and that there is neither morality nor law outside the state."[5] In fact, Hobbes recognizes three distinct sets of deontic principles operative in the state of nature: the laws of nature, natural rights, and justice.[6] The natural condition being a state of war, agents are not morally required to *act* upon the norms of justice and natural law if they judge that doing so would render them vulnerable to death and invasion (defeating the purpose of moral conduct; Hobbes 1969, 92–3; 1998, 53; 2012, 240; 1651, 79). When peace is deemed out of reach, each may avail themselves of blanket natural rights of self-defense: "*By all means we can, to defend our selves*" (2012, 200; 1651, 64). Moral laws are, in this sense, silent "in time of war, wherein every mans' being and well-being is the rule of his actions" (1969, 100; also 1998, 69; 2005, 34, 134). The laws of nature, prescribing the socially necessary means to establish peace, nevertheless ceaselessly bind *in conscience* and are, to that extent, operative even in conditions of war. The dispensation clause of the duty to practice justice and natural law – each agent equally having the right to assess for themselves whether present conditions permit harm-free performance – applies to international actors as well: "against Enemies, whom the Common-wealth judgeth capable to do them hurt, it is lawfull by the originall Right of Nature to make warre" (2012, 494; 1651, 165).

Commonwealths and pre-statist individuals face different *empirical* conditions, making the international state of war a less wretched condition for subjects than the pre-statist war of all against all. The latter dramatically immiserates individuals, precluding all industry, agriculture, and trade; international hostility, on the other hand, stimulates arms production and military employment, thereby upholding "the Industry of their Subjects" (2012, 196; 1651, 63). Humans are by nature highly vulnerable and roughly equal in power – the weakest being able to kill the strongest (Hobbes 1998, 26; 2012, 188; 1651, 60). Neither postulate is true for states, rendering international war less existential. The *normative* positions of commonwealths and pre-statist individuals appear at first sight structurally identical: both are endowed with the same right of nature and governed by the same laws of nature. However, what these principles in practice permit, require, and prohibit is contingent on the empirical situation agents are in. All agents must seek peace yet may avail themselves of armed force when deemed imperiled. But the prescribed means for establishing security differ for nations and pre-statist individuals.[7]

Consider wars of conquest. There being strength in numbers, individuals have a natural right to engage in anticipatory attacks to coerce others, including innocents, to join their sides (their personal slave army, if you will), thus amplifying their power and hence their personal security:

> there is no way for any man to secure himselfe, so reasonable, as Anticipation; that is, by force, or wiles, to master the persons of all men he can, so long, till he see no other power great enough to endanger him: And this is no more than his own conservation requireth, and is generally allowed. (2012, 190; 1651, 61)

Natural right permits conquering other people not just to thwart *their* future attacks, but also to fortify oneself against third-party threats. After all, if they "should not by invasion increase their power, they would not be able, long time, by standing only on their defence, to subsist. And by consequence, such augmentation of dominion over men, being necessary to a mans conservation, it ought to be allowed him" (2012, 190; 1651, 61). While imperialist strategies are both permissible and reasonable at the individual level, at the international level they are generally not so. In internally stable and peaceful commonwealths, sovereigns can heighten external security by encouraging industry and commerce and by investing in public defense – options not available to individuals in the state of nature (Hobbes 1998, 144–6; 2012, 514; 1651, 173). Sovereigns have the right to attack and conquer other states if they judge this necessary for national security (2005, 135–6). Yet military adventurism is a risky strategy and therefore generally imprudent (Hobbes 1998, 150).[8] In sum: among nations violent conquest does not generally promote security – unlike in the all-out war among individuals. This helps explain why "in wars between nations a degree of restraint has normally been observed" (1998, 69).

Informing another moral dissimilarity, some laws of nature arguably apply only to individuals, others only to states. Only individuals are, by the second law of nature, obliged to be willing to renounce their right to everything and submit themselves to a common sovereign. There is no textual evidence that Hobbes expected the same of states.[9] *Elements* 16.12 includes a specific law of nature forbidding discrimination in passage and trade, akin to the WTO's "most-favored-nation" principle.

> It is also a law of nature, *That men allow commerce and traffic* [i.e., trade] *indifferently to one another*. For he that alloweth that to one man, what he denieth to another, declareth his hatred to him, to whom he denied; and to declare hatred is war. And upon this title was grounded the great war between the Athenians and the Peloponnesians. For would the Athenians have condescended to suffer the Megareans, their neighbours, to traffic in their ports and markets, that war had not begun. (Hobbes 1969, 87)[10]

This law will, in practice, apply to states alone. It has little purchase in the interpersonal state of nature, where the *bellum omnium contra omnes* precludes trade (2012, 192; 1651, 62). Hobbes's inclusion under natural law of a principle sanctioning free trade is indicative of his attempt to naturalize the law of nations, to which I turn now.

15.2 A Naturalistic Conception of the Law of Nations

Hobbes's reduction of *jus gentium* to natural law is one of his signature contributions to modern international thought (Armitage 2013, 67–9; Boucher 2018, 141–8). Earlier theorists had made *jus gentium* partly, or wholly, a matter of tacit international agreement (i.e., of positive/voluntary/customary law). Positive international law – being morally arbitrary, mutable, and of conventional origin – was regarded as categorically distinct from natural law. For the Spanish theologian Francisco Suárez (1548–1617), the law of nations was entirely a matter of human agreement: "*ius gentium* properly so called ... differs from the natural law because it is based upon custom rather than upon nature" (2015, 399; also, 2015, 384, 397). Hugo Grotius (1583–1645) concurred.[11] Sharply as it breaks with this tradition, Hobbes's naturalistic conception of *jus gentium* is curiously undermotivated. *Elements* simply ends upon the assertion: "As for the law of nations, it is the same with the law of nature. For that which is the law of nature between man and man, before the constitution of commonwealth, is the law of nations between sovereign and sovereign, after" (Hobbes 1969, 190). Can we glean any arguments from Hobbes's works to justify this equation?

One implicit argument derives from Hobbes's conception of "law." Laws, properly understood, are commands addressed to someone previously bound to obey the lawgiver (Hobbes 1969, 185–6; 1998, 154; 2012, 414; 1651, 137; 2005, 31). Natural law counts as law proper only *qua* authoritative commands issued to subjects by God or by civil sovereigns (Hobbes 1998, 56–7; 2012, 242; 1651, 80; 2012, 418; 1651, 138). Agreements are not laws (Hobbes 1969, 185; 1998, 154–5). And customary law is law only by tacit consent of the civil sovereign (2012, 416; 1651, 138; 2005, 117). Hobbes's conception of law as binding commands issued by a sovereign precludes the existence of customary international law. *Jus gentium* can be truly law only qua divine decrees (i.e., as natural law; 2012, 552; 1651, 185–6). While Hobbes nowhere explicitly called the positive law of nations an oxymoron,[12] he strongly implied the same:

> All *human law* is *civil law*. For the state of man outside the commonwealth is a state of enmity; and because in that state no one is subject to anyone else, there are no laws beyond the dictates of right reason, which is divine law. (Hobbes 1998, 156)

Hidden within Hobbes's texts is another set of moves to support his anti-positivist conception of *jus gentium*. Hobbes silently subsumed under natural law various principles previously associated with the voluntary law of nations. Take the inviolability of ambassadors of peace (Hobbes 1969, 87; 1998, 51; 2012, 236; 1651, 78; cf. 2012, 382; 1651, 126). For Grotius (2005 [1625], 898), as for Vitoria (1991, 281) and Suárez (2015, 400), all "the Rights of Embassy" fall under "that Law of Nations which we call voluntary." These include that "Law of Nations, which renders the Persons of Embassadors sacred and inviolable" (Grotius 2005 [1625], 913).[13] As Samuel Rachel (1628–1691) argued: "that Ambassadors who come even from enemies, and may be bringing a declaration of war from a quarter already guilty of wrongdoing, should be entitled to security so unique and solemn ... this must unquestionably be attributed not to the Law of Nature, but to the deliberate choice of Nations" (1916 [1676], 215).[14] Tellingly, some of Hobbes's scathing criticisms of received criteria for transgressions of natural law (whatever "is against the consent of all nations, or the wisest and most civil nations") typically concerned *jus gentium* (Hobbes 1969, 75; also Hobbes 1998, 32–3).[15]

To support his naturalization of the law of nations, Hobbes could also have categorized some of its received elements under civil law. Clear examples of this are lacking. Most principles standardly subsumed under the positive law of nations he rather dispenses with by silence (e.g., rights of hospitality and of postliminy). Some may think of the institution of private property, which Hobbes insists is an effect of civil law.[16] Yet this institution was only considered part of the law of nations in its loose sense ('non-morally required widely observed human practices'); not in the strict sense central in this chapter ('moral norms governing international relations').[17]

Scholars have hitherto overlooked Hobbes's concomitant naturalistic conception of rights of war (*jus belli*) – justifying both preventive attacks and outright conquest. *De cive* 5.1 calls the natural right to everything a right of war: "as long as a person has no guarantee of security from attack, his primeval *Right* remains in force to look out for himself in whatever ways he will and can, i.e., a *Right to all things*, or a *Right of war* [*Ius in omnia*, sive *Ius belli*]" (Hobbes 1998, 69; also Hobbes 1998, 12). Hobbes accords pre-statist individuals and commonwealths virtually unrestrained rights to wage war. Any actor in the state of nature may by natural right defend themselves in any way they deem useful. Rights to wage defensive wars were traditionally regarded as due by nature and held by pre-statist individuals (e.g., Suárez 2015, 13.2.1; Vitoria 1991, 299). Hobbes substantially enlarged these natural rights of war by granting individuals a natural right to enslave the vanquished (aggressors and innocents alike). Previous thinkers regarded rights to enslave and govern those conquered in war as introduced by the common usage of humanity, and hence due by the positive law of nations (e.g., Gentili 1933 [1598], 332; Grotius 2005 [1625], 1360–80; Suárez 2015, 375, 402; Vitoria 1991, 281). Hobbes, by contrast, argued that rights of self-defense grant each "lawful title to subdue or kill, according as his own conscience and discretion shall suggest unto him for his safety and benefit" (1969, 130). Each human by nature has right to rule all others (Hobbes 1998, 173; 2012, 558; 1651, 187). Consequently, he could claim that "*slaves* are acquired by war just like other things" (Hobbes 1998, 105). Natural rights being mere liberty-rights, dominion arises only when subjects covenant to submit themselves to another (2012, 312; 1651, 104). All sovereign rule, whether obtained by institution or by conquest, involves natural rights to rule rendered effective by subjects' pacts of submission.

15.3 *De cive*: States as Rights-Bearing Persons

Only one explicit argument for his naturalistic conception of international ethics is found in Hobbes's works – the Assimilation Argument in *De cive* 14.4: "because commonwealths once instituted take on the personal qualities of men, what we call a *natural law* in speaking of the duties of individual men is called the *law of nations* [*jus gentium*], when applied to whole commonwealths, peoples or nations" (Hobbes 1998, 156). Armitage calls this "the clearest statement Hobbes would ever give of his rationale for identifying the law of nations with the law of nature" (2013, 64). Tuck glosses the same passage as attesting that Hobbes morally assimilated pre-statist individuals to sovereign states.[18] Boucher agrees: "In order to establish the efficacy of the equation of the law of nature and the law of nations, which differ only in the subjects they regulate, it is necessary that individuals and states somehow be equated" (2018, 149).[19] The Assimilation Argument for identifying the law of nations with natural law does not require sovereign states to be like pre-statist individuals in all respects; nor does it deny differences between the international and interpersonal state of nature. The argument merely has states somehow "take on" the moral rights and duties individuals possess by nature. The Assimilation Argument thus captures only part of the "domestic analogy" ascribed to Hobbes by international relations scholars (Beitz 1999 [1979], 36–50; Bottici 2009 [2004], 39–51; Bull 2012 [1977], 44–9; Cavallar 2002, 179–89).[20] (Modelling international relations on the interpersonal state of nature, the analogy denies the uniqueness of international society.)

The Assimilation Argument gains plausibility from other passages morally likening states to pre-statist individuals. In the natural condition "of Absolute Liberty, such as is theirs, that neither are Soveraigns, nor Subjects" (2012, 554; 1651, 186), each agent equally has the right to follow their own judgment, beholden to no one but God. "So in States, and Common-wealths not dependent on one another, every Common-wealth ... has an absolute Libertie, to doe what it [i.e. its sovereign representative] shall judge ... most conducing to their benefit" (2012, 332; 1651, 110). More succinctly, "sovereign power [is] no less absolute in the commonwealth, than before commonwealth every man was absolute in himself to do, or not to do, what he thought good" (Hobbes 1969, 113; also Hobbes 1998, 88).

Upon reflection, the Assimilation Argument proves problematic: the reasons why natural law is normative for individuals do not straightforwardly hold for commonwealths. Hobbes's interpersonal ethics are standardly regarded as being normatively grounded in the value of self-preservation. The right of nature allows individuals to use their powers and abilities in whatever way they deem fit to preserve their lives; while the law of nature prohibits self-destructive acts and requires each to adopt the surest means to self-preservation (2012, 198; 1651, 64). Does natural law likewise direct states (the multitude incorporated into one body politic)[21] to pursue self-preservation, either of itself or of its composite members? Why would states have self-preservation-based rights and duties? (Beitz 1999 [1979], 52). Further argument is needed to account for the normativity of natural law as applied to commonwealths.

Compounding this quandary, Hobbesian laws of nature are idiosyncratic in binding by nature in conscience alone (Hobbes 1998, 64). In the natural condition of equality, each person is beyond moral reproach by anyone but God, having a natural right to determine for themselves how best to seek personal security: "the Civill Law ceasing, Crimes cease: for there being no other Law remaining, but that of Nature, there is no place for Accusation; every man being his own Judge, and accused onely by his own Conscience, and cleared by the Uprightnesse of his own Intention" (2012, 454; 1651, 152; also 2012, 214; 1651, 70). As God alone can know our conscience, only he can hold us accountable for abiding by natural law outside the state (Hobbes 1969, 146; 2012, 866; 1651, 300). Commonwealths have no inner consciences and are not the kind of entities God can keep in line by threats of otherworldly torment. In what way, then, is natural law normative for states?

Other early modern theorists maintained that the law of nations is at least in part enforceable by international society. Emer de Vattel (1714–1767) maintained that many duties imposed by the law of nations are binding in conscience alone, on the Hobbesian grounds that "every nation [is] free, independent, and sole arbitress of her own actions" (2008 [1758], 266). Other nations can have no enforceable right "when the correspondent obligation depends on the judgment of the party in whose breast it exists" – each state being free to determine themselves what "the dictates of his own conscience" require (2008 [1758], 75).[22] However, states can enforce their perfect rights not to be injured and to protect themselves from blatant injustice (2008 [1758], 296–8). Hobbes's laws of nature are exceptional in being *entirely* unenforceable by humans outside the state. Beyond moral reproach by other human beings, rational individuals are instead motivated to abide by natural law to secure self-preservation and heavenly bliss. Neither rationale can be ascribed unproblematically to states. How, then, can states be bound by the same moral principles? How to render intelligible the assertion that commonwealths "take on" the rights and duties of pre-statist individuals? Perhaps readers can come up with creative solutions to this puzzle, in line with Hobbes's principles. Significantly, Hobbes made no attempt at explanation himself. On the contrary, perhaps in recognition of these difficulties, he abandoned the Assimilation Argument altogether in *Leviathan*, altering the normative underpinnings of *jus gentium* along the way.

15.4 *Leviathan*: *Jus Gentium* and the Office of the Sovereign

Both the English and Latin *Leviathan* reiterate the earlier equation of *jus gentium* with natural law. It has hitherto gone unnoticed, however, that the discussion of international law is moved from the chapter on laws to that on the sovereign's duties (cf. Hobbes 1969, 190; 1998, 156; 2012, 552; 1651, 185). This shift, I contend, is highly significant. Amending his earlier view, Hobbes now emphasizes that the duties of *jus gentium* really apply to sovereigns (bearing the person of the commonwealth). As the laws of nations bind in conscience only outside the state, they should be understood to apply "to Common-wealths, that is, to the Consciences of Soveraign Princes, and Soveraign Assemblies; there being no Court of Naturall Justice, but in the Conscience onely; where not Man, but God raigneth" (2012, 552; 1651, 185).[23] One commentator has remarked that this passage "left implicit what Hobbes had made explicit in *De cive*: that the commonwealth once constituted as an artificial person took on the characteristics and the capacities of the fearful, self-defensive individuals who fabricated it" (Armitage 2013, 64). I disagree. As signaled by its new textual location, Hobbes turns abiding by international ethics into a role-specific duty of sovereigns, for which they are accountable to God alone. That role-specific duty, I contend, undergirds and alters the normativity of Hobbes's international ethics from *Leviathan* onward.

Commonwealths are as free and equal vis-à-vis other commonwealths as individuals are vis-à-vis each other in the state of nature. Yet sovereigns are normatively positioned in relation to one another differently than pre-statist individuals are. Sovereigns have been contractually entrusted with a distinct set of duties, owed to God alone.[24] "The Office of the Soveraign ... consisteth in the end, for which he was trusted with the Soveraign Power, namely the procuration of *the safety of the people*; to which he is obliged by the Law of Nature, and to render an account thereof to God, the Author of that Law, and to none but him" (2012, 520; 1651, 175; also Hobbes 1969, 179; 1998, 143). Pre-statist individuals lack such role-specific duties of care. One of the sovereign's main tasks is to protect the people against foreign enemies. Defense against external enemies is a prime good of citizens (Hobbes 1969, 179, 184; 1998, 144–5) and a key reason for instituting the commonwealth (Hobbes 1969, 108; 2012, 406; 1651, 134). Indeed, the right of making war and peace with other nations is an essential mark of sovereignty (Hobbes 1998, 79; 2012, 274; 1651, 92). My contention is that the law of nations dictates to sovereigns *how* they should procure the people's safety against foreign enemies. For instance, its principles prohibit national wars of aggrandizement, waged "out of ambition, or of vain-glory" (Hobbes 1969, 184; also Hobbes 1998, 150; 2012, 518; 1651, 174; 2005, 16). A sovereign initiating war for glory flouts his role-specific duties by contravening the moral duty to seek external peace.

The sovereign is obliged by natural law to fulfil his role-specific duties to his best endeavor. Which law(s) of nature underpins these duties? Some specific sovereign duties track separate laws of nature (such as moral duties of equity and mercy); others do not.[25] Following suggestions by Murphy (1994, 284) and Malcolm (2002, 447; 2005, 126), I contend that the natural law of gratitude enjoins the sovereign to fulfil role-specific duties in general. Sovereigns are duty-bound to do their utmost to provide external defense on pain of acting "in contravention of the trust of those who put the sovereign power in their hands" (Hobbes 1998, 144).[26] Duties of gratitude spring from free gifts, as duties of justice from mutual covenants. The sovereign's duties are not assigned to him by the people, but a moral upshot resulting from having freely received supreme power from them. Sovereigns are morally obliged to give subjects "no reasonable cause to repent" their good will by discharging their office well (2012, 230; 1651, 75; also 2012, 492; 1651, 165). Should they breach the trust, then this is "not to be called injury; it hath another name (viz.) ingratitude" (Hobbes 1969, 85; also Hobbes 1998, 47–8; 2012, 230; 1651, 76; 2012, 390; 1651, 128). Again, sovereigns owe this natural law duty to God alone.

Leviathan's novel foundation of the principles of international ethics entails two further revisions. First, the right of nations allows sovereigns to wage war with foreign enemies – yet not to secure their own self-preservation but to protect their people. "And every Soveraign hath the same Right, in procuring the safety of his People, that any particular man can have, in procuring the safety of his own Body" (2012, 552; 1651, 185).[27] Individual rights to wage war are essentially rights of *self*-defense. By contrast, the sovereign's right to wage war against enemies of the commonwealth are at bottom rights of *other*-defense. Second, the principles of international ethics determine *how* the sovereign ought to protect the people from external enemies: "the people's safety dictates the law by which Princes come to know their *duty*" (Hobbes 1998, 143). The laws of nations dictate to rulers the surest means to international peace. Gratitude imposes an additional duty on the sovereign regarding sound foreign policy. Brazenly belligerent sovereigns hence do double wrong: violating *jus gentium* generally as well as the specific natural law duty of gratitude.

Sovereigns are accountable to God alone for fulfilling these moral duties. The deity kindly takes the endeavor for the deed; meaning that objectively disastrous decisions are justified if done in good faith. "In the judgement of the person actually doing is, what is done is rightly done, even if it is a wrong, and so is rightly done" (Hobbes 1998, 29; also Hobbes 1998, 54). To support his contention that the law of nations binds in conscience alone, I have suggested, *Leviathan* ditches the earlier Assimilation Argument. The common contention that *states* are bound by Hobbes's law of nations/nature should hence be rejected. In *Leviathan*, *jus gentium* binds the sovereign representative directly – not the commonwealth whose person he carries. The concluding section argues that international principles of justice and of just war are likewise matters of conscience alone.

15.5 Justice and Just War as Merely Requiring Right Intention

Hobbes is commonly read as a realist about war: moral categories would be inapplicable during armed conflict (e.g., Walzer 2015 [1977], 10–13). In fact, an ethical theory of war is present in Hobbes's works – albeit a highly idiosyncratic one (Thivet 2008). Rights to wage war are foundational to Hobbes's political theory. They explain why "before the Institution of Common-wealth, every man had a right to every thing, and to do whatsoever he thought necessary to his own preservation; subduing, hurting, or killing any man in order thereunto" (2012, 482; 1651, 161).[28] For this "right of all men to all things ... is the right of War" (Hobbes 1998, 12; also Hobbes 1998, 69). Sovereigns wield the same right of war when defending their people against domestic and foreign enemies: "the commonwealth retains its original Right against the dissenter, i.e. the *right of war*, as against an enemy" (Hobbes 1998, 77; also Hobbes 1998, 166; 2012, 494; 1651, 165).

The *Dialogue* contains Hobbes's most extensive engagement with received just war doctrines (cf. Hobbes 1998, 133; 2012, 386; 1651, 127). It stresses that decisions about war and peace are a sovereign prerogative, morally restrained only by the positional requirement to protect the people in any way deemed effective. Consider the passage on the lawfulness of armed intervention in foreign conflicts. "If the War upon our Neighbours [by a third country] be Just, it may be question'd whether it be Equity or no to Assist them against the Right." In response, the philosopher – supposedly Hobbes's spokesperson – tersely waives away any moral qualms about assisting unjust belligerents. "For my part I make no Question of that at all, unless the Invader will, and can put me in security, that neither he, nor his Successors shall make any Advantage of the Conquest of my Neighbour, to do the same to me in time to come; but there is no Common Power to bind them to the Peace" (Hobbes 2005, 23). Whether enemies have just cause for war is morally irrelevant for the sovereign. When dealing with "Enemies, whom the Common-wealth judgeth capable to do them hurt... the Sword Judgeth not, nor doth the Victor make distinction of Nocent, and Innocent, as to the time past; nor has other respect of mercy, than as it conduceth to the good of his own People" (Hobbes 2012, 494; 1651, 165).

Across his works, Hobbes insists that preventive wars are permissible, not just to avert imminent attacks but to heighten security generally. "And as their preservation, so also is their security a just pretence of invading those whom they have just cause to fear, unless sufficient caution be given to take away their fear, which Caution (for any thing I can yet conceive) is utterly impossible" (Hobbes 2005, 135–6; also 2012, 190; 1651, 61; 2012, 450; 1651, 150). Indeed, "Necessity, and Security are the principle justifications, before God, of beginning War" (Hobbes 2005, 136). In morally endorsing preventive wars aimed at security and in portraying them as essentially defensive in character, Hobbes followed Alberico Gentili (1552–1608) and Francis Bacon (Hoekstra 2012; Reichberg 2007; Tuck 1999, 126–39). Gentili sanctioned anticipatory warfare against any "probable and possible" attack (1933 [1598], 62), adding that a "just cause for fear is demanded; suspicion is not enough" (1933 [1598], 66). "Now a just fear is defined as the fear of a greater evil, a fear which might properly be felt even by a man of great courage" (1933 [1598], 66). Bacon similarly held that "a just feare (without an actuall invasion or offence) is a sufficient ground of a Warre, and in the nature of a true defensive" (1629, 8). A fear is just when prompted by "cleare foresight of imminent danger."

Hobbes concurred that war is defensive (and hence just) if motivated by considerations of national security. Yet he departed from his two bellicose predecessors in subjectivizing the just-fear criterion through his postulate of natural equality of right: "in the condition of meer Nature, where all men are equall, and judges of the justnesse of their own fears" (2012, 210; 1651, 68). Within conditions of war, each agent may by right rely on their own strength and judgment to determine how best to secure themselves. That natural right of personal judgement establishes immunity to human accusations of misconduct (2012, 214; 1651, 70). Only God can judge whether agents sincerely endeavor to abide by the natural law duty to pursue peace. Hobbes thereby effectively made having a right intention the sole criterion for permissible resort to armed force:

> to make War upon another like Soveraign Lord, and dispossess him of his Lands ... is Lawful, or not Lawful according to the intention of him that does it. For, First, being a Soveraign Ruler, he is not subject to any Law of Man; and as to the Law of God, where the intention is justifiable, the action is so also. (Hobbes 2005, 135)

Consequently, the laws of nations, prescribing the means to international peace, are duties of conscience alone, each sovereign equally having the right to follow their own judgment as to how their people is best protected.

The same holds true for obligations of justice to keep international pacts and truces. Commentators have rightly pointed out that Hobbes neither denies the possibility nor the benefits of international cooperation.[29] "Leagues between Common-wealths, over whom there is no humane Power established, to keep them all in awe, are not onely lawfull, but also profitable for the time they last" (2012, 370; 1651, 122).[30] However, such temporary leagues are by their very nature insufficient to guarantee enduring peace: "an association formed only for mutual aid, does not afford to the parties ... the security which we are looking for, to practice, in their relations with each other, the *laws of nature*" (Hobbes 1998, 70). Lacking a common power to keep members' wills aligned amidst inevitable disagreements, associations are inherently unstable (Hobbes 1998, 72). The *Dialogue* voices skepticism about the viability of "a constant Peace ... between two Nations, because there is no Common Power in this World to punish their Injustice: mutual fear may keep them quiet for a time, but upon every visible advantage they will invade one another" (Hobbes 2005, 12). Any newly arising just fear invalidates international pacts, retriggering hostilities: "And if a weaker Prince, make a disadvantageous peace with a stronger, for feare; he is bound to keep it; unless ... there ariseth some new, and just cause of feare, to renew the war" (2012, 212; 1651, 69; also Hobbes 1998, 145).

International leagues by definition lack a judge to settle conflicts and enforce rulings. They hence leave its members in a state of nature, where each party has right to judge for themselves the safety of continued cooperation. Whether a covenant of mutual trust can safely be kept hence "is for the fearful party to decide" (Hobbes 1998, 37). Outside the state, each person reneging on their covenants out of fear does so rightfully since they themselves are by natural right the judge of the justness of their fears. Just as each individual "may lawfully rely on his own strength and art, for caution against all other men" absent a functioning system of law enforcement, so may "Cities and Kingdomes ... upon all pretences of danger, and fear of Invasion ... endeavour as much as they can, to subdue, or weaken their neighbours, by open force, and secret arts, for want of other Caution, justly" (2012, 256; 1651, 85). Indeed, sovereigns are ex officio obliged to weaken enemies by any means possible: "They may also do anything that seems likely to subvert, by force or by craft, the power of foreigners whom they fear; for the rulers of commonwealths are obliged to do all they can to ensure that the calamities they fear do not happen" (Hobbes 1998, 146).

15.6 Conclusion

In this chapter I have analyzed Hobbes's reductionism about the principles of international ethics. Across his works, Hobbes insists that the law of nations equals the law of nature, and *jus belli* the right of nature. These continuities in substance notwithstanding, I have argued that Hobbes profoundly alters his account of international ethics in *Leviathan*. There, *jus gentium* spell out how the sovereign ought to fulfil his role-specific duty to safeguard the people from foreign threats. Violations of the law of nations are wrong both in itself and as transgressions of the natural law duty of gratitude.

In normatively grounding principles of international ethics in the sovereign's positional duties to promote *salus populi*, *Leviathan*'s theory resembles some modern realist theories of international relations. With this qualification: Hobbes's principles of international ethics exclusively concern defense against external enemies, rather than pursuit of national interest generally (Donnelly 2008; cf. Coady 2005). The proffered analysis provides some clues about the extent to which Hobbes's account of international ethics is: (1) merely an extrapolation of what individuals are morally permitted, required, and prohibited to do in the state of nature; (2) determined by role-specific duties of sovereigns; (3) informed by demands of political absolutism; or (4) a set of self-standing doctrines, developed by engaging with contemporary theories of *jus gentium* and *jus belli*. His account is perhaps best characterized as interlacing at various levels all four strands.

Notes

1 For insightful feedback on earlier versions of this chapter, I am indebted to Marcus Adams, Laurens van Apeldoorn, Alexandra Chadwick, and Ben Holland. Thanks to Peter Schröder for helpful conversations on the topic.

2 This chapter otherwise makes no inroads into the province of international relations theory. Hobbes's theoretical conjectures on the empirical conditions of and constraints on interactions between states are left undiscussed, as are considerations of mere prudence in international affairs. On Hobbes on international relations, compare the contrasting readings of Beitz (1999 [1979], 27–59), Malcolm (2002), Boucher (2018, 186–219).

3 For further depictions of the internal arena as a state of war, see e.g., 1998, 4, 126; 2012, 196; 1651, 63; 2012, 332; 1651, 110; 2005, 12. On Hobbes's idiosyncratic conception of peace, see 1998, 29–30; 2012, 192; 1651, 62; 2012, 272; 1651, 91.

4 For discussion, see Hoekstra 2012, 51–4. Tuck (1999, 127) ventures to speculate that "Hobbes actually drafted the treatise for his master [Bacon]".

5 For an elaborate critique of the moral relativist reading of Hobbes found in the older realist literature, see Malcolm 2002, 433–40.

6 Though itself a law of nature, justice is best regarded as a deontic principle qualitatively distinct from natural law. For justice and natural law regulate different kinds of moral obligations, with diverging conceptual features and metaethical statuses (Abizadeh 2018).

7 Vattel (2008 [1758], 8–9, 68–9) was hence uncharitable when accusing Hobbes of failing to realize that natural law changes its requirements when applied to nations. "[T]he *law of nations* is originally no other than the *law of nations applied* to nations. But as the application of a rule cannot be just and reasonable unless it be made in a manner suitable to the subject, we are not to imagine that the law of nations is precisely and in every case the same as the law of nature ... the same general rule, applied to two subjects, cannot produce exactly the same decisions, when the subjects are different".

8 While Hobbes's imperialism about private warfare is generally overlooked, anti-imperialist readings of Hobbes on international affairs proliferate (see, e.g., Christov 2015, 128–35; Malcolm 2002, 441–3; Springborg 2015; Tuck 2013, 107–10).

9 Gauthier (1969, 207–12) argues that the second law of nature, as applied to nations, requires pursuing mutual disarmament.

10 Cf. Thucydides 1998, 1.67 (= EW VIII.71). Gentili (1933 [1598], 88) had condemned the Athenians for closing their ports to the Megareans as contravening the law of nations. On duties of non-discrimination in international trade, see also Vitoria (1991, 279–80); Grotius (2005 [1625], 451–2).

11 E.g., Grotius (2005 [1625], 107, 112–13, 124).

12 Cf. Pufendorf (1729 [1672], 2.3.23): "Nor do we conceive, that there is any other Voluntary or Positive Law of Nations, properly invested with a true and legal Force, and obliging as the Ordinance of a Superior Power".

13 For an overview of early modern ideas on diplomatic immunity, see Young (1964, 148–67).

14 Pufendorf (1729 [1672], 2.3.23) followed Hobbes in subsuming the law of embassies under natural law. Van Velthuysen (2013 [1651], 72) distinguished between a natural and customary law of nations, while likewise following Hobbes in subsuming the law of ambassadors under the former.

15 Cf. *Justinian's Digest* 1.1.4: "*Jus gentium*, the law of nations, is that which all human peoples observe." (Watson 1985, 1).

16 E.g., Hobbes 1969, 138–40; 1998, 85, 136; 2012, 220; 1651, 72; 2012, 388; 1651, 128; 2005, 13–14, 34.

17 The last was labelled "*jus inter gentes*" by Zouche (1911 [1650], 1). On this distinction, see, e.g., Suárez (2015, 401).

18 Hobbes "accepted ... the Grotian assimilation of individuals to sovereign states" (Tuck 1999, 129). Tuck's study of early modern theories of rights of war traces the legacy of Grotius's putative moral identification of pre-statist individuals with sovereign states: "Grotius had thus made the claim that an individual in nature (that is, before transferring any rights to a civil society) was morally identical to a state, and that there were no powers possessed by a state which an individual could not possess in nature" (1999, 82; also 85, 95, 108, 228).

19 Also, e.g., Cavallar (2002, 179–80). *De cive*'s Assimilation Argument left a long legacy in international thought. E.g., Spinoza (2016, 522): "since the Right of the supreme power is nothing more than the Right itself of nature, it follows that two states are related to one another as two men are in the state of nature." Later theorists – including Vattel (2008 [1758], 73) and Reid (2007, 95) – combined a similar line of reasoning with Pufendorf's notion of the state as a moral person, endowed with joint capacities of reason and will. Their conception of moral state personality differs from Hobbesian state personality (Holland 2017, 91, 210–12).

20 Malcolm has criticized realist interpretations of Hobbes for advancing a "complete parallelism between individuals and states, so that anything he said about the psychology and the predicament of the former in the state of nature must equally apply to the latter" (2002, 443; 2005). Malcolm challenges both empirical and normative parallels between states and individuals, arguing that the parallelism holds true only partially, namely at the "jural level" of interpersonal rights and duties (2002, 446). He highlights Hobbes's reduction of *jus gentium* to natural law without explaining it.

21 On Hobbes's conception of the state, see Olsthoorn (2021).

22 Vattel attributes duties of consciences to states on grounds similar to those adopted in *Leviathan*: "The law of nations is the law of sovereigns" (2008 [1758], 18).

23 The reconceptualization of *jus gentium* as applying to sovereigns, rather than to states, is arguably facilitated by *Leviathan*'s novel theory of representation. Clarifying their relation as one of representation, the sovereign is now defined as he who acts on behalf of the commonwealth.

24 The sovereign is a third-party beneficiary in the original covenant, receiving the benefit (i.e., sovereign power) of the mutual exchange between citizens (May 2013, 48–66).

25 Eleanor Curran (2007, 113–16) argues, rightly, that at least some office-specific duties of sovereigns are irreducible to natural law duties. Their violation is hence not wrong in itself. Curran leaves unexplained what makes performance of such morally arbitrary offices mor-

ally binding. She overlooks that the sovereign is obliged by natural law to abide by the entire set of duties.

26 According to *De cive* 13.4, only sovereigns by institution are bound by this duty of trust; sovereigns by acquisition – who have conquered each subject separately – are not (Hobbes 1998, 144). *Leviathan* lacks a statement to this effect.

27 The parallel passage in Latin *Leviathan* 30.30 is more ambiguous: "Nam *Ius Gentium & Ius Naturae* idem sunt. That which every man could do before the institution of commonwealths, every commonwealth can do by the law of nations [or right of nations: *jus gentium*]" (2012, 553; 1668, 166).

28 On the natural right of self-preservation as warranting defensive killing, see also Hobbes 1969, 130; 1998, 40, 105; EW V.152; EW V.184–5, 2005, 135.

29 For Hobbesian defenses of an international legal order, see May (2013, 173–223) and Dyzenhaus (2014).

30 For further evidence of international agreements, see 2012, 308; 1651, 130; 2012, 346; 1651, 114; 2012, 495; 1668, 149; 2010, 301.

References

Abizadeh, Arash. 2018. *Hobbes and the Two Faces of Ethics*. Cambridge: Cambridge University Press.

Armitage, David. 2013. "Hobbes and the Foundations of Modern International Thought." In *The Foundations of Modern International Thought*, 59–74. Cambridge: Cambridge University Press.

Bacon, Francis. 1629. *Considerations Touching a Warre with Spaine*. London: n.p.

Beitz, Charles. 1999 [1979]. *Political Theory and International Relations*. Princeton, NJ: Princeton University Press.

Bottici, Chiara. 2009 [2004]. *Men and States: Rethinking the Domestic Analogy in a Global Age*, translated by Karen Whittle. New York: Palgrave Macmillan.

Boucher, David. 2018. *Appropriating Hobbes: Legacies in Political, Legal, and International Thought*. Oxford: Oxford University Press.

Bull, Hedley. 2012 [1977]. *The Anarchical Society: A Study of Order in World Politics*, 4th ed. New York: Palgrave Macmillan.

Cavallar, Georg. 2002. *The Rights of Strangers: Theories of International Hospitality, the Global Community, and Political Justice since Vitoria*. Aldershot: Ashgate.

Christov, Theodore. 2015. *Before Anarchy: Hobbes and His Critics in Modern International Thought*. Cambridge: Cambridge University Press.

Coady, C.A.J. (Tony) 2005. "The Moral Reality in Realism." *Journal of Applied Philosophy* 22 (2): 121–36.

Curran, Eleanor. 2007. *Reclaiming the Rights of Hobbesian Subjects*. New York: Palgrave Macmillan.

Donnelly, Jack. 2008. "The Ethics of Realism." In *The Oxford Handbook of International Relations*, edited by Christian Reus-Smit and Duncan Snidal, 150–62. Oxford: Oxford University Press.

Dyzenhaus, David. 2014. "Hobbes on the International Rule of Law." *Ethics and International Affairs* 28 (1): 53–64.

Gauthier, David. 1969. *The Logic of Leviathan: The Moral and Political Theory of Thomas Hobbes*. Oxford: Clarendon Press.

Gentili, Alberico. 1933 [1598]. *De Jure Belli Libri Tres*, 2 vols., edited by John C. Rolfe. Oxford: Clarendon Press.

Grotius, Hugo. 2005 [1625]. *The Rights of War and Peace*, 3 vols., edited by Richard Tuck. Indianapolis, IN: Liberty Fund.

Hobbes, Thomas. 1839–1845. *The English Works of Thomas Hobbes*, 11 vols., edited by Sir William Molesworth. London: John Bohn. Cited as EW.

Hobbes, Thomas. 1969. *The Elements of Law, Natural and Politic*, 2nd ed., edited by Ferdinand Tönnies. London: Frank Cass.

Hobbes, Thomas. 1998. *On the Citizen*, edited by Richard Tuck, translated by Michael Silverthorne. Cambridge: Cambridge University Press.

Hobbes, Thomas. 2005. *Writings on Common Law and Hereditary Right*, edited by Alan Cromartie and Quentin Skinner. Oxford: Clarendon Press.

Hobbes, Thomas. 2010. *Behemoth, or the Long Parliament*, edited by Paul Seaward. Oxford: Clarendon Press.

Hobbes, Thomas. 2012. *Leviathan*, 3 vols., edited by Noel Malcolm. Oxford: Clarendon Press. [First published 1651].

Hoekstra, Kinch. 2012. "Thucydides and the Bellicose Beginnings of Modern Political Theory." In *Thucydides and the Modern World*, edited by Katherine Harloe and Neville Morley, 25–54. Cambridge: Cambridge University Press.

Holland, Ben. 2017. *The Moral Person of the State: Pufendorf, Sovereignty and Composite Polities*. Cambridge: Cambridge University Press.

Malcolm, Noel. 2002. "Hobbes's Theory of International Relations." In *Aspects of Hobbes*, 432–56. Oxford: Oxford University Press.

Malcolm, Noel. 2005. "What Hobbes *Really* Said." *The National Interest* 81: 122–8.

May, Larry. 2013. *Limiting Leviathan: Hobbes on Law and International Affairs*. Oxford: Oxford University Press.

Morgenthau, Hans J. 1952. *American Foreign Policy: A Critical Examination*. London: Methuen.

Murphy, Mark C. 1994. "Deviant Uses of 'Obligation' in Hobbes' *Leviathan*." *History of Philosophy Quarterly* 11 (3): 281–94.

Olsthoorn, Johan. 2021. "*Leviathan* Inc.: Hobbes on the nature and person of the commonwealth." *History of European Ideas* 47 (1): 17–32.

Pufendorf, Samuel. 1729 [1672]. *Of the Law of Nature and Nations*, translated by Basil Kennett. London: printed for J. Walthoe et al.

Rachel, Samuel. 1916 [1676]. *Dissertations on the Law of Nature and of Nations*, edited by Ludwig von Bar. Washington, DC: Carnegie Institution.

Reichberg, Gregory M. 2007. "Preventive War in Classical Just War Theory." *Journal of the History of International Law* 9 (1): 5–34.

Reid, Thomas. 2007. *On Practical Ethics*, edited by Knud Haakonssen. Edinburgh: Edinburgh University Press.

Spinoza, Baruch. 2016. *The Collected Works of Spinoza, Vol. 2*, edited by Edwin Curley. Princeton, NJ: Princeton University Press.

Springborg, Patricia. 2015. "Hobbes, Donne and the Virginia Company: *Terra Nullius* and 'The Bulimia of Dominium'." *History of Political Thought* 36 (1): 113–64.

Suárez, Francisco. 2015. *Selections from Three Works*, edited by Thomas Pink. Indianapolis, IN: Liberty Fund.

Thivet, Delphine. 2008. "Thomas Hobbes: A Philosopher of War or Peace?" *British Journal for the History of Philosophy* 16 (4): 701–21.

Thucydides. 1998. *The Peloponnesian War*, edited and translated by Steven Lattimore. Indianapolis, IN: Hackett.

Tuck, Richard. 1999. *The Rights of War and Peace: Political Thought and the International Order from Grotius to Kant*. Oxford: Oxford University Press.

Tuck, Richard. 2013. "Grotius, Hobbes, and Pufendorf on Humanitarian Intervention." In *Just and Unjust Military Intervention: European Thinkers from Vitoria to Mill*, edited by Stefano Recchia and Jennifer M. Welsh, 96–112. Cambridge: Cambridge University Press.

Van Velthuysen, Lambert. 2013 [1651]. *A Letter on the Principles of Justness and Decency, Containing a Defence of the Treatise De cive of the Learned Mr Hobbes*, edited by Malcolm de Mowbray. Leiden: Brill.

Vattel, Emer de. 2008 [1758]. *The Law of Nations*, edited by Béla Kapossy and Richard Whatmore. Indianapolis, IN: Liberty Fund.

Vitoria, Francisco de. 1991. *Political Writings*, edited by Anthony Pagden and Jeremy Lawrance. Cambridge: Cambridge University Press.

Walzer, Michael. 2015 [1977]. *Just and Unjust Wars: A Moral Argument with Historical Illustrations*, 5th ed. New York: Basic Books.

Watson, Alan, ed. 1985. *The Digest of Justinian*, vol. 1. Philadelphia, PA: University of Pennsylvania Press.

Young, Eileen. 1964. "The Development of the Law of Diplomatic Relations." *British Yearbook of International Law* 40: 141–82.

Zouche, Richard. 1911 [1650]. *An Exposition of Fecial Law and Procedure, or of Law between Nations*, edited by James L. Brierly and Thomas E. Holland. Washington, DC: Carnegie Institution.

Part IV

Religion

16

Against Philosophical Darkness: A Political Conception of Enlightenment

LUC FOISNEAU

The title of Part 4 of *Leviathan*, "Of the Kingdom of Darkness," gives a good indication of the nature of Hobbes's contribution to Enlightenment thought. In the Bible, the expression "kingdom of darkness" refers to Satan's kingdom over demons, but Hobbes redefines this expression by calling demons "fantasies" and turning these fantasies into illusions or prejudices that darken men's minds about their political obligations. The kingdom of darkness is thus the name of an enterprise political by nature: it is a scheme for the usurpation of the power of the legitimate rulers by "a *Confederacy of Deceivers, that to obtain dominion over men in this present world, endeavour by dark, and erroneous Doctrines, to extinguish in them the Light, both of Nature, and of the Gospell; and so to disprepare them for the Kingdome of God to come*" (Hobbes 2012, 956; 1651, 333). Darkness and light thus form in Hobbes a chiaroscuro around the idea of sovereignty, which the exercise of critical judgment will have to dispel.

Whatever reservations one may have about Hobbes's belief concerning revelation, one must leave open, on first reading, the possibility that Hobbes be a supporter of moderate Enlightenment, compatible with the word of revelation, since it is the interpretative perspective that he himself claims.[1] The present chapter will not deal with this dimension of the question of Enlightenment in Hobbes, but with the role of the idea of sovereignty in the latter's critical thinking. The critique of Scholastic theology, to which Hobbes devoted original analyses, shall serve as an example. Hobbes does not only ask himself how to criticize the philosophical theses of Scholastic theologians, but also how to bring out the political dimension of theses that one would more readily describe as metaphysical. Since the Hobbesian Enlightenment wants to emancipate the minds of citizens subjected to theological prejudices, it does so by constructing an original hermeneutical device aiming to explain how metaphysical theses – the thesis of separate essences will be central to the demonstration – are likely to contribute to an enterprise of political domination.

A Companion to Hobbes, First Edition. Edited by Marcus P. Adams.

I shall try to show, first of all, that, for Hobbes, Scholastic theology comes under a specific institutional mode of functioning, that of the schools of philosophy whose long genealogy goes back to Greek and Jewish antiquity; I will show, then, in what way his critique of Scholastic arguments presupposes a critique of the language in which these arguments were formulated, and that this critique values the vernacular language of the sovereign State. After having analyzed this double move, I will show in what way the criticism of the apparently purely metaphysical thesis of the existence of separate essences belongs to a political context, that of the criticism of the domination over the minds of citizens by the Catholic Church.

16.1 Institutional Darkness: Why Schools Don't Matter So Much

The historical narrative through which Hobbes traces, in order to criticize it, the genesis of Scholastic philosophy takes the form of an institutional history of ideas. This story begins with a reminder of the definition of true philosophy, which is "the Knowledge acquired by Reasoning, from the Manner of the Generation of any thing, to the Properties; or from the Properties, to some possible Way of Generation of the same; to the end to bee able to produce, as far as matter, and humane force permit, such Effects, as humane life requireth" (Hobbes 2012, 1050; 1651, 367). Two things are important in this definition: first, that philosophy is knowledge through reasoning that deals with causes, and second, that philosophical knowledge is useful to men. Prudence, which is knowledge produced by experience, satisfies only the criterion of utility, but does not help discover truths of reason. Nor is the word of God philosophical, because it is not based on reasoning but on supernatural revelation. This definition of true philosophy is not sufficient, however, to understand the causes of the corruption of reasoning that made Scholastic theology possible. In order to understand it, it is necessary to add historical information: Scholasticism is that current of thought that sought to express Christian faith in the conceptual language of ancient philosophy. Hobbes intends to show that such a doctrinal conjunction cannot be explained by philosophical arguments alone but requires a political and juridical perspective. The method used to retrace the genesis of Scholastic philosophy in fact borrows from a theory of association, which gives a common legal status to the various forms of organization within which citizens of a state can come together. In order to show the dependence of associations with the sovereign state, Hobbes presents those associations as parts of the state, just as the muscles are parts of the natural human body (Hobbes 2012, 348; 1651, 115). The relationship with the idea of sovereignty is indeed direct, since a subordinate organization is the exact opposite of a sovereign organization, whose characteristics are to be "regular" (to have a representative body), "absolute" (not to depend on any other representative body), and "independent" (with no relationship of dependence on another organization) (Hobbes 2012, 348; 1651, 115). Compared to this sovereign organization, all other organizations are to be defined as "systems subject" (Hobbes 2012, 348; 1651, 115), or, in the Latin version, as "systemata civium" (Hobbes 2012, 349; 1651, 111), insofar as their legal status is dependent on the will of the sovereign; in other words, their status must be understood in relation to the only system that is not dependent on another system. If Hobbes does not use the notion of "institution," the notion of "system subject," which designates "any numbers of men joined in one Interest, or one Businesse" (Hobbes 2012, 348; 1651, 115), constitutes a prefiguration of it. Such a concept makes it possible to describe the legal status of the various forms of organization that can be found in a State, from public institutions to very informal gatherings of people in a market. From the point of view of the history of Scholastic philosophy, the interest of the notion of "system subject" is that it makes it possible to describe in political terms the logic that presided over the rapprochement between ancient philosophy and Christian dogma. Since "Scholastics" are men who belong to an organization responsible for teaching, the general idea is that it is not enough to read their texts, it is also necessary to take into account the fact that they are the products of specific institutions. If we want to characterize Hobbes's criticism of Scholasticism as accurately as possible, it must be said that it is a political history of educational institutions.

This genealogy of Scholasticism can be found in several works, in the fourth part of *Leviathan*, which offers the most complete exposition of it, but also in the *Historia ecclesiastica*,[2] in the Appendix to the Latin *Leviathan*,[3] and in *Behemoth*.[4] The prehistory of philosophy begins, in the exposition of chapter 46 of *Leviathan*, with the "Savages of America," who, although they had the faculty of reasoning, did not know how to make methodical use of it: if there "are not without some good Moral Sentences" and "have a little Arithmetick, to adde, and divide in Numbers not too great," "there are not therefore Philosophers" (Hobbes 2012, 1054; 1651, 368). One should not, however, relate this lack of method to a defect inherent in primitive thought, which has everything it needs as soon as it has language, but to the absence of a sovereign political order, or, as Hobbes says, to the absence of "great Common-wealths" (Hobbes 2012, 1054; 1651, 368; see also Hobbes 2008, 317). Considering that the study of philosophy requires the leisure that only civil peace makes possible, peaceful conditions thus appear to Hobbes to be decisive to the thriving of philosophy. He recalls that the Latin word *schola*, whose Greek etymon, σχολή, means "leisure," designates "the place where any of them [i.e., the Greek philosophers] taught, and disputed" (Hobbes 2012, 1056; 1651, 368): for all that, if it is true philosophy benefits from state politics, since the latter be a condition of leisure, it is also true that it suffers to be submitted to the rules of schools. As a negative proof of his thesis, Hobbes cites India, Persia, Chaldea, and Egypt, which experienced "philosophy" before Greece, not because of the genius of their philosophers, but because these countries benefited earlier from political stability through their monarchical regimes; these countries already formed great kingdoms at a time when Greece did not yet know civil peace because of the too small size of its cities and the incessant wars between them. Hobbes does not say so explicitly but he suggests it through a juxtaposition: "The Gymnosophists of India, the Magi of Persia, and the Priests of Chaldaea and Egypt, are counted the most ancient Philosophers; and those Countreys were the most ancient of Kingdomes" (Hobbes 2012, 1054; 1651, 368). Though implicit, the opposition with ancient Greece is crystal clear for the informed reader: contrary to the republican vulgate, Athens did not benefit but suffered from its democratic regime.[5] If Hobbes does not go into the nature of oriental philosophies – he merely repeats the commonplace that oriental wisdoms were the first manifestations of philosophical enlightenment before Greece – the important thing for him in this historical narrative is to make Greece lose the privilege of origin.

If, according to Hobbes, Greek philosophy does possess a historical singularity, it is not in the invention of philosophy that it resides. Greece's contribution to the history of philosophy lies, in fact, in a certain school practice that served as an institutional and social framework during the rise of Athenian hegemony in Europe and Asia. The school practice of Greek philosophy is an indirect effect of the expansionist policy of Athens, which gave the cities of the region relative stability and the philosophers the leisure they needed. However, the activity called by the Greeks "philosophy" is somewhat of a misnomer, since it consisted mainly in listening to news and reporting them, and talking about philosophy to the youth of the city. The institutional approach to Greek philosophy has very clearly, for Hobbes, a depreciative aim: it serves to underline that philosophical activity strictly speaking suffers from the predominance of school practices such as arguing and teaching. In order to give greater rhetorical weight to his criticism, Hobbes recalls that the famous name of the Academy comes very prosaically from the place where philosophical teaching took place. To destroy the myth of the Greek origin of philosophy, he remarks ironically that "they that followed *Plato*'s Doctrine, were called Academiques ... as if we should denominate men from *More-Fields*, from *Pauls-Church*, and from the *Exchange*, because they meet there often, to prate and loyter" (Hobbes 2012, 1056; 1651, 369; see also Hobbes 2008, 349). In order to tarnish the glory that surrounds them, Hobbes thus endeavors to underline the prosaic character of the context in which Greek philosophers carried out their activity: the Academy should be no more a myth than More-Fields or the Exchange in London. It is in this same spirit of demystification that Hobbes stresses that Greek philosophers are not the only ones to have invented the school practice of philosophy: Jews had also founded schools long before the opening of the Academy, the synagogues being less "Congregations of the People," as the etymology wrongly indicates, than places where the law was "read, expounded, and disputed" (Hobbes 2012, 1058; 1651, 370), that is, places that perform the function of public schools. There is little surprise, therefore, that it was in the synagogues that for the first time the texts of the Bible and Greek philosophy were mixed together: Hobbes seeks in the Jewish religion a prefiguration of Scholastic philosophy, since two elements that were mixed together in the latter, the text of revelation and ancient philosophy, could already be found in the Jewish schools. The description of the ancient Jewish teaching is no more laudatory than that of Greek philosophy: it is only "a Phantasticall kind of Philosophy, concerning the incomprehensible nature of God, and of Spirits; which they [i.e., the learned Jews] compounded of the Vain Philosophy and Theology of the Graecians, mingled with their own fancies, drawn from the obscurer places of the Scripture, and which might most easily bee wrested to their purpose; and from the Fabulous Traditions of their Ancestors" (Hobbes 2012, 1060; 1651, 370).

In this rewriting of the history of ancient philosophy, both Greek and Jewish, the important point is that, from its birth in Greece onward, school philosophy already possessed the two main features that it would retain in Christian Scholasticism, namely, the practice of *disputatio* and the practice of *lectio*. After his account of the beginnings, Hobbes comes to critically question the philosophical schools as a mode of organization of knowledge that opposes the development of true philosophy – what was not yet called "Enlightenment." If the formation of powerful republics has made the development of methodical reasoning possible, the associations of citizens (*systems subject/systemata civium*) in schools constitute a break on such progress. Far from having favored the exercise of reason, the school practice of philosophy has led to its stagnation, or even its regression, in all fields of knowledge. From this point of view, Hobbes encourages his readers to consider the invention of philosophical schools as a moment all the more critical in the history of philosophy that none of the parts of ancient philosophy, physical, logical, and moral, did benefit from it. The school structure appears, in any case, as a source not of progress but of intellectual regression – it constitutes the distant source of the darkness that reigned, according to Hobbes's account, over Christian Europe through the fault of Scholastic philosophy.

This reading, it should be stressed, presents all the features of a reconstruction. Hobbes forces Antiquity and the Middle Ages to fit into the frame of his reading at the service of the Enlightenment that he promotes. One proof among others of this forced appropriation of the past is given to us by Hobbes's proposed rereading of Plato's formula, "Let no one enter here unless he is a geometrician":

> That wee have of Geometry, which is the Mother of all Natural Science, wee are not indebted for it to the Schools. *Plato* that was the best Philosopher of the Greeks, forbad entrance into his Schoole, to all that were not already in some measure Geometricians. There were many that studied that Science to the great advantage of mankind: but there is no mention of their Schools; nor was there any Sect of Geometricians; nor did they then passe under the name of Philosophers (Hobbes 2012, 1058; 1651, 369).

The famous Platonic inscription on the pediment of the Academy of Athens signifies for the English philosopher the uselessness of the school structure, with its classes and disputes, since the geometricians managed very well to do without schools. What we have in geometry, the mother of all natural sciences, was obtained outside schools. Many studied this science for the benefit of mankind, without claiming for themselves the title of philosopher. Since geometry excludes formal argument and does not need to take the form of a didactic exposition, the mathematician has no need of the Academy within which Plato wished to confine him. Hobbes's interpretation is fanciful to say the least: it totally neglects the role that Plato intended mathematics to play in the training of philosophers. Thus reformulated in a way that introduces distortions, the history of ancient philosophy and the history of Jewish thought are supposed to help Hobbes's readers to understand the drawbacks of Scholasticism in the Christian era.

The invention of universities, an institutional contribution of medieval Christianity, consists according to Hobbes in a systematization of the system of ancient schools: "That which is now called an Vniversity, is a Joyning together, and an Incorporation under one Government of many Publique Schools, in one and the same Town or City" (Hobbes 2012, 1074; 1651, 370; see also Hobbes 1969, 40). Furthermore, Scholastic philosophy is only admitted to the university "as a handmaid to the Romane Religion" (Hobbes 2012, 1074; 1651, 370). All the less autonomous since it is reduced to the teaching of Aristotle's doctrine alone, philosophy ceases by the same token to deserve its name, to deserve rather, given the predominance of Aristotle, that of "Aristotelity" (Hobbes 2012, 1074; 1651, 370).

At the end of this analysis of the institutional sources of Catholic darkness, Scholastic philosophy appears as a theoretical artefact at the service of the extension of the power of the Church of Rome: the institutional organization of universities is supposed to give an account of the hold of a way of thinking hostile to the sovereignty of Christian states. It must be stressed that the re-reading of ancient and medieval thought that Hobbes proposes to his readers is made from the point of view of an idea of sovereignty, which is posterior to them. We could therefore say that, in this account of the origin of Scholastic philosophy, the theory of sovereignty takes over in a cavalier manner the ancient and medieval sources in the service of the foundation of a first version of the Enlightenment.[6] If Hobbes promotes Enlightenment, it could be therefore called an Enlightenment by the State: great cities are a condition of the development of philosophy, which should benefit from the limitation of the power of schools. Universities that impose a common rule for schools under the guidance of the pope should be reminded that they should be submitted to the rule of the sovereign.

To the criticism of the school institution that we have just analyzed, Hobbes associates a criticism of the language of the Scholastics, a neo-Latin untranslatable in the vernacular languages. Since English is also the language of the British state, in the next section I shall try to show how the role given by Hobbes to translation in his critique of Scholastic philosophy is likely to support the idea that the Hobbesian Enlightenment is, as we suggest, an Enlightenment by the state.

16.2 Linguistic Darkness: The Language of the State Against Scholastic Neo-Latin

If Scholastic philosophy has a specific institutional form, that of the university, it also has its own language, a Neo-Latin, in which all the treatises of Catholic Scholasticism were written (see Waquet 2001). Of Latin which he himself uses to write his treatises on philosophy and which is an essential part of his humanist training, Hobbes has a very sharp political vision: "The *language* also, which they use, both in the Churches, and in their Publique Acts, being *Latine*, which is not commonly used by any Nation now in the world, what is it but the *Ghost* of the Old *Romane Language*?" (Hobbes 2012, 1118; 1651, 386). From this perspective, Latin would not primarily be the language of humanism or modern natural science, but of a political organization that had long disappeared, the Roman Empire; it is characterized as a language that continued to be used even though no one spoke it any longer. Basically, it is the ecclesiastical use of Latin that would explain why this language continued to be used by Scholastic philosophers within the walls of universities and convents. For Hobbes, this use of Latin reinforced the idea of the ghostly character of the Papacy, of which he says in a famous formula that it is the "Ghost of the deceased Romane Empire, sitting crowned upon the grave thereof," adding that "the Papacy start[ed] up on a Sudden out of the Ruines of that Heathen Power" (Hobbes 2012, 1118; 1651, 386). Since Latin is the language of a dead political body, that of the Roman Empire, it can be deduced by contrast that English is the proper language of the British kingdom, and French of the French kingdom. Sensitive to the theme of the ordinary man for normative reasons,[7] Hobbes is also sensitive to it for political reasons: the vernacular being the language of the ordinary citizen, it is also the language by which sovereign power has to be exercised.

Hobbes thus reproaches Scholastic philosophy for a use of the Latin language where he sees a source of confusion and obscurity for thought, which is all the easier to introduce since Latin "is not commonly used by any Nation now in the world" (Hobbes 2012, 1118; 1651, 385). To the obscurity of Scholastic Neo-Latin distinctions, Hobbes opposes the supposed clarity of ordinary languages, including classical Latin.

The praise of ordinary languages and the correlative critique of Scholastic neo-Latin find their origin in the defense by humanists of the classical form of Latin against barbarous uses associated to Middle Age. This critique of Neo-Latin as a heritage of humanism is reformulated by Hobbes through a critique of Scholastic "jargon." Hobbes's numerous references to the common use of the English language are therefore intended to underline the fact that Scholastic distinctions are often nothing else than unintelligible expressions, which he calls "jargon."

It is to be noted that the substantive use of the word "jargon" to designate an incomprehensible learned idiom arises in Hobbes's work at the very moment it appears in the English language. As the *Oxford English Dictionary* mentions the date of 1651 for the substantive use of this word,[8] the latter is no older than the publication of the English version of *Leviathan*. Among other examples, Hobbes describes as "jargon" the Scholastic distinction used by Bramhall between *liberty of exercise only* and *liberty of specification and exercise* (EW V.56). Bramhall, who expresses surprise at Hobbes's criticism, returns to the technical meaning of the term "*jargon*," saying that he would not wonder that a "raw divine out of the pulpit declare against School Divinity to his equally ignorant auditors," but that it troubles him "to see a Scholar, one who hath been long admitted into the innermost closet of Nature, and seen the hidden secrets of more subtil learning, so far to forget himself as to stile School-learning no better than a plain *Jargon*, that is, a senseless gibrish, or a fustian language, like the chattering noyse of *Sabots*" (Hobbes 1656, 44; EW V.58–9). Hobbes's reply, in which he reaffirms his criticism, clarifies how he intends to use the term:

> It troubles him much that I stile School-learning *Jargon*. I do not call all School-learning jargon. I do not call all School-learning so, but such as is so, that is, that which they say in defending of untruths, and especially in the maintenance of Free-will, when they talk of *liberty of exercise, specification, contrariety, contradiction, acts elicite* and *exercite*, and the like; Which, though he go over again in this place, endeavouring to explain them, are still both here and there but *Jargon*, or that (if he like it better) which the Scripture in the first *Chaos* calleth *Tohu* and *Bohu*. (1656, 47; EW V.63)

If the substantive use of "jargon" is new in English, the polemics against an obscure and confusing use of Latin is not; it goes back to a long tradition of criticism of Scholastic Neo-Latin that was widespread among Renaissance authors such as Vives, Pierre de La Ramée, or Lorenzo Valla; Gianni Paganini has established a direct link between the use of the expression "all those barbarous expressions (*omnisque illa barbaries*)" in *De corpore* (Hobbes 1999, 34) and in the dedicatory letter to Candido Decembrio that opens Lorenzo Valla's *Dialecticae* (Valla 1540; see Paganini 2007, 341). But the originality of Hobbes lies not in the negative but in the positive side of the critic. The critique of neo-Latin depends indeed on a positive criterion of intelligibility: a proposition in a learned idiom is intelligible if it can be translated into a vernacular language such as English or

French. Otherwise, the criterion of intelligibility proposed by Hobbes in his criticism of Scholasticism is based on the idea that what cannot be translated into a vernacular language has no meaning:

> I shall only adde this, that the Writings of Schoole-Divines, are nothing else for the most part, but insignificant Traines of strange and barbarous words, or words otherwise used, then in the common use of the Latine tongue; such as would pose Cicero, and Varro, and all the Grammarians of ancient Rome. Which if any man would see proved, let him (as I have said once before) see whether he can translate any Schoole-Divine into any of the Modern tongues, as French, English, or any other copious language: for that which cannot in most of these be made Intelligible, is not Intelligible in the Latine (Hobbes 2012, 1098; 1651, 379).

Ordinary language thus appears as the medium of true philosophy: shared by all, it offers an easily applicable criterion of intelligibility. Thus, rather than engaging in an interminable examination of Scholastic distinctions, it suffices to invalidate them by showing, as Hobbes does in *The Questions concerning Liberty, Necessity and Chance*, that their translation into ordinary language is meaningless: "As for the distinction itself, because the terms are Latine, and never used by any Author of the Latine tongue, to shew their impertinence, I expounded them in English, and left them to the Readers judgment, to find the absurdity of them himself" (1656, 233–4; EW V.296–7). An English translation of Scholastic Latin thus exposes to the judgment of all the absurdity of a discourse that its extreme technicality was meant to keep hidden; the impossibility of returning to the ordinary language is said to be a sufficient formal criterion to establish the inanity of a philosophical argument. This criterion aims in particular at criticizing a certain use of ancient languages, as sources of anomalies within modern languages: "And therefore you shall hardly meet with a senslesse and insignificant word, that is not made up of some Latin or Greek names. A Frenchman seldome hears our Saviour called by the name of *Parole*, but by the name of *Verbe* often; yet *Verbe* and *Parole* differ no more, but that one is Latin, the other French" (Hobbes 2012, 60; 1651, 17). Obscure theological terms, such as the French word *Verbe* to designate the word of God, find in the strangeness of their linguistic form an alibi; recourse to a Latin lexicon forged from scratch can be an effective means of escaping the requirement of a rigorous definition of terms. The use of an unusual vocabulary is explained, then, not by a praiseworthy concern for rigor, but by the desire to artificially increase the gap between the thought of scholars and the thought of ordinary men. Ordinary language, even if it happens to be unfaithful to its initial intention, is subject to the univocity of definition, and as such includes the means of making the terms of scholars intelligible.

A first meaning of translation is the ordinary sense of the word, since the example cited is none other than the passage from learned Latin to everyday English. However, this ordinary translation needs also a more solid foundation that Hobbes finds in his theory of a translation of mental discourse into verbal discourse, which he has already defined in his *Elements of Law*: "And men desiring to shew others the knowledge, opinions, conceptions, and passions which are within themselves, and to that end having invented language, have by that means transferred all that discursion of their mind mentioned in the former chapter (i.e. chapter 4), by the motion of their tongues, into discourse of words" (Hobbes 1889, 23). Common English is valid as a criterion of intelligibility because it goes back to what Hobbes calls mental "discursion."[9]

The logical error of the Scholastic authors is that they have not respected the principles of the translation of the discourse of the mind into verbal discourse. Instead of translating mental contents into verbal denominations, the Scholastic proceeded to the opposite operation, which consisted, starting from the words of an artificial language, Scholastic Latin, to search for the representation that would correspond to them. The error induced by such an operation consists in naturalizing the link between the denomination and the associated representation, instead of revealing its artifice; the meaning of the words is then thought to be inherent to the words themselves, and the representation, which constitutes this meaning, as the product of the expressive force of the word. This reproach feeds, on its logical side, the polemic of Hobbes and Bishop John Bramhall on freedom and necessity. When Hobbes criticizes the Scholastic distinction between *actus imperatus* and *actus elicitus* by stating that these terms "are but words" (Hobbes 1656, 218; EW V.274), Bramhall responds to his objection that those who invented this distinction understood its meaning better than those who criticized it: "They knew there are mentall terms which are only conceived in the mind, as well as vocal terms, which are expressed with the tongue" (Hobbes 1656, 235; EW V.282). To the distinction between mental terms and vocal terms, Hobbes objects that such a distinction proceeds from a logical mistake: "In this place the Bishop hath discovered the ground of all his errors in philosophy, which is this, that he thinketh, when he repeateth the words of a proposition in his mind, that is, when he fancieth the words without speaking them, that then hee conceiveth the things which the words signifie, and this is the most general cause of false opinions" (Hobbes 1656, 235; EW V.299). In this passage, the Bishop would have revealed the origin of all his errors in philosophy. The mental term, which Bramhall conceives as a word that we only use in thought, is, in this case, for Hobbes a verbal term, to which we randomly associate the representation suggested to us by the sounds that compose it. By pretending to discover a pre-existing meaning in words, the bishop refuses to acknowledge that men arbitrarily fix the meaning of words. Hobbes's critique of Bramhall's use of mental terms can thus be understood as a critique of the naturalistic illusion of language.

The alternative appears clearly posed: either language is the translation of a discourse of the mind, which is not a proper language, and it proceeds from a kind of linguistic convention, or it is the illusory translation of a pre-existing language into present language. By opting for the theory of the translation of discourse of the mind into verbal discourse,[10] Hobbes refutes the late avatars of Cratylism. This choice has a philosophical significance, since the rule of univocity in definition that applies to ordinary language applies *a fortiori* to the discourse of philosophy. Similar to ordinary terms, concepts must give rise to an assignable representation in the mind of the person who hears them: it is only on this condition that they can be understood.

The distinctions, which are untranslatable in ordinary language, render the philosophical discourse of those who use them unintelligible. On this point, Hobbes finds material for developing his linguistic criticism of Scholasticism as a source of unintelligible discourse: many philosophers who claim to be Scholastics have, in his view, confused the rhetoric of school teaching with the concepts of philosophy. Although the didactic use can be justified, it should be rigorously limited to its own purpose: it should serve to facilitate the learning of logic through mnemonic means, as in the well-known *Barbara, Celarent, Darii, Ferio*, etc. that help remember the forms of syllogism. But certain terms of logic such as terms of *first* and *second intention, abstract*, and *concrete* names, etc., are by no means terms of art for Hobbes. While a philosopher is free to give words the meaning he or she likes, the philosopher is also obliged to do so by means of a definition formulated in a language that can be understood by all.

Hobbes's designation of the language of Scholastic theologians as a "jargon" is all the more interesting that it is linked by him to a political analysis of the hegemonic will of ecclesiastical powers. The meaning of those humanist and institutional critiques that we have just seen is to allow us to escape from a purely hermeneutical approach to Scholastic philosophy. For all that, Hobbes aims at situating particular Scholastic theses, such as the thesis of separate essences, in institutional and linguistic contexts. In the next section, I will show how he manages to understand the political stakes of the metaphysical discussion on separate essences.

16.3 Metaphysical Darkness: Essences Are Not Separate Entities

To understand the nature of the metaphysical theses of Scholasticism, Hobbes reminds us that the latter is the product of a mixture of Aristotle's metaphysics and Scripture. The dedicatory epistle of *De corpore* gives the following explanation of the origin of this synthesis:

> The first doctors of the Church, next the Apostles, born in those times, whilst they endeavoured to defend the Christian faith against the Gentiles by natural reason, began also to make use of philosophy, and with the decrees of Holy Scripture to mingle the sentences of heathen philosophers; and first some harmless ones of Plato, but afterwards also many foolish and false ones out of the physics and metaphysics of Aristotle; and bringing in the enemies, betrayed unto them the citadel of Christianity. From that time, instead of the worship of God, there entered a thing called *school divinity*, walking on one foot firmly, which is the Holy Scripture, but halted on the other rotten foot, which the Apostle Paul called *vain*, and might have called pernicious philosophy; for it hath raised an infinite number of controversies in the Christian world concerning religion, and from those controversies, wars. (EW I.x; Hobbes 1999, 4–5)

While it is supposed to contribute to the defense of Christianity, the pagan philosophy introduced into the Church during the Patristic era substitutes for divine worship the theses of Greek philosophy, which obscure its message of salvation.[11] This is the case of the thesis of separate essences (see Wright 2007, 398). To understand this thesis and its political consequences, Hobbes recommends, following Luther, that we go back to Thomas Aquinas: "Moreover, the same Luther in another place of his works saith thus, 'School-theology is nothing else but ignorance of the truth and a block to stumble at, laid before Scriptures.' And of Tho. Aquinas in particular he saith, that 'was he that did set up the Kingdome of Aristotle, the destroyer of godly Doctrine'" (Hobbes 1656, 48; EW V.64). What Hobbes calls, in order to contest its existence, "separated essence" or "*essentiis [et] formis substantialibus separatis*" translates, indeed, Thomas Aquinas' *substantia separata*. Aquinas, who is not the author of this doctrine, is however the first to give a formulation of it, which insists on the fact that *substantia separata* is a purely formal substance, in other words, without matter. Since existing (*esse*) does not imply possessing spatial dimensions, that is, having a body, but participating in the act of existing, there is nothing to prevent non-body substances from existing. The proof that Thomas Aquinas gives of the immateriality of separate substances (i.e., souls, intellects or angels, and God) connects them with the fact that God is not a corporeal being:

> And it is easy to see how this can be the case. For if two things are related in such a way that one of them is the cause of existence of the other, then the cause can exist without the other, but not conversely. But this is the relationship between matter and form, because form gives existence to matter; therefore, matter cannot exist without a form, but it is not impossible for a form to exist without matter. For a form, insofar as it is a form, does not have to depend on matter, but if one finds forms that cannot exist without matter, this happens to be the case because of their distance from the first principle, which is the first, pure actuality. So, those forms that are the closest to the first principle are forms subsisting without matter, for the whole genus of forms does not require matter, as has been said, and forms of this sort are the intelligences; so, the essences or quiddities of these substances do not have to be other than their form itself (Aquinas 2007, 239).

The series of causes and effects refers each term to its primary cause, but also each substance in its place, according to an ontological hierarchy, which is a function of the distance that separates each substance from the *causa prima*. In such a conception, the materiality of bodily substances can be interpreted as a sign of their distance from God, whereas the immateriality of spiritual substances is the index of their proximity to the first principle. The analogy thus conceived allows one not only to think of the relationship of creatures in general to God, but also to justify the non-material existence of certain substances. Since these substances are free of materiality and since the essence of bodily substances resides in the union of form and matter, the essence of non-material (or separate) substances will reside solely in their form. Aquinas can thus conclude that "the essences or quiddities of these substances do not have to be other than their form itself" (Aquinas 2007, 239). The distinction between *ens* and *esse* and the materialist or, rather, corporalist redefinition of the term *ens* are the remedies chosen by Hobbes to combat the perverse effects of Aquinas's doctrine of separate forms (see Pécharman 1992, 35–44). However, Hobbes intends to make it clear that these effects are political and not ontological in nature:

> But to what purpose (may some man say) is such subtility in a work of this nature, where I pretend to nothing but what is necessary to the doctrine of Government and Obedience? It is to the purpose, that men may no longer suffer themselves to be abused, by them, that by this doctrine of *Separated Essences*, built on the Vain Philosophy of Aristotle, would fright them from Obeying the Laws of their Countrey, with empty names; as men fright Birds from the Corn with an empty doublet, a hat, and a crooked stick (Hobbes 2012, 1082; 1651, 372–3).

In a striking shortcut from metaphysics to politics, Hobbes establishes the political significance of the issue of separate essences. Elaborated by Scholastic theologians in an extremely subtle way, this question has, according to the English philosopher, a very concrete political meaning: depending on whether the beings subject to political power are defined by their bodies or by their souls, political power is exercised over them according to the principle of sovereignty or according to a spiritual principle claiming its superiority above the latter. Because the idea of separate essences provides a theoretical basis for the idea of non-corporeal beings, it opens the way to a purely spiritual conception of authority. *Leviathan*'s abbreviated version of Hobbes's first philosophy aims at proving that subordination of the temporal to the spiritual power lies in a wrong conception of being. If one wants to avoid this dreadful political error, Aristotelian notions in first philosophy must be reinterpreted.[12]

Of this thesis, Hobbes gives a telling example in his criticism of the theory of the indirect power of the popes, developed by Cardinal Bellarmine in his *De summo Pontifice*:

> When it is said, the Pope hath not (in the Territories of other States) the Supreme Civill Power *Directly*; we are to understand, he doth not challenge it, as other Civill Soveraigns doe, from the original submission thereto of those that are to be governed. [...] He ceaseth not for all that, to claime it another way; and that is, (without the consent of them that are to be governed) by a Right given him by God, (which hee calleth *Indirectly*,) in his Assumption to the Papacy (Hobbes 2012, 910; 1651, 314).

The distinction between a right based on the consent of the subjects and a God-given right maintains intact the Papacy's claim to exercise effective power over Christians in the name of God, regardless of the kingdom to which they belong. This claim presupposes that there is a real distinction between body and soul, and that the power over souls is of a higher order than the power over bodies. The distinction between temporal power and spiritual power is thus derived from the metaphysical distinction between the soul, considered as a separate essence, and the body, considered as animated matter. It is this distinction on the basis of which the pope, according to Hobbes, claims eminent power over the souls of Christians, while recognizing other rulers as having subordinate power over the bodies of their Christian subjects. Thus, endowed with the "Sole Power to Judge" whether something is suitable or not "to the Salvation of men's Souls," the Supreme Pontiff can "depose Princes and States, as often as it is for the Salvation of Soules, that is, as often as he will" (Hobbes 2012, 910; 1651, 314). The right to depose unfaithful princes, a consequence of the attribution of indirect power to popes, was expressed in the form of decisions that could be read as undermining a politics of sovereignty. In this regard, Hobbes recalls, among other examples, the deposition of Chilperic, King of the Franks, and the excommunication of Henry of Navarre, king of France, by Pope Sixtus V in 1585 (see Hobbes 2012, 912; 1651, 315). Hobbes's criticism of the distinction between temporal and spiritual power thus proceeds directly from his criticism of the metaphysics of separate essences.

The main argument used by Hobbes to refute the existence of a double power is that "*Temporall* and *Spirituall* Government, are but two words brought into the world, to make men see double, and mistake their *lawfull Soveraign*" (Hobbes 2012, 732–4; 1651, 248). This distinction, which gives the Papacy a decisive political advantage, is however based on a prior error, which consists in considering "*that the present Church now militant on Earth, is the Kingdome of God*, (that is, the Kingdome of glory, or the Land of Promise; not the Kingdome of Grace, which is but a Promise of the Land)" (Hobbes

2012, 1104; 1651, 381). For this statement to be true, the men over whom spiritual power is exercised would have to be spiritual and eternal bodies from this life on. But this is impossible because the faithful will only be endowed with an eternal spiritual body after the resurrection of the bodies.[13] On earth, the bodies of the faithful being "grosse, and corruptible," we must conclude that there "is therefore no other Government in this life, neither of State, nor Religion, but Temporall" (Hobbes 2012, 734; 1651, 248).

The temporal nature of public power is clearly related to the material nature of the human body. Conversely, because it makes the immortality of the soul a fundamental dimension of human existence, the thesis of the existence of separate essences provides metaphysical support for the papal claim to spiritual power in this world. If there were separate spiritual beings in this life, the popes would indeed be justified in claiming a government of a properly spiritual nature. As princes exercise their power over corruptible bodies, so the popes would exercise their power over incorruptible souls. The doubling of power structures – a temporal one and a spiritual one – would then correspond to the dualism of human nature, divided between a mortal part, the body, and an immortal part, the soul. This doubling is however invalidated by the falsity of the doctrine of separate essences.

16.4 Conclusion

I have shown, in this chapter, that the metaphysical critique of the doctrine of separate essences was inseparable in Hobbes from a critique of the political conditions of Scholastic philosophy in the Catholic Church. This critique takes an institutional form when Hobbes reminds us that we must not forget the practical conditions in which a philosophical theory develops. These conditions are those of universities, which certainly provide the leisure of reflection but do so in particular political conditions, for example, those of the Catholic church. The leisure of σχολή is not neutral, since a Catholic university is an organization subject to the supervision of the Papacy, which imposes on it its rules, and the defense of theses that contribute to the justification of the pope's power over foreign citizens. Political criticism of Scholasticism also takes a linguistic form, since Hobbes imposes on philosophy a norm of translation into vernacular language that casts systematic doubt on the possibility of expressing oneself clearly in the Neo-Latin of Scholasticism.

These two conditions of Hobbes's re-reading of Catholic Scholasticism give a clue to understand Hobbes's contribution to the nascent Enlightenment: that contribution rests on a forced appropriation of the resources of ancient and medieval philosophy, in order to show that there can be no enlightened thought outside the framework set by the sovereign state, which values institutions subject to its sole power and the national language of the state. The strength of Hobbes's demonstration is proportional to its ability to set the limits of philosophy within the framework of the sovereign state. What I would call Enlightenment by the State is a too often forgotten dimension of modern Enlightenment thinking, of which Hobbes can be considered as the first, and maybe the best, representative. The study of his critique of Catholic Scholasticism is therefore important not only for its own sake, but also for what it teaches about the sources of Enlightenment in seventeenth-century Europe and the role of the theory of sovereignty in it.

Notes

1 In the 1930s, Leo Strauss forcefully tried to present Hobbes as a radical, albeit hidden, critic of revelation, and thus as a defender of radical Enlightenment. His analyses can be found in one chapter of his *Spinoza's critique of religion* (Strauss 1965), but mainly in "Die Religionskritik des Hobbes" (1933/1934) where he traces a direct link between the Socinian critique of revelation and Hobbes unbelief in revelation (Strauss 2001, 323–38).

2 *Historia ecclesiastica* stresses also the importance of the State in the development of philosophy: "From this source originated power for kings and leisure for the people; and leisure was the wellspring of the liberal arts" (Hobbes 2008, 317).

3 The Appendix was added to the Latin version of *Leviathan* in 1668: the second chapter, "On Heresy," has quick descriptions of the formation of sects in ancient Greece and Judaism (see Hobbes 2012, 1190–2).

4 The description of the universities in the first Dialogue of *Behemoth* tends to show the responsibility of the pope in the whole project: "A. What other design was he like to have, but (what you heard before) the advancement of his own authority in the countries where the Universities were erected? There they learned to dispute for him [i.e., the pope], and with unintelligible distinctions to blind men's eyes, whilst they encroached upon the rights of kings" (Hobbes 1969, 40), with a strong thrust against the inventors of school-divinity: "For the first Rector of the University of Paris (as I have read somewhere) was Peter Lombard, who first brought in them the learning called School-divinity; and was seconded by John Scot of Duns, who lived in, or near the same time; whom any ingenious reader, not knowing it was the design, would judge to have been two of the most egregious blockheads in the world, so obscure and senseless are their writings" (Hobbes 1969, 40–1).

5 On the function of majority rule in Hobbes's approach to democracy, see Foisneau (2016, 27–47). For a defense of Hobbes as defender of radical democracy, see Tuck (2006, 171–90). For a critique of the previous thesis, see Hoekstra (2006, 191–218).

6 Catherine König-Pralong (2019, 15) speaks of a "colonization of the past" about the uses of the history of philosophy in eighteenth and nineteenth centuries, but the case of Hobbes could justify to widen the perimeter of the thesis to the seventeenth century.

7 The notion of ordinary language in Hobbes can also be considered in a normative perspective (see Foisneau 2013, 47–63).

8 Jargon: "5. Applied contemptuously to the language of scholars, the terminology of a science or art, or the cant of a class, sect, trade, or profession 1651" (OED 1987, 1127). The verbal form of the term is much older: "2. intr. To utter jargon; to talk unintelligibly 1570," coming from the old French, "jargonner."

9 Hobbes insists in using the expression "mental discursion" instead of "mental discourse." His explanation of this choice is the following: "The succession of conceptions in the mind, their series or consequence of one after another, may be casual and incoherent, as in dreams for the most part; and it may be orderly, as when the former thought introduceth the latter; and this is discourse of the mind. But because the word discourse is commonly taken for the coherence and consequence of words, I will (to avoid equivocation) call it DISCURSION" (Hobbes 1889, 13).

10 The word "translation" is not used in chapter 5, § 14, but in the chapter's summary (Hobbes 1889, 17): "14. Translation of the discourse of the mind into the discourse of the tongue, and of the errors thence proceeding."

11 In the line of Saint Paul's warning against "vain philosophy," a critique similar to Hobbes's had already been formulated by Francis Bacon in 1605: "I have digressed because of the extreme prejudice which both religion and philosophy hath received and may receive by

being commixed together; as that which undoubtedly will make an heretical religion, and an imaginary and fabulous philosophy" (Bacon 1893, II, VI). For Hobbes's interpretation of Saint Paul's critique – "Beware lest any man spoil you through philosophy and vain deceit" (Colossians 2: 8) – see the epistle dedicatory to *De corpore* (Hobbes 1999, 5), and Leijenhorst's comments on it (1998, 29–38).

12 For an analysis of the reinterpretation of the concepts of matter, form, and essence in Hobbes's first philosophy, Leijenhorst's thesis is that Hobbes "propounds a systematic reinterpretation of traditional Aristotelian hylemorphism along the line of his mechanistic theory of representation. While Aristotelians still generally held that corporeal substances are matter – form compounds, Hobbes claims that they are material entities only, which exist independently of the substantial form" (Leijenhorst 1998, 197).

13 On the link between the interpretation of the Bible and the defense of sovereignty, see Foisneau (1997, 303–5; 2016, 314–16).

References

Aquinas, Thomas. 2007. "Thomas Aquinas on Being and Essence." In *Medieval Philosophy: Essential Readings with Commentary*, edited by Gyula Klima, 227–49. Oxford: Blackwell Publishing.

Bacon, Francis. 1893. *The Advancement of Learning*. London: Cassell.

Foisneau, Luc. 1997. "Obéissance politique et mortalité humaine selon Hobbes." In *Politique, droit et théologie chez Bodin, Grotius et Hobbes*, edited by Luc Foisneau, 283–305. Paris: Éditions Kimé.

Foisneau, Luc. 2013. "Common People as Individuals: Hobbes's Normative Approach to the Ordinary Mind." In *In Praise of Ordinary People: Early Modern Britain and the Dutch Republic*, edited by Margaret C. Jacob and Catherine Secrétan, 47–63. New York: Palgrave Macmillan.

Foisneau, Luc. 2016. *Hobbes: La vie inquiète*. Paris: Gallimard.

Hobbes, Thomas. 1656. *The Questions Concerning Liberty, Necessity and Chance. Clearly Stated and Debated Between Dr. Bramhall Bishop of Derry, and Thomas Hobbes of Malmesbury*. London: Andrew Crooke.

Hobbes, Thomas. 1839–1845. *The English works of Thomas Hobbes*, 11 vols., edited by Sir William Molesworth. London: John Bohn. Referred to as EW.

Hobbes, Thomas. 1889. *The Elements of Law Natural and Politic*, edited by Ferdinand Tönnies. London: Simpkin, Marshall, and Co.

Hobbes, Thomas. 1969. *Behemoth, or, the Long Parliament*, 2nd edn., edited by Ferdinand Tönnies. Introduction to the second edition by Maurice M. Goldsmith. London: Frank Cass.

Hobbes, Thomas. 1999. *De corpore*, edited by Karl Schuhmann. Introduction by Karl Schuhmann and Martine Pécharman. Paris: Librairie philosophique J. Vrin.

Hobbes, Thomas. 2008. *Historia Ecclesiastica*, edited and translated by Patricia Springborg, Patricia Stablein, and Paul Wilson. Paris: Éditions Champion.

Hobbes, Thomas. 2012. *Leviathan*, 3 vols., edited by Noel Malcolm. Oxford: Clarendon Press. [First published 1651].

Hoekstra, Kinch. 2006. "A Lion in the House: Hobbes and Democracy." In *Rethinking the Foundations of Modern Political Thought*, edited by Annabel Brett and James Tully, 191–218. Cambridge: Cambridge University Press.

König-Pralong, Catherine. 2019. *La colonie philosophique: Écrire l'histoire de la philosophie aux XVIIIe et XIXe siècles*. Paris: Éditions EHESS.

Leijenhorst, Cornelis H.. 1998. *Hobbes and the Aristotelians. The Aristotelian Setting of Thomas Hobbes's Natural Philosophy*. Utrecht: Zeno Institute of Philosophy. The Leiden-Utrecht Research Institute.

Paganini, Gianni. 2007. "Hobbes's Critique of the Doctrine of Essences and Its Sources." In *The Cambridge Companion to Hobbes's Leviathan*, edited by Patricia Springborg, 337–57. New York: Cambridge University Press.

Pécharman, Martine. 1992. "Le vocabulaire de l'être dans la philosophie première: *ens, esse, essentia*." In *Hobbes et son vocabulaire: Études de lexicographie philosophique*, edited by Yves Charles Zarka, 31–59. Paris: Librairie philosophique J. Vrin.

Strauss, Leo. 1965. *Spinoza's Critique of Religion*, translated by Elsa M. Sinclair. Chicago: University of Chicago Press.

Strauss, Leo. 2001. "Die Religionskritik des Hobbes. Ein Beitrag zum Verständnis der Aufklärung (1933/1934)." In *Leo Strauss, Gesammelte Schriften, Vol. 3*, edited by Heinrich Meier, 263–373. Stuttgart: J.B. Metzler Verlag.

Stevenson, Angus, Lesley Brown, and Georgia Hole. 1987. *The Shorter Oxford English Dictionary on Historical Principles*, 3rd edn. Oxford: Clarendon Press. Referred to as OED.

Tuck, Richard. 2006. "Hobbes and Democracy." In *Rethinking the Foundations of Modern Political Thought*, edited by Annabel Brett and James Tully, 171–90. Cambridge: Cambridge University Press.

Valla, Lorenzo. 1540. "Dialecticae Disputationes." In *Opera*, edited by Lorenzo Valla. Basel: Apud Henricum Petrum.

Waquet, Françoise. 2001. *Latin, or, the Empire of a Sign: From the Sixteenth to the Twentieth Centuries*. London: Verso.

Wright, George. 2007. "The 1668 Appendix and Hobbes's Theological Project." In *The Cambridge Companion to Hobbes's Leviathan*, edited by Patricia Springborg, 392–409. New York: Cambridge University Press.

17

Hobbes on Submission to God

MICHAEL BYRON

17.1 Kingdom of God by Nature

In chapter 31 of *Leviathan*, Hobbes introduces the "Kingdom of God by Nature," or natural kingdom. A number of recent studies examine this chapter,[1] yet none considers the question that interests me: namely, how exactly does one become a subject in this kingdom? Hobbes does not address this question. He is clear about one thing: not everyone is a subject in the natural kingdom, or natural subject. Hobbes excludes atheists and deists.

The fact that Hobbes excludes some people from the natural kingdom helps resolve a puzzle from earlier in *Leviathan* concerning whether justice is possible in a state of nature. Hobbes appears to offer conflicting answers: at 13.13, he says no:

> To this war of every man against every man, this also is consequent: that nothing can be unjust. The notions of right and wrong, justice and injustice, have there no place. Where there is no common power, there is no law; where no law, no injustice (Hobbes 2012, 196; 1651, 64).

In the very next chapter (14.7), Hobbes provides an account of how injustice is possible after all in a state of nature. When one renounces or transfers a right to something, then one is,

> Obliged or Bound not to hinder those to whom such right is granted or abandoned from the benefit of it; and that he ought, and it is his DUTY, not to make void that voluntary act of his own, and that such hindrance is Injustice (Hobbes 2012, 200; 1651, 65).

I have proposed resolving the apparent conflict by adopting a modified version of the distinction Martinich draws between primary and secondary states of nature.[2] A

A Companion to Hobbes, First Edition. Edited by Marcus P. Adams.

primary state of nature is one inhabited only by atheists, and this situation is truly natural: it has no sovereign whatever – including God – and thus no law – including laws of nature – and no justice, as Hobbes remarks in chapter 13. The sense in which justice is impossible in such a state of nature is that nothing can count as law or violating law: with no sovereign whatever, people have no legal obligations. With no legal obligations, neither obedience to nor violation of the law is possible; and this seems to be the sense in which Hobbes intends in chapter 13 to claim that justice is impossible in a state of nature.

A secondary state of nature contains theists, and its inhabitants are subjects of God's natural kingdom (we will refine this account and consider the situation of deists below). They have no civil sovereign, however, and so are still in a state of nature. At the end of chapter 15 (15.41), Hobbes distinguishes between two roles for the precepts of the laws of nature (Hobbes 2012, 242; 1651, 80). They are rationally deducible, and so he says that they are "natural theorems." But they gain the normative status of proper law – and become obligatory – only for God's subjects.[3] God's natural subjects are obligated by the laws of nature as proper laws in virtue of their submission to God. And so, in a secondary state of nature, justice (and injustice) are possible in virtue of the possibility of obeying or violating the law (as such). The distinction between subjects and non-subjects in God's natural kingdom provides a basis for explaining the apparent problem about justice.

Previously (Byron 2015, 90), it seemed to me that if not believing in a providential God excluded one from God's natural kingdom, then believing should be sufficient for inclusion. Following Hobbes, I call the act of making oneself a subject of a commonwealth or kingdom (one kind of commonwealth) "submission." So it seemed to me that one submitted to God by having faith (with perhaps some constraints on the object thereof). I now refine this position: Hobbes says that belief, including religious faith, is involuntary; yet submission, for reasons I address below, must be voluntary. But still: the distinction between theists and atheists seems to be belief in God. And this problem brings me to the questions I hope to answer here, namely: how exactly does one submit to God, and what role does belief in God play in that submission?

Hobbes explains in considerable detail how one submits to a civil (human) sovereign, whether in a commonwealth by acquisition or by institution. Regardless of the method of commonwealth building, I submit when I covenant with others and thereby transfer (most of) my right of self-governance to another, who becomes my sovereign. The methods of commonwealth building differ regarding my covenant partners. In what Hobbes calls a commonwealth by acquisition, I covenant with the one who has vanquished me: the victor agrees to spare my life, and I agree to obey that person as my sovereign. In a commonwealth by institution, I covenant with others who are also willing so to submit, and we agree to treat someone (or some assembly) as our sovereign (Hobbes 2012, 262; 1651, 88). Either way, the covenant entails a transfer of right to another person, thus creating the (vast) disparity of right characteristic of the relation between Hobbesian sovereigns and subjects, and the correlative obligation to obey.

This account cannot be correct for the natural kingdom. The reason is that the required disparity of right between sovereign and subject already exists, independent of anyone's submitting to God.[4] Because Hobbes defines (14.9) the constitutive purpose of any covenant as a transfer of right,[5] we cannot explain submission to God and God's constitution as sovereign of the natural kingdom in terms of a covenant.[6] Hobbes consistently maintains that God's omnipotence – God's "irresistible" power – confers on God "dominion" over the world. Further, no covenant I might make with other people is relevant to the question of whether I am God's natural subject. So the model of submission built on a covenant with another human being is inadequate to account for submission to God.

Hobbes simply does not explain submission to God. We can reconstruct his thinking by building on what he does say, especially on his exclusion of atheists and deists from the natural kingdom.

17.2 Exclusion from the Natural Kingdom

The argument begins with the claim that not everyone is a natural subject. Hobbes explains exclusion from the natural kingdom by contrasting the proper sense in which God reigns with God's omnipotence. God's omnipotence follows from God's providence – traditionally held to be God's infinite power, knowledge, and goodness – which entails that God has causal power over everything.[7] If $O_p g$ represents the statement that God is omnipotent, $O_k g$ that God is omniscient, and $O_b g$ that God is omni-benevolent, Hobbes's assumption of a providential God can be represented, following the traditional formula, as follows.

1. $O_p g \cdot O_k g \cdot O_b g$ — Premise

The premise that God's omnipotence entails causal power over everything (S_p, or being subject to God's causal power) is:

2. $O_p g \rightarrow (\forall x) S_p x$ — Premise

And from (1) and (2) it follows that God has causal power over everything (everything is subject to God's causal power).

3. $(\forall x) S_p x$ — (1, 2)

Crucially, however, this (mere?) causal power does not entail that God literally "reigns" over everything. Hobbes remarks at 31.2, "But to call this power of God (which extendeth itself not only to man, but also to beasts, and plants, and bodies inanimate) by the name of kingdom is but a metaphorical use of the word" (Hobbes 2012, 554; 1651, 186). What "beasts," plants, and inanimate objects lack is the power of language and the related capacity to be addressed and commanded. They cannot be motivated by promised rewards for compliance or threatened punishments for disobedience.[8] God is properly said to reign only over creatures who can understand and respond to promises and threats. Thus those who cannot be subjected to God's commands (S_c) cannot be subjects in God's natural kingdom (S_n).

4. $(\forall x)(\neg S_c x \rightarrow \neg S_n x)$ — Premise

The contrapositive of (4) provides a necessary (but not sufficient) condition of being a subject in the kingdom of God by nature, namely the capacity to be the subject of God's commands (and thus responsive to God's promised rewards and threatened punishments).

5. $(\forall x)(S_n x \rightarrow S_c x)$ (4)

The criterion of being a natural subject is not complete, because having the power of speech is not sufficient: Hobbes excludes atheists and deists, who have the power of speech and so far seem to be capable of understanding rewards and punishments.

17.3 Omnipotence and Subjects

Before discussing the place of atheists and deists in the argument, it is worth delving into some important consequences of Hobbes's excluding plants, non-human animals ("beasts"), and inanimate objects from the natural kingdom. The basis for this exclusion is the assumption that these things are not apt recipients of God's commands. Non-humans are not apt subjects of God's commands, which we may represent as follows, where H is the set of human beings.[9]

6. $(\forall x \notin H)\neg S_c x$ Premise

As a result, we have that non-humans are excluded from being God's natural subjects.

7. $(\forall x \notin H)\neg S_n x$ (4, 6)

God does not literally reign over them with promised rewards and threatened punishments, so saying God "reigns" over such things is merely a figure of speech.

Assuming that something exists besides human beings, it follows that there are beings who are subject to God's causal power, but who are not subjects in the natural kingdom.

8. $(\exists x)(S_p x \cdot \neg S_n x)$ (Given $x \notin H \neq \varnothing$, 3, 7)

And this statement in turn entails that being subject to God's causal power is not sufficient for being God's natural subject.

9. $\neg(\forall x)(S_p x \rightarrow S_n x)$ (8)

Because God's causal power over everything is a consequence of God's omnipotence,[10] it follows that God's omnipotence is also not a sufficient condition for being a natural subject.

10. $\neg[O_p g \rightarrow (\forall x)(S_n x)]$ (2, 8)

To summarize so far: assuming that God is omnipotent and that omnipotence is or entails that God has causal power over everything, Hobbes introduces a necessary condition for reign and so for being a subject in the natural kingdom. Reigning involves promising rewards and threatening punishments, so being capable of understanding those promises and threats – the capacity to be commanded – is necessary for being a subject in the kingdom of God by nature. Not everything satisfies this condition, which is thus non-trivial.

17.4 Atheists and Deists

Before continuing to unpack Hobbes's argument, it will be useful to define some terms. Theists (T) believe in the existence of God (B_g).

11. $(\forall x)(Tx \leftrightarrow B_g x)$ Def. T

Atheists ($\neg T$) deny the existence of God and are thus the complement of the set of theists. Deists (D) are theists who do not acknowledge or recognize God as providential (I explain acknowledgment below).

12. $(\forall x)[Dx \leftrightarrow (B_g x \cdot \neg A_g x)]$ Def. D

Note that being a deist is sufficient for being a theist.

13. $(\forall x)(Dx \rightarrow Tx)$ (11, 12)

It is worth distinguishing theism – a term Hobbes does not employ – or (mere) belief in the existence of God from what Hobbes often (though inconsistently) calls "faith."[11] The distinctive, salvific faith of Christians is the belief that Jesus is God or the Christ, and having faith obviously entails theism. But Jews, Muslims, and deists as well as Christians are theists. Deists, who adopt what some describe as a "clockmaker" view of God, maintain that God created the universe and laws of nature and then left it alone. Specifically, deists deny God's revelation and providential involvement in the affairs of human beings.[12]

Hobbes explicitly excludes atheists and deists from the natural kingdom, and he does so because they lack the capacity to be commanded.

> Subjects, therefore, in the kingdom of God are not bodies inanimate, nor creatures irrational (because they understand no precepts as his), nor atheists, nor they that believe not that God has any care of the actions of mankind (because they acknowledge no word for his, nor have hope of his rewards, or fear of his threatenings) (Hobbes 2012, 554; 1651, 186).

Although atheists and deists, like everything else, are subject to God's causal power, they are not subject to God's commands because they do not *acknowledge* them as such. This notion of acknowledgment plays a key role in the argument. What atheists and deists share is not being subject to God's commands.

14. $(\forall x)[(\neg Tx \vee Dx) \rightarrow \neg S_c x]$ Premise

And so they are not subjects in the natural kingdom.

15. $(\forall x)[(\neg Tx \vee Dx) \rightarrow \neg S_n x]$ (4, 14)

It follows from (15) that deists are not natural subjects.

16. $(\forall x)(Dx \rightarrow \neg S_n x)$ (15)

If there are deists (as there were in Hobbes's time at least), then at least some theists are not natural subjects.

17. $(\exists x)(Tx \cdot \neg S_n x)$ (Given $(\exists x)Dx$, 13, 16)

In turn, we may infer that theism, or belief in God's existence, is not sufficient for being a natural subject.[13]

18. $\neg(\forall x)(Tx \rightarrow S_n x)$ (17)

Moreover, because theists are human beings, it follows that omnipotence is not sufficient for people to be natural subjects.

19. $\neg[O_p g \rightarrow (\forall x \in H)(S_n x)]$ (10, 18)

Note that though (19) is similar to (10), its domain is restricted to human beings. (10) relies on the fact that non-human animals and inanimate objects lack reason and "understand no precepts as" God's to claim that some things are not subjects of God's reign, properly so called. (19) relies on the fact that there are people who reject God's commands. Such people, Hobbes declares, are God's *enemies*.[14]

17.5 Natural Subjects and Acknowledgment

We noted in (5), $(\forall x)(S_n x \rightarrow S_c x)$, that being an apt subject of God's promises and threats (S_c) is a necessary condition of being a natural subject (S_n). The key to understanding why it is not also sufficient is supplied by Hobbes's exclusion of atheists and deists from the natural kingdom. It is, in short, a further necessary condition of being a natural subject that one not be an atheist or deist.

20. $(\forall x)[S_n x \rightarrow \neg(\neg Tx \vee Dx)]$ (15)

It follows from this exclusion that atheists are excluded,

21. $(\forall x)(S_n x \rightarrow \neg\neg Tx)$ (20)

and in turn, given the relation between theism and atheism, that theism is a necessary condition for being a natural subject.

22. $(\forall x)(S_n x \rightarrow Tx)$ (21)

As we have seen, however, theism, or belief in the existence of God, is not sufficient for being a natural subject. If theism were sufficient for being a natural subject, then deists would be natural subjects and not enemies. Natural subjects must therefore be theists who are not deists.

23. $(\forall x)[S_n x \rightarrow (Tx \cdot \neg Dx)]$ (20)

By the definition of deists, we have:

24. $(\forall x)S_n x \rightarrow [Tx \cdot \neg(B_g x \cdot \neg A_g x)]$ (12, 23)

Using the definition of theists as those who believe in God's existence, we can simplify this expression.

25. $(\forall x)S_n x \rightarrow [Tx \cdot \neg(Tx \cdot \neg A_g x)]$ (11, 24)

26. $(\forall x)[S_n x \rightarrow (Tx \cdot A_g x)]$ (25)

Now we may observe that acknowledging God's providence is a sufficient condition for theism:

27. $(\forall x)(A_g x \rightarrow Tx)$ From def. A_g

We can accordingly simplify the right side of (26) to yield:

28. $(\forall x)(S_n x \rightarrow A_g x)$ (26, 27)

(28) states that a necessary condition of being a natural subject is acknowledging God's providence. Because this acknowledgment entails the other conditions of being a natural subject (being subject to God's commands and being a theist), and assuming that the only categories of people Hobbes excludes from the natural kingdom are atheists and deists, it follows that acknowledgment is the criterion of being a natural subject.[15]

29. $(\forall x)(S_n x \leftrightarrow A_g x)$ (28)

And that is the result we have been seeking. Submission to God in the natural kingdom must be an act of acknowledging God's providential involvement with the world, which only atheists – who deny God's existence – and deists – who believe in God's existence but deny God's providence – fail to do.

17.6 God's Dominion

We might worry that this conclusion is in tension with Hobbes's views about God's dominion over people. If God has dominion over all of creation, how could some of us not be God's natural subjects? Further, how could some fail to be obligated by the laws of nature, even in a primary state of nature? God's dominion is not mere causal power: it is the *right* to rule.[16] So if God has a right to rule everyone, what sense can it make to exclude anyone from the natural kingdom?

Hobbes claims that God's omnipotence grounds God's dominion ($D_m g$) over all (see note 4).

30. $O_p g \rightarrow (\forall x) D_m gx$ Premise

So because Hobbes presupposes the existence of an omnipotent God, God has dominion over everyone.

31. $(\forall x) D_m gx$ (1, 30)

We may detach the consequent of (30) given God's omnipotence.

Dominion is the right to rule, and Hobbes conceives of rights as liberties.[17] What we have liberty to do, we may do without wrong or injustice. Thus, what we have a right to do to others we may do without wronging them.

32. $(\forall x, y, a, x \neq y)(D_m xy \leftrightarrow Lxay)$ Def. of D_m

33. $(\forall x, y, a, x \neq y)(Lxay \rightarrow \neg Wxay)$ Def. of L

(32) states that for any two distinct people, x and y, and for any act a, x has dominion over y just in case x has the liberty to do a to y ($Lxay$). And (33) expresses the idea that having the liberty to do a to y entails that it is not wrong for x to do so ($\neg Wxay$).

Dominion over others thus entails that, whatever we do to those others, we do not wrong them.

34. $(\forall x, y, a, x \neq y)(D_m xy \rightarrow \neg Wxay)$ (32, 33)

In light of the fact that God has dominion over all, God may do anything to anyone without wronging them. Hence, we have:

35. $(\forall x, a) \neg Wgax$ (31, 34)

Whatever God does to God's creatures, God is not wrong to do so and commits no injustice. This consequence is a crucial feature of Hobbes's conception of God's dominion.

17.7 Obligation

Having this conception of God's dominion over creation, we are in a better position to resolve the apparent tension between the exclusion of some people from the natural kingdom and God's dominion over all. To do that, we must examine the idea of obligation.

First, it might seem that dominion, or the right to rule, must impose correlative obligations on those who are ruled. Hobbes discusses both together when he introduces his account of obligation in chapter 14. But there, of course, he is arguing for the civil commonwealth, and human sovereigns are crucially different from God: they are not omnipotent. God has the right to rule by nature. Human sovereigns acquire dominion only by voluntary transfer of right. And that voluntary transfer, not the right to rule per se, entails obligation.

Hobbes claims that obligation most generally is the result of a voluntary transfer of right, for example, in a contract or covenant.[18] He is quite explicit there that obligations are undertaken only voluntarily. Legal obligations in particular are undertaken by a covenant of a specific kind, namely a promise to obey commands. This promise is a voluntary act and, under the right circumstances, part of a covenant that those who join a commonwealth offer in the sovereign-constituting act of submission.

In chapter 26, Hobbes notes that law is a species of command.[19] Its differentiae include that the commanded is "formerly obliged" or has previously promised to obey. Those whom I have not promised to obey may command but cannot legally obligate me. Whatever the grammatical form of their imperatives to me, those will not constitute laws or entail obligations. In the context of commonwealths, including the natural kingdom, the promise to obey partly constitutes the act of submission. So we may write Hobbes's general conditions for legal obligation as:

36. $(\forall x, y, a, x \neq y)[Oxya \rightarrow (Cyxa \cdot Sxy)]$ Premise

This premise states roughly that, for any distinct persons x and y and for any act a, it is a necessary condition for x to be (legally) obligated to y to do a ($Oxya$) that y has commanded x to do it ($Cyxa$) and that x has submitted to y (Sxy).[20]

It follows from the conception of natural subjects that all and only those who submit to God are subjects in God's natural kingdom (already labeled S_n). We may represent this premise thus:

37. $(\forall x)(S_n x \leftrightarrow Sxg)$ (Def. of S_n)

And, because natural subjects are all and only those who acknowledge God's providence, it follows that submission is that act of acknowledgment.

38. $(\forall x)(Sxg \leftrightarrow A_g x)$ (29, 37)

We know further that some people do not acknowledge God's providence, are not natural subjects, and are rather God's "enemies," so we have:

39. $(\exists x)\neg S_n x$ (17)

Hence, some people have not in fact submitted to God.

40. $(\exists x)\neg Sxg$ (37, 8)

Submission is a condition of a command constituting law and imposing obligation. It follows from the necessary conditions for obligation and the fact that some people have not submitted to God that some are not obligated to obey God's commands.[21]

41. $(\forall x, a, x \neq g)[Oxga \rightarrow (Cgxa \cdot Sxg)$ (36)

42. $(\exists x, a)(Cgxa \cdot \neg Oxga)$ (40, 41)

This seems to be the point where we run up against the worry about dominion: how can God have dominion over everyone, and yet some not be obligated to obey God's commands as laws?[22]

The answer is that God's dominion concerns God's right to command, not whether those commanded are obligated by the commands as laws. God's right to rule is grounded in God's omnipotence, not a transfer of right. The transfer of right, not mere possession of the right, entails obligations. Hence, God's act of commanding those who are not God's subjects is not wrong, but also does not entail obligations for them.[23]

$$43.\ (\forall x, a)[(c = Cgxa \cdot \neg Sxg) \rightarrow (\neg Wgcx \cdot \neg Oxga)] \qquad (35, 41)$$

This statement says roughly that for any person x and act a, if God commands, c, that x do a, and if x is not God's subject, then it is not wrong for God to issue command c, but God's doing so also does not impose an obligation on x to do a.

This conclusion might seem perplexing, but Hobbes says something analogous about civil sovereigns who punish subjects. If the punishment concerns a right that Hobbes regards as inalienable, such as the right to life, then a sovereign's command to forfeit my life cannot obligate me.[24] I cannot possibly have promised to obey such a command. And yet, as I am a subject of this sovereign the command is rightful. The case of God's enemies is parallel: God's commands to enemies are rightful because God has dominion over them; yet the enemies are not bound by a legal obligation to obey them because they have not submitted to God.

We may draw two further conclusions. First, the fact that God has dominion over all and commands certain precepts for all – the laws of nature – is not sufficient to make all God's subjects.

$$44.\ \neg(\forall x, a)[(D_m gx \cdot Cgxa) \rightarrow Sxg] \qquad (31, 40)$$

In turn, because being obligated to obey God's commands as laws depends on having submitted to God, God's having dominion and issuing commands are not sufficient to make those precepts obligatory for all.

$$45.\ \neg(\forall x, a)[(D_m gx \cdot Cgxa) \rightarrow Oxga] \qquad (41, 44)$$

God's dominion thus does not entail obligations, in particular the obligation to obey the laws of nature as laws.

17.8 Acknowledgment

It remains to be shown that Acknowledging God's providence is a voluntary act of promising to obey. The argument here must change tacks. Though Hobbes uses the verb "acknowledge" in various forms throughout *Leviathan*,[25] and seemingly consistently, he does not address the relationships among faith, belief generally, submission, and this act of Acknowledgment. The argument to this point has been a rational reconstruction of the position to which Hobbes commits himself with his account of natural subjects in chapter 31. Some of that reconstruction has been interpretative, as when I interpreted Hobbes's notion of atheists and deists in a particular way. I need a different kind of argumentation for this more interpretative section of the chapter, and will deploy a cumulative case argument.[26]

17.8.1 *"Voluntary"*

Hobbes uses "acknowledge" and its cognates throughout *Leviathan*, and his usage seems to satisfy his definition of "voluntary." To acknowledge is not to know or believe scientifically, nor to believe or have faith religiously, but rather to express something (I will be more specific about the content below) in speech or action. For example, in chapter 7 (7.5) Hobbes discusses belief and faith generally (not specifically or exclusively to do with religion) (Hobbes 2012, 100; 1651, 31). Hobbes contrasts believing a "saying" or statement with belief or faith "in" a person. In the following paragraph (7.6), he considers "believing in a doctrine."

> But by *believing in*, as it is in the creed, is meant, not trust in the person, but *confession and acknowledgment* of the doctrine. For not only Christians, but all manner of men, do so believe in God as to hold all for truth they hear him say, whether they understand it or not; which is all the faith and trust can possibly be had in any person whatsoever; but they do not all believe the doctrine of the creed. (Hobbes 2012, 102; 1651, 31; latter emphasis added)

Clearly, acknowledgment here means more than merely believing (or "believing in"): it entails confession, assertion, or recognition.

Such an expression in speech or writing is a performative speech act: like apologizing, promising, or forbidding, acknowledging names a kind of action performed by its own expression. Just as I apologize to you by saying "I apologize," so I acknowledge, say, your owning a piece of land by saying, "I acknowledge that you own this land." Acknowledging God's providence, which I will distinguish by capitalizing the word, need not be explicit. Other performatives that tacitly Acknowledge God's providence include honoring God, worshiping, going to church, praying, and swearing an oath.[27] And just like other performatives, Acknowledgment must be sincere. Insincere statements cannot be performatives because they do not constitute the actions that they purport to express.

Hobbes defines (6.1) voluntary motion as synonymous with "animal motion," or movement of the limbs or body caused by the mind, in particular, the passions (Hobbes 2012, 78; 1651, 23). He defines (6.53) deliberation as the interaction of (possibly contrary) motives prior to action. The will is the last motive before action (Hobbes 2012, 92; 1651, 28), and because Hobbes understands the etymology of "voluntary" (from the Latin *voluntas* or will), any motivated act will count as voluntary. "For a *voluntary act* is that which proceedeth from the *will*, and no other.... *Will* therefore *is the last appetite [or aversion] in deliberating*" (Hobbes 2012, 92; 1651, 28).

Performative speech acts satisfy this conception of voluntary action because they are motivated, deliberate actions and so result from will. When we explicitly Acknowledge God, then, such action is voluntary in virtue of being a performative speech act. Even when we tacitly Acknowledge God, in prayer, worship, or other form of honoring God, these acts are also voluntary. So Acknowledgment, which constitutes submission to God, satisfies the definition of "voluntary."

17.8.2 *Faith*

Acknowledgment and faith are species of different genera. As we just saw, Acknowledgment is a performative speech act that is the causal result of our motives. Hobbes regards faith as a cognitive state that is set apart from our motives, and so is not a causal consequence of the will. Faith is thus not voluntary, which Hobbes often, though not consistently, maintains.

Curley remarks that "It's not clear to me that Hobbes has a consistent view on the extent to which faith may be a voluntary act on the part of the believer" (Hobbes 1994, 527, n. 17). He mentions four passages in this context, including the one (40.2) most commonly cited to support the claim that Hobbes thought faith was not voluntary. "As for the inward *thought* and *belief* of men, which human governors can take no notice of (for God only knoweth the heart), they are not voluntary, nor the effect of the laws, but of the unrevealed will, and of the power, of God, and consequently fall not under obligation" (Hobbes 2012, 738; 1651, 249).[28] Hobbes seems to be clear, at least very often in *Leviathan*, that belief is not voluntary. If we assume that faith is a species of belief or thought, then it follows that faith, too, is involuntary. In that case, faith cannot be the act of submission that constitutes people as natural subjects.

17.8.3 *Submission*

God's natural subjects are obligated to obey the laws of nature in virtue of their submission to God and its (perhaps tacit) promise to obey. If Acknowledgment constitutes voluntary submission to God, then it must include a promise to obey.

Hobbes links acts of worship, prayer, and sacrifice to submission and obedience in chapter 31. The context of these passages is the claim (31.29) that it is a "general precept of reason" that divine worship must be "signs of the intention to honour God" (Hobbes 2012, 568; 1651, 191). First, consider what he says (31.34) about "heathen" religions: he explains that the heathens "did absurdly to worship images," but that their songs and prayers honored their gods appropriately and thus were "reasonable" and satisfied this general precept of natural reason.

> Also that the beasts they offered in sacrifice, and the gifts they offered, and their actions in worshipping, were *full of submission*, and commemorative of benefits received, was according to reason, as proceeding from an intention to honour him. (Hobbes 2012, 570; 1651, 192; emphasis added)

Hobbes thinks that the heathens had false religion; but their acts of acknowledging their gods were rational, not least because they properly expressed submission to their gods. Had they been Christians Acknowledging God, they presumably would also be submitting, and doing so correctly.

Hobbes goes on to add (31.36) that, "obedience to his laws (that is, in this case, to the laws of nature) is the greatest worship of all. For as obedience is more acceptable to God than sacrifice, so also to set light by his commandments is the greatest of all contumelies" (Hobbes, 2012, 570; 1651, 192). He seems to say here that worship and its attendant forms of honoring God includes a promise of obedience, in particular to the laws of nature (which are, of course, the laws of the natural kingdom). If worship is a form of Acknowledgment, and the "greatest worship" is obedience, then it follows that those who voluntarily Acknowledge and submit to God thereby commit themselves to obeying the laws of nature.

Conclusion

I conclude by tying Acknowledgment to the account of justice in states of nature with which we began. A primary state of nature includes atheists, or so says (Martinich 1992, 76ff.). We are now in a position to be more precise: a primary state of nature is inhabited by God's enemies, both atheists and deists. Those are the people for whom there is no justice or injustice (13.13): "where there is no common power, there is no law; where no law, no injustice" (Hobbes 2012, 196; 1651, 63). God's enemies have no common power because they Acknowledge none, and so they submit to no one. They can have little hope of escaping the state of nature.[29]

It would, of course, be irrational to choose to be an enemy of an omnipotent being. Hobbes here underscores the irrationality of God's enemies by condemning them to a permanent and irredeemable state of war in a primary state of nature. The best that they may hope for is to use whatever powers of reason they possess to discern the rational theorems given by God in the precepts of natural law, and to accept those principles on purely rational grounds (not as commanded by God). Doing so might enable these unhappy souls to avoid what Hobbes calls (31.40) God's "natural punishments" for those who violate the laws of nature (Hobbes 2012, 572; 1651, 193).

In contrast, those who Acknowledge God's providence fare no worse than a secondary state of nature. In that state, though still having no civil sovereign or law, nor civil commonwealth, all are God's natural subjects. They are accordingly obligated by the laws of nature as laws, and their submission to God by Acknowledgment affords them the possibility of justice and injustice. Once the inhabitants of a secondary state of nature Acknowledge God and thereby submit, they constitute themselves as natural subjects and become obligated to obey the laws of nature as God's commands.

Distinguishing between a primary and secondary state of nature allows us to avoid attributing a blatant contradiction to Hobbes. Jones (2019, 452) contends that Hobbes has higher priorities than mere logical consistency: "Hobbes is often willing to appeal to different values and assumptions—even contradictory ones—in an effort to persuade a broad range of readers to accept those conclusions as necessary for peace."[30] Beyond being a hermeneutical last resort in general, we should be especially loath to find contradictions in Hobbes on methodological grounds. Hobbes claims, after all, to have shown *deductively* that the commonwealth is the only way for people to live in peace. Attributing a contradiction to him regarding so basic a premise as the state of nature threatens to trivialize his conclusion. Fortunately, with a proper understanding of Acknowledgment and submission to God in the natural kingdom, we can do justice to the text.

Notes

1 See for example Jones (2019), Martinich (2018), and Abizadeh (2017). Far more attention has been paid to the questions of whether Hobbes was an atheist or had a natural theology. See Tuck (1992), Stauffer (2013), and Lupoli (2016). For convenience, I convert Hobbes's Roman numeral chapter numbers to Arabic numerals.

2 Martinich (1992, 76ff.) proposes the distinction for the same purpose, but draws it on a different basis. See Byron (2015, ch. 1) for the details of my appropriation of this distinction.

3 I defend this normative analysis of the laws of nature in Byron (2015, ch. 2).

4 "To those, therefore, whose power is irresistible, the dominion of all men adhereth naturally by the excellence of power; and consequently it is from that power that the kingdom over men, and the right of afflicting men at his pleasure, belongeth naturally to God Almighty, not as Creator and gracious, but as omnipotent" (Hobbes 2012, 558; 1651, 187).4

5 "The mutual transferring of right is that which men call CONTRACT" (Hobbes 2012, 204; 1651, 66). Two paragraphs later Hobbes defines a covenant as a species of contract in which the performances of the two parties occurs at different times.

6 Compare God's prophetic kingdom, which is built on God's covenant with Abraham, in which God rules one particular nation for his subjects by positive laws (Hobbes 2012, 556; 1651, 187).

7 "Whether men will or not, they must be subject always to the divine power. By denying the existence or providence of God, men may shake off their ease, but not their yoke" (Hobbes 2012, 554; 1651, 186). Cf. the cognate passage in *De cive*, 15.2 (Hobbes 1998, 172). It is worth pointing out that Hobbes tends to emphasize divine power and knowledge, mentioning divine goodness far less in *Leviathan*. Still, nothing in the text hints that he rejects any elements of the traditional conception. Hobbes might have issues with "infinite" power, knowledge, etc. given his nominalism and psychology. These concerns will not affect my argument, and might be finessed if Hobbes learned the modern distinction between infinite and indefinitely large quantities.

8 "For he only is properly said to reign that governs his subjects by his word, and by promise of rewards to those that obey it, and by threatening them with punishment that obey it not" (Hobbes 2012, 554; 1651, 186).

9 Note that I capture Hobbes's negative point: non-humans are excluded from the set of those who are subject to God's commands. From this it does not follow that all humans are included, as we see below.

10 A "consequence" because God's omnipotence arguably includes the capacity to do all logically possible acts, not only all nomologically possible acts. If those sets coincide, then God's causal power over everything *is* omnipotence.

11 See for example 42.11, where Hobbes refers to "faith in Christ" (Hobbes 2012, 784; 1651, 271). Chapter 42, by far the longest chapter in *Leviathan*, is especially rich with additional examples.

12 Hobbes does not use the term "deist," but instead refers to those who deny God's revelation and providence. See 31.2 (Hobbes 2012, 554; 1651, 186), cited just below. And again from chapter 31 (31.17): "they who attributing (as they think) ease to God take from him the care of mankind, take from him his honour; for it takes away men's love and fear of him, which is the root of honour" (Hobbes 2012, 564; 1651, 190). Hobbes's friend, Herbert of Cherbury, was an early deist who made these very claims in *De Veritate* (1624); see the discussion in Springborg, 2016.

13 This point begins to refine the claim I have made (Byron 2015, 90), where I stated that theism was sufficient for being a natural subject. Although mere belief in God's existence is not sufficient for being a natural subject, Christian faith is, as it entails both theism and acknowledgment of God's providence.

14 "They, therefore, that believe there is a God that governeth the world, and hath given precepts, and propounded rewards and punishments to mankind, are God's subjects; all the rest are to be understood as enemies" (Hobbes 2012, 554; 1651, 186).

15 Here we may assume that the set of those with the capacity to Acknowledge already excludes people Hobbes thinks are not natural subjects: "natural fools, children, and madmen" (Hobbes, 2012, 422; 1651, 140).

16 In a passage already quoted, Hobbes writes (31.5), "To those, therefore, whose power is irresistible, the dominion of all men adhereth naturally by the excellence of power; and consequently it is from that power that the kingdom over men, and the right of afflicting men at his pleasure, belongeth naturally to God Almighty, not as Creator and gracious, but as omnipotent" (Hobbes 2012, 558; 1651, 187).

17 See 26.44: "For *right* is *liberty*, namely that liberty which the civil law leaves us; but *civil law* is an *obligation*, and takes from us the liberty which the law of nature gave us" (Hobbes 2012, 450; 1651, 150).

18 See 14.7 (Hobbes 2012, 200; 1651, 65), quoted in Section 17.1 (this chapter).

19 See 26.2: "And first, it is manifest that law in general is not counsel, but command; nor a command of any man to any man, but only of him whose command is addressed to one formerly obliged to bey him" (Hobbes 2012, 414; 1651, 137).

20 I defend this reading of Hobbes on obligation in (Byron 2015, ch. 3).

21 Martinich (2018, 40, n.61) points out that Hobbes had argued in *De cive* (15.7) that omnipotence entails an obligation to obey (Hobbes 1998, 174–5). But Hobbes famously *omitted* this claim and its supporting argument from both the English and Latin texts of *Leviathan*: his mature view is that omnipotence and dominion do *not* entail obligations, as I have shown.

22 I say "obligated to obey God's commands as laws" because the precepts commanded may (and according to Hobbes do in fact) have a distinct normative standing. The very same precepts, Hobbes notes at the end of chapter 15 (15.41) (Hobbes 2012, 242; 1651, 80), are both rational theorems and divine laws. As rational theorems, their status is prudentially binding. Reason requires that we follow these precepts. But the same precepts become laws only where the commanded are subjects who have promised to obey. I defend this view in Byron 2015, ch. 2.

23 We all have, of course, *prudential* reasons to follow the precepts of the laws of nature because those are rational theorems. It does not follow that the laws are obligatory for all.

24 See 28.2: "[N]o man is supposed bound by covenant not to resist violence, and consequently, it cannot be intended that he gave any right to another to lay violent hands upon his person. ... But to covenant to assist the sovereign in doing hurt to another, unless he that so covenanteth have a right to do it himself, is not to give him a right to punish" (Hobbes 2012, 482; 1651, 161).

25 Relevant examples of "acknowledge" and its cognates include: 10.21, 12.7, 15.21, and 26.24 (Hobbes 2012, 136, 166, 234, 434; 1651, 43, 53, 77, 144).

26 Cumulative case arguments are common in criminal prosecution. Prosecutors often argue, for example, that defendants had the motive to commit the crime, that they had the means, and the opportunity, and that they lacked an alibi, and that there was an eyewitness, and that there was DNA evidence. These arguments together aim to demonstrate the guilt of defendants beyond a reasonable doubt. The metaphor usually invoked to explain cumulative case arguments is that of the legs of a table: though no one leg may be sufficient to support the table, together they do so. Similarly, though none of the arguments I present in this section on their own might be sufficient to establish my conclusion, together they make it highly probable.

27 See 10.21 (Hobbes 2012, 136; 1651, 43) for example, and especially 45.12 (Hobbes 2012, 1028; 1651, 357): "Therefore, to pray to, to swear by, to obey, to be diligent and officious in serving—in sum, all words and actions that betoken fear to offend or desire to please—is

worship, whether those words and actions be sincere or feigned; and because they appear as signs of honouring, are ordinarily also called honour."

28 The other passages Curley mentions are 26.41, 42.11, and 46.38 (Hobbes 2012, 444, 784, 1096; 1651, 149, 271, 378; though latter's relevance is unclear). Curley's footnote quoted earlier is a note to the Appendix 2.31 (Hobbes 2012, 1202; 1651, 351), where Hobbes refers to "a man whose faith is chosen," which seems to undercut his view that faith is involuntary.

29 Hobbes remarks in the Latin Appendix (2.38) that "in every commonwealth the law commands religion and the recognition of the divine power, and it is essential to every commonwealth that people keep faith in covenants, especially if their faith is confirmed by an oath. Therefore, because an atheist cannot be obliged by swearing, he ought to be cast out of the commonwealth, not as someone who is obstinate, but as someone who is harmful to the public" (Hobbes 2012, 1206; 1651, 352). I have shown (Byron, 2019) that Hobbes's Foole must be an atheist on related grounds.

30 Jones attributes this interpretative approach to Hoekstra (2006).

References

Abizadeh, Arash. December 2017. "Hobbes's Conventionalist Theology, the Trinity, and God as an Artificial Person by Fiction." *The Historical Journal* 60 (4): 915–41.

Byron, Michael. 2015. *Submission and Subjection in Leviathan: Good Subjects in the Hobbesian Commonwealth.* Basingstoke: Palgrave Macmillan.

Byron, Michael. 2019. "Hobbes's Confounding Foole." In *Interpreting Hobbes's Political Philosophy*, edited by S. A. Lloyd, 206–222. Cambridge: Cambridge University Press.

Hobbes, Thomas. 1994. *Leviathan: With Selected Variants from the Latin Edition of 1668*, edited by E. M. Curley. Indianapolis: Hackett.

Hobbes, Thomas. 1998. *Hobbes: On the Citizen*, edited by Richard Tuck and Michael Silverthorne. Cambridge: Cambridge University.

Hobbes, Thomas. 2012. *Leviathan*, 3 vols., edited by Noel Malcolm. Oxford: Clarendon Press. [First published 1651.]

Hoekstra, Kinch. 2006. "The End of Philosophy (The Case of Hobbes)." *Proceedings of the Aristotelian Society* 106 (1): 25–62.

Jones, Ben. 2019. "The Natural Kingdom of God in Hobbes's Political Thought." *History of European Ideas* 45 (3): 436–53.

Lupoli, Agostino. 2016. "Hobbes and Religion Without Theology." In *The Oxford Handbook of Hobbes*, edited by Aloysius P. Martinich and Kinch Hoekstra, 453–480. Oxford: Oxford University Press.

Martinich, Aloysius P. 1992. *The Two Gods of Leviathan: Thomas Hobbes on Religion and Politics.* Cambridge: Cambridge University Press.

Martinich, Aloysius P. 2018. "Natural Sovereignty and Omnipotence in Hobbes's Leviathan." *Hobbes on Politics and Religion*, edited by Laurens van Apeldoorn and Robin Douglass, 29–44. Oxford: Oxford University Press.

Springborg, Patricia. 2016. "Hobbes's Materialism and Epicurean Mechanism." *British Journal for the History of Philosophy* 24 (5): 814–35.

Stauffer, Devin. 2013. "Hobbes's Natural Theology." In *Political Philosophy Cross-Examined*, edited by Thomas L. Pangle and J. Harvey Lomax, 137–51. New York: Palgrave Macmillan.

Tuck, Richard. 1992. "The 'Christian Atheism' of Thomas Hobbes." In *Atheism from the Reformation to the Enlightenment*, edited by Michael Hunter and David Wootton, 111–30. Oxford: Oxford University Press.

18

Thomas Hobbes and the Christian Commonwealth

JEFFREY COLLINS

When *Leviathan* appeared as the third version of Thomas Hobbes's civil science, it was notable in several respects: its rhetorical strategies, its political implications, and its appeal to an anglophone audience. Its primary thematic innovation, however, was its greatly augmented consideration of ecclesiological and theological topics. Hobbes gathered the bulk of this new material into the third and fourth parts of *Leviathan*: "On the Christian Commonwealth" and "On the Kingdom of Darkness." The former of these, the subject of this chapter, constituted the longest of the four parts of *Leviathan*, filling twelve chapters and one hundred and twenty five folio pages in the first edition of the work.

There has been much scholarly attention paid to Hobbes's religious writing, but little specifically to his use of the phrase the "Christian Commonwealth." His use of the term "commonwealth" is itself of considerable interest, but cannot be fully explored here. Suffice it to say that Hobbes's deployment of that word demonstrates its flexibility, and its availability to those uninterested in evoking the sense of "social justice" or popular reformism that at times attached to the term (Knights 2011, 667–9). Nor did Hobbes accept that incorporated cities might form "city commonwealths" (*communitates*; Withington 2005, 8–15). These he derided as "lesser Common-wealths in the bowels of a greater, like worms in the entrails of a natural man" (Hobbes 2012, 516; 1651, 174). Hobbes was no advocate for a "godly reformed Commonwealth," though, given the popularity of the term and its attachment to the post-regicidal regimes, he may well have been engaged in a piece of persuasive re-description with his own Commonwealth (Knights 2011, 679–81). The term was closely related to the equally ambiguous Latin word *respublica*, and like it could simply denote a polity or state (as in Bodin's writing), though both *respublica* and "Commonwealth" became increasingly associated with non-monarchical or mixed-monarchical government during the seventeenth century. As Raleigh had complained, the term "commonwealth" had become a "usurped nickname" to refer to the "government of the whole multitude." Hobbes's persistence with the traditional terminology is in some ways puzzling (Skinner 1989, 120–6).

A Companion to Hobbes, First Edition. Edited by Marcus P. Adams.

Nevertheless, his "commonwealth/state/sovereign was the embodiment of all the men who had, to paraphrase [Thomas] Smith, freely united under a set of common rules" (Knights and Burgess 2011, 671, 675). Hobbes wrote of "that great LEVIATHAN called a COMMONWEALTH, or STATE (in Latin CIVITAS), which is but an artificial man" (Hobbes, 2012, 16; 1651, 1). In his own 1668 Latin translation of *Leviathan*, Commonwealth was translated not into *respublica*, but *civitas*.

What of Hobbes's "Christian Commonwealth"? The phrase was common in early modern texts, and generally incidental. In the decades before *Leviathan*, it can be found in hundreds of printed works, though much less commonly than the ubiquitous phrase "Christian King" or monarch. It was more common than the rare phrase "Christian Republic," though when Christian Commonwealth is found in a work translated from Latin, it was usually a translation of the phrase *Christiana respublica*.[1]

"Christian Commonwealth" was typically unproblematic, synonymous with yet another very common phrase, "a Christian state." This later phrase could denote a sovereign Christian polity or a Christian "estate," such as the "Christian state of marriage." Used in the former manner, a Christian Commonwealth or state was usually a simple, neutral descriptor, distinguishing such states from pagan or Muslim polities. Also common were usages militating for practices that should be enforced in rightly ordered Christian communities. These usages could be little more than moralizing bromides, as when Lawrence Humphrey pronounced that slothful and licentious nobles had "no place in a right and Christian Common wealth" (Humphrey 1563, unpaginated), or when Oliver Cromwell chastised parliament that "it was not to be endured in a Christian Commonwealth, that some should so enrich and greaten themselves in the ruine of others" (Wharton 1658).

The Reformation introduced a divisive edge into any inventory of the notes of a true Christian polity. The first hints of what we might call the Hobbesian resonances of the term emerged in anti-Catholic polemics of the late sixteenth century. This was a context in which the term Christian Commonwealth carried contestable interpretive weight. In pre-Reformation and Roman Catholic usage, the Christian Commonwealth often denoted the transnational civilization elsewhere called Christendom. In this sense there was only the single entity, "the Christian Commonwealth," reaching wherever political communities had embraced Christianity. For some decades even early Protestants wrote in this way, as when Raphael Holinshed recorded Robert, Duke of Normandy "abroade in the service of the Christian common wealth agaynstt the Infidels," or when the translator of Johannes Sleidanus wrote of the general interests of the "whole Christian Commonwealth" (Holinshed 1577, 338; Sleidanus 1689, 165). John Foxe wrote in this manner (Foxe 1683, 299, 301–3, 425). But during the age of confessionalization, the notion of a single Commonwealth of Christendom appealed primarily to Catholics, who avowed "that the Church taken either for the whole companie of the faithfull, or for the Christian Common-wealth, is contented with her sole only head, and essentiall foundation our Lord Jesus Christ" (Richer 1612, unpaginated). In this sense any individual Christian state (or temporal commonwealth) could be distinguished from the generality of the "Christian Common-wealth" (De Tourval 1611, 49). It was this usage, for instance, that was found throughout English translations of the decrees of the Council of Trent (Anon 1687, 2, 17, 81–2). The single Christian Commonwealth might refer to the universal jurisdiction of the Holy Roman Emperor. More commonly, it was a conception of unity that buttressed the spiritual and potential temporal authority of Rome. At its height during the Middle Ages, the concept of the Christian Commonwealth entailed an expansive understanding of *ecclesia*, according to which "all Christians and potentially all men formed a single corporate political entity." For more uncompromising papalists this was "not merely a spiritual unity" but a "civil society, a universal body politic" (Wilks 1963, 18–19).

Reformation texts abandoned this notion of a single "commonwealth of Christendom," with its suggestion of a universal *ecclesia*. They began to speak of individual Christian states, in the plural. The "Christian commonwealth" was broken up into particular entities that might be distinguished from others, or spoken of as part of the collection of Christian commonwealths, potentially divided by particular confessions. It was not incidental that Hobbes, for instance, used the indefinite article rather than the definite article when he composed "Of a Christian Commonwealth." By the seventeenth century discussion of Christian commonwealths could be swept up in the turn to sovereignty, and folded into the reason of state literature and the writings of *politiques*. One illustrative example of this was Jean Bodin, who elevated the spiritual authority of sovereigns for political, rather than spiritual purposes. In English translations of his *Six Bookes of the Commonwealth* are found fulminations at the pretended sovereignty of the "Bishop of Rome," and the excommunications and interdicts "which the popes used as firebrands to the firing of the Christian Commonweales" (Bodin 1606, 145). Or consider Juan de Santa Maria's 1615 *Tratado de republica y policia christiana*, translated in 1632 into the popular work *Christian Policie, or, The Christian Common-wealth published for the good of Kings and Princes* by Edward Blount (who was likely known to Hobbes).[2] This mirror for princes text (first written for Philip III) anticipated quite a lot of Hobbesian rhetoric and argument. Hobbes's Mortal God paralleled its description of a monarch as an "image of God upon earth," and both Hobbes and Santa Maria use the image of a tennis match to describe the task of counselling monarchs (Hobbes 2012, 410; 1651, 136). More substantively, the Spaniard anticipated aspects of Hobbes's account of sovereignty in his definition of a Commonwealth:

> A Republick, or Common-wealth, is a Congregation of many men, subject to the same Lawes and Government, which is not possible to be conserved, if Justice therein shall be wanting. Which gives to everyone, that which is his owne, keepes men within the bounds of good Order and Discipline, and bridles those by reason, which transported by their unruly appetites, (like headstrong jades) would live without it, admitting no curbe ... If Men would but observe that first rule of the Law natural, consecrated by the mouth of our divine Master Christ ... Offer not that to another which thou wouldst not have donne to thyselfe ... And for this cause, they resolved to leade a joynt life together, submitting themselves to one and the same Lawes, and subjecting themselves to one and the same King (Santa Maria 1632, 177–8).

Indeed, Juan de Santa Maria's *Christian Commonwealth* characterized sovereigns as "sole Commanders of the whole Kingdome like unto that great Leviathan, or huge Whale in the Sea, of whom Job saith: Before his face is povertie and want, for he spoyleth and devoureth all that stands in his way, and trusteth that he can draw up Jordan into his Mouth" (Santa Maria 1632, 137–9).

Tantalizing though this is, the possible influence over Hobbes of Blount's translation of the *Christian Commonwealth* must remain a matter of speculation. The work, in any case, did not anticipate the Erastian ecclesiological dimensions of Hobbes's thought that were the chief subject of *Leviathan*'s Christian Commonwealth. As a Catholic, Juan de Santa Maria – even in a "reason of state" text celebrating Christian sovereigns – asserted the superiority of spiritual to temporal things, and insisted that monarchs be guided in their ecclesiastical policy by the "ancient canons and counsels" of the church. This dualism of parallel temporal and spiritual authorities served as one of Hobbes's principle political targets in all of his works. His chief polemical foil in this context was the great counter-Reformation theologian Robert Bellarmine.

18.1 The Christian Commonwealth in Hobbes's Major Texts

Hobbes's first invocation of the notion of the Christian Commonwealth was found in his early *Elements of Law* (hereafter *Elements*). Having defined the nature and extent of political sovereignty, Hobbes dedicated a chapter to rebutting the claim that subjects were "bound to follow their private judgements in controversies of religion." Advising the earl of Newcastle during the religious controversies before the Civil War, Hobbes insisted that "in Christian commonwealths obedience to God and man stand well together." He spoke of Christian Commonwealths in the plural in the *Elements*, and he explicitly contrasted them to ancient polities among the Jews, Greeks, Romans, and "other Gentiles," where spiritual and temporal authority was never divided. His target were those "Christians only, to whom it is allowed to take for the sense of the Scripture that which they make thereof, either by their own private interpretation, or by the interpretation of such as are not called thereunto by public authority" (Hobbes 1994, 141).

Hobbes conceded that Peter had pronounced it better to obey God than Man, but noted that this was said to the Jewish council. There was a distinction between living as a Christian under a Christian sovereign, as opposed to a pagan or infidel sovereign. His main concern was to secure the "obedience to public authority" of Christians living in Christian polities, and thus the "Christian Commonwealth" found in the *Elements* was primarily distinguished from non-Christian polities. His problem was to define the minimum conditions of a Christian Commonwealth:

> And under a Christian sovereign we are to consider, what actions we are forbidden by God Almighty to obey them in, and what not. The actions we are forbidden to obey them in, are such only as imply a denial of that faith which is necessary to our salvation; for otherwise there can be no pretence of disobedience (Hobbes 1994, 144).

Hobbes here introduced his opinion that assent to the claim "Jesus is the Messiah" represented a fundamental article of faith. In the *Elements* Hobbes also avowed that belief in scripture and in the immortality of the soul were necessary fundamentals. But all other points of doctrine were mere "superstruction" (Hobbes 1994, 144).

The *Elements* marshalled scriptural evidence supposedly affirming the minimal nature of essential Christian doctrines. Hobbes swept away contested theological subtleties that had, in recent generations, caused turmoil and sectarianism (particularly controversies over free will). But Hobbes was also concerned to define the parameters of the Christian Commonwealth. The more limited his slate of theological fundamentals was, the broader these parameters could be. Any polity that upheld his minimal fundamentals qualified as a Christian Commonwealth. The many other points of doctrine, ecclesiology, and practice that divided Christian churches were placed under sovereign authority: subjects were required to obey them by the laws of nature. "These things considered," Hobbes wrote, drawing the threads of his argument together:

> it will easily appear: that under the sovereign power of a Christian commonwealth, there is no danger of damnation from simple obedience to human laws; for in that the sovereign alloweth Christianity, no man is compelled to renounce that faith which is enough for his salvation; that is to say, the fundamental points. And for other points, seeing they are not necessary to salvation, if we conform our actions to the laws, we do not only what we are allowed, but also what we are commanded, by the law of nature, which is the moral law taught by our Saviour himself (Hobbes 1994, 152–3).

To those construing such subservience as a violation of conscience, Hobbes appealed to the distinction of inner conscience (or individual opinion) and outer practice. "The difficulty therefore of obeying both God and man, in a Christian commonwealth is none," concluded Hobbes. More problematic, he conceded, was any Christian submitting to the sovereignty of an "Infidel." In a somewhat convoluted passage Hobbes held out the option of martyrdom in such contexts (Hobbes 1994, 154).

In sum, the *Elements* deployed the notion of Christian Commonwealths narrowly, to distinguish them from pagan or infidel states and to establish the broad terms that minimally defined states sufficiently Christian to merit the unquestioned obedience of Christian subjects. The distinctions between eastern and western Christianity, between Catholic and Protestant, and among species of Protestant, mattered not at all in defining the Christian Commonwealth. Hobbes thus discredited any early modern resistance theory that hung on such distinctions. His understanding of the category of Christian Commonwealths was pluralistic and ecumenical. Hobbes's "Christian State," writes one authority, was "designed to accommodate people's desire to be *saved* and neutralize the politically destabilizing thrust of the desire" (Farneti 2007, 291).

In the Latin *De cive*, Hobbes similarly defined the Christian Commonwealth according to this minimal theology. States were due obedience in spiritual causes if they "profess themselves Christian" and did not require subjects to deny Christ. And again in *De cive*, Hobbes conceded that in religious matters Christians might follow the church rather than an infidel sovereign, but must also spurn resistance and accept martyrdom if required (Hobbes 1998, 245).

In both texts Christian Commonwealths belong to a broad category of state that enjoyed – according to the scriptures – the unreserved obedience of Christian subjects. Necessarily the Christian "mysteries" (such as the Trinity) took on a different status as part of the law of Christian Commonwealths (Martinich 1992, 221). Hobbes's main concern was to distinguish them from non-Christian states, which also enjoyed full spiritual authority, but might discomfit conscientious Christians more seriously. In both texts Hobbes was certainly concerned to defuse corporate, clerical rivals to sovereignty, but where he deployed the language of the Christian Commonwealth, he targeted conscientious sectarians and grandiose notions of explicit political covenants with God (Lessay 2007, 243–65). These texts did not directly engage with the alternate, more universal definition of a single Christian Commonwealth offered by Catholic authors. Indeed, in the *Elements* Hobbes avowed that the problem of ungovernable conscience, not found among either ancient pagans or Jews, was also absent among "Christians that dwell under the temporal dominion of the bishop of Rome" (Hobbes 1994, 142). Certainly he did not ascribe to a single Christian commonweal under papal jurisdiction, but Hobbes did admit Catholic states into his pluralistic understanding of "Christian Commonwealths."

In all of his writings, Hobbes would maintain this minimal understanding of a Christian Commonwealth. But in *Leviathan*, he was more exercised by the threat of corporate clerical power, and his much more extensive discussion of Christian Commonwealths in this text was clearly directed at Catholic definitions of a single *Christiana respublica*. *Leviathan* made greater use of the notion of the Christian Commonwealth, as an umbrella concept covering the longest of the work's four parts. A description of Hobbes's understanding of the Christian Commonwealth might thus encompass all of his theological and ecclesiological doctrines. More useful in the present context is to map where, and how, *Leviathan* directly deployed the phrase. As in the *Elements*, Hobbes introduced the religious portions of *Leviathan* by asking whether obedience to civil law might ever be "repugnant to God." We should neither offend the "Divine Majesty" with obedience to civil law, nor could we disobey civil law out of an overly scrupulous conscience. Hobbes thus prepared to again demonstrate that natural law and divine law agreed in requiring obedience from Christians to sovereigns (Hobbes, 2012, 554; 1651, 187). The accord of reason, law, and revelation on this point was fundamental to the constitution of the "Kingdom of God" (Jones 2018, 446–7). The Christian Commonwealth existed within the more expansive and prophetic realm of this "divine Kingdom." Hobbes's aim was to preserve maximum authority both temporal and spiritual for Christian polities and sovereigns (Johnston 1986, 164–84). He characterized this effort as an implication of "the principles of Christian politiques":

> I Have derived the Rights of Soveraigne Power, and the duty of Subjects hitherto, from the Principles of Nature onely ... that is to say, from the nature of Men, known to us by Experience, and from Definitions (of such words as are Essentiall to all Politicall reasoning) universally agreed on. But in that I am next to handle, which is the Nature and Rights of a CHRISTIAN COMMON-WEALTH, whereof there dependeth much upon Supernaturall Revelations of the Will of God; the ground of my Discourse must be, not only the Naturall Word of God, but also the Propheticall (Hobbes 2012, 576; 1651, 195).

Hobbes again sought to expansively define the "rights of a Christian Commonwealth." Sovereignty, defined according to natural reason, would now be measured according to Christian scripture. This was reminiscent of the *Elements*, and Hobbes was again concerned to refute any who might disobey the state out of "pretence of private Inspiration, or Revelation ... their own Dreams, and extravagant Fancies, and Madnesse" (Hobbes 2012, 606; 1651, 205).

However, *Leviathan* was the first of Hobbes's text to explicitly deploy the terminology of the Christian Commonwealth within an attack on sovereignty's clerical rivals. Hobbes asserted that "the Church, if it be one person, is the same thing with a Common-wealth of Christians; called a Common-wealth, because it consisteth of men united in one person, their Soveraign; and a Church, because it consisteth in Christian men, united in one Christian Soveraign." A church that did not participate in this unified authority had no "Will, Reason, nor Voice," and was not a public power at all but merely a private assembly. On the other hand, if "the whole number of Christians" worldwide were understood as "one Common-wealth, then all Christian Monarchs, and States are private persons, and subject to be judged, deposed, and punished by an Universall Soveraigne of all Christendome." The question was whether Christian sovereigns were "absolute in their own Territories, immediately under God; or subject to one Vicar of Christ, constituted of the Universall Church; to bee judged, condemned, deposed, and put to death, as he shall think expedient, or necessary for the common good" (Hobbes 2012, 606; 1651, 206).

Though it built on longstanding concerns of his political theory, this context for Hobbes's consideration of the *Christiana respublica* was substantially new in his writing. For the first time he explicitly rejected the Catholic understanding of the Christian Commonwealth as a single, universal entity, a Christendom ruled by Rome. His usage echoed Reformation discourse in speaking of plural Christian commonwealths. His own science of sovereignty endowed these polities with an absolute authority derived in the first instance from natural law but also from scripture and thus "Christian."

We do not need to seek far to surmise why Hobbes made this rhetorical move. It parried the language of the textual foil most commonly cited in *Leviathan*: the counter-Reformation theologian Cardinal Robert Bellarmine.

18.2 Hobbes and the Christian Commonwealths of Rome and Canterbury

Bellarmine's diverse writings participated in a disruptive effort – both between Protestants and Catholics and among different species of counter-Reformation Catholics – to define the *Christiana respublica* during the age of confessionalism. Stefania Tutino has established the critical importance of Bellarmine's ecclesiology as a contested position within a series of fraught political conflicts well known to Hobbes: the Venetian Interdict crisis; the controversies surrounding Gallican Catholicism; and the polemics attending the Jacobean Oath of Allegiance. In these contexts Bellarmine promoted an ecclesiology defining the church as a single "theo-political organism," the "*respublica Christiana*" (Bourdin 2010). This position countered Protestant efforts to establish national Christian churches, but it also rejected more ambitious defenses of the papacy's temporal political power. Both Protestantism and ultra-papalism accommodated, problematically in Bellarmine's view, the "consolidation of the early modern state," which tended toward the fusion of spiritual and temporal jurisdiction (Tutino 2010, 14). In all of his works, but notably in the three books of his *Disputationes de controversiis Christianae Fidei*, the Thomist Bellarmine adapted medieval notions of the Christian Commonwealth found within the canon law tradition. Central to his view was the incommensurability of temporal and spiritual authority (Tutino 2010, 28, 63–4). Bellarmine remained hostile to any endowment of Rome with temporal power, and this earned him the Vatican's hostility. But the spiritual *Christiana respublica* was no mere invisible communion of believers. National states were plural, differently organized to provide temporal goods according to different customs and traditions. "Christian kings," wrote Bellarmine, "rule Christian people not as Christians, but as political men." Only the church retained any global authority as an empire. "This empire, however, is a supernatural one, an empire of the consciences, outside of and beyond the boundaries of the political condition" (Tutino 2010, 66–7). Bellarmine preserved considerable autonomy for political states, who enjoyed "dominium not founded in grace or faith, but in free will and reason." Temporal power did not rest on divine law but the law of nations. Even infidel sovereigns wielded sovereignty on these terms. But Bellarmine's famous doctrine of the Papacy's "indirect power" granted it a universal authority to govern the external religious practices of Christendom. This authority over the "empire of souls" was what Bellarmine called, following medieval usage, the *Christiana respublica*. It extended universally, wherever professing Christians were found. All of this followed neo-Thomist thinking, particularly Vitoria, where natural law thinking – rather than grace or divine law – grounded temporal power. But Bellarmine was particularly determined to limit the temporal power claims of Rome. Vitoria, Suarez, and de Molina tended to maintain some authority over temporal affairs for the Papacy in order to preserve the earthly church through all human time. "The difference, then," writes Tutino, "between Suárez, Vitoria, Molina, and Bellarmine is in the nuances of this spiritual intervention, which for Bellarmine must remain spiritual, while for the others such intervention assumes a quasi-temporal character." For this entire neo-Thomist tradition, both the state and the church were "perfect Commonwealths" in their respective spheres, the former of subjects united according to natural law for temporal goods, the latter of Christians united underneath the papal monarchy for spiritual goods. Only the latter, however, was global in reach. Only the latter, furthermore, could properly be called the "Christian Commonwealth" (Tutino 2010, 40–6).

Bellarmine's version of the Christian Commonwealth could be mobilized against Gallican Catholics, against the independent authority of Venice's church, and of course against Protestant Erastians. But it also undermined the papal monarchy, and earned the enmity of Pope Sixtus V. Bellarmine stirred opposition by presenting clerical exemptions from temporal law as matters of human, rather than divine, law. This provoked more uncompromising defenders of papal authority, such as Francisco Peña, whose 1611 treatise *De regno Christi* held that the kingdom of Christ was a single perfect Commonwealth encompassing spiritual and temporal authority, with princes subordinated to the superior authority of the papacy. It could also provoke Catholic defenders of the divine right of Kings. The Scottish Catholic William Barclay tangled with Bellarmine in his *De Potestate Papae* of 1609, which augmented the spiritual authority of sovereigns by denying that there existed two Commonwealths, one spiritual and one temporal. There was, rather, but one *Christiana respublica*, ruled by two authorities (Barclay 1609, 104, 135–50; Tutino 2010, 150–1). Christian "authorities" (*potestates*) had been separated in pagan antiquity, and were in modern infidel states, but were conjoined in Christian polities, where the only true *Christiana respublica* could be found.

This had the effect of augmenting the equal authority of Kings and popes, rejecting Bellarmine's effort to secure an authority for Rome that was universal but apolitical.

The sustained attack on Bellarmine in *Leviathan* effectively intervened in this debate (Springborg 1995). Hobbes's insistence that natural and divine law were mutually reinforcing and undergirded the full temporal and spiritual authority of sovereigns was a direct rebuke to Bellarmine's dualism of divine law and the law of nations. Hostility to Bellarmine's scheme of diverse, plural states constituting a single spiritual Commonwealth explains Hobbes's remark, quoted earlier, that any Commonwealth encompassing all the world's Christians would empower the pope as a sovereign and make mere "private persons" of states (Malcolm 2002, 453–5). Hobbes's theory was closer to the unified sovereignist positions of Barclay and Peña (Sommerville 1992, 116). Where many Protestants presented the papal states as evidence of the corruption of Rome, Hobbes was notably sanguine about the Vatican's direct temporal rule.

The Christian Commonwealth of *Leviathan* was thus an absolute political entity achievable wherever a sovereign state espoused Hobbes's minimal theology. In the primitive church, before the conversion of Rome, there had been "no Christian Common-wealth" (Hobbes 2012, 776; 1651, 267). Likewise, while an infidel state clearly was no Christian Commonwealth, Christians within such a state were mere private persons, and their church did not constitute any sort of spiritual commonwealth at all. All states enjoyed full supremacy over public religious practice and doctrine, and in Christian Commonwealths this meant that they enjoyed the power to define revelation, judge prophecy, order sacraments, excommunicate, and govern the clergy. Wrote Hobbes: "whosoever in a Christian Common-wealth holdeth the place of Moses, is the sole Messenger of God, and Interpreter of his Commandements" (Hobbes 2012, 774; 1651, 252). Likewise, "in every Christian Common-wealth the Civil Sovereign is the Supreme Pastor, to whose charge the whole flock his subjects is committed, and consequently it is by his authority, that all other pastors are made, and have power to teach" (Hobbes 2012, 852; 1651, 295).

Bellarmine's *De summo Pontifice* provoked Hobbes as the most able defense of the pope's "Supreme Ecclesiastical Power." In using Bellarmine as his chief foil, rather than a more uncompromising papal sovereignist such as Peña, Hobbes was not condemning clerical figures wielding sovereignty (which was theoretically acceptable to him), but the dangerous division of sovereignty between spiritual and temporal powers. This, he believed, set up a rivalry that caused all civil wars in Christendom (Hobbes 1998, 80–1).

Much of the anti-Catholic rhetoric of *Leviathan* should also be read to condemn the usurpations of authority effected by the Laudian Church of England (Collins 2000, 229–31). Hobbes's high view of the state's ecclesiastical authority could find some parallels in the "Anglican" tradition, not least in Richard Hooker (Sommerville 1992, 117). But Hobbes's Erastianism far outstripped that of Hooker, and the Laudian revolution in the Caroline church was widely taken to have abandoned such deferential Reformation Erastianism. In both Hooker and Laud, the Commonwealth and the Church were each understood as a "collective body" with a distinct end, and neither was permitted to "swallow up" the other (Laud 1847–1860, 1: 6). In a sermon before the first parliament of Charles I, Bishop Laud declared it "not possible in any Christian Commonwealth that the church should 'melt' and the state stand firm" (Laud 1847–1860, 1: 112). Laud was fond of quoting the fourth century Saint Optatus, bishop of Milevis, that the

"Church is in the commonwealth, not the commonwealth in the Church" (Laud 1847–1860, 2: 125, 223).

Bellarmine's particular dualist notion of the *Christiana respublica* was obnoxious to Hobbes on its own terms, but also approximated the ecclesiology of the Laudian church. The Laudians threatened an internal division of sovereignty, as Bellarmine's ecclesiology represented a division that empowered the clerical estate universally. The national and global dimensions of the question could be intertwined. Hobbes, for instance, agreed with Bellarmine that bishops did not enjoy authority *jure divino*. But empowering and depriving bishops belonged to the pope only "in his own Dominions, or in the Dominions of any other Prince that hath given him that Power; but not universally, in Right of the Popedome: For that power belongeth to every Christian Soveraign, within the bounds of his owne Empire, and is inseparable from the Soveraignty" (Hobbes 2012, 906; 1651, 313). Hobbes thus used Bellarmine's papalism against the Laudian bishops, but his own account of unified sovereignty against Bellarmine's papalism. He directly assailed Bellarmine's notion of the pope's "indirect" temporal authority (as when a heretical prince was dethroned by Rome). Bellarmine conceded that popes did not enjoy direct temporal power because they did not enjoy temporal sovereignty by the consent or compact of the governed. Hobbes ratified this point (which worked to undermine more thoroughgoing arguments for the temporal authority of the Papacy), but he rejected the Cardinal's subsequent claim that God had granted popes jurisdiction over the "salvation of souls," and that this might necessitate an "indirect" meddling in temporal affairs. As Harro Höpfl has put it, Bellarmine held that "once Christianity had been established in a commonwealth, Christian subjects may not tolerate the accession of a heretical King ... For it now became incumbent upon Christian Commonwealths and rulers to pursue an end which is not that of secular authority and commonwealths as such." This was Bellarmine's inlet for admitting "indirect" spiritual power (Höpfl 2004, 364). To Hobbes this amount to hair splitting: "For this distinction of Temporall, and Spirituall Power is but words. Power is as really divided, and as dangerously to all purposes, by sharing with another Indirect Power, as with a Direct one" (Hobbes 2012, 912; 1651, 314).

Hobbes and Bellarmine differed over the extent and quality of a/the "Christian Commonwealth" in part because they espoused different soteriologies. Here Hobbes's minimal theological fundamentals again came into play, and informed an understanding of the notes of a Christian Commonwealth sufficiently minimal to credibly empower temporal rulers spiritually. "That a Common-wealth," wrote Hobbes,

> to defend it selfe against injuries, may lawfully doe all that he hath here said, is very true ... And if it were also true, that there is now in this world a Spirituall Common-wealth, distinct from a Civill Common-wealth, then might the Prince thereof, upon injury done him, or upon want of caution that injury be not done him in time to come, repaire, and secure himself by Warre; which is in summe, deposing, killing, or subduing, or doing any act of Hostility. But by the same reason, it would be no lesse lawfull for a Civill Soveraign, upon the like injuries done, or feared, to make warre upon the Spirituall Soveraign; which I beleeve is more than Cardinall Bellarmine would have inferred from his own proposition. But Spirituall Common-wealth there is none in this world: for it is the same thing with the Kingdome of Christ; which he himselfe saith, is not of this world; but shall be in the next world, at the Resurrection, when they that have lived justly, and beleeved that he was the

> Christ, shall (though they died Naturall bodies) rise Spirituall bodies; and then it is, that our Saviour shall judge the world, and conquer his Adversaries, and make a Spirituall Commonwealth (Hobbes 2012, 918; 1651, 317).

A particular, universal polity tasked with safeguarding the sacraments, doctrine, revelation, and full Christian practice was unnecessary given the minimal requirements of salvation. The Kingdom of God would only become a Spiritual Commonwealth with the Second Coming. One of Hobbes's most forceful assertions that the confusion of divine and human authority in any "Christian Common-wealth" was the cause of civil war is found at the start of *Leviathan's* chapter 43, "on what is necessary for a mans reception into the Kingdome of Heaven" (Hobbes 2012, 928; 1651, 321). It was here where he again asserted his own minimal slate of theological fundamentals.

18.3 Hobbes and the Christian Commonwealth of the Sects

Hobbes's theological minimalism raises another possible context in which Hobbes seems to have grappled with the discourse of a Christian Commonwealth: sectarian debate over the compatibility of toleration and the *Christiana respublica*. If the most direct context for Hobbes's definition of a Christian Commonwealth was his engagement with counter-Reformation ecclesiology, the proliferating sectarianism of the 1640s and 1650s surely provided another. Printed invocations of the Christian Commonwealth spiked around the time *Leviathan* appeared, responding no doubt to the post-regicidal regime's formal designation of itself as a Commonwealth, but also to the general ferment of politicized, providential religiosity, and competing efforts to define an English Godly republic. Thus could John Eliot invoke "the Prophecies and Promises of holy Scripture" foretelling that "Lord Jesus will bring down all people, to be ruled by the Institutions, Laws, and Directions of the Word of God; not only in Church-Government and Administrations, but also in the Government and Administration of all affairs in the Commonwealth" (Eliot 1656, preface). Eliot's was not the only such effort to extract patterns of church and temporal governance directly from the scriptures. In offering his own account, which subordinated scripture to civil science, Hobbes was undoubtedly targeting not just Catholics and Laudians but overly zealous radical Protestants of this stripe. He had no interest in any understanding of the Kingdom of God, or the Christian Commonwealth, saturated with providential or apocalyptic zealotry. (On this point, he went so far as to agree with Bellarmine that the pope could not be identified as the Antichrist [McQueen 2018, 127]).

Hobbes was not alone in such hesitancy. Anthony Norwood, for instance, offered a more spare understanding of the Christian Commonwealth that detached it from both *jure divino* monarchy and episcopacy but also theocratic rule by the "saints" (Norwood 1652, 18). Hobbes also kept his distance from those opponents of radical sectarians who primarily looked to the clergy to uphold the godly polity. He would have had little time for those assorted orthodoxy moderates who in the Worcestershire Petition pronounced: "No Ministry, no Christian Magistracy; no Christian Magistracy, no Christian Commonwealth" (Baxter 1653, 23; Smith 1655, 43–4). Hobbes would not give to a Presbyterian or episcopalian clerical order the pride of place he had denied to the

Catholics. He scorned assertions, such as that made by the Presbyterian provincial assembly of London, that an ordained ministry was fundamental to a "well-ordered Christian Commonwealth" (Calamy 1654, 192).

Hobbes's direct invocations of the Christian Commonwealth chiefly occur in his disputes with Bellarmine. But a few seemingly responded to one particular dimension of revolutionary debate: namely, whether or not a properly Christian Commonwealth was required to enforce fundamental orthodoxy, or should instead protect conscience freedom. Thomas Edwards, for instance, was in no doubt that "Christian Common-wealths" should "throw downe all things contrary to faith and the true worship of Christ, and positively by outward acts promote and command the outward worship of God, have a care of the Ecclesiasticall Discipline, and of all the parts of Religion that they may be preserved" (Edwards 1647, 43–4). Tolerationist sectarians countered by upholding the freedom of the Christian man as the true note of Christian Commonwealths (Price 1645, 15, 31). This rhetoric spilled over into related debates over the freedom of the press. "Far be it from a Christian Commonwealth to suffer weekly Advocates to write for Satan," wrote one orthodox author (Cheynell 1652, 11; Jenkyn 1652, 11).

When measured against the tightly structured Catholic debate over the Christian Commonwealth, English protestant usages from the 1640s and 1650s were cacophonous and diverse. It is tempting to suggest that with *Leviathan*, and its use of the terminology of the Commonwealth, Hobbes was intervening in these debates. But he had used the term Commonwealth frequently, as early as the *Elements of Law*, long before the governors of the formal English Commonwealth had appeared as possible patrons of his work. Nevertheless, at a few junctures of *Leviathan* his discussion of the Christian Commonwealth touched on issues relevant to debates over toleration, where the term had been prominently deployed on both sides. As often with his discussions of toleration and conscience, there was an ambiguity to Hobbes's intervention. In a well-known passage on the importance of uniformity in "public worship," Hobbes wrote that "where many sorts of Worship be allowed, proceeding from the different Religions of Private men, it cannot be said there is any Publique Worship, nor that the Common-wealth is of any Religion at all" (Hobbes 2012, 570; 1651, 570). The suggestion here was that a polity allowing a plurality of voluntary religious practices would sacrifice the very status of a Christian Commonwealth. In another invocation of the Christian Commonwealth, Hobbes asked how a Muslim subject in such a polity should respond to a requirement that he attend Christian worship. His answer was that outer obedience did not compromise conscience, which was an aspect of inner belief. Like Naaman in the House of Rimmon, he could obey without sin (Hobbes 2012, 784; 1651, 271). Later in *Leviathan*, Hobbes referenced the best practices of "Christian Commonwealths" when he commended Paul and the primitive Christians for their obedience to heathen rulers. "It is not therefore for want of strength, but for conscience sake, that Christians are to tolerate their Heathen Princes, or Princes (for I cannot call any one whose Doctrine is the Publique Doctrine, an Haeretique) that authorize the teaching of an Errour" (Hobbes 2012, 922; 1651, 318).

In sum, Hobbes's definitions of the Christian Commonwealth established minimal conditions for that status, definitively ruled out the necessity of any clerical authority, and rejected the arguments of some sectarians that free religious exercise was essential to the Christian polity. To be sure, in much of *Leviathan* and in his later writings, a new deference to conscience seems to represent Hobbes's considered view (Curley 2007; Tuck 2016). His theological minimalism pushed against the enforcement of complex systems of theological belief and practice. But such toleration of individual religious practice that Hobbes did recommend he allowed as a matter of prudent governance: a freedom gifted to individual believers that might also free sovereigns from usurping clerical advisors. Free outward religious practice, and freedom of philosophical speculation, were certainly wise policies. They were not, however, rights, nor a necessary feature of a Christian Commonwealth.

18.4 Conclusion

The extensive discussion of Christian Commonwealths in *Leviathan* redirected the history of the concept and the English resonance of the phrase. There is a notable spike in printed discussion of the Christian Commonwealth during and after the 1650s, doubtless in part reflecting the immense response that Hobbes's masterpiece provoked. Bishop Bramhall spoke for both Catholic and Church of England critics when he objected to Hobbes's doctrine that "if the whole number of Christians be not contained in one Commonwealth, they are not one Person, nor is there an Universal Church, that hath any Authority over them" (Hobbes 1682, 70). This, to Bramhall, vitiated the Creed's avowal of a "Catholick or Universal Church." He continued: "All other Men distinguish between the Church and the Common-wealth; only T[homas] H[obbes] maketh them to be one and the same thing." Hobbes responded with a brazen concession that there was indeed, no "Universal Church on Earth." The spiritual laws and practices of "Christian Common-wealths" did indeed "contradict one another," Hobbes conceded, "but contradict not the Law of God (Hobbes 1682, 70–1)."

Bramhall's objection to Hobbes's pluralistic and minimal understanding of Christian polities, shorn of all clerical authority, would persist in high church and particularly Catholic ecclesiology. Protestant nonconformists, however, would come to object to Hobbesian Erastianism no less forcefully. Their revolutionary efforts to define the Christian Commonwealth as a godly polity came to grief after 1660. Most tolerationist sectarians, furthermore, became increasingly unwilling to accept their religious freedom as a mere gift of sovereigns. What is surely the most famous, if only implicit, riposte to Hobbes's Christian Commonwealth is thus found in Locke's *Epistola de Tolerantia*:

> But there is absolutely no such thing under the Gospel as a Christian commonwealth [*respublica Christiana*]. I admit that there are many kingdoms and cities which have been converted to the Christian faith, but they have retained and preserved their ancient form of government, on which Christ enjoined nothing in his law ... nor did he arm any magistrate with a sword with which to force men into the faith or worship he prescribed for his people, or prevent them from practicing another religion (Locke 1968, 117).

Hobbes's Christian Commonwealth was rejected by traditionalist clericalists and by nonconformists, who preserved spiritual autonomy for churches or for individual consciences respectively (Collins 2020, chapter 5). On its own terms and in its own context, however, Hobbes's Christian Commonwealth – defined as a sovereign state enjoying full spiritual authority, but counselled to enforce only a minimal theology – was a central component of the political project advanced in *Leviathan*. It lacked a permanent constituency, but it enjoyed a durable influence, if only as an ineluctable foil.

Notes

1 *Early English Books* online presents about 600 instances of variations of "Christian Commonwealth" across the sixteenth and seventeenth centuries. There are only a few dozen occurrences of a "Christian Republic," and thousands of a "Christian King".

2 Blount was perhaps the most important book publisher of his day, and printed the *Horae Subsecivae* probably written by William Cavendish under Hobbes's tutelage.

References

Anon. 1687. *The Canons and Decrees of the Council of Trent*. London.

Barclay, William. 1609. *De Potestate Papae: An & quatenus in Reges & Principes seculares ius & imperium habeas*. London.

Baxter, Richard. 1653. *The Worcester-shire Petition to the Parliament*. London.

Bodin, Jean. 1606. *Six Bookes of a Commonweale*. London.

Bourdin, Bernard. 2010. *The Theological-Political Origins of the Modern State. The Controversy Between James I of England and Cardinal Bellarmine*, translated by Susan Pickford. Washington: Catholic University of America Press.

Cheynell, Francis. 1652. *The Beacon Flameing with a Non Obstant*. London.

Collins, Jeffrey. 2000. "Christian Ecclesiology and the Composition of *Leviathan*: A Newly Discovered Letter to Thomas Hobbes." *Historical Journal* 43: 217–31.

Collins, Jeffrey. 2020. *In the Shadow of Leviathan: John Locke and the Politics of Conscience*. Cambridge: Cambridge University Press.

Curley, Edwin. 2007. "Hobbes and the Cause of Religious Toleration." In *The Cambridge Companion to Leviathan*, edited by Patricia Springborg, 309–34. Cambridge: Cambridge University Press.

De Tourval, Jean Loiseau. 1611. *The French Herald Summoning All True Christian Princes to a General Croisade*. London.

Edwards, Thomas. 1647. *The Casting Down of the Last and Strongest Hold of Satan; or a Treatise Against Toleration*. London.

Eliot, John. 1656. *The Christian Commonwealth: Or, the Civil Policy of the Rising Kingdom of Jesus Christ*. London.

Farneti, Roberto. 2007. "Hobbes on Salvation." In *The Cambridge Companion to Leviathan*, edited by Patricia Springborg, 291–308. Cambridge: Cambridge University Press.

Foxe, John. 1683. *Actes and Monuments*. London.

Hobbes, Thomas. 1682. *An Answer to a Book Published by Dr. Bramhall...* London.

Hobbes, Thomas. 1994. "Elements of Law." In *Human Nature and de Corpore Politico*, edited by John C.A. Gaskin. Oxford: Oxford University Press.

Hobbes, Thomas. 1998. *On the Citizen*, edited and translated by Richard Tuck and Michael Silverthorne. Cambridge: Cambridge University Press.

Hobbes, Thomas. 2012. *Leviathan*, 3 vols., edited by Noel Malcolm. Oxford: Oxford University Press.

Holinshed, Raphael. 1577. *Laste Volume of the Chronicles of England*. London.

Höpfl, Harro. 2004. *Jesuit Political Thought: The Society of Jesus and the State, c. 1540–1630*. Cambridge: Cambridge University Press.

Humphrey, Lawrence. 1563. *The Nobles or of Nobilitye the Original Nature, Dutyes, Right, and Christian Institucion*. London.

Jenkyn, William. 1652. *An Exposition of the Epistle of St Jude, Together with Many Large and Useful Deductions*. London.

Johnston, David. 1986. *The Rhetoric of Leviathan: Thomas Hobbes and the Politics of Cultural Transformation*. Princeton, NJ: Princeton University Press.

Jones, Ben. 2018. "The Natural Kingdom of God in Hobbes's Political Thought." *History of European Ideas* 45: 436–53.

Calamy, Edmund. 1654. *Jus Divinum Ministerii Evangelici; or the Divine Right of the Gospel-Ministry*. London.

Knights, Mark. 2011. "Commonwealth: The Social, Cultural, and Conceptual Contexts of an Early Modern Keyword." *Historical Journal* 54: 659–87.

Laud, William. 1847–1860. *The Works of the Most Reverend Father in God, William Laud*, edited by James Bliss and William Scott (7 vols). Oxford.

Lessay, Frank. 2007. "Hobbes's Covenant Theology and Its Political Implications." In *The Cambridge Companion to Hobbes's Leviathan*, edited by Patricia Springborg, 243–65. Cambridge: Cambridge University Press.

Locke, John. 1968. *Epistola de Tolerantia*, edited by Raymond Klibansky, translated by John W. Gough. Oxford: Oxford University Press.

Malcolm, Noel. 2002. "Hobbes's Theory of International Relations." In *Aspects of Hobbes*, 432–56. Oxford: Oxford University Press.

Martinich, Aloysius P. 1992. *The Two Gods of Leviathan: Thomas Hobbes on Religion and Politics*. Cambridge: Cambridge University Press.

McQueen, Alison. 2018. *Political Realism in Apocalyptic Times*. Cambridge: Cambridge University Press.

Norwood, Anthony. 1652. *New Errors Made Palpable by an Old Light*. London.

Price, John. 1645. *Independency Accused by Nine Severall Arguments*. London.

Richer, Edmund. 1612. *A Treatise of Ecclesiasticall and Politike Power...* London.

Santa Maria, Juan de. 1632. *Christian Policie, Or, The Christian Common-Wealth Published for the Good of Kings and Princes*. London.

Skinner, Quentin. 1989. "The State." In *Political Innovations and Conceptual Change*, edited by Terence Ball, James Farr, and Russell Hanson, 90–131. Cambridge: Cambridge University Press.

Sleidanus, Johannes. 1689. *The General History of the Reformation of the Church*. London.

Smith, George. 1655. *God's Unchangeableness, or God's Continued Providence*. London.

Sommerville, Johann. 1992. *Thomas Hobbes: Political Ideas in Historical Context*. New York: St Martin's Press.

Springborg, Patricia. 1995. "Thomas Hobbes and Cardinal Bellarmine: Leviathan and the 'Ghost of the Roman Empire'." *History of Political Thought* 16: 503–31.

Tuck, Richard. 2016. "Hobbes, Conscience, and Christianity." In *The Oxford Handbook of Hobbes*, edited by Aloysius P. Martinich and Kinch Hoekstra, 481–99. Oxford: Oxford University Press.

Tutino, Stephania. 2010. *Empire of Souls: Robert Bellarmine and the Christian Commonwealth*. Oxford: Oxford University Press.

Wharton, Sir George. 1658. *A Second Narrative of the Late Parliament (So Called)*. London.

Wilks, Michael. 1963. *The Problem of Sovereignty in the Later Middle Ages*. Cambridge: Cambridge University Press.

Withington, Phil. 2005. *The Politics of the Commonwealth: Citizens and Freemen in Early Modern England*. Cambridge: Cambridge University Press.

19

Hobbes and Toleration

JOHANN SOMMERVILLE

Hobbes argued for absolute sovereignty, and claimed that in Christian countries the sovereign was fully empowered to govern the church as well as the state. The "Supreme Pastor," he declared, is "the Civill Soveraigne" (Hobbes 2012, 934; 1651, 323). He held that sovereigns could and should make and enforce laws concerning religion, and that they ought to control what was taught and published in their lands. The universities, he contended, were the prime sources of learning in every country: "the Instruction of the people, dependeth wholly, on the right teaching of Youth in the Universities" (Hobbes 2012, 532; 1651, 180). Since "the Universities are the Fountains of Civill, and Morall Doctrine" he suggested that his own *Leviathan* should be taught there (Hobbes 2012, 1140; 1651, 395). In *Behemoth*, claims David Wootton, Hobbes "wanted to impose a state religion on a country where there was a measure of toleration, and to impose a state ideology on universities in which a certain amount of intellectual diversity was permitted" (Wootton 1997, 240). He believed (Wootton continues) "that force, indoctrination, and coerced consent can produce a stable political order" (Wootton 1997, 241). There are grounds, then, for seeing Hobbes as a staunch opponent of religious toleration, and a number of scholars support some variation of this position (e.g., Kabala 2019; Tralau 2011).

Some commentators, however, have argued for a more tolerant Hobbes. Alan Ryan put forward that interpretation more than 30 years ago (Ryan 1983, 1988). Others have taken a similar line, sometimes with interesting and important modifications (Abizadeh 2013; Bejan 2016; Collins 2007; Curley 2007; Lessay 2018; Owen 2005; Remer 1992; Sreedhar 2017). Richard Tuck has perhaps most forcefully contended that *Leviathan* was a defense of toleration (Tuck 1990). Late in *Leviathan*, Hobbes said that in the course of the history of Christianity three "knots" had come to be placed upon the "Christian liberty" of individual believers. The first arose when the pastors or presbyters of a number of different congregations met together in an assembly, and agreed that they and their flocks would henceforth be bound by the

A Companion to Hobbes, First Edition. Edited by Marcus P. Adams.

assembly's decisions, thus creating new duties unmentioned in the original Christian message. Two further knots were imposed when bishops took power over the assemblies of presbyters, and then the pope seized authority over bishops. Hobbes welcomed the later untying of the knots, pointing out that in England the pope had lost power in the time of Queen Elizabeth, while the bishops and Presbyterians had been deprived of their authority much more recently (Hobbes 2012, 1114; 1651, 384–5). Tuck argues that this passage about the knots is "in blatant support of religious toleration" (Tuck 2016, 498).

When Hobbes talked about the tying and untying of the knots, he was evidently discussing things that had been done by (and later to) churchmen – presbyters or Presbyterians, the bishops and Episcopalians, and the pope and Catholics. But when scholars contend that Hobbes opposed or severely limited toleration they generally discuss his views on the power of the state. What follows surveys the case for and against the idea of the tolerant Hobbes, beginning with his views on the clergy, and the historical context of those views, especially in the debates on church–state relations that preoccupied his English contemporaries. As we shall see, he favored a large degree of liberty in religious matters, though empowering the sovereign to restrict freedom of action when the security of the state required such a course. In what follows, we shall concentrate on *Leviathan*. On Hobbes's own later account (*Answer to Bramhall*; EW IV.355), there was no sovereign or church in England when he wrote *Leviathan*. He was therefore free to write what he pleased. But when he penned *De cive* and the *Elements of Law*, there was a sovereign and he had to tailor his remarks to accord with the sovereign's views, which may not have accorded precisely with his own ideas.

19.1 Sin and Godly Rule: Hobbes, Toleration, and the Clergy

The English Civil War, said Hobbes, began as a struggle between people who "disagreed in Politiques" but later developed into a contest "about the liberty of Religion" (Hobbes 2012, 278; 1651, 93). For a while it looked as though the Presbyterians would win the dispute, and impose their ideas of godly rule upon the population as a whole. Civil War between the King and parliament broke out in England in 1642, and in the following year parliament negotiated a treaty with the Scots, who sent them military aid in return for which they wanted the English to adopt a Presbyterian system of church government on the Scottish model. Parliament set up the Westminster Assembly of clerics and a few laymen to work out the details of a religious settlement. It sat from 1643, and duly endorsed Presbyterianism. Ultimately, that recommendation was not fully enforced. Some members of parliament had qualms about it. In 1647–1649 the New Model Army intervened against the Presbyterians, and untied Hobbes's third knot. Hobbes's later enemy John Wallis served as a secretary to the Assembly (Malcolm 1994, 1.313n9).

Enthusiasts for Presbyterianism commonly insisted that it was the divinely appointed form of church government. They claimed that pastors and elders had been instituted to rule over local congregations, and that synods or councils had authority over larger areas. The church, they said, was independent of the state. Church officers were empowered by God to discipline the laity, and use coercive means to turn them from sin and toward righteousness. The archetypal Scottish Presbyterian George Gillespie, who was a member of the Westminster Assembly, strongly urged the English to accept and enforce the "sin-searching, sin-discovering, and sin-censuring discipline" that already existed in Scotland (Gillespie 1646, 587). He insisted that "the Civil and Ecclesiastical powers" each derived its authority from God. "Both Civil Magistrates and Church Officers are Fathers and ought to be honoured and obeyed according to the fifth Commandment." Secular magistrates and church officials had governing power by divine appointment (Gillespie 1646, 184). In the case of the civil magistrate, power was to be exercised by legislation and physical coercion. Ecclesiastical officers, on the other hand, were to make rulings on religious doctrine and on the "such particulars" of the church's affairs as "are not determined in Scripture," and to employ "corrective discipline or censures to be exercised upon the scandalous and obstinate" (Gillespie 1646, 185–6).

The principal means by which church officers were to discipline sinners in the Presbyterian system was excommunication, in the form of suspension from the sacrament of the Lord's Supper or Eucharist (which was technically known as lesser excommunication). Gillespie was typical in arguing that "the Sacrament is not a converting, but a confirming and sealing Ordinance." In other words, taking the bread and wine did you good if you had already been converted to godliness, but not otherwise. This was "why prophane and scandalous persons are to be kept off from the Sacrament, and yet not from hearing the Word" (Gillespie 1646, 489). So it made sense to have sinners subjected to the preaching God's word, because hearing sermons was potentially very good for them, as it might convert them from sin to righteousness. But until they were in fact converted it would do them no good to receive the sacramental bread and wine. Indeed, "the admission of scandalous and notorious sinners to the Sacrament" "is a profanation or pollution of that Ordinance" (Gillespie 1646, 542). In short, people that church officers deemed wicked ought to be subjected to godly preaching, but forbidden from receiving the sacrament. In practice, this would mean that other members of the congregation would be aware of just who were the notorious sinners among their neighbors, and could shun them accordingly.

Presbyterians recommended a system in which "the censure of mens manners, was in the power of the Presbytery" and argued that "in the Christian Church" there "ought to be an Ecclesiastical Government distinct from the Civil" (Gillespie 1646, 284). They acknowledged the power of the secular magistrate over civil questions, but supplemented it with the extensive power of church officers over morals and doctrine. As S.R. Gardiner, the great Victorian liberal historian of the English Civil War put it, the Scottish Presbyterians "strove by means of church discipline, enforced in the most inquisitorial manner, to bring a whole population under the yoke of the moral law" and strictly to enforce doctrinal orthodoxy (Gardiner 1901, 1.226). In Presbyterian theory, the civil authorities enforced law, but it was the church that led the fight against sin.

In *Leviathan*, Hobbes adopted positions diametrically opposed to those of the Presbyterians on key points. He argued that a church and a commonwealth (or state) are one institution: "a Church, such a one as is capable to Command, to Judge, Absolve, Condemn, or do any other act, is the same thing with a Civil Common-wealth" (Hobbes 2012, 732; 1651, 248). "*Temporall* and *Spirituall* Government, are but two words," he proceeded, "brought into the world, to make men see double, and mistake their *Lawfull*

Soveraign" (Hobbes 2012, 732–4; 1651, 248). "There is," he declared, "no other Government in this life, neither of State, nor Religion, but Temporall; nor teaching of any doctrine, lawfull to any Subject, which the Governour both of the State, and of the Religion, forbiddeth to be taught." That governor was the "one chief Pastor," namely "the Civill Soveraign" (Hobbes 2012, 734; 1651, 248). So the Presbyterian contention that there are separate and independent secular and ecclesiastical jurisdictions was false, as was the notion that by divine right Presbyterian church officers held any power over the laity. After the Resurrection, he said, "the bodies of the faithful" will be "not onely Spirituall, but Eternall" (Hobbes 2012, 734; 1651, 248), but in this life there was no such thing as spiritual power.

Presbyterians argued that sinners should be disciplined by being suspended from receiving the sacrament of the Lord's Supper. In Hobbes's opinion, that sacrament was a commemoration of "our Blessed Saviours death upon the crosse." His death led to the salvation of people who believe he is Christ, and who strive to obey the law (Hobbes 2012, 648; 1651, 221). Failing to commemorate his death would not affect our prospects of salvation. So being suspended from the sacrament would provide no corrective discipline. Taking the bread and the wine would have no effect on us, and the same applied to not taking them.

Hobbes did talk about excommunication, by which he meant marking out Christians as sinners, whose company was to be avoided by the faithful (Hobbes 2012, 798; 1651, 276). He said that "the sentence of Excommunication, importeth an advice, not to keep company, nor so much as to eat with him that is Excommunicate." It followed that sovereigns could never be excommunicated, since the law of nature requires us to keep company with them when they require it. Nor can people depart from the sovereign's dominion "without his leave; much lesse (if he call them to that honour,) refuse to eat with him" (Hobbes 2012, 804; 1651, 278). Excommunication, Hobbes argued, would be pointless against non-believers, who held non-Christian opinions, but might work to improve the conduct of some errant Christians. We saw that Gillespie contended that "the censure of mens manners" (Gillespie 1646, 284) was a key part of the godly discipline that he wanted to see enforced in England. Hobbes said that people who claimed to be Christians could fall into evil ways. A true Christian "beleeveth Jesus to be the Christ" and strives to obey the law. But a hypocrite might perform actions that deviated from "the rule of Manners." In Gillespie's theory, the rule of manners was the moral code that the Presbyterian church authoritatively gleaned from Holy Scripture. Hobbes took a rather different approach, asserting that the law of the sovereign is the rule of manners. He stated that "the Church cannot judge of Manners but by externall Actions, which Actions can never bee unlawfull, but when they are against the Law of the Commonwealth" (Hobbes 2012, 804; 1651, 278).

Presbyterians affirmed that sin was a breach of moral rules and that it was subject to the jurisdiction of church officers. Civil laws, enforced by the secular authorities, were only a subset of the more extensive category of sin, which fell under the control of the church and not the state. Hobbes rejected such views. He held that "without Authority from the Civill Soveraign, to excommunicate any person" was "to take from him his Lawfull Liberty, that is, to usurpe an unlawfull Power over their Brethren."

"The Authors ... of this Darknesse in Religion," he declared, "are the Romane, and the Presbyterian Clergy" (Hobbes 2012, 1106; 1651, 382).

According to Hobbes, sin and lawbreaking were generally the same thing. "A *Sinne*," he said, "is not onely a Transgression of a Law, but also any Contempt of the Legislator." It consisted in committing acts or speaking words forbidden by law, or omitting what the law required, and also "in the *Intention*, or purpose to transgresse" (Hobbes 2012, 452; 1651, 151). Intentions as well as words and deeds could be sinful, if what was intended was illegal. But merely to imagine an event, without actually intending to bring it about, was not sinful in Hobbes's estimation. "To be delighted in the Imagination onely, of being possessed of another mans goods, servants, or wife, without any intention to take them from him by force, or fraud, is no breach of the Law, that sayth, *Thou shall not covet*." It was also fine to imagine or dream "of the death of him, from whose life he expecteth nothing but dammage, and displeasure" (Hobbes 2012, 452; 1651, 151). The Bible contained some material that might seem to constrict the actions of a freedom-loving person. However, Hobbes argued that Christ had not made any new laws, but just given advice (Hobbes 2012, 762–4; 1651, 262). Many of the precepts contained in the Bible were suggestions, not commands. For instance, St. Paul said "*Drink no longer water, but use a little wine for thy healths sake*," but this was a recommendation rather than a law (Hobbes 2012, 894; 1651, 309). The Bible, said Hobbes, was "there onely Law, where the Civill Soveraign hath made it so; and in other places but Counsell; which a man at his own perill, may without injustice refuse to obey' (Hobbes 2012, 932; 1651, 322).

In Hobbes's theory, then, no one except the sovereign has any authority over what we do or say in religious or in other matters (except our parents if we are children, and those parents are themselves likely to be the sovereign's subjects; Hobbes 2012, 526–8; 1651, 178). People in all states enjoy liberties that "depend on the Silence of the Law." So liberties vary in accordance with changes in the law. But "where the Soveraign has prescribed no rule, there the Subject hath the Liberty to do, or forbeare, according to his own discretion" (Hobbes 2012, 340; 1651, 113). No one apart from the sovereign has any power whatsoever to order or forbid us to do or say anything. Clerics, teachers, or others might try to shape our conduct, and dissuade us from error, but we are free to ignore them. The extent of our liberty reflects the extent of the law. In modern times the number of laws in force is enormous. In 1667, a volume was published in London entitled *A Collection of all the Statutes at Large, now in force* (Anon 1667). It included all the acts of parliament passed since 1640. The text ran to a mere 456 pages. The English state in Hobbes's time was small and meagerly financed. Hobbes noted that clerics were commonly funded by tithes, which were a tenth of the incomes of the laity to whom they catered. An ancient King of Athens, he remarked, had defrayed all public expenses by taking in taxes amounting to just one-twentieth of his subjects' earnings, and nevertheless had been "esteemeed a tyrant" (Hobbes 2012, 964; 1651, 336).

Of course, government could be small and cheap, but still intolerant. So far, we have seen that Hobbes protected individual freedom from the clergy, and, indeed, from everyone other than the sovereign. But what safeguards did people have against a sovereign or state determined to persecute?

19.2 The State and Religious Liberty: Belief

The purpose of the state, in Hobbes's theory, was to secure its members' welfare. He argued that this can be achieved only if there is an absolute sovereign in charge. The sovereign, as we have seen, had authority in ecclesiastical as well as civil matters. Christian sovereigns "oblige themselves (by their Baptisme) to teach the Doctrine of Christ" (Hobbes 2012, 882; 1651, 305). The only "Article of Faith, which the Scripture maketh simply Necessary to Salvation, is this, that JESVS IS THE CHRIST" (Hobbes 2012, 938; 1651, 324), or the King who will reign with God eternally over the Jews and other believers. Christians were also bound to obey – or at least seriously to endeavor to obey – God's laws, which "are none but the Laws of Nature, whereof the principall is, that we should not violate our Faith, that is, a commandement to obey our Civill Soveraigns, which wee constituted over us, by mutuall pact one with another" (Hobbes 2012, 932; 1651, 322).

According to Hobbes, the Bible says that we will be saved if we obey the law and have faith in Christ. He held that sovereigns possess the power to enforce the laws, but not to compel us to have beliefs. Addressing the question of what would happen if the state forbade "us to believe in Christ," he replied that "such forbidding is of no effect; because Beleef, and Unbeleef never follow mens Commands." "Faith," he declared, "is a gift of God, which Man can neither give, nor take away by promise of rewards, or menaces of torture" (Hobbes 2012, 784; 1651, 271). However, if the sovereign commands us to say that we do not believe in Christ, we must obey even if we do in fact believe in him. In this case, the act of expressing disbelief is the sovereign's, not the obedient subject's: "whatsoever a Subject ... is compelled to in obedience to his Soveraign, and doth it not in order to his Own mind., but in order to the laws of his country, that action is not his, but his Soveraigns" (Hobbes 2012, 784; 1651, 271).

In fact, Hobbes argued, the sovereign ought not to pry into people's beliefs. Discussing the false philosophy of the Scholastics, he noted that they extend

> the power of the Law, which is the Rule of Actions onely, to the very Thoughts, and Consciences of men, by Examination, and *Inquisition* of what they Hold, notwithstanding the Conformity of their Speech and Actions: By which, men are either punished for answering the truth of their thoughts, or constrained to answer an untruth for fear of punishment. (Hobbes 2012, 1096; 1651, 378)

The state was empowered to promote the safety and welfare of the public by enforcing the laws, which concerned outward actions. It had no authority to poke its nose into private beliefs. True, a magistrate can ask someone he is thinking of appointing to a teaching position whether he is willing to teach certain doctrines, and if he is not may refuse to appoint him. But "to force him to accuse himselfe of Opinions, when his Actions are not by Law forbidden, is against the Law of Nature" (Hobbes 2012, 1096; 1651, 378).

Punishments and rewards, Hobbes argued, have the effect of shaping our wills, so that we avoid illegal actions in the future, and perform praiseworthy ones. But beliefs were not subject to the will: "As for the inward *thought*, and *belief* of men, which humane Governours can take no notice of, (for God onely knoweth the heart) they are not voluntary, nor the effect of the laws, but of the unrevealed Will, and of the power of God; and consequently fall not under obligation" (Hobbes 2012, 738; 1651, 249–50). However, beliefs are affected by teaching, and the sovereign is in charge of education. The reason why people tended to believe the Christian message in Christian countries was that they had been taught it there: "in Christian Common-wealths they are taught it from their infancy; and in other places they are taught otherwise." True, not everyone ended up believing what they had been taught, and Hobbes explained this by arguing that "Faith is the gift of God, and hee giveth it to whom he will," though normally this happens through the mechanism of teaching (Hobbes 2012, 936; 1651, 324). But it was still the case that beliefs are in general profoundly influenced by education, and Hobbes placed education under the sovereign's control. His theory appears at first to leave individuals free from the sovereign's intervention in matters of religious belief (if not practice) but on closer inspection he arguably grants the state a substantial role in the formation of our thinking. David Wootton sees him as advocating "a politics of censorship and brainwashing" (at least in *Behemoth*) (Wootton 1997, 242). Gary Remer similarly speculates on "whether Hobbes would have permitted inquisitions, had he been aware of the effectiveness of 'brainwashing"' (Remer 1992, 31n117).

But the beliefs on religious matters that Hobbes wanted Christian sovereigns to encourage were remarkably few. In fact, there was only one – namely that Jesus is the Christ. The state could order the teaching of other doctrines and erroneously claim that we need to believe them if we are to be saved. But this was not what Hobbes recommended, though he implied that it in fact happened – for example, in Catholic countries (Hobbes 2012, 868; 1651, 300). The claim that Jesus is the Christ cannot be proved or disproved, since it is a matter of faith or belief (which rely on our trust in other people: Hobbes 2012, 100; 1651, 31), and not on demonstrable knowledge. A sovereign who believed it, and who tried to teach it to his subjects, would be fulfilling the duty to promote their welfare. This would arguably not limit their freedom in any drastic fashion, unless he introduced brainwashing or similar techniques to force belief. It is unclear that God (on Hobbes's reading of the Bible) would have accepted coerced or brainwashed faith as his own gift, or the effect of his unrevealed will and power.

In addition to believing that Jesus is the Christ, said Hobbes, we also need to obey the law. This, he argued, was part of the Christian message. It was also made clear by natural law, and was demonstrated at length by Hobbes in his political writings – to this own satisfaction, at least. Christianity did not add any new duties to the obligations that the law of nature gave subjects toward their sovereigns. But it did add a new incentive to obey them – namely that by doing so we could obtain salvation, provided that we also believed that Jesus was the Christ. In his discussion of the foundation of new commonwealths among non-Christians, Hobbes stated that their "first Founders, and Legislators" "have had a care, to make it believed, that the same things were displeasing to the Gods, which were forbidden by the Lawes" (Hobbes 2012, 176–8; 1651, 57). Among non-Christians as well as Christians, then, the state exploited religious beliefs to encourage obedience.

In non-Christian commonwealths, legislators tried to "imprint" in the people's minds the divine origins of the "precepts which they gave concerning Religion" (Hobbes 2012, 176; 1651, 57). In Christian countries, too, the ordinary people were susceptible to persuasion by those in authority. Indeed, Hobbes declared, "the Common-peoples minds" "are like clean paper, fit to receive whatsoever by Publique Authority shall be imprinted in them" (Hobbes 2012, 524; 1651, 176; a valuable discussion of Hobbes's use of the metaphor of imprinting is in Bejan 2018). So ordinary people could easily be propagandized into accepting things that the authorities found it convenient for them to believe, however unfounded they in fact were. In this way "millions of men" had been made to "believe, that the same Body may be in innumerable places, at one and the same time, which is against Reason" – but which was regarded as true by Catholics who (in their doctrine of transubstantiation) endorsed the idea of the real presence of Christ's body and blood in the bread and the wine during the sacrament of the Lord's Supper. Imprinting this kind of belief upon impressionable minds by appealing to authority might not quite be brainwashing, but it was not wholly different from that activity. It was also something of which Hobbes heartily disapproved.

Hobbes argued that if people could be persuaded of things that were contrary to reason, they could much more readily be brought to believe things that were "so consonant to Reason, that any unprejudicated man, needs no more to learn it, than to hear it" – as were the principles he himself put forward in *Leviathan* (Hobbes 2012, 524; 1651, 177). This applied at least to the common people, though not so much perhaps to "Potent men" who had difficulty digesting "any thing that setteth up a Power to bridle their affections" and so were disinclined to favor absolute sovereignty, nor to "Learned men" who were unhappy with "any thing that discovereth their errours, and thereby lesseneth their Authority" (Hobbes 2012, 524; 1651, 176). The learned among the clergy had acted especially perniciously in stifling philosophical and scientific progress from ancient times to the condemnation of Galileo. The last two parts of *Leviathan* had a great deal to say – and to condemn – about the ways in which greedy and ambitious clerics had undermined the truth by introducing false beliefs concerning religion and the church.

Hobbes recorded that the ancient Romans "made no scruple of tollerating any Religion whatsoever in the City of *Rome* it selfe; unlesse it had somthing in it, that could not consist with their Civill Government" (Hobbes 2012, 178; 1651, 57). It has been suggested that he "applauded the model of the Romans" in this passage, and that like them he favored granting a wide measure of toleration (Champion 2006, 233). We have seen that he recommended that sovereigns take no action to discover or discipline beliefs. But did he allow liberty of *action* in religious matters?

19.3 The State and Religious Liberty: Action

In Hobbes's day the main religious groups to be found in the lands where he lived – England and France, with a few excursions to neighboring countries – were Protestant and Catholic Christians. Jews were officially readmitted to England in 1656, after a long expulsion. Muslims were rarely seen but well-known, especially those who lived in the Ottoman or Turkish Empire. In *Leviathan* Hobbes observed that "where the Popes Ecclesiasticall power is entirely received, Jewes, Turkes, and Gentiles, are in the Roman Church tolerated in their Religion, as farre forth, as in the exercise and profession thereof they offend not against the civill power." But "in a Christian, though a stranger, not to be of the Roman Religion, is Capitall; because the Pope pretendeth that all

Christians are his Subjects" (Hobbes 2012, 964–6; 1651, 336–67). In other words, where the pope ruled, it was fine to practice your religion as a Turk, Jew, or some other variety of non-Christian (Gentile), provided that you did not break laws on civil matters. But it was a capital offense to profess non-Catholic Christianity. Hobbes criticized this situation not because it was too tolerant – in granting religious freedom to Jews and Turks – but because it was not tolerant enough – since it persecuted Christians who were not Catholic. It was, he said, against the law of nations (which was the same as the law of nature: Hobbes 2012, 552; 1651, 185) for the pope to persecute Jews or Turks, and at least "as much ... or rather more" against it to persecute fellow-Christians (Hobbes 2012, 966; 1651, 336–7).

So Hobbes regarded toleration of non-Christians as compatible with natural law. Of course, the sovereign might command the Turk to profess belief in Christ. As we saw, if the Turk obeyed, the act would be the sovereign's, not the Turk's (in the discussion of the state, religious liberty and belief above, we noted that Hobbes said that "whatsoever a Subject ... is compelled to in obedience to his Soveraign ... that action is not his, but his Soveraigns" (Hobbes 2012, 784; 1651, 271). He addressed the question of what should happen if a Christian sovereign required a subject who was "inwardly in his heart of the Mahometan Religion" to "bee present at the divine service of the Christian Church, and that on pain of death." In this case, it made sense to argue that the subject "ought to obey that command of his lawfull Prince." To claim that "he ought rather to suffer death" was in effect to authorize "all private men, to disobey their Princes, in maintenance of their Religion, true, or false" (Hobbes 2012, 786; 1651, 271). If we permit subjects to refuse to comply with the state's orders whenever they happen to think those orders conflict with their own religious views, we may license wide disobedience and unleash anarchy.

Many English Protestant supporters of toleration drew the line at tolerating Roman Catholicism. John Milton wanted "toleration for all Protestant sects, whatever their aberrations" but "would have prohibited Roman Catholics from exercise of their conscience" by celebrating mass even "in private homes" (Wolfe 1961, 834). Oliver Cromwell expressed general support for freedom of conscience, but added that "if by liberty of conscience, you mean liberty to exercise the Mass, I judge it best to use plain dealing, and to let you know, Where the Parliament of England have power, *that* will not be allowed of' (quoted in Carlin 1996, 216). John Locke denied Catholics toleration on the grounds that they paid allegiance to a foreign power (Horton and Mendus 1991, 46). Hobbes, by contrast, permitted the sovereign to delegate the management of ecclesiastical affairs to the pope. Sovereigns, he said, "may (as many Christian Kings now doe) commit the government of their Subjects in matters of Religion to the Pope," though in this case the pope exercises power in subordination to the civil sovereign (Hobbes 2012, 866; 1651, 300).

Of course, much of the second half of *Leviathan* was taken up with the refutation of the ideas of Cardinal Bellarmine and some other Catholics on the powers of the pope over sovereigns, and of the misguided teachings of ambitious clerics that served to boost their wealth and power while obscuring the truth in science and philosophy. Hobbes vigorously rejected such ideas. But he was happy enough with an arrangement whereby the secular authorities retained sovereignty but permitted the pope and the Catholic clergy to have the everyday running of the church under supervision – an arrangement that the secular power could, of course, end whenever it pleased. This was arguably a reasonable description of the way things worked in France, where *Leviathan* was written. There, Gallican thinkers affirmed the king's sovereignty and rejected the claims of Bellarmine, but Catholicism was the state religion, the Protestant Huguenots were tolerated, and some of Hobbes's Catholic friends, such as Mersenne and Gassendi, were at the forefront of innovatory scientific and philosophical research.

Where Catholics were in charge of the church, Catholic ceremonies were used in church services, and Catholic doctrines were taught. People who were commanded by the sovereign to use Catholic ceremonies were obliged to do so. Some of the Catholic doctrines, such as transubstantiation, were (in Hobbes's view) contrary to reason, and it would make no sense for anyone who recognized this to believe them. Irrational doctrines might be based on misinterpretations of the Bible. Hobbes held that the Bible contained nothing contrary to reason, but that there were passages in it which were "above Reason." In these cases we should not try to understand them – or to sift out of them "a Philosophicall truth by Logick" – but instead simply swallow them whole, like pills for the sick (Hobbes 2012, 576–8; 1651, 195). The Bible, on Hobbes's account, tells us that the one belief we must have if we are to be saved is that Jesus is the Christ. The sovereign might "draw some false consequences" from this, or (and here Hobbes alluded to I Corinthians 3: 12) "make some superstructions of Hay, or Stubble, and command the teaching of the same." So sovereigns could order the teaching of transubstantiation, as they did in Catholic countries. They might be mistaken in doing this, but they and not their subjects, had the authority to decide what should be taught. "Christian Kings may erre in deducing a Consequence, but who shall Judge?" It was not for "any man" to judge "but he that is appointed thereto by the Church, that is, by the Civill Soveraign that representeth it." Subjects were to obey (Hobbes 2012, 952; 1651, 330), but did not need to believe in transubstantiation or any other non-essential doctrine.

In the early Christian period, said Hobbes, practice ran strongly against "the Casting out of the Church faithfull men, such as beleeved the foundation, onely for a singular superstructure of their own, proceeding perhaps from a good & pious conscience." The rule in those times had been that pastors should not "make new Articles of Faith, by determining every small controversie, which oblige men to a needlesse burthen of Conscience, or provoke them to break the union of the Church" (Hobbes 2012, 802; 1651, 277–8). In other words, deviations on small points had then commonly been tolerated. So people had then been free to express – and not merely to believe – deviant viewpoints on minor matters concerning the Christian religion. Mere unexpressed belief would not have led to controversies, however small. The early Christians, then accepted the foundation – the belief that Jesus was the Christ – but felt free to discuss other points of religion. There is little reason to suppose that Hobbes held that modern Christians should be any less free to debate such questions now than their ancestors were then, provided that in doing so they obeyed the law. Christian sovereigns had a duty to provide for the teaching of their subjects on the fundamentals of Christianity. Additionally, sovereigns in general had an obligation to manage education more broadly, and "by good Lawes to encourage men to the study" of "the Sciences Mathematicall" in particular (Hobbes 2012, 574; 1651, 193). The state, Hobbes argued, ought also to arrange for the education of the people in their duties to the sovereign, and assemble them so that they can publicly worship God. To what extent did the requirement for public worship undermine religious liberty?

19.4 Public Worship, the Untying of the Knots, and Religious Liberty

Hobbes contended that "there is a *Publique*, and a *Private* Worship" (Hobbes 2012, 564; 1651, 189). He argued that "seeing a Common-wealth is but one Person, it ought also to exhibite to God but one Worship; which then it doth, when it commandeth it to be exhibited by Private men, Publiquely." So private individuals should be assembled in public places to worship. There they should all worship God in a single, uniform way: "And this is Publique Worship; the property whereof, is to be *Uniforme*" (Hobbes 2012, 570; 1651, 192). The precept that states should establish the uniform, public worship of God stemmed, in his opinion, from reason and nature. But they did not cease to apply once sovereigns became Christian.

Another task for the sovereign was to organize the instruction of subjects in their civil obligations. The state, claimed Hobbes, should set aside "some certain times" for the people to "attend those that are appointed to instruct them." After "prayers and praises given to God, the Soveraign of Soveraigns," they should "hear those their Duties told them, and the Positive Lawes, such as generally concern them all, read and expounded" (Hobbes 2012, 528; 1651, 178). It is not clear whether Hobbes thought that the same people who took charge of praising God should also manage the instruction of the people. Perhaps he would have given the former job to clerics, and the latter to scholars trained at the universities in the teachings of *Leviathan*. Or perhaps he believed that church services could usefully be combined with civics lessons, all managed by pastors.

As we have seen, toward the end of *Leviathan* Hobbes argued that in early Christian times the clergy had reduced the liberties of believers by imposing new obligations upon them. At first, individuals had been free to believe what private conscience prompted and to do what public conscience required. Their "Words and Actions" were "subject to none but the Civil Power" (Hobbes 2012, 1114; 1651, 384). Hobbes held that in our actions we must follow the sovereign's decree; it is the "publique Conscience" by which we have "already undertaken to be guided" in joining the commonwealth (Hobbes 2012, 502; 1651, 169; Hobbes's ideas on conscience are discussed in Hanin 2012). Later, pastors associated together in assemblies and agreed to enforce the decrees of those bodies, though neither the people nor the civil magistrate had consented to that. This tied "the first knot" on the people's liberty. Then the presbyters of leading cities took authority over other pastors (and styled themselves bishops), thus tying the second knot. The third knot came into being when the pope took power from the bishops. Then the three knots were untied, culminating in the overthrow of Presbyterianism by the English parliamentarian army in 1647–1649. One consequence was the full restoration of civil power over church affairs. Another was that individual congregations again became autonomous, as they had been in ancient times, and Hobbes welcomed this as "perhaps the best" arrangement, though with some reservations.

For most of Hobbes's lifetime, English subjects were by law required to worship regularly at their local parish churches. But on September 27, 1650 parliament passed

"An Act for the Repeal of several Clauses in Statutes imposing Penalties for not coming to Church" (Firth and Rait 1911, 3:423–5). This repealed penalties for infringing various earlier laws on church attendance (Firth and Rait 1911, 423–4) but stipulated that on Sundays and days of public thanksgiving everyone had to "resort to some publique place where the Service and Worship of God is exercised" or to "be present at some other place in the practice of some Religious Duty" such as prayer, preaching, or reading Scriptures (Firth and Rait 1911, 425). So people had a choice on how to spend their Sundays. They could, as Hobbes said, opt to follow any of various preachers or pastors, "every man as he liketh best" (Hobbes 2012, 1116; 1651, 385). Indeed, there was no reason to select preachers of any particular order or training – such as (say) ordained, university educated ministers. It would be wrong, he said, to "impropriate the Preaching of the Gospell to one certain Order of men, where the Laws have left it free" and he spelled out that this meant that if "the State give me leave to preach, or teach; that is, if it forbid me not, no man can forbid me" (Hobbes 2012, 1098; 1651, 378). On any given Sunday, Hobbes would therefore arguably have been entitled to preach to himself.

When discussing the dissolution of the third knot, Hobbes remarked that it was "perhaps best" but added that this would be so only if it occurred "without contention" (Hobbes 2012, 1116; 1651, 385). Jon Parkin notes that it is "possible that Hobbes' claim here is satirical (on the grounds that the practical chances of such pluralism existing without contention are zero)" but concludes that Hobbes in this passage was defending "extensive prudential toleration" though "only with the precondition that the beliefs so permitted are absolutely consistent with the persistence of the state" (Parkin 2013, 620). Using religion as an excuse for disobeying the sovereign was never permissible.

It is not wholly clear whether Hobbes saw the autonomous congregations that emerged after the demise of Presbyterianism as institutions for public or for private worship (for a discussion of Hobbes's ideas on toleration, which usefully emphasizes the public-private distinction, see Abizadeh 2013). In either case, the sovereign could command or forbid what might be said and done in them, and their members would be bound to obey. He claimed that the three knots had reduced "Christian Liberty" and that their untying served to revive the practice of "the primitive Christians," so it is evident that he had in mind groups that consisted of Christians (Hobbes 2012, 1114–16; 1651, 384–5). But it is hard to see why his arguments would not apply to other types of association. On Hobbes's principles, citizens can surely establish "private churches ... just as they can create private businesses and football clubs" (Olsthoorn 2018, 23). It is difficult to see why a Hobbesian sovereign would not similarly permit the formation of private non-Christian churches, and tolerate them provided that they did not break the law or threaten the security of the state.

19.5 Conclusion

Scholars debate whether Hobbes was a supporter or an opponent of religious toleration. He advocated absolute sovereignty and state control of education, and some have linked this to intolerant authoritarianism. Others view him as an adherent of toleration. This chapter surveys the case for both claims, concluding that in many but not all ways he favored toleration.

Hobbes granted the sovereign in every state absolute power. Sovereigns, he held, could make and enforce laws on all matters, including religion. A sovereign who believed that the public good required the prohibition of certain religious activities or groups would be fully justified in acting accordingly. No religious group had a permanent and inalienable right to toleration by the state. In Hobbes's day, the most vocal opponents of religious toleration were religious denominations. In the 1640s, Presbyterian clerics asserted authority over moral and religious matters in England, and argued that their powers were independent of the state. Hobbes rejected all such claims. He contended that the state alone was empowered to control education and religious actions. Sovereigns, he said, ought not to pry into private beliefs, and he permitted religious actions and organizations that did not break the law or threaten state security.

References

Abizadeh, Arash 2013. "Publicity, Privacy, and Religious Toleration in Hobbes's *Leviathan*." *Modern Intellectual History* 10: 261–91. DOI:10.1017/S1479244313000012

Anon. 1667. *A Collection of All the Statutes at Large, Now in Force*. London, in the Savoy: English & Welsh Royal (or State) Printers.

Bejan, Teresa M. 2016. "Difference without Disagreement: Rethinking Hobbes on 'Independency' and Toleration." *The Review of Politics* 78: 1–25. DOI:10.1017/S0034670515000856.

Bejan, Teresa M. 2018. "First Impressions: Hobbes on Religion, Education, and the Metaphor of Imprinting." In *Hobbes on Politics and Religion*, edited by Laurens van Apeldoorn and Robin Douglass, 45–62. Oxford: Oxford University Press. DOI:10.1093/oso/9780198803409.003.0004.

Carlin, Norah 1996. "Toleration for Catholics in the Puritan Revolution." In *Tolerance and Intolerance in the European Reformation*, edited by Ole Peter Grell and Bob Scribner, 216–30. Cambridge: Cambridge University Press.

Champion, Justin A. I. 2006. "*An Historical Narration Concerning Heresie*: Thomas Hobbes, Thomas Barlow, and the Restoration Debate over 'Heresy'." In *Heresy, Literature, and Politics in Early Modern English Culture*, edited by David Loewenstein and John Marshall, 221–53. Cambridge: Cambridge University Press.

Collins, Jeffrey 2007. *The Allegiance of Thomas Hobbes*. Oxford: Oxford University Press.

Curley, Edwin 2007. "Hobbes and the Cause of Religious Toleration." In *The Cambridge Companion to Hobbes's Leviathan*, edited by Patricia Springborg, 309–34. Cambridge: Cambridge University Press. DOI:10.1017/CCOL0521836670.014.

Firth, Charles H. and Robert S. Rait eds. 1911. *Acts and Ordinances of the Interregnum*. 3 vols. London: His Majesty's Stationery Office.

Gardiner, Samuel Rawson 1901. *History of the Great Civil War 1642–1649*, 4 vols. London: Longmans, Green, and Co.

Gillespie, George 1646. *Aarons Rod Blossoming, Or, the Divine Ordinance of Church-government Vindicated*. London: E.G. for Richard Whitaker.

Hanin, Mark 2012. "Thomas Hobbes's Theory of Conscience." *History of Political Thought* 33: 55–85.

Hobbes, Thomas. 1839–1845. *The English Works of Thomas Hobbes*, 11 vols., edited by Sir William Molesworth. London: John Bohn. Cited as EW.

Hobbes, Thomas. 2012. *Leviathan*, 3 vols., edited by Noel Malcolm. Oxford: Clarendon Press. [First published 1651.]

Horton, John and Susan Mendus eds. 1991. *John Locke: A Letter Concerning Toleration in Focus*. London: Routledge.

Kabala, Boleslaw Z. 2019. "The Return of the Intolerant Hobbes." *History of European Ideas* 45: 785–802. DOI:10.1080/01916599.2019.1628581.

Lessay, Franck 2018. "Tolerance as a Dimension of Hobbes's Absolutism." In *Hobbes on Politics and Religion*, edited by Laurens van Apeldoorn and Robin Douglass, 63–78. Oxford: Oxford University Press. DOI:10.1093/oso/9780198803409.003.0005.

Malcolm, Noel. 1994. The Clarendon Edition of the Works of Thomas Hobbes, Vol. 6: *The Correspondence, Vol. 1: 1622–1659*. Oxford: Clarendon Press.

Olsthoorn, Johan 2018. "The Theocratic Leviathan: Hobbes's Arguments for the Identity of Church and State." In *Hobbes on Politics and Religion*, edited by Laurens van Apeldoorn and Robin Douglass, 10–28. Oxford: Oxford University Press. DOI:10.1093/oso/9780198803409.003.0002.

Owen, Judd. 2005. "The Tolerant *Leviathan:* Hobbes and the Paradox of Liberalism." *Polity* 37: 130–48. DOI:10.1057/palgrave.polity.2300004.

Parkin, Jon 2013. "Toleration." In *The Oxford Handbook of British Seventeenth Century Philosophy*, edited by Peter Anstey, 609–25. Oxford: Oxford University Press. DOI:10.1093/oxfordhb/9780199549993.913.0027.

Remer, Gary 1992. "Hobbes, the Rhetorical Tradition, and Toleration." *The Review of Politics* 54: 5–33. DOI:10.1017/S0034670500017162.

Ryan, Alan 1983. "Hobbes, Toleration and the Inner Life." In *The Nature of Political Theory*, edited by David Miller and Larry Seidentop, 197–218. Oxford: Clarendon Press, 1983.

Ryan, Alan 1988. "A More Tolerant Hobbes." In *Justifying Toleration*, edited by Susan Mendus, 37–60. Cambridge: Cambridge University Press. DOI:10.1017/CBO9780511735295.004.

Sreedhar, Susanne 2017. "Rethinking Hobbes and Locke on Toleration." In *Politics, Religion and Political Theology*, edited by C. Allen Speight and Michael Zank, 39–56. Boston Studies in Philosophy, Religion and Public Life, volume 6, Dordrecht: Springer.

Tralau, Johan 2011. "Hobbes Contra Liberty of Conscience." *Political Theory* 39: 58–84. DOI:10.1177/0090591710386698.

Tuck, Richard 1990. "Hobbes and Locke on Toleration." In *Thomas Hobbes and Political Theory*, edited by Mary G. Dietz, 153–71. Lawrence: University Press of Kansas.

Tuck, Richard 2016. "Hobbes, Conscience, and Christianity." In *The Oxford Handbook of Hobbes*, edited by Aloysius P. Martinich and Kinch Hoekstra, 481–500. Oxford: Oxford University Press. DOI:10.1093/oxfordhb/9780199791941.013.29.

Wolfe, Don M. 1961. "Limits of Miltonic Toleration." *The Journal of English and Germanic Philology* 60 (4): 834–46.

Wootton, David 1997. "Thomas Hobbes's Machiavellian Moments." In *The Historical Imagination in Early Modern Britain. History, Rhetoric, and Fiction, 1500–1800*, edited by Donald R. Kelley and David Harris Sacks, 210–42. Cambridge: Woodrow Wilson Center Press and Cambridge University Press. DOI:10.1017/CBO9780511721052.011.

20

Hobbes, Rome's Enemy

FRANCK LESSAY

The exceptional length of *Leviathan*'s chapter 42, "Of Power Ecclesiastical," is in itself a striking feature. The space devoted to a critique of Cardinal Bellarmine's thought in that chapter may also appear puzzling. The Roman prelate (1542–1621) had died thirty years before the publication of *Leviathan*. The topics dealt with by Hobbes in his commentaries, both theological and ecclesiological, did not seem directly related to the immediate context of the Interregnum period. The importance of the Catholic community in the events of the time was no longer such as to justify, apparently, that lengthy attack against a Jesuit's conceptions, however prestigious the theologian Hobbes chose to confront. The fact remains that Bellarmine's writings were yet to inspire Catholic doctrines for several centuries (they still do to a large extent). The Church of Rome's lasting and at times virulent hostility to Hobbes's thinking also suggests that the controversy in which the English philosopher engaged against Bellarmine, in support of his own political theory, touched upon key aspects of Catholic (and possibly Christian) politics. It is this chapter's hypothesis that the opposition between those two philosophies of the State in its relation to religion might shed some additional light on the situation of Hobbes in the field.

20.1 Bellarmine as Hobbes's Target

The choice of Bellarmine as a target could be explained by the Cardinal's prominence among late Renaissance Catholic theologians.[1] It had another advantage which was that the criticisms aimed at Bellarmine could apply to a wide range of the positions held by Anglicans. After all, Bishop John Bramhall, against whom Hobbes conducted a twenty-year long controversy (see the treatises *Of Liberty and Necessity*, *Questions Concerning Liberty, Necessity and Chance*, and *An Answer to a book Published by Dr. Bramhall, late Bishop of Derry called "The Catching of the Leviathan"*), claimed

A Companion to Hobbes, First Edition. Edited by Marcus P. Adams.

that Catholics err in no point necessary to salvation and that, to that extent, they "do not differ from us in fundamentals."[2] Moreover, the abundance of Bramhall's explicit and implicit references to Aquinas, Peter Lombard, and Saint Anselm (among other medieval authors) clearly evinced his indebtedness to scholastic literature, in which Bellarmine was steeped. Conversely, the heterodox theology defended by Hobbes had been condemned equally by Rome and Canterbury on several essential points, such as the corporeal nature of God and the soul, the mortality of the soul, the denial of Hell's eternal punishments, and the implicit rejection of the Trinity.

Bellarmine was a scholar of international reputation.[3] He was the author of *Institutiones Linguae Hebraicae* (1578), which Hobbes seems to quote approvingly about a Hebrew phrase in *An Answer to Bishop Bramhall's Book, called "The Catching of Leviathan"* (EW IV.317). He had taken an active part in the publication of the definitive version of the Vulgate (1592). His decisive interventions in the three great ideological crises of the early seventeenth century (on the Oath of Allegiance in England, the Interdict of Venice, and the assassination of Henri IV in France) and the enormous number of polemical books and pamphlets his pronouncements had sparked off had made him "the voice of Rome" in England and Europe at large (Springborg 1995, 516). As a student at Oxford and as tutor to two young gentlemen (William Cavendish, 1591–1628, and his son, also named William Cavendish, 1617–1684), who were educated at Cambridge, where "anti-Bellarmine lectures and sermons had been a staple for decades" (Rose 2015, 44), Hobbes was inevitably acquainted with the Cardinal's writings. Later, he had direct access to them in the rich Hardwick/Chatsworth Library, which was largely constituted for his benefit by his patrons, the Cavendish family (see Talaska 2014). The ring of his personal friends included several Catholic priests with whom years of fruitful intellectual exchanges, especially during his exile in France, could very well have increased his familiarity with Bellarmine's doctrines: Gassendi (1592–1655), Mersenne (1588–1648), and Thomas White (1592–1676) in particular.[4] His travels on the continent at different periods of his life, especially when he accompanied his pupils on their "grand tour," gave him many occasions of contacts with Catholic institutions and individuals, including Jesuits. It even appears that, together with William Cavendish, his second pupil in the Cavendish family, Hobbes had dinner at the Jesuits' English College in Rome in 1636 (Hobbes 1994, 805).

Apart from Bellarmine, Hobbes seldom mentions other members of the Society of Jesus or the Jesuits at large. He stigmatizes what he regards as Suarez's incomprehensible jargon in chapter 8 of *Leviathan* (through an allusion to his "first book, *Of the Concourse, Motion, and Help of God*"; 2012, 122; 1651, 147). He reiterates his criticism in *An Answer to Bishop Bramhall's Book, called "The Catching of Leviathan"*[5] and again in *Behemoth.*[6] In the latter book, he denounces the agitation entertained by Jesuits in the Catholic aristocracy under Elizabeth and in the early Jacobean period.[7] The *Dialogue of the Common Laws* contains another allusion to the Gunpowder Plot and the participation (although an indirect one) taken in the conspiracy by the Jesuit Henry Garnet.[8] Bellarmine is definitely Hobbes's primary target among Jesuits. Described as "the champion of the Papacy against all other Christian princes and states" (Hobbes 2012, 926; 1651, 609), he is repeatedly mentioned in *Leviathan's* chapter 42, and again, although more sparingly or allusively, in chapters 44 and 46, and in the Appendix to the Latin version of the treatise. Bellarmine's main work cited or referred to by Hobbes is taken from the *Tertia Controversia Generalis de Summo Pontifice*, first published at Ingolstadt in 1577 and later included in the first volume of the *Disputationes de Controversiis Christianae Fidei adversus hujus temporis Haereticos*, which went through several successive editions, also at Ingoldstadt, the first of which appeared in three volumes between 1581 and 1583.

Early in *Leviathan's* chapter 42, Hobbes observes that "Cardinal Bellarmine, in his third generall Controversie, hath handled a great many questions concerning the Ecclesiasticall Power of the Pope of Rome" (2012, 778; 1651, 524). Hence, probably, the length of that chapter, which can also be explained by Hobbes's determination to strike at the heart of the Jesuit's plea in defense of papacy and to leave none of its essential aspects untouched (and intact). The demonstration broadly follows the order in which Bellarmine's main arguments are presented and tends to assume a somewhat meandering course. Its contents can be reconstructed by distinguishing seven angles in Hobbes's attack.

1) **Church government**. Bellarmine examines the question of the form of government characterizing the Church. That, according to Hobbes, is a vain enterprise since all political regimes have one fundamental feature in common, which is that they are coercive (Hobbes 2012, 778; 1651, 525). As to the best form of government, supposedly a synthesis of the three basic *régimes*, which would precisely correspond to the Church, it is based on another illusion. Power is always identical in essence. Moreover, the present form of government is always preferable (Hobbes 2012, 868; 1651, 577).
2) **Church power**. The power of the Church results from her origin, which Bellarmine ascribes to the designation of Peter by Christ at her head. But that claim is wrong. All that is proved by Christ's word, "Thou art Peter, and upon this Rock I will build my Church" (Matthew 16:18), is that the Church has one single foundation, which is the article of faith that "[Jesus] was the Christ—all other articles requiring faith no otherwise than as founded on that" (Hobbes 2012, 870; 1651, 578). Peter was not made bishop of Rome by Christ. Neither did he transmit any authority thus acquired to supposed successors who later became popes. The first bishop of Rome was Constantine, who occupied that function as the first Christian emperor. Hobbes specifies: "emperor of the Roman Empire, not of all Christendom" (2012, 874; 1651, 580).
3) **Mission of the Church**. Contrary to Bellarmine's assertions, the only task assigned by Christ to the apostles and through them to the Church was to teach, in other words "a Power to proclaim the Kingdom of Christ, and to perswade men to submit themselves thereunto, and by precepts and good counsell, to teach them that have submitted, what they are to do, that they may be received into the Kingdom of God when it comes," so that "the Apostles, and other Ministers of the Gospel, are our Schoolmasters, and not our Commanders, and their Precepts not Laws, but wholesome Counsells" (Hobbes 2012, 780; 1651, 525). In short, "the Power of the Pope, though he were S. Peter, is neither Monarchy, nor hath any thing of *Archicall*, nor *Craticall*, but only of *Didacticall*; For God accepteth not a forced, but a willing obedience" (Hobbes 2012, 904; 1651, 596).

4) **Field of action**. The pope can hardly be described as an "ecclesiastical prince," enjoying as such the same power, although on a universal scale, as civil sovereigns. To the extent that the notion of "ecclesiastical princes" has any meaning, it applies to princes whose authority is restricted to the limits of their respective territories: "without those bounds, though they may be received for Doctors they cannot be acknowledged for Princes" (Hobbes 2012, 892; 1651, 589). Moreover, whatever the nature of the power popes exercise, it is one of Bellarmine's two "grosse errours" to claim that "all Christian Kings, Popes, Clergy, and all other Christian men, make but one Common-wealth: For it is evident that France is one Common-wealth, Spain another, and Venice a third, &c. And these consist of Christians; and therefore also are severall Bodies of Christians, that-is-to-say, severall Churches: And their severall Soveraigns Represent them, whereby they are capable of commanding and obeying, of doing and suffering, as a naturall man; which no Generall or Universall Church is, till it has a Representant; which it hath not on Earth" (Hobbes 2012, 914–916; 1651, 602). Given that situation, Hobbes writes sarcastically, it is in fact conceivable that civil sovereigns "(as many Christian Kings now doe) commit the government of their Subjects in matters of Religion to the Pope; but then the Pope is in that point subordinate to them" (Hobbes 2012, 866; 1651, 575).

5) **Modes of action (1), infallibility**. As proof of the supremacy that ought to be granted to the pope in matters of faith and manners, Bellarmine cites the infallibility of his judgments. If it were true, Hobbes replies, this proposition would make the pope "*the absolute Monarch of all Christians in the world*" (Hobbes 2012, 878; 1651, 582; emphasis original), implicitly an impossibility in the absence of a universal commonwealth. All the passages in Scripture alleged by Bellarmine fail to prove it. This is clear when one considers the two standard passages: "Thou art Peter, and upon this Rock I will build my Church" (as already argued) and "Feed my sheep" (John 21:16), "which contains no more than a Commission of Teaching" (Hobbes 2012, 882; 1651, 584). On that capital point, not surprisingly, Hobbes returns to a theme that he discusses several times in *Leviathan*. In the next chapter, chapter 43, he confirms that "there is nothing in the Scripture, from which can be inferred the Infallibility of the Church; much lesse of any particular Church; and least of all, the Infallibility of any particular man" (Hobbes 2012, 934; 1651, 613–614). In earlier chapters, he has repeatedly stated that only methodical reasoning can produce infallible assertions. That is why it is in science alone that infallibility can be found, as shown by arithmetic, which is "a certain and infallible Art" (Hobbes 2012, 66; 1651, 111). The same description applies to geometry, which possesses "infallible rules" (Hobbes 2012, 406; 1651, 308). Those are expressions of "that skill of proceeding upon generall, and infallible rules, called Science, which very few have, and but in few things" (Hobbes 2012, 188; 1651, 183).

6) **Modes of action (2), the indirect power**. A corollary of infallibility, the pope's indirect power in temporal matters was the subject of what came to be considered as Bellarmine's main doctrinal innovation, and a major source of his lasting international fame and influence in the Church of Rome down to the twentieth century.[9] It receives due critical treatment from Hobbes, who points out that

although Bellarmine's exposition of the theory starts from a denial that the pope claims a direct universal jurisdiction empowering him to interfere in the temporal affairs of all States, this apparent renunciation is only a skillful ploy designed to justify a so-called "indirect power" possessed of exactly the same effects as the direct one. Again sarcastically, Hobbes assumes Bellarmine's concession could hardly mean that the pope had acquired this new form of jurisdiction "by indirect means." What is once more at stake, according to Hobbes, is the basis and nature of the pope's power. The renunciation of a direct universal jurisdiction masks the admission that the pope does not detain "the Right of all Soveraigns [which] is derived originally from the consent of every one of those that are to be governed" (Hobbes 2012, 910; 1651, 599). The pope's claim to an indirect power has the same object as that of a direct one, although it is grounded on "a right given him by God (which he calleth *indirectly*) in his Assumption to the Papacy" (2012, 910; 1651, 599; emphasis original). The pope means (through his spokesman) that "such Temporall Judisdiction belongeth to him of Right, but that this Right is but a Consequence of his Pastoral Authority, the which he could not exercise unless he have the other with it: And therefore to the Pastoral Power (which he calls Spirituall) the Supreme Power Civill is necessarily annexed" (Hobbes 2012, 908; 1651, 598). It thus appears that "by what way soever he pretend, the Power is the same." The practical consequence is that "he may (if it bee granted to be his Right) depose Princes and States, as often as it is for the Salvation of Soules, that is, as often as he will" (Hobbes 2012; 1651, 910). In this, Hobbes remarks, Bellarmine just reiterates an old argument of the Roman Church, formally expressed in a decree adopted at the fourth council of Lateran under Pope Innocent the Third, in 1215, and illustrated through numerous papal decisions to depose European kings, a practice that had started even before that council, since Hobbes's list of examples includes Childéric III of France (improperly renamed Chilperique), who died in 755.

For reasons difficult to establish, Hobbes's list mentions Henry, King of Navarre, the future Henry IV of France, assassinated in 1610, but does not refer to the deposition of Queen Elizabeth of England by Pius V in the Bull *Regnans in Excelsis*, in 1570 (Hobbes 2012, 912; 1651, 600). However that may be, Hobbes concludes his short historical survey with a striking understatement ("I think there be few Princes that consider not this as Injust, and Inconvenient"; 2012, 912; 1651, 600) and gives a commentary that puts into relief two crucial and closely related points of his own political theory. First, sovereignty cannot be divided ("Men cannot serve two Masters"), a truth Bellarmine's doctrine of the indirect power tends to obfuscate in order to legitimize the Pope's unrestricted supremacy over all civil authorities. That is why kings ought to choose between "holding the Reins of Government wholly in their own hands," and "wholly delivering them into the hands of the Pope" (Hobbes 2012, 912; 1651, 600). Secondly, the analysis of Bellarmine's invention of a God-given indirect papal power confirms that the "distinction of Temporall and Spirituall Power is but words" (Hobbes 2012, 912; 1651, 600). Thus, it further illustrates what Hobbes had stated even more forcefully in a previous chapter of *Leviathan*, chapter 39, about the exclusively temporal nature of government, whoever is in charge of it, and (again) the absolute necessity of placing the commonwealth's supreme authority in the hands of a single sovereign:

> *Temporall* and *Spirituall* Government, are but two words brought into the world, to make men see double, and mistake their *Lawfull Soveraign*. It is true, that the bodies of the faithfull, after the Resurrection, shall be not only Spirituall, but Eternall; but in this life, they are grosse and corruptible. There is therefore no other Government in this life, neither of State, nor Religion, but Temporall; nor teaching of any doctrine, lawfull to any Subject, which the Governour both of the State, and of the Religion, forbiddeth to be taught: And that Governour must be one; or else there must needs follow Faction, and Civil War in the Common-wealth, between the Church and State; between *Spiritualists* and *Temporalists*; between the *Sword of Iustice* and the *Shield of Faith*; and (which is more) in every Christian mans own brest, between the *Christian*, and the *Man*.(2012, 732–734; 1651, 498–499)

7) **"Consolidation of the right politic and ecclesiastic."** The discussion of Bellarmine's papalist plea unsurprisingly proves the validity of Hobbes's political theory. Conducted as part of Hobbes's "endeavour to advance the civil power" (to quote *Leviathan*'s dedication to Francis Godolphin), it completes his demonstration by rational, scriptural, and historical arguments that "the Civill Soveraigne if a Christian, is head of the Church in his own Dominions," and leads to a conclusion that leaves no place to any degree of autonomy for the Church in the commonwealth, let alone to any form of preeminence over the sovereign:

> From this consolidation of the Right Politique, and Ecclesiastique in Christian Soveraigns, it is evident, they have all manner of Power over their Subjects, that can be given to man, for the government of mens externall actions, both in Policy, and Religion; and may make such Laws, as themselves shall judge fittest, for the government of their own Subjects, both as they are the Common-wealth, and as they are the Church: for both State, and Church are the same men. (Hobbes 2012, 864, 1651, 575)

Church and State being coextensive, and the temporal/spiritual distinction being declared meaningless (in keeping with Hobbes's materialism, which denied that the word "spirit" could refer to an incorporeal being), the justification of a sovereignty including the qualification of the sovereign as the commonwealth's "supreme pastor," invested with full powers of nomination and interpretation in the Church, and able to perform all pastoral functions by himself, received confirmation from the refutation of Bellarmine, while it helped strengthening it. Hobbes could legitimately write of that sovereign, in words strongly reminiscent of both the 1559 Elizabethan Act of Supremacy and the 37th of the Church of England's 39 Articles of Religion, adopted in 1571: "In Summe, he hath the Supreme Power in all causes, as well Ecclesiasticall, as Civill" (Hobbes 2012, 866; 1651, 576). Hobbes, however, defended a far more radical and diminutive view of the Church than his co-religionists did, and one proper to scandalize many if not all of them. The purely legalistic definition of the Church that underlay his critique of Bellarmine, as "a Congregation assembled, of professors of Christianity, whether their profession be true, or counterfeit" (Hobbes 2012, 730; 1651, 497), logically led (in a Hobbesian perspective) to the assertion that this congregation could not exist as such, that-is-to say "be taken for one Person," "without warrant from the civil sovereign" and unless it was subjected to the latter's control (Hobbes 2012, 732; 1651, 498). The Church was a civil institution, regardless of creed or faith; a Christian Church was one that happened to be composed of Christians. Ecclesiology appeared as a function in the theory of the State. One can hardly be surprised by Bishop Bramhall's protest, in *The Catching of Leviathan or the Great Whale,*[10] nor by the fact that the Church of Rome put *De cive* on the Index in 1654 and *Leviathan* in a second stage (in 1703), a major motive for the censors' condemnation being that Hobbes's ecclesiological doctrine, based on the principle "*una est Ecclesia et Civitas Christiana,*" disregarded the difference of essence between Church and State (see Baldini 2001).

From that viewpoint, Bellarmine embodied an ancient and constant Christian tradition (which may be why Hobbes attacked his doctrines). His political theology was aimed at three targets: the advocates of Venice at the time of the interdict (1606–1607), who defended the right of the Republic to restrict the papacy's jurisdiction in matters of faith and property;[11] James I of England (VI of Scotland) who had attempted to impose an Oath of Allegiance on his Catholic subjects, meant to oblige them to solemnly profess their loyalty to the King of Great Britain and their rejection of the pope's right to depose heretic sovereigns and absolve them of their duty of obedience (see Patterson 2000); the Gallicans who, in defense of the liberties of the French Church, challenged the pope's authority over their ecclesiastical institutions and clergy (see Bouwsma 1990; Colosimo 2019; Salmon 1987). That was the background to the interventions of European Jesuits in support of the pope's international role, as defined at the Council of Trent that had started in 1545 and ended, after several interruptions, in 1563 (see Höpfl 2004). Bellarmine and Francisco Suarez were two leading figures in that battle fought to defend an extensive conception of papal power, judged necessary to counter the rise of Protestantism. The indirect power stigmatized by Hobbes was a central element in Bellarmine's conceptual arsenal. It did not refer to a mode of acquisition or exercise of power, as conceded by Hobbes, but to the object of the pope's jurisdiction. Direct power concerned matters of faith, belief, or dogma. In that spiritual field, the pope possessed an unrestricted (and infallible) authority. In the temporal field, which naturally covered politics, the pope did not claim any supremacy, which would have meant a usurpation of the civil rulers' sovereignty. However, it had to be admitted that the boundary between spiritual and temporal was occasionally (*casu*) impossible to establish and that some temporal subjects (as in law or the treatment of heresies) spilled over into the spiritual. It was the pope's duty to determine whether such was the case and make the right decisions for the salvation of souls. These might include the deposition of incompetent, heretical or tyrannical kings whose action threatened their subjects' spiritual welfare (see Bourdin 2004; Murray 1948).

20.2 Papal Indirect Power between Nostalgia and Innovation

Some twentieth-century commentators have pointed out, long after Hobbes, what looked like a sleight of hand on the part of Bellarmine, enabling him to disguise a reaffirmation of the pope's limitless jurisdiction thanks to the rhetorical trick of an indirect power that implied an apparent renunciation of supremacy over civil rulers (see de Lubac 1932; Lecler 1944, 101–104; Murray 1948, 500–501). In that regard, several points deserve to be underlined.

As far as the practical effects of the indirect power are concerned, such as the right of deposition, they resulted from a jurisdiction that popes had claimed since the early Middle Ages. Hobbes rightly mentions, as recalled above, the fourth council of Lateran of 1215. A dogmatic pillar of the Church of Rome, the bull *Unam Sanctam* promulgated in 1302 by Pope Boniface VIII in the course of his conflict with the French King Philip the Fair (1268–1314), distinguished between the spiritual and the temporal swords, proclaimed that "one sword ought to be subordinated to the other and temporal authority, subjected to spiritual power," and deduced from this assertion that "if the terrestrial power err, it will be judged by the spiritual power,"[12] coming close, as a result, to excommunicating the king and imposing an interdict on his kingdom.[13]

As clearly appears in that capital document, the argument for the pope's superiority over kings rested on a unitary concept of society. The two swords represented two distinct functions existing within a single body, which was the Church. It was stated in *Unam Sanctam* that "We are informed by the texts of the gospels that in this Church and in its power are two swords; namely, the spiritual and the temporal," but that "of the one and only Church there is one body and one head, not two heads like a monster." Bellarmine was still intellectually dependent on that vision when he wrote: "The fact is that the political commonwealth and the ecclesiastical commonwealth make one Church, not two; and of that one Church the head is the Vicar of Christ, the successor of St. Peter."[14] In the words of one of his ablest commentators, J.C. Murray, S.J., he was referring to "the one *ecclesia* that was both Church and State," and "the operative principle of its unity was the spiritual unity of the Church herself; in fact, political unity was but an aspect of Christian unity." Murray adds:

> In the oneness of the head the dualism was reduced to unity; and this reduction of all things to unity was the ineluctable medieval drive. To Bellarmine, as to Boniface VIII, the prince is not "head" of a "body" politic; for there is only the one body, and it is mystical, and it cannot have two heads but only one. The subordination of prince to Pope is therefore a necessity, in order that the body may be one. Thus the celebrated *argumentum unitatis* appears even in Bellarmine ... It is the premise of Bellarmine's theology of the indirect power; it sets the framework within which he vindicates the two cardinal conclusions of his theory – the papal right to depose princes, and the prince's duty to exterminate heresy. (Murray 1948, 513)

Needless to say that an ardent supporter of national Churches like Hobbes could hardly accept this nostalgic vision of a Christendom united under papal rule, which had lost much of its relevance to the fractured religious landscape of seventeenth-century Europe.

What was innovative in Bellarmine's sleight of hand of the indirect power was the insistent recognition that civil States possessed full autonomy in their own sphere (and therefore that it was only incidentally [*casu*] that the pope could intervene in their affairs). From that standpoint, States enjoyed a complete equality of status. This view did not make it any easier to specify the type of relations that must prevail between temporal sovereigns and the Church. But it had several important consequences.

Bellarmine and other Jesuit theologians justified the autonomy of the State by arguing from the natural character of its missions. In keeping with the teaching of Aristotle and Aquinas, they emphasized the practical necessity and legitimacy of temporal government as such, irrespective of any religious grounds (although as part of a God-ordered universal structure). Paradoxically, their theory pointed in the direction of a secularization of the concept of the State. In his perceptive essay on Jesuit thought, J.N. Figgis commented on the disappearance, in Bellarmine's days, of "the great Church-State with its twin heads," by stating: "the theory of the 'indirect power' marks the change from the idea of one commonwealth with different officers to the modern conception of Church and State as two distinct social entities. In this sense, it is epoch-making" (Figgis 1907, 182–3).

The Jesuit theologians' influential reinterpretation of Catholic doctrines about the State paved the way for other capital evolutions. It justified, at a later stage in Church history, the conclusion of *concordats*, that-is-to-say formal agreements or treaties between two independent entities (Church and State) meant to regulate their mutual relations, on the model of what was achieved in France in 1802. It led the Church to acknowledge the legitimacy of the modern liberal State and of a policy of religious tolerance, witness the 1885 encyclical *Immortale Dei*.[15] It gave rise to a school of international law that was deeply indebted to thinkers sharing in Bellarmine's doctrines.[16] Besides that historical development, there seems to be a case for arguing that the contemporary debates over a right of international interference – its ethical justifications in terms of the protection of populations in grave danger, and the obstacles it encounters due to the strict application of the principle of State sovereignty – contains definite echoes of the philosophical confrontation over the indirect power, such as reconstructed through the Bellarminian and Hobbesian positions (see Havercroft 2012).

20.3 Varieties of Anti-Romanism

Bellarmine and Hobbes embodied two separate roads to modernity. This, however, is not to say that their political theologies had much in common or pointed towards the same conclusions. The critique of papalism connected Hobbes with a powerful anti-Roman current within the Catholic Church, which remained a central target of the pope's advocates for a long time. One was conciliarism, which had emerged in the Middle Ages and argued for the superior authority of general councils over that of popes.[17] It had found its most forceful expression in the decree *Haec Sancta* adopted in 1415 at the council of Constance (1414–1418), which asserted that the general council possessed a power that bound the pope in matters of faith, schism, and reform. The validity of that decree had been denied by Bishop Torquemada, whose arguments were to be taken up later by Bellarmine in his defense of papal supremacy (Izbicki 1986). But conciliarist ideas left lasting traces in Church circles, as suggested by the fact that they were repeatedly condemned in dogmatic constitutions down to the nineteenth century. Their influence was clearly perceptible in England, where they were a source of weapons to attack the pope in the contexts of Henry VIII's divorce and then of the Oath of Allegiance controversy (Oakley 1994). It could also be felt in Scotland (Burns 1963). They represented a form of constitutionalism articulated around the rejection of autocracy and a collegial exercise of power that could easily be transposed from ecclesiology into the field of politics, which explains why they were again found serviceable at the time of the English revolutions, in the parliamentary cause (see Oakley 1962).[18] They largely inspired, during the Interdict crisis, the Venetian opponents to Pope Paul V, whose main contender, Fra Paolo Sarpi (1552–1623), crossed swords with Bellarmine and stigmatized papal lust for power and Church corruption in terms closely resembling those of Hobbes (see De Franceschi 2013; Dompnier and Viallon 2019; Oakley 1996; Reverso 2016; Viallon 2010).

From the beginning of their movement down to their latter-day manifestations, conciliarists formed a common front with another category of anti-Roman critics, the French Gallicans. The glorification of French ecclesiastical liberties and the support to royal policies directed against papal interference in the affairs of the national Church had crystallized during the conflict between Philip the Fair and pope Boniface VIII. A key moment in the history of the movement was the 1614 Estates-General (held in the wake of King Henri IV's assassination and in a climate of violent hostility to the Jesuits, Bellarmine and Suarez in particular), during which the third Estate submitted to the assembly an article declaring as a "fundamental law of the kingdom" that the King of France "receives his crown from God alone" and that "there is no power on earth, whether spiritual or temporal, which has a right in his kingdom to deprive the sacred persons of our Kings of their crown nor to dispense or absolve their subjects of the allegiance and obedience they owe him for whatever cause or pretext" (Blet 1955, 92; my translation from the French). Gallicanism reached its apex with the Four Articles approved by the Assembly of the Clergy of France in 1682 (largely drafted by Bossuet). In a succession of statements containing evident allusions to the controversies in which Bellarmine and Hobbes had taken an active part, this last document affirmed the validity of the Constance decrees and proclaimed "that Kings and Sovereigns are subjected to no ecclesiastical power by God's ordinance in temporal matters, that they cannot be deposed directly or indirectly by the authority of the leaders of the Church," and repeated "that their subjects cannot be dispensed of the submission and obedience they owe them, or absolved of the oath of allegiance."[19]

In spite of their English sympathies, Gallicans stopped short of promoting the idea of a French schism.[20] Hobbes very much regretted that attitude.[21] The Venetians also chose to remain part of that Roman Church whose tyrannical practices they denounced. The specificity of the anti-papal line followed by Hobbes is further confirmed when one considers the important issue of infallibility. Like Hobbes, conciliarists challenged the papalists' claim that the pope could not err in his pronouncements, but they did in no way reject the idea of an infallible power in the Church, which they ascribed to the council. This was the stance defended by one of their main spokesmen at the time of the council of Constance, the chancellor of the University of Paris Jean Gerson (1363–1429).[22] It was again advocated by the radical exponent of conciliarism Edmond Richer (1559–1631) (see Oakley 1999). Fra Paolo Sarpi, on the Venetian side, engaged in a protracted duel of publications with Bellarmine over Gerson's writings on the subject (Foucault 2010) and the related issue of excommunication. According to the Four Articles of the Clergy of France in 1682, the pope's judgment in matters of faith "is not irreformable unless it receives the consent of the Church," which implied its conditional infallibility.[23]

20.4 Rome v. Hobbes

Judging by her repeated condemnations of Hobbes, the Church of Rome obviously recognized the singular radicalism of his system. The censors of the Holy Office have already been quoted. Later strictures were more elaborate. The article "Civil Authority" published in the 1907 volume of the *Catholic Encyclopedia*, signed Joseph Rickaby, selects two philosophers, Hobbes and Rousseau, to present closely associated theories that contradict the teachings of the Church in the political field, derived from Aristotle and Aquinas essentially. One reads that "Hobbes is rigidly logical; such inconsistencies as appear in him come from a certain timidity in speaking out, and a humility that approaches nigh to hypocrisy." However, while Rousseau, to the philosopher, is "contemptible," "Hobbes is an antagonist worthy of any man's steel." His philosophy being "tinged with the calvinism of his day," "he took it that man is of himself 'desperately wicked.'" As a consequence, in the state of nature, "Hobbesian man is a savage, solitary, sensual, and selfish." He has therefore every reason for getting out of this situation, which he does by a pact that enables him to live in society, "the social body thus formed having all the rights of the individuals contributing to form it." As a result, the State, termed the Leviathan, "is omnipotent, containing in its one self absolutely all the rights of the citizens who compose it." Hobbes saw "with laudable perspicacity" that "tyranny is better wielded by one man than by a multitude" and favored the resignation of all the contracting individuals' power "into the hands of a Single Person." This theory, like that of Rousseau that it inspired, was bound to legitimize despotism because it started from "a false supposition, that the natural state of man is savage solitude, not civil society," and proceeded "through the false medium of the 'Social Contract', false because society is not a thing of convention," and "false again, because it is out of all keeping with the evidence of history" (Rickaby 1907).

This article ended with references to the Syllabus of Pius IX (1864), which had condemned the fundamental errors – based on individualism and rationalism – leading to the dangerous modern theories, and to the encyclical *Immortale Dei* (1885), in which Leo XIII had recalled the Church's proper social doctrines. The rejection of all that Hobbes represented from a Catholic viewpoint took a more virulent turn with Joseph Vialatoux's book, *La Cité totalitaire de Hobbes*, first published in 1935. Imbued with Jacques Maritain's personalist philosophy, Vialatoux (1880–1970) denounced Hobbes's materialist anthropology, which denied the existence of man's spiritual nature and, by giving voice to the "sovereignty of the temporal dimension," ineluctably led to a political absolutism embodying the typically modern idolatry of the all-powerful State. Through a succession of historical stages, the reduction of ethics to considerations of individual interest and of law to the exclusive preoccupation with personal security assumed the shapes of enlightened despotism, of the liberal State, and ultimately of totalitarianism in its Fascist and socialist versions. Hobbes was the totalitarian thinker *par excellence* because of his radical individualism which replaced, in European conscience, the notion of the human person by that of an anonymous and self-centered individual willing to accept all kinds of oppression in exchange for peace. His political system revealed the tragic essence of political sovereignty when cut off from any transcendent source. His naturalism was the cause of a "total integration of man into the Leviathan-State" (Vialatoux 1952, 178).[24]

Some years later, Jacques Maritain in his turn decried Hobbes's dangerous politics by arguing that its fundamental vice was the very notion of sovereignty, another word for absolutism (Maritain 1951). The tone was more measured, but the philosophy the same as that of Vialatoux. Absolutism was understood in a definitely negative way. What it meant was the denial – best exemplified by Hobbes – that there exists a power above that of the sovereign (although the latter detains an unrestricted authority in the temporal sphere) and that sovereignty is fully legitimized by its supernatural basis. It was the Church's vocation and unique privilege to embody that transcendent dimension of politics and offer (or impose) her guidance to rulers and citizens at large, derived from her interpretation of Revelation and the tradition she summarized. What was left of her ancient authority was still relevant to modern societies insofar as it could effectively protect them against immorality and abuses of authority. Hobbes's materialism might indeed have been admissible (some Fathers of the Church had been materialists) if it had not served to discredit the very idea of a spiritual power, separate from the temporal one. According to the English philosopher's bleak world-picture, politics referred to a self-contained life experience in which the last word was a purely human one and which, for that reason, could be called "totalitarian."

Yet, when Bellarmine claims, quoting St. Bernard, that "the Pope is not the lord of the world, but the whole world pertains to him" (Bellarmine 2012, 173), he also formulates what could be regarded as a form of absolutism. The exclusive responsibility for the salvation of men's souls that he attributes to the head of the Church, and the infallibility he invests him with in matters of faith and manners reinforces that interpretation. Hobbes certainly felt that way (although the word "absolutism" did not yet exist in his day) judging by his statement, already quoted, that Bellarmine thus makes the pope "*the absolute monarch of all Christians.*" The Hobbesian sovereign, whatever the extent of his power, has no such responsibility. The sole motive for his control of religion is the preservation of civil peace. Private beliefs are so far from falling within his competence that even atheists must be considered as eligible to citizenship (see Lessay 2018). Leviathan has none of the crypto-theological features that Carl Schmitt (2004) and Ernst Kantorowicz (1957), in their different fashions, ascribe to the modern State.[25] It is not modelled on the Church, while the Church is identifiable as a "subordinate political system" according to Hobbes's definitions of such bodies in *Leviathan*'s Chapter 22.[26]

20.5 Conclusion

Two absolutisms were in competition in Bellarmine and Hobbes. They seemed to be incompatible. It would be presumptuous to say whether one of the two, and which, has triumphed over time. One was the absolutism of an institution that has gone through deep adaptations, although its doctrines have remained fundamentally the same. The other was the absolutism of a single philosopher who decoded the making of a modern State that has also developed, although it has retained many of the basic characters he construed. Both deserve to be also approached in the context of our century, to which they have kept much of their relevance.

Notes

1 On the Bellarmine–Hobbes relationship, see Springborg (1995) and Rose (2015).
2 See *A Replica to the Bishop of Chalcedon* (1654) in volume 2 of Bramhall's *Works* (1842, 204).
3 On Bellarmine, see Tutino (2010).
4 Mersenne, a Minim friar, probably gave Hobbes further access to the works of Bellarmine and other Catholic theologians by allowing him to use the library of the Minim convent in Paris (see Malcolm's introduction to Hobbes 2012, 107). White, alias Blacklo, defended theological and political views that met with the strong disapproval of the Church of Rome (all of his writings were consigned to the Index) and the English Parliament. Hobbes wrote a refutation of White's treatise *De mundo* (Hobbes 1973).
5 "for the multitude, Suarez and the Schoolmen will never gain them, because they are not understood" (EW IV.330).
6 Hobbes ridicules, in *Behemoth*, school-divines who "wrote great books of school-divinity, which no man else, nor they themselves, were able to understand; as any man may perceive that shall consider the writings of Peter Lombard, or Scotus, or of him that wrote commentaries upon him, or of Suarez, or any other school-divine of later times" (EW VI.185).
7 Those members of the nobility, Hobbes writes, "as they were not much molested in points of conscience, so they were not by their own inclination very troublesome to the civil government; but by the secret practice of the Jesuits and other emissaries of the Roman Church, they were made less quiet than they ought to have been. and some of them to venture on the most horrid act that ever had been heard of before, I mean the Gunpowder Treason" (EW VI.189).
8 "if a subject should counsel any other man to kill the King, Queen, or heir-apparent to the Crown, it would at this day be adjudged high-treason; and yet it is no more than bare words. In the third year of King James, Henry Garnet, a Jesuit priest, to whom some of the gunpowder traitors had revealed their design by way of confession, gave them absolution without any caution taken for their desisting from their purpose, or other provision against the danger, and was therefore condemned and executed as a traitor, though such absolution was nothing else but bare words" (EW VI.77).
9 See De Franceschi (2002).
10 The bishop writes on that point: "All other men distinguish between the Church and the Commonwealth; only T. H. maketh them to be one and the same thing ... Upon which account there was no Christian Church in these parts of the world for some hundreds of years after Christ, because there was no Christian sovereign" (*The Catching of Leviathan or the Great Whale* (1658), in Bramhall 1844, 531–532).
11 As a result of the Interdict imposed by Pope Paul V. See Bouwsma (1992).
12 Papal Encyclical Online, https://www.papalencyclicals.net/bon08/b8unam.htm, accessed 26 October 2020.
13 An interdict forbade the celebration of Church rites in a certain place or country.
14 Robert Bellarmine, *Tractatus de potestat. Summi Pontificis in rebus temporalibus adversus Gulielmum Barclaeum* (*Opera Omnia*, Naples, 1856, V, Pars 2, 280), quoted in Murray (1948, 510).
15 This point was again made by Figgis (1907). For a recent restatement, see Mull (2018).
16 The School of Salamanca, in Spain, saw the first systematic theorizing of international law in the Renaissance. Francisco Suarez was one of its leading figures, after the Dominican Francisco de Vitoria (c. 1480–1546) had launched that new field of thinking. See Azevedo and Moreira (2013).
17 See chapter 1 of Sère (2019, 21–66).

18 For a criticism of Francis Oakley's methodology and interpretation, see Nederman (1996). For a general reflection on the subject, see Fombaustier (2014).

19 At the site http://louisxiv.over-blog.com/article-23-mars-1682-47161670.html, accessed 26 December 2020. My translation from the French.

20 According to a French historian, "no doubt gallicanism was for much in the preservation of orthodoxy in the kingdom" (Fliche 1942, 147).

21 In *Behemoth*, one of the two interlocutors wonders that "the Kings and States of Christendom" seemed indifferent to "the progress of the Pope's power" in Elizabethan and Jacobean times, bringing the answer that "if they would have freed themselves from his tyranny, they should have agreed together, and made every one, as Henry VIII did, head of the Church within their own respective dominions. But not agreeing, they let his power continue, every one hoping to make use of it, when there should be cause, against his neighbour" (EW VI.190).

22 See Figgis (1899). Figgis underlines the fact that "it was because the conciliar party was able to find in the infallibility of the Church a religious sanction of its authority, that it could assert, and for the time being make good, its claim to superiority over the Pope, and declare the entire subjection of any individual, however exalted, to the community" (1899, 112–113).

23 1682 Four Articles of the Assembly of the Clergy of France. At the site http://louisxiv.over-blog.com/article-23-mars-1682-47161670.html, accessed 19 November 2020. My translation.

24 On Vialatoux, see Soubbotnik (1997), and on Vialatoux's circle, see Chenaux (1999).

25 See chapter 2 of Sère (2019, 67–95).

26 Commonwealths belong to the category of "*absolute* and *independent* systems," which are "subject to none but their own Representative." Churches obviously belong to an essentially different category, which is that of "subordinate systems." Hobbes distinguishes as follows in *Leviathan* 22: "Of Systemes subordinate, some are *Politicall*, and some *Private*. *Politicall* (otherwise Called *Bodies Politique*, and *Persons in Law*) are those, which are made by authority from the Soveraigne Power of the Common-wealth" (Hobbes 2012, 348; 1651, 274).

References

Azevedo, André Alves and Jose Manuel Moreira. 2013. *The Salamanca School*. New York and London: Continuum.

Baldini, Artemio Enzo. 2001. "Censures de l'Eglise romaine contre Hobbes: *De Cive* et *Léviathan*, *Bulletin Hobbes XIII*." *Archives de Philosophie* 64 (2): 2–7.

Bellarmine, Robert. 2012. "On the Temporal Power of the Pope. Against William Barclay." In *On Temporal and Spiritual Authority: Political Writings of Robert Bellarmine*, ed., trans., and with an introduction by Stefania Tutino. Indianapolis: Liberty Fund. Accessible at the site: https://oll.libertyfund.org/title/on-temporal-and-spiritual-authority#lf1607_head_036.

Blet, Pierre, S. J.. 1955. "L'article du Tiers aux Etats généraux de 1614." *Revue d'histoire moderne et contemporaine* 2 (2): 81–106.

Bourdin, Bernard. 2004. "La théorie bellarminienne du pouvoir temporel indirect des papes: une ecclésiologie politique." In *La genèse théologico-politique de l'Etat moderne*, 109–34. Paris: Presses Universitaires de France.

Bouwsma, William. 1990. "Gallicanism and the Nature of Christendom." In *A Usable Past: Essays in European Cultural History*, 308–24. Berkeley and Los Angeles: University of California Press.

Bouwsma, William J. 1992. *Venice and the Defence of Republican Liberty: Renaissance Values in the Age of the Counter-Reformation*. Berkeley and Los Angeles: University of California Press.

Bramhall, John. 1842. *The Works of John Bramhall*, Vol. 2. Oxford: Parker.

Bramhall, John. 1844. *The Works of John Bramhall*, Vol. 4. Oxford: Parker.

Burns, James H. 1963. "The Conciliarist Tradition in Scotland." *The Scottish Historical Review* 42 (134): 89–104.

Chenaux, Philippe. 1999. *Entre Maurras et Maritain. Une génération intellectuelle catholique (1920–1930)*. Paris: Cerf.

Colosimo, Jean-François. 2019. "Le pas de deux gallican" and "Zéro dissidence." In *La religion française*, 216–232. Paris: Cerf.

De Franceschi, Sylvio Hermann. 2002. "Le pouvoir indirect du pape au temporel et l'antiromanisme catholique des âges pré-infaillibiliste et infaillibiliste." *Revue d'Histoire de l'Eglise de France* 88: 103–49.

De Franceschi, Sylvio Hermann. 2013. "Entre antiromanisme catholique et républicanisme absolutiste. Paolo Sarpi (1552–1623) et la défense du bien public au temps de la crise de l'interdit vénitien (1606–1607)." In *Les clercs et les princes. Doctrines et pratiques de l'autorité ecclésiastique à l'époque moderne*, edited by Patrick Arabeyre and Brigette Basdevant-Gaudemet, 323–37. Paris: Études et rencontres de l'École des chartes, 41.

de Lubac, Henri, S. J. 1932. "Le pouvoir de l'Eglise en matière temporelle." *Revue des Sciences Religieuses* 12: 329–54.

Dompnier, Bernard and Marie Viallon. 2019. *L'Habit religieux du penseur politique. Une biographie de Paolo Sarpi*. Paris: Garnier.

Figgis, John Neville. 1899. "Politics at the Council of Constance." *Transactions of the Royal Historical Society* 13: 103–15.

Figgis, John Neville. 1907. "The Jesuits." In *Studies of Political Thought: From Gerson to Grotius 1414–1625*, 167–190. Cambridge: Cambridge University Press.

Fliche, Augustin. 1942. "Les origines du gallicanisme." Review of *Les origines du gallicanisme*, by Victor Martin, *Journal des savants* October–December: 145–158.

Fombaustier, Laurent. 2014. "L'influence des modèles ecclésiologiques et des institutions de l'Eglise sur les modèles et institutions étatiques." *Droits* 59 (1): 123–44.

Foucault, Didier. 2010. "Sarpi, l'interdit de Venise et la France d'après la correspondance de l'ambassadeur Canaye de Fresne." In *Paolo Sarpi: Politique et religion en Europe*, edited by Marie Viallon, 189–208.Paris: Éd Classiques Garnier

Havercroft, Jonathan. 2012. "Was Westphalia 'All That'? Hobbes, Bellarmine, and 17th-Century Debates over Intervention." *Global Constitutionalism* 1 (1): 120–40.

Hobbes, Thomas. 1839–1845. *The English Works of Thomas Hobbes*, 11 vols., edited by Sir William Molesworth. London: John Bohn. Cited as EW.

Hobbes, Thomas. 1973. *Critique du De Mundo de Thomas White*, edited by Jean Jacquot and Harold W. Jones. Paris: Vrin-CNRS.

Hobbes, Thomas. 1994. *The Correspondence of Thomas Hobbes*, edited by Noel Malcolm, Vol. II. Oxford: Clarendon.

Hobbes, Thomas. 2012. *Leviathan*, 3 vols., edited by Noel Malcolm. Oxford: Clarendon Press. [First published 1651.]

Höpfl, Hanno. 2004. *Jesuit Political Thought: The Society of Jesus and the State, c. 1540–1630*. Cambridge: Cambridge University Press.

Izbicki, Thomas M. 1986. "Papalist Reaction to the Council of Constance: Juan de Torquemada to the Present." *Church History* 55 (1): 7–20.

Kantorowicz, Ernst. 1957. *The King's Two Bodies*. Princeton: Princeton University Press.

Lecler, Joseph, S. J. 1944. *L'Eglise et la souveraineté de l'Etat*. Paris: Flammarion.

Lessay, Franck. 2018. "Tolerance as a Dimension of Hobbes's Absolutism." In *Hobbes on Politics and Religion*, edited by Laurens van Apeldoorn and Robin Douglass, 63–78. Oxford: Oxford University Press.

Maritain, Jacques. 1951. *Man and the State*. Chicago: University of Chicago Press.

Mull, Nathaniel. 2018. "Divine Right and Secular Constitutionalism: The Jesuit-Absolutist Debates, 1580–1620." *History of Political Thought* 39 (4): 606–33.

Murray, John Courtney, S.J. 1948. "St. Robert Bellarmine on the Indirect Power." *Theological Studies* 9: 491–535.

Nederman, Cary J. 1996. "Constitutionalism – Medieval and Modern: Against Neo-Figgisite Orthodoxy (Again)." *History of Political Thought* 17 (2): 179–94.

Oakley, Francis. 1962. "On the Road from Constance to 1688: The Political Thought of John Major and George Buchanan." *Journal of British Studies* 1 (2): 1–31.

Oakley, Francis. 1994. "Constance, Basel and the Two Pisas: The Conciliarist Legacy in Sixteenth and Seventeenth-Century England." *Annuarium Historiae Conciliorum* 26: 87–118.

Oakley, Francis. 1996. "Complexities of Context: Gerson, Bellarmine, Sarpi, Richer and the Venetian Interdict of 1606–1607." *The Catholic Historical Review* 82 (3): 369–96.

Oakley, Francis. 1999. "Bronze-Age Conciliarism: Edmond Richer's Encounters with Cajetan and Bellarmine." *History of Political Thought* 20 (1): 65–86.

Patterson, William B. 2000. *King James VI and I and the Reunion of Christendom*. Cambridge: Cambridge University Press.

Reverso, Nicla. 2016. "Paolo Sarpi: The Hunted Friar and His Popularity in England." *Anali d'Italianistica* 34: 297–318.

Rickaby, Joseph. 1907. "Civil Authority". In *The Catholic Encyclopedia*, Vol. 2. New York: Robert Appleton Company. At the site: http://www.newadvent.org/cathen/02137c.htm, accessed 14 September 2020.

Rose, Matthew. 2015. "Hobbes contra Bellarmine." *Journal of Moral Theology* 4 (2): 43–62.

Salmon, John Hearsey McMillan 1987. "Gallicanism and Anglicanism in the Age of the Counter-Reformation." In *Renaissance and Revolt: Essays in the Intellectual and Social History of Early Modern France*, 155–88. Cambridge: Cambridge University Press.

Schmitt, Carl. 2004. *Political Theology*. Chicago: University of Chicago Press. [First published 1922.]

Sère, Bénédicte. 2019. *L'invention de l'Eglise*. Paris: Presses Universitaires de France.

Soubbotnik, Michael A. 1997. "Hobbes années trente: l'absolutisme et l'Etat total." *Revue Française d'Histoire des Idées Politiques* 6: 311–27.

Springborg, Patricia. 1995. "Thomas Hobbes and Cardinal Bellarmine: Leviathan and the 'Ghost of the Roman Empire'." *History of Political Thought* 16 (44): 503–31.

Talaska, Richard. 2014. *The Hardwick Hall Library and Hobbes's Early Intellectual Development*. Charlottesville: Philosophy Documentation Center, www.pdcnet.org.

Tutino, Stefania. 2010. *Empire of Souls: Robert Bellarmine and the Christian Commonwealth*. Oxford: Oxford University Press.

Vialatoux, Joseph. 1952. *La Cite totalitaire de Hobbes, théorie naturaliste de la civilisation. Essai sur la signification de l'existence du totalitarisme*. Lyon: Chronique Sociale de France. [First published 1935.]

Viallon, Marie, ed. 2010. *Paolo Sarpi: Politique et religion en Europe*. Paris: Garnier.

21

Hobbes and the Papal Monarchy

PATRICIA SPRINGBORG

21.1 Hobbes and the Papal Monarchy, a Neglected Subject

The papal monarchy is not only the model for the Leviathan of Hobbes's *Leviathan*, I hypothesize, but also the subject of its last book, Book 4 on the "Kingdom of Darkness." It is also the subject of Hobbes's *Historical Narration concerning Heresy*, much of *Behemoth*, and his long Latin poem, the *Historia Ecclesiastica*. How is it then that Hobbes's account of the papal monarchy has for so long been overlooked as a subject for systematic treatment? Hobbes wrote about religion, the history of the church, and the papacy, in highly polemical works and in enormously heightened polemical contexts. And that is how on the whole they have been read, to some extent rightly (Springborg 1994). So *Leviathan* and *Behemoth* are given primacy over later and sometimes less polemical works like the *Historia Ecclesiastica*, which as a Latin poem in the elegiac mode, is in any case relatively inaccessible. We have superb recent treatments of Hobbes the polemicist by Jeffrey Collins, Franck Lessay, Quentin Skinner, Johann Sommerville, and others. Jeffrey Collins, in his excellent essay on the *Historia Ecclesiastica* even projects the poem forward, as a proto-Enlightenment essay, citing volume 2 of J.G.A Pocock's monumental study of Edward Gibbon, *Barbarism and Religion* (1999):

> Hobbes's ecclesiastical history strongly prefigured what J.G.A. Pocock has called the "Enlightenment narrative," which posited a post-Constantinian "Christian millennium" of "barbarism and religion" as a foil for the Enlightenment's own intellectual revolution. (Collins 2016, 542)

But let us leave aside the polemics of the day, as well as Hobbes's history as a pre-Enlightenment narrative, and assume for the moment that Hobbes is ignorant of the future and innocent of the burden with which he has been saddled. Then, given that *Leviathan* is about sovereignty, and that for nearly a thousand years the papal monarch

A Companion to Hobbes, First Edition. Edited by Marcus P. Adams.

was the most salient universal monarch in Christendom, it is startling that Hobbes on the papal monarchy has still not yet been systematically treated, as I first observed long ago (Springborg 1995). Hobbes wrote before Gibbon cast his long shadow over the history of the Roman Empire east and west, which means that he wrote in a certain state of innocence. What he has to say about the institutional history of the papacy in the context of the history of the Roman Empire, first the united empire, then the divided empire, and finally the Holy Roman Empire, closely parallels some of the most authoritative modern accounts, now that the shadow of Gibbon has more or less passed. Modern historians of the late Middle Ages could agree that church and empire cannot be seen as separate entities, for "the medieval Church was a State (in fact, the only State there was), with courts, laws, and with *sovereignty*," so that "the imperial struggle occurred within a single conception of society, a quarrel over who rightly ordered the unified *societas Christiana*" (Luman 1963, 478).

There were reasons to neglect Hobbes's ecclesiastical history. Commentators have long puzzled over Hobbes's famous claim in the *Elements of Law* 27.7 (hereafter *Elements*) to be the first to understand the meaning of "this word 'body politic', and how it signifieth not the concord, but the union of many men." When Hobbes spells out what he means by "body politic," his claim seems most implausible:

> And though in the charters of subordinate corporations, a corporation be declared to be one person in law, yet the same hath not been taken notice of in the body of a commonwealth or city, nor have any of those innumerable writers of politics observed any such union. (*Elements* 27.7; 1889, 138)

Such a claim suggests that Hobbes was ignorant of the elaborate concepts of corporation crafted from the twelfth century by Bologna-educated civil and canon lawyers for religious orders and ecclesiastical educational communities or *universitates* (Olsthoorn 2020; Ribarevic 2017). And yet it is clear that he was well acquainted with these concepts, and even seems to have borrowed from Pope Innocent IV, one of the cleverest lawyer popes, the notion of "fictitious person," or *persona ficta* to designate as *universitas*, or corporation, the legal person of the state.

It is true that the Hardwick Hall Library, which Hobbes tells us his patron assembled on his recommendations for his use in the 1630s, and for which we have the booklist, MS E.1.A. in Hobbes's own hand, was light on Roman Law. It contains only the *Corpus Juris Civilis*, and Justinian's *Institutes* and none of the works of the great Italian Roman Law commentators, Bartolus de Saxoferrato (1313–57), or Baldus de Ubaldis (1327–1400); not even the *De Legibus et Consuetudinibus Angliae* ("On the Laws and Customs of England"), attributed to the Norman English jurist, Henry of Bracton (1210–1268), which treats medieval legal fictions of crown and corporation. However, there were libraries where Hobbes could have read these works, for instance in Paris in the 1640s where, through his mentor Marin Mersenne, he had access to the great library of the Minim Fathers on the Port Royal (Malcolm 2007; 2012, 119–28). As I argue, Hobbes's legal research was probably done in London in the 1660s, in the library of Chief Justice Lord Vaughan, where he also researched his works on heresy.

It is worth noting however that what the Hardwick Hall Library lacked in Roman Law was well-compensated in terms of its holdings in canon law, ecclesiastical histories, and histories of the popes. To take ecclesiastical histories alone, in the theological section of Hobbes's booklist, Part 2: E.1.A. "Old Catalogue," we find the works of Epiphanius, Bishop of Salamis (d. 402 CE), listed as item 170 (most likely the two-volume Basel folio edition of 1544); the ecclesiastical history of Eusebius, Bishop of Caesarea (260–340 CE) collected together with the ecclesiastical histories of Socrates Scholasticus of Constantinople (c. 380–450) and the Syrian Evagrius Scholasticus (536–90) in an English edition translated from the Greek, listed as item 171; the ecclesiastical history of the Syrian Theodoret of Cyrrhus (c. 393–458) listed as item 428, and cross-referenced under Eusebius, item 171, as items 429 and 430; and the ecclesiastical history of Sozomen of Constantinople (c.400–50), are also cross-referenced (Springborg 2008, Appendix B, 282–92; Talaska 2013, 50, 64, and 68).

21.2 Hobbes and the Ghost of the Roman Empire

Hobbes's *De cive* (Hobbes 1998) and *Leviathan* reflect his time in France more than we have reckoned, I believe, being his response to the new style of civil science represented by Jean Bodin; an administrative science based on a division of competencies that did not however diminish the undivided sovereignty of the absolute state (Lee 2013; 2016). Bodin's focus coincided with parallel but different concerns in England in the lead up to the civil war, which Hobbes's famous works written in France, as an unintended consequence, served to enhance. Johann Olsthoorn in a recent essay (2020) argues persuasively that Hobbes had already formulated his thesis "on the nature and person of the state" in the *Elements* and *De cive*; but that in those works he speaks of "civil persons" and not of "representation," which he introduces only in *Leviathan*. Olsthoorn also does not fail to note that we have a premonition of Hobbes's mature thesis of incorporation in his disclosure in *Elements* (27.7; 1889, 138) that he believes he has made a great advance in civil science by taking the incorporation of towns and cities as a model for the "body politic." If we add to this anticipation the clever research of Noel Malcolm (2007; 2012, 28) into Hobbes's possible use of Leviathan as a figure for incorporation as found in Jesuit and Capuchin commentaries that he could have read in the Minim Friar's Library in Paris, we have the etiology of the very compelling image of the *Leviathan* frontispiece.

Leviathan, much more than *De cive*, represented a new post-reformation science based on the Tudor settlement and the accommodation of Protestant doctrines that built on the Jewish kingdom of the Hebrew Bible, contract and covenant as models for church-state relations. In this spirit Hobbes's treatment of the papacy in the last book of *Leviathan*, as the kingdom of the fairies and its doctrines as fairy stories, is relentlessly satirical. Only in his later works of the 1660s, written in response to heresy charges that the Parliament laid against him, does Hobbes seriously examine the history of the papal monarchy, specifically in the *Historia Ecclesiastica*. So it would come as a surprise to those who have only read the English *Leviathan* that Hobbes had a more considered view of the institutional role of the papacy in the history of the Roman Empire.

Jeffrey Collins is right to point out that in the Restoration Hobbes becomes an increasingly serious historian. This was because of a sea change in history writing generally: "The polemic needs of the Reformation [had] launched sacred history projects of industrial scale, often collaboratively written and grounded on innovative archival research (if not always on scrupulous critical judgment)" (Collins 2016, 523–4). Here Collins cites Johannes Sleiden's widely translated *De statu reigionis et reipublicae* of 1555, a history of religion and the state from Luther to the Diet of Augsburg, and the works of the "hard-line Lutheran Hebraist," Matthias Flacius; along with the 12 volume Catholic response to the Reformation genre of historiography, Cardinal Cesare Baronius's *Annales Ecclesiastici*, published from 1588 to 1607. These were all works held in the Hardwick Hall Library, and named in Hobbes's book list, Sleiden's both in Latin, item 407, and in English translation, item 391; Flacius as items 101 and 179; and Cardinal Cesare Baronius, as item 48. The sea change between the Tudor Reformation and the Stuart Restoration, between the polemics of the Reformation, and the work of the antiquarians once the immediate religious crisis had past, is registered also in Hobbes's historiography. For, Hobbes followed the trajectory of the antiquarians John Aubrey and John Selden, in England, his friends; and on the Continent, the historians Johann Cluver, and the great polymath, Gerard Vossius (Springborg 1996); whose works are also included in Hobbes's book list of the Hardwick Hall Library.

Hobbes's was not the only account in his day of the papal monarchy as a history of iniquity, or even as "the ghost of the Roman Empire." Pierre Du Moulin, in his reply to Robert Bellarmine of 1614, *De Monarchia temporali pontificis Romani*, a work held in Hobbes's patron's library, had declared that "[t]he Papal monarchy was born from the ruins of the Roman Empire," memorably rephrased by Hobbes as "the *Ghost* of the deceased *Romane Empire*, sitting crowned upon the grave thereof" (Sommerville 1992, 114, 194 n. 14; Springborg 1995). Du Moulin, a Huguenot supporter and co-author of James I, who produced the original French version of James's *Remonstrance* against Cardinal Du Perron of 1615 and approved his case against Bellarmine, very likely provided Hobbes with the thesis of his history of the papal monarchy, as Sommerville notes. Besides Du Moulin's history of the papacy, the Hardwick Hall Library lists Philippe de Mornay's, *The Mysterie of Iniquitie: That is to Say, the Historie of the Papacie* (London 1612). Mornay's history is among the most learned of the monarchomach treatises, citing the early Greek and Latin Fathers and early Church Histories in Greek and Latin, and documenting the outcome of specific Councils. But it is still basically a chronicle, full of the Whore of Babylon, the Devil, the Book of Daniel, and Anti-Christ, and lacking any serious analysis. Curiously, when in the *Historia Ecclesiastica* Hobbes again rephrases the thesis of the pope as the "the *Ghost* of the deceased *Romane Empire*," he appears to compound both the theses of Moulin and Mornay, borrowing Mornay's governing idea of the papacy as *the Mysterie of Iniquitie*, to which he adds Moulin's thesis to yield his own: "Rome, which is nothing but a great sepulcher, and the Pope a menacing ghost at Caesar's tomb, ruling in the shadows which he himself made, and continues to make; and seeking by verbal trickery, royal rights" (Hobbes 2008, lines 1581–4, 502–3).

But Hobbes is not content to elaborate this thesis with a catalogue of satanic tricks, the Whore of Babylon, the Anti-Christ, and so on. The tricks of the papacy were cleverer than that, and Hobbes spells them out in terms of three institutional strategies: first, papal claims to imperial power by means of the *translatio imperii*, or transmission of power from imperial Rome; second, the co-optation of Roman Law as canon law, which enabled the Roman *pontiff* to claim the rights of the Roman *princeps*; and third, the creation of an ecclesiastical system of offices that paralleled the administrative system of the old Roman Empire. To take them in turn, it is important to recognize that Hobbes's thesis of "the Pope [as] a menacing ghost at Caesar's tomb," by contrast with Moulin's, refers to explicit medieval claims of *translatio imperii*, the notion of a linear succession of empires which, by means of "legitimate" transfer, could claim to inherit the *imperium* of the old Roman Emperor. Claims of *translatio imperii* were famously made to connect both the Byzantine and the Holy Roman Empires – the latter the German Empire – to the ancient Roman Empire. Among the most notable legitimations of the Holy Roman Empire in terms of *translatio imperii*, were those of tenth-century Adso of Montier-en-Der, who claimed the sequence of translations to be from the Roman Empire, via the Carolingian Franks to the Saxons; and twelfth-century Otto of Freising, who claimed the sequence from Rome to be via Byzantium, the Franks, the Longobards, and thence to the Germans under the Holy Roman Empire (Pocock 2003, ch. 7). But claimants were not exclusively German, and the twelfth-century French author of Arthurian romances, Chrétien de Troyes, listed the translations differently: from Greece to Rome to France. Not surprisingly, the *translatio imperii* was claimed not only for secular rulers, but also by the Church at the height of its powers in the thirteenth and fourteenth centuries; and this is the particular translation to which Hobbes refers with his theory of papacy as "the *Ghost* of the deceased *Romane Empire*."

Hobbes's analysis of the second papal strategy, the co-optation of Roman Law as canon law, is complicated, and we will return to it. But the third, the papal creation of a parallel system of offices in the late Roman and Holy Roman Empires is of immense institutional importance. It is this analysis that allows Hobbes to sustain his bold claim of the *Elements* 27.7, to be a first to apply the new Bodinian administrative science to the modern state (see Springborg forthcoming). Moreover, Hobbes was one of the first to consider the role of the Church in the development of Western philosophy of mind, which is why his account of the heresies is so important. For, what was "ghostly" about the papacy as "the *Ghost* of the deceased *Romane Empire*," was the fact that it ruled not primarily by coercive force, but by imposing a belief system, and by defending that belief system legally, and against all comers. This belief system was based on ontological and epistemological principles concerning human nature, mind and body, and man's relation to the cosmos, adopted from Greek philosophy. The Church ruled this "ghostly" empire, not only through a system of offices, but also by means of councils called to deal with dissent in the form of heresies; and through courts. These heresies aired serious alternatives to the philosophy of mind that the Church taught, and sprang up in provinces of the Empire where non-Greek or pre-Greek religions and philosophical systems were indigenous. Some of these heresies, like the Arian and the Monophysite heresies, which were concerned with the attributes of persons, and specifically the persons of the Godhead in the Trinity, lasted centuries, and were eventually responsible for the loss of provinces of the Eastern Roman Empire, Syria, Egypt and Palestine, to Islam, which was a direct heir to the indigenous pre-Greek philosophical systems they enjoyed, as Hobbes is clearly aware (Hobbes 2008, lines 1039–1100, 428–41).

21.3 Hobbes's Analysis of the Papal Monarchy

Hobbes's account of both the institutional and philosophical consequences of the papal monarchy is surprisingly congruent with some of the most authoritative modern accounts. Besides the works of the memorable Frederic Maitland (1898, 1911), I include the histories of Michael Wilks (1963), Harold Berman (1983), and Colin Morris (1991). As Hobbes tells it, the institutional power of the Church grew from Council to Council, for there were some 19 General Ecumenical Councils and innumerable regional councils and synods over a thousand years between the Christianization of the Empire under Constantine and the Protestant Reformation. The recodification of Roman Law under Justinian gave legal footing to this institutional power, upon which Papal legitimacy depended, and allowed it to establish itself as the beneficiary of the *translatio imperii* from ancient Rome.

But because the *Historia Ecclesiastica* is a Latin poem in the elegiac mode, it tends to express institutional facts in coded language. For instance, when he portrays the papacy, having reached its acme in the twelfth and thirteenth centuries, the pope challenging the Roman emperor in his power to command peoples of the entire Eurasian continent, Hobbes depicts him as a sun-king, with the power to summon up wealth from the four corners of the earth (Hobbes 2008, lines 1231–4, 456–7). Hobbes's invocation of sun-king imagery was not innocent, however. The simile of "the sun and moon," renowned in the history of the medieval papacy, was made famous by Pope Innocent III in a letter of October 30, 1198, addressed to those Italian cities that had acknowledged papal lordship: "Now just as the Moon derives its light from the Sun and is indeed lower than it in quantity and quality, in position and in power, so too the royal power derives the splendor of its dignity from the pontifical authority" (Innocent III, 1198). The "sun and moon" theory was made universal Catholic doctrine by the Fourth Lateran Council of 1215; and in Pope Boniface VIII's papal bull, *Unam sanctam*, of 1302, it was married to the allegory of the "Two Swords," secular and religious. Dante Alighieri discusses it in in his *De Monarchia* of 1312–1313, book 3, chapter 4, in line with his rejection of the Church's theocratic claims, with which Hobbes was undoubtedly familiar. Hardwick Hall Library holdings of works by popes, according to MS E.1.A., include, "Innocentij Papae. oper. fol.," item 239 (Talaska 2013, 54), probably the Cologne folio 1552 edition of Pope Innocent III's works: *Innocentii III, Romani Pontificis Opera Omnia*. While part III of the Catalogue, listing works in the vernacular European languages, lists two works by Dante (Talaska 2013, 121), the first, item 1310. 'Dante. Canzoni. 8o.', which could be any of the many editions of Dante's lyric poetry; and the second, item '1314, Dante,' otherwise unidentified, which could indeed be *De Monarchia*.

In the longest digression of the *Historia Ecclesiastica* on the power of the papacy at its peak (Hobbes 2008, lines 1229–1300, 455–67), Hobbes explores several famous tropes in terms of which this power was historically portrayed, of which the sun-king imagery of Innocent III is only the first. The second is "Leviathan" imagery where "the popes by their own cunning overcame all the monsters that the earth produces" (Hobbes 2008, lines 1237–8, 456–7). Hobbes depicts the pope as "the shrewd fisherman," who "does not neglect his customary skill, however great the prey entangled in his nets," perhaps "mending his nets if at some point a great whale has forced its way through"

(Hobbes 2008, lines 1245–8, 458–9). But, in fact, Leviathan is incidental to this story, although apparently amplified by the insertion of two lines that tie the poem closer to Hobbes's works, *Leviathan* and *Behemoth*, an interpolation that we have established was certainly not made by Hobbes, but perhaps by his printer, to help sell the earlier books! (Hobbes 2008, Malcolm Appendix C, 277; Springborg forthcoming):

> Leviathan, like Behemoth had again taken the hook in the nose;
> both the king and people were slaves.
>
> (Hobbes 2008, lines 1229–30, 454–5)

Setting these two lines aside, in fact the fishing imagery most closely tracks the famous treatment of clerical power by Hobbes's contemporary, Isaac Walton, in *The Compleat Angler* of 1653. The digression on papal power continues, weaving back and forth, to the practice of beatification and the selling of indulgences, before returning to the nepotism of the Renaissance popes (Hobbes 2008, lines 1279–1300, 464–7). Finally, in an elaborate coda on idol worship rich in classical references, Hobbes explores Christian statue cults, which allowed "idolatry ... to travel as the companion of true Faith" (Hobbes 2008, lines 1300–21, 466–71); an account that follows closely that of statue cults in the English and Latin editions of *Leviathan*. Over 100 lines of the poem are devoted to the syncretism of Christian idol worship, incorporating pagan practices of various sorts, a practice which "no prince dared attack" (Hobbes 2008, lines 1321–1426, 470–81). Hobbes notes an early and unsuccessful intervention by the Emperor Leo, probably Leo I, the Thracian (457–74), the first to receive his crown from the Patriarch of Constantinople (Springborg et al. 2008, 471 n. 421). This nod to the iconoclasm of the Eastern Church prefaces another long digression, this time on images, idols, phantasms, and the problem of unexamined sense data (Hobbes 2008, lines 1375–1426, 1474–81). It weaves between the Bible, classical references such as the *simulacra* of Lucretius, and the *Idolum* of Francis Bacon's *Novum Organum* (Springborg et al. 2008, 479 n. 444; c.f. Schuhmann 2004, 25).

These digressions, the surfeit of allusions, and the admittedly loose structure of the *Historia Ecclesiastica*, easily divert attention from the serious content of the poem. For, what is most extraordinary about Hobbes's account of the papal monarchy, complicated and spread over such different works, is the degree to which he understood the church precisely as a state with characteristic legal institutions, which governed by rule of law. Frederic Maitland summarized his own thesis in words that could well apply to Hobbes: "When the medieval church is regarded as a political organization, as a state, it becomes very interesting"; because although "[a]s a whole the constitution of this state may be unique, ... there is hardly a feature in it for which we may not find analogies elsewhere"; moreover, "[a]t various points it becomes a model for the constitution of other and secular states, while [it] itself reproduces many traits of the ancient Roman Empire" (Maitland 1898, 100–1). Rule of law was not incidental to the papal monarchy, then. It was precisely because "[i]t has laws, lawgivers, law courts, lawyers"; because "[i]t uses physical force to compel men to obey its laws"; and "[i]t keeps prisons," that the church is a state (Maitland 1898, 101). And it was self-consciously a state that governed by rule of law: for, "the canonists, since they have had Justinian's books before them, have been fostering this resemblance, and applying to the pope whatever has been said of the *princeps*" (Maitland 1898, 101).

21.4 Hobbes and the *Corpus Mysticum*

In the *Historia Ecclesiastica* we have Hobbes's most systematic account of the papal monarchy, which displays his considerable knowledge of the gradual development of imperial and ecclesiastical parallel structures within the *societas Christiana*. It is a history of doctrinal developments and the Church Councils designed to settle them. But it is also a history of papal Decretals and the adaptation of Roman Law that provided the juridical underpinning of the papacy as the continuator of the Roman Empire by virtue of *translatio imperii*, the translation of power from the pagan Roman Empire to the Christianized Roman Empire, divided into western and eastern parts. Ecclesiastical history proper, as the history of the church as a parallel structure with imperial ambitions, post-dates the move of the imperial capitol to Constantinople, and is therefore post-Constantine (Roman Emperor 306 to 337 CE). For, it was only under the Christianized empire that the possibility of papal territorial power arose, leading to an eventual struggle over investiture, or the appointment to offices, between the pope and the emperor, due to papal claims to jurisdiction in the East. Pre-Constantine, however, important concepts of the Christian community as a corporation, or *corpus mysticum*, were developed by the Church Fathers, which made its later territorial claims possible.

Foremost among these developments was the Neoplatonist realism of Augustine (354–430 CE). Under the early Church Fathers, particularly Augustine, the *corpus mysticum* was developed as a construct deemed to represent the body of Christ as a Platonic ideal, a *polis* laid up in heaven like the true Pauline *respublica*, whose spiritual person was none other than Christ himself (Wilks 1963, 20). *Corpus mysticum*, a term first applied to the Eucharist, was not transferred to the *ecclesia* as such until the twelfth century. It was even later, under Pope Boniface VIII (1292–1303), that the church was officially decreed to be the mystical body of Christ, *corpus Christi mysticum*; and it was Boniface VIII who at the same time, officially declared the *ecclesia* to be a corporation, that is to say, a *universitas*, or juridical person in Roman Law (Wilks 1963, 23). Already latent in the twelfth-century *Decretals* of the canonist Gratian (fl. 1150), the concept of the church as corporation had been elaborated by Pope Innocent IV (c.1195–1254), who declared the *ecclesia* to be a *persona ficta* (Wilks 1963, 23–4), the famous term that Hobbes seems to borrow for his sovereign in *Leviathan*. The papal publicists, in their interpretation of the *lex regia*, the Roman law whereby the people first transferred their power to a sovereign, were the first to formulate a theory of "social contract" – the notion that Hobbes in the *Elements* and *De cive* already takes over. Again it was the papal publicists, discussing the corporate nature of the ruler, who first pointed out that "when the whole community is in its corporate nature represented by one man, that one man becomes himself a corporation," achieving in one stroke "a direct transfer to the papacy of the Roman law theory of corporation sole: '*papa solus totius Ecclesiae gestat personam*'" (Wilks 1963, 32). Wilks translates it: "In his solitude the pope epitomizes the oneness of the *universitas fidelium*, and contains all that is necessary for the functioning of the universal body." As Hobbes well knew, the Tudor Reformation settlement had seen the co-optation of the medieval "corporation sole" to express the double incorporation of church and realm in the person of the king (Maitland 1911). An idea which the *Leviathan* frontispiece with the king wielding sword and crozier seems to express.

It had thus taken some 700 years for the "combination of Roman Law and Pauline teaching ... already adopted by Augustine" to be realized, and then only as a fiction; but the fiction designed to allow the corporation to act as a legal person was no less important for being a fiction, for, as Augustine had declared, and Aquinas repeated, "it is the fiction that is the mark of truth."[1] It was this form of philosophical realism, attributing greater reality to the fiction than the individual items that fell under it and, correspondingly, more importance to corporate entities than to individual persons, that characterized the thinking of the hierocratic papal publicists. Papal absolutism at its height thus became vulnerable on philosophical grounds to the nominalism and skepticism, as well as the humanist individualism of the late medieval period, which brought about its eventual decline. The most fanatical hierocrats and defenders of the papal plentitude of power were the fourteenth-century Augustinus Triumphus (1243–1328), Aegidius Romanus, or, Giles of Rome (1247–1316) and Alvarus Pelagius (1280–1352; Wilks 1963, 2–3). Augustinus Triumphus, premier among them, was a Hermit of St. Augustine, and author of the influential *Summa de potestate ecclesiastica*, first printed in 1473 and frequently reprinted in the sixteenth century, but significantly referred to by Bellarmine as an "egregious" work because of its apparent absolutism (Wilks 1963, 6). Aegidius Romanus, or Giles of Rome, associated with him, was an Augustinian, and produced *De regimine principum* for Philip IV, first printed in Augsburg in 1473. The third of the trio, all roughly contemporary, Alvarus Pelagius, was a Franciscan from Galatia and Bologna-educated canonist, author of *Statu et planctu ecclesiae duo libri*, 1330–1340, first printed in Ulm in 1474.

The hierocratic theorists of papal plenipotentiary power came late in the history of the church. Their antagonists, whose nominalism and skepticism are attributed to bringing hierocratic theory down, came late also and were contemporaries, with whom the publicists sometimes interacted. Ptolemy of Lucca (1236–1327), a Dominican and confessor of Thomas Aquinas (1225–1274), who produced the *Historia Ecclesiastica Nova* in 24 books, and *De regimine principum*, was one. Another was Marsilius of Padua (1275–1342), who studied medicine at the University of Padua before becoming an Aristotle scholar at the University of Paris, to which he was appointed Rector in 1313, and was author of the renowned *Defensor pacis* in support of Ludwig of Bavaria against Pope John XXII. His colleague, William of Ockham (1287–1347), the Oxford educated Franciscan theologian and logician, author of the *Summa logicae* of 1323 on the problem of universals, had joined Marsilius at Ludwig of Bavaria's court, where he contributed a number of works to his campaign. Not surprisingly, it was their nominalism and skepticism, fatal for the fictions on which the hierocratic publicists relied, that appealed to Hobbes, a nominalist and skeptic himself. But the ground between the protagonists and antagonists on papal plenitude was not as great as might be supposed. The conciliarist arguments of Ockham and Marsilius, so abhorred by Hobbes despite his endorsing their nominalism and skepticism, had been anticipated by Aquinas, the papal moderate, and even by the hierocratic fanatic Augustinus Triumphus (Luman 1963, 478–9).

It is noteworthy that none of the works of the hierocratic papal publicists, or of their adversaries, was held in the Hardwick Hall library: no Augustinus Triumphus, no Aegidius Romanus or Giles of Rome, no Alvarus Pelagius, no Ptolemy, no Marsilius, no Ockham and no Suarez. Talaska notes that "[a] surface study of the contents of MS E.I.A" suggests that "the great exponents of Scholastic philosophy and logic" were represented: "Aquinas, Scotus, Keckermann," the latter a Protestant adversary; and even "the Oxonian Aristotelian John Case" (Talaska 2013, 20). But, I would add, those that were missing were at least as important to Hobbes as the works it contained. It is possible that he read the missing works earlier, in the library of the Minim Friars in Paris, to which he had access through Mersenne in the 1640s (Malcolm 2007, 39; 2012, 28). Hobbes was clearly familiar with the arguments of Ockham, Marsilius, and Suarez, the latter whom he even quotes, but the rest he may not have read systematically at all, their ideas being common currency in his day.

It is nevertheless possible that Hobbes did read them, perhaps later, after the atheism charges the parliament laid against him in 1666–7, when he wrote the series of works on heresy to which the *Historia Ecclesiastica* belongs. They include: his *Response to Bramhall's "The Catching of Leviathan,"* written in 1666–7; his *Historical Narration Concerning Heresy* of 1668; *De Haeresi*, his Appendix to the Latin *Leviathan* of the same year; the *Dialogue Concerning the Common Laws*, written after 1668 (given the section on heresy relating to the Scargill affair of 1669); *Behemoth*, written between 1668 and 1670; and the Chatsworth MS on Heresy of 1673. I would hypothesize that Hobbes researched these works in the London library of Lord John Vaughan (1603–1674), "his great acquaintance," Aubrey tells us, whom he delighted to visit thrice weekly during his London period (Aubrey 1898, 1.369). At this time Hobbes lived at Little Salisbury House in the Strand, the house of his patron, William Cavendish, third earl of Devonshire. We could assume that Lord Vaughan, as Chief Justice of the Court of Common Pleas, and therefore the second most senior common law judge in the land, had a well-stocked library. Significantly, it was in Lord Vaughan's library, that the fair copy of the *Historia Ecclesiastica* made by Hobbes's amanuensis, James Wheldon, which provided the copy text for the printed edition of 1688, was deposited sometime between 1671 when it was completed, and 1674, when Vaughan died, for which we also have Aubrey's testimony (Aubrey 1898, 1.364; Springborg 2008, 87).

21.5 Decline of the Papal Monarchy, Aristotelianism, and Islam

That the papal monarchy began to decline once it reached the limits of absolutism under Innocent III (1198–1216), Innocent IV (c.1243–1254), and Boniface VIII (1294–1303), was not only due to over-reach. It was because its philosophy of mind seemed to have failed it, or at least was superseded, as Hobbes realized. This was due to factors to some extent exogenous, that can be summed up as the development of Aristotelian humanism, with which all the parties to the power struggle between pope and emperor became infected. Aristotelian humanism in turn grew out of the reception of the Arabic Aristotle commentaries from the twelfth century on. For, the turning point in the development of late medieval and early modern conceptions of sovereignty, today often subsumed under Quattrocento "Renaissance Humanism," or even "Classical

Republicanism," happened a couple of centuries earlier, in what has become known as the European twelfth-century Renaissance (Haskins 1927). With very few exceptions this has been air-brushed out of modern histories – even the exemplary medieval historian Wilks (1963), makes passing references to Avicenna (980–1037), the Persian polymath, and Averroes (1126–1198), the Andalusian philosopher, but no substantial case for the Arabic commentaries and their reception as being the turning point. The renowned German medieval historian and canon lawyer, Peter Landau, in his review critical of Berman's *Law and Revolution* (1983), is an exception. Berman argues for the Gregorian Reforms of Hildebrand, Pope Gregory VII (1015–1085) as being the turning point, but Landau protests: "The great event in the articulation of the concept of the State and the origins of political science was the translation of Aristotle's writings around 1260" (Landau 1984, 941). Landau sees Berman setting the turning point far too early: "The first treatise on the Church as a separate entity was written at the beginning of the fourteenth century by James of Viterbo," author of the *De regimine christiano* (*On Christian Government*); "while the first treatise on the State was probably Dante's *De Monarchia*" (Landau 1984, 941).

James of Viterbo's *De regimine christiano* (*On Christian Government*), was written in 1302 during the bitter conflict between Boniface VIII and the king of France, Philip IV (the Fair), to which Giles of Rome had also contributed; while Dante, who is believed to have been in Paris between 1307 and 1309, wrote *De Monarchia* at that time to celebrate the election of Henry of Luxemburg as emperor Henry VII in November, 1308. Viterbo's treatise was the work of a University of Paris-educated Augustinian hierocratic theorist, and often compared to Giles of Rome's *De ecclesiastica potestate* (*On Ecclesiastical Power*). For, in the words of *De regimine*'s editor, Viterbo hoped "to formulate a theory of papal monarchy that is every bit as imposing and ambitious as that of [Giles]" (Côté 2014, citing *De regimine christiano*: xxxiv). Wherever we look, in fact, the connection is either to the University of Paris, which became the hub for the reception of the Arabic Aristotle commentaries in the twelfth century, or Padua, to which the Averroist Aristotelians fled once 219 philosophical theses attributed to Averroes were proscribed by Etienne Tempier, Bishop of Paris, in 1277.

The fourteenth-century hierocratic publicists belonged as much to the reception of Averroist Aristotelianism as their contemporary antagonists, Ockham and Marsilius, and they had the same connections. William of Ockham, the Franciscan theologian and publicist, and Marsilius of Padua, the jurist, were both refugees from the University of Paris at the court of Ludwig of Bavaria, who was advancing the imperial cause against the pope in Avignon. Both Ockham and Marsilius produced a nominalist metaphysics and a materialist ontology of matter-in-motion that owe their genesis to the reception of the Aristotle commentaries of Averroes, whose work so excited scholars at the University of Paris. And they too were among the refugees who fled to Padua. Even the most extreme papalist, Augustinus Triumphus was educated at the University of Paris, studying under Aquinas from whom he took his mastership in 1270, and was even delegated by Aquinas to replace him at the Council of Lyons of 1274, but died on the way (Wilks 1963, 4). In sum, our protagonists on both sides of the debate over papal plenitude have connections to Paris, Padua, or Bologna, as well as to one another.

Although the philosophical and scientific importance of the reception of the Arabic Aristotle commentaries is by now well recognized among specialists (Akasov and

Giglioni 2013; Gutas 1998), their implications for political theory are less clear, given that the political works of Aristotle were relatively neglected by the *Falasifa*. In terms of political theory and the development of state sovereignty, Aristotelian naturalism of the type introduced by the Arabic commentaries could *by implication* not support hierocratic absolutism and the fictions that had grown out of Augustinian Platonism and Neoplatonism. But this is only a presumption and can only be filled out by further presumptions. It is my thesis that it in fact fell to the protagonists in the late medieval European debate on imperial versus papal power whom we are considering to make the connection to the political Aristotle, producing a type of Aristotelianism that was in fact new and took on a life of its own; and that this is what so excited students at the University of Paris, and subsequently, Padua. Furthermore, it is possible that this is the reason why the role of the Arabic commentators is absent in what has become "Renaissance humanism" and "classical republicanism," terms that have long been convicted of lacking in definition, to which we can now give greater specificity. For I am suggesting that the Arabic commentaries produced a political reception immensely important in the contest between the empire and the papacy out of which the modern state was born, falling into the hands of a learned clerical elite which was able to extrapolate from Aristotelian naturalism weapons against Augustinian Platonism; weapons that they honed so that parties to both sides of the debate shared assumptions and concepts that were new, but entirely indispensable.

None of the parties to the struggle between pope and emperor appears to have been immune to the Aristotelianism of the Arabic commentators. Marsilius and Ockham, are acknowledged to be profoundly influenced by Averroes. Augustinus Triumphus, the hierocratic publicist par excellence, was also a student at the University of Paris. Aegidius Romanus, Giles of Rome, an Augustinian and disciple of Aquinas at the University of Paris between 1269 and 1272 and author of Aristotle commentaries himself, had been caught up in the condemnations of 1210–1277 and had to flee Paris for Italy. Forced to retract his Aristotelianism under Pope Honorius IV, he was vindicated by his order and by Pope Boniface VIII and made Archbishop of Bourges in 1295. The connections of the canonist Alvarus Pelagius, reputed to be a student of Duns Scotus who taught at Oxford, to which the Franciscan Friars Minor had moved once the University of Paris was dispersed in 1229–1230 due to proscriptions, also had connections to Bologna, where he had studied canon law. One can only assume that the hierocratic monarchists knew the structure of the Roman and Hellenistic empires sufficiently to understand their differentiated layers, divided between Eastern and Western provinces, city and municipality and their characteristic forms of government. They were undoubtedly able to extrapolate the connection to the Aristotle, supporter of limited government, to which the Arabic commentators subscribed, but perhaps for pragmatic reasons, did not discuss. And they were certainly able to apply the nominalism and scientific naturalism of the *Falasifa* to the destruction of the Augustinian Platonist fictions upon which the foundations of papal monarchy were built. So Al-Ghazali (1058–1111), whose attack on Neoplatonism that argued for faith over reason in *The Incoherence of the Philosophers* had attracted the decisive rebuttal of Averroes, *The Incoherence of the Incoherence*, advancing a defense of Aristotelianism and the "double truth" of faith and reason, which became the hallmark of Renaissance Averroists, Marsilius, Dante and, I would dare to suggest, even Hobbes himself.

21.6 Hobbes Roman Law and the *Persona Ficta*

As Luka Ribarevic (2017) has pointed out in his excellent essay on Hobbes's *Leviathan* and the medieval *universitas*, it was not the Roman Law concept of legal personality to which Hobbes appealed when he claimed to have invented the fictitious person of the state, redeeming his claim of *Elements* 27.7 to have created an entirely new civil science. It was rather the Canon Law concept of *universitas*. It is well known that a concept of legal personality was what Roman law lacked, but canon law could supply. Hobbes's corporation theory attempts a delicate balancing act. Addressed to "those who contend on one side for too great liberty, and on the other side for too much authority," as Hobbes notes on the opening page of his short Dedicatory letter, it aimed to put the state out of the reach of its creators – and also potential wreckers – both the people and the sovereign (Skinner 2018). As Ribarevic (2017) demonstrates, *persona ficta*, as formulated by the great lawyer pope, Innocent IV, provided Hobbes with a vehicle that Roman law could not. Roman law, it is true, contained the elements necessary to a theory of authorization, *auctors* (authors) and *actors* (agents), which by the legal delegation of authority allow the creation of contracts, and legal representation for towns and communities; concepts on which Hobbes importantly draws for his theory of representation. But it was only the church, with its long experience of incorporated communities, religious orders, and colleges, that could supply the notion of an endowment in perpetuity, enjoying legal autonomy and even powers beyond the control of its initial founders. That Hobbes fully appreciated the significance of his move is clear from the examples of corporations he gives, "a church, an hospital, a bridge" (Hobbes 2012, 246; 1651, 81), typical medieval ecclesiastical foundations that satisfy all the conditions of autonomy in perpetuity.

We did not have to wait for *Leviathan*, in fact. Hobbes had already delivered on his claim of *Elements* 27.7 to be the first to apply to "the body of a commonwealth or city" the notion of corporation, as "declared to be one person in law," in the *Elements* itself. "Not a 'fictive person', in the sense of that abomination of metaphysics, medieval corporation theory," as I have recently argued, "but a corporation whose charters people were familiar with and which were commonly litigated in the courts, like the 'subordinate corporations' with which he introduces his claim" (Springborg 2019, 32). That "famous claim can now be reread as foreshadowing Hobbes's deflationary 'artificial person' of the state of *Leviathan*" designed to avoid the Platonist realism of the ecclesiastical *persona ficta* and all its metaphysical hazards. As Olsthoorn (2020) demonstrates, the vehicle, which *Elements* and *De cive* were lacking and *Leviathan* supplied, was admirably suited to the task. It was the Ciceronian author/actor model taken from the stage, where "natural" person is simply the person acting for himself, and "artificial" person simply the person acting for another, which avoided any further metaphysical claims about personation, representation, or the generation of corporations. It is all the more curious, then, that the Leviathan frontispiece should be appear to be a perfect realization of the medieval *persona ficta*, identifiable by incorporation of the body politic in its head; and not some depiction from the stage! Except for one consideration that Olsthoorn (2018) had earlier maintained, and reiterates (2020, 12). It so happens that for Hobbes the Reformed church enjoys the same structure as a commonwealth: "*A company of men professing Christian Religion, united in the person of one*

Sovereign" (Hobbes 2012, 732; 1651, 248). Church and state are identical and overlapping, as incorporated in the person of the sovereign, in what Olsthoorn (2018) describes as Hobbes's "theocratic turn." Hobbes thus accepted the master-stroke of the Tudor jurists, co-opting for his Leviathan the very same theocratic structure pioneered by the papal monarchy, which the jurists had taken over. This the frontispiece faithfully represents.

Although the *Historia Ecclesiastica* adds nothing to the elaborate exegesis of the "artificial person of the state" of *Leviathan*, nor is the term *persona ficta* ever mentioned, Hobbes is able to portray the papal monarchy as a formidable actor, enjoying dominion from east to west and even in the New World, apparently in perpetuity. That the papal monarchy had pioneered the "body politic" that became known as the early modern European state, historians, Maitland, Wilks, Berman, Morris, and others, have already argued. But without noticing that Thomas Hobbes had already observed this, co-opting the papacy as a model for his *Leviathan*, and supplying its *Ecclesiastical History* in his long Latin poem. That he did so at the risk of popularizing the very fiction, the *corpus mysticum*, which *Leviathan* sought to destroy, has also not been noticed. Hence the ambiguity of the *Leviathan* frontispiece (Springborg forthcoming). It is ironic that Hobbes should be immortalized for an iconic image, reinterpreted as representing "The King's Two Bodies," "the Corporation Sole," even "the Crown" (Kantorowicz 1957; Maitland 1911); legal fictions in the creation of which the papacy was complicit, but that Hobbes's materialist and mechanistic metaphysics quite simply forbade.

21.7 Conclusion

Earlier in this chapter I suggested that we set aside "Hobbes's history as a pre-Enlightenment narrative, and assume for the moment that Hobbes is ignorant of the future and innocent of the burden with which he has been saddled," in order to look at the *Historia Ecclesiastica* with fresh eyes. We must avoid further systematic anachronism, as I have elsewhere warned, by refusing "to treat Hobbes as metonymizing the long process by which the system of offices was established in medieval Europe, structured in terms of the transfer of legal personality ... from individuals (natural persons) to collectivities (fictive persons) which are accorded corporate status" (Springborg 2019, 34, citing Runciman 1997, 2000). As I go on to note: "To see Hobbes's political theory as a gloss on this history is, on the face of it, far-fetched, and involves the fallacy of retrospectivity, because it requires at least in part the hindsight yielded only when the Holy Roman Empire was dead and the modern nation state was flourishing, which was long after Hobbes's demise" (Springborg 2019, 34–5). In the German Hobbes tradition of Pufendorf and von Gierke (1900), who were engineering nationalist projects and were guilty of this fallacy, there is a sense of predestination or inevitability, such that the irresolvable antinomies to which Hobbes's project gives rise, and which we have stressed, are elided. The legacy of this tradition is still pervasive, and it is to this legacy that my cautionary tale is addressed.

Notes

1 Wilks (1963, 24) citing Augustine, *De quaestionibus evangelistarum*, ii, 51 (PL, xxxv. 1362; cited by Aquinas, *Summa theologica*, III. lv. 4 ad I).

2 For a fuller treatment of the Greek into Arabic and Arabic into Latin translation movements and the Aristotle commentaries of the Falasifa that catalyzed Medieval European Scholasticism, see Springborg, 2018, sections 3, "Constitutionalism and Antiquity Transformation" (11–15), and section 4, "Antiquity Transformation and Islamic Jurisprudence" (16–20); and Springborg, 2019a, section 2, "The Twelfth Century Renaissance in the Norman Kingdoms of England and Sicily" (5–12), and section 3, "English Seventeenth Century Scientific Culture, Arabic MSS, the Bodleian Library and Royal Society" (12–17).

References

Akasov, Anna. and Guido Giglioni 2013. *Renaissance Averroism and its Aftermath: Arabic Philosophy in Early Modern Europe*. Dordrecht: Springer Verlag.

Aubrey, John 1898. *"Brief Lives," Chiefly of Contemporaries, Set down by John Aubrey between the Years 1669 & 1696*, edited from the author's Mss. by Andrew Clark. 2 vols. Oxford: Oxford University Press.

Berman, Harold J. 1983. *Law and Revolution, the Formation of the Western Legal Tradition*. Cambridge, MA: Harvard University Press.

Collins, Jeffrey 2016. "Thomas Hobbes's Ecclesiastical History." In *The Oxford Handbook of Hobbes*, edited by Aloysius P. Martinich and Kinch Hoekstra, 520–44. Oxford: Oxford University Press.

Côté, Antoine. 2014. James of Viterbo. Entry in the *Stanford Encyclopedia of Philosophy*. https://plato.stanford.edu/archives/spr2014/entries/james-viterbo

Gierke, Otto von. 1900. *Political Theories of the Middle Ages* translated by Frederic William Maitland. Cambridge: Cambridge University Press.

Gutas, Dmitri 1998. *Greek Thought, Arabic Culture: The Graeco-Arabic Translation Movement in Baghdad and Early 'Abbasaid Society*. London: Routledge.

Haskins, Charles Homer 1927. *The Renaissance of the Twelfth Century*. Cambridge, MA: Harvard University Press.

Hobbes, Thomas. 1889. *The Elements of Law Natural and Politic*, edited by Ferdinand Tönnies. London: Simpkin, Marshall and Co. online at https://doi.org/10.4324/9780429030772.

Hobbes, Thomas. 1998. *On the Citizen (De cive)*, translated by Richard Tuck and Michael Silverthorne. Cambridge: Cambridge University Press.

Hobbes, Thomas. 2008. *Historia Ecclesiastica: Critical Edition*, edited by Patricia Springborg, Patricia Stablein and Paul Wilson. Paris: Honoré Champion.

Hobbes, Thomas. 2012. *Leviathan*, 3 vols., edited by Noel Malcolm. Oxford: Clarendon Press.

Innocent III; Letter to Acerbius. 1198, *Medieval Sourcebook: Innocent III: Letters on Papal Polices*. Fordham.edu: https://sourcebooks.fordham.edu/source/inniii-policies.asap.

Kantorowicz, Ernst. 1957. *The King's Two Bodies: A Study in Mediaeval Political Theology*. Princeton, NJ: Princeton University Press.

Landau, Peter. 1984. "Review of *Law and Revolution* by Harold J. Berman." *University of Chicago Law Review* 51 3: 937–43. Accessed September 3, 2020. https://chicagounbound.uchicago.edu/uclrev/vol51/iss3/8.

Lee, Daniel. 2013. "'Office Is a Thing Borrowed': Jean Bodin on Offices and Seigneurial Government." *Political Theory* 41 (3): 409–40.

Lee, Daniel. 2016. *Popular Sovereignty in Early Modern Constitutional Thought*. Oxford: Oxford University Press.

Luman, Richard. 1963. "Review of *the Problem of Sovereignty in the Later Middle Ages* by M. J. Wilks." *Church History* 32 (4): 478–9. DOI: 10.2307/3163296.

Maitland, Frederic. 1898. "William of Drogheda and the Universal Ordinary." In *Roman Canon Law in the Church of England*, 100–31. London: Methuen.

Maitland, Frederic. 1911. "'The Corporation Sole,' and 'The Crown as Corporation'." In *Maitland, Collected Papers*, edited by Herbert A.L. Fisher. Cambridge: Cambridge University Press, Vol. 3, 210–43, and 244–70.

Malcolm, Noel. 2007. "The Name and Nature of Leviathan: Political Symbolism and Biblical Exegesis." *Intellectual History Review* 17 (1): 29–58. DOI: 10.1080/17496970601140196.

Malcolm, Noel. 2012. *Hobbes's Leviathan*, Vol. 1, Introduction. Oxford: Clarendon Press.

Morris, Colin. 1991. *The Papal Monarchy: The Western Church from 1050 to 1250*. Oxford: Oxford University Press.

Olsthoorn, Johann. 2018. "The Theocratic *Leviathan*: Hobbes's Arguments for the Identity of Church and State." In *Hobbes on Religion and Politics*, edited by Laurens van Apeldoorn and Robin Douglass, 10–28. Oxford: Oxford University Press.

Olsthoorn, Johann. 2020. "*Leviathan* Inc.: Hobbes on the Nature and Person of the State." *European History of Ideas* 1–16. DOI: 10.1080/01916599.2020.1779466.

Pocock, John G.A. 1999. *Barbarism and Religion: Volume 2, Narratives of Civil Government*. Cambridge: Cambridge University Press.

Pocock, John G.A. 2003. *Barbarism and Religion: Volume 3, the First Decline and Fall*. Cambridge: Cambridge University Press.

Ribarevic, Luka. 2017. "*Leviathan* and the Medieval *Universitas*: Hobbes's Debt to Canon Law." *History of Political Thought* 38 (1): 92–109.

Runciman, David. 1997. *Pluralism and the Personality of the State*. Cambridge, MA: Cambridge University.

Runciman, David. 2000. "What Kind of Person is Hobbes's State? A Reply to Skinner." *Journal of Political Philosophy* 8 (2): 268–78.

Schuhmann, Karl. 2004. "Phantasms and Idols: True Philosophy and Wrong Religion in Hobbes." *Revista di Storia della Filosofia* 59 (1): 15–31.

Skinner, Quentin. 2018. "Hobbes on Political Representation." In *From Humanism to Hobbes; Studies in Rhetoric and Politics*, 190–221. Cambridge: Cambridge University Press.

Sommerville, Johann P. 1992. *Thomas Hobbes: Political Ideas in Historical Context*. London: Palgrave Macmillan.

Springborg, Patricia. 1994. "Hobbes, Heresy, and the *Historia Ecclesiastica*." *Journal of the History of Ideas* 55: 553–71.

Springborg, Patricia. 1995. "Thomas Hobbes and Cardinal Bellarmine: Leviathan and the Ghost of the Roman Empire." *History of Political Thought* 16 (4): 503–31.

Springborg, Patricia. 1996. "Writing to Redundancy: Hobbes and Cluverius." *The Historical Journal* 39 (4) (December 1996): 1075–8.

Springborg, Patricia. 2008. "Introduction." In *Thomas Hobbes Historia ecclesiastica*, critical edition, edited by Patricia Springborg, Patricia Stablein, and Paul Wilson, 17–267. Paris: Honoré Champion.

Springborg, Patricia. 2018. "Constitutionalism and Antiquity Transformation," *Global Intellectual History*, DOI: 10.1080/23801883.2018.1527516.

Springborg, Patricia. 2019a. "Raylor's Revisionist Humanist Hobbes," *Global Intellectual History*, DOI: 10.1080/23801883.2019.1606692.

Springborg, Patricia. 2019b. "Quentin Skinner and Hobbes's Artificial Person of the State Redux. Review Essay of Quentin Skinner, *From Humanism to Hobbes*." *Global Intellectual History* 2019 47 pp. Accessed October 30, 2020. https://doi.org/10.1080/23801883.2019.1677282.

Springborg, Patricia. forthcoming. "Hobbes's Leviathan has Feet of Clay". '*Hobbes Studies*, special issue, Festschrift for Johann Sommerville, edited by Daniel Kapust and Brandon Turner.

Springborg, Patricia, Patricia Stablein, and Paul Wilson ed. 2008. *Thomas Hobbes Historia ecclesiastica*, critical edition. Paris: Honoré Champion, 729 pp.

Talaska, Richard, ed. 2013. *The Hardwick Hall Library and Hobbes's Early Intellectual Development*. Charlottesville, VA: Philosophy Documentation Center. Available as an e-book from http://www.pdcnet.org

Wilks, Michael. 1963. *The Problem of Sovereignty in the Later Middle Ages*. Cambridge: Cambridge University Press.

Part V

Controversies and Reception

22

Body and Space in Hobbes and Descartes

EDWARD SLOWIK

As is well-known, Hobbes's natural philosophy of body and space, although influential in his own day, has largely been overshadowed in the contemporary historical literature by the system developed by his chief rival in the mechanical philosophy, Descartes. Part of the reason for this neglect might stem from the obvious success and continuing interest generated by Hobbes's social and political philosophy, an accomplishment that overshadows other parts of his philosophical oeuvre. But, there is also a suspicion that the oversight is due to the fact that the type of "matter and motion" physics that Hobbes developed is just too similar to the Cartesian program, and that the benefits of a close comparison of the two will bear meagre fruit. In this chapter, Hobbes's theories of space and body will be contrasted with the Descartes's hypotheses, a comparison that is intended to reveal several conceptual issues that distinguish Hobbes's work from the Cartesian system, and thereby dispel any lingering doubts concerning the uniqueness and merits of Hobbes's approach. As will be demonstrated, there are a host of intriguing differences between the rival camps as regards body and space, from Hobbes's application of his empirically based notion of phantasms and imaginary space to his analysis of the material constitution of bodies. Yet, the close similarities between the two systems on various other issues will also be addressed, such as the rejection of void space and the emphasis on extension. The focus of the investigation, furthermore, will largely center on their most significant and influential achievements in natural philosophy, Descartes's *Principles of Philosophy*, and Hobbes's *De corpore*, although other texts will factor into the analysis as well. In the first section, after a short summary of Hobbes's system, several aspects of Descartes and Hobbes's respective hypotheses of body will be compared and evaluated. The second section will focus on their assessments of void space, while the third section will examine their relationship to Scholastic and non-Scholastic imaginary space hypotheses, with the ancient neo-Platonist, John Philoponus, serving as a framework by which to appraise Descartes' and Hobbes's divergent conceptions. In the fourth section, a few concluding observations will be

A Companion to Hobbes, First Edition. Edited by Marcus P. Adams.

offered on the function of experimental evidence, as opposed to *a priori* reasoning, in Hobbes's natural philosophy of body and space.

22.1 Body

22.1.1 *Hobbes on Body and Accident, Real and Imaginary Space*

In *De corpore*, Hobbes declares that "SPACE *is the phantasm of a thing existing without the mind simply*" (EW I.94), an inference that he reaches by way of a thought experiment involving the annihilation of the world: "If therefore we remember, or have a phantasm of any thing that was in the world before the supposed annihilation of the same; and consider, not that the thing was such or such, but only that it had being without the mind, we have presently a conception of that we call *space*: an imaginary space indeed, because a mere phantasm" (EW I.93). A phantasm pertains to "the memory and imagination of [bodily] magnitudes, motions, sounds, colours, &c. as also of their order and parts" (EW I.92); and, since memory and imagination are implicated, phantasms obviously require sensation: "SENSE *is a phantasm, made by reaction and endeavor outwards in the organ of sense, caused by an endeavor inwards from the object, remaining for some time more or less*" (EW I.391). In short, phantasms would appear to involve the cognitive processes associated with sense, imagination, and understanding (where understanding is obtained through imagination; Hobbes 2012, 36; 1651, 7). In what follows, an analysis of these specific cognitive processes, as well as the role that nominalism and language play, will not be examined at length (but see, e.g., Slowik 2014 on these issues). Since the context of our investigation concerns various ontological hypotheses regarding space that were developed by Hobbes, Descartes, and other natural philosophers of the period, only those aspects of phantasms that pertain to bodily and spatial ontology will be investigated in depth. Nevertheless, by associating phantasms with "imaginary space" in the first quotation provided above, where the latter term as employed in the later medieval and renaissance periods normally signified something more than a mere cognitive process, it thus follows that important aspects of Hobbes's notion of a phantasm cannot be entirely sidelined in our ensuing analysis either.

Unlike imaginary space, body "is *a thing subsisting of itself*," and "is called the subject, because it is so placed in and *subjected* to imaginary space, that it may be understood by reason, as well as perceived by sense. The definition, therefore, of *body* may be this, a *body is that, which having no dependence upon our thought, is coincident or coextended with some part of space*" (EW I.102). If body is "subjected to imaginary space," so that it can "be understood by reason," then at least part of Hobbes's conception of imaginary space would appear to involve cognitive faculties that go beyond mere sense and imagination, such as reason's ability to abstract or generalize. Space also plays a central role in Hobbes's approach to accidents. After defining "an *accident* to be *the manner of our conception of body*" (EW I104), a description that has led some commentators to a transcendental idealist interpretation (see Herbert 1987), Hobbes offers a conception that upholds the traditional substance/accident scheme that he inherited from the Scholastics, namely, that accidents "inhere" in a subject: "as magnitude, or rest, or motion, is in that which is great, or which resteth, or which is moved, ... so also, it is to be understood, that every other accident *is in* its subject" (EW I.104). Bringing all of these themes together, he concludes: "The *extension* of a body, is the same thing with the *magnitude* of it, or that which some call *real space*. But this *magnitude* does not depend upon cogitation, as imaginary space doth; for this is an effect of our imagination, but *magnitude* is the cause of it" (EW I.105).

22.1.2 Contrasting Hobbes and Descartes on Body

Given the similarities between Hobbes's and Descartes' respective programs in natural philosophy, especially their mechanistic approach and anti-Scholasticism, it is thus not surprising that their differences on the nature of body, space, and motion are often quite subtle or difficult to discern. Indeed, while both claim to have overthrown the Aristotelian heritage for a mechanical modernism, they nonetheless often rely on Scholastic conceptions and arguments in advancing their respective systems. For example, Hobbes refers to Descartes' conception of body in the following: "I find space to be falsely defined by certain philosophers, who infer ... that the world is infinite (for taking *space* to be the extension of bodies, and thinking extension may encrease continually, he infers that bodies may be infinitely extended)" (EW I.93). While Hobbes's argument against the infinity of space will be examined later, his assertion that Descartes takes bodily extension to be the same as space is not far removed from Hobbes's own conception. As noted above, Hobbes defines "real space" as bodily extension, while Descartes declares that "the same extension which constitutes the nature of body also constitutes the nature of space, and that these two things differ only in the way that the nature of the genus or species differs from that of the individual" (Descartes 1983, 44). In a similar vein, Hobbes contends that "that there are certain accidents which can never perish except the body perish also; for no body can be conceived to be without extension, or without figure" (EW I.104).

Another issue upon which both Hobbes and Descartes agree is the inadequacy of the Aristotelian hypotheses relating to rarefaction and condensation, as well as heaviness. "Condensed, is when there is in the very same matter, less quantity than before; and rarified, when more," Hobbes explains, but he retorts, "[a]s if there could be matter, that had not some determined quantity; when quantity is nothing else but the determination of matter" (EW I.679). Descartes responds similarly: "it is clearly contradictory for anything to be increased by new quantity or new extension, unless a new extended substance, that is, a body, is added to it: for it cannot be understood that any increase in extension or quantity can occur except by the addition of a substance which has extension and quantity" (Descartes 1983, 42).

Turning to the phenomenon of gravity, Descartes and Hobbes both focus on the unhelpful and uninformative role that the form of "heaviness" assumes in the Aristotelian-Scholastic account. Descartes singles out its erroneous status or function as a type of goal-directed mental property: "what makes it especially clear that my idea of gravity was taken largely from the idea I had of the mind is the fact that I thought that gravity carried bodies towards the centre of the earth as if it had some knowledge of the centre within itself. For this surely could not happen without knowledge, and there can be any knowledge except in a mind" (Descartes 1984, 298). Hobbes, on the other hand, illuminates the vacuous nature of the proposed explanation afforded via heaviness: "the Schools will tell you out of Aristotle, that the bodies that sink downwards, are *heavy*; and that this heaviness is it that causes them to descend. But if you ask what they mean by *heaviness*, they will define it to be an endeavour to go to the centre of the earth. So that the cause why things sink downward, is an endeavour to be below: which is as much as to say, that bodies descend, or ascend, because they do" (EW IV.678). On both Descartes' and Hobbes's respective schemes for natural philosophy, only a mechanical explanation that relies on matter and motion alone can be an acceptable hypothesis.

A charge that has often been levelled at Descartes' material system is that it is compromised by a circularity that lies at the heart of his accounts of body and motion (see, e.g., Slowik 2002, 168–9), but this problem may also have a correlate in Hobbes's scheme. In the *Principles of Philosophy*, his most important work on natural philosophy, Descartes defines motion as "*the transference of one part of matter or of one body, from the vicinity of those bodies immediately contiguous to it and considered as at rest, into the vicinity of others*. By *one body*, or *one part of matter*, I here understand everything which is simultaneously transported" (Descartes 1983, 51). The circularity in this account of both motion and body is easily discernible: after defining motion as a transfer of a body from its neighboring bodies, he then proceeds to define body as that which is simultaneously transported. Hobbes's alleged circularity problem, put forward in Brandt (1928), would seem to comprise an equivalent phantasm-based version. As discussed above, a motion ("endeavor") from a body conveyed by way of a person's sense organs brings about a phantasm, an hypothesis that prompts Brandt to comment that "hence the idea of magnitude [i.e., a phantasm of "real space"] is also 'in reality' motion—but motion cannot be conceived without space and magnitude" (Brandt 1928, 253).[1] He concludes that this circularity demonstrates that Hobbes "drops the idea of an entirely 'phantastic' space" and embraces instead the view that "body, which occupies space, really does exist apart from our consciousness" (1928, 253).

But even granting this justifiable inference, there is a significant difference between the two cases that Brandt considers, with the upshot being that Hobbes's circularity predicament would appear to be much less onerous than Descartes' similar quandary, if there is a problem at all. For the latter, the circularity pertains to the same object – *this* body moves because it is one, and it is one body because it moves simultaneously – whereas the former invokes the phantasm-inducing motions in the sense organs that were brought about by the body; i.e., the circularity of the definition does not involve the same object (or event) alone. Put differently, the motion that is caused in the mind/sense organ is not directly associated with the *material* identity of the body that causes the motion in the mind/sense organ, whereas motion is directly linked to the body's identity in that way for Descartes. This point would seem to be related to an insightful observation that Jesseph makes regarding the spatiality intrinsic to Hobbes's explication of phantasms: given that a sensation is a phantasm "*made by reaction and endeavor outwards in the organ of sense, caused by an endeavor inwards from the object*" (EW I.391), he points out that "the very concept of a phantasm presupposes such spatial orientations such as 'inward' and 'outward'" (Jesseph 2015, 195); i.e., Hobbes's explanation assumes that there is a spatial distinction, or separation, between the body and the sense organs/mind prior to the phantasm-inducing motions. Finally, and more importantly, the analysis of body in Part II of *De corpore*, which lays out Hobbes's physical ontology, does not employ motion to define body, but instead appeals to the occupation of space by body (see EW I.102 above), whereas Descartes does directly employ motion in his description of body.

22.2 Space and Void

22.2.1 Hobbes and Descartes on Void Space

One of the central, as well as most discussed, differences between Hobbes and Descartes concerns the possibility of a void space. In the *Principles*, it automatically follows that a vacuum is impossible since "space does not in fact differ from material substance" (Descartes 1983, 44), and thus he declares that "[t]hat it is contradictory for a vacuum, or a space in which there is absolutely nothing, to exist" (1983, 46). Following the precedent set by such medieval thinkers as Marsilius of Inghen (see Grant 1981, 122–3), Descartes concludes that "if anyone asks what would occur if God removed the whole body contained in any vessel and did not permit anything else to take the place of the body which had been removed, the answer will have to be that the sides of the vessel would thereby become contiguous to each other. For, when there is nothing between two bodies, they must necessarily touch each other; and it is manifestly contradictory for them to be apart" (Descartes 1983, 48).

Given his identification of real space and bodily magnitude, one would think that Hobbes would likewise regard a void space as a contradiction in terms. Yet, Hobbes offers a different assessment, a reply that would seem to be specifically directed at Descartes and his followers: "[T]hough between two bodies there be put no other body, and consequently no magnitude, or, as they call it, real space, yet if another body may be put between them, that is, if there intercede any imagined space which may receive another body, then those bodies are not contiguous.... For can any man that has his natural senses, think that two bodies must therefore necessarily touch one another, because no other body is between them?" (EW I.108–9). In an earlier passage, furthermore, he offers a distinction between a full and empty space that would seem to concede the possibility of a void: "Space, or place, that is possessed by a body, is called *full*, and that which is not so possessed, is called *empty*" (EW I.107). Following the analysis in Sylla (2002), Leijenhorst summarizes the problem with Hobbes's stance: "Hobbes defines imaginary space as nothing but a phantasma, a mental representation of real space or the real extension of external bodies. In the above-mentioned passage, however [EW I.108–9], imaginary space is considered to be a physical entity that can be interposed between two natural bodies. In other words, Hobbes seems to confound our representation of a void space with a physical void" (Leijenhorst 2002, 124). Or, put differently, a mental image of bodily extension, derived from sense alone, cannot provide information on what must occur if a body is removed from the material world. One would need to supplement the sense-based phantasm with a theory that details the behavior or operation of bodies under these circumstances – but a theory of that type transcends the content of a phantasm, and must therefore be a physical hypothesis that is based, at least in part, on reason, and not sensation alone. For Descartes, on the other hand, the rejection of a vacuum follows directly from his contention, which is clearly ontological in nature, that three-dimensional extension is identical with corporeal substance (and so the extended region of the void is really matter). As will be examined, Hobbes does reject the void in *De corpore*, but the basis of his dismissal does not follow from the very definitions of body and space, as it does for Descartes.

The inconsistency in Hobbes's treatment of a void space can be usefully contrasted with his analysis of an infinite world, for the latter discussion would appear to remain more consistent with the allegedly empirical nature of his phantasm methodology than the former. In a passage that criticizes those natural philosophers that accept an infinitely extended world, such as Descartes (see section 22.1.2), Hobbes reasons: "Whatsoever we know that are men, we learn it from our phantasms; and of the infinite, whether magnitude or time, there is no phantasm at all; so that it is impossible either for a man or any other creature to have any conception of infinite.... But whether we suppose the world to be finite or infinite, no absurdity will follow. For the same things would now appear, might appear, whether the Creator had pleased it should be finite or infinite" (EW I.411–12). In this context, Hobbes is content to leave open the ontological question of the world's actual extension, so that either scenario (finite or infinite) is possible, since there are no phantasms of the infinite. Accordingly, if Hobbes had employed the same reasoning to his hypothetical case of a void space brought about the removal of a body from its neighboring contiguous bodies, then he should have reached the same conclusion, i.e., that either scenario, the bodies becoming contiguous or remaining non-contiguous, is possible after the removal of the intermediate body. Just as there are no phantasms of the infinite in *De corpore*, his stipulation that there are no vacua entails that there can be no phantasms of a void space either, and so he should have remained as neutral as regards the outcome of his hypothetical void space scenario as in the parallel case of an infinite world. In response, one could argue that these two cases, a phantasm of the infinite and a phantasm of the void, are dissimilar on the grounds that it is conceptually impossible to experience the infinite (i.e., one can only experience finite things on Hobbes's estimation), whereas it would be possible to experience a void if one did exist. Some philosophers, such as Hume,[2] denied that one could actually experience a void, it should be noted, although the case of a body-sized void situated between other bodies (as in Hobbes's example) might possibly allow such an experience (or phantasm). Under those circumstances, the absence of the body would presumably stand out against the material surroundings. Another possible rejoinder to the criticism raised above (that Hobbes unwarrantedly treats phantasms of the void differently than the infinite) might focus on his claim in the passage above (EW I.411–12) that "no absurdity will follow" if the world is either finite or infinite because "the same things would now appear, might appear." That is, we would experience the same finite objects in both cases, for an infinite object cannot be experienced. Presumably, this form of reply would contend that an absurdity would follow if the surrounding bodies became contiguous after the deletion of the in-between body, but what is that absurdity (maybe a lessening of the world's material contents)?

22.2.2 Hobbes's Case Against Void Space

As recounted in Leijenhorst (2002, 124–5), Hobbes began to posit a plenum (matter-filled) world around 1648, reversing his earlier endorsement of small interworld vacua that were instrumental to his account of light in several works on optics up through the mid-1640s. The production of light by the sun was conceived as analogous to the pumping motion of the heart, a dilation and contraction that exerted pressure on the medium and which thus necessitated small vacua in order to accommodate the dilation process. Yet, since he also conceived light as a pulse through a medium, any discontinuity in that medium, such as a void space, would appear to undermine the propagation of the pulse. This dilemma may have been the rationale behind Hobbes's decision to opt for a plenum, although the textual evidence is ambiguous on this specific point. Descartes advanced a similar optical hypothesis at roughly the same time, i.e., that light is propagated by pressure through a medium (see Descartes 1983, 117), it is important to note; but there are important differences between their respective models, and it is highly doubtful that Hobbes's views were directly based on, or inspired by, Descartes' similar system.

Among the several arguments that Hobbes deploys against the void, one of the more informative for the content of his physics pertains to the ancient atomist's contention that a plenum would prevent motion from occurring since there would be no empty places for a body to occupy. Hobbes objects that there does not "appear any cause, why the matter of the world should, for the admission of motion, be intermingled with empty spaces rather than full; I say full, but withal fluid," and adds that "whilst they contemplate the nature of fluid, they conceive it to consist, as it were, of small grains of hard matter, in such a manner as meal is fluid, made so by grinding of the corn; when nevertheless it is possible to conceive fluid to be of its own nature as homogenous as either an atom, or vacuum itself" (EW I.417). This last observation may be an allusion to the Cartesian hypothesis of elementary matter, since Descartes does treat his first element of matter, following Hobbes's homespun analogy, more like meal than grain. While the microscopically small, spherical second element of matter functions somewhat like an atom, and the third element comprises much larger chunks of matter, Descartes explains that the first element "has so much force of agitation that, by colliding with other bodies, it is divided into particles of indefinite smallness, and which adapts its shapes to fill all the narrow parts of the little angles left by the others [second and third element matter]" (Descartes 1983, 110). As the debris left over from the collisions of the other two elements, first element matter primarily serves, as Descartes remarks, to fill in the gaps between those other elements; but it is still an extended material "particle" that collides "with other bodies," and thus the only significant difference when compared with the second and third element is its "indefinite smallness."

Hobbes, on the other hand, rejects these types of atomistic or corpuscularian accounts and simply appeals to a fluid body that has "its own nature" and is as "homogenous as either an atom, or vacuum itself." Drawing upon our common experience of solid bodies in fluids, he infers that a fluid would not hinder the motion of a solid body that moves through it: "Bodies moved, and also the mediums in which they are moved, are of two kinds. For either they have their parts coherent in such a manner, as no part of the moved body will easily yield to the movent, except the whole body yields also, and such things we call *hard*: or else their parts, while the whole remains unmoved, will easily yield to the movent, and these we call *fluid* or *soft* bodies" (EW I.334). Yet, as another ancient, Archimedes, was possibly the first to discover, a submerged body displaces an equal volume of fluid, and so Hobbes has only resolved the ancient atomist's argument if his solid object is already assumed to be present in the plenum world: i.e., in a world filled with fluid matter, such that no fluid could be displaced, a solid object could not even enter the world.[3] Hobbes's criterion for distinguishing solid and fluid bodies is, moreover, quite problematic. Fluid bodies do not always "easily yield to the movent," as anyone who has skipped stones on a pond's surface can affirm, and soft bodies exhibit behavior that is generally much closer to solid bodies than to fluid bodies. In short, even if it has "its own nature," the specific ontological details of a fluid body are not explained in sufficient detail, especially as regards the difference between the intrinsic structure and constitution of his fluid body as compared with a solid material body. A fluid, or hydrostatics, orientation is a central feature of many of the hypotheses that comprise Descartes' mechanical system, it is important to stress (see Slowik 2002, ch. 5). But the Cartesian conception of the world's most basic material entities, the three elements of matter, aligns more naturally with an atomistic or corpuscularian collision model, with fluid or hydrostatic explanations often relegated to the behavior of a whole system or ensemble. Hobbes, in contrast, would appear to invoke a fundamental distinction between an extended material body and a fluid body at the ground floor of his mechanical system.

Probably the most discussed argument that Hobbes wields against the void concerns the well-known Torricellian experiment that centers upon the behavior of the mercury that fills an inverted tube. When the bottom of the tube is opened while submerged in a pool of mercury (and the top is sealed), the mercury in the tube will descend, with the empty space at the top of the tube now revealing the presence of a void, or so argued the opposing camp in this dispute. Hobbes rebuts this attempted proof by declaring that the pressure of the mercury descending in the tube forces the air to ascend through the silver into the top portion of the tube: "if the force with which the quicksilver descends be great enough, ... it will make the air penetrate the quicksilver in the vessel, and go up into the cylinder to fill the place which they thought was left empty" (EW I.421–2). Descartes offers a similar proposal, but utilizes his first element of matter as the substance that fills the top of the tube, and with small pores in the glass's structure serving as the point of entry rather than through the mercury (see Garber 1992, 138).

22.3 Imaginary Space and Immobility

Hobbes's use of the term "imaginary space" inevitably draws comparisons with a host of Scholastic and non-Scholastic hypotheses in the late Medieval and Renaissance periods that bear the same name. The problems associated with Aristotle's analysis of place and void prompted the development of these imaginary space conceptions, especially his contention that place is the motionless innermost surface of the contiguous bodies that surround the contained body in a plenum (and not the three-dimensional extension within, and bounded by, that two-dimensional surface; Aristotle 1949, 57).

In addition, Aristotle raises the objection that if the void possessed dimensional extension, then the dimensionality of a body, such as a wooden cube, and the dimensionality of the void space that the cube enters, would both coincide – an outcome that, apparently, undermines the identity of the body, or, at the least, proves that the dimensionality of the void space is a superfluous addition: "How then will the body of the cube differ from the void or place that is equal to it?" (1949, 65).

Many later philosophers were not content with the Aristotelian conception of place, such as the sixth-century neo-Platonist, John Philoponus, whose arguments against Aristotle would foreshadow, and directly inspire, the development of various imaginary space theories in the sixteenth and seventeenth centuries. In his *Corollaries*, Philoponus insists that the interpenetration of bodily extension and void extension is neither superfluous nor impossible: "it [does] not follow that body is in body, since the void is not a body at all ..., neither will the body qua extension be in another [bodily] extension: rather, qua bodily-extension it will be in place-extension" (Philoponus 1991, 61). He also presents several well-known criticisms against the hypothesis that motion is merely the reciprocal change of Aristotle's two-dimensional containing surface (1991, 24); e.g., a body at rest could still be judged to be in motion if the surrounding air (in contact with the body's surface) is constantly changing, a counter-intuitive outcome that that also undermines Aristotle's insistence that place is immobile. As an alternative, Philoponus contends that place is "a certain extension in three dimensions, different from the bodies that come to be in it, bodiless in its own definition" (1991, 28), and that "there could be no motion in place at all if there were not such an extension [i.e., place-extension]" (1991, 67).

The imaginary space hypotheses developed in the sixteenth and seventeenth centuries would offer a scheme similar to Philoponus' place-extension concept in order to ensure the immobility of place (and thus refute the counter-intuitive consequences associated with Aristotelian motion). Toletus, the sixteenth-century Scholastic whose internal and external place distinction mirrors Descartes' use of those terms, employed imaginary space for that purpose (Toletus 1589, 122–3), i.e., place's immobility, along with the Coimbra Jesuits and many others. Toletus likewise claimed that our conception of imaginary space is obtained through a process of abstraction from our experience of extended bodies, somewhat in the manner of mathematical abstraction: "since [space] seems to remain the same while bodies are always changing, one thinks that it [i.e., space] remains numerically the same, although it is only the same in species and in equality" (1589, 123; translated in Garber 1992, 150). Descartes, following Toletus, declares that "internal place is exactly the same as space; while external place can be taken to be the surface which most closely surrounds the thing placed" (Descartes 1983, 46), and that "we attribute a generic unity to the extension of the space, so that when the body which fills the space has been changed, the extension of the space itself is not considered to have been changed or transported but to remain one and the same; as long as it remains of the same size and shape and maintains the same situation among certain external bodies by means of which we specify that space" (1983, 43–4).

While Descartes appeals to both internal and external space, Hobbes favors the former over the latter: "the nature of *place* does not consist in the *superficies of the ambient*, but in *solid space*; for the whole placed body is coextended with its whole place, ... [and] it cannot be understood to be coextended with superficies," and he offers various arguments, some akin to Philoponus' versions, to demonstrate the inadequacy of external place (EW I.106–7). In a well-known passage, Hobbes incorporates the accounts of immobility by both Descartes, based on internal place (as above), and Thomas White (White 1643, 32–3), employing external place, within his own interpretation based on phantasms:

> And as for those, that, by making *place* to be of the same nature with *real space*, would from thence maintain it to be immovable, they also make place, though they do not perceive they make it so, to be a mere phantasm. For whilst one affirms that place is therefore said to be immovable, because space in general is considered there; if he had remembered that nothing is general or universal besides names or signs, he would easily have seen that that space, which he says is considered in general, is nothing but a phantasm, in the mind or the memory, of a body of such magnitude and such figure. And whilst another says: real space is made immovable by the understanding; as when, under the superficies of running water, we imagine other and other water to come by continual succession, that superficies fixed there by the understanding, is the immovable place of the river: what else does he make it to be but a phantasm, though he do it obscurely and in perplexed words? (EW I.106)

Following the precedent of Toletus and Descartes, who ascribe the immobility of place/space to a conceptual abstraction ("same in species" for Toletus, "generic unity" for Descartes), Hobbes connects immobility to his language-based nominalist scheme. "Names are signs not of things, but of our cogitations" (EW I.17), he insists, and thus one possible interpretation of the passage above, (EW I.106), is that space "in general" is a name that signifies a cognitive process or item (phantasm) – but, since names or cogitations do not literally move, the immobility of "space in general" is therefore guaranteed.[4] If this is the intended meaning of Hobbes's argument, then it is problematic on the grounds that some signs or names associated with space, such as "real space" or "magnitude," refer to more than mere phantasms, as was discussed in Section 23.1; e.g., "*magnitude* does not depend upon cogitation," and "*place* is feigned extension, but *magnitude* is true extension" (EW I.105). Yet, if bodily magnitude does not depend on cogitations (since it's an independently existing entity), then how can he be certain that place, which is closely linked to bodily magnitude, is nothing more than a cogitation (phantasm)?

Hobbes has other arguments to offer for the immobility of place, however: "if place were moved, it would also be carried from place to place, so that one place must have another place, and so on infinitely, which is ridiculous" (EW I.106). One can find this form of argument advanced by other natural philosophers, both prior and subsequent to Hobbes, but it would seem only to establish the conclusion that place cannot be a property of individual bodies, whereas it could still be either a property of all matter or an independently existing entity. Both Newton and Clarke would opt for the latter (see Slowik 2011), employing a version of the argument to defend absolute space, while Philoponus' concept of place-extension might fit the former, namely, that space is a property of all material substance. As regards the fact that many bodies can fill the same place, he reasons that "[j]ust as, in the case of matter, when form [properties] are destroyed, another form at once takes over [e.g., whiteness is replaced by another color property], so too in this case the exchange of bodies never leaves the space empty" and thus "quantity cannot subsist without substance. For the void can never exist in separation from body" (Philoponus 1991, 41). Utilizing the Aristotelian substance/property dichotomy, Philoponus classifies the quantity of place-extension as a property of substance ("quantity cannot subsist without substance"), an interpretation that accords with the assessment of both Descartes ("it is entirely contradictory for that which is nothing to possess extension," Descartes 1983, 47) and Hobbes (see Section 23.1). Yet, Philoponus' "space as property of all body" hypothesis might represent a more robust ontological conception than either Descartes or Hobbes would accept, for he also rejects the view that place-extension can be derived conceptually from three-dimensional bodily-extension, i.e., as an abstraction from body: "[that] place-extension is like bodily-extension without bodily qualities, is altogether far from the truth. For that extension [bodily-extension without qualities] is nothing but quality-less body" (Philoponus 1991, 39). In other words, abstraction only secures a conception of body without qualities, and not space.

Edward Grant characterizes Philoponus' theory as a "void space always occupied by body," and that "he distinguished between material body and immaterial three-dimensional extension; the former is a substance, the latter is not" (Grant 1981, 19–20). A number of non-Scholastic sixteenth- and seventeenth-century natural philosophers would be inspired by Philoponus' work to create their own hypotheses that rely on a three-dimensional void space that is always filled with some type of matter, such as Telesio, Patrizi, Bruno, and Campanella. Yet, it was the spatial hypotheses of many Scholastics, starting roughly in the thirteenth and fourteenth centuries with the work of De Ripa, Bradwardine, and Oresme, that would usher in the imaginary space concept that informs the similar theories of Suárez, Fonseca, Amicus, and many others in the centuries prior to Descartes' and Hobbes's time. Whereas Philoponus rejected the possibility of extracosmic void space outside the material world, Scholastic imaginary space hypotheses were partly motivated by that very possibility, with an immobile, God-grounded, incorporeal and non-dimensional void space serving as the basis for any God-induced motions of the world through the extracosmic void. Oresme, for example, stipulates that "outside the heavens, then, is an empty incorporeal space quite different from any other plenum or corporeal space.... Now this space of which we are talking is infinite and indivisible, and is the immensity of God and God Himself" (Oresme 1968, 176). The exact ontological details concerning how imaginary space was linked to God's immensity often varied among these theorists. Suárez, the seventeenth-century Scholastic who greatly influenced both Hobbes and Descartes (and accepted the internal and external place distinction as well), described imaginary space as the way we understand God's immensity (Suárez 1965, 95–111), an interpretation that he hoped would circumvent the difficulties involved with associating this peculiar form of non-entity with God: i.e., imaginary space was often regarded as a pure privation, or a mere capacity to receive bodies, lacking corporeal dimension but somehow linked to, and congruent with, God's immensity. One can only "imagine" such a non-dimensional space via our experience of extended body, hence the sobriquet, "imaginary space."

In his critique of White's *De mundo*, Hobbes provides a description of the extracosmic void that mirrors the Scholastic imaginary space tradition: "What lies outside the world is surely able to contain body. We must call this ability either space or absence [*privatio*] of space .... Before the Creation, however, it was possible to contrive a world and to place it in a spot different from that occupied by our own world; so there exists outside the world an ability to receive body" (Hobbes 1976, 152–3). If the description and function of Hobbes's version of imaginary space follows the Scholastic model, it nonetheless lacks its ontological grounding in God's immensity, an incorporeal being whose immobility was often regarded as the source of space's immobility; e.g., De Ripa (see Sylla 1998, 216), and, later, the Cambridge neo-Platonism of More and Newton (see Slowik 2011). Indeed, God and angels are excluded from *De corpore*, "and all such things as are thought to be neither bodies nor properties of bodies" (EW I.10), and *Leviathan* mocks the notion of an incorporeal substance as a contradiction in terms (Hobbes 2012, 610; 1651, 207). Descartes' philosophy, needless to say, is predicated on a sharp distinction between corporeal and incorporeal substance (Descartes 1983, 23), along with a God that recreates or conserves the world at every moment (1983, 57), but his indefinitely extended world does not admit the extracosmic void, and thus imaginary space plays no role in his natural philosophy: "I cannot but conceive a space beyond whatever bounds you assign to the universe; and on my view such a space is a genuine body. I do not care if others call this space imaginary and thus regard the world as finite; for I know what are the preconceived opinions that gave rise to this error" (Descartes 1991, 375).

22.4 Conclusion

If one were to venture a pithy encapsulation of Hobbes's natural philosophy of body and space, a plausible candidate might single out his adoption of an empiricist or cognitive centered approach as a means of handling various ontological and theological disputes on the nature of body and space, i.e., his unique phantasm and imaginary space hypotheses. One might argue, consequently, that his handling of the issues pertaining to body and space points forward to the later British Empiricist school, especially Locke and Hume, who typically offered very restricted or tentative pronouncements due to the simple fact that many ontological items, such as substance or space, cannot be directly experienced. As Jesseph has pointed out (Jesseph 2015, 200), some of the important conclusions that Hobbes reaches are likewise hesitant or limited, the most notable being his uncertainty on the world's size, finite or infinite. On the rejection of a vacuum, Jesseph has similarly concluded that "[i]n Hobbes's view, the question of whether there is a vacuum is an empirical one, to be decided on the basis of experiment rather than a priori reasoning" (2015, 202). While this assessment has much merit, especially when compared to Descartes's *a priori* rejection of a void based on his identification of spatial extension and body, the contention that evidence is the determining factor underlying Hobbes's position is much harder to accept. Hobbes sudden reversal on the existence of intercosmic vacua, for instance, probably stems from his adoption of a new theory of light, and not on any experimental evidence. As Leijenhorst notes regarding Hobbes's dismissal of the Torricellian experiment, where it is alleged that the air filters back into the tube through the mercury, "this explanation has all the marks of an *ad hoc* escape route" (Leijenhorst 2002, 126). Ad hoc hypotheses are still tied to experimental evidence, it could be argued, but one could also plausibly infer that one of Hobbes's central claims, that "all mutation is motion" (EW I.126), is as empirically irrefutable as any of Descartes' *a priori* stipulations. Indeed, if there is any issue on which both Hobbes's and

Descartes' competing systems exhibit a profound similarity, it is that both incorporate a hodgepodge of empirically based and non-empirically based hypotheses, although that paltry observation might qualify as empirically irrefutable as well!

Notes

1 Or, as Jesseph (2015) puts it: "In other words, rather than taking space as a basic concept in terms of which to define motion, Hobbes took motion as basic and defined space in terms of it".

2 Hume claims in the *Treatise* that "we can form no idea of a vacuum, or space, where there is nothing tangible or visible" (Hume 2007, 40), and "we have no idea of any real extension without filling it with sensible objects" (2007, 47).

3 He does argue that "when [a] space is enclosed, and both bodies be fluid, they will, if they be pressed together, penetrate one another" (EW I.336), but the case he cites involves two fluids that interpenetrate without losing any volume (and so this section of *De corpore* would not seem to suggest that a fluid body could be condensed so as to allow the motion of a solid body in an enclosed space).

4 A more elaborate version of the argument is in his earlier critique of White's *De Mundo*: "[White] ought to have said that [i] the imaginary surface caused by the sight of the running water was an image of the water, not as water, but as body, and that [ii] the image therefore represents not that particular water but any water, or air, or body of the same size and shapes. Hence it is the surface which was in the mind, i.e. the imaginary surface, that is immobile, not the surface associated with the water by chance" (Hobbes 1976, 53).

References

Aristotle. 1949. *Physics*, translated by Robert Purves Hardie and Russell Kerr Gaye. Oxford: Oxford University Press.

Brandt, Frithiof. 1928. *Thomas Hobbes' Mechanical Conception of Nature*. London: Librairie Hachette.

Descartes, René. 1983. *Principles of Philosophy*, translated by Valentine R. Miller and Reese P. Miller. Dordrecht: Kluwer.

Descartes, René. 1984. *The Philosophical Writings of Descartes, Vol.2*, edited and translated by John Cottingham, Robert Stoothoff, and Dugald Murdoch. Cambridge: Cambridge University Press.

Descartes, René. 1991. *The Philosophical Writings of Descartes, Vol.3, The Correspondence*, edited and translated by John Cottingham, Robert Stoothoff, and Dugald Murdoch. Cambridge: Cambridge University Press.

Garber, Daniel. 1992. *Descartes' Metaphysical Physics*. Chicago: University of Chicago Press.

Grant, Edward. 1981. *Much Ado About Nothing: Theories of Space and Vacuum from the Middle Ages to the Scientific Revolution*. Cambridge: Cambridge University Press.

Herbert, Gary. 1987. "Hobbes's Phenomenology of Space." *Journal of the History of Ideas* 48: 709–17.

Hobbes, Thomas. 1839–1845. *The English Works of Thomas Hobbes*, 11 vols., edited by Sir William Molesworth. London: John Bohn. Cited as EW.

Hobbes, Thomas. 1976. *Thomas White's De Mundo Examined*, translated by Harold Whitmore Jones. London: Bradford University Press.

Hobbes, Thomas. 2012. *Leviathan*, 3 vols., edited by Noel Malcolm. Oxford: Clarendon Press. [First published 1651.]

Hume, David. 2007. *A Treatise of Human Nature*, edited by David Fate Norton and Mary J. Norton. Oxford: Clarendon Press.

Jesseph, Douglas. 2015. "Hobbes's Theory of Space." In *Mathematizing Space: The Objects of Geometry from Antiquity to the Early Modern Age*, edited by Vincenzo De Risi, 193–208. Cham: Springer.

Leijenhorst, Cees. 2002. *The Mechanization of Aristotelianism*. Leiden: Brill.

Oresme, Nicolas. 1968. *Le Livre Du Ciel et Du Monde*, edited and translated by Albert D. Menut and Alexander J. Denomy. Madison: University of Wisconsin Press.

Philoponus, Johannes. 1991. *Corollaries on Place and Void*, translated by David J. Furley. London: Bloomsbury.

Slowik, Edward. 2002. *Cartesian Spacetime*. Dordrecht: Kluwer.

Slowik, Edward. 2011. "Newton, the Parts of Space, and the Holism of Spatial Ontology." *HOPOS: The Journal of the International Society for the History of Philosophy of Science* 1: 249–72.

Slowik, Edward. 2014. "Hobbes and the Phantasm of Space." *Hobbes Studies* 27: 61–79.

Suárez, Francisco. 1965. *Disputationes Metaphysicae*, Vol. 2. Hildesheim: Verlag.

Sylla, Edith. 1998. "Imaginary Space: John Dumbleton and Isaac Newton." In *Raum Und Raumvorstellungen Im Mittealter*, edited by Jan A. Aertsen and Andreas Speer, 202–26. Berlin: W. de Gruyter.

Sylla, Edith. 2002. "Space and Spirit in the Transition from Aristotelian to Newtonian Space." In *The Dynamics of Aristotelian Natural Philosophy from Antiquity to the Seventeenth Century*, edited by Cornelis Leijenhorst, Christoph Lüthy, and Johannes Thijssen, 249–87. Leiden: Brill.

Toletus, Franciso. 1589. *Commentaria una cum quaestionibus in Octo Libros Aristotelis de Physica Auscultatione*, 4th edn. Venice: Iuntas.

White, Thomas. 1643. *De mundo dialogi tres*. Paris: D. Moreau.

23

Hobbes's Mechanical Philosophy and Its English Critics

JOHN HENRY

23.1 Hobbes's Mechanical Philosophy

The mechanical philosophy was a new system of natural philosophy developed in the early part of the seventeenth century, and which soon came to be seen as the best replacement for the natural philosophical system of scholasticism (based largely on Aristotelian precepts), which dominated university teaching, but was increasingly seen to be moribund and fundamentally misconceived. Based in large measure on the Ancient atomistic physics of Epicurus, the mechanical philosophy was developed to explain all physical phenomena in terms of the motions and physical interactions of countless invisibly small particles of matter, which were supposed to constitute all bodies. Where the Ancient atomists referred all phenomena to "atoms and the void," the new mechanical philosophers summed up their philosophy in terms of "matter in motion." Their emphasis was upon kinematics – the science of motion – and mechanics – the understanding of impacts and collisions. United in assuming the particulate nature of matter, they remained divided as to whether the particles moved in void space or were jostled together in a plenum, and whether the particles of matter were indivisible (as atomists claimed) or (at least in principle) infinitely divisible (as those who have come to be designated "corpuscularists" claimed).

This new approach to understanding the natural world was prefigured in the work of Galileo (Henry 2011) but was developed in its most powerful, systematic, and historically influential form by René Descartes, in his *Principia philosophiae* of 1644 (Gaukroger 2002). Although the rival system of mechanical philosophy of Thomas Hobbes did not appear in fully developed form until 1655, in his *De corpore*, Hobbes was recognized long before that as a leading exponent of this new style of natural philosophy (Brandt 1928). Interacting with Sir Kenelm Digby (who would publish the first system of mechanical philosophy in English in 1644) and other English pioneers in the new

A Companion to Hobbes, First Edition. Edited by Marcus P. Adams.

philosophy in the 1630s, and with Descartes himself as well as other rival mechanical philosophers, such as Pierre Gassendi, Gilles Personne de Roberval, and Thomas White in the 1640s (Malcolm 2002, 11–18), Hobbes was working throughout on his own distinctive system, and was recognized by other new natural philosophers to be one of the most powerful of this new breed of thinkers who sought to explain all physical phenomena in terms of matter in motion.

Hobbes's mechanical philosophy was by no means merely derivative from Descartes's *Principia philosophiae*; indeed, Hobbes came closer than anyone else to developing a mechanistic system to match it. Like Descartes, Hobbes rejected any suggestions that bodies might have powers or other occult abilities, and explained all phenomena as the results of nothing more than the motions, impacts, and combinations, or disaggregations of the particles of bodies (EW I.531; Descartes 1644, 304–5). Where Descartes insisted that extension was matter, Hobbes recognized a clear distinction between extension and the thing extended (EW I.105; Descartes 1644, 20). While Descartes was a committed dualist, exempting immaterial substances, such as souls or God, from his materialist physics, Hobbes insisted that only material substance was real: "every part of the universe is body, and that which is not body, is no part of the universe: and because the universe is all, that which is no part of it, is nothing" (Hobbes 2012, 1076; 1651, 371).

One of the most characteristic aspects of Descartes's system was his use of three laws of nature as the starting point for his physics; from these three laws, all else followed. Descartes's laws had to be underwritten by God (since inanimate bodies cannot obey laws), and Hobbes, who preferred to keep his science and his religion separate (EW I.10; Leijenhorst 2004, 76–81), never adopted physical laws but based his physics on what he called "principles," which were modeled on logical or geometrical precepts (Psillos and Goudarouli 2019). Descartes considered motions as the result of collisions, and had to develop a new theory of causation (involving God) to accommodate his radically new assumption that motion could be *transferred* from one body to another (Henry 2004). Hobbes avoided commitment to a new theory of causation simply by defining motion as "a continual relinquishing of one place, and acquiring of another," and collisions as merely a case of one body moving into the place of another. So, a body continually changing its place may take over the place previously occupied by a stationary body, and "by having taken its [the stationary body's] place renders it unable to any longer stay at rest" (EW I.109; EW I.115; Psillos and Goudarouli 2019, 102–4).

Although it seems likely that Hobbes's concept of *conatus*, or "endeavour," was inspired by Descartes's earlier notion of *conatus*, it is clearly different, and fulfils a significantly different function in Hobbes's system (Jesseph 2016, 72–3). *Conatus*, for Descartes, was the name he gave to the centrifugal tendency of rotating bodies, and he used this tendency to explain the propagation of light. For Hobbes, *conatus* signified the inertial motion that a body possessed, even though that motion might not be sensible ("motion made in less space or time than can be given; that is, less than can be determined"), and Hobbes used it to explain pressure and similar phenomena, in which a body was exerting an action (which according to Hobbes it could only do by moving) even though it did not seem to be moving (EW I.206, and I.333; Brandt 1928, ch. 9; Barnouw 1992; Jesseph 2016). *Conatus*, or endeavor, plays a role too in Hobbes's geometry, psychology, and political theory, and has been seen, therefore, as a uniquely

Hobbesian concept that enables a unity of approach across all the elements of his philosophy (Jesseph 2016).

Hobbes himself suggested that his kinematic philosophy was inspired by the work of Galileo, and it is clear that this was not just an attempt to disguise what was really a Cartesian influence (EW I.viii). Hobbes's concept of "simple circular motion," which was a mainstay of his physics, was clearly derived from Galileo and had no equivalent in Cartesianism (Henry 2016). Hobbes supposed that any particle of matter, once set in motion in a circle, would continue to move circularly until another body or bodies happened to prevent that movement. Moreover, a body in simple circular motion could set another body moving the same way by making contact with it. This clearly derived from Galileo's belief in what has been called "circular inertia" – the belief that circular motion is somehow natural and perpetual and once initiated will continue until surrounding physical circumstances prevent it (Henry 2016). Although Descartes's cosmology depended upon the assumption that the planets were driven around the Sun by a vast whirlpool, or vortex, of particulate matter, the vortexes were not considered to be in natural perpetual motion, but to be forced into circularity by surrounding vortexes, all of which were expanding outward as a result of the centrifugal tendency caused by their circular motion (Gaukroger 2002). If it were not for the fact that our Sun's vortex was hemmed in, in this way, the particles constituting the vortex would move naturally in straight lines and would dissipate. So, for Hobbes each individual particle has its own circular motion, but for Descartes particles only move circularly in mass, when forced into circularity by surrounding pressure from other moving particles. Robert Boyle, the leading English natural philosopher and committed opponent of Hobbes, recognized this difference when he wrote:

> the *Cartesians* will think it at least as allowable for them to suppose the Motion he will not grant in their *Materia subtilis*, as for Mr. *Hobbs* to assume it in his *Particulæ terreæ*: especially since he seems to make each such Atom put into and kept in a regular motion; whereas they assume but the having of one general impulse given to the whole mass of Matter. (Boyle [1662] 1999, vol. 3: 134)

Hobbes's system was a carefully thought-out and uniquely original system of mechanical philosophy, and none of his contemporaries, not even his staunchest critics, ever considered it to be simply derived from Cartesianism. Almost as soon as Hobbes's *De corpore* appeared, however, his reputation as a leading mechanical philosopher went into steady decline (Malcolm 2002, 498–500). This was largely the result of the introduction of his idiosyncratic geometry into his physics.

Seeking to present his system of philosophy as superior to any that had gone before, Hobbes began *De corpore* by establishing "the true foundations of natural philosophy" (EW I.xi) with sections on logic, "the most common notions by accurate definition," and geometry (EW I.xiii–xiv). Hobbes felt justified in claiming, therefore, that "in the three former parts of this book all that I have said is sufficiently demonstrated from definitions; and all in the fourth part [his mechanical natural philosophy] from suppositions not absurd" (EW I.xi). The crucial thing about the first three parts was that they could be claimed to be demonstrable and certain because they were established by human minds: "Geometry therefore is demonstrable for the lines and figures from which we reason are drawn and described by ourselves" (EW VII.184; see also OL II.93–4). Hobbes knew that the same could not be said about natural bodies because they are created by God, not by humankind (hence natural philosophy had to be based on "suppositions not absurd"), but geometrical reasoning played a crucial role for Hobbes in establishing secure foundations for philosophical speculation.

This might have been fine if it was not for the fact that Hobbes did not rely on tried and tested Euclidean principles, but introduced his own idiosyncratic notions about geometry into the *De corpore*. Unfortunately, Hobbes seems to have believed that to bolster his monistic claims that all that exists is corporeal he must also develop a materialistic geometry. Moreover, such a materialistic approach to geometry, he believed, would finally result in the solution of longstanding mathematical problems (Jesseph 1999, 73–4). Instead of regarding geometry as a purely abstract science applying to conceptual idealized versions of physical objects, Hobbes wanted to suggest that even the fundamentals of geometry themselves, points, lines, surfaces, and solids, were material objects generated by the motion of bodies (a moving material point creates a line, a moving line creates a surface, and so forth; EW I.70–1; Jesseph 1999, 77–85, 94–100). The results were disastrous, and Hobbes went from being the much-respected mathematician he had been in the 1640s, to a laughingstock among continental mathematicians (Jesseph 1999, 276, see also 280, 352).

Robert Boyle's sources were perhaps correct, therefore, when they suggested that continental readers would not require a refutation of Hobbes's natural philosophy: "I was ... informed by learned men (some of whom keep great Correspondences with the *Virtuosi* abroad) that my publishing any thing against his Objections [to Boyle's work] would not be necessary, nor was much expected" (Boyle [1662] 1999, vol. 3: 111). The otherwise unknown Flemish writer, G. Moranus (1655), published a short critique of *De corpore*, including its bizarre mathematics (Clucas 2017); and the Cartesian Louis de La Forge (1666) included him very briefly alongside Gassendi and Henricus Regius as a significant anti-Cartesian; but no others felt a refutation was worth the effort (Malcolm 2002, 498–9). In the remainder of this chapter, therefore, we shall focus on the English response to Hobbes as a mechanical philosopher.

23.2 English Critics of Hobbes's Mechanical Philosophy

After the publication of *De corpore*, Hobbes was acknowledged as a leading mechanical philosopher, and one whose theories should be taken into account, even if only as a foil to alternative approaches. Among the members of the Royal Society of London, founded in 1660 as one of the earliest formal institutions devoted to the study and promotion of natural philosophy, Hobbes knew he had admirers: "As for the Members, I haue amongst them for the most part a sufficient reputation" (Malcolm 1994, 751). He was never proposed as a fellow, however, and Hobbes attributed this to a number of leading members who were implacably opposed to him and his teachings. He wrote in *Dialogus physicus* (1662) of the "masters of the rest" in the Society, all of whom "are my enemies" (OL IV.237, quoting the translation in Shapin and Schaffer 1985, 348). Hobbes would have been thinking of John Wilkins, Bishop of Chester, and Seth Ward, Bishop of Exeter and Salisbury, who had dismissed his criticisms of the English universities in *Leviathan*

(Hobbes 2012, 1074–6; 1651, 370–1; rejected in Ward 1654, 6–7 [in the Prefatory epistle by Wilkins], and 51–61; Parkin 2007, 145–53), Robert Boyle, and John Wallis, unyielding critic of Hobbes's mathematics.

Their enmity toward Hobbes undoubtedly stemmed from their efforts to defend their new philosophy from accusations of atheism. These four mainstays of the Society were all too aware that for many of their contemporaries the mechanical philosophy was identified with Epicureanism and therefore atheism (Hunter 1990; Parkin 2007, 170). Always striving to show that the mechanical philosophy was compatible with sound religious belief, they saw Hobbes, and his reputation, as compromising all their efforts (for more on Hobbes and the Society, see Jesseph 1999, 274–81; Malcolm 2002, 317–35; Parkin 2007, 215–22).

Even those who respected Hobbes as a mechanical philosopher, recognized that his reputation in politics and religion made it expedient to distance themselves from him. Accordingly, we do not see works expounding, digesting, or popularizing Hobbes's mechanical philosophy. The field was left clear, therefore, for those who wished to dismiss the validity of his natural philosophy. The religious and anti-atheistic motivations underlying those dismissals can be seen clearly, for example, in both of the two most prominent critics of Hobbes's mechanical philosophy, Robert Boyle and Henry More.

23.3 Robert Boyle and Hobbes

An important aspect of the dispute between Boyle and Hobbes was concerned with the correct method to arrive at knowledge of the natural world (Shapin and Schaffer 1985). Boyle was a pioneer of the use of experiment in natural philosophy, while Hobbes clung to the traditional view that the aim of natural philosophy was to provide a proposed theoretical account capable of giving a causal explanation of physical phenomena. Hobbes's speculative approach was essentially the method deployed in the scholastic natural philosophy of the universities (Grant 2002), and was also embraced by Descartes in his alternative system of natural philosophy (Gaukroger 2002). The experimental philosophy was radically different. For Boyle, experiments could establish details of how nature really operated, and they could do so without invoking unconfirmable speculations about possible causes. For Hobbes experiments were of no consequence because they could not indicate the causes of natural phenomena; causes were a matter of rational speculation. As Hobbes wrote in his *Dialogus physicus de natura aeris*, his response to Boyle's *New Experiments Physico-Mechanical* (1660), discussing Boyle's notion of a "spring" of the air, "if they [fellows of the Royal Society] wish to be taken for physicists, they would have to assign some possible cause for it" (OL IV.271, see also 278; Shapin and Schaffer 1985, 377, 383). There was no requirement that the proposed cause had to be proven to be true, all that was required of the natural philosopher was "that all things that are supposed must all be of a possible, that is conceivable nature" (OL IV.247; on this aspect of Hobbes's methodology see Malcolm 2002, 178–84; Shapin and Schaffer 1985, 146–54). Occasionally Hobbes allowed himself to boast about the authenticity of his physics; in the *Dialogus*, for example, he suggested that Boyle's experiments with the air-pump seem to have been "made intentionally by nature to confirm my physics" (OL IV.236). For the most part, however, he was more cautiously probabilistic: declaring that the air-pump showed "that the hypotheses of Hobbes, which indeed were probable enough beforehand, may by this be rendered more probable" (OL IV.273; see also EW I.65–6; EW VII.184).

Boyle subscribed to the very different approach to natural philosophy first developed by Francis Bacon. One of the major reasons for the failure of previous natural philosophy to properly understand the world, according to Bacon, was

> because of the premature and precipitate onrush of the intellect and its tendency to jump the gun and fly off towards the generalities and principles of things, terrible danger may well arise from philosophies of this kind. (Bacon 2004 [1620], 101; see also 45)

The danger, of course, was to fix too soon on incorrect causal explanations that as well as being misconceived would also put a stop to any further attempts to discover the truth. Accordingly, as a convinced Baconian, Boyle avoided ascribing causal explanations to the phenomena he demonstrated experimentally. In his *Examen* (1662), his reply to the *Dialogus*, Boyle stands his ground:

> whereas Mr. *Hobbs* is pleas'd to find much fault with the Society, and me, for not assigning the Cause of Springs in general; that Omission seeming to him very unworthy of Philosophers: I answer, that the Society having hitherto, for weighty Reasons, forborn to determine the particular Causes of Things, there was no Reason they should alter their Method ... And as for me, the Title of my Book promises some *Experiments* touching the Spring of the Air and its Effects, not Speculations of the Causes of Springs in general. (Boyle [1662] 1999, 121)

Underlying these differences were deeper concerns about the usefulness of natural philosophy – in particular its role in establishing what Boyle referred to as "higher Truths" about the relationship between God and the world (Boyle [1662] 1999, 112), and even, it has been argued, about the correct way to maintain social order (Shapin and Schaffer 1985, 21, 332, *passim*).

Boyle points out that Hobbes, in his *Dialogus*,

> endeavoured to disparage unobvious Experiments themselves, and to discourage others from making them. Which if he could by his Dialogue effect, I dare be bold to say, he would far more prejudice Philosophy by this one Trace, then He ... can promote it by all his other Writings. (Boyle [1662] 1999, 111; see also, [1674] 2000, 163; and OL IV.273, 278; Shapin and Schaffer 1985, 379, 383)

The prejudices to philosophy Boyle had in mind are certain opinions of Hobbes "about some important, if not fundamental, Articles of Religion" (Boyle [1662] 1999, 112). Acknowledging that this is hardly the place to discuss religious matters, Boyle insists that Hobbes started it:

> I should scarce in the Introduction to a Dispute about the Air have at all mentioned any thing of this nature, but that Mr. *Hobbs* in the Preface to his Dialogue is pleased ... to speak without limitation or distinction ... of the things said in the Books of Naturalists concerning immaterial substances. (Boyle [1662] 1999, 112, see also 111; OL IV.238)

Hobbes's method allows him to declare that "Nature does all things by the conflict of bodies pressing each other mutually with their motions" (OL IV.238; Shapin and Schaffer 1985, 348), and to go on to deny the existence of incorporeal substance as a contradiction in terms. It was clearly perceived at the time that the new mechanical philosophies, whether Epicurean, Cartesian, or Hobbesian, were increasingly embraced by those who rejected religious belief (Hunter 1990). One of Boyle's guiding principles was to demonstrate to his contemporaries that the mechanical philosophy could be, indeed, if understood properly *must* be, a support to Christian faith. One way of seeing Boyle's voluminous writings in natural philosophy is as a sustained attempt to show that the strictly kinematic versions of the mechanical philosophy, as developed exclusively by Descartes and Hobbes, were unworkable and therefore that other physical factors had to be taken into account to properly understand the way the world worked. The crucial point about such seemingly non-mechanical factors was that they indicated the hand of Providence. The so-called "spring" of the air was just such a phenomenon.

Boyle's experiments with the air-pump demonstrated that the air had an ability to spontaneously expand itself, and indeed to do so to a remarkable extent. Accordingly, as Hobbes summed it up, "there is an elastic force in the air," and the air consists of parts "endowed with a power or principle of dilatation, by whose strength ... [it] restores itself with a spontaneous motion" (OL IV. 246–7). Hobbes scorned these non-mechanical assumptions. Nevertheless, it was clear that a sealed deflated bladder suspended in the chamber of the air-pump would spontaneously inflate itself as the chamber was evacuated of air – even to the point of eventually bursting the bladder. For Boyle this seemed to expose as false mechanist claims that all physical phenomena are the result of impacts from other moving particles. The air particles in the bladder spread themselves out to take up a larger space; there are no candidate moving particles in the experimental setup that could be the cause of this expansive "spring." Furthermore, believing that particles of matter are according to their own nature completely passive and inert, as Boyle does (here agreeing with Descartes and Hobbes), he concluded that this power of spontaneous expansion must have been bestowed upon the particles by God:

> Mr Hobbs ... must allow ... that God put them into a Motion not included in their Nature. From which it will necessarily follow, that at least some Bodies may have Motion though it be not given them by any Body contiguous and moved. (Boyle [1662] 1999, 122; EW I.124)

Boyle did not restrict his discussion to his own discovery of the "spring" of the air; but also insisted that Hobbes has had to smuggle into his own philosophy concepts that cannot simply be referred back to motions caused "by a Body contiguous and moved." Boyle objected that Hobbes's concept of *conatus* suggests that bodies have motion which is "an unlooseable [*sic. i.e.* unloseable] Property, congenit to Matter" (Boyle [1662] 1999, 122). Hobbes, like Boyle, therefore, must accept that God has put into bodies motions that are not part of their nature (Boyle [1662] 1999, 123, 122). Similarly, Boyle objected to Hobbes's concept of "simple circular motion" as another example of unexplained motion of a particle that is not caused by another moving body, but is "*naturæ suæ congenitus*" (Boyle [1662] 1999, 134; see OL IV.253). Again, this is seen by Boyle as something that only God could superadd to matter: "For Philosophers that are known to wish very well to Religion, and to have done it good service, have been very shy of having recourse, as he [Hobbes] has, to Creation, for the explaining of particular *Phænomena*" (Boyle [1662] 1999, 134). Boyle is claiming here that by introducing *conatus* and simple circular motions, Hobbes is recurring to Creation, that is, to the intervention of God.

It is at least possible to argue that these criticisms are unfair. Taken on their own terms in Hobbes's system of philosophy, both *conatus* and "simple circular motion" are justified in mechanistic terms. Simple circular motion, for example, is regarded as inertial (once a body is set moving in a circle that motion will continue indefinitely), and although it is not clear how the simple circular motion of one particle can set up a simple circular motion in another particle, it is perhaps no more dubious than some of Descartes's starting assumptions. Hobbes presents his principles of circular motion in chapter 21 of *De corpore*, and simply makes it axiomatic that simple circular motions can be transferred from one body to another: "Such things as are moved with simple circular motion beget simple circular motion" (EW I.329). Boyle objects that "'tis not likely they [Hobbes's supposed particles] should be permitted to exercise such a regular motion as he attributes to them; but hitting against one another, they must in probability be put into almost as various and confused a motion as *Des-Cartes* ascribes to his Terrestial Particles swimming in the Atmosphere" (Boyle [1662] 1999, 134). But Boyle is simply disregarding Hobbes's axioms here. What is required from Boyle is a demonstration that the transfer of simple circular motion from one body to another does not fit Hobbes's criterion of being "of a possible, that is, conceivable, nature" (OL IV.247). Boyle does not do this (to do so, he would have to take on Galilean physics; see Henry 2016), although he does insist that there is "not any unquestionable Example or Experiment whereby it can be made out, that any small parcel of matter has such a *motus circularis simplex*" (Boyle [1662] 1999, 133). Given that Hobbes regards experimental "evidence" as irrelevant, Boyle's argument again lacks cogency. After all, Hobbes could easily point out that there is no experiment whereby it can be made out that bodies are composed of invisibly small corpuscles of matter (Henry 2016; Shapin and Schaffer 1985).

The main aim of Hobbes's *Dialogus* was to show how his concept of simple circular motion can explain the results of all the air-pump experiments performed by Boyle. Where Boyle suggested it is lack of air that puts out a candle or kills a small creature in the air-pump, Hobbes said these things are the result of greatly exacerbated circular motion of the air, caused by operating the pump: "The very violent motion [of the air] by which the enclosed bladders are distended and broken kills those animals contained in the receiver" (OL IV.259). Boyle responded by pointing out that a fish's bladder suspended in the air-pump, or a compass needle delicately balanced on another needle, "betrayed no such motion as Mr. *Hobbs* here supposes" (Boyle [1662] 1999, 146; see also, [1674] 2000, 196).

Indeed, it is this aspect of Hobbes's *Dialogus* that Boyle could most tellingly examine. Boyle did not just respond with arguments, but conducted further experiments to show that Hobbes's speculative claims could not be correct. Hobbes insisted that if air is removed from the chamber of the air-pump by moving its piston outward, then other air from outside the pump must enter the chamber through a supposed tiny gap between the piston and its cylinder. Being a plenist, Hobbes assumed that there was no room for the air being sucked out of the chamber, unless some of the air already outside the chamber made way for it. But in a plenum, where could this air go? Clearly, it must go where there is room for it: in the chamber of the air-pump (OL IV.245–6). So, as soon as the piston draws out some air, more re-enters through the gap between the piston and its cylinder. Boyle responded by submerging the air-pump in water, whereupon it can be seen that air is expelled from the pump by the bubbles in the water, but no water enters the pump (Boyle [1662] 1999, 13536).

Boyle anticipated that Hobbes would simply say that air invisibly re-enters the submerged pump:

> he will here say ... That the Air passes thorough the body of the water to fill up that deserted space, that must otherwise be void: But then I appeal to any rational man, whether I am obliged to believe so unlikely a thing upon Mr. *Hobbs*'s bare affirmation. If I be, I must almost despair to prove things by Experiments. (Boyle [1662] 1999, 137–8)

Boyle summed it up: "either his Explication or a Vacuum *must* be admitted" (Boyle [1662] 1999, 138; see also, [1674] 2000, 189). Boyle also pointed out that Hobbes's account depended upon air entering the water "so strangely and unperceivedly." After all, Boyle noted, wind on water normally causes a commotion of the surface, or we might expect to see bubbles of air converging on the cylinder of the submerged air-pump. Moreover, when the chamber's stopper is removed under water, water rushes in, in a way it would not if the chamber was full of air (Boyle [1662] 1999, 138).

Boyle's experimental method increasingly came to be seen as the proper way to conduct investigations of the natural world, and to reach sound conclusions about how the world and its parts worked together to constitute the *machina mundi*. Hobbes, by contrast, was already arguing, at the time of their dispute, in a way that increasingly seemed inadequate. When Boyle defended the experimental approach against Hobbes's dismissive attitude toward it, he was defending it as a way of disregarding merely hypothetical, or speculative attempts to explain nature. The dangers of the speculative approach could be seen in Hobbes's *ipse dixit* that there was no such thing as incorporeal substance, and that only material bodies were real (Hobbes 2012, 1076; 1651, 371). As Boyle's mentor, Bacon had insisted with regard to speculative philosophies, "if the notions themselves (and this is the heart of the matter) are confused, and recklessly abstracted from things, nothing built on them is sound" (Bacon 2004 [1620], 69). Boyle believed that the experimental method could not only dismiss Hobbes's recklessly abstracted notions (as he saw them), but could also demonstrate that some physical phenomena (such as the "spring" of the air – its ability to spontaneously spread itself out to fill whatever empty space might be available to it) required the existence of God. Only a divinity could endow "spring," "gravitational attraction," and other active powers on naturally inert matter. Boyle saw these two aspects of the experimental method as capable of delivering fatal blows against Hobbesianism.

For his part, by contrast, Hobbes simply believed that if he could show that all the phenomena produced by the air-pump could be explained by the "circular wind" created as particles of air moved with simple circular motion, he had done enough to show that the experiment was irrelevant, and that the Royal Society should adopt his principles (OL IV.236, 273). It is difficult not to conclude that Hobbes was simply stuck in a rut – a leading natural philosopher of an earlier generation, who had not just failed to see the importance of the experimental method but also resolutely refused to believe that it had any significance.

23.4 Henry More and Hobbes

The Cambridge Platonist Henry More was primarily what we would call a philosophical theologian, and he put all his philosophy into combating the rise of atheism that he perceived all around him (Leech 2013). This led him into making novel claims in natural philosophy, and in turn to reject Hobbes's materialism (Grant 1981, 226–7; Parkin 2007, 197–9). More's overriding strategy was to accept the Cartesian assumption that matter or bodies were completely passive and inert, and were not (and for More *could* not be – not even by God) endowed with powers, or any other active principles. From here, he went on to demonstrate that some physical phenomena could not be explained in mechanistic terms, and therefore that there must be, in addition to inert matter, a principle of activity at work in the world, which More called the "Spirit of Nature" (Gabbey 1990). Clearly, since matter is passive, this self-active Spirit of Nature must be immaterial, and More went on to insist that only immaterial spirit can be inherently active (Grant 1981, 221–8; Henry 1990; Mintz 1962, 84–95). The aim was to persuade atheists that immaterial substance must be required to keep the world system working. More believed that once the atheist conceded that the Spirit of Nature must exist, they would accept that the incorporeal human soul and God must also exist.

Clearly, More could not allow Hobbes's monistic materialism to go unchallenged. In his *Immortality of the Soul* (1659), therefore, he took pains to refute Hobbes's philosophy. As More noted, Hobbes sees

> so little into the nature of Spirits, that defect is compensated with an extraordinary Quick sightedness in discerning of the best and most warrantable ways of salving all Phaenomena from the ordinary allowed properties of Matter. (More 1662, 58)

He dismissed Hobbes's claim that incorporeal substance is a contradiction in terms as a mere assertion. He insisted that the "Order of things" led to the conclusion that there must be a "higher Principle" at work, and presented this as the origin of the concept of immaterial substance, rather than Hobbes's claim that such substances only originated in "Dreams, fears, and superstitious fancies" (More 1662, 40; cf. Hobbes 2012, 1014; 1651, 352–3). He argued that Hobbes's materialist account of sensation, in terms of motion and reaction, leads to the conclusion that all bodies must have sensation, even gold or lead bars (although they might require stronger motions for them to register a reaction; More 1662, 48). Similarly, he dismissed Hobbes's account of memory as a decaying version of sense experience by suggesting that the decaying vibrations of a struck bell would have to count as a memory. As More concluded, "Matter is utterly uncapable of such operations as we find in our selves, and that therefore there is Something in us Immaterial or Incorporeal" (Duncan 2012, 392–5; More 1662, 66).

He also pointed out that Hobbes's account of gravity falsely implies that bodies fall to the axis of the Earth's rotation, not to its center, and therefore concluded that, in spite of his claims, "he does not produce so much as possible Corporeal causes of the most ordinary effects in Nature" (More 1662, 198; cf. EW I.513).

The most significant way that More asserted the reality of incorporeal substances against Hobbes, however, should perhaps be seen as something of a concession to Hobbes's way of thinking. More's great innovation in seeking to establish "that the Notion of a Spirit is as naturally conceivable as the Notion of a Body," was to reject the Cartesian claim that immaterial entities could not be considered to occupy space (More 1662, 41). More evidently recognized an increasing tendency among his contemporaries to assume that real things occupied space – if something was said to have no place or location, but to be nowhere, it was all too easy to dismiss it as not really existing. More could see their point and simply insisted that immaterial entities, incorporeal spirits, must be extended and occupy space (Reid 2003). The difference between corporeal and incorporeal was not defined by extension or lack of it, but by impenetrability and penetrability. Bodies were impenetrable to one another, while spirits could penetrate one another and bodies as well (More 1662, 32). More easily dismissed the age-old insistence that incorporeal spirits had to be dimensionless to ensure their indivisibility by pointing out that it is impossible to separate out part of a light beam, even though it occupies space, and indeed it is impossible to divide space itself (Grant 1981, 221–8; More 1662, 25–6; Reid 2003).

More was able to use this against Hobbes:

> he would infer that the whole Universe is Corporeal, ... because there is nothing but has Length, Breadth and Depth. This therefore is the very last ground his Argument is to be resolved into. But how weak it is I have already intimated, it being not Trinal Dimension, but Impenetrability, that constitutes a Body. (More 1662, 42)

In spite of More's assertion, however, at that time three-dimensionality *was* routinely regarded as being entirely characteristic of body, and inapplicable to incorporeal spirit. More's concept of spirit, therefore, would have looked to his contemporaries as a strange hybrid, evidently material because it was extended, but claimed, paradoxically, to be immaterial (Gabbey 1990; Henry 1990).

Indeed, there are remarkable similarities between Henry More's supposedly *immaterialist* philosophy of spirit, and the *materialist* theology that Hobbes discussed in print for the first time in the Latin *Leviathan* of 1668, and posthumously in his *Answer to Bishop Bramhall* (1682). More's God had to exist in space (Grant 1981, 223–5; More 1662, 24), but so did Hobbes's corporeal God (Hobbes 2012, 1076; 1651, 371). As Hobbes wrote in *Decameron Physiologicum* (1678), the jumbled motions of particles could never result even momentarily in producing a void space because "he that created them is not a Fancy, but the most real substance that is; who being Infinite, there can be no place empty where he is, nor full where he is not" (EW VII.89). Answering Bishop Bramhall, perhaps as early as 1668 (Leijenhorst 2004, 74), he insisted that God was "a most pure, simple, invisible spirit corporeal." He went on to say that "By corporeal I mean a substance that has magnitude, and so mean all learned men, divines and others" (EW IV.313, see also 393). Perhaps Hobbes was making a point against More: if

More's God occupies space he has magnitude and thereby is corporeal. In accordance with this view, Hobbes held that spirits were not immaterial, as More tried to claim, but were composed of highly attenuated matter (EW IV.313; Gorham 2013; Leijenhorst 2004).

It seems, then, that Hobbes held God to be an extremely thin and subtle material spirit that filled all of infinite space. Indeed, he went so far as to say God, as a spirit, was *infinitely* subtle:

> If I should ask any the most subtile distinguisher, what middle nature there were between an infinitely subtile substance, and a mere thought or phantasm, by what name could he call it? He might call it perhaps an incorporeal substance; and so incorporeal shall pass for a middle nature between *infinitely subtile* and *nothing*, and be less subtile than infinitely subtile, and yet more subtile than a thought. (EW IV.313)

The "subtile distinguisher" Hobbes might have had in mind, could well have been Henry More. Hobbes again seems to be suggesting that More's claims about incorporeal spirit are absurd (less subtle than infinitely subtle), and unnecessary ("He might call it perhaps ... incorporeal").

There is even a remarkable similarity between the concept of God that Hobbes describes in his *Answer*, and More's Spirit of Nature. For More, wishing to maintain a level of transcendence for his God, the Spirit of Nature was merely the "Vicarious power of God" and, as such, it filled all of infinite space, and was responsible for all physical changes in the world (Henry 1990; More 1662, 203). Defending his view of God as a spirit that is "thin, fluid, transparent, invisible body," Hobbes presented an analogy:

> I have seen ... two waters, one of the river and the other mineral water, so that no man could discern one from the other from his sight; yet when they are both put together the whole substance could not be distinguished from milk. Yet we know the one was not mixed with the other, so as every part of the one to be in every part of the other, for that is impossible, unless two bodies can be in the same place. How then could the change be made in every part, but only by the activity of the mineral water, changing it everywhere to the sense and yet not being everywhere and in every part of the water. If such gross bodies have such great activity what then can we think of spirits, whose kinds be as many as there are kinds of liquor, and activity greater? Can it then be doubted that God, who is infinitely fine spirit, and withal intelligence, can make and change all species and kinds of bodies as he pleaseth? (EW IV.309–10)

Hobbes was no chemist and so he is merely providing his own account here. His assumption is that the two fluids cannot become one fluid because that would violate the principle that bodies cannot occupy the same space at the same time. The fluids must somehow intermingle, therefore, alongside each other in the same area of space (easy to envisage if we assume both fluids are composed of particles). Meanwhile, the activity of the mineral water (presumably Hobbes means its chemical activity, but perhaps he thinks this can be reduced to motion of the particles) changes the fluids somehow to give the milky appearance. If something as gross as mineral water can do this, then the infinitely fine spirit of God intermingled with his Creation can bring about any and all changes. Because of the materiality of God and the world, Hobbes cannot take the same line as More, who simply insists immaterial spirits can penetrate matter (More 1662, 19–20). Evidently, Hobbes is thinking of God as more like the concept of aether, as assumed in both contemporary scholasticism and Cartesianism.

The aether was always held to be an all-pervasive material entity, which was highly rarefied and subtle. Generally invoked as a material medium between bodies to explain phenomena that might otherwise look like actions at a distance (actions not involving material contact between the interacting bodies, such as magnetism or gravity), the aether could be, and was, enlisted at need for various etiological purposes. It was supposed to fill all empty space; including the supposed pores or channels between the particles composing the various bodies. So, the aether was all around bodies, and inside them too, but without ever occupying exactly the same space that was taken up by the particles of bodies. It seems that Hobbes was thinking in the same way about his God. As an infinitely subtle spirit corporeal, God was assumed to occupy all unoccupied space, even inside the cavities or pores of all other bodies in the universe. Bearing in mind that Hobbes's physics was corpuscularian, it should be acknowledged that his God could be effectively ubiquitous; God's infinite subtlety enabled him to seep into every nook and cranny between every one of the countless particles of Hobbes's world system. Moreover, as Hobbes suggested in his *Answer*, God "can make and change all species and kinds of bodies as he pleaseth," although, as he went on to point out, just how he changes things is beyond our apprehension (EW IV.310; but the same could be said of More's Spirit of Nature, cf. More 1662, 32–3).

This might seem implausible to modern readers; if Hobbes's world was a plenum and already full of matter, surely there is no room for a corporeal God? Certainly, this was Boyle's opinion: "it seems difficult to conceive, how in a World that is already perfectly full of body, a Corporeal Deity, such as he maintains ... can have that access even to the minute parts of the Mundane Matter that seems requisite to the ... Operations that belong to the Deity" (Boyle 2000 [1674], 162). Boyle was no plenist, but he must surely have known that Descartes and other plenists routinely invoked an all-pervasive material aether in their supposedly already full world systems. Skepticism about this was a major reason for Boyle's vacuist approach. Aethers were developed and promoted by plenists for plenists, however, and were always envisaged as pervading the spaces between all the other bodies of the universe. Hobbes's corporeal God was just like the subtle material aethers found in other plenist philosophies, except that his aether had intelligence (EW IV.310). We should not forget also Hobbes's comment that "there can be no place empty where he is, nor full where he is not" (EW VII.89).

So, whereas More's Spirit of Nature was held to be all-pervasive because incorporeal spirit could penetrate matter, Hobbes's material God could not be in the same place as another body. Nevertheless, by being present in between the corpuscles of other bodies in an infinitely subtle way, his God could be said to be as effectively ubiquitous as More's Spirit (Gorham 2014, 38–9). But More's Spirit of Nature was self-active, activity was part of its nature and enabled it (somehow) to move otherwise inert matter. For Hobbes matter was also inert and could only move if it was moved by something that was itself already in motion: "when any body is moved which was formerly at rest, the immediate efficient cause of that motion is in some other moved and contiguous body" (EW I.205). The matter that composed Hobbes's God, however, was the exception that proved the rule. Hobbes's God was "eternally moving" and, being corporeal, could initiate motion in other bodies (EW I.412; OL I.336; see also Gorham 2013, 248–55; Hobbes 2012, 160; 1651, 51).

Hobbes had resolutely refused to discuss the nature of God before 1668; always insisting instead that "he is Incomprehensible; and his greatness and power are unconceivable", and that the "signification of Spirit ... falleth not under humane Understanding" (Hobbes 2012, 46, 614; 1651, 11, 208; Leijenhorst 2004, 76–81). It is possible, therefore, that in the earlier part of his career Hobbes did not know how to reconcile his materialist philosophy with his belief in God. The infinitely subtle corporeal God of 1688 and after has been seen, then and now, as deriving from the Ancient Stoic concept of *pneuma* (EW IV.309; Gorham 2014; Sellars In press). But the similarity is by no means as close as it is with More's Spirit of Nature. If Hobbes heard that More's *Immortality of the Soul* offered a critique of his philosophy and was thereby led to read it, he would have seen everything he needed in More's Spirit of Nature, *mutatis mutandis*. More's three-dimensional view of God has been seen as an "incredibly bold and unheard of step" (Grant 1981, 223), so it may well have surprised Hobbes as a very welcome innovation, which was just what he needed for his own theology. Regarding More's three-dimensional Spirit as necessarily corporeal, in spite of anything More said to the contrary, Hobbes only had to change More's Spirit into God himself, rather than the intermediary "great Quartermaster-General of Divine Providence" as it was for More (More 1662, 203). If he had done so, Hobbes immediately would have had a well worked-out theory of a corporeal God.

More's earliest biographer, Richard Ward, reported that

> even Mr Hobbs himself, as I have been informed, hath been heard to say, That if his own Philosophy was not True, he knew of none that he should sooner like than More's of Cambridge. (Ward 1710, 80)

Although he gave no source for this suggestion, and it is anyway mere hearsay, it is by no means completely implausible (Parkin 2007, 199). Given the close similarities between More's Spirit of Nature, and Hobbes's corporeal God, it is plausible that Hobbes found More's ideas a convenient source for his own arguments. In works written in 1668, both Hobbes and More alluded to the comment in Acts 17: 28, "For in him we live, and move, and have our being" (Hobbes 2012, 1228, 1229; 1668, 360; More 1668, 107). For both men, it encapsulated their views on the nature of God.

23.5 Conclusion

Hobbes acquired an international reputation as a promising contributor to efforts to develop a new philosophy to replace Aristotelianism in the 1640s. His system of mechanical philosophy, as developed in *De corpore*, was arguably second only to Descartes's *Principia philosophiae* in its philosophical consistency and forcefulness, and was recognized as such by contemporaries. It failed to have anything like the impact of the Cartesian system, however, because it attracted vigorous opposition from leading thinkers opposed to Hobbes's religious and political ideas. The close affiliation between the church and Aristotelian natural philosophy that had developed since the foundation of the medieval universities, and the perceived atheism of ancient atomism that formed the basis of the new mechanical philosophies, meant that the new philosophers had to work hard to counter contemporary perceptions that their philosophy was subversive to religion. Hobbes's uncompromising commitment to materialism was seen as undermining these efforts, and thus the leading defenders and promoters of the mechanical philosophy insistently rejected his philosophy; and even those less directly concerned about its religious implications felt the need to distance their own thinking from that of Hobbes. Additionally, the persuasiveness of Hobbes's philosophy was drastically weakened by his idiosyncratic approach to geometry, which signaled to other mathematically minded natural philosophers (who were more numerous amongst mechanical philosophers than amongst scholastic natural philosophers) that Hobbes was merely incompetent. Similarly, his failure to recognize the value of the new emphasis upon experimentation developed in the Royal Society and more generally throughout Europe, only reinforced contemporary views of him as a dogmatic thinker, and a dangerous one at that, committed to his own unproven speculations. Hobbes was by no means the only philosopher adhering to the more traditional speculative approach, however, and judged on their own terms Hobbes's philosophical claims were comparable in consistency and cogency with those of contemporary Cartesianism. Furthermore, the distinctions between the thought of Hobbes and his critical contemporaries were often by no means as stark as his critics wanted to maintain, but were highly nuanced. This can be seen most strikingly, perhaps, in the marked similarity between Hobbes's concept of a corporeal God, and Henry More's influential concept of a supposedly immaterial but nonetheless three-dimensionally extended God.

References

Bacon, Francis. 2004 [1620]. *The Instauratio Magna Part II: Novum Organum*, edited and translated by Graham Rees and Maria Wakely. Oxford: Oxford University Press.

Barnouw, Jeffrey. 1992. "Le Vocabulaire Du *Conatus*." In *Hobbes Et Son Vocabulaire: Études De Lexicographie Philosophique*, edited by Yves-Charles Zarka, 103–24. Paris: Vrin.

Boyle, Robert. 1999 [1662]. "An Examen of Mr. T. Hobbes His Dialogus Physicus De Naturâ Aëris." In *The Works of Robert Boyle*, edited by Michael Hunter and Edward B. Davies, Vol. 3, 109–88. London: Pickering & Chatto.

Boyle, Robert. 2000 [1674]. "Animadversions upon Mr. Hobbes's Problemata De Vacuo." In *The Works of Robert Boyle*, edited by Michael Hunter and Edward B. Davies, Vol. 8, 159–202. London: Pickering & Chatto.

Brandt, Frithiof. 1928. *Thomas Hobbes' Mechanical Conception of Nature*. Copenhagen: Levin and Munksgaard.

Clucas, Stephen. 2017. "An Early European Critic of Hobbes's *De corpore*." *Hobbes Studies* 30: 4–27.

Descartes, René. 1644. *Principia Philosophiae*. Amsterdam: Elsevier.

Digby, Sir Kenelm. 1644. *Two Treatises in the One of Which, the Nature of Bodies; in the Other, the Nature of Mans Soule; Is Looked Into: In Way of Discovery, of the Immortality of Reasonable Soules*. Paris: Gilles Blaizot.

Duncan, Stewart. 2012. "Debating Materialism: Cavendish, Hobbes, and More." *History of Philosophy Quarterly* 29: 391–409.

Gabbey, Alan. 1990. "Henry More and the Limits of Mechanism." In *Henry More (1614–1687): Tercentenary Studies*, edited by Sarah Hutton, 55–76. Dordrecht: Kluwer.

Gaukroger, Stephen. 2002. *Descartes' System of Natural Philosophy*. Cambridge: Cambridge University Press.

Gorham, Geoffrey. 2013. "The Theological Foundations of Hobbesian Physics: A Defence of Corporeal God." *British Journal for the History of Philosophy* 21: 240–61.

Gorham, Geoffrey. 2014. "Mixing Bodily Fluids: Hobbes's Stoic God." *Sophia* 53: 33–49.

Grant, Edward. 1981. *Much Ado About Nothing: Theories of Space and Vacuum from the Middle Ages to the Scientific Revolution*. Cambridge: Cambridge University Press.

Grant, Edward. 2002. "Medieval Natural Philosophy: Empiricism without Observation." In *The Dynamics of Aristotelian Natural Philosophy*, edited by Cees Leijenhorst, Christoph Lüthy and Johannes M. M. H. Thijssen, 141–68. Leiden: Brill.

Henry, John. 1990. "Henry More Versus Robert Boyle: The Spirit of Nature and the Nature of Providence." In *Henry More (1614–1687): Tercentenary Studies*, edited by Sarah Hutton, 55–76. Dordrecht: Kluwer.

Henry, John. 2004. "Metaphysics and the Origins of Modern Science: Descartes and the Importance of Laws of Nature." *Early Science and Medicine* 9: 73–114.

Henry, John. 2011. "Galileo and the Scientific Revolution: The Importance of His Kinematics." *Galilaeana* 8: 3–36.

Henry, John. 2016. "Hobbes, Galileo, and the Physics of Simple Circular Motions." *Hobbes Studies* 29: 9–38.

Hobbes, Thomas. 1839–1845a. *The English Works of Thomas Hobbes*, 11 vols., edited by Sir William Molesworth. London: John Bohn. Cited as EW.

Hobbes, Thomas. 1839–1845b. *Thomæ Hobbes malmesburiensis opera philosophica*, 5 vols., edited by Gulielmi Molesworth. London: John Bohn. Cited as OL.

Hobbes, Thomas. 1994. *The Correspondence of Thomas Hobbes*, edited by Noel Malcolm, 2 vols. Oxford: Clarendon Press.

Hobbes, Thomas. 2012. *Leviathan*, 3 vols., edited by Noel Malcolm. Oxford: Clarendon Press. [First published 1651.]

Hunter, Michael. 1990. "Science and Heterodoxy: An Early Modern Problem Reconsidered." In *Reappraisals of the Scientific Revolution*, edited by David C. Lindberg and Robert S. Westman, 437–60. Cambridge: Cambridge University Press.

Jesseph, Douglas M. 1999. *Squaring the Circle: The War Between Hobbes and Wallis*. Chicago, IL: University of Chicago Press.

Jesseph, Douglas M. 2016. "Hobbes on 'Conatus': A Study in the Foundations of Hobbesian Philosophy." *Hobbes Studies* 29: 66–85.

Leech, David. 2013. *The Hammer of the Cartesians: Henry More's Philosophy of Spirit and the Origins of Modern Atheism*. Leuven: Peeters.

Leijenhorst, Cees. 2004. "Hobbes' Corporeal Deity." *Rivista di Storia della Filosofia* 59: 73–95.

Malcolm, Noel. 2002. *Aspects of Hobbes*. Oxford: Clarendon Press.

Mintz, Samuel I. 1962. *The Hunting of Leviathan*. Cambridge: Cambridge University Press.

More, Henry. 1662. "The Immortality of the Soul." In *A Collection of Several Philosophical Writings of Dr. Henry More*. London: James Flesher.

More, Henry. 1668. *Divine Dialogues, Containing Sundry Disquisitions & Instructions Concerning the Attributes and Providence of God*. London: James Flesher.

Parkin, Jon. 2007. *Taming the Leviathan*. Cambridge: Cambridge University Press.

Psillos, Stathis and Eirini Goudarouli. 2019. "Principles of Motion and the Absence of Laws of Nature in Hobbes's Natural Philosophy." *HOPOS* 9: 93–119.

Reid, Jasper. 2003. "Henry More on Material and Spiritual Extension." *Dialogue* 42: 531–58.

Sellars, John. In press. "The Early Modern Legacy of the Stoics." In *The Oxford Handbook of Hellenistic Philosophy*, edited by Nathan Powers and Jacob Klein. New York: Oxford University Press.

Shapin, Stephen and Simon Schaffer. 1985. *Leviathan and the Air-Pump: Hobbes, Boyle, and the Experimental Life*. Princeton, NJ: Princeton University Press.

Ward, Richard. 1710. *The Life of the Learned and Pious Dr. Henry More*. London: Joseph Downing.

Ward, Seth. 1654. *Vindiciae Academiarum... Together with an Appendix Concerning What M. Hobbs and M. Dell Have Published on This Argument*. London: Thomas Robinson.

24

Cudworth as a Critic of Hobbes

STEWART DUNCAN

24.1 Introducing Cudworth

Ralph Cudworth (1617–1688) was the son of a fellow of Emmanuel College, Cambridge, where he himself studied and was later elected as a fellow. He became in 1645 Master of Clare College and Regius Professor of Hebrew, and in 1654 Master of Christ's College. As a philosopher, he has never quite become a canonical figure, but was also never quite forgotten, being mentioned in such places as Hegel's lectures on the history of philosophy and Ueberweg's *Grundriss der Geschichte der Philosophie*, as well as histories of British Moralists and Cambridge Platonists.

Cudworth's major philosophical publication in his lifetime was *The True Intellectual System of the Universe: The First Part; Wherein, All the Reason and Philosophy of Atheism is Confuted; And its Impossibility Demonstrated* (henceforth, *System*).[1] The one modern edition in English of a work of Cudworth's presents his *Treatise Concerning Eternal and Immutable Morality* (henceforth, *Treatise*) and his *Treatise of Freewill* (henceforth, *Freewill*).[2] Neither of those was published in Cudworth's lifetime, but they correspond to parts of a plan of writing reported in the Preface to the *System*. There Cudworth says that he aimed to write three books: one "Against *Atheism*"; one "For such a *God* as is not meer *Arbitrary Will Omnipotent, Decreeing, Doing*, and *Necessitating* all Actions, *Evil* as well as *Good;* but *Essentially Moral, Good* and *Just*"; and one "Against *Necessity Intrinsecall* and *Essentiall* to all *Action;* and for such a *Liberty*, or *Sui-Potestas*, in *Rational Creatures*, as may render them *Accountable*, capable of *Rewards* and *Punishments*, and so *Objects* of *Distributive* or *Retributive Justice*."[3] The *True Intellectual System* is the first part of this, the *Treatise* corresponds roughly to the projected second book, and *Freewill* (and other manuscripts on that topic) to the third.

Reading Cudworth's philosophical works, one finds many references to other philosophers, often ancient philosophers. Consider, for example, the first chapter of the

A Companion to Hobbes, First Edition. Edited by Marcus P. Adams.

Treatise, which introduces the view that nothing is good or evil, just or unjust "naturally and immutably" (Cudworth 1996, 9). It does this by noting mentions of this view in Plato's works, then in Aristotle's; looking for evidence in Plato, Diogenes Laertius, and Plutarch of who the ancient proponents of this view were; and by observing the Epicurean history of the view. Only then does Cudworth come to a "late writer of ethics and politics," whom he quotes but does not name: Hobbes (Cudworth 1996, 13). The survey does not end there, however, but moves to theological versions of the view, mentioning Ockham and others following him, before turning to "some [more recent] late authors," most of whom Cudworth does not name (Cudworth 1996, 15).[4]

In that chapter, as elsewhere in Cudworth's philosophical writings, there is a great deal of engagement with ancient philosophy. Indeed, some scholars have thought of Cudworth largely as a historian or philologist. Cudworth was, however, consistently engaged with the philosophical views of his contemporaries.[5] As we read his work, we see him criticizing Descartes, Gassendi, and Spinoza.[6] But the one contemporary philosopher he comes back to again and again, even more than Descartes, is Hobbes.

It would be an exaggeration to say that the *System* is just a giant argument against Hobbes. Many views that are distant from Hobbes's are considered there. But Cudworth did see Hobbes as a representative of exactly the three views he was attacking: atheism, determinism, and the denial that morality is eternal and immutable. Moreover, he did not just criticize Hobbes by assuming that a general critique of those views applied to Hobbes's particular case. Rather, he singled out Hobbes, often by quoting him, and argued against the distinctively Hobbesian positions he had identified.[7] In this chapter, I look at Cudworth as a critic of Hobbes in two of the three central areas, atheism and ethics, focusing on passages where we see him explicitly picking out Hobbes.[8]

24.2 Hobbes and Atheism in the *True Intellectual System*

Cudworth's *System* is a defense of theism against atheism. The arguments of that defense often appear to be aimed at types of position, rather than at the views of particular individuals. Moreover, when individuals are named, they are usually ancient philosophers, rather than Cudworth's contemporaries. There is, for example, a general attack upon atomic (or Democritick or Epicurean) atheism. There are also attacks on other types of atheism, which Cudworth calls hylozoic, hylopathian, and cosmo-plastick atheism. We might reasonably take the attack on the Epicurean view to be aimed in part at Hobbes.[9] But there is also a more specific attack on Hobbes, in passages that are clearly aimed at him in particular. In those passages, Cudworth quotes and criticizes a "modern writer," who is Hobbes.[10] Those passages are the main focus of my discussion in this section.

The passages that quote Hobbes are in chapter 2, where Cudworth is presenting arguments for atheism, and in chapter 5, where he is responding to them. In those passages, six themes emerge: (1) the argument for atheism from our having no idea of God (which connects to Hobbes's deflationary account of apparent descriptions of God's attributes); (2) the explanatory role of fear in Hobbes's view; (3) arguments from principles of motion and causation; (4) the role of politicians; (5) knowledge, understanding, and nominalism; and (6) materialism about the mind.[11] In this section I concentrate on the first of these themes, which is the one about which Cudworth has most to say. Looking at what he says about it shows us how he understands Hobbes's views, as well as how he wants to criticize them.

24.2.1 An Argument for Atheism

My starting point here comes from the beginning of Cudworth's exposition of arguments for atheism:

> The grounds of Reason alledged for the Atheistical *Hypothesis* are chiefly these that follow. First, That we have no *Idea of God*, and therefore can have no Evidence of him; which Argument is further flourisht and descanted upon in this manner. That Notion or Conception of a Deity, that is commonly entertained, is nothing but a Bundle of Incomprehensibles, Unconceivables, and Impossibles; it being only a compilement of all Imaginable Attributes of Honour, Courtship, and Complement, which the Confounded Fear, and Astonishment of Mens minds, made them huddle up together, without any Sence or Philosophick Truth. (*System* 63)

Cudworth follows that with two passages from Hobbes: a paraphrase of a discussion of the attributes of God early in the *Questions Concerning Liberty, Necessity, and Chance* (EW V.6), and a quote from chapter 46 of *Leviathan* on the same topic (Hobbes 2012, 1086; 1651, 374).[12]

In the discussion of this first argument for atheism we find an allegedly Hobbesian argument for atheism from the claim that we have no idea of God; the connection of that argument to Hobbes's views about divine attributes; an explicit connection to Hobbes himself by quotation; and then, after the quotes, a mention of the role that Hobbes gives to fear and astonishment in explaining religious belief.

The argument for atheism itself seems to have this structure:

(1) We have no idea of God;
(2) If we can have no idea of something, then it does not exist; so
(3) God does not exist.

Note what the conclusion here says about Cudworth's understanding of Hobbes. First, Cudworth believes that Hobbes is an atheist, in the sense that he denies the existence of God.[13] Secondly, by associating this conclusion with Hobbes, Cudworth commits himself to a suspicious reading of Hobbes, on which Hobbes does not mean what he says.[14] Hobbes, after all, does not say that God does not exist – indeed he keeps saying that He does.[15]

In his initial presentation, Cudworth gives us no quotation to connect the first premise to Hobbes, but it clearly is a claim Hobbes makes. Consider, for example, Hobbes's Objections to Descartes's *Meditations*. In the *Meditations*, Descartes offers two arguments for the existence of God, both of which begin by focusing on the meditator's idea of God. Hobbes objects to those arguments by denying that we have an idea of God.[16]

Premise 2 is more puzzling. Cudworth himself seemingly grants the acceptability of the premise, but does Hobbes believe or assert it?[17] Hobbes seems to grant the existence of things of which we have no idea, most obviously God. Indeed, Hobbes believes we have a way to think about God that does not involve having an idea of him – a way of thinking of God relationally, with no conception of his intrinsic features.[18] Cudworth, however, is inclined to take Hobbes as deriving non-existence from inconceivability. Perhaps Cudworth thought that a version of the argument from inconceivability to non-existence was a good one, and thus an uncontroversial attribution. But it is a little tricky to pin this on Hobbes, and this makes a significant difference to how one understands Hobbes. With this premise at hand, Hobbes has an obvious argument for atheism. Without it, he has a point about the extreme limits of our ability to think about God.

24.2.2 Cudworth's Arguments That We Do Have an Idea of God

In responding to this argument for atheism, Cudworth's focus is on the first premise. He replies to the view that there is no idea of God, and to various arguments for it. Indeed, all of chapter 4 of the *True Intellectual System* is devoted to arguing that we do indeed have an idea of God. That is a long and complex chapter, filling over 400 pages. Much of it is occupied by discussions of pagan polytheism, and the question of what, if any, ideas of divinities those pagans had. Before that however, we find discussion of what the idea of God is: "the true and genuine *Idea* of *God* in general, is this, *A Perfect Conscious Understanding Being* (or Mind) *Existing of it self from Eternity, and the Cause of all other things*" (*System* 195).[19] Even before that, Cudworth gives us two arguments that we do have an idea of God. He argues first that people who speak different languages all think about God, so there must be some idea they share (*System* 192). His second argument is that atheists have an idea of God, which they rely on in denying the existence of God (*System* 194).

These arguments succeed, at least, in pointing out that we seem to have some way of thinking of God. Given certain assumptions, it might seem obvious to conclude from that that we have an idea of God. But Hobbes has another way of accounting for the phenomena. We can, he grants, think about God relationally, as the cause of the world. This does not involve having an idea of God or any grasp on God's intrinsic features, because an idea of God would be an (impossible) image of God. Cudworth thus seems off target in his criticism of Hobbes here, or at least to need to say more. Indeed, there is an ambiguity about what it is to have an idea of God.[20] If it is just to have some way of thinking about God, Hobbes and Cudworth agree that we have it. If it is to have an image of God, they agree that we do not. If it is to have an idea of "*A Perfect Conscious Understanding Being* (or Mind) *Existing of it self from Eternity, and the Cause of all other things*," then Cudworth thinks we have it, and Hobbes disagrees. Indeed, if it is to have any positive conception of the attributes of God, then again, Cudworth thinks we have it, and Hobbes disagrees.[21]

24.2.3 Cudworth's Response to Arguments That We Have No Idea of God

Aside from responding to the view that there is no idea of God, Cudworth also responds to arguments for it. We see these responses in his reply to the first argument for atheism at the start of chapter 5 of the *System*. There he lists arguments for the claim that we have no idea of God.

> First, *That we have no Idea nor Thought of any thing not Subject to Corporeal Sense; nor the least Evidence of the* Existence *of any thing, but from the same.* Secondly, *That Theists themselves acknowledging God to be Incomprehensible, he may be from thence inferred to be a Non-Entity.* Thirdly, *That the Theists Idea of God including Infinity in it, is therefore absolutely Unconceivable and Impossible.* Fourthly, *That Theology is an Arbitrarious Compilement of Inconsistent and Contradictious Notions;* And Lastly, *That the* Idea *and* Existence *of God ows all its being, either to the Confounded Non-Sence of Astonish'd Minds; or else to the Fiction and Imposture of Politicians.* (*System* 634)

Note three arguments here. Argument 1 is based on the view that all our ideas, thoughts, and evidence derive from our senses. Argument 2 is based on the observation that theists say God is incomprehensible. Argument 3 moves from observing the claim that God is infinite, through the view that the infinite is inconceivable, to the conclusion that we have no idea of (such an infinite) God.[22]

Argument 1. Ideas come from sense. Cudworth associates this sub-argument directly with Hobbes (*System* 634–7).[23] Our ideas, Hobbes says, come from sensation and are image-like. They are ideas or phantasms of the imagination. We see a set of connected views here: that ideas are images, that they come from sense, and that we possess sense and imagination but not a further faculty of intellect. From this Cudworth draws the conclusion that, for Hobbes, things of which we can have no images, no sense-derived ideas, cannot be conceived.

Cudworth's reply to this argument starts with the thought that there is a higher faculty than sense (or, indeed, than imagination). The allegedly Hobbesian view makes sense the judge of all existence, but according to Cudworth there is a higher faculty, reason, which is a judge of these things, and leads us to things that sense cannot reach. More basically, on Cudworth's view, there are ideas that are not phantasms or images, and do not have phantasms "belonging to" them (*System* 636). Cudworth indeed gives the idea of God as an example here. This was of course a contested example, but Cudworth does offer a supporting argument.[24] To simplify slightly: suppose we think of God as an absolutely perfect substance; we have no phantasm of absolutely perfect, nor do we have one of substance; therefore, we have no phantasm of God.

Argument 2. Theists say God is incomprehensible. More than once in the Third Objections, Hobbes appeals to the Christian view that God is inconceivable in support of his view that we have no idea of God.[25] That is, Hobbes does indeed appear to have given this argument that Cudworth discusses.

Cudworth responds to this argument at some length, but his key move is to deny that the incomprehensible is inconceivable. God is incomprehensible, which is to say that we cannot have a conception of God that is "fully *Adequate* and *Commensurate* to" God (*System* 638). But this is not to say that we cannot conceive of God at all, only that we cannot fully understand God. Indeed, Cudworth argues, this is not such an unusual situation. It is common for us to be unable to grasp the essences of things: "even *Body* it self ... hath such puzzling Difficulties and Entanglements in the Speculation of it, that they can never be able to extricate themselves from" (*System* 639). But that does not show that we have no ideas of those things, or that we cannot think about them at all. The same goes for God, even though God "is more *Incomprehensible* to us than any thing else whatsoever" (*System* 639).

Argument 3. God is said to be infinite. In considering the third argument, we find an even clearer connection to Hobbes. For in replying to this argument – which involves the claim that God is inconceivable because infinite – Cudworth again quotes Hobbes.[26]

In discussing this argument, Cudworth grants to the atheist that there is no phantasm (or imagistic idea) of the infinite. But this is of course not what he thinks the main issue is, as he does not think all ideas are phantasms. Cudworth also grants that we cannot fully comprehend the infinite. Indeed, he goes further and grants that there are some infinites of which we have no idea: "That as for those *Infinities*, of *Number*, of *Corporeal Magnitude*, and of *Time* or *Successive Duration*, we have not only no *Phantasm*, nor *Full Intellectual Comprehension* of them, but also no manner of *Intelligible Idea, Notion* or *Conception*" (*System* 643). His central reason is that in these cases there are no actual infinites, only potential ones. If we think we have an idea of actual infinite space, for example, we are merely confused. Cudworth takes it, however, that the case of God is different.[27] We have some notion of God as an infinite being, though we do not fully understand the infinity of God. This connects, then, to the general question of how, and to what degree, we can think about or understand God. Cudworth grants we do not have a complete understanding, but he does think that we have ideas that represent God's nature, above and beyond the merely relational conception Hobbes thinks we have.

Cudworth's criticism of Hobbes's view that we have no idea of God is closely connected to his criticism of Hobbes's theory of the language we apparently use to describe the attributes of God. These two issues also have a close connection in Hobbes's thought. Our inability to form an idea of God is our inability to form a positive, non-relational conception of him. If we had such a conception, it would involve conceiving some of God's attributes. For example, if we had an idea of God as an omniscient being, it would involve a conception of God's omniscience. The absence of such an idea involves, indeed basically just is, the absence of a positive conception of God's attributes.

Such conceptions may be absent, but people clearly do use language that seems to describe God's attributes. What is such language doing, in the absence of those conceptions? Hobbes's response to that situation is to argue that such language has a purpose, but the purpose is not to describe God's attributes. Language can be used to praise and honor God, without describing him.

Cudworth was well aware of this theory of Hobbes's.[28] He himself had a very different approach, and a significant part of his reply to Hobbes's view consists in stating his view that we do have an idea of God as a perfect being. On the one hand, this idea is simple. On the other, we can demonstrate that a perfect being has indeed the various divine attributes. Cudworth grants, again, that we lack full understanding in this realm. Moreover, he suggests that talking in terms of multiple divine attributes is itself a sign of our lack of understanding in this realm. God's attributes are, on this story, "but so many *Partial* and *Inadequate Conceptions*, of *One and the Same, Simple Perfect Being*, taken in as it were by piecemeal: by reason of the Imperfection of our Humane Understandings, which could not fully Conceive it all together at once" (*System* 652). But this is not to say that talk of God's attributes is insignificant, or not descriptive at all. It may involve limited and imperfect descriptions but they are indeed, contrary to Hobbes, descriptions.

24.3 Morality in the *Treatise on Eternal and Immutable Morality*

24.3.1 The Structure and Topics of the *Treatise*

In the scheme announced at the start of *System*, Cudworth's second book is supposed to tell us that there is such a "*God* as is not meer *Arbitrary Will Omnipotent, Decreeing, Doing,* and *Necessitating* all Actions, *Evil* as well as *Good;* but *Essentially Moral, Good* and *Just*."[29] From that, one might expect a book focused on God. From the title of the *Treatise Concerning Eternal and Immutable Morality* (which corresponds, if anything does, to that projected second book) one might expect it to be a book focused on morality. On reading *Treatise*, what one finds is a book focused on epistemology and psychology, where there is a lot of material on, for instance, the distinction between sense and intellect.

Though much shorter than the *System*, the *Treatise* is divided into four books. The first, and probably best-known, focuses on the question whether morality can depend on decision alone, human or divine. That leads Cudworth to a discussion in the second book of the view that there are no immutable natures or essences, a view he connects to Protagoras, among others. At the end of that book, Cudworth concludes that there is "another principle in us superior to sense, which judges what is absolutely and not fantastically or relatively only true or false" (*Treatise* 48). Starting from there, the third book discusses the difference between sense and knowledge, sensitive and intellectual cogitation. The fourth book continues that discussion, finding that the mind can, by its active powers, know the intelligible, immutable natures of things. Moral good and evil, just and unjust must themselves, according to Cudworth, have such natures.

Where does Hobbes fit in that long epistemological discussion? Cudworth's arguments about the nature and role of intellect are anti-Hobbesian, but they do not usually pick Hobbes out or argue against him explicitly. One notable exception is an explicit argument against Hobbes's nominalism (*Treatise* 116ff.). Hobbes of course thinks there are such things as reason and knowledge, but he understands them very differently than Cudworth does. His account does not include the thing that Cudworth emphasizes, the active mind that can grasp intellectual natures. Hobbes does think there is universal thought, and science, but he thinks those can be enabled by adding the power of language to an underlying psychology of imagistic representation. Cudworth thinks that is not enough to get us genuine knowledge. Meanwhile, Hobbes believes that the epistemic activity Cudworth finds most important, the active mind cognizing immutable natures, simply does not exist, so does not need to be explained.

24.3.2 *Against the View That Morality Depends on Decision*

Book 1 of Cudworth's *Treatise* contains a relatively short, and apparently free-standing, argument that morality cannot arise merely from decisions, either human or divine. In recent decades, this has perhaps been the most-discussed part of Cudworth's work.[30]

The question that connects the beginning and end of the *Treatise* is whether morality depends on God's will or his intellect. Those who think it depends on his will (thus, on decision making) are Cudworth's primary target in the first book, before he starts to build his case that morality in fact depends on God's intellect. Hobbes – despite

Cudworth's general interest in arguing against him – is rather an incidental target of the early argument. Hobbes agrees with Cudworth's main targets that morality depends on decision, but thinks that human decisions, not divine ones, are what's important (on Cudworth's reading of Hobbes, and many others).[31]

The central passage in Cudworth's argument is the following.

> Wherefore in the first place, it is a thing which we shall very easily demonstrate, that moral good and evil, just and unjust, honest and dishonest (if they be not mere names without any signification, or names for nothing else but willed and commanded, but have a reality in respect of the persons obliged to do and avoid them) cannot possibly be arbitrary things, made by will without nature; because it is universally true, that things are what they are, not by will but by nature. As for example, things are white by whiteness, and black by blackness, triangular by triangularity, and round by rotundity, like by likeness, and equal by equality, that is, by such certain natures of their own. Neither can Omnipotence itself (to speak with reverence) by mere will make a thing white or black without whiteness or blackness; that is, without such certain natures, whether we consider them as qualities in the objects without us according to the Peripatetical philosophy, or as certain dispositions of parts in respect of magnitude, figure, site, and motion, which beget those sensations or phantasms of white and black in us. (*Treatise* 16)[32]

Some commentators have thought this argument fails, because it is merely tautological.[33] Cudworth does rely on the claim that "things are white by whiteness, and black by blackness, triangular by triangularity, and round by rotundity, like by likeness, and equal by equality," which sounds like a list of tautologies. His talk about natures is relevant though. Something cannot be made white, he says, without also being given the nature of a white thing – even God cannot simply declare something to now be white. Taking the talk about natures in a mechanical way, even God would have to arrange the small parts of the object so as to make it white.[34] That new arrangement of the small parts then explains why the object is now white.

Thus, when Cudworth says "things are white by whiteness," 'white' and 'whiteness' name two different things. On the one hand there's a way the object is: in this case, white. On the other hand, there's the underlying nature – what Cudworth calls the 'whiteness' – that explains why the object is that way. Sticking with the mechanical explanation, the whiteness is, roughly, the arrangement of the small parts of the object. Saying that the whiteness makes the thing white is giving an abbreviated explanation, not stating a tautology.

More generally, Cudworth claims that things do not acquire features just by decision, even by divine decision, except by acquiring the nature of a thing with that feature. Applying this principle to the case of goodness, even God cannot make a thing good just by deciding it shall be good, for even God has also to give it the underlying nature of a good thing, whatever that may be.

In thinking about this argument, several possible objections might come to mind. First, note that Cudworth is assuming that the principle about natures that holds in the examples above, about whiteness and so on, also holds of goodness. Perhaps it does, but it is open to someone to respond that it does not – that being good works differently, for there is no underlying nature that makes an object good, aside from simply being good. (Nothing stands to being good in the way that, according to the mechanist, having a surface texture that reflects light in a certain way stands to being green.) This non-reductive sort of response seems not open to Hobbes, though.

Secondly, there is a question about what the underlying nature is that makes something good. For Cudworth's purposes here, however, we do not need to know what the nature is, just to recognize that there must be one (and that it does not just consist in having been decided).[35]

Thirdly, one might argue in response to Cudworth that not all obligations arise from the natures of the things we are obliged to do. For instance, if I promise to do X, there may be nothing in X considered alone that makes it obligatory. It nevertheless is obligatory, but just because I promised to do it.

Cudworth responds to that sort of objection, granting that in some cases a command can make a thing obligatory, when before we were obliged neither to do it nor to refrain from it. However, he says, this cannot be the source of all obligations. A command to do X would not create an obligation to do the intrinsically morally neutral X unless one were already obliged to obey the command. Thus:

> we shall find that even in positive commands themselves, mere will doth not make the thing commanded just or obligatory, or beget and create any obligation to obedience; but that it is natural justice or equity which gives to one the right or equity of commanding, and begets in another duty and obligation to obedience. (*Treatise* 18)

Cudworth's view is that, although some obligations may arise from commands or decisions, not all obligations may do so. Any obligation that arises from a command or decision must ultimately depend on an obligation that does not so arise. In a simple case, the dependence will be easy to see. Suppose we are obliged to obey the monarch's command because of the nature of the monarch, and the monarch commands that we do X. We become, thus, obliged to do X. The obligation to do X is not ultimately explained by the decision alone. The explanation requires, rather, that the monarch be such you should obey their decisions.[36] More complicated cases are possible, but still, Cudworth says, there must be that basic obligation, one not grounded in a mere command, for the whole scheme to work.[37]

Evaluating this argument as criticism of Hobbes is tricky, insofar as it requires us first to say something about how exactly Hobbes thinks obligation arises. The question of where to locate the origin of normativity in Hobbes's system is not my topic here. Cudworth does however point us toward the difficult questions in that area. There are ways of reading Hobbes that find there is one basic obligation in Hobbes's system, from which others derive.[38] If there is one basic obligation in the system, what is it and where does it come from? If there is none – if there really are just decisions at the base, and nothing else – why is there any normativity in the system at all?

24.4 Conclusion

Cudworth engaged repeatedly with Hobbes's philosophical writings. Hobbes, whom Cudworth saw as an atheist who denied the eternal and immutable nature of morality, was a representative of all that Cudworth thought was bad in philosophy. But he was not just a representative of a broader trend – Cudworth picked out particular Hobbesian texts by quotation, and engaged with them in some detail.

We can see some of the broader disagreements of Hobbes and Cudworth, by looking at what they say about whether we have an idea of God. Most simply, Cudworth says we do, while Hobbes says we do not. Looking a little further, we see two different views about what ideas are, with Hobbes thinking they are all images, and Cudworth denying that. Looking beyond that, we see two different pictures of knowledge and the mind: Hobbes's view that relies just on the imagination and language being opposed by Cudworth's view of the intellect as an active being, capable of grasping eternal natures.

Sticking more closely to the question about God, we see Cudworth as an early suspicious reader of Hobbes: not accepting him as giving an account of our very limited ability to conceive of God, but taking him to deny God's existence, and to argue for that on the basis of our having no idea of God.

Issues about eternal natures arises again when we think about morality. Hobbes may not be the main target of Cudworth's argument that morality is not a matter of decision, but he is one of Cudworth's targets. Cudworth's criticism here points us to a recurring and difficult question about Hobbes, the question of how there can be any normativity in the Hobbesian system.[39]

Notes

1 Other publications of Cudworth's include *A Discourse Concerning the True Notion of the Lord's Supper* (1642), *A Sermon Preached Before the Honourable House of Commons* (1647), and *A Sermon Preached to the Honourable Society of Lincons-Inne* (1664).

2 The edition is Cudworth (1996). A short extract from *System* appears in Clarke and Collins (2011), and there is a modern German translation of Cudworth's sermon preached before the House of Commons (Cudworth 2018). The *Treatise* was not published until the eighteenth century, and *Freewill* not until the nineteenth.

3 *System*, "Preface to the Reader," third unnumbered page.

4 The one who is named is Joannes Szydlovius. Cudworth (1996, 15) refers to his "book published at Franeker," Szydlovius (1643). On Szydlovius (or Szydłowski) see Cudworth (1996, 15 n. 31); Kiedroń (2013, 223); Kronen (2015, 239); and Wojcik (1997, 193 n. 9).

5 Locke suggested that Cudworth's book could be used as a textbook of ancient Greek philosophy (Locke 1823, 9.185–6). More recently, Levitin (2016, 16) has described Cudworth "as a cutting-edge European philologist".

6 In *System*, there are about a dozen references to Descartes by name (*System* 39, 54, 161, 174–5, 646, 672, 684, 721, 724, 761, 843, 863, 882), Gassendi's views are noted and criticized (*System* 462, 641, 697, 769), and one passage criticizes Margaret Cavendish's views (*System* 137–8). Cudworth also cites chapters 19 (*System* 656) and 6 (*System* 707) of Spinoza's *Tractatus Theologico-Politicus*. This second reference, to the chapter on miracles, is noted by Colie (1963) and Israel (2006, 446), who both also argue that Cudworth's criticism of hylozoic atheism was intended as criticism of Spinoza. Cudworth describes hylozoic atheism as a view "that attributes to all Matter, as such, a certain *Living* and *Energetick Nature*, but devoid of all *Animality*, *Sense* and *Consciousness*" (*System* 135), and says in the Preface to the *System* that he has "certain Knowledge of [this view's] being of late *Awakened* and *Revived*" (ninth unnumbered page). Passmore (1990, 6) adds that "In one of his manu-

scripts Cudworth refers to Spinoza as 'a kind of hylozoic atheist'," referring to British Library MS 4982, p. 55.

7 The notes provided by Mosheim, who translated *System* into Latin, are helpful in identifying what passages in Hobbes's work Cudworth is referring to (Cudworth 1733, 1820).

8 Space being limited, I do not here discuss Cudworth's criticisms of Hobbes on freewill. On Cudworth on freewill, see Leisinger (2021) and Passmore (1990). On Cudworth's criticisms of Hobbes's determinism, see Irwin (2007, 247–9).

9 See Duncan and LoLordo (Forthcoming). Sarah Hutton says that Hobbes is a hylopathian atheist, not an atomic one (Hutton 1996, 2013). She argues that "Hobbes, by denying the existence of spirit altogether, but not denying the existence of God is a material atheist of the hylopathian variety" (Hutton 1996, 27). Cudworth, however, thought that Hobbes denied the existence of God. Beyond that, Cudworth's main contrast between hylopathian and atomic atheism seems to lie in the conception of matter, not in a different view about the existence of God. Thus, he distinguishes "the *Hylopathian* or *Anaximandrian*, that derives all things from Dead and Stupid Matter in the way of *Qualities and Forms*, Generable and Corruptible" from "the *Atomical* or *Democritical*, which doth the same thing in the way of *Atoms* and *Figures*" (*System* 135).

10 It depends a little on how one counts, but there something like 17 such passages with identifiable direct references.

11 For relevant texts in *System* on the explanatory role of fear, see *System* 63–4, 68–9, 96–7, 650–1, 655–6, and 891–2; on the role of politicians, 96–7, 697–9, and 891–2; on principles of motion and causation, 76–7 and 667–9; on knowledge, understanding, and nominalism, 730–2 and 853–4; and on materialism about the mind, 760–2 and 840–1.

12 Cudworth gestures towards there being other passages; we might add *De cive* 15.14 and a passage in chapter 31 of *Leviathan* (Hobbes 2012, 566; 1651, 190).

13 That is, Cudworth does not just use 'atheist' to describe heterodox views about the nature of God, or as a mere term of abuse.

14 Note the related suspicious reading of Gassendi, "another Learned *Well-willer* to *Atheism*" (*System* 641).

15 This is not the place to talk at length about the pros and cons of suspicious readings of philosophers. I note however that Hobbes said plenty of controversial things, even if we take him at face value. If we are to give a suspicious reading of Hobbes, we will need a fairly complex theory of what he was up to – what he certainly did not do, was to hide a controversial view behind a conventional facade. For examples of suspicious readings of Hobbes, see Curley (1992, 1995, 1996a, 1996b) and Jesseph (2002). In opposition, see Martinich (1992; 1996).

16 A note on terminology: Cudworth talks of ideas, and Hobbes uses that language when talking with Descartes, but generally prefers other terms elsewhere, such as 'phantasm.' I use 'idea' throughout the discussion in this chapter.

17 Cudworth grants the claim "That what is so Utterly *Unconceivable*, as that no man can frame any manner of *Idea* or *Conception* of it, is therefore either in it self, or at least to us, *Nothing* (*System* 638). Why should one think this? Here Cudworth tells us that there is "some Truth in that of *Aristotle*, that ... *the Rational Soul or Mind, is in a manner All things*; it being able to frame some *Idea* and *Conception* or other, of whatsoever is in the *Nature of things*, and hath either an *Actual* or *Possible Existence*, from the very Highest to the Lowest. Mind and Understanding is as it were a *Diaphanous* and *Crystalline Globe*, or a kind of *Notional World*, which hath some *Reflex Image*, and correspondent Ray, or Representation in it, to whatsoever is in the *True and Real World of Being* And upon this account may it be said, that whatsoever is in its own Nature Absolutely *Unconceivable*, is indeed a *Non-Entity*" (*System* 638). Whatever else we say about this, we can agree that it does not give us a Hobbesian reason to endorse premise 2.

18 Hobbes illustrates this claim with the example of a man born blind who thinks of fire as the cause of warmth he feels. We are supposed, analogously, to think of God as the cause of the things in the world. We see this in the Third Objections (AT 7.180; CSM 2.127) and later in *Leviathan* (Hobbes 2012, 160; 1651, 51).

19 Although "none should be condemned for *Absolute Atheists*, merely because they hold *Eternal Uncreated Matter*, unless they also deny, an *Eternal Unmade Mind*, ruling over the Matter, and so make *Sensless Matter* the Sole Original of all things" (*System* 199).

20 Similarly, Cudworth had begun this discussion by invoking "Modern Atheists" who "stick not to maintain, That the *Word God* hath no *Signification*" (*System* 192), which sounds vaguely Hobbesian, but it is not quite Hobbes.

21 This is much the same as the situation in Hobbes's Objections to Descartes's *Meditations*: Hobbes and Descartes agree that we have some way to think about God, and that we have no image of God, but disagree about whether we have the idea of God that Descartes's meditator claims to have, and indeed about whether we have any positive conception of the attributes of God.

22 A final thought involves giving alternative, deflationary explanations of our thoughts of God, explanations that may be psychological or political. This consideration works in a different way than the others – it is not really an argument that we have no idea of God – and I do not discuss it here.

23 Thus, he quotes the final paragraph of chapter 3 of *Leviathan*: "Thus a Modern *Atheistick Writer; Whatsoever we can conceive, hath been Perceived first by Sense, either at once or in parts; and a man can have no Thought representing any thing not Subject to Sense*. From whence it follows, that whatsoever is not *Sensible* and *Imaginable*, is utterly *unconceivable* and to us *Nothing*" (*System* 634).

24 "But to prove that there are *Cogitations* not subject to *Corporeal Sense*, we need go no further than this very *Idea* or *Description* of God; *A Substance, Absolutely Perfect, Infinitely Good, Wise and Powerful, Necessarily Self-existent, and the Cause of all other things*. Where there is not One Word unintelligible, to him that hath any Understanding in him, and yet no Considerative and Ingenuous Person can pretend, that he hath a *Genuine Phantasm* or *Sensible Idea*, answering to any one of those words; either to *Substance*, or to *Absolutely Perfect*, or to *Infinitely*, or to *Good*, or to *Wise*, or to *Powerful*, or to *Necessity*, or to *Self-existence*, or to *Cause*; or indeed to *All*, or *Other*, or *Things*" (*System* 636).

25 Note a comment in Hobbes's fifth objection – "this is why we are forbidden to worship God in the form of an image; for otherwise we might think that we were conceiving of him who is incapable of being conceived" (AT 7.180, CSM 2.127) – and one in his eleventh – "Since it has not been demonstrated that we have the idea of God, and since the Christian religion obliges us to believe that God cannot be conceived of (which means, in my view, that we can have no idea of him), it follows that no demonstration has been given of the existence of God, let alone the creation" (AT 7.189, CSM 2.133).

26 Cudworth quotes *De corpore* 26.1 and chapter 3 of *Leviathan* (Hobbes 2012, 46; 1651, 11). We see this thought back in the Third Objections as well (AT 7.186, CSM 2.131).

27 Cudworth thinks that God has infinite duration – though infinite duration "cannot possibly belong to any *Successive Being*" (*System* 645), it can belong to God.

28 He quotes several relevant passages: two from chapter 46 of *Leviathan*, one quoted at *System* 650 (Hobbes 2012, 1078; 1651, 371) and later one (in Hobbes's text) quoted at *System* 63–4 (Hobbes 2012, 1086; 1651, 374); *De corpore* 7.12, quoted at *System* 641; and the *Questions concerning Liberty, Necessity, and Chance* (EW 5.6), quoted at *System* 63.

29 *System*, "Preface to the Reader," third unnumbered page.

30 These discussions include Prior (1949, 13–25), Passmore (1990, 40–51), Zagorin (1992), Schroeder (2005), Irwin (2003; 2006, 2007, 249–63).

31 Here as elsewhere, Cudworth includes Hobbes among his atheistic opponents, not those with (merely) the wrong theological views. Thus, as far as Cudworth's reading of Hobbes goes, I disagree with Irwin (2007, 250), who says "Hobbes accepts voluntarism by treating the laws of nature as the commands of God." That is not an implausible reading of Hobbes, but it is not Cudworth's reading of him.

32 On the Platonic heritage of this argument of Cudworth's, see Irwin (2003; 2006). But see also Irwin's comments on Cudworth as defending certain Scholastic views about the will and morality against Hobbes's criticisms (Irwin 2007, 240).

33 Zagorin (1992, 131–2). Compare Passmore (1990, 41–2).

34 Cudworth thinks the argument would work equally well, if one took the talk about natures in a "Peripatetical" way. The key thought is that the presence of a feature must have an underlying explanation (which does not merely state an efficient cause).

35 On Cudworth on the nature of goodness, see Irwin (2007, 254).

36 We might even say the obligation is grounded in the nature of X, if having been commanded by the monarch counts as part of the nature of X. See Prior (1949, 21). More generally, there are questions about what is to be included in the natures of things here. For instance, does the relevant nature here include some fact about the monarch's relation to you, which explains why you must obey this monarch and not another?

37 For a possible response to this objection from Hobbes's perspective, see Irwin (2007, 258).

38 See Darwall (1995, 188–9) on "a single background moral fact." The one basic obligation might be an egoistic one. Thus, one might, as Shaver (1999) does, describe Hobbes as a rational egoist, even if Shaver is right that Hobbes has no good argument for that view. Alternatively, one might take the basic obligation in Hobbes's view to be an obligation to obey God, basing this on Hobbes's claim at the end of chapter 15 of *Leviathan* that the laws of nature are only "properly called Lawes" if they are considered "as delivered in the word of God" (Hobbes 2002, 242; 1651, 80). The most famous version of this sort of interpretation is that found in Warrender (1957) but see also Martinich (1992).

39 I thank Antonia LoLordo and Marcus Adams for their comments on earlier versions of this chapter.

References

Clarke, Samuel and Anthony Collins. 2011. *The Correspondence of Samuel Clarke and Anthony Collins, 1707–1708*, edited by William Uzgalis. Peterborough, ON: Broadview.

Colie, Rosalie L. 1963. "Spinoza in England, 1665–1730." *Proceedings of the American Philosophical Society* 107 (3): 183–219.

Cudworth, Ralph. 1642. *A Discourse Concerning the True Notion of the Lord's Supper*. London: Richard Cotes.

Cudworth, Ralph. 1647. *A Sermon Preached before the Honourable House of Commons*. Cambridge: Roger Daniel.

Cudworth, Ralph. 1664. *A Sermon Preached to the Honourable Society of Lincons-Inne*. London: Richard Royston.

Cudworth, Ralph. 1678. *The True Intellectual System of the Universe*. London: R. Royston.

Cudworth, Ralph. 1733. *Radulphi Cudworthi Systema Intellectuale Hujus Universi*, translated by Johann Mosheim. Leiden: Samuel and Johannes Luchtmans.

Cudworth, Ralph. 1820. *The True Intellectual System of the Universe*. London: Richard Priestly.

Cudworth, Ralph. 1996. *A Treatise Concerning Eternal and Immutable Morality*, edited by Sarah Hutton. Cambridge: Cambridge University Press.

Cudworth, Ralph. 2018. *Predigt Vor Dem Unterhaus Und Anderen Schriften*, edited by Alfons Fürst and Christian Hengstermann. Münster: Aschendorff Verlag.

Curley, Edwin. 1992. "'I Durst Not Write so Boldly' Or, How to Read Hobbes's Theological-Political Treatise." In *Hobbes E Spinoza*, edited by Daniela Bostrenghi, 497–593. Naples: Bibliopolis.

Curley, Edwin. 1995. "Hobbes versus Descartes." In *Descartes and His Contemporaries*, edited by Roger Ariew and Marjorie Grene, 97–109. Chicago, IL: University of Chicago Press.

Curley, Edwin. 1996a. "Calvin and Hobbes, Or, Hobbes as an Orthodox Christian." *Journal of the History of Philosophy* 34: 257–71.

Curley, Edwin. 1996b. "Reply to Professor Martinich." *Journal of the History of Philosophy* 34: 285–87.

Darwall, Stephen. 1995. *The British Moralists and the Internal Ought*. Cambridge: Cambridge University Press.

Duncan, Stewart and Antonia LoLordo. Forthcoming. "Early Modern Accounts of Epicureanism". In *The Oxford Handbook of Hellenistic Philosophy*, edited by Jacob Klein and Nathan Powers. Oxford: Oxford University Press.

Hobbes, Thomas. 1839–1845. *The English Works of Thomas Hobbes*, 11 vols., edited by Sir William Molesworth. London: John Bohn. Cited as EW.

Hobbes, Thomas. 2012. *Leviathan*, 3 vols., edited by Noel Malcolm. Oxford: Clarendon Press. [First published 1651.]

Hutton, Sarah. 1996. "Lord Herbert and the Cambridge Platonists." In *British Philosophy and the Age of Enlightenment*, edited by Stuart Brown, 20–42. Abingdon, UK: Routledge.

Hutton, Sarah. 2013. "The Cambridge Platonists." In *The Stanford Encyclopedia of Philosophy (Winter 2013 Edition)*, edited by Edward N. Zalta. https://plato.stanford.edu/archives/win2013/entries/cambridge-platonists

Irwin, Terence. 2003. "Morality and Immutability: A Platonic Contribution to Meta-Ethics." In *Perspectives on Greek Philosophy*, edited by Robert W. Sharples, 19–37. Aldershot: Ashgate.

Irwin, Terence. 2006. "Socrates and Euthyphro: The Argument and Its Revival." In *Remembering Socrates: Philosophical Essays*, edited by Lindsay Judson and Vassilis Karasmanis, 58–71. Oxford: Oxford University Press.

Irwin, Terence. 2007. *The Development of Ethics. Volume 2: From Suarez to Rousseau*. Oxford: Oxford University Press.

Israel, Jonathan. 2006. *Enlightenment Contested*. Oxford: Oxford University Press.

Jesseph, Douglas. 2002. "Hobbes's Atheism." *Midwest Studies in Philosophy* 26: 140–66.

Jesseph, Douglas. 2016. "Hobbes on the Foundations of Natural Philosophy." In *The Oxford Handbook of Hobbes*, edited by Aloysius P. Martinich and Kinch Hoekstra, 134–48. Oxford: Oxford University Press.

Kiedroń, Stefan. 2013. "Jan Makowski (1588–1644). Polish Theologian in Frisian Franeker." *Odrodzenie i Reformacja w Polsce*. special issue. http://dx.doi.org/10.12775/OiRwP.SI.2013.10.

Kronen, John. 2015. "Suárez's Influence on Protestant Scholasticism: The Cases of Hollaz and Turretín." In *A Companion to Francisco Suárez*, edited by Victor M. Salas and Robert L. Fastiggi, 221–47. Leiden: Brill.

Leisinger, Matthew A. 2021. "Cudworth on Freewill." *Philosophers' Imprint* 21 (1): 1–25.

Levitin, Dmitri. 2016. *Ancient Wisdom in the Age of the New Science: Histories of Philosophy in England, c. 1640–1700*. Cambridge: Cambridge University Press.

Martinich, Aloysius P. 1992. *The Two Gods of Leviathan: Thomas Hobbes on Religion and Politics*. Cambridge: Cambridge University Press.

Martinich, Aloysius P. 1996 ."On the Proper Interpretation of Hobbes's Philosophy." *Journal of the History of Philosophy* 34: 273–83.

Passmore, John Arthur. 1990. *Ralph Cudworth*. Bristol: Thoemmes Antiquarian Books. A reprint of the 1951 edition.

Prior, Arthur N. 1949. *Logic and the Basis of Ethics*. Oxford: Clarendon.
Schroeder, Mark. 2005. "Cudworth and Normative Explanations." *Journal of Ethics and Social Philosophy* 1 (3): 1–27.
Shaver, Robert. 1999. *Rational Egoism: A Selective and Critical History*. Cambridge: Cambridge University Press.
Szydlovius, Johannes. 1643. *Vindiciae Quęstionum Aliquot Difficilium Et Controversarum in Theologia*. Franeker: Uldericum Balck.
Warrender, Howard. 1957. *The Political Philosophy of Hobbes: His Theory of Obligation*. Oxford: Clarendon Press.
Wojcik, Jan. 1997. *Robert Boyle and the Limits of Reason*. Cambridge: Cambridge University Press.
Zagorin, Perez. 1992. "Cudworth and Hobbes on Is and Ought." In *Philosophy, Science, and Religion in England, 1640–1700*, edited by Richard Kroll, Richard Ashcraft, and Perez Zagorin, 128–48. Cambridge: Cambridge University Press.

25

Cavendish and Hobbes on Causation

MARCY P. LASCANO

This chapter examines the connections between Hobbes's and Cavendish's accounts of causation. Eileen O'Neill and Marcus Adams have argued that Hobbes and Cavendish share the same notion of entire causes as necessary and sufficient for producing their effects. While this account is well-suited to Hobbes's mechanical account of causation, O'Neill worries that this claim collapses Cavendish's account of occasional causation into full-on occasionalism. I argue that a close analysis of Cavendish's views on perception shows that the external object makes a causal contribution that precludes occasionalism. Karen Detlefsen has argued that Cavendish's account of causation requires libertarian freedom and the denial of nature as a principal cause. This would put Cavendish at odds with both Hobbes's account of causes and his account of freedom. I argue that Cavendish's occasional causation only requires self-motion, that self-motion does not require libertarian freedom, and that matter is the principal or entire cause of all the effects in nature. This not only goes a long way in reconciling Cavendish's views with those of Hobbes, but also provides a more natural reading of her texts.

25.1 Natural Philosophy and Causation

The study of natural philosophy was of central concern to both Cavendish and Hobbes. Both philosophers thought that philosophy consisted in determining the causes of natural effects. For instance, Cavendish writes that "natural philosophy is no more but a rational inquisition into the causes of natural effects" (2001, 158). Hobbes too thought that we used reason in order to ascertain the causes from their effects. In *De corpore*, he defines philosophy as follows:

A Companion to Hobbes, First Edition. Edited by Marcus P. Adams.

> Philosophy is such knowledge of effects or appearances, as we acquire by true ratiocination from the knowledge we have first of their causes or generation: And again, of such causes or generations as may be from knowing first their effects. (EW I.3)

Both Cavendish and Hobbes have wholly materialistic conceptions of nature and so they both agree that the subject of natural philosophy is bodies in motion. Given that the knowledge of causes and their effects is the aim of philosophy for both Cavendish and Hobbes, it makes sense that they both would provide an analysis of the relationship between causes and effects. This chapter will analyze Cavendish's views on causation while pointing out similarities and differences between her views and those of Hobbes. We know that Cavendish was familiar with Hobbes's views from reading the English versions of *De corpore* and *Leviathan* in addition to the fact that he was a frequent guest in the Cavendish household.[1]

When it comes to Cavendish's views on the nature of causation, there has been a fair amount of discussion in the secondary literature. For instance, both Eileen O'Neill and Marcus Adams claim that Cavendish, like Hobbes, holds that all causes must be "entire causes," that is all causes are necessary and sufficient for their effects (Adams 2016, 196; O'Neill 2001 xxxiii). In addition, O'Neill goes on to claim that in the case of perception, where Cavendish holds an occasionalist account, the external object is merely a "moral cause" while the perceiver is the "principal cause" of the perception (2001, xxiii). Likewise, Karen Detlefsen has also argued that in the case of perception the external object is a mere moral cause (2006, 15–19). Detlefsen argues that not only are perceiving individuals the principal cause of their own perceptions, but that individuals within nature are the only principal causes; thus, she denies that nature as a whole is a principal cause. Here, I will examine the claims in the secondary literature and point out some of the tensions that arise. I will argue that the distinction between patterning and figuring can mitigate some of the issues, and show that Cavendish holds that matter, or self-moving matter, is the only prime or principal cause in nature. This will lead to a new understanding of Cavendish's system, which has consequences for her views on freedom. I begin with a brief overview of Cavendish's general views on causation.

Cavendish holds that there are two distinct types of causation. The first is what we might call "substance transfer" and the second type is occasional causation. Like Hobbes, Cavendish holds that causation involves change in a body's motions. So, for instance in substance transfer, Cavendish holds that a part of one body will divide from that body and compose with another body, as happens during digestion, generation, and respiration.[2] According to Cavendish, motion can be transferred this way because the motion moves with the matter. So, for instance, when a child is conceived, matter from both the parents, along with the motions that cause human development, are transferred into the mother's womb. Substance transfer can also happen by impact or the force of one body upon another, but it is important to remember that Cavendish maintains if motion transfers from one body to another body matter must also be transferred because motion is not separable from matter. For Cavendish, this type of causation is an instance of the composition and division of parts, which occurs whenever a body grows or decays and does involve contact between bodies. In positing substance transfer, Cavendish seems to depart from Hobbes. She discusses Hobbes's example from *De corpore*:

> [Hobbes says] *that, when the hand, being moved, moveth the pen, the motion doth not go out of the hand into the pen, for so the writing might be continued, though the hand stood still, but a new motion is generated in the pen, and is the pens motion*: I am of his opinion, that the motion doth not go out of the hand into the pen, and that the motion of the pen, is the pens own motion. (Cavendish 1664, 54; Hobbes *DCo* VIII.21; EW I.117; OL I.104)

That Cavendish agrees with Hobbes that the motion is not transferred from the hand to the pen might make one think she does not have a substance transfer view. But as I have emphasized, her account of the transfer of motion is really the transfer of moving *matter* from one body to another and this only occurs in the sorts of cases already mentioned. In the passage just cited, Cavendish agrees with Hobbes that the motion from the hand does not transfer to the pen because she sees this as an instance of her second type of causation.[3] This second sort of causation – occasional causation – is due to the self-moving nature of composed bodies and does not involve the transfer of matter and motion nor does it require contact between bodies. Cavendish provides an example in which a hand moves a string or ball. She writes,

> Therefore when a man moves a string, or tosses a ball, the string or ball is no more sensible of the motion of the hand, than the hand is of the motion of the string or ball; but the hand is only an occasion that the string or ball moves thus or thus. I will not say, but that it may have some perception of the hand, according to the nature of its own figure; but it does not move by the hand's motion, but by its own: for, there can be no motion imparted, without matter or substance. (2001, 140)

In occasional causation, one object serves as the occasion for another object to move via its own self-motion in reaction to the first object. Of course, this is just a general statement of how it works – exactly what the exterior object does to trigger the self-motion of the other object is what is crucial for an understanding of her account. It is true that in the case of the hand and ball, the ball moves by its own self-motion. But as Eileen O'Neill has pointed out, if the external object, the hand in this case, plays no role in the causal process, how is Cavendish not committed to full occasionalism? Hobbes might have a similar problem. In his denial of motion transfer, he argues that when a hand moves a pen, the hand does not transfer its motion to the pen, "but that one accident perisheth, and another is generated" (Hobbes *DCo* VIII.21; EW I.117; OL I.104). But what does the hand do to cause the generation of a new accident in the pen? Since Hobbes denies self-motion, it seems he has no answer to this question.[4] But as we will see, Cavendish, in subscribing to both self-motion and Hobbes's account of entire causes can provide a more satisfactory account.[5]

25.2 Entire or Principle Causes

As noted earlier, commentators have already shown that Cavendish accepts Hobbes's account of "entire causes."[6] In *De corpore*, Hobbes writes

> But a cause simply, or an entire cause, is the aggregate of all the accidents both of the agents how many soever they be, and of the patient, put together; which when they are all supposed to be present, it cannot be understood but that the effect is produced at the same instant. (*DCo* IX.3; EW I.121–2)

Here, we have Hobbes's account of entire cause, which includes all the properties of both the external object and the perceiver. Cavendish, of course, rejects Hobbes's account of the perceiver as a patient, as well as his view that perception occurs as a result of mechanical pressure relayed to the senses by movements from the external object. However, Cavendish does agree that causation occurs as a result of motions in both bodies. But since Cavendish holds that every body has its own self-motion, she denies that any bodies are merely passive or that all perception is caused by pressure or contact. As Adams notes, he, O'Neill, and Michaelian subscribe to Cavendish's acceptance of this account of causes. And they all rightly note that Cavendish takes the fact that causes must be necessary and sufficient for their effects to show that external bodies cannot be the entire cause of a perception. Adams writes,

> With this understanding of *causa integra*, for Cavendish the internal self-motions of patterning and figuring are both necessary and sufficient causes for human visual perception or for self-motions that are indistinguishable from human visual perception, like dreaming. Another way of putting this point is that since causes are always necessary for their effects on the *causa integra* view, external bodies cannot be the cause of patterning since patterning can occur without any such external objects being present. (Adams 2016, 196)

I too agree that Cavendish subscribes to the Hobbesian account of entire causes, but there are two important modifications I want to add to this general account. First, while it is true that Cavendish does not think that the external object is the entire cause of perception, she does think that it plays an important role in perception. Consider the following:

> The Sensitive motion and matter in the Ears receives Words or Sounds, as the Sensitive matter and motion in the Eye doth receive Objects, *for the Motion of the Objects are not the only Cause* of Hearing or Seeing, or the Effects of the other Senses, but the Motions in the Senses make such Motions as the Objects. (1663, 299; emphasis added)[7]

Here, Cavendish tells us that the motions of outward objects are *not the only cause* of perception, and she means that they are a cause in conjunction with the self-motion of the perceiver. But what exactly do external objects do that distinguishes Cavendish's occasional causation from full occasionalism? One obvious answer is that they are causes in virtue of their power of self-motion. According to Cavendish, individual bodies are not causally inert so that some other entity – God, for instance – needs to be the sole cause of motion.[8] So, Cavendish is not a full occasionalist. But then one might worry that Cavendish's view is closer to Leibniz's Pre-established Harmony where the individuals are all self-moving but have no real external relations between them.[9] However, I do not think this is true. In order to see why we first have to understand that for Cavendish the entire cause is not just the sentient, or in the case of perception, the perceiver. Rather, like Hobbes, Cavendish holds that the entire cause involves both the bodies.[10] In addition to the passage cited earlier, evidence for this view is that Cavendish believes that in cases of perception whenever we are presented with external objects and our senses are working properly, we pattern those object *as they are*.

> But I will conclude this Chapter of Colours with an Answer to Two Questions, the First is, Whether all Creatures see all Objects alike? My Answer is, that if the Sight be Perfect, and without Imperfection, they do, but if the Sight be Imperfect, either by Nature or Accident, or be Over-powered, they do not... but Particulars are no Objection against the General, for surely an Eye is Nature's Press, to Print all Outward Objects that are Presented to it, the like are all the rest of the Senses. (1663, 217–18)

> It is the perceptive motions of the eye, which pattern out an object as it is visibly presented to the corporeal motions in the eye; for according as the object is presented, the pattern is made, if the motions be regular. (1664, 510–11)

> So soon as the object is removed, the sensitive perception is altered. (2001, 33)

> For the effects flow from the cause; and as the cause is, so are its effects. (1664, 197; see also 1664, 269)

In these and many other passages, Cavendish seems to hold that our sense organs insofar as they are working normally produce adequate copies of exterior objects. She does spend some time discussing how this otherwise reliable system can make mistakes and errors, but she notes these particular issues do not violate the general rule that our senses are such that they pattern external objects "as they are." When my eyes are open and functioning properly (as human eyes) I cannot help but pattern the objects in my visual array, and the same goes for my other sense organs. If the objects are removed or changed, so does my perception of them. This shows the dependence of my perceptions on the actual objects presented. However, one might worry that cases of optical illusion might undermine this claim. Kourken Michaelian has argued that Cavendish holds that illusions are due to mistakes in the senses.[11] He claims that this occurs when "the sensitive motions in the perceiving thing, although 'regular', make an incomplete copy of the figurative motions of the perceived thing" (2009, 43). He quotes the following passage from Cavendish as an example:

> According as the object is presented, the pattern is made, if the motions be regular; for example, a fired end of a stick, if you move it in a circular figure, the sensitive corporeal motions in the eye pattern out the figure of fire, together with the exterior or circular motion, and apprehend it as a fiery circle ...; so that the sensitive pattern is made according to the exterior corporeal figurative motion of the object, and not according to its interior figure or motions. (Cavendish 1664, 511; Michaelian 2009, 43)

Michaelian claims the fiery circle is an optical illusion, and he writes that "in this case, the exterior motions of the object are patterned out but its interior motions are not, giving rise to an inaccurate (because incomplete) copy" (2009, 44). The quotation he presents might lead one to think that the perception of the circular figure of fire is incomplete because the interior figure or motions of the stick are not patterned. If Michaelian believes perceptions are incomplete due to a lack of patterning of interior natures, then he is mistaken. For Cavendish is clear that we never perceive or pattern the interior natures of things, as to pattern the interior nature of something is to become that thing.[12] Cavendish writes:

> Nor can I believe, that the exterior parts of objects are able to inform us of all their interior motions; for our human optic sense looks no further than the exterior and superficial parts

> of solid or dense bodies, and all creatures have several corporeal figurative motions one within another, which cannot be perceived neither by our exterior senses, nor by their exterior motions: as for example, our optic sense can perceive and see through a transparent body; but yet it cannot perceive what that transparent body's figurative motions are, or what is the true cause of its transparentness. (2001, 59)

Michaelian points out that patterning cannot entail that something becomes the thing patterned according to Cavendish. He writes,

> Although patterning out is a sort of copying, it is an imperfect copying: when the figurative motions of a thing pattern out those of another thing, the former does not come to instantiate the very same figure as the latter, any more "than when a painter draws a fire or light, the copy should be a natural fire or light"; there is always a difference between the copy and the original of which it is a copy (2001, 187). This allows Cavendish to account for the possibility of multiple, distinct perceptions of the same thing (1664, 74), and, more importantly, to avoid saying that perceiving a thing is a matter of coming to resemble it. (Michaelian 2009, 39–40)

So, these perceptions are not incomplete because they do not include perceptions of the interior natures of things. In truth it seems that Cavendish is not all that concerned with optical illusions as the term "illusion" does not appear in her philosophical essays. Rather, she seems to think that the fiery circle is a true perception of the phenomena and is not a mistake. However, Cavendish does cite two examples that do seem to be illusions – the case of a person on a moving ship who believes it is the shore moving rather than the ship, and a person looking in a mirror while walking backward from it who believes the image in the mirror is going further inward. These cases Cavendish says are "neither perfect mistakes, nor delusions, but onely want of a clear and thorow perception" (1664, 510). The problem, as she sees it, is not that we do not pattern the interior of objects, but rather due to the limitations of human sight, we cannot pattern the motions of the distance or medium between us and a perceived object.

> The cause of it is, That the perception in the eye perceives the distanced body, but not the motion of the distance or medium; for though the man may partly see the motion of the visible parts, yet he doth not see the parts or motion of the distance or medium, which is invisible, and not subject to the perception of sight; and since a pattern cannot be made if the object be not visible, hence I conclude, that the motion of the medium cannot make perception, but that it is the perceptive motions of the eye, which pattern out an object as it is visibly presented to the corporeal motions in the eye; for according as the object is presented, the pattern is made, if the motions be regular. (1664, 510–11)

Illusions are due to a lack of patterning of the subtle matter of air, light, or reflective mediums, according to Cavendish. But since illusions result from not patterning those objects imperceptible to human sight, we cannot say that they provide evidence for the claim that exterior objects are neither necessary nor sufficient for perception. We can only perceive the perceivable objects and no account of perception should say otherwise. So, now we must turn to the cases that are more often cited as proving that external objects are not necessary of sufficient for perception – dreaming and being pinched without noticing it.

25.3 External Objects as Necessary and Sufficient for Proper Perception

Due to the case of dreaming, Adams claims that Cavendish holds that "external bodies cannot be the cause of patterning since patterning can occur without any such external objects being present" (Adams 2016, 196). In addition, Karen Detlefsen has claimed that "the constraint exercised [by the occasional cause] is neither necessary nor sufficient for the action to occur" (Detlefsen 2006, 234). O'Neill also claims that the cases of dreaming or distraction indicate that the external object is neither necessary nor sufficient for perception (2001, xxxiii). However, once we dig a bit deeper into Cavendish's account we will see that these cases do not justify these claims.

In the case of dreams, Cavendish tells us that the rational parts move *by rote*, that is, they move by a pattern (or at least by a very similar pattern to one) that they have made before. Like memory, the motions of dreams require prior experience of the object. So, the object need not be present when we remember or dream about it, but we cannot produce a thought of an object without having patterned it, or something like it, before. Cavendish calls these motions "figuring" motions rather than patterning. She writes,

> Working by rote, and by Sensible remembrance, they Work falsly, which causes the Rational motions to move Erroneously in Sleep, by reason the Rational moves according, for the most part, to the Sensitive Prints or Pictures; but sometimes the Sensitive, and so the Rational, moves just to those Objects, that have been formerly Printed on the Outside of the Sensitive passages, and then those Sensitive motions cause Perfect Dreams. (1663, 283)

> But Dreaming is, when they move in Figures, making such Figures, as these Objects, which have been Presented to them by the Sensitive motions, which are only Pictures or Copies of the Original Objects, which we call Remembrance, for Remembrance is nothing but a Waking Dream, and a Dream is nothing but a Sleeping Remembrance. (1663, 286)

> But Dreams, according to my opinion, are made by the Sensitive and Rational Corporeal Motions, by figuring several objects, as awake; onely the difference is, that the Sensitive motions in Dreams work by rote and on the inside of the Sensitive organs, when as awake they work according to the patterns of outward objects, and exteriously or on the outside of the sensitive Organs, so that sleep or dreams are nothing else but an alteration of motions, from moving exteriously to move interiously, and from working after a Pattern to work by rote. (1664, 28–9)

> When outward objects present themselves to the optic sense to be perceived, the perception of the sentient is an occasioned perception; but *whensoever, either in dreams, or in distempers, the sensitive motions of the same organ, make such or such figures, without any presentation of exterior objects, then that action cannot properly be called an exterior perception*; but it is a voluntary action of the sensitive motions in the organ of sight, not made after an outward pattern, but by rote, and of their own accord. (2001, 20; emphasis added)

> But it is well to be observed, that, besides those exterior perceptions of objects, there are some other interior actions both of sense and reason, which are made without the

> presentation of exterior objects, voluntarily, or by rote; *and therefore are not actions of patterning, but voluntary actions of figuring*: ... And therefore it is well to be observed, that figuring and patterning are not one and the same; figuring is a general action of nature: for, all corporeal actions are figurative, whenas patterning is but a particular sort of figuring. (2001, 170; emphasis added)

> For though the Animate motions oftentimes move and work as Actively to Sleep, and in Sleep, yet it is easier to move Voluntarily, than when they are Bound to Outward objects, as to Work upon Constraint and Necessity. (1663, VI.XIX, 280)

As Michaelian notes, "Dreaming, for example, will not count as perception" because dreaming is not patterning, but rather one of the motions made by rote (2009, 41). So, the fact that we can have a figurative motion that creates images in our sleep without external objects does not mean that perception properly so called can happen without exterior objects. Thus, the claims that dreaming shows that exterior objects are not causally necessary for proper perception are false.

The claim that exterior objects are not sufficient for perception are largely based on passages where Cavendish claims that a person can be pinched, but not notice it. She explains the case as follows:

> Suppose a man be in a deep contemplative study, and somebody touch or pinch him, it happens oft that he takes no notice at all of it, nor doth feel it; whenas yet his touched or pinched parts are sensible, or have a sensitive perception thereof; also a man doth often see or hear something, without minding or taking notice thereof, especially when his thoughts are busily employed about some other things; which proves, that his mind, or rational motions, work quite to another perception than his sensitive do. (2001, 150; cf. 1663, 293)

However, in the case of the pinch that goes unnoticed, Cavendish thinks that the sensitive matter does pattern the pinch, so patterning does occur. It is simply the case that the rational matter is so preoccupied that the sensitive patterning went unacknowledged (the double-perception that normally occurs fails in this case). This is similar to cases when one has been driving for a while and realizes that they have not been paying attention. The driving was still happening – the eyes were looking at the road, the foot was pressing the gas – but the mind was elsewhere. As Cavendish concludes:

> [t]herefore it may very well be, that a man in a deep contemplative study, doth not always feel when he is pinched or touched; because all the rational motions of his body concur or join to the conception of his musing thoughts; so that only the sensitive motions in that part, do work to the perception of touch; whenas the rational, even of the same part, may work to the conception of his thoughts. (2001, 152)

These cases only show that the mind can be so preoccupied that we do not notice our sensations. They do not show that "The principal cause acts entirely on its own" without exterior objects (Detlefsen 2006, 234). Rather, in the case of the pinch, the object does cause the appropriate perception in the sensitive matter, but the rational matter fails to pattern the sensitive perception as it normally does. These often-cited cases do not prove that the external object is neither necessary nor sufficient for perception.[13] Of course, it is true that actions made by rote in memory, dreams, or delusions, do not require the external object's presence, but since these are cases of figuring rather than patterning – that is they are not cases of proper perception at all – the claim that external objects constitute part of the entire cause of perception stands.

But there is a further advantage to interpreting Cavendish's account this way. The cases of delusion and dreaming can help us to understand the causal role of the occasional cause. In the case of dreaming, as noted earlier, Cavendish tells us that the external sensory organs of the perceiver do not pattern an external object; rather they move by "rote" or memory (actions she associates with voluntary motions). In dreams, as the quotes above indicate, motions begin in the interior parts of the body and are figured on the inside of the sensory organs, while in cases of proper perception the motions begin on the outside of our sensory organs and move inward to the nerves and brain. Cavendish writes:

> yet the sensitive corporeal motions having their proper organs, as Work-houses, in which they work some sorts of perceptions, those perceptions are most commonly made in those organs, and are double again; *for the sensitive motions work either on the inside or on the out-side of those organs, on the inside in Dreams, on the out-side awake* .... (1664, 19; emphasis added; see also 1996, 20)

> The Difference between Sleeping and Waking, is, that in Sleep the Sensitive Animate matter and motions Work on the Inside of the Sensitive passages, as they do when as Awake on the Outside of the Sensitive passages, and when as the Sensitive motions Work on the Inside of the Sensitive passages, they Work by Rote, that is, they Work as to make Prints and Figures on the Inside of the Sensitive passages, without the Help or Patterns of Outward objects. (1663, 282)

Cavendish's accounts of dreaming are usually given in contrast to cases of proper perception, in which the exterior object is the occasion of the patterning of the exterior parts of our sensory organs, which information is then relayed inward to the brain.[14] Thus, we can conclude that in cases of proper perception the existence of the exterior occasional cause determines the *direction* of the causal process from exterior to interior. Without the occasional cause, the figurative motions, if any, would move in a different direction – from the brain to the inside of the sense organs. In this way, we can claim that *the occasional cause does do something.* It does affect the perceiver as it brings about a direction of causality within the perceiver that would not occur if it were absent. If the external object does determine the direction of causation, it would seem that the individual is not completely self-determining with respect to their perceptions. Although it is still true that the perceptive motions in the perceiver's sensory organs and mind are self-motions, these motions are affected by the presence or absence of the exterior object. Moreover, this explains why Cavendish calls occasioned action, "necessary" or "forced." For example, she writes, "that exterior body is the occasion that it moves after such a manner or way, and therefore this motion of the line, although it is the lines own motion, yet in respect of the exterior body that causes it to move that way, it may be called a forced, or rather an occasioned motion" (1664, 443). In addition, in her criticism of Hobbes's account of voluntary motions, she writes, "they cannot properly be called voluntary, but are rather necessitated, at least occasioned by the Mind or Fancy; for I oppose voluntary actions to those that are occasioned or forced" (1666, 55). I will return to this issue.

I have here argued that, for Cavendish, the external object is an occasion for the perceiver to pattern via its own power of self-motion the external object, but in addition I have argued that this occasional cause is part of the entire cause in cases of proper perception. The external object contributes in two ways: first, the external object's proprieties (Cavendish's term) determine the content of the perception of the perceiver when the perceiver's organs are in normal working order; second, the external object determines the direction of causation within the perceiver. Without the external object, the sensitive and rational matter may move figuratively to create dreams, imaginings, or fancies, but these are not cases of proper perception. In addition, in cases of dreaming, the figuring is done on the inside of the sensory organs rather than on the outside.

The picture painted so far looks to be in keeping with Hobbes's causally deterministic view of the world. But we might still claim that because perceivers have self-motion, they are still self-determining and so Cavendish's system allows for non-deterministic processes in a way that Hobbes's account does not. Next, I will consider Karen Detlefsen's argument that individuals are not subject to any sort of causal determinism.

25.4 Nature as the Principal Cause

As we have seen, for Cavendish, perception involves occasional causation, which Cavendish calls patterning. The ball patterns the motions of the hand and moves itself in accordance with this perception, and the seemingly conclusive cases of dreams and delusions (which I have argued against) provide reason for Detlefsen to think that the "principal cause" (in this case the ball) is completely free. Detlefsen argues there are three reasons for believing that occasional causation supports libertarian freedom. She writes:

> Principal causes that are encouraged to act in a specific way by occasional causes are free, of course, for the following reasons: the constraint exercised is neither necessary nor sufficient for the action to occur; the principal cause is self-moved; and the principal cause acts in accordance with its own reasons. But the occasional cause exercises some constraining influence – a moral influence – over the actions of the principal cause. (Detlefsen 2006, 234)[15]

So, the principal cause must be radically free because the occasional cause is neither necessary nor sufficient for the action of the principal cause, the principal cause moves itself, and the principal cause acts by its own reasons. I have already shown that the occasional cause is necessary and, when acting as part of the entire cause, sufficient for cases of proper perception. But Detlefsen claims in several places that self-motion and reason are sufficient for libertarian freedom. However, it seems that this is not so. Having the power to move oneself and the power of reason are compatible with determinism. After all, there are many compatibilist accounts that hold that we are self-moving and (at least somewhat) reasonable – Locke's, Leibniz's, etc.[16] In addition, I nowhere find Cavendish discussing a part moving "in accordance with its own reasons." Nevertheless, we should still examine the parts of Detlefsen's argument that do not depend just on occasional causation. In a passage claiming the parts of nature are not necessitated, she implies that if nature were a principal cause and the parts of nature "mere effects" necessitation would hold. She writes:

> The theory of occasional causation supports a view of nature in which natural parts themselves act as principal causes and are not necessitated to behave in a certain way. They are necessitated neither by nature as a whole imposing, from the top down, specific interrelations among the parts (which then become mere effects and not causes at all), nor by occasional causes necessitating that the principal cause act in a specific fashion. That is, they are free from extrinsic control. (Detlefsen 2006, 234)

Cavendish seems to use the language of principal causes and prime causes interchangeably, and she is pretty clear about what counts as a prime or principal cause.

> But there is but one onely chief and prime cause from which all effects and varieties proceed, which cause is corporeal Nature, or natural self-moving Matter, which forms and produces all natural things. (1664, 237)

> Matter is the prime cause of Figure, but not Figure of Matter, for Figure doth not make Matter, but Matter Figure, no more than the Creature can make the Creator, but a Creature may make a Figure. (1663, 93)[17]

> But, to conclude, human sense and reason perceiveth, that from Few, indeed, but from One Principle, (as the Only matter) Infinite Effects do proceed. (1663, 8)

> But, in my opinion, Water, and the rest of the Elements, are but effects of Nature, as other Creatures are, and so cannot be prime causes. (1664, 234)

According to Cavendish, the prime cause is matter, which is all of nature. She is also pretty clear about what the effects of matter are – everything in nature. She notes that these effects, however, are also causes.

> There are Infinite effects and every produced effect, is a Producing effect, which Effect produces Effects, and the only matter is the cause of all Effects.(1663, 100)

> To treat of Infinite Effects, produced from an Infinite Cause, is an endless Work, and impossible to be performed, or effected; only this may be said, That the Effects, though Infinite, are so united to the material Cause, as that not any single effect can be, nor no Effect can be annihilated; by reason all Effects are in the power of the Cause. But this is to be noted, That some Effects producing other Effects, are, in some sort or manner, a Cause. (1996, 15)

Detlefsen claims that we must choose whether we want to say that Nature is the principal cause and that all causation is "top-down" or whether individuals are the real principal causes. She goes for the latter claim saying that "we need to deny that nature is principal cause in a natural, physical sense" in order to hold that individuals are principal causes (2006, 236). Instead of holding that nature is a principal physical cause, Detlefsen argues that Cavendish must hold that nature is merely a moral cause.[18] Detlefsen acknowledges that this goes well beyond the text. There is nowhere in Cavendish's corpus where she speaks of moral causes. But, as noted earlier, there are places where Cavendish calls nature the prime and principal cause. In addition to claiming that nature or only matter is the prime cause of all her effects, Cavendish also claims that all these effects constitute the body of nature.

> for my opinion is, that they are all but one matter, and *one material body of nature*. And this is the difference between the cause or principle, and the effects of nature, from the neglect of which, comes the mistake of so many authors, to wit, that they ascribe to the effects what properly belongs to the cause, making those figures which are composed of the aforesaid animate and inanimate parts of matter, and are no more but effects, the principles of all other creatures. (2001, 206; emphasis added)

> there is infinite nature, which may be called general nature, or nature in general, which includes and comprehends all the effects and creatures that lie within her, and belong to her, as being *parts of her own self-moving body*. (2001, 197; emphasis added)

Detlefsen says that she takes Cavendish's claim that nature is one body seriously, but she seems to think that it implies top-down causation. However, I think that this is not the case. It is obvious that living bodies do not operate in a completely top-down manner. Rather, there is some degree of top-down causation, but there is also bottom-up causation, and lateral causation within the systems and structures of the body. Cavendish holds that there are bodies within bodies in nature, and each of these bodies have their own particular figurative motions that form causal systems that perform the functions of various organs, circulate blood, push oxygen into the lungs, and expel waste through the intestines. The fact that nature works like a body explains why Cavendish's texts sometimes look like she is positing a top-down system and sometimes a bottom-up system – both are included.

This brings us to Cavendish's holism, which is closer to what we might now call biological holism than metaphysical holism. For Cavendish, causal relations happen at every level of the organism (or whole of nature). Just as in a human being there are bodily commands that come from the mind and direct the whole organism in certain ways, as when we might flee a perceived danger, but there are also causal relations that occur within parts of the body as when our heart beats, and across parts as when we digest food. This is not to say that nature is a person or a human, but that nature is a living organism.[19]

So, while contemporary metaphysicians might speak of holism as the view that there are properties of nature that are not the result of the fundamental parts and their relations and that the whole is something over and above the parts, this is not Cavendish's view. Rather, Cavendish's view most closely resembles the sort of holism we see in the living sciences. This, of course, makes sense. According to this sort of holistic view, we cannot fully understand a single organism without reference to the whole system as all the parts of the system are interconnected in such a way that individuals are, in some sense, incomplete when abstracted away from the whole. Cavendish frequently stresses the interdependence of the parts of nature. If nature is the principal cause of all the effects in nature, then we can see that while Cavendish may not be committed to top-down causal laws, she is still committed to the parts of nature being effects in a complex system of causal interrelations.

25.5 Determinism?

We may not think that appeals to causation are the correct way to argue about determinism today due to issues about what counts as a cause. However, in the seventeenth century, being committed to causes as necessary and sufficient for their effects was the leading way to argue that the world was deterministic in nature. For instance, Hobbes writes that "An entire cause is always sufficient for the production of its effect, if the effect be at all possible" (EW I.122). And "a necessary cause is defined to be that, which being supposed, the effect cannot but follow" (EW I.123). From these claims he argues that determinism follows. He writes,

> For whatsoever is produced, in as much as it is produced, had an entire cause, that is, had all those things, which being supposed, it cannot be understood but that the effect follows; that is, it had a necessary cause. And in the same manner it may be shewn, that whatsoever effects are hereafter to be produced, shall have a necessary cause; so that all the effects that have been, or shall be produced, have their necessity in things antecedent. (EW I.123)

Cavendish does not argue for determinism, although her account of causation would make Hobbes's argument available to her. Even though she does not argue for determinism, we should not ascribe libertarian free will to her either.[20] Deborah Boyle correctly notes that Cavendish's texts cut both ways with respect to free will. Boyle also notes, I believe correctly, that freedom is not a central theme in Cavendish's writing (2019, 37). I think this is probably good reason not to saddle her with a radical libertarian account that most of her contemporaries did not hold.

It seems likely that Cavendish does not develop an account of freedom because she does not take it to be an important part of natural philosophy. This would be a more radical line of what should be included in the study of bodies than Hobbes takes. Hobbes claims that natural philosophy excludes theology (the study of the nature of God), the study of spirits and immaterial entities, divine revelation, and issues of worship and faith (EW I.10–11). However, Cavendish seems to think that the question of whether we have free will or not is one that is more suited for theologians and moral philosophers. Writing in response to Hobbes's claims about voluntary motions she writes that Hobbes "is much for necessitation, and against free-will, which I leave to Moral Philosophers and Divines" (1664, 96). Cavendish does write about moral and political issues as well as the occasional references to religion and God's nature (as does Hobbes), but her most robust discussions of moral and political issues are kept separate from her works on natural philosophy. It is still worthwhile to examine briefly what she says in response to Hobbes regarding voluntary motions and freedom since her acceptance of his views on causation make it more likely that she would also hold something similar to his views on determinism and freedom.

In his discussion of gravity, Hobbes claims that inanimate bodies cannot move themselves to a place because they "have no appetite at all," and so it is "ridiculous to think that by their own innate appetite they should preserve themselves, not understanding what preserves them" (EW I.510). He goes on to claim that even humans "who have both appetite and understanding" cannot leap more than three or four feet above the ground to save their own lives (EW I.510). Cavendish responds to this passage in her

Philosophical Letters by arguing that if God gave humans who are just parts of nature a "power and free will of moving himself, why should God not give it to Nature?" (1664, 95). She continues:

> I do not say, That man hath an absolute Free-will, or power to move, according to his desire; for it is not conceived, that a part can have an absolute power: nevertheless his motion both of body and mind is a free and self-motion, and such a self-motion hath every thing in Nature according to its figure or shape ... Yet do I not say, That there is no hindrance, obstruction and opposition in nature; but as there is no particular Creature, that hath an absolute power of self-moving; so that Creature which hath the advantage of strength, subtilty, or policy, shape, or figure, and the like, may oppose and over-power another which is inferior to it, in all this; yet this hinderance and opposition doth not take away self-motion. (1664, 95–6)

Here, Cavendish seems to claim that self-motions are free. Of course, what matters is how she understands the term "free." It seems that she thinks that one is free if one is able to move as one desires and that this holds for every part of nature.[21] But bodies are sometimes necessitated by exterior objects. These objects can necessitate responses from other objects through either occasional causation or substance transfer. When this occurs, the action is not voluntary or free. Cavendish criticizes Hobbes's account of voluntary actions because they are "caused and depend upon our Imagination," and she wonders "how can they be voluntary motions, being in a manner forced and necessitated to move according to Fancy or Imagination?" (1664, 96). In a section explaining "obscure and doubtful passages" in her prior works, which is appended to the end of the 1666 edition of *Observations Upon Experimental Philosophy*, she clarifies her criticism writing:

> When, contradicting the opinion of Mr. Hobbes concerning voluntary motions ... My meaning is not as if those actions were not self-actions, nor as if there were no voluntary actions at all; for to make a balance between Natures actions, there are voluntary, as well as occasioned actions, both in sense and reason; but because Mr Hobbs says, that those actions are depending upon Imagination and Fancy, and that Imagination is the first internal beginning of them, which sets them a going, as the prime wheel of a Watch does the rest: My opinion is, that after this rate they cannot properly be called voluntary, but are rather necessitated, at least occasioned by the Mind or Fancy; for I oppose voluntary actions to those that are occasioned or forced; which voluntary actions are made by the self-moving parts by rote, and of their own accord; but occasioned actions are made by imitation, although they are all self-actions, that is, move by their own inherent self-motion. (1666, 54–5)

According to Cavendish, occasioned actions are not voluntary or free because they involve an exterior cause. Only actions that have their origin in the desire or will of the individual – those actions done by rote – will count as voluntary or free, and these in a compatibilist sense. It is also interesting that sometimes when Cavendish talks about the movements of the parts of nature, she uses Hobbes's phrase, which she quotes from *Leviathan* – "knowing what they do, or why and whither they move" (1666, 308; 1996, 139, 207, 258). The echoing of this language is surely intentional on

Cavendish's part and belies an affinity with Hobbes's account of liberty – according to which one is at liberty if one is able to move as one desires, rather than will as one pleases. While we cannot say that Cavendish argues for determinism or a compatibilist account of freedom, it does seem that her views on causation lead one to believe that she held such a view.

25.6 Conclusion

I have argued that Cavendish's system is more deterministic and closer to that of Hobbes than other commentators have thought. In doing so, I have argued that her account of perception does not entail that perceivers are the entire cause of their perceptions and that Cavendish thought that matter was the only prime and principal cause in nature. This interpretation is more naturalistic than others on offer and eschews any teleological or normative structure in Cavendish's system of nature. This, I take to be more in keeping with her aims of constructing a natural philosophy that adequately accounts for the movements of the organic bodies in nature.

Notes

1 Cavendish claimed that she never spoke more than 20 words to Hobbes, but his influence on her philosophy is widely recognized. For more on the relationship between Hobbes and the Cavendish family, see Detlefsen (2012), Duncan (2012), Hutton (1997) and Whitaker (2002).

2 As Eileen O'Neill points out "Cavendish insists that transeunt causation takes place all the time in animal generation and the varieties of 'respiration'" (2001, xxxv; 2013, 323–4).

3 Cavendish's criticisms of Hobbes in this letter seem additionally odd because instead of talking about her own view of causation, she discusses Hobbes's claim that accidents (which she claims are just ways matter moves) are generated (a process she believes requires substance transfer) and perish (something that she thinks cannot happen in nature because all motions are repeatable). Cavendish does address the possibility of motion transfer a few pages later. There she argues that if the motion is incorporeal, then it is a mere nothing or a Devil, Angel, or supernatural soul, which she thinks have better things to do. If the motion is corporeal, she argues, the hand would lose strength with every effort because it must lose matter as well. So, there must be an additional sort of causation (1664, 77–9).

4 According to Hobbes, "That which rests, is understood to rest always, unless some other body is together with it, by which assumption, it is not able to rest any longer" (OL I.102). Hobbes argues in the continuation of this passage that without a sufficient cause to move in any particular direction a body will remain at rest. But he does not explain how it is that a body can cause another body that is at rest to generate motion.

5 I would like to thank Marcus Adams for bringing this to my attention.

6 Note that O'Neill calls them "principal causes," even though she is referring to Hobbes's account of entire causes.

7 Compare to *Philosophical Letters*: "But yet I do not say, that the motion of the hand doth not contribute to the motion of the bowl; for though the bowl hath its own natural motion in itself, ... nevertheless the motion of the bowl would not move by such an exterior local motion, did not the motion of the hand, or any other exterior moving body give it occasion

to move that way; *Wherefore the motion of the hand may very well be said to be the cause of that exterior local motion of the bowl*, but not to be the same motion by which the bowl moves" (1664, 447–8; emphasis added).

8 Occasional causation, as defined by Steven Nadler (1994, 39) "denotes the entire process whereby one thing, A, occasions or elicits another thing, B, to cause e. Even though it is B that A occasions or incites to engage in the activity of efficient causation in producing e, the relation of occasional causation links A not just to B, but also (and especially) to the effect, e, produced by B." This is in contrast to Occasionalism of the sort attributed to Malebranche.

9 For the account of Leibniz's Pre-established harmony see Leibniz (1997).

10 I will focus on cases of perception which is an instance of occasional causation since she discusses these cases more frequently than non-perceptual causal relations.

11 For further discussions of perceptual errors in Cavendish, see Boyle (2015 and 2019) and Adams (2016).

12 Cavendish holds that every object has exterior and interior figure and motions. The interior figures and motions make a thing what it is. "And it is to be observed, that in composed figures, there are interior and exterior parts; the exterior are those which may be perceived by our exterior senses, with all their proprieties, as, colour, magnitude, softness, hardness, thickness, thinness, gravity, levity, etc. *But the interior parts are the interior, natural, figurative motions, which cause it to be such or such a part or creature*: As for example, man has both his interior and exterior parts, as is evident; and each of them has not only their outward figure or shape, *but also their interior, natural, figurative motions, which did not only cause them to be such or such parts; (as for example, a leg, a head, a heart, a spleen, a liver, blood, etc.) but do also continue their being*" (2001, 162; emphasis added).

13 It should be noted that David Cunning (2020, 153) agrees that the external object is sufficient for changes in the "direction of motion" in the perceiver. However, Cunning also notes that the amount of motion in the perceiver is not changed by the causal process. It is difficult to know how, for instance, a ball can accelerate or a person running into a wall is stopped without an increase or decrease of motion.

14 Consider a passage that may cast doubt on this reading: "It is true, by Experience we find, that without an Eye we cannot see Outward objects as they are without us, yet we see those Objects as they are without us in our Sleep, when our Eyes be shut: Thus the Sense of Seeing is not lost, although the Eyes were out, and the Optick Nerves stop'd up" (1663, 294–5). The context of this passage is Cavendish's objection to the idea that all figures in the mind come in through the eyes. Cavendish argues in the quote above that (1) we "see" figures in our minds when we dream, but when we dream our eyes are closed and our optic nerve is "stop'd up." She goes on to argue that (2) the motions of the brain are motions of rational matter and those motions are always figurative whether it is thinking, imagining, dreaming, or receiving non-optical sensory information (1663, 259–99).

15 O'Neill also claims that the exterior object is merely a moral cause (2001, xxx–xxxiii).

16 Boyle (2018; 2019) follows Detlefsen on these points.

17 Note this interesting exception to the rule: "Was not God able to give self-motion as well to a Material, as to an Immaterial Creature, and endow Matter with a self-moving power? I do not say, Madam, that Matter hath motion of it self, so, that it is the prime cause and principle of its own self-motion; for that were to make Matter a God, which I am far from believing; but my opinion is, That the self-motion of Matter proceeds from God, as well as the self-motion of an Immaterial Spirit; and that I am of this opinion, the last Chapter of my Book of Philosophy will enform you, where I treat of the Deitical Centre, as the Fountain from whence all things do flow, and which is the supream Cause, Author, Ruler and Governor of all" (1664, 179).

18 Detlefsen's argument follows O'Neill's discussion of occasional causes being principal causes (2001, xxx–xxxiii).

19 See Anker (2003) for a discussion of how Cavendish holds that Nature is a *human* body.

20 Cunning (2016, 214) argues that libertarian freedom does not follow from Cavendish's use of free will and freedom in her works. Cunning argues that Cavendish's commitment to the plenum means that parts of nature will not always be allowed to move as they will. Thus, he assigns a compatibilist account of freedom to Cavendish.

21 Cavendish will often say that Nature as a whole is free because she is always able to move as she pleases. For example, "although nature is free, and all her parts self-moving; yet not every part is free to move as it pleases" (OEP, 244), and "as nature is full of variety of motions or actions, so are her parts; or else she could not be said self-moving, if she were bound to certain actions, and had not liberty to move as she pleases" (2001, 138–9).

References

Adams, Marcus. 2016. ""Visual Perception as Patterning: Cavendish against Hobbes on Sensation."." *History of Philosophy Quarterly* 33 (3): 193–214.

Ankers, Neil. 2003. "Paradigms and Politics: Hobbes and Cavendish Contrasted." In *A Princely Brave Woman: Essays on Margaret Cavendish Duchess of Newcastle*, edited by Stephen Clucas, 242–54. Aldershot: Ashgate.

Boyle, Deborah. 2015. "Margaret Cavendish on Perception, Self-Knowledge, and Probable Opinion." *Philosophy Compass* 10 (7): 438–50.

Boyle, Deborah. 2018. *The Well-Ordered Universe: The Philosophy of Margaret Cavendish*. Oxford: Oxford University Press.

Boyle, Deborah. 2019. "Informed by 'Sense and Reason': Margaret Cavendish's Theorizing about Perception." In *The Senses and the History of Philosophy*, edited by Brian R. Glenney and Filipe Pereira da Silva, 231–48. London and New York: Routledge.

Cavendish, Margaret. 1663. *Philosophical and Physical Opinions*. London: William Wilson.

Cavendish, Margaret. 1664. *Philosophical Letters: Or, Modest Reflections upon Some Opinions in Natural Philosophy, Maintained by Several Famous and Learned Authors of This Age....* London: n.p..

Cavendish, Margaret. 1666. *Observations upon Experimental Philosophy*. London: A. Maxwell.

Cavendish, Margaret. 1996. *Grounds of Natural Philosophy: Divided into Thirteen Parts: With an Appendix Containing Five Parts*. West Cornwall, CT: Locust Hill Press. Cited as GNP followed by page number.

Cavendish, Margaret. 2001. *Observations upon Experimental Philosophy*, edited by Eileen O'Neill. Cambridge: Cambridge University Press.

Cunning, David. 2016. *Cavendish*. New York: Routledge.

Cunning, David. 2020. "Cavendish on Causation and Cognition." In *Causation and Cognition in Early Modern Philosophy*, edited by Dominik Perler and Sebastian Bender, 145–70. New York: Routledge.

Detlefsen, Karen. 2006. "Atomism, Monism, and Causation in the Natural Philosophy of Margaret Cavendish." *Oxford Studies in Early Modern Philosophy* 3: 199–240.

Detlefsen, Karen. 2012. "Margaret Cavendish and Thomas Hobbes on Freedom, Education, and Women." In *Feminist Interpretations of Thomas Hobbes*, edited by Nancy J. Hirschmann and Joanne H. Wright, 149–68.

Duncan, Stewart. 2012. "Debating Materialism: Cavendish, Hobbes, and More." *History of Philosophy Quarterly* 29 (4): 391–409.

Hobbes, Thomas. 1839–1845a. *The English Works of Thomas Hobbes*, 11 vols., edited by Sir William Molesworth. London: John Bohn. Cited as EW.

Hobbes, Thomas. 1839–1845b. *Thomæ Hobbes malmesburiensis opera philosophica*, 5 vols., edited by Gulielmi Molesworth. London: John Bohn. Cited as OL.

Hutton, Sarah. 1997. "In Dialogue with Thomas Hobbes: Margaret Cavendish's Natural Philosophy." *Women's Writing* 4 (3): 421–32.

Leibniz, Gottfried. W. 1997. *Leibniz's 'New System' and Associated Contemporary Texts*, translated and edited by Roger S. Woolhouse and Richard Francks. Oxford: Oxford University Press.

Michaelian, Kourken. 2009. "Margaret Cavendish's Epistemology." *British Journal for the History of Philosophy* 17: 31–53.

Nadler, Steven. 1994. "Descartes and Occasional Causation." *British Journal of the History of Philosophy* 2: 35–54.

O'Neill, Eileen. 2001. "Introduction." In *Observations upon Experimental Philosophy*, edited by Eileen O'Neill, x–xxxvi. Cambridge: Cambridge University Press.

O'Neill, Eileen. 2013. "Margaret Cavendish, Stoic Antecedent Causes, and Early Modern Occasional Causes." *Revue Philosophique* 3: 311–26.

Whitaker, Katie. 2002. *Mad Madge*. New York: Basic Books.

26

Striving, Happiness, and the Good: Spinoza as Follower and Critic of Hobbes

JUSTIN STEINBERG

It is often noted that among the ways that Spinoza's philosophy reflects the influence of Hobbes is in terms of his conception of striving (*conatus*).[1] While this is undoubtedly true, in this chapter I wish to analyze one important way in which Hobbes and Spinoza differ in their understanding of "striving" and to show that this difference goes some distance in accounting for their remarkably different normative philosophies. I argue that Spinoza's commitment to an essentialist reading of striving helps to explain his profound, and somewhat underappreciated, break with Hobbes not only in terms of his views of right and obligation, but also in terms of his conceptions of happiness and the good.

The structure of this chapter is as follows: I open by examining the similarities between Hobbes's and Spinoza's views on motivation. This is followed by an analysis of the distinct ways in which they understand striving, and in turn agency and artifice, showing how these differences are reflected in their conceptions of civil life. Finally, I consider how the differences described in the preceding sections yield fundamentally different views of goodness, happiness, liberty, and the function of the state.

Fundamentals of Moral Motivation

Though Spinoza's debt to Hobbes is widely acknowledged in the scholarly literature,[2] the striking ways in which Spinoza's account of motivation resembles Hobbes's has not been fully charted. In this section I survey of some of the important connections. To appreciate their accounts of moral motivation, we must situate them in relation to the Scholastic model that they both sought to supplant.

A Companion to Hobbes, First Edition. Edited by Marcus P. Adams.

Critique of Scholasticism

The Scholastic account of human action assigned an irreducible and ineliminable explanatory role to final causes. Final causes were not only distinct from and irreducible to efficient causes, they explained the efficacy of efficient causes themselves. As Aquinas puts it: "the end is the cause of the causality of the efficient cause, for it makes the efficient cause to be an efficient cause."[3] For humans, goodness is the end of action, or that towards which the will is directed and which consequently shapes the particular desires by which we act. Even when we desire something that is not really good, we still pursue things under the appearance of the good, with goodness itself – along with our capacity to be apprehend and be drawn by its power – grounding any explanation of why we choose what we do.[4] Goodness, as the end of action or the object of the will, enables us to apprehend courses of action as choiceworthy in some respect.

Still, Scholastics did not think that the apprehension of goodness alone fixes action, as this would imply an execrable form of intellectual determinism. Instead, they maintained that we possess another power – i.e., the liberty of exercise – by which we can perform or refrain from performing the action specified by the intellect.[5] The liberty of exercise is a self-determining power, a two-way ability to do or forebear. The Scholastic conception of action thus depended both on the explanatory independence (and priority) of final causes and a libertarian freedom of the will.

Hobbes and Spinoza reject both of these elements. Hobbes categorically denies the existence of a free will, claiming that it is flatly incompatible with the notion of a cause, which is such that when all of the contributing factors are present "it cannot be understood but that the effect is produced at the same instant; and if any one of them be wanting, it cannot be understood but that the effect is not produced" (EW I.122).[6] Since nothing exists for which there is not a total and sufficient cause, Hobbes infers that "whatsoever is produced is produced necessarily ... and therefore also voluntary actions are necessitated" (EW V.380). To appeal to a free will to explain action would be to invite an untenable regress: "a man can no more say he will will, than he will will will, and so make an infinite repetition of the word will; which is absurd and insignificant" (EW IV.69).

Hobbes also rejects the view of final causes as grounding the efficacy of efficient causes. In response to Bramhall, he writes that any attempt to show that human action is "moved not by an efficient [cause], is nonsense" (EW V.77; cf. EW I.131–2). Still, he admits that human actions can be explained in terms of ends, provided that we concede that the representation of an end "is entirely the same as an efficient cause," since the imagination of some pleasure gives rise to "motion towards the desired object" (1976, 315; EW I.131–2). He inverts the priority relationship between appetites and goodness: we do not desire things because they are good; rather "good" and "evil" are just terms that denote that which we desire or imagine with pleasure (2012, 80–2; 1651, 24; see also EW IV.32).

Spinoza denies free will and final causation on similar grounds. He asserts that "in nature there is nothing contingent, but all things have been determined from the necessity of the divine nature to exist and produce an effect in a certain way" (1p29; 1985, 433).[7] The view that everything that exists is necessary follows in part from his commitment to a robust version of the principle of sufficient reason (e.g., 1p11 alt. dem;

1985, 417). On the basis of his necessitarianism, he straightforwardly rejects the notion of the will as a two-way power or faculty (see 2p48 [1985, 483]; 2p35s [1985, 473]; 1 Appendix [1985, 440]).

Spinoza also rejects the standard view of final causes. *Ethics* 1 Appendix includes a protracted diatribe against natural teleology in which he claims that: "all the prejudices I here undertake to expose depend on this one: that men commonly suppose that all natural things act, as men do, on account of an end ... Nature has no ends set before it ... all final causes are nothing but human fictions" (1985, 439, 442). But while he denies that end-directed explanations are distinct from efficient causal explanations, he, like Hobbes, allows for reductive sense of final causation: "What is called a final cause is nothing but a human appetite in so far as it is considered as a principle, or primary cause, of some thing ... It is really an efficient cause, which is considered as a first cause, because men are commonly ignorant of the causes of their appetites" (4 Preface; 1985, 544). Consequently, he also inverts Scholastic explanatory order, explaining "ends" in terms of appetites, rather than the other way around (1 Appendix [1985, 442]; 3p9s [1985, 500]).

We see then that Hobbes and Spinoza not only reject these fundamental elements of Scholastic accounts of motivation, they do so for similar reasons. They are both determinists who deny the existence of free will on the grounds that it jars with causal sufficiency, and in place of the view of final causes as explaining the efficacy of efficient causes, they reduce final causes, or ends, to efficient causes. This clears the ground for their positive, naturalistic accounts of motivation.

Hobbes on Motivation

At the foundation of Hobbes's account of human motivation is the concept of endeavor – or *conatus* in Latin – which is defined as the "small beginning of motion" (2012, 78; 1651, 23). The notion of conatus figures into nearly every aspect of Hobbes's philosophy, from his physics to his account of sense perception.[8] Unsurprisingly, then, it is the foundation of his account of motivation: "This endeavour, when it is toward something which causes it, is called appetite, or desire ... And when the endeavour is from ward something, it is generally called aversion" (2012, 78; 1651, 23). Endeavor is the fount of action.

Appetites and aversions are not blind impulses, but rather "depend always upon a precedent thought of *whither, which way*, and *what*" (Hobbes 2012, 78; 1651, 23; see also 1972, 55). The specific thoughts that direct one's endeavor are anticipations of "good and evil consequences" (2012, 94; 1651, 29; cf. EW V.357–8), or hedonic or painful representations of various courses of action (2012, 82; 1651, 25; see also EW IV.32). And to represent something as pleasant is to perceive it as good, representations of goodness being nothing apart from pleasure, appetite, or love (EW V.390; EW IV.32; 1972, 47; EW II, 196; 2012, 80; 1651, 24; 2012, 242; 1651, 79). Ultimately, Hobbes folds a number of affective and motivational dimensions into his conceptions of pleasure and pain, claiming that pleasure and pain are themselves appetitive and aversive motions and that passions like love, hate, hope, and fear are mere permutations of pleasure and pain. As he baldly puts it in *Elements of Law*, "pleasure, love, and appetite, which is also called desire, are divers names for divers considerations of the same thing" (EW 4, 32; cf. 2012, 80; 1651, 23–4). Hobbes thus advances a stripped-down account of motivation: appetitive pleasure and aversive pain are motions that lead us toward or away from some object, and the representations of goodness and evil are simply manifestations of appetitive pleasure or aversive pain (EW V.358; 2012, 90; 1651, 28; EW I.409–10).

Finally, to get the full picture of Hobbes on the metaphysics of motivation, we may observe that pleasure and pain are themselves rooted in a system's functioning:

> This Motion, which is called Appetite, and for the apparence of it Delight, and Pleasure, seemeth to be, a corroboration of Vital motion, and a help thereunto; and therefore such things as caused Delight, were not improperly called Jucunda, (A Juvando,) from helping or fortifying; and the contrary, Molesta, Offensive, from hindering, and troubling the motion vital. (2012, 82; 1651, 25; cf. EW IV.31)

Ultimately, then, human motivation depends on how one's vital, preservational motions are affected.

Spinoza on Motivation

Striving is also at the root of Spinoza's account of motivation: "each thing, as far as it is it in itself [*quantum in se est*], strives [*conatur*] to persevere in its being" (3p6; 1985, 498; translation modified). Striving is a thing's fundamental motive tendency: insofar as we are in ourselves,[9] we will do things that promote our being. This is the ground of everything that we do.

But what one does is not determined by one's conatus *simpliciter*, but rather by one's affective state, or how one's conatus is constituted (3 DA 1, expl; 1985, 531). There are three basic classes of affect: joy (*laetitia*), sadness (*tristitia*), and desire (*cupiditas*). Joy and sadness are for Spinoza what pleasure and pain are for Hobbes: they are the fundamental springs of action that reflect changes to our vital activity. Joy marks an increase in one's power of acting, while sadness marks a decrease of this power. Not only does Spinoza follow Hobbes in explaining basic affects in terms of changes to one's preservational activities, he also accepts Hobbes's view that these basic affective states are complex intentional states, not blind, raw feelings.[10] Because affects are representational, they direct our striving so that we pursue things that we imagine with joy and avoid things that we imagine with sadness (3p12–13; 1985, 502).

As for desire, it is simply one's essence or striving insofar as this essence is constituted by a form of joy or sadness (3p56d [1985, 527]; cf. 3 DA I, expl. [1985, 531]).[11] On this view, the same "mode" may be understood either as a form of joy (e.g., a love of an object) or as a desire (a striving for an object), depending on whether or not one is attending to the way in which this mode orients one's striving. Desire is just an emotion considered *strivingly*. This reveals yet another way in which Spinoza's position resembles Hobbes's. Just as Hobbes thinks that pleasure and pain are motivational, such that pleasure itself is an appetite and pain an aversion, Spinoza thinks that modes that constitute joy and sadness are motivational, with the distinction between emotions like joy and sadness and desires being merely aspectual. For Spinoza, as for Hobbes, there is no gap between how we are affected and how we are determined to act.

Finally, to get the comparison with Hobbes in full view, let us consider how evaluative judgments fit into this account of motivation. Having rejected the Scholastic view that good and evil are features of the world that compel our will, Spinoza embraces the Hobbesian view that judgments of the good are grounded in our desires: "[W]e neither strive for, nor will, neither want, nor desire anything because we judge it to be good; on the contrary, we judge something to be good because we strive for it, will it, want it, and desire it" (3p9s [1985, 500]; cf. 3p39s [1985, 516–17]). The specific nature of the dependency relationship between evaluative judgments and desire is fleshed out in *Ethics* 4, where Spinoza maintains that that the ideas of good and evil are nothing but affects themselves (4p8 [1985, 550]; 4p19d [1985, 556–7]).[12] Like Hobbes, Spinoza denies that judgments of good and evil play any independent explanatory role in human motivation, treating them instead as motivational just insofar as they are affects.

We see from this that Spinoza and Hobbes advance remarkably similar accounts of motivation. They both reject free will and the traditional conception of final causes and along with it the explanatory independence of evaluative judgments. Instead, they offer mechanistic accounts according to which: we strive to persevere in our being; joy/pleasure and sadness/pain are responses to how one's vital functioning is impacted; these basic affective states are also motivational; evaluative appraisals are constituted by affects or desires.

In light of how similar their views are, it seems fair to conclude that Spinoza, an eager and astute reader of Hobbes, was strongly influenced by his predecessor in developing his account of moral motivation. But while Spinoza and Hobbes adopt similar motivational frameworks on which they base their moral and civil philosophies, they nevertheless arrive at fundamentally different normative conclusions. In this next section, I will explore one notable difference in their accounts of motivation, a difference that is the wedge that drives their views apart.

Striving and Essence

The crucial difference between Hobbes and Spinoza concerns the role that essences play in their respective conceptions of striving. Put simply, Spinoza is committed to the explanatory significance of essences, whereas Hobbes is not.

Spinoza on Striving and Essence

Essences figure into Spinoza's account of striving in a couple of ways. On the one hand, Spinoza claims that striving is "the actual essence of the thing" (3p7; 1985, 499). It is what one does and cannot but do. As one's essential activity, striving not only generates, but informs, particular desires. In other words, all desires in some sense express, or inherit the very character of, that essential tendency.[13]

Moreover, it has plausibly been argued that to strive is to realize one's essence as far as possible.[14] Although striving to "persevere in its being [*in suo esse*]" (3p6; 1985, 498) is sometimes glossed as a principle of mere existential inertia, in fact such a reading jars with other claims in the *Ethics*.[15] Just as existence should not be measured in terms of persistence over time (2p45s [1985, 482]; 1D8 exp [1985, 409]), neither should striving. Rather, striving is the tendency to increase one's power or perfection, both of which are to be understood in terms of one's essence or nature:

> By virtue and power I understand the same thing, that is (by IIIP7), virtue, insofar as it is related to man, is the very essence, or nature of man, insofar as he has the power of bring about certain things, which can be understood through the laws of his nature alone. (4D8; 1985, 547)
>
> [W]e understand by perfection the very essence of the thing. (3 GDA; 1985, 542–3)
>
> [B]y perfection in general I shall, as I have said, understand reality, that is, the essence of each thing insofar as it exists and produces an effect, having no regard to its duration. (4 Preface; 1985, 546)

In light of this understanding of power and perfection, we see that striving to increase one's power or perfection is tantamount to striving to realize one's essence more completely.[16]

Hobbes on Striving and Essence

Spinoza's essentialist account stands in sharp contrast to Hobbes's view of striving. Hobbes is generally skeptical about the explanatory role of essences or natures. In *Elements of Law*, he reduces a thing's nature to its powers, rather than treating it as the ground of powers (EW IV.2). And in *Leviathan*, he rails against Aristotelian real essences, claiming that "an essence, therefore, is not a thing, either created or uncreated; it is, rather, a name invented for the sake of their craft. It is only Aristotle who has given birth to new, bastard and empty *beings* of this kind" (2012, 1079; 1651, 320 – Curley's translation; cf. 2012, 80; 1651, 24; 2012, 1076–82; 1651, 371–3). By denying real (irreducible) essences, Hobbes also eschews the view of striving as one's essential activity. So, while one's vital motions figure into the generation of voluntary motions, it is not the case that appetites and aversions are conceptually tied to self-preservation (more below); nor can this vital activity be conceptualized as "essence realizing." Put simply, essences play no role in Hobbes's account of motivation.

To be sure, Hobbes does invoke the notion of a human *nature*. However, this conception of nature does not delimit one's range of activity in the way that it does for Spinoza. As S. A. Lloyd and Susanne Sreedhar have stressed, for Hobbes, the mere fact that an impulse or desire arises from one's nature does not make it effective. So, for instance, while the aversion to death may be in us by nature, such that in the absence of other impulses we will tend to preserve ourselves, humans commonly "create countervailing forces to thwart the effectiveness of their natural impulses" (Lloyd 2009, 63).[17] Bernard Gert also argues that we must distinguish between what "human beings naturally avoid and what actual human beings (those who have been subject to education and training, good or bad) avoid" (Gert 2010, 45). On such readings, one's nature may be roughly understood as something like one's *biological* nature. But, as Lloyd puts it, we are "as much creatures of our cultural nurture as we are of our abstract nature"

(2009, 66). Indeed, according to Hobbes, in order to live in peace, humans must in some sense transcend or overcome our nature, which would not be possible on an essentialist reading.

From the preceding analysis, we see that while Hobbes and Spinoza both accord to striving a pride of place in their theories of motivation, they conceive of the character and role of striving quite differently. Most notably, Spinoza regards striving as tied to a metaphysics of essences, while Hobbes does not.

This entails that, for Spinoza, while we can desire all sorts of particular things – namely, anything that we represent as the object of joy – these ends are always expressive of our striving to persevere in our being. We might distinguish between the superficial and the deep content of desires. The superficial content – or immediate object – of desire is always conditioned and underwritten by the deep content of striving to persevere in one's being.[18] Because the striving to persevere does not merely generate desires, but is expressed in all desires, Spinoza can only offer a rather tortured analysis of suicide, claiming that apparently voluntary acts of self-destruction are really just instances of destruction by "hidden external causes" (4p20s [1985, 557]; cf. 4p18s [1985, 556]).

By contrast, Hobbes has no such difficulty accounting for suicidal and self-sacrificial behavior (2012, 116; 1651, 37; see also EW VI.281; 1972, 48–9). While we have a natural aversion to death, this aversion can be overridden by stronger passions that we cultivate (EW II.82–3). The fact that a desire or aversion is natural does not mean that it occupies a privileged status in Hobbes's motivational scheme; and it certainly does not mean that all other motives reflect this impulse. For Hobbes, the reasons for which we intentionally or voluntarily act – that is, the aspect or description under which we act – need not appeal to one's striving: one can act for love, glory, charity, salvation, fear of damnation, or any other number of other ends, even at the cost of bodily preservation. So, despite his popular reputation as a psychological egoist, Hobbes was a pluralist about motivation. It is Spinoza, not Hobbes, who is something of a motivational monist, at least in the limited sense that he is committed to the view that desires are always ultimately expressive of striving to realize one's essence.[19]

In the next section we will begin to explore the ethical and political implications of Hobbes's and Spinoza's distinct views of motivation by examining the relationship between their respective views of striving and their accounts of action and artifice. We will see that while Hobbes will have no truck with real essences, Spinoza will have no truck with the notion of overcoming one's nature or creating a realm of artifice.

Action, Artifice, and Civil Life

As noted above, Hobbes thinks that we construct selves beyond our natures. To see how, we must examine Hobbes's views of activity and artifice, which turn on his conception of language. As Philip Pettit puts it: "Language, in Hobbes's story, provides the magic that enables us to jump the limitations of the natural, animal mind" (2008, 25). Hobbes conceives of speech as a kind of technology, calling it "the most noble and profitable invention" (2012, 48; 1651, 13) and claiming that on its basis our faculties "may be improved to such a height, as to distinguish men from all other living creatures" (2012,

48; 1651, 11. cf. EW IV.25). Language augments cognition, facilitates the exercise of deliberative control and agency, and enables us to create social realities through the declaration of will.[20]

Spinoza adopts a fundamentally different conception of action and agency, one that is rooted, unsurprisingly, in his conception of essence. Action, for Spinoza, does not require transcending one's nature; indeed, it is precisely a matter of producing effects *from* one's nature. Spinoza spells this out in the very beginning of *Ethics* 3, where he claims that we act when we are the adequate cause of something, that is, when we produce effects that are explicable through our nature alone (3D1–3D2). By contrast, we are passive when we produce effects only in conjunction with the natures of other things. One exercises one's agency not, *per impossible*, by transcending one's nature,[21] but precisely by bringing it about that one's nature is more efficacious.

Hobbes's and Spinoza's distinct views of action and activity figure directly into their respective analyses of civic life. For Hobbes, speech enables us to construct new social realities, most notably the commonwealth.[22] The artificiality of the state is so prominent in Hobbes's account that I needn't belabor this point. I note it simply to set up the contrast with Spinoza, who, when prompted by his friend Jarig Jelles to explain how his view differs from Hobbes's, responded: "As far as Politics is concerned, the difference you ask about, between Hobbes and me, is this: I always preserve natural Right unimpaired and I maintain that in each State the Supreme Magistrate has no more right over its subjects than it has greater power over them" (Ep. 50; 2015, 206). For Spinoza, right is coextensive with power, which, *as one's very essence*, is not something from which one can be alienated or which one can transfer like a piece of property. So, whereas Hobbes thinks that authority is constructed through the transfer of right or declaration of will, Spinoza thinks that authority is a fully natural (*de facto*) condition that is established only insofar as dependency relations obtain (TP 2/10 [2015, 512]; TTP 17.5–6 [2015, 512]).[23] This point of contrast between Spinoza and Hobbes is rooted in their distinct views of one's nature or essence: for Hobbes, one's nature is merely the starting point of human life, whereas for Spinoza one's nature is one's inalienable power that defines all that one is and does.

These different conceptions of right yield correspondingly distinct views of obligation. For Hobbes, transferring right through declaring one's will entails incurring obligation, so that to violate a covenant is to have conflicting wills, or to contradict oneself (EW IV.96). By contrast, Spinoza denies that contracts oblige independent of perceived utility (TTP 16.20 [2015, 512]; TTP 16.9 [2015, 512]; TP 2/12 [2015, 512–13]). This follows from his view that right is coextensive with power: being obligated entails lacking the right to something; but anything one *can* do – including breaking pledges – one does by right (TP 2/12; 2015, 512–13). Like authority, obligation is a *de facto* condition: it consists in actually being held to something, which in the case of contracts or promises is a matter of remaining motivated to comply with them.[24]

On the basis of their distinct understandings of right, authority, and obligation, Hobbes and Spinoza adopt very different views about how the commonwealth should be structured and what sovereign absolutism entails.[25] But rather than lingering on these juridical differences, I want to turn in this final section to a set of concepts that have received comparatively less attention as a point of contrast, namely, their respective conceptions of goodness and happiness.

Striving, Happiness, and the Good

Hobbes and Spinoza both claim that the concepts of good and evil depend on the motivational states of the agent. But, as we will see in this section, their distinct views about motivation yield different views of value (e.g., good and evil) and happiness.

Hobbes on Happiness and the Good

We saw in the first section that Hobbes thinks that the concepts of good and evil refer to our affective responses to things rather than to mind-independent properties. We call things good insofar as they please us and we desire them, and we call things evil insofar as they displease us and we are averse to them. This is not just a point about we happen to use language, it is a claim about the very meaning of the concepts of good and evil: they are terms we ascribe to things based on how they affect us – things that delight us or impel us are good, while things that displease us or repel us are bad. In presenting good and evil as affect-dependent concepts, Hobbes calls attention to their variability. Not only are there differences between individuals in their axiological appraisals, but the very same individual may adopt different evaluative stances at different times in relation to one and the same thing (see e.g., 2012, 242; 1651, 80). The instability of evaluative standards contributes to disputes and antagonisms. The remedy, of course, is to establish a public standard of good and evil in the form of a sovereign or authorized legislator (see 2012, 1090; 1651, 376).

By establishing a common standard of right, wrong, good, and evil, the commonwealth functions to reduce conflict, while providing the security that everyone desires. The state is thus the "the greatest of human powers" (2012, 132; 1651, 41), powers being means for obtaining other goods or desires (2012, 132; 1651, 41). Other powers include friendship, riches, wisdom, the arts and sciences, and honor (1972, 47–51; EW IV.37–8; *Leviathan* chapter 10). Such things are useful irrespective of one's particular intrinsic ends and may consequently be regarded as common goods in Hobbes's sense (1972, 47). The fact that there are common goods and that the state supplies a public standard of good and evil might lead us to think that Hobbes has a desire-independent conception of good. In fact, though, Hobbes insists that "whatever is good, is good for someone or other" (1972, 47; EW V.193) and that public standard of the civil law and the goodness of powers are parasitic on the intrinsic desires of individuals. Consequently, nothing in Hobbes's account of the public standard or of common goods implies a disavowal of his desire-dependent conception of the good.

Nevertheless, not everything that one desires is good. Hobbes is keen to distinguish real from apparent goods (1972, 48; EW IV.25), claiming that one can desire something the obtainment of which would actually be, on balance, bad for the agent. For instance, he claims that emotions "militate against the real good, and in favor of the apparent and most immediate good, which turns out frequently to be evil when everything associated with it hath been considered" (1972, 55). One might wonder how Hobbes, who rejects any conception of proper functioning, can distinguish desires that aim at "real goods" from those that do not. The answer is that, unlike merely apparent goods, real goods are things that one pursues insofar as one is rational, in the sense of properly reckoning long-term consequences (1972, 48; cf. EW IV.34). Emotions "obstruct right reasoning" because they prompt one to pursue lesser proximate goods without regard to long-term consequences (1972, 55; cf. EW II.47–8; 2012, 282; 1651, 94). This is consistent with the good being desire-dependent, since what counts as a real good ultimately depends on what one desires, or what one would desire if one were adequately informed. Nothing in the account presupposes the existence of substantive, desire-independent ends.

Just as real goods vary from person to person, so does felicity or happiness. Felicity is defined in explicitly desire-dependent terms as: "continuall successe in obtaining those things which a man from time to time desireth" (2012, 96; 1651, 29). This is one way in which Hobbes sets his account of felicity apart from the eudaimonist tradition: he denies that it consists in something like proper human functioning, claiming instead that what makes one happy varies according to one's desires (2012, 150; 1651, 47).[26] Another way that Hobbes breaks from classical eudaimonism is in his denial that happiness consists in perfecting of one's capacities, whether intellectual or moral.[27] And whereas, on a classical conception, to perfect one's capacities is, in a sense, to acquire all that one lacks, Hobbes emphatically insists that because human desires are never fully satiated, happiness consists in *prospering*, not having prospered (2012, 150; 1651, 47; see also 1972, 53). We should not, therefore, take happiness to be the contentment that arises from self-perfection: "the felicity of this life consisteth not in the repose of the mind satisfied. For there is no such *Finis ultimus* (utmost aim) nor *Summum Bonum* (greatest good)" (2012, 150; 1651, 47).

Let me conclude by noting a couple of significant consequences of Hobbes's desire-dependent conceptions of goodness and felicity. First of all, it limits the moral ambitions of the state. To be sure, the sovereign is enjoined to govern so as to promote peace, preservation, and the "commodious life" of citizens. However, as Bernard Gert puts it, the "positive goal" of promoting felicity "has no specific content" (2010, 50), since it depends on desires. So, while Hobbes advocates the establishment of a rather robust conception of safety that facilitates the procurement of "all other contentments of life, which every man by lawful industry, without danger or hurt to the commonwealth, shall acquire to himself" (2012, 520; 1651, 175; cf. 2012, 196; 1651, 63; EW II.167–8), he acknowledges that such contentments will vary from person to person. Consequently, although Hobbes does think that the state can and should seek to supply the means for contentment or commodious living, it remains the case that individuals retain their own particular sets of desires and conceptions of the good and felicitous life, the obtainment of which lies somewhat beyond the ambit of state power.[28]

Moreover, since Hobbes rejects appeals to essences or proper functioning, he also abjures the ideal of positive liberty as self-realization. Instead, in *Leviathan* 21 he famously conceives of liberty in terms of the absence of physical or "artificial" impediments, rendering one free to the extent that one is not prevented from doing what one wills. His novel "negative" conception of liberty is to some extent an outgrowth of his desire-relative conception of goodness and his corresponding rejection of perfectionism.

Spinoza on Happiness and the Good

The contrast with Spinoza on goodness, happiness, liberty, and the aims of the state could hardly be starker. For Spinoza, while goodness is, in some sense, motivation-dependent, the relevant motivation here is one's essential, invariant striving. This serves as a fixed standard of evaluation: things really are good or evil relative to how they impact one's striving or essence.

Spinoza advances his revisionist accounts of good and evil in *Ethics* 4, where, after again denying that predicates like good, evil, imperfect, and imperfect are intrinsic properties of things, he proposes that we understand good and evil in terms of how things affect one's essence or power of acting (4p8d; 1985, 550). Things are good insofar as they increase one's power or aid one in realizing one's power and are evil insofar as the diminish one's power or prevent one from realizing one's power. This fits with the other prominent way in which Spinoza construes the concepts of good and evil, namely, in terms of whether something brings one closer to, or renders one further from, the "model of human nature" (4 Preface; 1985, 545) The model of human nature is a paradigm of human power or "reality" – that is, it is a model of a fully realized human essence.

So, while Spinoza's conception of the good is motivation-dependent, it is *in some sense* mind-independent, in that it does not hinge on one's perceptions or on the superficial content of one's desires. Things really are good insofar as they conduce to essence realization, even if they are not overtly pursued or represented as good. Put somewhat differently, Spinoza thinks that while some ways of striving are fully one's own, or authentic, there are also ways of striving that reflect the influence of external natures.

We can elucidate this point via the distinction between action and passion. We will recall from the previous section that, according to Spinoza, one acts in the strict sense when and only when one is the adequate cause of something. In *Ethics* 4, Spinoza casts this notion in a few interchangeable ways. For instance, he defines virtue as one's essence or power of bringing about effects from one's nature (4D8; 1985, 547), from which he infers that to act from virtue is to act from the laws of one's nature, or to act in the strict sense (4p24d; 1985, 558). Moreover, having previously argued that one acts in the strict sense when and only when one has adequate ideas (3p1, 3p3; 1985, 493, 497), he claims that one acts from the laws of one's own nature – or, acts in the strict sense – when one is guided by reason: "acting from reason is nothing else but to do what follows from the necessity of our own nature considered solely in itself" (4p59d [1985, 579]; cf. 4p24 [1985, 558]; 4p35d/c1 [1985, 563]; 4p37s1 [1985, 565–6]; 4p52 [1985, 575]).[29] To strive from reason, or to act from rational desires, is to act authentically, from desires that spring from one's nature, which he groups under the rubric "strength of character" [*fortitudo*] (3p59s; 1985, 529). By contrast, to strive from passions or confused ideas, is to be "guided by things outside [oneself]" and to be "determined by them to do what the common constitution of external things demands, not what his own nature, considered in itself, demands" (4p37s1; 1985, 565–6).

On the basis of this analysis, we see that while Spinoza and Hobbes agree that things are really good insofar as they satisfy rational desires, this resemblance cloaks a much deeper division. Hobbes operates with a functional distinction between reason and desire, taking reason to be a cognitive ability that, among other things, enables us to calculate consequences so as to satisfy our desires, whatever they happen to be. By contrast, Spinoza regards acting from reason as simply acting from the laws of one's nature, or acting authentically, which consists in forming adequate ideas that beget further adequate ideas, producing effects that are intelligible through one's nature alone (see Rutherford 2008). Rational desires follow from one's nature alone and enable one to further realize this very nature. So, while Hobbes and Spinoza agree that what we rationally desire is really good, for Hobbes this is because reason helps us to satisfy our variable desires, whereas for Spinoza this is because acting from reason is just acting from, and more fully realizing, one's essence.

We find a corresponding contrast in their views on happiness. While Hobbes conceives felicity in terms of desire-satisfaction, forsaking any appeal to proper functioning, Spinoza advances a view that is far more congenial to the eudaimonist tradition. He construes "happiness" [*felicitas*] as successful striving (4p18s; 1985, 556), asserting that "if we pass the whole length of our life with a sound mind in a sound body, that is considered happiness" (5p39s; 1985, 614). Happiness is a kind of flourishing that comes from the exercise of virtue (2p49s; 4p20s [1985, 557]), that is, the realization of one's essence. And one's "highest happiness," or blessedness, consists in perfecting one's intellect and coming to know and love God (4 App. Cap IV [1985, 588]; 5p36s [1985, 612–13]; TTP 3.2 [2015, 111]), resulting in a form of reflective self-contentment or "satisfaction of mind" [*acquiescentia mentis*] (4 App. Cap IV [1985, 588]; 5p27 [1985, 609]; 5p32 [1985, 611]; 5p36s [1985, 612–13]). Not only, then, does Spinoza conceive happiness as flourishing or the realization of one's essence, he also represents the affective condition that results from self-realization in terms of something like the very mental repose that Hobbes declared unachievable.

Unlike Hobbes, Spinoza also connects happiness with doing good for others, treating "nobility" [*generositas*], or the desire "to aid other men and join them to him in friendship," as one family of rational desire (3p59s; 1985, 529–30).[30] Indeed, he maintains that "men who are governed by reason ... want nothing for themselves that they do not desire for other men. Hence, they are just, honest, and honorable" (4p18s; 1985, 556; cf. 4p37; 1985, 559). Underwriting the rational pursuit of others' power is, once again, Spinoza's essentialism. Because humans agree in their nature,[31] one who acts from reason, or from the laws of our nature, will strive for, and rejoice in, the realization of our common nature: "Man, I say, can wish for nothing more helpful to the preservation of his being than that ... that all should strive together, as far as they can, to preserve their being; and that all, together, should seek for themselves the common advantage of all" (4p18s). Leaving aside the reasoning in support of this view, we may note that the resulting picture is that there are goods that are common not merely in the weak sense of being rational for each person to desire, but in the much stronger sense that their promotion is directly beneficial to all. Knowledge or understanding in particular is "a good that is common to all men, and can be possessed by all" (4p36d; 1985,564), and so insofar as one is rational one will promote the understanding of all humans, and in so doing more fully realize one's own essence (4p37d; 1985,559).[32]

Spinoza's account of happiness and the agreement of essences profoundly shapes his view of the function of the state. In the *Political Treatise*, he claims that the purpose of the state is peace, explicating peace in a way that is plainly critical of Hobbes's construal of peace as the absence of war (2012, 192; 1651, 62; see also EW II.11):

> Peace isn't the privation of war, but a virtue that arises from strength of mind [*animi fortitudine*] ... the best state is one where men pass their lives harmoniously, I mean that they pass a human life, one defined not merely by the circulation of the blood, and other things common to all animals, but mostly by reason, the true virtue and life of the Mind...peace does not consist in the privation of war, but in a union or harmony of minds. (TP 5/4–5/5 [2015, 530]; TP 6/4 [2015, 533])

While Hobbes thinks that the state fosters conditions in which individuals can pursue their own individual happiness, Spinoza regards it as the aim of the state to cultivate reason, and to bring about a "harmony of minds," which would directly contribute to human happiness.

His account of the purpose of the state in TTP is at least as robust: "The end of the Republic, I say, is not to change men from rational beings into beasts or automata, but to enable their minds and bodies to perform their functions safely, to enable them to use their reason freely ... So the end of the Republic is really freedom" (TTP 20.11–12 [2015, 346]). Freedom, for Spinoza, consists in the ability to act and exist from the necessity of one's own nature (1D8 [1985, 409]; Ep. 58 [2015, 427–30]). And, while God alone is fully free, since no finite thing exists from its own nature, human beings are free to the extent that we are able to act from reason, or from our nature alone. The freedom that he promotes in the politics is this very liberty of acting or essence realization: "I call a man completely free just insofar as he is guided by reason, because to that extent he is determined to action by causes which can be understood adequately through his own nature alone" (TP 2/11 [2015, 512]; cf. TP 2/7 [2015, 510]; TP 3/6–3/7 [2015, 519–20]). So, while Hobbes conceives of political liberty as the absence of impediments, Spinoza adopts a positive conception of liberty as self-realization, or acting from one's essence alone, and he maintains that it is the function of the state to promote this positive good as far as possible.

Conclusion

Hobbes's influence on Spinoza's conception of motivation is unmistakable and profound. But while both Hobbes and Spinoza see goodness as in some sense motivation-dependent, Hobbes takes this to imply that goodness and the content of one's happiness depend on the variable content of one's desires, Spinoza regards the motivational tendency on which goodness depends as one's *essential* striving for self-realization, providing a firm standard for evaluating goodness and happiness.

On Spinoza's account, things that aid one's essence or power really are good, while things that inhibit it really are evil, irrespective of how they related to the superficial content of one's desires, which only masks one's deep, essential striving for power. Rational desires are authentic, following from one's essence or striving alone, while passions are not. And insofar as we act from these authentic, rational desires, we will not only act in ways that are empowering to ourselves, but also in ways that are empowering to other human beings, who agree with us in nature. The more one is able to develop one's own mind and to promote human understanding more generally, the more one will have realized one's essence, and the happier one will be.

On the basis of all of this, one sees that Spinoza's normative ethical philosophy has considerably more in common with traditional eudaimonism than Hobbes's does. Ultimately, Spinoza builds a modern form of eudaimonism on the basis of a mechanistic moral psychology that is deeply indebted to Hobbes. Like Hobbes, he rejects the intrinsic reality of evaluative predicates and the irreducible efficacy of final causes. But he insists on the explanatory power of non-teleological essences,[33] which anchor a conception of goodness and flourishing that, while in some sense mind-independent, remains firmly motivation-dependent.

Acknowledgment

Thanks to Marcus Adams and Karolina Hübner for very helpful comments on an earlier draft.

Notes

1 Curley (1988); Jesseph (2016); Malinowski-Charles (2017).
2 See Curley (1992); Malcolm (2002); Wernham (1958).
3 Aquinas, *Opera omnia*, xvi. 340 (cited in Carriero 2005).
4 For a characteristic account of the explanatory role of goodness, see Suarez *Metaphysical Disputations*, disputation 23, Section 5, §15, Opera vol. 25, 867, in Suarez (1856–1870) (cited in Pink 2018, 7).
5 See Pink (2018); Sleigh, Chappell, and Rocca (1998, 1197–1198); Stump (2005), 22.
6 Cf. Spinoza 1A3; 1985, 410.
7 I adopt the following abbreviations for the *Ethics*: Numerals refer to parts; "p" denotes proposition; "c" denotes corollary; "d" denotes demonstration; "D" denotes definition; "DA" denotes Definition of the Affects; "s" denotes scholium (e.g. 3p59s refers to *Ethics*, part 3, proposition 59, scholium). References to the Tractatus Theologico-Politicus (TTP) denote the chapter and section in the Curley translation. For instance, TTP 3.28 refers to chapter 3, Section 28. References to the Tractatus Politicus (TP) denote the chapter and section. For instance, TP 4/1 refers to chapter 4, Section 1.
8 For a sense of the scope of application, see Jesseph (2016).
9 For a discussion of what it means to be *in se*, see Garrett (2018a).
10 See for instance 2A3 (1985, 448) as well as 3 GDA explication (1985, 542–3) and 3p56/d (1985, 526–7), where Spinoza claims that affects are individuated by their affecting objects.
11 For a defense of this reading, see J. Steinberg (2016).
12 For more, see J. Steinberg (2016).
13 Desires express one's striving in Spinoza's technical sense of expression that involves property inheritance. See Karolina Hübner and Róbert Mátyási on "Spinoza on Expression and the Grounds of Intelligibility" (n.d.).
14 See e.g., Garrett (2018a); Viljanen (2011, 125–32).
15 It fails, for instance, to explain the inference from the initial formulation of the doctrine (3p6; 1985, 498) to the "progressive" claim that all things strive to increase their power of acting (3p12–13; 1985, 502). It fails to make sense of his claim that the foundation of virtue is "striving to preserve one's being" (4p18s [1985, 555–6]; 4p22 [1985, 558]) *and* "the striving for understanding" (4p26d; 1985, 559), since understanding goes well beyond

merely enduring. And it cannot easily be squared with the claim that the free man avoids deception even on pain of death (4p72s; 1985, 587). For a helpful discussion, see Youpa (2003).

16 One might worry that the claim that one's essence consists in striving to realize one's essence is circular. While a full response to this worry would require entering the deep waters of Spinoza's metaphysics, I will simply indicate why I don't think that this is a problem. Striving is one's actual essence. However, Spinoza allows for another way of thinking of essences – sometimes flagged as one's *formal* essence – which is something more like a thing's blueprint, an eternal description or structure from which certain properties or effects necessarily follow (2p8/c [1985, 452]; 5p22 [1985, 607]; 5p23/d [1985, 607]; 5p29/d [1985, 609–10]; see Garrett 2018b). One's striving or actual essence consists in tending to realize this (formal) essence and all that follows from it as far as possible.

17 Cf. Sreedhar (2010, 36).

18 This may be one respect in which Spinoza's psychology anticipates Freudian psychotherapy (see Neu 1977).

19 This is not to say that he is an egoist, since he thinks that striving to persevere in one's being entails striving to aid others (discussed in the final section).

20 Recent scholarship has emphasized the ways in which speech facilitates human agency. For instance, Laurens van Apeldoorn has pushed back against the view that Hobbes has an impoverished view of agency, claiming that, for Hobbes, language enables us to order our thoughts, record past experiences, draw inferences on the basis of general rules, and make informed, careful judgments about consequences, thereby exercising deliberative control (Van Apeldoorn 2012, 2014). Arash Abizadeh advances a similar view, according to which language transforms reasoning such that our deliberation may be at once "active" and "strongly cognitive" (Abizadeh 2017).

21 And certainly not though the exercise of language, which Spinoza relegates to the lowest kind of cognition (2p40s2; 1985, 477–8).

22 Without speech, there is "neither commonwealth, nor society, nor contract, nor peace" (2012, 48; 1651, 12).

23 For a full defense of this claim, see Steinberg (2018a). For readings of Hobbes that bring his view closer to Spinoza's, see Field (2014); Hoekstra (2004).

24 For a more complete, and more nuanced, analysis of these points, see Steinberg (2018a, ch. 2).

25 Steinberg (2018b).

26 See Gert (2010, 51); Hamilton (2016, 142).

27 On the severance of happiness and moral virtue, see Hamilton (2016, 146); Rutherford (2003, 380).

28 Again, this is not to deny that Hobbes thinks that the state ought to do more than establish basic physical security. For a discussion of the political significance of felicity, see Rutherford (2003). I find Rutherford's analysis generally compelling, though I think that Hobbes's break with eudaimonism is sharper than Rutherford does.

29 While Spinoza initially introduces reason [*ratio*] as comprising a subset of adequate ideas, namely, those formed from "common notion and adequate ideas of the properties of things" (2p40s2), in *Ethics* 4 he seems to operate with a more expansive conception of reason, comprising *all* adequate ideas (4p26d [1985, 559]; 4p37s1 [1985, 565–6]; 4p52 [1985, 575]).

30 See Curley (1994), xxxii on this point of distinction.

31 For accounts of how to square this with his nominalism, see Hübner (2016); Steinberg (1984).

32 For some analysis of the problems with the reasoning here, and how they might be overcome, See Della Rocca (2004); Steinberg (1984); Steinberg (2019).

33 For good discussions of this point, see Carriero (2005); Viljanen (2011).

Works Cited

Abizadeh, Arash. 2017. "Hobbes on Mind: Practical Deliberation, Reasoning, and Language." *Journal of the History of Philosophy* 55 (1): 1–34.

Carriero, John. 2005. "Spinoza on Final Causality." *Oxford Studies in Early Modern Philosophy* 2: 105–47.

Curley, Edwin. 1988. *Behind the Geometrical Method*. Princeton, NJ: Princeton University Press.

Curley, Edwin. 1992. "'I Durst Not Write so Boldly' or, How to Read Hobbes' *Theological-Political Treatise*." In *Hobbes e Spinoza*, edited by Daniela Bostrenghi, 497–593. Naples: Bibliopolis.

Curley, Edwin. 1994. "Notes." In *A Spinoza Reader: The Ethics and Other Works*, edited and translated by Edwin Curley. Princeton, NJ: Princeton University Press.

Della Rocca, Michael. 2004. "Egoism and the Imitation of Affects in Spinoza." In *Spinoza on Reason and the 'Free Man,'* edited by Yirmiyahu Yovel and Gideon Segal, 123–47. New York: Little Room Press.

Field, Sandra. 2014. "Hobbes and the Question of Power." *Journal of the History of Philosophy* 52 (1): 61–85.

Garrett, Don. 2018a. "Spinoza's Conatus Argument." In *Nature and Necessity in Spinoza's Philosophy*, 352–90. New York: Oxford University Press.

Garrett, Don. 2018b. "Spinoza on the Essence of the Human Body and the Part of the Mind that is Eternal." In *Nature and Necessity in Spinoza's Philosophy*, 243–62. New York: Oxford University Press.

Gert, Bernard. 2010. *Hobbes: Prince of Peace*. Cambridge, UK: Polity Press.

Hamilton, James J. 2016. "Hobbes on Felicity: Aristotle, Bacon, and Eudaimonia." *Hobbes Studies* 29: 129–47.

Hobbes, Thomas. 1839–1845. *The English Works of Thomas Hobbes*, 11 vols., edited by Sir William Molesworth. London: John Bohn. Cited as EW.

Hobbes, Thomas. 1972. *Man and Citizen*, translated by Charles T. Wood, Thomas S. K. Scott-Craig, and Bernard Gert, edited by Bernard Gert. Garden City, NY: Anchor.

Hobbes, Thomas. 1976. *Thomas White's De Mundo Examined (Anti-White)*, translated by Harold Whitmore Jones. London: Bradford University Press.

Hobbes, Thomas. 2012. *Leviathan*, 3 vols., edited by Noel Malcolm. Oxford: Clarendon Press. [First published 1651.]

Hoekstra, Kinch. 2004. "The De Facto Turn in Hobbes's Political Philosophy." In *Leviathan after 350 Years*, edited by Tom Sorell and Luc Foisneau, 33–73. Oxford: Oxford University Press.

Hübner, Karolina. 2016. "Spinoza on Essences, Universals, and Beings of Reason." *Pacific Philosophical Quarterly* 97 (1): 58–88.

Hübner, Karolina and Róbert Mátyási. (n.d.) "Spinoza on Expression and the Grounds of Intelligibility." Manuscript.

Jesseph, Douglas. 2016. "Hobbes on 'Conatus': A Study in the Foundations of Hobbesian Philosophy." *Hobbes Studies* 29 (1): 66–85.

Lloyd, S.A. 2009. *Morality in the Philosophy of Thomas Hobbes*. Cambridge: Cambridge University Press.

Malcolm, Noel. 2002. *Aspects of Hobbes*. Oxford: Clarendon Press.

Malinowski-Charles, Syliane. 2017. "Reason and Desire: Hobbes and Spinoza on Conatus, Reason and the Emotions." In *Reason and No-Reason from Antiquity to the Modern Times*, edited by Loredana Cordullo and Francesco Coniglione, 151–68. S. Augustin: Academia Verlag.

Neu, Jerome. 1977. *Emotion, Thought and Therapy*. Berkeley, CA: University of California Press.

Pettit, Philip. 2008. *Made with Words: Hobbes on Language, Mind, and Politics*. Princeton, NJ: Princeton University Press.

Pink, Thomas. 2018. "Agents, Objects, and their Powers in Suarez and Hobbes." *Philosophical Explorations* 21 (1): 3–24.

Rutherford, Donald. 2003. "In Pursuit of Happiness." *Philosophical Topics* 31: 369–93.

Rutherford, Donald. 2008. "Spinoza and the Dictates of Reason." *Inquiry* 51 (5): 485–511.

Sleigh, Robert, Jr., Vere Chappell, and Michael Della Rocca. 1998. "Determinism and Human Freedom." In *The Cambridge History of Seventeenth-Century Philosophy*, Vol. 2, edited by Dan Garber and Michael Ayers, 1195–278. Cambridge: Cambridge University Press.

Spinoza, Benedict de. 1985, 2015. *The Collected Works of Spinoza*, Vols. 1–2, translated and edited by Edwin Curley. Princeton, NJ: Princeton University Press.

Sreedhar, Susanne. 2010. *Hobbes on Resistance*. Cambridge: Cambridge University Press.

Steinberg, Diane. 1984. "Spinoza's Ethical Doctrine and the Unity of Human Nature." *Journal of the History of Philosophy* 22: 303–24.

Steinberg, Justin. 2016. "Affect, Desire, and Judgement in Spinoza's Account of Motivation." *British Journal for the History of Philosophy* 24 (1): 67–87.

Steinberg, Justin. 2018a. *Spinoza's Political Psychology: The Taming of Fortune and Fear*. Cambridge: Cambridge University Press.

Steinberg, Justin. 2018b. "Spinoza and Political Absolutism." In *Spinoza's Political Treatise: New Assessments*, edited by Hasana Sharp and Yitzhak Melamed, 175–89. Cambridge: Cambridge University Press.

Steinberg, Justin. 2019. "Spinoza on Civil Agreement and Bodies Politic." In *Spinoza and Relational Autonomy: Being with Others*, edited by Aurelia Armstrong, Keith Green, and Andrea Sangiacomo, 132–48. Edinburgh: Edinburgh University Press.

Stump, Eleonore. 2005. *Aquinas*. London: Routledge.

Van Apeldoorn, Laurens. 2012. "Reconsidering Hobbes's Account of Practical Deliberation." *Hobbes Studies* 25: 143–65.

Van Apeldoorn, Laurens. 2014. "Rationality and Freedom in Hobbes's Theory of Action." *History of European Ideas* 40 (5): 603–62.

Viljanen, Valtteri. 2011. *Spinoza's Geometry of Power*. Cambridge: Cambridge University Press.

Wernham, A.G. 1958. "Notes and Introduction." In *Spinoza: The Political Works*. Oxford: Clarendon Press.

Youpa, Andrew. 2003. "Spinozistic Self-Preservation." *The Southern Journal of Philosophy* 41 (3): 477–90.

27

Hobbes and Astell on War and Peace

JACQUELINE BROAD

Throughout her political writings, Mary Astell (1666–1731) presents both positive and negative arguments to demonstrate that rebellion and civil war are never morally justified. In keeping with her devout Anglican beliefs, Astell's positive arguments typically rely on religious injunctions. Christianity, she says, "does no where allow Rebellion ... he that bawls out the Liberty of Conscience and Loss of Religion to vindicate his Rebellion, has too much of Atheism in him, to be a true Christian" (Astell 1996b, 169). Her negative arguments are formulated in opposition to several principles that were upheld in her time as "just causes" of the civil wars in England (1642–1651), including appeals to the broken social contract, the natural right of self-preservation, and the people's right to depose unjust or tyrannical rulers. In this chapter, I interpret Astell's critique of these principles as engagements with the political philosophy of Thomas Hobbes (1588–1679). In the past few decades, scholars have examined Astell's writings in relation to the Hobbesian concept of the state of nature and Hobbes's theory of the social contract. Ruth Perry has highlighted Astell's critique of Hobbes's denial of human interdependence in the natural state (Perry 1990, 454, 457); Penny Weiss has provided a useful contrast between Astell and Hobbes's conceptions of political authority and the "miserable condition" (Weiss 2009, 146–7); and Patricia Springborg and Karen Green have analyzed Astell's rejection of Hobbesian contractarianism (Green 2012, 173–7; Springborg 2005, 122–30). These commentators have connected Astell's criticisms of Hobbes to the early feminist views of her best-known works, *A Serious Proposal to the Ladies, Parts I and II* (1694; 1697) and *Some Reflections upon Marriage* (1700). They point to her anticipation of recent liberal feminist critiques of social contract theory.

My own analysis will trace Astell's engagement with Hobbesian ideas concerning war and peace in her three political pamphlets of 1704: *Moderation Truly Stated, A Fair Way with the Dissenters*, and *An Impartial Enquiry into the Causes of Rebellion and Civil War*. Together these anonymous Tory pamphlets constitute Astell's contribution to the

A Companion to Hobbes, First Edition. Edited by Marcus P. Adams.

"occasional conformity" debates of 1702–4, an ongoing controversy about the dissenter practice of taking occasional communion in Anglican churches solely in order to qualify for public office. In what follows, I begin by highlighting Astell's explicit references to Hobbes in her first two pamphlets. Springborg has claimed that Hobbes was "never named by Astell" (2005, 39), but in *Moderation Truly Stated*, Astell speculates that "*a State of Nature was a meer figment of* Hobbs's *Brain*" (1704, xxxv), and in *Fair Way with the Dissenters*, she claims that rebellious principles follow "by a Chain of Mr. *Hobbes's* Consequences" (1996a, 97). These named references are useful for revealing how Hobbesian ideas concerning war and peace were received by Astell; they also show that her challenges to Whigs and dissenters of her time can be interpreted as challenges to so-called Hobbesian principles. But my main purpose will be to demonstrate that Astell had more in common with Hobbes than she would have liked to admit. While Astell explicitly vilifies Hobbes as a proponent of just cause theory, in these political pamphlets she implicitly adopts salient aspects of his views concerning the maintenance of peace. More than this, she follows through on the logical implications of his principles, to suggest that sexist opinions about female sovereigns (namely Queen Elizabeth I and Queen Anne), and women's susceptibility to seditious opinion, pose significant threats to the social order. Her writings are thus valuable for demonstrating how Hobbesian ideas concerning war and peace were embraced – and extended – by a feminist pioneer of the early modern era.

27.1 Astell on Hobbes and "Just Causes"

Astell's first explicit reference to Hobbes comes in the "Prefatory Discourse" of her *Moderation Truly Stated*, a long essay written in response to Charles Davenant's *Essays upon Peace at Home, and War Abroad* (1704). Davenant wrote this work to provide Queen Anne with advice about how to avoid the political instability caused by dissenting religious and political views in the early years of her reign (see Broad 2011, 11–13; Perry 1986, 197–202). In one part, he suggests that human beings find fault with political authority because they can somehow recall the liberty that they experienced in the state of nature, the natural condition of human beings prior to civil society (Davenant 1704, 352, 355). In order to attain "Ease, Plenty, and Protection," Davenant says, men gave up this state of nature, relinquished their natural rights, and entered into a contract "for the Benefit of Society" (Davenant 1704, 355). Without openly supporting Hobbes, Davenant appeals to elements of his famous theory to explain how political conflict arises. He alludes to Hobbes's view that in the state of nature, every man has the right to preserve his life and must be allowed "the *right to use any means and to do any action by which he can preserve himself*" (Hobbes 1998, I.8, 27; see also, 2012, 198; 1651, 64).[1] According to Hobbes, this condition brings with it an enormous amount of misery and unhappiness; in the state of nature, men are tormented by continual fear of a sudden, violent death (Hobbes 1998, I.13, 30; 2012, 192, 1651, 62). To obtain peace and security, rational men endeavor to get out of this state as quickly as possible. Reason tells them that they must enter into a voluntary agreement with other men: they must either relinquish their right to all things or transfer it to another. To achieve lasting peace, a supreme power with the right of commanding all men is required, and this authority must have the requisite power to compel men to perform their covenants by threat of punishment (Hobbes 1998, V.11, 73; 2012, 210; 1651, 68). Davenant evinces a familiarity with these views, but emphasizes that a man retains a claim on his rights if ever the political authorities break the contract, that is, "if he is neither Happy, nor Safe, through their Fault who rule" (Davenant 1704, 355; see Hobbes 2012, 344; 1651, 114). Davenant suggests that Hobbes's principles support a citizen's right to resist those rulers who cannot ensure his peace and safety. When faced with rulers who "have no Right to command him," a man "is return'd to the full Liberty his Progenitors enjoy'd in the free State of Nature, and ... may act for himself, and take all the Ways of Consulting and Compassing his own Safety" (Davenant 1704, 355). As a response to dissent, therefore, Davenant advises Queen Anne to avoid having a "loose and weak" administration (1704, 355), to be a strong and decisive leader, and to stamp out political faction whenever it arises (1704, 56, 58).

With characteristic irony, Astell makes the following response to Davenant's remarks:

> *Sir, I am to thank you for a Discovery, alas! I have hitherto thought, that according to* Moses, *we were all of* Adam's *Race, and that a State of Nature was a meer figment of* Hobbs's *Brain, or borrow'd at least from the Fable of* Cadmus, *or Æacus his Myrmidons, till you were pleas'd to inform me* 'of that Equality wherein the Race of Men were plac'd in the free State of Nature. ['] *How I lament my Stars that it was not my good Fortune to Live in those Happy Days when Men sprung up like so many Mushrooms or* Terræ Filii, *without Father or Mother or any sort of dependency!* (Astell 1704, xxxv)

Here Astell recalls a memorable statement in Hobbes's *De cive*, first printed in Latin in 1642, and then translated into English in 1651 as *Philosophicall Rudiments concerning Government and Society*. In chapter 8 of *De cive*, Hobbes invites us to "return once again to the natural state and to look at men as if they had just emerged from the earth like mushrooms and grown up without any obligation to each other" (Hobbes 1998, VIII.1, 102). This remark appears in the context of his explanation of how "the right of Dominion [*Dominium*] is acquired over men's *persons*" (VIII.1, 102). There are three ways in which such a right might be acquired – by contract, conquest, or generation. The first of these is made by mutual contract or agreement between men to give up their natural rights to a supreme power "for the sake of peace and mutual defence" (VIII.1, 102). Through her sarcasm and scorn, Astell challenges the initial step in Hobbes's account of dominion – she repudiates the idea that there could ever have been a state of equality in which human beings were not somehow dependent on other human beings (on this topic, see Perry 1990, 454, 457).[2]

Astell's reference to the mushroom men of *De cive* echoes those of her contemporaries who took up Hobbes's remarks and drew similarities between Hobbes's natural men and Cadmus's mercenary soldiers in Ovid's *Metamorphoses* (see Goldie 1991, 604–5). In book three of Ovid's classic work, Cadmus kills a serpent and then sows its teeth into the ground; shortly thereafter, several armed men rise from the earth and fight one another to the death. Edward Hyde, the first Earl of Clarendon, notes that in developing his theory of the state of nature Hobbes must have appealed to "the autority of *Ovids Metamorphosis*, of the sowing of *Cadmus*'s teeth"; he could not have appealed to divine authority to support such a theory (Clarendon 1676, 38–9). The royalist pamphleteer

John Nalson likewise says that Hobbes's assertion that all men desire to do mischief to one another

> is false to every Reason; unless he will revive the old Fable of *Cadmus* in *Ovid*, and slurr it upon us for an Historical Truth; and suppose all Mankind to be like the Harvest sprung from the Serpents Teeth; unnatural Sons of the Earth, born in Arms. (Nalson 1677, 6)

In a dialogue with a Hobbesian, John Eachard's speaker mockingly refers to "*your Mushroom state of Men suddainly springing out of the Earth*, without any kind of engagement to each other" (Eachard 1672, 63–4), and he too alludes to "*Cadmus*, that had a *Plantation* of *Armed Men*" (1672, 67). Astell's own references to Cadmus and *terræ filii* ("sons of the earth") recall these late seventeenth-century commentaries. Like these authors, she casts scorn on Hobbes's negative conception of human beings as naturally unsociable and belligerent.

Astell's second named reference to Hobbes comes in her *Fair Way with the Dissenters*, a pamphlet written against Daniel Defoe's anonymous polemic, *More Short-Ways with the Dissenters* (1704). In his work, Defoe attacks a sermon by the High-Church Tory Henry Sacheverell (1704) for upholding a "Whiggish Principle," the idea that "The Regular Administration of Justice, is the Grand End and Design both of Government and Law" (Defoe 1704, 8). Somewhat mischievously, Defoe argues that this notion lends support to resistance because:

> If this be true it follows that Justice which is the End, is Superior to the King, that Executes, who is the Means, for the End is always Superior to the Means, and if this be true, Deposing Tyrannick evil Administrating Princes cannot be Criminal, because they Overturn and Destroy the end of Government. (Defoe 1704, 8)

In response, Astell defends Sacheverell against Defoe's spurious reasoning. "Who but a Dissenter," she exclaims, "could ever have had Brains enough to pick this out of Mr. *Sacheverel's* Sermon!" Yet she concedes that the conclusion – that it is permissible to depose tyrants – "follows most undeniably by a Chain of Mr. *Hobbes's* Consequences" (Astell 1996a, 97). Here it is difficult to determine exactly what Astell means by "a Chain of Mr. *Hobbes's* Consequences." In *Leviathan*, Hobbes asserts that human beings desire to contract out of the state of nature, and set up civil government, so that they might be assured of peace and safety. To uphold the safety of the people, the sovereign power is obliged to ensure that "Justice be equally administred to all degrees of People; that is, that as well the rich, and the mighty, as poor and obscure persons, may be righted of the injuries done them" (Hobbes 2012, 534; 1651, 180). Thus it might be said (loosely speaking) that, according to Hobbes, the administration of justice is the *end* of government, while the supreme power (whether it be monarchic, democratic or aristocratic) is merely the *means* for bringing about that end.[3] We might also surmise, along with Astell, that this theory implies that a supreme power can be overthrown if it ever fails to uphold its obligation to preserve the peace and security of the commonwealth.

Astell was not the only one among her contemporaries to see such hidden consequences in Hobbesian contractarianism. Clarendon comes to similar conclusions in his examination of *Leviathan*, when he identifies a major weakness in Hobbes's theory of political obligation (see Goldie 1991, 604; Parkin 2007, 318). Despite asserting that civil subjects have divested themselves of liberty, and transferred their rights to an absolute sovereign, Clarendon points out, Hobbes allows that they retain an inalienable right to defend themselves (Clarendon 1676, 39). In Clarendon's view, this is antithetical to the maintenance of peace, since this liberty gives subjects "a wonderful latitude" to challenge their sovereigns and destroy the peace whenever they feel threatened (1676, 100). The problem, as one of Eachard's speakers notes, is that by Hobbes's principles, a subject may give up his power to the sovereign, only to "call for't again, when he thinks it for his advantage" (Eachard 1673, 242–3). Hobbes's theory leaves it open for any individual to be his own judge of when the sovereign constitutes a danger to his life. Astell raises similar concerns about the same Hobbesian principles, when she wryly observes against Davenant that:

> *truly who can blame a Man who finds himself not at* Ease, *or so well as he would be, if he reassumes a Fundamental Right, a Privilege of which no Man can divest himself, and so soon as he can get more Men of his Mind to make his Party strong enough, declares the* Contract broken. (Astell 1704, xxxvi)

Like the earlier English writers, Astell points to the inherent risks and dangers in Hobbes's theory that civil society originates in a covenant between men. If subjects retain their right to protect themselves, this leaves the door open for them to break the contract and return to a state of war.[4]

These brief allusions to Hobbes thus give us a fair indication of how Astell perceives Hobbesian political thought. First, for Astell, Hobbes is the originator of the absurd hypothesis of the state of nature, a supposedly natural condition in which men are born equal, with no dependence upon (or subordination to) other human beings, including their own parents. Her dismissive tone suggests that she believes that this state of nature has never existed among men, and that it also fails to provide a useful theoretical tool for thinking about prepolitical society. Second, Astell associates Hobbes with a "chain of consequences" in which the rebellion of subjects against their rulers is sometimes justified. According to this Hobbesian logic, if rulers do not arbitrate justice for the sake of peace and safety, then the people might exercise their inalienable right to defend themselves (their right of self-preservation) by force. Once again, Astell's tone suggests that she finds this contractarian logic deplorable.

In Astell's third political pamphlet of 1704, *An Impartial Enquiry*, her explicit targets are Whigs and dissenters of her own time, but these same "Hobbesian" principles come under repeated attack. In this work, Astell responds to Bishop White Kennett's *Compassionate Enquiry into the Causes of the Civil War* (1704), a sermon presented on the anniversary of Charles I's execution. In his sermon, Kennett laments the fact that the King did not allay public fears about tyranny and arbitrary power during his reign. If the people had thought themselves secure in their rights, he says, then they would not have resorted to war and rebellion. But instead they were led to believe that their liberties and estates were endangered, and "under that Prospect and Persuasion they must have been drawn in for the *Meaning* at least of Self-preservation" (Kennett 1704, 18–19). Astell takes issue with Kennett's presupposition that the right of self-preservation is a just reason for going to war in the first place (Astell 1996b, 141–3). Her point is that, if perceived violations (or even *real* violations) of the right of self-preservation are always just causes, then they can be used as pretexts in any situation (1996b, 189). The same excuses have been used to justify war and rebellion against good men (such as Charles I, in her opinion) as well as bad ones. "The Peoples Right to shake off their Oppressor," she says, has been "equally destructive of the Best, as well as the worst Princes" (1996b, 148); so we cannot rely on such precepts for moral guidance. In Astell's view, it is inevitable that some unscrupulous men will have a vested interest in making pre-emptive strikes against a regime, for the sake of ambition or avarice or to gratify their passion for revenge (1996b, 147). They will cry up "liberty" and "self-preservation" against the sovereign, merely to serve their own interests.

In this pamphlet, Astell's argumentative strategy is to depict the Whigs as proponents of a long historical tradition of resistance theory, as well as the holders of principles that led to civil war and the execution of the "Royal Martyr," Charles I. But her comments against Davenant and Defoe – about Hobbes's state of nature and "a Chain of Mr. *Hobbes's* Consequences" – suggest that she also means to associate the Whigs with reviled Hobbist principles. Astell frequently recalls Hobbes's hypothesis about men "giving up their liberties" in order to contract out of the hateful state of nature. "They discover Plots which themselves have made," she says of rebellious men, and "they give up Liberties upon a valuable consideration, and when time shall serve, know how to procure to themselves the Honour of Retrieving them" (Astell 1996b, 196). She also challenges the moral status of the "right of self-preservation" as the right to preserve one's body, civil liberties, and material property. "Beware of every one," she says, who would "draw you in by the old Cant of *Self-Preservation*" (1996b,141; see also 142, 143, 189, 196). These are the same dangers that Astell identified in the Hobbesian state of nature and Hobbesian contract theory in her previous pamphlets.

27.2 Astell and Hobbes on the Maintenance of Peace

Astell's named references to Hobbes are reflective of a popular if somewhat distorted conception of Hobbesian politics in her time. As we have seen, her English contemporaries, Clarendon, Eachard, and Nalson, also presented Hobbes as the advocate of natural human aggression and self-interestedness (see Goldie 1991, 602–5; Parkin 2007, 288–98, 313–22). More recently, however, scholars have presented us with a different Hobbes – not the proponent of rampant psychological egoism, but rather someone whose major concern was the avoidance of civil war and the maintenance of peace and social order (Gert 2010; see also Jaede 2018; Thivet 2008). I turn now to Astell's own views about how to avoid civil war, to demonstrate that she has much in common with this peace-theorist Hobbes of modern-day scholarship. We will see that Astell's dismissive references to Hobbes cloak her more positive engagements with Hobbesian principles concerning the maintenance of peace.

There are, to be sure, many important and fundamental differences between Astell and Hobbes (for details, see Green 2012; Perry 1990; Springborg 2005; Weiss 2009). They wrote their polemics in vastly different periods, in response to radically different political concerns. Hobbes wrote during the tumultuous periods of the Fronde, the Thirty Years' War, and the English civil war; while Astell wrote in the period following the (relatively bloodless) Glorious Revolution of 1688–9 and during the early reign of Queen Anne. Hobbes has a secular and conventional theory of the origins of political obligation; Astell has a religious or natural one. Hobbes claims that the ultimate basis of allegiance to our rulers is the pursuit of good for ourselves; Astell maintains that the ultimate basis of submission to our rulers is the deference that we owe to the divine authority of the office. Hobbes was a supporter of absolutist monarchism; Astell was an advocate of constitutional monarchy. Yet despite these differences, the two thinkers share common ground in their practical theories concerning the maintenance of peace.[5]

The most striking similarity is in their view that the spreading of false and seditious opinions – including both political and religious beliefs – poses the most significant threat to peace and stability in civil society. In Hobbes's state of nature, according to Richard Tuck (1996; 1999), the war of every man against every man is essentially an *epistemic* conflict or "a conflict of *belief*" (Tuck 1996, xxvii). In this natural state, conflict arises because each man is his own judge about the best means to his self-preservation, and people inevitably form incompatible judgements about what really matters (Tuck 1999, 131). Controversies result from the differing opinions of men about "*mine* and *yours*, *just* and *unjust*, *useful* and *useless*, *good* and *bad*, *honourable* and *dishonourable*, and so on" (Hobbes 1998, VI.9, 79; see also, 2012, 196; 1651, 63). In civil society, such disagreements are avoided because the power of judging the best means to our preservation lies with the sovereign alone. This supreme power provides the ultimate arbitrator and preventative for epistemic controversies, because only this power may decide whether any future action is just or unjust, good or bad, and so on (Hobbes 1998, VI.8–9, 79; 2012, 220; 1651, 71–2). The sovereign thus shows us "the royal road" or the "high-way" to peace (Hobbes 1998, preface, 10). Toward this end, it is crucial that the sovereign's power be single and uncontested. Simplicity and unity of rule is a necessary condition for reaching consensus about what might be considered just and unjust. "[I]t is required," according to Hobbes, "that there be a *single will* [*una voluntas*] among all of them in matters essential to peace and defence. This can only happen if each man subjects his *will* to the *will* of the *single* other ... that is, of one *Man* [*Hominis*] or of one *Assembly* [*Concilium*]" (Hobbes 1998, V.6, 72). In civil society, every man has given up his power to judge the best means to his self-preservation to the supreme power. Private citizens do not have the power to judge for themselves what is a "just" or an "unjust" means anymore. When they submit to a governing authority, its judgements about the best means to their preservation – and the preservation of the commonwealth as a whole – must thereafter become their own. For Hobbes, this is the best safeguard against the war of all against all. Sovereigns have the right to govern according to their own judgement, and citizens must not challenge or rebel against those judgements.

Along similar lines, Astell affirms that no citizen has the right to judge for themselves about the justness of rebellion against their sovereigns. In one part of her *Impartial Enquiry*, Astell explains why she holds this view with reference to Henry Foulis's *History of Romish Treasons and Usurpations* (2nd edn, 1681). In that work, Foulis says that

> If we allow that People may lawfully Rebel against Princes, and at the same time be Judges of the justness of the Reason; to be in Authority will be a Slavery, the Word Monarch absolute Nonsense, the King oblig'd to obey every man's Passion and Folly; nor Peace nor

> Justice can be expected, the Nation being in a perpetual Hurly-burly every other day. (Foulis 1681, 74; quoted in Astell 1996b, 168–9)

Foulis's point about judgement is crucial for Astell's case against civil war in the *Impartial Enquiry*. If citizens have the right to judge for themselves about the best means to their preservation, she suggests, the nation would be in "a perpetual Hurly-burly," a state of chaos and confusion. They would be throwing the monarch "out of the Saddle" on the slightest pretext and all political stability would be lost (Astell 1996b, 168). For the sake of peace and quiet, the power of judgement must lie solely with the supreme political authority. In *Moderation Truly Stated*, Astell puts this same sentiment in her own words. She says that in civil society an "Absolute or Unaccountable Power, or which is the same thing, a last Appeal, must be lodg'd some where; otherwise there is, there can be, no Government, whatever Men may talk, but all is in Confusion" (Astell 1704, xxxviii). To attain political stability, "the only way is for the Supreme Power wherever it is Lodg'd, to Govern it self, and to take all its Measures according to the Direction of the Laws; which, tho' they may not be Infallible, are yet the Supreme Wisdom of the State" (1704, xxxviii). Like Hobbes, Astell regards obedience to a common power as a practical necessity, to avoid epistemic conflict and maintain peace and harmony in society. In language that is partly reminiscent of Hobbes, Astell declares:

> allowing that the People have a Right to Design the Person of their Governour; it does by no means follow that they Give him his Authority, or that they may when they please resume it. None can give what they have not: The People have no Authority over their own Lives, consequently they can't invest such an Authority with their Governours. And tho' we shou'd grant that People, when they first enter into Society, may frame their Laws as they think fit; yet these Laws being once Establish'd, they can't Legally and Honestly be chang'd, but by that Authority in which the Founders of the Society thought fit to place the Legislature. (Astell 1996b, 170)

Despite her ridicule for Hobbes's state of nature, Astell concedes that if human beings do contract to "enter into Society," they do not retain any authority to challenge the supreme power later. Similarly, while Hobbes maintains that civil war and "the right of the *private Sword*" are much worse than subjection to any kind of civil authority (Hobbes 1998, VII.4, 93), Astell asserts that acts of rebellion are "perhaps more Grievous than Tyranny, even to the People; for they expose us to the Oppression of a multitude of Tyrants" (Astell 1996b, 197). Astell suggests that the people give up their right to stand in judgement on "tyrannical" rulers, in return for the long-term stability offered by a single sovereign power.

Astell and Hobbes also share similar ideas about the importance of encouraging a *disposition* toward peace in citizens. According to Hobbes, a state of war does not consist in the act of fighting alone, but rather a period of time in which individuals are known to have a certain attitude or disposition to fight: the "will to contend by force," as Hobbes says (Hobbes 1998, I.12, 29–30; see also, 2012, 192; 1651, 62). It follows from his definition of the state of war that, for Hobbes, peace is not merely the absence of violent conflict, but rather a state of affairs or "a tract of time" in which we are assured that our fellow human beings have a peaceful disposition toward us (Hobbes 2012, 192; 1651, 62;

see also Lee 1989, 189; Thivet 2008, 703). For Hobbes, a lasting state of peace requires more than just the suppression of violence by a powerful sovereign; it requires the kind of security that is promoted through public education and increased knowledge (Jaede 2018, 35, 96). In *De cive*, Hobbes outlines those laws of nature that can be derived from the first fundamental law of nature, "*to seek peace*" (Hobbes 1998, II.2, 34, 2012, 200; 1651, 64). One law is mercifulness or forgiveness for those who repent their past actions (Hobbes 1998, III.10, 48); another is the law that revenge and punishment should be inflicted only for the sake of future good and never without reason (III.11, 49); and other laws recommend against pride in favor of humility and modesty, which require recognition of the moral equality of human beings (III.13–14, 50). Hobbes suggests that the cultivation of the virtues of mercy, forgiveness, humility, and modesty will ensure that individuals are inclined to be accommodating to one another, and thereby bring about an enduring peace.

In her later work, *The Christian Religion* (1705), Astell also recommends the cultivation of forgiveness, humility, and meekness, and the avoidance of unnecessary resentment and revenge, for the sake of peace. "The peace of the world," Astell says, "is promoted by nothing so much as by the meek, forgiving, and ... 'passive' doctrines which are in a most peculiar manner the doctrines of the gospel" (Astell 2013, 285). She says that

> [w]e imagine the world will trample on us unless we resent injuries; but the lamb of God assures us, that the way to be happy, even in this world, is to be "meek"; that revenge will continue and increase injuries, and that he who passes them by, both possesses his own soul in patience, whereby he is an impregnable fortress. (Astell 2013, 107)

Astell emphasizes the importance of taming the passions, especially those of pride, anger, and resentment, since these are the main causes of quarrel (Astell 2013 196–9; see Broad 2015, 164). Like Hobbes, Astell places emphasis on what kind of moral character should be cultivated in order to avoid the principal causes of conflict. She agrees with Hobbes that while the threat of punishment by the sovereign might provide an external motive for human beings to overcome their disposition to quarrel, only a concomitant change in the general human character can give the assurance of long-lasting peace. In this respect, Hobbes's and Astell's recommendations regarding moral virtue and peace are surprisingly similar, despite the fact that Astell offers a somewhat religious theory, while Hobbes offers an outwardly naturalist one.

27.3 Astell on Women and Peace

We will now see that Astell takes these Hobbesian ideas further by highlighting (1) the need to challenge prejudicial opinions concerning female sovereigns, and (2) the importance of educating women to avoid being persuaded by "Seditious Demagogues, and Popular Haranguers" (Astell 1704, 93). Unlike Hobbes, Astell maintains that a failure to recognize women's moral and intellectual equality might precipitate the kind of civil unrest that arises from the spreading of seditious opinion.

First, Astell suggests that sexist opinions about female sovereigns can constitute seditious tools in the hands of unscrupulous men. In *Moderation Truly Stated*, she takes offence at Davenant's remark that Elizabeth I enjoyed a successful reign because she had "a Mind above her Sex," and his later suggestion that Elizabeth demonstrated that, to practice good government, "no more Skill, no more Policies are requisite than what may be comprehended by a Woman" (Davenant 1704, 180, 364). In Astell's view, these prejudicial statements are not only incompatible with each other, they are insulting to Elizabeth's political authority. Elizabeth enjoyed such success in her reign, Astell suggests, not because she had the mind of a man or because Elizabethan statecraft was a simple art form. Rather, "the Felicity of Queen *Elizabeth*'s Reign is generally ascrib'd to the goodness of her Ministry, and her excellent choice of all the hands that she imploy'd" (Astell 1704, 29), and because the queen was "Constant in her Maxims of State, and firm in executing her Resolutions" (Astell 1704, 82). Elizabeth was an active and decisive political leader. If one were to object that Elizabeth's good governance was due to her male counsellors rather than herself, Astell responds by citing Machiavelli's maxim that princes can never be well advised if they have no wisdom of their own; good counsellors will be ineffectual if their advice is never heeded (Astell 1704, 30). Astell defends Elizabeth against the view that, as a woman, she did not have the intellectual capacity to rule in her own right.

Astell then applies these lessons concerning Elizabeth to the reign of Anne, the first English queen to rule independently since Elizabeth's time. In a crucial passage of *Moderation Truly Stated*, Astell imagines a scene in which a female speaker intervenes in a conversation between two male opponents, each of whom uses Davenant's words to defend his case. The woman says:

> *Whatever other Arts ... you gentlemen may excel in, methinks you have not given your selves much trouble in studying the Art of* Decorum *and good Manners, since in a Lady's Reign, and even in Books that you Dedicate to Her Majesty, you take upon you to tell the World that* in this Kingdom no more Skill, no more Policies are requisite, than what may be comprehended by a Woman [Davenant 1704, 364]. *As if there were* any *Skill*, any *Policy that a Woman's Understanding could not reach! So again, if Women do any thing well, nay should a hundred thousand Women do the Greatest and most Glorious Actions, presently it must be* with a Mind *(forsooth)* above their Sex! ([Davenant 1704, 180.]) *Now if Women be such despicable Creatures, pray what's the plain* English *of all your fine Speeches and Dedications to her Majesty, but* Madam we mean to Flatter you*?* (Astell 1704, lii–liii)

Astell's speaker criticizes Davenant for his condescending attitude toward Anne's intellect. While Davenant pretends to tell the queen "*what is* Right and Safe, *and what her* Gracious Wisdom and Noble Compassion *ought to do*" (Davenant 1704, dedication), in reality his opinions undermine her political authority by highlighting her apparently inferior status as a woman. By making sexist judgements on her decision-making skills, Davenant is no better than the seditious demagogues he condemns. In response, Astell asserts that the queen herself is "*better able to discern what is fit for Her to do, than these Wise Men are to inform Her*" (Astell 1704, liii). To ensure peace and unity in her reign, the best path forward is for men such as Davenant to

> *leave Her Majesty to Her* own *Superior Judgment, and the Integrity of Her* own English Heart ... *let Her exert Her Self, according to Her own Good Sense, Right Principles, and Generous Inclinations, with that undaunted Courage and Royal Magnanimity, that has never been wanting to those Ladies that have adorn'd the English Throne.* (Astell 1704, liv–lv)

Davenant's conflicting advice does nothing but "perplex" the case: it introduces an instability where there would have been none if only he had trusted the sovereign's judgement. The instability that results from continual assaults on Anne's authority can have only pernicious consequences for the commonwealth as a whole. These can serve only to render a government "weak," "despicable," and "Contemptible" (Astell 1704, 30, 31); they lead to "the Majesty and Authority of Government" losing "its Reverence in the Peoples hearts" (Astell 1704, 31). Astell says:

> And since by the continual Struggle of contending Parties, the Government is render'd uneasy and precarious, the Prince whose true Grandeur consists in the Prosperity and Dutiful Affections of his People, by being made uneasy on his Throne, finds himself unable to attend the Publick Good as a Wise and Vertuous Prince desires, and is forc'd to apply himself only to provide for his own Security. The People are alarm'd and harrass'd, the Benefit of Society is in a great measure lost, it being better to Live alone, than to always in fear, always in Arms and upon the Guard; and much more easy to have only wild Beasts to contend with, than to be ever at variance with those of the same Nature, nay it may be with our nearest Relations. (Astell 1704, 117)

Astell's references to the "Prince" here allude to Queen Anne (the word is typically gender-neutral in the period). In Hobbesian terms, Astell suggests that repeated assaults on Anne's sovereignty rob the people of that "common Power to keep them all in awe," and drive them to become antisocial out of fear of their fellow citizens (Hobbes 2012, 192; 1651, 62). They lead to situations in which "the Common Safety is neglected" and subjects are no longer afforded the protection that they ought to receive from their sovereign (Astell 1704, 39). For the sake of peace and quiet, Astell implies, Davenant should keep his sexist opinions to himself.

Astell also recalls Hobbes's sentiments when she warns of the dangers of seditious opinion among female citizens. Like Hobbes, she seeks to avoid the political instability that arises when citizens believe they are entitled to make private judgements about their preservation. It is a short step from holding this opinion, in Hobbes's view, to taking up arms in defense of it. As a safeguard against conflict, the sovereign power must be the sole "Judge of what Opinions and Doctrines are averse, and what conducing to Peace." In the "well governing of Opinions," Hobbes says, "consisteth the well governing of mens Actions, in order to their Peace, and Concord" (2012, 272; 1651, 91). Astell elaborates on this idea by highlighting the need to govern the opinions of women, and to improve their reasoning skills, to help them resist the arguments of popular opinion makers. In *Moderation Truly Stated*, Astell's speakers discuss those "noisy *Women*" whom Davenant singles out for forming cabals and intrigues against the government (Astell 1704, li; Davenant 1704, 200). One speaker, "Nokes," complains that:

> if the Young and the Handsom, the Witty and the Gay, the Intriguing and Politick Ladies are all on the Factious Side; and only the Old and the Ugly, the Praying and the Women of

> Thought, are on the other, the former without Controversie will have much the stronger Party, and greatest number of Followers; and alas what shall the Government do? its Friends are not an equal Match! (Astell 1704, li)

Adapting Davenant's words, Nokes claims that "whoever has a Mind to disturb the State will always Court" such women (Davenant 1704, 254); seditious men will always find it in their interests to bring attractive women over to their side, to gain additional followers to their cause. The other speaker, "Styles," also observes that the dissenters have among them "not a few of the Female Sex," and that "*if the Ladies should put themselves in the Head of* these Multitudes, *what a formidable Insurrection would it make!*" (Astell 1704, xlix). Astell highlights the danger of foolish women being seduced into becoming battering rams at the doors of authority.

In response, Astell highlights the importance of all citizens learning to distinguish true beliefs from falsehoods, so that truth "*might Triumph over that painted* Syren, *Popular Eloquence, and all those pernicious Arts with which Falshood and Cunning bewitch Mankind*" (Astell 1704, lxv). The people must be taught to be wary of the snares and traps of wicked men, to realize that the people might throw their sovereign out of the saddle only to "*become in a little time mere Slaves to the Arbitrary Rule of some of the worst of their Fellow Subjects, those Popular Demagogues who drove them into these pernicious ways*" (Astell 1704, xxxvii–xxxviii). To avoid the misery that accompanies rebellion and civil war, Astell advises her reader:

> to take nothing upon Trust, but to see with his *own* Eyes, and to judge according to his *own* Understanding; to be of no Party, no Opinion, because this Relation, or that great Man are of it; because it is popular or plausible, because it will serve a present Turn, or make a Fortune, or even because one has been of this Opinion formerly. (Astell 1704, 3–4)

It is crucial, in her view, that the people vow to call "no Man Master upon Earth" and refuse to follow popular speakers and party leaders who urge them to swallow seditious principles only in order to achieve their own ends (Astell 1996b, 177).

Although Astell does not say so explicitly, this advice in her pamphlets is consistent with her earlier calls for women to receive a proper education in reason and religion. In her *Serious Proposal to the Ladies*, Astell argues for the establishment of a learned academy in which women might study the Christian religion and Cartesian rules of reasoning, to cultivate virtuous habits and critical-thinking skills. This higher education, she says, will keep women safe from those designing men who court and flatter them for selfish purposes. In *The Christian Religion*, she also reminds her female readers "to receive no man's opinion on his bare word, nor to swallow his arguments without examining them" (Astell 2013, 309); rather, she insists that women assert their "just and natural" right to judge for themselves (Astell 2013, 49). In her political pamphlets, these same themes re-emerge in Astell's suggestion that all citizens must be alert to the specious arguments of rebellious men. If they are not taught to resist the eloquence of popular speakers, then their actions might precipitate the ruin of the state. Without an education in critical thinking – without learning to think for themselves – female citizens, too, might be led into rebellion whenever they are persuaded that someone other than the supreme power can ensure their safety and protection.

27.4 Conclusion

We have seen that Astell's explicit criticisms of Hobbes conceal an implicit endorsement of Hobbesian ideas concerning war and peace. While Astell openly rejects Hobbes's state of nature and his contractarian logic concerning the origins of civil society, she echoes Hobbes's sentiments when she warns her readers about the dangers of epistemic conflict and of descending into a state in which we are "always in fear, always in Arms and upon the Guard" (Astell 1704, 117). While Astell cautions that the "Cant of *Self-Preservation*" is often used as an alluring "bait" that covers the "hook" of rebellion (Astell 1996b, 141, 168), like Hobbes, she agrees that long-term preservation can be attained only when citizens have cultivated a standing disposition toward peace and pledged unquestioning obedience to the sovereign. But she takes these ideas even further than Hobbes, to suggest that a failure to recognize women's moral and intellectual equality is pernicious for the state, since it is likely to lead to civil unrest. To attain lasting peace and security, we should be intolerant of prejudices about female sovereigns and we should realize that, without a proper education, female citizens are susceptible to seditious opinion. Astell builds on Hobbes's views by suggesting that recognition of women's moral and intellectual competence can play a positive role in the maintenance of peace.[6]

Notes

1 References to Hobbes (1998) will provide chapter and section numbers (e.g., I.8 refers to chapter I, section 8).

2 To be fair to Hobbes, there is evidence that he too regards the state of nature as a mere theoretical state of affairs, and that his "mushroom men" are simply an imaginative device to explain social contract theory (on this point, see Gert 2010, 63, 113). A key difference between Astell and Hobbes, however, is that Astell regards this device as offering an unrealistic and therefore unhelpful conception of human beings in the natural state.

3 It must be allowed, however, that this interpretation is open to question, given Hobbes's assertion that nothing can be just or unjust in the natural condition (2012, 196; 1651, 63), and so justice cannot strictly be the goal of entering into the social contract.

4 To be fair, it should be noted that, according to Hobbes, subjects have the right to defend themselves only in those cases in which the sovereign poses an imminent threat to their lives (see 2012, 202; 1651, 66). It is not clear that Hobbes grants subjects the right to resist any perceived threats to their long-term self-preservation, as Astell and her contemporaries imply.

5 Weiss also identifies similarities between the views of Astell and Hobbes on the "significance of security," observing that they "look with equal alarm at resistance, disobedience, and revolution as threats to the state" (Weiss 2009, 151, 143). She says that Astell's *Reflections on Marriage* suggests that "inattention to gender may unwittingly invite into the commonwealth the potential for revolt Hobbes sought to eliminate" (Weiss 2009, 152). My analysis takes these observations further by investigating Astell's theory of peace in her political pamphlets.

6 A much earlier version of this chapter was presented at the International Peace Research Association Conference at the University of Sydney in July 2010. I owe a debt of gratitude to

Michael Deckard, both for inviting me to that event and for sharing his conference paper "Hobbes on Peace" with me – that paper provided much of the initial inspiration for this chapter. I am also grateful to the Australian Research Council, who provided me with financial support to complete the research and writing for this chapter (project IDs: FT0991199; DP190100019), and to Marcus Adams, who provided helpful comments on the draft.

References

Astell, Mary. 1704. *Moderation Truly Stated: Or, a Review of a Late Pamphlet, Entitul'd. Moderation a Vertue*. London: R. Wilkin.

Astell, Mary. 1996a. "*A Fair Way with the Dissenters and Their Patrons* (1704)." In *Astell: Political Writings*, edited by Patricia Springborg, 81–127. Cambridge: Cambridge University Press. DOI:10.1017/CBO9780511802164.

Astell, Mary. 1996b. "*An Impartial Enquiry into the Causes of Rebellion* (1704)." In *Astell: Political Writings*, edited by Patricia Springborg, 129–97. Cambridge: Cambridge University Press. DOI:10.1017/CBO9780511802164.

Astell, Mary. 2013. *The Christian Religion, as Professed by a Daughter of the Church of England*, edited by Jacqueline Broad. Toronto, ON: Centre for Reformation and Renaissance Studies and Iter Publishing.

Broad, Jacqueline. 2011. "Mary Astell's Machiavellian Moment? Politics and Feminism in *Moderation Truly Stated*." In *Early Modern Englishwomen Testing Ideas*, edited by Jo Wallwork and Paul Salzman, 9–23. Farnham, NY: Ashgate. DOI:10.4324/9781315578446.

Broad, Jacqueline. 2015. *The Philosophy of Mary Astell: An Early Modern Theory of Virtue*. Oxford: Oxford University Press. DOI:10.1093/acprof:oso/9780198716815.001.0001.

Davenant, Charles. 1704. *Essays upon Peace at Home, and War Abroad. In Two Parts*, 3rdedn. London: James Knapton.

Defoe, Daniel. 1704. *More Short-Ways with the Dissenters*. London: n.p.

Eachard, John. 1672. *Mr Hobbes's State of Nature*. London: E. Blagrave.

Eachard, John. 1673. *Some Opinions of Mr Hobbs Considered in a Second Dialogue between Philautus and Timothy*. London: J. Macock.

Foulis, Henry. 1681. *The History of Romish Treasons and Usurpations*. London: Thomas Basset et al.

Gert, Bernard. 2010. *Hobbes: Prince of Peace*. Cambridge: Polity Press.

Goldie, Mark. 1991. "The Reception of Hobbes." In *The Cambridge History of Political Thought 1450–1700*, edited by James H. Burns and Mark Goldie, 589–615. Cambridge: Cambridge University Press. DOI:10.1017/CHOL9780521247160.022.

Green, Karen. 2012. "When Is a Contract Theorist Not a Contract Theorist? Mary Astell and Catharine Macaulay as Critics of Thomas Hobbes." In *Feminist Interpretations of Thomas Hobbes*, edited by Nancy J. Hirschmann and Joanne H. Wright, 169–89. University Park, PA: Pennsylvania State University Press.

Hobbes, Thomas. 1998. *On the Citizen*, edited by Richard Tuck and Michael Silverthorne. Cambridge: Cambridge University Press. DOI:10.1017/CBO9780511808173.

Hobbes, Thomas. 2012. *Leviathan*, edited by Noel Malcolm, 3 vols. Oxford: Clarendon Press [first published 1651].

Hyde, Edward, Earl of Clarendon. 1676. *A Brief View and Survey of the Dangerous and Pernicious Errors to Church and State, in Mr. Hobbes's Book, Entitled Leviathan*. Oxford: Printed at the Theater.

Jaede, Maximilian. 2018. *Thomas Hobbes's Conception of Peace: Civil Society and International Order*. Cham: Springer. DOI:10.1007/978-3-319-76066-7_1.

Kennett, White. 1704. *A Compassionate Enquiry into the Causes of the Civil War*. London: A. and J. Churchil.

Lee, Steven. 1989. "A Positive Concept of Peace." In *The Causes of Quarrel: Essays on Peace, War, and Thomas Hobbes*, edited by Peter Caws, 183–92. Boston, MA: Beacon Press.

Nalson, John. 1677. *The Common Interest of King and People*. London: Jonathan Edwin.

Parkin, Jon. 2007. *Taming the Leviathan: The Reception of the Political and Religious Ideas of Thomas Hobbes in England 1640–1700*. Cambridge: Cambridge University Press.

Perry, Ruth. 1986. *The Celebrated Mary Astell: An Early English Feminist*. Chicago: University of Chicago Press.

Perry, Ruth. 1990. "*Mary Astell and the Feminist Critique of Possessive Individualism*." *Eighteenth-Century Studies* 23: 444–57.

Sacheverell, Henry. 1704. *The Nature and Mischief of Prejudice and Partiality Stated in a Sermon Preach'd at St Mary's in Oxford*. Oxford: Leon, Lichfield for John Stephens.

Springborg, Patricia. 2005. *Mary Astell: Theorist of Freedom from Domination*. Cambridge: Cambridge University Press. DOI:10.1017/CBO9780511499203.

Thivet, Delphine. 2008. "Thomas Hobbes: A Philosopher of War or Peace?" *British Journal for the History of Philosophy* 16 (4): 701–21. DOI:10.1080/09608780802407407.

Tuck, Richard. 1996. "Introduction." In Thomas Hobbes *Leviathan*, edited by Richard Tuck, ix–xlv. Cambridge: Cambridge University Press. DOI:10.1017/CBO9780511808166.001.

Tuck, Richard. 1999. *The Rights of War and Peace: Political Thought and the International Order from Grotius to Kant*. Oxford: Oxford University Press. DOI:10.1093/acprof:oso/9780199248148.001.0001.

Weiss, Penny A. 2009. *Canon Fodder: Historical Women Political Thinkers*. University Park, PA: Pennsylvania State University Press.

28

Hobbes and Hume on Human Nature: "Much of a Dispute of Words?"

ALEXANDRA CHADWICK

According to Hume, the question of the "dignity" or "meanness" of human nature comes down to a comparison of its "different motives or actuating principles": that is, whether "our selfish and vicious principles" are "predominant above our social and virtuous" (Hume 1987, 84). Hume was responding in part to Hobbes, and comparison between the two philosophers on this question is common, with Hobbes placed on the "selfish" side, and Hume on the other.[1] But, as Hume immediately goes on to say, "There is much of a dispute of words in all this controversy." The implication is that the distinction at the heart of the dispute contains fairly little of substance.[2] I shall argue that this is indeed an appropriate description of the difference between Hobbes and Hume on the subject of human selfishness when we consider the former's psychological writings in *Leviathan*. Nevertheless, words matter when writing about human motivation because, by carrying connotations of praise or blame, they influence human actions. Accordingly, I shall suggest that the emphasis on self-regarding motives in Hobbes's political writings results from a judgement about which image of human nature it is most useful to present.

Hume certainly acknowledged a great deal of selfishness in human beings, particularly in the *Treatise*, where we read that men are "naturally selfish, or endow'd only with a confin'd generosity" (Hume 2011, 3.2.5.8). One Hume scholar accordingly contrasts Humean selfishness, in which "one's circle of immediate concern includes family members," with selfishness in "the Hobbesian sense," which is said to consist in "holding one's personal interest above all others" (Baillie 2000, 151–2). In this way, a clear distinction is maintained between the two philosophers on the grounds that Hobbes presents humans as "fundamentally self-interested" (Buckle 2018, 32), or gives a "strictly egoistic account of human nature" (McArthur 2016, 490). Yet it is not at all clear that such a picture of Hobbesian human nature is correct, raising the question of how a distinction between Hobbes and Hume can accurately be drawn.

A Companion to Hobbes, First Edition. Edited by Marcus P. Adams.

Part of the reason for this lack of clarity is that the terms of the contrast themselves are slippery. The picture of Hobbes as a psychological egoist has been somewhat undermined in Hobbes scholarship, but there is no clear consensus on this point.[3] This difference in opinion no doubt partly results from disagreement about what counts as "psychological egoism" (Slomp 2019, 113). In any case, merely adjudicating whether the label applies to one or both philosophers is insufficient to resolve the question of the difference between them, since it is possible to distinguish between more and less "selfish" positions within theories that fall under the umbrella of psychological egoism. I shall begin, then, with a brief consideration of some pertinent forms of psychological egoism, and relate these to Hobbes's theory of motivation. This will clarify some definitions and distinctions that will help us identify two possible psychological differences between Hobbesian and Humean individuals that might lead to a greater degree of selfishness in the former. I shall then consider the evidence for each of these possible psychological differences, and conclude that neither leads to a clear distinction between Hobbes's and Hume's views of human nature. Next, I shall elaborate an alternative position: Hobbes and Hume differ most not in their "scientific" anatomies of human nature, but in which "rhetorical" image of human nature they consider most beneficial to present to their readers. The final section suggests why this matters for thinking about Hobbes's ideas.

28.1 Selfishness and Psychological Egoism

One form of psychological egoism is equivalent to what we might call egoistic psychological hedonism: the thesis that when we act, we act to secure what appears to us the most pleasurable outcome for ourselves. This is the most relevant sense for our discussion, not only because of the role of pleasure in Hobbes's and Hume's accounts of motivation – which I come to shortly – but also because this "Epicurean" link between motivation and pleasure was fundamental to characterizations of "selfish" motives in the eighteenth century. For example, when attempting to establish the existence of benevolent desires in human beings, Francis Hutcheson contests the claim (which he attributes to Epicurus and his followers) "that all our Desires are *selfish*: or, that what every one intends or designs ultimately, in each Action, is the obtaining Pleasure to *himself*, or the avoiding his own *private Pain*" (Hutcheson 2002, 22–3).

In the *Treatise*, Hume writes that "pain and pleasure" is "the chief spring and moving principle of all [the human mind's] actions" (Hume 2011, 1.3.10.2).[4] There will be grounds to qualify this later on in this chapter, but for now we can grant that, at least in the *Treatise*, Hume understands most human actions as originating in aversion to pain and desire for pleasure. In this way, Hume agrees with Hobbes, as we shall see. The latter, however, ties his account of motivation to a mechanical model of nature by embedding it in a particular physiology, which gives it some distinctive features. I shall first explain Hobbes's model of motivation, then consider how the language of selfishness, psychological egoism, and related terminology might be applied to it.[5] This will then allow us to identify more precisely where Hume's account would have to differ if Humean individuals were to be less selfish than their Hobbesian counterparts.

According to Hobbes, an appetite (also called a desire), or an aversion, is an internal bodily movement ("endeavour"), distinguished by whether it has a positive or negative effect on the functioning of the body. It occurs when a thought, understood as a movement of matter, impacts on the body's "Vitall motion" and either "fortif[ies]" or "trouble[es]" it. Pleasure or pain is a sensation that accompanies an appetite or aversion respectively: it is the "apparence" of that fortification or troubling of the body (Hobbes 2012, 78, 82; 1651, 23, 25). A motive for action is the last appetite or aversion that results from a process of "deliberation," in which the potential actor imagines possible outcomes (Hobbes 2012, 90; 1651, 28). Each imagined outcome gives rise to appetite or aversion, and hence to pleasure or pain. The final appetite that results from the process of deliberation – the appetite that immediately causes the action – will necessarily be the greatest endeavor, accompanied by the greatest amount of pleasure. Thus, humans always choose the option that appears most pleasurable. But it is perfectly possible, within Hobbes's theory, that the outcome that appears most pleasurable to the actor is one that brings about *somebody else's* pleasure.

To illustrate this, imagine being faced with a choice between either going out for dinner, or looking after a friend who is ill. To choose the first option would be "selfish" in an everyday sense: it would be, as the *Oxford English Dictionary* puts it, "Concerned chiefly with one's own advantage or welfare, to the exclusion of consideration for others." But Hobbes's psychology does not entail that the first option is chosen. It *does* entail that if the second option is chosen, the thought of helping the friend must have given rise to the greatest appetite, and thus appeared more pleasurable than going to the restaurant. Which option generates the greatest appetite and pleasure will be determined by previous experience: "Appetites of particular things, proceed from Experience, and triall of their effects upon themselves, or other men" (Hobbes 2012, 80; 1651, 24). For example, parental rewards for kindness to others in childhood could form an association between pleasure and helping others, which motivates this behavior in later life (Kavka 1986, 36). Far from suggesting a universal tendency toward "selfish" motives in the everyday sense, it is a consequence of the role of experience in forging links between pleasure and benevolence that human motives must be considerably dependent on personal history, and hence subject to a great deal of variation.

Neither is it the case that Hobbesian motives must necessarily conform to Hutcheson's definition of "selfish" desires. Hobbes's model of motivation does fit the bill for psychological hedonism: since we necessarily act on the greatest appetite, we necessarily choose that action that brings with it the greatest pleasure. Yet it is not obviously the case that what one "intends or designs ultimately" is one's own pleasure. Pleasure is involved in explaining how the action arises, rather than the intention of the actor. Gregory Kavka (1986: 35–6) calls this "causal egoism." For Kavka, causal egoism is not a "genuine" form of psychological egoism, but only "pseudo-egoistic"; psychological egoism proper is understood as a thesis about the *objects* not the *causes* of desires.[6] Desires are genuinely egoistic if their object is some benefit to oneself, i.e., the desire is self-regarding, as opposed to an other-regarding desire, which has benefit to another as its object. Hobbes recognizes a "Desire of good to another" (Hobbes 2012, 84; 1651, 26), which he calls "Benevolence" and places in his list of "*Pleasures of the Mind*," lending further support to the conclusion that he is not a genuine egoist.[7]

The preceding discussion now gives us a picture of where Hume's account of motivation might differ from Hobbes's, if Humean human nature is to be less selfish. One or both of the following two claims must be true:

(A) Humean individuals have a natural capacity to feel pleasure when other people feel pleasure, and/or pain when other people feel pain, which Hobbesian individuals do not possess.
(B) Humean individuals can be motivated by benevolent desires that are not caused by one's own pleasure or pain.

The significance of both claims lies in building a tendency toward benevolence (i.e., the "Desire of good to another") into human nature, ensuring that the existence of other-regarding desires need not depend solely on personal history. In the first case, which stays within a hedonistic motivational framework, naturally feeling pleasure or pain at the pleasure or pain of others removes the need for such associations to be made by experience. In the second case, benevolent desires need not depend on personal pleasure at all. Neither factor would be decisive in determining whether the "selfish" principles would be less predominant in a population of Humean than Hobbesian creatures, but they might tilt the balance in that direction, by providing an innate disposition to benevolence.

The following two sections discuss each claim in turn, drawing on recent literature that provides support for them.

28.2 Selfishness and Sympathy

Hume's idea of "sympathy" provides an obvious example of a natural capacity to feel another's pleasure or pain. Sympathy refers to a mechanism through which humans "receive by communication" the "inclinations and sentiments" of others (Hume 2011, 2.1.11.2). On one reading, recently put forward by Paul Sagar (2018), sympathy enables a major departure from Hobbesian psychology, within a shared hedonistic framework.[8] According to this view, Hobbesian humans, unlike their Humean equivalents, are to a large degree "sentimentally closed off" from one another and "driven by private appetites and aversions" (Sagar 2018, 67–8). In a similar vein, Angela Calvo de Saavedra (2020, 75) writes that "selfish theories" of the sort Hume attributed to Hobbes deny "our capacity to be affected by human happiness or misery." We shall see, however, that the sharpness of this contrast depends on an inaccurate presentation of Hobbesian humans. Indeed, there is little evidence that Humean sympathy, at least as presented in his *Treatise*, goes beyond what is psychologically possible for Hobbesian individuals.

The building blocks of Humean sympathy are present also in Hobbes. For Hume, sympathy relies on a fundamental similarity between human beings: "The minds of all men are similar in their feelings and operations; nor can only one be actuated by any affection, of which all others are not, in some degree, susceptible" (Hume 2011, 3.3.1.7; see also 2.1.11.5). This similarity allows us accurately to interpret the emotional states of others by observing behavioral signs:

> When I see the *effects* of passion in the voice and gesture of any person, my mind immediately passes from these effects to their causes, and forms such a lively idea of the passion, as is presently converted into the passion itself ... No passion of another discovers itself immediately to the mind. We are only sensible of its causes or effects. From *these* we infer the passion: And consequently *these* give rise to our sympathy. (Hume 2011, 3.3.1.7)

Hobbes makes similar remarks in the Introduction to *Leviathan* concerning "the similitude of the thoughts, and Passions of one man, to the thoughts, and Passions of another" which allows us to "read and know ... the thoughts, and Passions of all other men" (Hobbes 2012, 18; 1651, 2). Important and much-discussed aspects of Hobbes's political theory are based precisely on the view that humans are influenced by the emotions of others, conveyed by behavioral signals: they take pleasure in the honor given to them by others, and get angry at signs of contempt.[9] Men "work upon each other's minds" through "signs, by which one taketh notice of what another conceiveth and intendeth" (Hobbes 2007, "The Order," description of ch. 13; I.13.1). These signs might be linguistic, or they might be "actions and gestures" – such as laughter and weeping.[10]

Certainly, Hobbes's treatment of how men work upon each other's minds focuses mainly on the transmission of honor and contempt. But Hume also emphasizes the value men place on other people's opinion of them: "Our reputation, our character, our name are considerations of vast weight and importance, and even the other causes of pride; virtue, beauty and riches; have little influence, when not seconded by the opinions and sentiments of others." In fact, sympathy is introduced specifically "In order to account for this phaenomenon" (Hume 2011, 2.1.11.1). For Sagar, however, any Hobbesian capacity to share others' sentiments is without "meaningful other-regarding content." This is exemplified by Hobbes's concept of pity (Sagar 2018, 68):

> *Griefe*, for the Calamity of another, is PITTY; and ariseth from the imagination that the like calamity may befall himselfe; and therefore is called also COMPASSION, and in the phrase of this present time a FELLOW-FEELING. (Hobbes 2012, 90; 1651, 27)

Jean Hampton (1997, 81), however, points out that pity here *is* other-regarding, since it is "*for* and *about*" the other, not the imagined self. This observation, along with Hobbes's definition of benevolence mentioned earlier, strongly suggest that Hobbes did recognize other-regarding sentiments.[11] However, might there nevertheless be an important difference in the *way* pity is formed for Hobbes – involving "the imagination that the like calamity may befall himself" – which entails that a Hobbesian individual remains "closed-off" to the pain of another?

To consider the steps in Hobbes's account of pity formation, take the story presented in the following well-known passage from Aubrey's life of Hobbes:

> One time, I remember, goeing in the Strand, a poor and infirme old man craved his [Hobbes's] almes. He, beholding him with eies of pitty and compassion, putt his hand in his pocket, and gave him 6*d*. (Aubrey 1898)

Leviathan's account of pity, applied to this situation, would go something like this:

(1) Hobbes sees a poor and infirm old man in the street.
(2) Hobbes imagines himself in that condition.
(3) Hobbes feels pain (pity).

Why does Hobbes feel pity and not, for example, disgust, when he sees the old man? The answer must lie in the insertion of step (2): "the imagination that the like calamity may befall himselfe." This step allows him to perceive the old man as suffering (rather than as, say, dirty and diseased), prompting him to feel "*Griefe*, for the calamity of [the old man]," rather than a different passion (such as disgust). Recall that for Hobbes all appetites and aversions result from images in the mind: "Imagination is the first internall beginning of all Voluntary Motion" (Hobbes 2012, 78; 1651, 23). In the case of pity, we have a combination of two images: the old man's condition, and oneself in the same condition. Absent either of these, the passion produced would be different.

Hume's account of the production of pity through sympathy also involves the image of oneself, or specifically in Hume's terminology, the "impression" of oneself, which is "always intimately present with us" (2011, 2.1.11.4).[12] Impressions are one of two kinds of perceptions, distinguished from ideas by having greater "force and liveliness" (Hume 2011, 1.1.1.1). Using the same example of the poor old man, we can construct Hume's account of pity as follows:

(1) Hume sees a poor and infirm old man.
(2) This produces in Hume an *idea* of the old man's pain, because the "external signs in the countenance and conversation ... convey an idea of it" (Hume 2011, 2.1.11.3). In other words, we are able to understand the emotional state of the old man by receiving and interpreting behavioral signs.
(3) The idea of the old man's pain becomes associated with Hume's ever-present *impression* of himself, because "All human creatures are related to us by resemblance" (Hume 2011, 2.2.7.2).[13]
(4) Through its association with the impression of himself, the idea of pain takes on greater force, and is converted from an *idea* of pain into an *impression* of pain (Hume 2011, 2.1.11.3–4). The result is that Hume now feels pain (pity).

In Hume's case too, then, the insertion of the image (impression) of the self is a necessary intermediate step in the formation of pity. In Hobbes's case, we might speak of a process of "imaginative identification" (Hampton 1997, 81); in Hume's case, this is fleshed out through the sympathy mechanism.

Hume is sometimes taken to be directly opposing Hobbes's account of pity (e.g., recently Merivale 2019, 58) when he attacks "Those philosophers, who derive this passion from I know not what subtile reflections on the instability of fortune, and our being liable to the same miseries we behold" (Hume 2011, 2.2.7.4). Whether or not Hume had Hobbes in mind here, the force of his objection is against an idea that pity might depend on "subtile reflections"; hence he deals with it by arguing that pity "is deriv'd from the imagination." Yet Hume's argument here does not refute Hobbes's position, since the latter also relies on the imagination, and does not imply a long chain of reasoning.

Where does that leave us regarding claim A?

(A) Humean individuals have a natural capacity to feel pleasure when other people feel pleasure, and/or pain when other people feel pain, which Hobbesian individuals do not possess

Humean sympathy appears to be innate: it is a "quality of human nature," both "conspicuous in children" and in "men of the greatest judgement and understanding" (Hume 2011, 2.1.11.2). The Hobbesian capacity to feel pity, on the other hand, is not explicitly said to be natural. Further, Hobbes's example of pity concerns pain felt when confronted with someone's else's pain, but he is silent about the capacity to feel pleasure when confronted with someone else's pleasure; Hume, by contrast, gives several examples of the latter (e.g., Hume 2011, 2.1.11.2; 2.2.5.14). Nevertheless, on Hobbes's model, taking pleasure in another's pleasure must remain psychologically possible through a similar process of imaginative identification. All in all, it seems that we cannot rule out a sympathy-like natural capacity within the framework of Hobbes's psychology.

Another possibility remains for hanging a Humean tendency to benevolence on sympathy: that Humean sympathy is somehow stronger or of greater force than its Hobbesian alternative.[14] However, Hume himself acknowledges that when it comes to the formation of motives, sympathy's force is weak:

> we may easily remove any contradiction, which may appear to be betwixt the *extensive sympathy*, on which our sentiments of virtue depend, and that *limited generosity* which I have frequently observ'd to be natural to men, and which justice and property suppose ... My sympathy with another may give me the sentiment of pain and disapprobation, when any object is presented, that has a tendency to give him uneasiness; tho' I may not be willing to sacrifice any thing of my own interest, or cross any of my passions, for his satisfaction ... Sentiments must touch the heart, to make them controul our passions: But they need not extend beyond the imagination, to make them influence our taste. (Hume 2011, 3.3.1.23)

If Hobbesian humans were entirely emotionally separated from their fellows' pain, they would not even be capable of Hume's "limited generosity," and we would arrive at a clear-cut sympathy-based distinction between the two philosophers. But as we have seen, that atomistic picture of Hobbesian human nature does not hold up. Hence the grounds for using the *Treatise*'s account of sympathy to argue that selfish motives are less predominant amongst Humeans than Hobbesians are, if not fully removed, then at least called into serious doubt.

28.3 Selfishness and Innate Appetites

I turn now to the possibility that Hume avoids "Hobbesian" selfishness by stepping outside a psychological hedonist framework: that is, benevolent desires are not always caused by one's own pleasure or pain (claim [B]). Amyas Merivale (2019, 49–90) and Peter Millican (2020, 281–6) convincingly demonstrate that Hume is no longer committed to an exclusively hedonistic model of motivation in his second *Enquiry*.[15] The change becomes apparent in an argument presented in Appendix 2,

"Of Self-love," in which Hume targets the attempt of Epicureans and Hobbists to "explain every affection to be self-love, twisted and moulded ... into a variety of appearances" (Hume 1998, App. 2.4). This view that all passions resolve into self-love is referred to as "the selfish hypothesis" (Hume 1998, App. 2.6). Countering the selfish hypothesis involves, for Hume, establishing the existence of benevolence, both "*general*" and "*particular*":

> The first is, where we have no friendship or connexion or esteem for the person, but feel only a general sympathy with him or a compassion for his pains, and a congratulation with his pleasures. The other species of benevolence is founded on an opinion of virtue, on services done us, or on some particular connexions. (Hume 1998, App. 2.5, n. 60)

Both general and particular benevolence "must be allowed real in human nature," Hume continues, "but whether they will resolve into some nice considerations of self-love, is a question more curious than important." Nevertheless, he considers it worth "bestow[ing] a few reflections upon it" (Hume 1998, App. 2.5) to establish that benevolence *cannot* be resolved into self-love.[16]

Hume presents a number of arguments against the selfish hypothesis, three of which are unconvincing as a refutation of Hobbes's position, and need only a few words in response. First, Hume claims that the selfish hypothesis "is contrary to common feeling," "common language and observation," and to the "obvious appearance of things" (Hume 1998, App. 2.6). Since Hobbes's theory of motivation has been shown to recognize the existence of pity ("*Griefe*, for the calamity of another") and benevolence ("Desire of good to another"), rather than denying other-regarding emotions, it is not clear what aspects of his psychology should be challenged by this appeal to common experience and language. Second, Hume writes that "Animals are found susceptible of kindness ... Shall we account for all *their* sentiments too, from refined deductions of self-interest?" (Hume 1998, App. 2.8). This will not work as a refutation of Hobbes's position, for the reason given earlier: Hobbesian pity does not depend on "subtile reflections."[17] Third, Hume presents two situations that he suggests cannot be accounted for by the selfish hypothesis. One is the case of a "fond mother," "who loses her health by assiduous attendance on her sick child, and afterwards languishes and dies of grief, when freed, by its death, from the slavery of that attendance" (Hume 1998, App. 2.9). The other is a desire of a friend's welfare "even though absence or death should prevent us from all participation in it" (Hume 1998, App. 2.10). Again, however, neither of these cases poses a problem for Hobbesian motivation, since Hobbes takes into account the role of imagination in desire formation. On the Hobbesian model, we are able to desire the welfare of the friend, even if we will not be around to enjoy it, because the imagination of the friend's happiness is pleasurable (Hobbes 2012 152; 1651, 48: "any thing that is pleasure in the sense, the same also is pleasure in the imagination"). Similarly, the mother might die of grief because the *memory* of the sick child, remaining after the child's death, is so painful (imagination and memory being, for Hobbes, the same thing: Hobbes 2012, 28; 1651, 5).

But a fourth argument marks an apparent distinction with Hobbesian psychology by abandoning psychological hedonism. It is worth quoting at length:

> There are bodily wants or appetites ... which necessarily precede all sensual enjoyment, and carry us directly to seek possession of the object. Thus, hunger and thirst have eating and drinking for their end; and from the gratification of these primary appetites arises a pleasure, which may become the object of another species of desire or inclination that is secondary and interested. In the same manner, there are mental passions, by which we are impelled immediately to seek particular objects, such as fame, or power, or vengeance, without any regard to interest; and when these objects are attained, a pleasing enjoyment ensues, as the consequence of our indulged affections. Nature must, by the internal frame and constitution of the mind, give an original propensity to fame, ere we can reap any pleasure from the acquisition, or pursue it from motives of self-love, and desire of happiness ... If I have no vanity, I take no delight in praise: If I be void of ambition, power gives me no enjoyment ... In all these cases there is a passion, which points immediately to the object, and constitutes it our good or happiness ... [L]ikewise ... from the original frame of our temper, we may feel a desire of another's happiness or good, which, by means of that affection, becomes our own good, and is afterwards pursued, from the combined motives of benevolence and self-enjoyment[.] (Hume 1998, App. 2.12–13)

Millican (2020, 288) calls this the "cart before the horse" point: Hume's claim is that the desire for benevolence comes *before* the pleasure produced by its satisfaction.[18]

Key to this argument is an analogy between "bodily appetites" and "mental passions, by which we are impelled immediately to seek particular objects." These mental passions include benevolence as well as "fame, or power, or vengeance," all of which come from "the original frame of our temper." Yet Hobbes too identifies some bodily appetites as "born with men":

> Of Appetites, and Aversions, some are born with men; as Appetite of food, Appetite of excretion, and exoneration ... and some other Appetites, not many. The rest, which are Appetites of particular things, proceed from Experience, and triall of their effects upon themselves, or other men. (Hobbes 2012, 80; 1651, 24)

According to Hobbes's psychology, appetites "born with man" will be accompanied by pleasure, because pleasure simply is the "the apparence, or sense of that motion" (appetite) that fortifies the body (Hobbes 2012, 82; 1651, 25). But inborn appetites differ from others, in that they are originally pursued prior to any experience of the relevant kind of object, and hence prior to any association formed between a particular object and a sensation of pleasure. Therefore inborn appetites for Hobbes too can fall outside psychological hedonism. He does not (at least explicitly) include benevolence among the appetites born with man. Importantly, however, neither does he include such self-regarding passions as "vanity" or "ambition" there.

For the Hume of the second *Enquiry*, then, benevolence – and vanity, and ambition – are innate, in the same way as hunger and thirst. For Hobbes these appetites, both other and self-regarding, are (probably) the results of experiences an individual has had in life. When expanding on his claim that "Hume rejects Hobbes's strictly egoistic account of human nature," McArthur notes that Hume thinks we "naturally possess benevolent sentiments" (McArthur 2016, 489–90). This is true. But it does not amount to an explanation of a tendency toward benevolence in Humean men since, unlike the creatures described by Hobbesian psychology, they also naturally possess self-regarding mental passions. Which of Hume's innate appetites is "predominant" is unanswered by the "cart before the horse" argument, hence it cannot explain why Humean individuals would have a greater tendency toward benevolent desires than their Hobbesian counterparts.

28.4 Two Images of Human Nature

So far I have suggested that there is little evidence in Hobbes's psychological writings in *Leviathan* to support the stark contrasts drawn between Hobbes and Hume on the predominance of selfishness in human nature. Yet it is undoubtedly the case that Hobbes's political writings contain stark depictions of self-regarding motives. How might we explain this, if not by reference to features of Hobbesian psychology?

The strongest textual support for the absence of benevolence in Hobbesian individuals come from one passage: *De cive* I.2. In a typical extract, Hobbes writes:

> By nature ... we are not looking for friends but for honour or advantage [*commodum*] from them ... So clear is it from experience to anyone who gives any serious attention to human behaviour, that every voluntary encounter is a product either of mutual need or of the pursuit of glory. (Hobbes 1998, 22–3)

However, three factors advise against placing too much weight on *De cive* I.2 when examining Hobbes's view of human nature. First, it is not part of his psychological writings, but rather introduces his account of the state of nature in *De cive* (1642). Second, it is unparalleled in *The Elements* (1640) or *Leviathan* (1651), the two books in which Hobbes's psychology is presented prior to his moral and political theory. Third, it is targeted at the idea that love for one's fellow man, or as he also calls it "mutual human benevolence," might be a principle to rely on when considering the practical organization of human life (Hobbes 1998, 22, 24). Hence Hobbes's point in the passage is not that benevolence is absent in human nature, but that it is has little to do with the nature of political society.

In his essay "Of the Independency of Parliament," Hume notes that "Political writers have established it as a maxim, that, in contriving any system of government, and fixing the several checks and controuls of the constitution, every man ought to be supposed a *knave*, and to have no other end, in all his actions, than private interest." This, Hume asserts, is indeed "a just *political* maxim," but it is "false in *fact*" (Hume 1987, 42). For Hume, it is important that we do not lose sight of the facts, however, since he thinks there is great benefit in emphasizing benevolence in human nature. As he writes in the essay "Of the Dignity or Meanness of Human Nature," with which this chapter began:

> the sentiments of those, who are inclined to think favourably of mankind, are more advantageous to virtue, than the contrary principles, which give us a mean opinion of our nature. When a man is prepossessed with a high notion of his rank and character in the creation, he will naturally endeavour to act up to it, and will scorn to do a base or vicious action, which might sink him below that figure which he makes in his own imagination. (Hume 1987, 81)

In other words, emphasizing the "social and virtuous" rather than the "selfish and vicious" motives of which human beings are capable is morally "advantageous."

Hobbes, however, is particularly focused on highlighting the danger of attributing too much benevolence to human nature: not only because of the figure his reader might make of them*self* in their imagination, but also that which they might make of other people. The passages in which Hobbes apparently disparages human nature, I suggest, form part of his attempt to portray disreputable motives behind apparently noble activities. Amongst philosophers, for example – "those who profess to have more wisdom than other men" – "everyone wants to be thought a Master; otherwise not only do they fail, like other men, to love their companions, they actively pursue their resentments against them" (Hobbes 1998, 23). When men meet to discuss "public affairs," "it is sometimes the occasion of faction, but never of goodwill" (Hobbes 1998, 22). Such examples cohere with Hobbes's frequent reference to the ambitious motives driving those who claim to know better than the sovereign (for examples see Slomp 2000, 60–2). By presenting those people who claim to have the interests of the people at heart as driven by self-serving desires, Hobbes seeks to discourage citizens from listening to them.

For Hobbes, then, the danger was not that people thought too little of human nature, but that they thought too highly of it.[19] Arguably, his most negative portrayals of human motives were a contingent element of his argument, targeted to the politics of his time, in which (he thought) wannabe-statesman, philosophers in thrall to the Greeks and Romans, and ambitious priests were hoodwinking the people into supporting seditious ideas. We might therefore loosely term this picture of motivation part of Hobbes's "rhetorical" image of human nature, as opposed to the "scientific" account he presents in his psychology.

28.5 Conclusion

I began from Hume's remark that the question of whether our "selfish" principles outweigh our "social" contains little substantial disagreement. Noting that Hobbes is usually placed on the "selfish" side of the dichotomy, I asked how we might accurately pinpoint a difference between them. I identified two possible ways in which Humean individuals might be less selfish than Hobbesian men. One involves staying within a psychological hedonist framework, but attributing only to Humean men the capacity to feel pleasure when others feel pleasure, or pain when others feel pain. The other involves granting them benevolent desires that are not caused by personal pleasure or pain. Neither possibility ultimately provides a clear distinction between the motives of Hobbesian and Humean men, however. The first overlooks the way in which Hobbesian psychology allows for something like Humes's mechanism of sympathy in the formation of other-regarding desires. The second confers on Humean men an innate desire for benevolence, but also innate self-regarding desires, such as a desire for fame, leaving unexplained which if any of these desires are "predominant."

I suggested that the presence of passages in Hobbes's political writings portraying human motives as strongly self-interested, such as *De cive* I.2, reflects a distinction between "scientific" and "rhetorical" images of human nature in Hobbes. The latter I ventured to call a contingent element of Hobbes's argument. Whether it really is a contingent element, or whether aspects of Hobbes's moral theory and theory of the state depend upon his rhetorical rather than scientific image of man, is a question of great interest in interpreting Hobbes's philosophy, and one that further comparisons between Hobbes and Hume can help us to answer. I conclude with a brief explanation of why this is so.

Hume sets his moral theory in the second *Enquiry* against the "selfish system" of "HOBBES and LOCKE" (Hume 1998, App. 2.3), and he avoids Hobbes's conclusion that absolute sovereignty is necessary for peace (see, e.g., Hardin 2007, 214). But if, as I have argued here, their accounts of human motivation are not so dissimilar, how are apparent differences in ethics and politics to be accounted for? One answer might be that Hobbes's practical philosophy does not rely on his scientific view of man after all: this has certainly been the opinion of some Hobbes scholars, who have instead identified the relevant view of man as, for example, "moral" (humans are motivated by "vanity"), or "Christian" (humans are motivated by sin; Strauss 1963, 6–29; Glover 1966). Both characterizations are ultimately variations on the claim that for Hobbes "our selfish and vicious principles" are "predominant above our social and virtuous."

But an alternative answer, consistent with the view that the debate about human selfishness is "much of a dispute of words," is that the real divide between Hobbes and Hume – that which gives Hobbes's political philosophy its particular character – lies elsewhere. Considering where this might be – in other words, considering why Hume is not Hobbes – should give us a clearer image of the creature for whom Hobbes's ethics and politics was built.[20]

Notes

1 Hume does not refer to Hobbes in the essay from which this passage is taken ("Of the Dignity or Meanness of Human Nature"). However, Hobbes is identified in Appendix 2 of *An Enquiry Concerning the Principles of Morals* ("Of Self-Love") as a proponent of "the selfish hypothesis." Bernard Mandeville, another prominent figure on the selfish side of the eighteenth-century debate about human nature, is dismissed swiftly (Hume 1998, App. 2.1), with the rest of the appendix devoted to countering a position attributed to "An EPICUREAN or a HOBBIST" (Hume 1998, App. 2.4).

2 Hume refers to debates that are "merely" or "only" a "dispute of words" at three points in the *Treatise*: 1.4.6.7, 2.3.1.16 and 3.3.4.1. See also Hume 1998, App. 4.1; 2000, 8.3, 2007, 12.6 and 12.8, note.

3 For example, Bernard Gert (2001, 243) writes that "It is now generally recognised that although Hobbes had a pessimistic view of human nature, he did not hold an egoistic view," whereas C. D. Meyers (2013, 272) asserts that "Most scholars interpret Hobbes as holding a thoroughly egoistic psychology."

4 See also, for example, Hume 2011, 2.3.3.3; 2.3.9.1; 3.3.1.2.

5 I focus on *Leviathan*, leaving open the possibility that details of Hobbes's account change between his earlier and later works.

6 For Kavka's analysis of whether Hobbes can be labeled a psychological egoist in *Leviathan*, and references to other classic contributions to the debate, see Kavka (1986, 44–51). For a recent approach, see Arash Abizadeh (2018, 146–7) who regards Hobbes as a psychological egoist "of sorts," but not a "strong" psychological egoist (for whom the object of every desire is one's own pleasure).

7 The smoking gun of psychological egoism in *Leviathan* is sometimes taken to be the following passage: "of the voluntary acts of every man, the object is some *Good to himselfe*" (Hobbes 2012, 202; 1651, 66). However, this remark is not found in *Leviathan*'s psychological chapters, but in chapter 14, in a discussion of the rights that subjects can "be understood" to have transferred to their sovereign. The passage merits further analysis in that particular context, which would take us beyond the confines of the current discussion. Other relevant passages include Hobbes (2012, 222; 1651, 72), and Hobbes (2012, 398; 1651, 132), which are located in chapters 15 and 25. For now, however, it is sufficient to note that in his chapter on voluntary motion, Hobbes writes that "whatsoever is the object of any mans Appetite or Desire; that is it, which he for his part calleth *Good*" (Hobbes 2012, 80; 1651, 24), which is consistent with both an other-regarding and self-regarding object.

8 For arguments against the claim that sympathy (as understood in the *Treatise*) actually takes Hume *outside* a hedonistic motivational framework, see Millican (2020, 283 fn. 21).

9 See, for example, the literature on glory, such as Slomp (2000).

10 Such gestures "cannot easily be counterfeited ... especially if they be sudden." Language is a different case, since it can be used without sincerity, to deceive and manipulate.

11 "Sentiment" is not a Hobbesian term, however given the way that evaluative judgements are formed within his psychology ("whatsoever is the object of any mans Appetite or Desire; that is it, which he for his part calleth Good: And the object of his Hate, and Aversion, evill") we can use it as equivalent to his "desire" or "aversion" (Hobbes 2012, 80; 1651, 24).

12 There is a well-known tension between Hume's use of the impression of oneself in Book 2 of the Treatise and his remarks on the self in Book 1 (Hume 2011, 1.4.6).

13 "Resemblance" is one of Hume's three principles of association (Hume 2011, 1.1.4).

14 Hampton (1997) claims that for Hobbes "something analogous to Hume's operation of sympathy ... produces in us concern for others ... But [Hobbes] does not think that passions such as pity are significant or frequent motivators of human action".

15 On the possibility that Hume had started to have doubts about the hedonistic framework in the *Treatise* see Millican (2020, 283–5).

16 Note that until the 1777 edition of the second *Enquiry*, this discussion of self-love appeared in Section 2, rather than in an appendix.

17 Furthermore, there is no reason to believe that Hobbes would have been unwilling to extend pity to animals, given the similarities he was happy to grant between human and animal cognition (Hobbes 2012, 40; 1651, 9). I am grateful to Marcus Adams for this point.

18 In "Of the Dignity or Meanness of Human Nature," Hume says the following, which Millican (2020, 288–9) takes to be "the same key point": "The virtuous sentiment or passion produces the pleasure, and does not arise from it. I feel a pleasure in doing good to my friend, because I love him; but do not love him for the sake of that pleasure" (Hume 1987, 85–6). This makes things a bit more complicated, however, since it brings in the relationship between "love" and "benevolence," so I limit the discussion here to the argument as expressed in Appendix 2 of the second *Enquiry*.

19 This is in keeping with Hobbes's well-known opposition to pride and vainglory. However, existing literature on that theme in Hobbes tends to focus on an individual's view of them*self* and their abilities in relation to others, rather than their view of human nature: see, for example, Cooper (2010) and references therein.

20 For comments on the draft of this chapter, and many helpful suggestions, I am very grateful to Marcus Adams, Johan Olsthoorn, Peter Millican, Lodi Nauta, and Paul Sagar. Earlier versions were presented at the Institute of Historical Research (2019), the "Hume as a Reader" workshop at the University of Edinburgh (2019), the Oxford Hume Forum (2019), and University College Dublin (2020), and I am also grateful to the convenors and participants of those events.

References

Abizadeh, Arash. 2018. *Hobbes and the Two Faces of Ethics*. Cambridge: Cambridge University Press.

Aubrey, John. 1898. *Brief Lives*, edited by Andrew Clarke, Oxford: Clarendon Press. Accessed November 10, 2020: https://www.gutenberg.org/files/47787/47787-h/47787-h.htm#FNanchor_1785.

Baillie, James. 2000. *Routledge Philosophy Guide Book to Hume on Morality*. London and New York: Routledge.

Buckle, Stephen. 2018. "Hume's Philosophy and Its Modern British Debts." In *The Humean Mind*, edited by Angela M. Coventry and Alexander Sager, 23–36. Abingdon, UK and New York, NY: Routledge.

Calvo de Saavedra, Angela. 2020. "Benevolence and Self-Interest in Hume's Moral Philosophy." In *Reading Hume on the Principles of Morals*, edited by Jacqueline Taylor, 58–76. Oxford: Oxford University Press.

Cooper, Julie E. 2010. "Vainglory, Modesty, and Political Agency in the Political Theory of Thomas Hobbes." *The Review of Politics* 72: 241–69.

Gert, Bernard. 2001. "Hobbes on Reason." *Pacific Philosophical Quarterly* 82: 243–57.

Glover, Willis B. 1966. "Human Nature and the State in Hobbes." *Journal of the History of Philosophy* 4: 292–311.

Hampton, Jean. 1997. "The Hobbesian Side of Hume." In *Reclaiming the History of Ethics: Essays for John Rawls*, edited by Andrews Reath, Barbara Herman, and Christine M. Korsgaard, 66–101. Cambridge: Cambridge University Press.

Hardin, Russell. 2007. *David Hume: Moral and Political Theorist*. Oxford: Oxford University Press.

Hobbes, Thomas. 1998. *On the Citizen*, edited by Richard Tuck and Michael Silverthorne. Cambridge: Cambridge University Press.

Hobbes, Thomas. 2007. *The Elements of Law*, edited by Ferdinand Tönnies. Boston, MA: Elibron Classics [facsimile reprint].

Hobbes, Thomas. 2012. *Leviathan*, 3 vols., edited by Noel Malcolm. Oxford: Clarendon Press. [First published 1651.]

Hume, David. 1987. *Essays Moral, Political, and Literary*, edited by Eugene F. Miller. Indianapolis, IN: Liberty Fund.

Hume, David. 1998. *An Enquiry Concerning the Principles of Morals*, edited by Tom L. Beauchamp. Oxford: Oxford University Press.

Hume, David. 2000. *An Enquiry Concerning Human Understanding*, edited by Tom L. Beauchamp. Oxford: Clarendon Press.

Hume, David. 2007. *Dialogues Concerning Natural Religion and Other Writings*, edited by Dorothy Coleman. Cambridge: Cambridge University Press.

Hume, David. 2011. *A Treatise of Human Nature*, edited by David Fate Norton and Mary J. Norton. Oxford: Clarendon Press.

Hutcheson, Francis. 2002. *An Essay on the Nature and Conduct of the Passions and Affections, with Illustrations on the Moral Sense*, edited by Aaron Garrett. Indianapolis, IN: Liberty Fund.

Kavka, Gregory. 1986. *Hobbesian Moral and Political Theory*. Princeton, NJ: Princeton University Press.

McArthur, Neil. 2016. "Hume's Political Philosophy." In *The Oxford Handbook of Hume*, edited by Paul Russell, 489–504. Oxford: Oxford University Press.

Merivale, Amyas. 2019. *Hume on Art, Emotion, and Superstition: A Critical Study of the Four Dissertations*. New York, NY and London: Routledge.

Meyers, Chris D. 2013. "Hobbes and the Rationality of Self-Preservation: Grounding Morality on the Desires We *Should* Have." *The European Legacy* 18: 269–86.

Millican, Peter. 2020. "The Relation Between Hume's Two *Enquiries*." In *Reading Hume on the Principles of Morals*, edited by Jacqueline Taylor, 273–99. Oxford: Oxford University Press.

Sagar, Paul. 2018. *The Opinion of Mankind: Sociability and the Theory of the State from Hobbes to Smith*. Princeton, NJ: Princeton University Press.

Slomp, Gabriella. 2000. *Thomas Hobbes and the Political Philosophy of Glory*. Basingstoke: Macmillan.

Slomp, Gabriella. 2019. "On Benevolence and Love of Others." In *Interpreting Hobbes's Political Philosophy*, edited by Sharon A. Lloyd, 106–21. Cambridge: Cambridge University Press.

Strauss, Leo. 1963. *The Political Philosophy of Hobbes: Its Basis and Its Genesis*. Chicago, IL: University of Chicago Press.

29

He Shows "Genius" and Is "More Useful than Pufendorf": Kant's Reception of Hobbes

HOWARD WILLIAMS

In 1793, in the aftermath of the French Revolution, Kant published in the journal *Berlinische Monatsschrift* an article entitled "On the Common Saying: That may be correct in theory but it is of no use in practice." The journal was edited by a friend of Kant's Johann Biester, and it was very much an institution of the remarkable Berlin Enlightenment. The essay dealt with the question of the relationship between theory and practice in morals and politics. Kant's purpose was to undermine the view that neither politics nor morality could benefit from philosophical theory. The essay was divided into three sections. In the second section, Kant puts in question the political philosophy of Hobbes. The first section took issue with the contemporary German popular philosopher Christian Garve who questioned the applicability of Kant's moral theory to everyday problems. Garve was a long-time interlocutor of Kant. At times Kant greatly appreciated the interest Garve showed in his philosophy since it brought Kant's ideas to the attention of the German public, however in this instance he appears irritated with Garve's interventions. Garve was drawn to British empiricist philosophy and had published several volumes demonstrating his admiration of the standpoint, and had also translated William Paley's *The Principles of Moral and Political Philosophy*, which has a strongly utilitarian bent. Kant wanted particularly to distance himself from Garve's advocacy of utilitarian philosophy. In his response to Garve, Kant makes it abundantly clear that, unlike the utilitarians, he sees the highest ethical good as arising from our obedience to the call of duty rather than the mere pursuit of happiness. The third (briefest) part of Kant's critical essay deals with the views of Moses Mendelssohn. Mendelssohn was a key figure of the Berlin Enlightenment whom Kant knew personally and admired, but he could not accept the pessimistic view of history as a matter of ever recurring cycles, which Mendelssohn had put forward. Unlike Mendelssohn Kant argues, on the basis of his own critical philosophy, that we can discern a positive path in history in contrast to the ever-repeated fortune and misfortune that Mendelssohn portrayed.

A Companion to Hobbes, First Edition. Edited by Marcus P. Adams.

One of the main themes of the article "Theory and Practice" is, as its title suggests, that those engaged in moral and political activity have – despite appearances to the contrary – a great deal to gain from the study of philosophical theory. Indeed, it is Kant's belief, which he expresses in the second paragraph of the article, that far from being a hindrance to practice, moral and political theory are an undeniable necessity for its lasting success. To those who argue that achieving things in practice relies primarily on talent, ability, and everyday know-how, and so it is merely technical incompetence that makes things go wrong, Kant suggests that in many such instances the problem is not one of an excess of theory but rather of "there having been not enough theory" (8: 275). Kant defends the role of political theory in politics at a time where it was being questioned by those who were concerned about the disruptive role that political ideas appear to have played in the French Revolution. This disruptive role is highlighted in Edmund Burke's book *Reflections on The French Revolution*, which was published in German translation in the same year as Kant's article (Williams 2003, 42–3).

On the surface it might well appear that Hobbes should be seen as in agreement with Kant on the question of the role of theory in morals and politics. Hobbes's approach to political philosophy in his main works is nothing if not systematic. His political philosophy is part of a larger metaphysics, which Hobbes frequently reveals to his readers. Thus, mastering Hobbes's political philosophy could not be lightly done. His writings require systematic study. Thus, in terms of his main theme in "Theory and Practice" it would appear that Kant had chosen the wrong opponent in confronting his ideas in the political realm. For just as Kant aims to integrate his political theory into his wider critical metaphysics of transcendental idealism, so Hobbes's major writings *De cive* [On the Citizen] and *Leviathan* are integrated into his wider mechanistic materialism.[1] But what leads Kant ultimately to place Hobbes among those thinkers who put too little weight on theory in morals and politics is the authoritarian empiricist stamp of Hobbes's political philosophy. For it turns out that, in Kant's mind, Hobbes is insufficiently concerned with the disinterested and open enquiry he advocates in his philosophical method to be regarded as a true proponent of theory in morals and politics. Hobbes places philosophical enquiry too much in the hands of those holding political power in determining what is right or wrong. Whereas Kant wishes to encourage open debate and ensure that political leaders pay heed to the critical metaphysical ideas of philosophers, Hobbes gives to rulers the power to decide what opinions should be heard.

Through his scientific approach, Hobbes believes that he has discovered the only correct way in which human conduct should be regulated and that only the one truth should be tolerated by a human society if it is to flourish. Hobbes's lack of respect for scholarly debate in relation to politics stands in the way as a reliable advocate of theory. Despite Hobbes's own theoretical credentials Kant places him "at one in attacking the academic, who works on theory on behalf of them all and for their benefit, since they fancy that they understand matters better than he, they seek to banish to his school ... as a scholar who, spoiled for practice, only stands in the way of their experienced wisdom" (8: 277).[2] Not everything admittedly can be debated openly at every time. As subjects of a state, we must all pay our taxes when they are levied, and we are not entitled to argue about the appropriateness of paying them when they are due, and the sums agreed. However, as scholars who are independently pursuing research on the nature and feasibility of taxation, as modern economists often do, we are entitled to dispute the idea and type of taxation. Hobbes would not permit such scholarly debate or at least he would believe the sovereign entitled to silence those views that went contrary to existing policies. Hobbes particularly wanted to silence philosophical debate about religious questions and beliefs since in his view they led to unnecessary conflict and disorder (Martinich 1999, 245–6). We shall return to this later.

The section in "Theory and Practice" on Hobbes does not, as we might expect, provide a critical exegesis of Hobbes's writings on politics. Indeed there is very little direct mention of Hobbes at all. But we are presented with an exposition of Kant's own political philosophy, which in many regards runs directly contrary to Hobbes's views. Kant's two major writings on political philosophy *Toward Perpetual Peace* and the first part of the *Metaphysics of Morals* (1797), the "Doctrine of Right," were yet to come. Some writings published earlier than "Theory and Practice" may have hinted at Kant's principal political ideas but, possibly under the pressure of events in France and the reaction to them in Prussia, here Kant gives a very concise (if extraordinarily complex) summary of the main precepts of his political and legal doctrines. It is of immense significance that Hobbes's political thinking provides the backdrop for this exposition. We can see from the centrality of the social contract in the theory that Kant propounds, and the equivalent prominence given to the idea of the state of nature that in Kant's "Theory and Practice" essay that Kant does not lose sight of Hobbes's system. Indeed, Kant wants to confront systematically the challenges that Hobbes's political realism poses. And Kant regards this enterprise not merely as a matter of necessary scholarly debate but also as a matter of immediate ethical and political concern in facing up to the challenge posed by revolutionary France and the inherited monarchical political system that predominated in Europe at the time. At the time France and Britain were at loggerheads in seeking to determine the most appropriate political system for European states. Kant takes the side of the republican insurgents (while denying a right of political insurgency) in France against a monarchical Britain whose constitution met with greater approbation from the classical Hobbesian perspective.

Kant had studied Hobbes's political philosophy for a very long time. As I shall show here, Hobbes plays a major role in the formation of Kant's legal and political doctrines. The only figure to have a similarly profound influence upon Kant was Rousseau. Kant absorbed Rousseau's ideas as a contemporary whereas Hobbes was a significant figure from a former century. Some of Hobbes's ideas Kant was never going to repudiate, but he was drawn strongly to Rousseau's radicalism so that ultimately Kant's reception of Hobbes was colored by modern republican sentiments and enlightenment principles. Kant's judgment on Hobbes was always equivocal. He was both drawn to his ideas but also repelled by some of them. Kant was not generally attracted by rhetoric and emotion in presenting his theory of law and politics. Kant thinks we should be convinced, rather than enticed to accept the better political doctrine. Unlike Hobbes, Kant was not persuaded that sovereigns should enjoy unquestioned authority in the realm of ideas. While accepting Hobbes's view that the legal authority of the sovereign or sovereign body can never be resisted, Kant nonetheless believed that the policies and laws of sovereigns should be open to criticism from the law-abiding subject. In the essay "What is Enlightenment?" Kant explains his position by distinguishing between the "private use of freedom" and the "public use of freedom." The public use of reason takes place when subjects tested their ideas among others in critical and fully open debate, and should always be permitted, even encouraged, however the private use of reason, which is the use "one may make of it in a certain civil post or office with which he is entrusted" (8: 37/18) may be legitimately restricted. There are certain spheres of activity within a commonwealth where "a certain mechanism is necessary, by means of which some members must behave passively" so that an artificial social unity may prevail in order to realize "public ends" (8: 37/18). Kant sees Hobbes's writings as endangering the freedom of expression, which is so vital to the health of a society and its scientific and scholarly endeavors.

29.1 A Paradoxical Thinker in Whose Writing Genius Reigns

What was Kant's verdict on Hobbes looking on the work of a fellow philosopher from the unearned point of advantage of a future generation? From Kant's *Lectures on Anthropology* given in winter 1772/3 we can read one striking public assessment of Hobbes:

> A writing in which genius reigns, even if it at the same time with many mistakes, is much better than one which contains no mistakes, but none less only presents the most everyday or common or garden things. He who travels mistakenly is nonetheless travelled. Through a book of the former kind my understanding is brought into action, and in this situation it can itself come across new horizons. Hobbes is more useful than Pufendorf. Paradoxical writings are ones that stand opposed to generally accepted propositions. All new writings are paradoxical if they go into matters of which one otherwise is only generally hears the opposite maintained. Paradoxical writings deserve the closest attention. Terrasson notes that paradoxical writings are only written for the next generation, because they refute the general illusion according to which they are always and ever judged by their contemporaries. (Kant *AA* 25, II 1, 27)

As we have just shown the confrontation with Hobbes does not lead to the complete rejection of his views. The paradoxical nature of Hobbes's thinking stimulates Kant into absorbing some of his ideas while at the same time rejecting many others. In this way there is a strongly Hobbesian color to the political philosophy Kant adopts. Toward the very end of the section on Hobbes in "Theory and Practice" Kant, for example, denotes his agreement with one of the key principles of Hobbes's political thinking, namely, the acceptance and recognition of the sovereign's unchallengeable political authority within the state, but at the same time he insists on a principle of his own as a counterweight to this hegemony: that the right of publicity be accepted. What Kant means by publicity is the free and open exchange of ideas among the subject of the state as scholars. This is not a right of forceful dissent nor, least of all, is it a right of resistance but it is rather a right of communication. As Kant puts it,

> in every commonwealth there must be obedience under the mechanism of the state constitution to coercive laws (applying to the whole), but there must also be a spirit of freedom, since each, in what has to do with universal human duties, requires to be convinced by reason that this coercion is in conformity with right, lest he fall in contradiction with himself. (*AA* 8: 305)

Hobbes's principle of obedience has to be matched by a respect of the independence of each subject whose conformity with law has to be gained through persuasion and reason. Without such respect for freedom people would inevitably voice their dissatisfaction with the government secretly from closed societies, which itself would pose a threat to political order. Kant sees such open scholarly discussion as providing an indispensable aid to good government: "how else, again, could the government get the knowledge it requires for its own essential purpose" (*AA* 8: 305/303). Kant takes seriously Hobbes's view that the laws of the sovereign must always be obeyed, but for Kant this does not mean that the subject has always to agree with the views of the government on matters of public order. Kant holds that Hobbes's "mechanism of the state" indeed must have the last word but that last word has to be gained through listening to the engaged debate of law-abiding subjects.

Hobbes presents as the aim of the sovereign "the procuration of the safety of the people" (2012, 520; 1651, 175). Hobbes deploys the Latin phrase, *salus populi*, drawn from Cicero to describe the sovereign's main object of concern.[3] This is not an aim that is voluntarily chosen by the sovereign. It is an obligation, a law of nature for which the sovereign must answer always to God. Safety here is not to be narrowly understood as merely an obligation to preserve the life of the people, "but also other contentments of life which every man by lawful industry, without danger, or hurt to the commonwealth, should acquire to himself" (Hobbes 2012, 520; 1651, 175). We are all naturally drawn to our own happiness and the sovereign must fully provide for that "contained in public instruction, both of doctrine, and example; and in the making and the executing of good laws, to which individual persons may apply their cases" (Hobbes 2012, 520; 1651, 175). Kant concurs with Hobbes to an extent but not fully so, since Kant believes that the idea of state right cannot rest wholly on the idea of the well-being of the people. For "if one looks to the people's welfare, no theory at all is really valid" (8: 306, 304) because what brings happiness to human individuals is always different from one individual to the next. Our well-being can vary with the times, with taste, and with fashion. If state right is to mean anything it has to be "based on a priori principles (for experience cannot teach what is right)" (8: 306).

29.2 *Leviathan* and the Power of Analogy

The senses are a far more important touchstone for human behavior in Hobbes than they are with Kant. Hobbes in depicting his picture of the organization of human society that he most prefers has before him the human individual as a thinking being but also as a sensuous, natural being. Like Hobbes, Kant was strongly influenced by the rise of natural sciences as disciplines in the approach he took to philosophy. Kant strongly admired the precision and success of natural science and mathematics and took them as a model at which to aim in achieving philosophical rigor. But as with Hobbes, Kant did not translate the methods of those disciplines wholesale and unchanged into his philosophical writings. For Kant the conditions of those endeavors contrasted starkly with that of metaphysical subjects. Kant's *Critique of Pure Reason* was directed at the lack of cohesion of previous metaphysics. He believed that any impartial observer would regard the condition of metaphysics in the eighteenth century as resembling a battleground rather than a flourishing activity. The reputation of metaphysics was decidedly poor because of the number of seemingly unresolved disputes and the number of rival parties engaged in the discipline. Kant greatly laments this condition of disorder and in outlining what he himself thinks should be done about it in the section on "the discipline of pure reason" in the *Critique of Pure Reason* it is perhaps not surprising that he has recourse to Hobbes's political theory in expressing his views.

Kant sees himself as introducing "the critique of pure reason as the true court of justice for all controversies of pure reason" (A751/B779; 649). This critique is "set the task of determining and judging what is lawful in reason in general in accordance with the principles of its primary institution" (A751/B779; 649). Kant holds that there are limits to the use of pure reason, which had not properly been observed in previous metaphysics. And this lack of regard for the limits of reason accounted for many of its failures demonstrated most clearly in the factionalism that bedeviled philosophical enquiry. Those who practiced philosophy were far too ambitious in their aims. They all appeared to take the view that they had discovered the ultimate nature of reality and displayed it in such a way that was irrefutable. Because of this excess of ambition "reason is as it were in the state of nature, and it cannot make its assertions and claims valid or secure then except through war" (A751/B779; 649). Kant is hoping to make peace break out among the various adversaries. This peace should have a constitutional status "whose authority no one can doubt" (A751/B779; 649). Kant thinks that this would represent a big step forward for philosophy, bringing quarrel to an end in a manner that would lead not to "victory" for one side or another, but analogous to a state of law it would represent a "verdict" recognized and accepted by all the participants (A752/B780). Kant seeks a permanent peace in philosophy so that its enquiries might be carried out more calmly and more fruitfully for all concerned. Through his critical philosophy Kant hopes to bring to an end "the endless controversies of a merely dogmatic reason" (A752/B780). Significantly, he sees this as analogous to Hobbes's step of moving from the state of nature to civil society in his political philosophy.

> Just as Hobbes asserted, the state of nature is a state of injustice and violence, and one must necessarily leave it in order to submit himself to the lawful coercion which alone limits our freedom in such a way that it can be consistent with the freedom of everyone else and thereby with the common good. (A752/B780; 650)

Hobbes's depiction of the state as Leviathan has immense philosophical significance for Kant, so much so that it enters as an emblem of what he believes he has achieved in the *Critique of Pure Reason*. Not only does it provide an analogy that permits Kant to express most fully the purpose of the *Critique* but also symbolizes the systematic, undisputed, and fully recognized nature of knowledge at which he aims. The outcome of the painstaking, careful, and verifiable labor of philosophers should be recognized by all as legitimate. Philosophers in their turn should always be open to criticism, and older, previously accepted ideas, should only be removed when it has been fully established that they can be improved upon. The outcome should not be seen as merely the outcome of rhetorical debates but as sincere investigations that can be accepted in a verdict to which all can accede.

But recognizing the strength of Hobbes's analógy of the state as a Leviathan does not lead Kant to accept as a consequence the whole of Hobbes's account of the state and its origin. He entirely agrees with Hobbes that the irresistible power of the state in carrying out the rule of law introduces freedom for the first time to a society and "in such a way that it can be consistent with the freedom of everyone else" (A752/B780). However, for Kant this freedom has to go further than the freedom Hobbes grants. It has to be more than a freedom simply to do what the sovereign does not forbid. There has also to be room for the subject to enjoy a freedom to play a part in the shaping of the laws and the policies pursued. There has to be a counterpart to the unquestioned political authority of the state that Hobbes envisages as a Leviathan. As Kant sees it, "to this freedom there belongs also the freedom to exhibit the thought and doubts which one cannot resolve oneself for public judgement without thereupon being decried as a malcontent and dangerous citizen" (A752/B780). Subjects have to be permitted the freedom of enquiry and expression by rulers.

This view is, as we have seen, at the heart of the criticism that Kant makes of Hobbes in the article on "Theory and Practice." Kant has no place for the censorship of political and (public) religious views in his political philosophy. Kant thinks that open, public discussion must play a vital part in improving and maintaining the security of a society. Hobbes believes public debate has to be severely curtailed in the public interest. He presents in chapter 18 of *Leviathan* an account "Of the rights of sovereigns by institution representative" a list of the powers of the sovereign and includes as the sixth the right "to be the judge of what opinions and doctrines are averse, and what conducing to peace; and consequently, on what occasions, how far, and what, men are to be trusted withal, in speaking to multitudes of people, and who shall examine the doctrines of all books before they be published" (Hobbes 2012, 272; 1651, 91). Hobbes acknowledges that there may be some difficulty in judging what is disruptive peace, especially where "by negligence, or unskilfulness of governors, and teachers, false doctrines are by time generally received" (Hobbes 2012, 272; 1651, 91), however Hobbes still thinks it a matter for the sovereign to decide when the contrary truth should be heard. The goal of Hobbes's censorship is not primarily that only what is true is taught and publicized, rather the highest priority is that the sovereign should judge "to prevent discord and civil war" (Hobbes 2012, 272; 1651, 91). From Kant's perspective, Hobbes here is conveniently ruling out how significant questions about the nature of truth, the way in which it might be derived, and how public discourse is pursued should be resolved. In matters of public policy, for Kant everyone is entitled to express their views in learned journals and books, addressing the public with a view to everyone's enlightenment. The object of such discussion is not to decide what is public policy but to provide the information and knowledge with which those who hold sovereign authority can determine the best policy (Williams 2003, 228).

29.3 The Power of Psychology: Hobbes's Method

The focus of Hobbes's political philosophy is man. Hobbes believes that this takes him to the root of the subject of the moral sciences. He sets as his task in *Leviathan* "to describe the nature of this artificial man" government. To do this he proposes looking at the "artificer" and the "matter thereof," both of "which is man" (Hobbes 2012, 18; 1651, 2). In discovering what man is, Hobbes believes he has the best chance of prescribing how behavior is to be regulated. To understand man, Hobbes argues in the "Introduction" "that wisdom is acquired, not by reading of books, but of men" (Hobbes 2012, 18; 1651, 2). We have to observe people around us and elsewhere. But this observation of our fellow humans should be done in a critical manner, since following common assumptions and gossip in society may lead only to the most uncharitable of conclusions. To be successful this observation must begin with ourselves and focus throughout on a comparison of our own predispositions and responses with those of others. To "learn truly to read one another" the best prescription is to "read thyself" (Hobbes 2012, 18; 1651, 2). Since we are all similar in our opinions, hopes, and fears we can therefore "read and know, what are the thoughts of, and passions of all other men" (Hobbes 2012, 18; 1651, 2). Admittedly we are all different in the objects of our passions, which are affected by our particular "constitutions" and our "particular education" so we can only truly learn the purposes of others by "searching hearts" (Hobbes 2012, 18; 1651, 2). The only key we have to "decipher the hearts of others" is to compare their "actions" and "designs" with our own. This is an extraordinarily difficult task for political philosophy. But "he that is to govern a whole nation, must read in himself, not this or that particular man; but mankind: which thought it be hard to do, harder than to learn any language, or science" (Hobbes 2012, 20; 1651, 2). Hobbes however believes that he can rise to the challenge so much so that after his own "reading orderly, and perspicuously, the pain left to another, will be only to consider, if he also find not also the same in himself" (Hobbes 2012, 20; 1651, 2). In keeping with his own reflective method, Hobbes recommends that his own careful attempt at understanding should not be simply taken at face value but should be considered alongside the reader's own evaluation. He draws the stark conclusion that in political philosophy there is not alternative to this comparative psychological self-examination: "For this kind of doctrine admitteth no other demonstration" (Hobbes 2012, 20; 1651, 2).

This is the kind of observation of others and the observation of ourselves in our social interactions and our intentions that we are nowadays used to calling psychology. This is not a term that Hobbes much deploys; however, it is a term that Kant refers to often in his philosophy, but not generally in very favorable terms. As will be discussed, his broad concern is that psychology cannot in the end provide us with fully reliable knowledge. Thus, despite his deep respect for Hobbes's writings, Kant's assessment of the cognitive value of psychology represents a major sticking point in his reception. For Kant observation of the human being in its various behaviors and contexts, and equally our observation of our own dispositions and responses in acting cannot provide a reliable starting point for moral and political philosophy. Of course, they cannot be entirely discarded in considering our nature and the consequences of our actions, but they should not wholly set the framework for moral and political conduct. Thus, a central aim of Kant's political philosophy is – while respecting Hobbes's achievement – to move on from it.

One of the key lessons of the *Critique of Pure Reason* is that psychology is an unreliable discipline in seeking to discover systematic (coherent) principles on which to ground knowledge and morality (Altman 2017, 567–91). Kant divides psychology into rational psychology and empirical psychology. Rational psychology deals with the doctrine of the soul and it is given the closest attention by Kant in his discussion of the paralogisms (A341–2/B399–400; 411–12). There are important lessons to be learned from rational psychology, but they are not at all what the previous proponents of the doctrine believed them to be. Indeed, Kant believes that rational psychology unavoidably leads to a dialectical illusion that

> rests on the confusion of an idea of reason (of a pure intelligence) with the concept, in every way indeterminate of a thinking being in general. I think of myself, in behalf of a possible experience, by abstracting from all actual experience, and from this conclude that I could become conscious of my existence even outside experience and its empirical conditions. (B426–7)

Thus, for Kant we can conclude from rational psychology neither that the soul persists eternally nor that it subsists independently of the body. Indeed, the rational psychology of previous metaphysicians relied upon importing too readily into empirical psychology inferences that had significance only from a reflective transcendental point of view. We need to presuppose from a transcendental standpoint that our experience is drawn together into one thinking subject. But for Kant this thinking self is not necessarily experientially accessible to us. It is indeed a precondition for our experience but it is an intellectual precondition and not an empirical one.

> That the I of apperception, consequently in every thought, is a single thing that cannot be resolved into a plurality of subjects, and hence a logically simple subject lies already in the concept of thinking, and is consequently an analytic proposition; but that does not signify that the thinking I is a simple substance, which would be a synthetic proposition. (B407–8; 446)

Empirical psychology deals with our own immediate perception of ourselves through our senses and our understanding. In Kant's view "empirical psychology must" be "entirely banned from metaphysics, and is already excluded by the idea of it." By this Kant means that empirical psychology cannot be relied upon to supply any *a priori* principles of cognition, rather it has always to be combined with such principles to provide any knowledge whatsoever. For Kant empirical psychology can play a part only "on the side of applied psychology" (A848/B877; 700). What we observe about human beings and their thinking cannot then for Kant form a basis for consistent reasoning about the kind of knowledge we may gain, the kind of action we may be involved in, and the kind of expectations we should form of ourselves and the human species as a whole.

This is a very powerful conclusion to draw and one that has many important implications for how political philosophy might proceed. We cannot, first, look to psychology to provide us with dependable generalizations upon which to build a political theory. Quite clearly Kant's critical system rules out the approach adopted by those political philosophers such as Hobbes and Locke who begin their enquiries by precisely determining the nature of the human individual. Niccolo Machiavelli argues in a similar vein from his direct experience of politics in the Italian peninsula in the fifteenth century.[4] From Kant's perspective no such precise determination is possible simply by observing our own inner experience and the experiences of other human individuals, even if this is the experience of the human species as a whole. The nature of the human individual cannot be prescribed from what we discern of our own inner lives and the lives of others we observe. Secondly, if psychology is to be deployed in political philosophy, it can only be so after the main principles have been set out from the standpoint of human reason. The nature we observe and so also the human society we apprehend are from a Kantian perspective already the products of the structuring process of the mind, the "I think" or the "unity of apperception." To construct a political philosophy, we must step out of the theoretical mode of philosophy into the sphere of practice (moral philosophy). The *a priori* principles of political philosophy must be drawn from pure moral theory. Now this moral theory of politics cannot at all disregard the results of the enquiries of those who engage in empirical psychology, nor in the observation of the human species in general. In seeking to put into effect the requirements that practical reason places upon us as legal and political beings we have to consider what is already (albeit incompletely) known of human individuals and society.

Kant's doctrine of right and his political philosophy do not give precedence to the observation of human experience as the basis for his theory and recommendations. Practical philosophy, of which political philosophy is a part, has to begin from our own reasoning processes in deliberating upon action and our knowledge of others and the world. From Kant's critical idealist perspective, observation is itself as subject to rules that are brought to it from our cognitive process as it is to by what we may provide the initial stimulus to our senses. Political philosophy has to begin from our freedom and the capacity for reason which underlies it.

Hobbes is not so self-reflective about the observational process. He starts from a high opinion of science, and he believes that those who have inquired about government have shown too little respect for it.

> Science is the knowledge of consequences, and dependence of one fact upon another: by which, out of that we can presently do, we know how to do something else when we will, or the like, another time: because when we see how anything comes about, upon what causes, and by what manner; when the like causes come into our power, we see how to make it produce the like effects. (Hobbes 2012, 72; 1651, 21)

He deploys this consequentialist method, drawn from his observation of science in observing the human being and in recommending those policies that are best to deploy in governing them. Hobbes thinks we need to be strict empiricists who work in a consistent way on the evidence provided by our senses and understanding. Based upon his systematic enquiries he believes human action can be seen as similar to animal motion. "There be in animals, two sort of motions peculiar to them" one called vital "begun in generation and continued without interruption through their whole life; such as the course of the blood, the pulse, the breathing" and secondly "animal motion, otherwise called voluntary motion; as to go, to speak, to move any of our limbs, in such manner fancied by our minds" (Hobbes 2012, 78; 1651, 21). Like all other animals we are conditioned to respond to our circumstances and respond in a manner that enables our preservation. But we can also attest that we have mental powers, imagination in particular, that can affect our motion. The imagination recalls what our senses have imparted to us in the past and prompts us to motion. Human beings, like all other beings, are conditioned by a process that effects all other beings, namely, endeavor: "these small beginnings of motion, within the body of man, before they appear in walking, speaking, striking, and other visible actions, are commonly called endeavour" (Hobbes 2012, 78; 1651, 23).

Appetites or desires arise in us. Some appetites are born with us such "as appetite for food, appetite of excretion" and aversions (Hobbes 2012, 80; 1651, 24). And "the rest, which are appetites for particular things" come from experience "and trial effects upon" us or "other men" (Hobbes 2012, 80; 1651, 23). Desires are ever changing "because the constitution of a man's body is in in continual mutation" (Hobbes 2012, 80; 1651, 24) and not always shared. It is not possible to say that we share absolutely the same desire as another. We are as much subject to our desires as we are the masters of them. "Pleasure therefore, (or delight) is the appearance of a sense of good." All desire, 'appetite,' and 'love' is "accompanied with some delight more or less" (Hobbes 2012, 82; 1651, 25). They are brought about by a chain of causes for which the individual is the facilitator rather the full point of origin. We may conceive ourselves as deliberators in this process, but it is for Hobbes a restricted process as the choice is already determined. Deliberation is really "the last appetite, or aversion, immediately adhering to the action" (Hobbes 2012, 92; 1651, 28). This capacity for deliberation Hobbes considers we share with all other animals. We call the last act of deliberation willing and see it as exercised by our wills, but ultimately it can be seen always as the outcome of the many transient appetites that affect us.

Kant has an entirely different approach to human desire and action. He sees it as being brought about by the human will which, though affected by our senses and inclinations, nonetheless is able to deliberate independently. For Kant we know we are able to play a part in shaping our desires, since they are the product of our intelligence and imagination, rather than seeing our desires as controlling us, we can seek to control them. Kant makes a distinction between the negative and positive concept of freedom. This distinction cuts entirely against Hobbes's view of motion and desire in the human being. "Freedom of choice is this independence from being determined by sensible impulses; this is the negative concept of freedom. The positive concept of freedom is that of the ability of pure reason itself to be practical" (6: 213, 374). There is a sharp difference between Kant and Hobbes on this point. For Hobbes our appetites or desires mold us as active human beings. Our desires cause us to act from the stimulation of our imagination, which leads to animal motion. What distinguishes human action for Hobbes is that it is a product of endeavor that has its roots in the invisible capacity we have to envisage ourselves in new situations. This is a sensuous process to which the intellect contributes but does not wholly shape. With Hobbes reason is generally subject to appetite and desire. He does not grant reason the independence that is such a special feature of Kant's philosophy. Desire cannot of course be neglected if we are to express our freedom, but with Kant desire has to be led by reason and not command it. Kant has an active manner of conceiving desire rather than a merely reactive one: "the faculty of desire is the faculty to be, by means of one's representations, the cause of the objects of those representations" (MM 6: 211, 373). We do not live at the behest of our desires. We consciously shape them through our understanding and interpretation of our experience. As Katrin Flikschuh puts it:

> Kant does not entertain Hobbes' physiological conception of desiring as externally stimulated and internally transmitted vital motions which 'in pressing upon the brain and heart' etc. eventually issue in outward bodily movement. Kant does not think of agents as subject to the causality of their desires. Instead he regards human agents as "the causes of their

desires; at any rate they have the capacity to be the causes of their desires." (Flikschuh 2000, 100)

As Kant sees it, we are the instigators of our desires. It is laziness and cowardice, according to Kant, to suggest that we have no ability to shape them. Phrases like "I just had to have an ice cream" or "I need that new car" may easily trip of the tongue, but from Kant's perspective they are simply fictions that disguise our inability to take proper advantage of our freedom. Pleasure can indeed come before a desire and lead to our being animated to want something, but this wanting, if it is properly to become a human desire, has to be affirmed by our understanding and reason. Objects of desire can be of two kinds for Kant. Where the pleasure precedes the desire, "the practical pleasure must be called an interest of inclination"; where the pleasure follows on a prior "determination of the faculty of desire it is an intellectual pleasure, and the interest in the object can be called an interest of reason" (MM 6: 212). Human beings are capable of embracing both kinds of desire, but they enhance their humanity when they seek only to fulfil those desires that follow an interest of reason. Allowing our choice to be determined by our inclination would lead us only to exercising animal choice. The pleasures of our inclination would be shaping us rather than our personalities shaping our pleasures. In contrast to such animal choice "only that choice which can be determined by pure reason is called a free choice" (*AA* 6: 213).

From the standpoint of practical philosophy, as Kant sees it, we can be seen as producing our desires. An object of desire is not just a product of how our senses strike us, but is rather one that has already been transformed by our cognitive and aesthetic faculties into an object. Desire always presents a challenge to us. Kant believes from a legal and political perspective that we have to be permitted to seek to realize those desires that we have chosen ourselves. Thus, within a civil society we may even seek pleasures that reflect our inclinations only, so long as they do not hamper others in the pursuit of their freedom. However, from the ethical perspective of the moral law, which requires us to see ourselves and others not simply as means but always also as ends, we should act only upon those desires that are also affirmed by pure reason.

29.4 Conclusion

The evidence we have looked at suggests that Kant took very seriously Hobbes's political philosophy and the general metaphysical outlook that Hobbes advocated. From the metaphysical standpoint Kant appears to have grouped Hobbes together with the empiricist philosophers who stood opposed to the rationalist tradition from which Kant himself emerged. In the narrower terms of political philosophy, Kant regards Hobbes as a unique and stimulating thinker whose views need close consideration and, for Kant himself, powerful criticism. Hobbes and Kant have very different views on what philosophy can achieve. Hobbes holds that there can be a scientific philosophical approach that unites the realm of nature and society, natural science and political philosophy. The human being can be seen for Hobbes as an integral part of the natural order originally ordained by God. The laws that govern the natural order (motion) are also the laws of the human order. Kant differentiates, in contrast, between the realm of natural science and the human world. Some aspects of the study of natural science can be carried over into political philosophy, however with Kant humans can seek to achieve genuine voluntary action, so there is the opportunity (which can never be wholly proved) for us to shape the natural world and the social world. Political philosophy for Kant belongs to practical philosophy, which has as an unavoidable assumption the potential for human freedom. Kant is a philosopher of human emancipation whereas Hobbes is a philosopher for the reconciliation of human existence with a natural order regulated by fear, channeled positively by the laws of nature he has discovered.

Kant's objection to Hobbes's political theory in the article "Theory and Practice" is not merely the explicit one of rejecting Hobbes's power of censorship given to the ruler. The most philosophically significant objection Kant raises is distilled in the three major requirements he presents for an acceptable polity for its subjects: freedom, equality, and independence. These three principles lead in an entirely different direction from Hobbes's *Leviathan*. Equality for Kant only comes into existence where the conditions for freedom (set out in a social contract) are properly realized. Freedom requires the possibility of reciprocal coercion, enforced by a representative ruler or rulers. Equality for Kant is brought about not in the natural condition as with Hobbes but in a society regulated by law where no privilege is permitted that allows individuals to act above the law. Kant's principle of independence, though admittedly granted only to a minority of males, takes us well beyond the aspirations of Hobbes's theory of government. The independent citizens participate in the formation of governments through elections for the executive and legislature, and so can regard themselves as the indirect authors of the laws they have to observe. Kant's notion of independence (which all subjects should regard as the ideal) combines freedom with the responsibility of legislation, and an executive chosen by the citizens.

Notes

1 "Since knowledge is unified, ultimately, political philosophy rests on correct physics, which Hobbes tries to give in *De corpore*" (Martinich 1995, 233).

2 For Hobbes's contempt for the "schoolmen," see *Leviathan* 8.27 (2012, 122; 1651, 39) and *Leviathan* 12.31 (2012, 184; 1651, 59).

3 Kant makes a similar reference to the idea of the "safety of the people" in the "Doctrine of Right." The phrase he deploys however slightly misquotes Cicero. Whereas Cicero speaks of the safety of the people being the supreme law (*Salus populi suprema lex esto*) Kant cites the phrase as (*salus rei publicae suprema lex est*). This is to underline the point that "by the well being of a state is understood ... the condition in which its constitution conforms most fully to principles of right; it is that condition which reason, by a categorical imperative, makes it obligatory for us to strive after (*AA* 6, 318)." See also Williams (1983, 194–5).

4 See Williams (1992, 49–50).

References

References to Kant's works are made to: 1900 onward. *Gesammelte Schriften Akademieausgabe* Berlin: Prussian (later German) Academy Edition. Berlin. *AA* and volume number in the text. References to the *Critique of Pure Reason* are to the first (A) and second editions (B).

Altman, Mathew. 2017. *The Palgrave Kant Handbook*. London: Palgrave Macmillan.

Flikschuh, Katrin. 2000. *Kant and Modern Political Philosophy*. Cambridge: Cambridge University Press.

Hobbes, Thomas. 2012. *Leviathan*, 3 vols., edited by Noel Malcolm. Oxford: Clarendon Press. [First published 1651.]

Martinich, Aloysius P. 1995. *A Hobbes Dictionary*. Oxford: Blackwell.

Martinich, Aloysius P. 1999. *Hobbes: A Biography*. Cambridge: Cambridge University Press.

Williams, Howard. 1983. *Kant's Political Philosophy*. Oxford: Blackwell.

Williams, Howard. 1992. *International Relations in Political Theory*. Buckingham: Open University Press.

Williams, Howard. 2003. *Kant's Critique of Hobbes*. Cardiff: University of Wales Press.

30

Catharine Macaulay and the Reception of Hobbes During the Eighteenth Century

KAREN GREEN

There is a surprising disconnect between the central place that Hobbes's works now occupy in the presumed history of democratic republicanism and the fortunes of those same works during the period that led up to the American and French revolutions. For, although democratic republicanism is grounded in social contract theory, and modern accounts of the history of social contract theory characteristically begin with Hobbes, and in particular, *Leviathan*, his philosophy was very little discussed in Great Britain during the eighteenth century. As David Hume observed, while Hobbes had been celebrated during the seventeenth century, in the eighteenth he was "much neglected" (Hume 1757, 126). Even during the seventeenth century Hobbes's philosophy had been more often rebutted than celebrated, while during the eighteenth century almost every reference to his political views was negative. One of the few writers to engage directly with his political philosophy was Catharine Macaulay, whose highly critical *Loose Remarks on certain positions to be found in Mr. Hobbes's Philosophical rudiments of government and society* appeared in 1767 and was reissued with a letter from Benjamin Rush in 1769 (Macaulay 1767). As an influential republican historian, Macaulay was at the center of radical opinion in England, corresponded with important political players in the lead up to the American Declaration of Independence, and was fêted by friends in France, in particular Jacques-Pierre Brissot de Warville, who encouraged Mirabeau to take up the task of translating her *History of England* into French (Macaulay 1763–1783, 1791–1792).[1] Her critical reception of Hobbes's philosophy should remind us that the historical genesis of contemporary liberal, democratic institutions was rather different from that often assumed. Radical critics of liberal democracy, from C.B. Macpherson to Carole Pateman have represented it as grounded in Hobbesian psychological egoism, possessive individualism, and rational self-interest (Green 2012; Macpherson 1962; Pateman 1991). Macaulay, by contrast, looked forward to a democratic commonwealth, in which the common good would be the common care, and based her advocacy of democratic institutions in natural law, rational religion, Christian

A Companion to Hobbes, First Edition. Edited by Marcus P. Adams.

eudaimonism, and rational altruism (Green 2018; Withey 1976). Nevertheless, I suggest that subsequent philosophical developments, which eroded religious belief and promoted secularism, help explain how it was possible for Hobbes to take on the central philosophical position that he currently occupies, despite his political writings having had almost nothing to do with the actual process that resulted in the democratic revolutions of the late eighteenth and nineteenth centuries.

In the first section I look at the broader reception of Hobbes during the eighteenth century, and the background to Macaulay's critique. In the next, I offer an account of that critique. In conclusion I show how Macaulay's critique of Hobbes in fact tends to result in a way of reading him that has become standard for contemporary social contract theory. The standard reading that I have in mind goes something like this. In 1651 Hobbes argued that legitimate government "is founded on an agreement or a social contract made by individuals who are endowed with natural rights," John Locke and Jean-Jacques Rousseau "like Hobbes before them ... imagine human beings in a state of nature, an original condition which is prior to and outside of government" (Taylor 2019, 36). This reading minimizes the conflict between Locke's political philosophy and Hobbes's, thus suggesting that, since Locke's political philosophy was influential, Hobbes was also a significant figure in the genesis of liberal democracy. Already in the eighteenth century, there were readings of Locke that might be interpreted along these lines; Hume, for instance, mentions Hobbes and Locke in the same breath as maintaining "the selfish system" (Hume 1751, 13). But turning back to more radical eighteenth-century writers than did Hume reveals a quite different situation. The promoters of democratic republicanism during the eighteenth century rightly regarded Hobbes as their ideological enemy. Although they followed Locke, they rejected Hobbes. Nevertheless, aspects of Macaulay's refutation and rejection of Hobbes's views suggest why it has been easy for the standard account to prosper during the twentieth century.

30.1 Hobbes in the Eighteenth Century

Very few editions of Hobbes's political works or discussions of his philosophy appeared in English between 1700 and 1800. An edition of his collected political works was published in 1750, which included biographies, but it cannot have met with great success, since there was a single edition and few exemplars survive (Hobbes 1750). His translation of Thucydides was reissued in 1723, and *A true ecclesiastical history* in 1722. Apart from these, Hobbes appears to have been an almost forgotten author, whose works were not worthy of republication, so that, when she came to refute him, Macaulay relied on a reprinting of the 1651 English translation of the Latin *De cive* (1642) published with the title *Philosophical rudiments concerning government and society* and given the false date of 1751 (Gunther-Canada 2006; Hobbes 1651). Although references to the "atheistical Hobbes" are scattered throughout her works, she does not mention *Leviathan* either in this early refutation or anywhere else in her published works, perhaps because it is not so clearly a defense of monarchy, or possibly because she did not have access to it. While Hobbes's own works were generally neglected, one major discussion and refutation of Hobbes's views was translated three times during the century, indicating the generally negative attitude that then prevailed. This was Richard Cumberland's *De legibus naturae disquisition philosophica*, which had originally appeared in 1671. In 1727 a translation by John Maxwell was published, with the title, *A Treatise of the Laws of Nature*, while a later translation, heavily footnoted and called *A Philosophical Enquiry* was the work of John Towers, and came out in 1750, the same year as the edition of Hobbes's works (Cumberland 1727, 1750). Cumberland's Latin treatise had also provided the basis of James Tyrrell's *A Brief Disquisition of the Law of Nature*, this earlier translation, adaptation, and abridgement of Cumberland's work was undoubtedly known to Locke, who counted Tyrrell among his friends (Locke 1954, 9–10; Tyrrell 1701). Since, despite his friend Tyrrell's urging, Locke chose not to publish his own early *Essays on the Law of Nature* it is difficult to determine to what extent he would, later in life, have disagreed with Cumberland's views, though elements of the *Essay Concerning Human Understanding* imply that his view of human nature was more jaundiced than Cumberland's. For Cumberland, "the object of the will is Good," but at least by the time he came to revise the *Essay* for a second edition, Locke had come to emphasize the role of "uneasiness" in the determination of the will, rather than desire for the good (Locke II.xxi.31–41, 250–8; Cumberland 1727, 45; 1750, 20; Darwall 1995, 158). Nevertheless, both authors claim that moral principles are as demonstrable as those of mathematics, while rejecting Platonist theories of innate knowledge, so their positions are, in this respect, similar (Beiser 1996, 271 n. 9; Cumberland 1750, xvi; Locke 1975, IV.iii.18, 549, IV.iv.7, 565). Cumberland asserts:

> By Laws of Nature, we understand some Propositions of unchangeable Truth and Certainty, which are to direct and govern the voluntary Motions of rational free Agents, in the Election of Good, and in the avoiding of Evil: Which Laws lay Obligations upon all outward acts of Behaviour, even in a State of Nature, prior and antecedent to all Laws of human Imposition whatever. (Cumberland 1750, 2–3; 1727, 39)

Locke agrees that the state of nature has a law of nature to govern it and identifies the law of nature with a law of reason (Locke 1988, II.2.6, 270–1).

Locke was in turn a major influence on Macaulay, and she endorses his desire to see "the fixing moral truths on such grounds of apparent certainty, as shall render them capable of as clear a demonstration as mathematical problems" but she is rather ecumenical in relation to the nature of our capacity to carry out such demonstrations (Macaulay 1767, 9; 1783, 17, 30–2). Her acquaintance, Richard Price, had argued that, in order for there to be knowledge of immutable moral truths residing in the natures of things, it was necessary to reject Locke's epistemology and to reintroduce innate knowledge of universals. His ethical rationalism turned back from Locke toward that of the earlier Cambridge Platonists (Beiser 1996, 266–7; Price 1758).

For Macaulay, the mechanisms whereby we can come to know the immutable moral truths are less important than their existence and knowability. Nevertheless, she believes that our flourishing as progressive beings depends on the discovery of and adherence to such moral principles, which cannot be reduced to rational self-interest, narrowly conceived, and which oblige quite independently of actual positive law, which must be subject to the tribunal of the immutable moral principles. Although not published until many years after her critique of Hobbes, her *Treatise on the Immutability of Moral Truth* shows that she believed that God has created us with free will so that by struggling with our passions and increasing our understanding we can collectively attain perfection and come to live in accord with his moral law (Macaulay 1783; Withey 1976). In her *Loose Remarks* she criticizes, from the perspective of natural law, those cultures that have accepted the exposure of infants and elsewhere she objects to the treatment of women in China and other polygamous societies from the same perspective (Macaulay 1783, 155–8). Given the perfectionism that lies behind her reformist aspirations, it is important that there exists an ethical standard independent of established custom, for, as she remarks to Hume, were there no such standard, all attempts at significant political reform would, "involve all reformers in unavoidable guilt" (Green 2019, 39).

Cumberland's fundamental statement of the law of nature is that "the fullest, most vigorous Endeavour, of each and all rational Agents, in promoting the Common Good of the whole rational System, contributes effectually to the Good of every single Part in such a System" (Cumberland 1750, xxvi). This results in the universal precept,

> That the greatest Benevolence, of each and every one individual Agent in the rational System, fully exercised and exerted towards all, essentially forms the happiest State which each (single Person or Individual) from his own free Capacities and Powers is capable of: which (Benevolence) is moreover, the only Method or means indispensably necessary, towards effectually promoting the happiest State, which each can possibly enjoy. (Cumberland 1750, 9)

He sets out to prove this precept on the basis of the nature of things, including the fact that humans "are so weak and insignificant as to want many Helps, many Assistances of many Agents, necessary to the Enjoyment of an happy Life" (Cumberland 1750, 64). One might wonder whether this principle can be true, since in aiding one's friends one may disadvantage, or at least not offer help to, others who are in need. Cumberland rejects the suggestion that there really is any such conflict. For he claims that there is no better method for bringing about both universal benevolence and private friendship than that

> everyone really and in fact shall show himself affected towards all, just in the same Way that he himself could wish all to appear and really to be affected towards himself; that is, with an Universal Benevolence upon all proper Occasions and Opportunities exerted towards all; but with a more intense, though not contrary Propensity, when exerted towards a few select Persons, chosen as Friends. (Cumberland 1750, 48)

This attitude may seem optimistic, yet it does seem plausible that, were everybody to actually act benevolently toward all, this would bring about the greatest possible happiness. The real-life problem for humans lies in the difficulty of trusting others to act benevolently. Were we able to trust everybody to act as benevolently, in the circumstances in which they find themselves, as we would like others to act towards us, in like circumstances, this would, surely, result in the greatest possible happiness. So, Cumberland, like Macaulay, is committed to the rationality of benevolence or altruism, and although she does not explicitly mention him (so far as I can determine) they share a commitment to the promotion of universal benevolence and the rationality of altruism.

Unsurprisingly, since he was Bishop of Peterborough, Cumberland unashamedly bases his demonstration of the truth of the law of nature, as he understands it, on the demonstrability of the existence of a God, who is the first cause, and who has made us in his image (Cumberland 1750, xxvii). Part of his critique of Hobbes turns on the widespread accusation of atheism, and more generally inconsistency, for Hobbes both claims to accept that God exists, but also claims that there are no non-corporeal substances, which, since Cumberland does not allow that materialist pantheism could be anything but atheism, implies that there is no God. Cumberland refers to passages where Hobbes seems to allow that God is the first cause yet, "we find many Passages, wherein he both contradicts the being of God, proved from these Principles, and also, the Divine Authority of natural Laws established upon the very same Foundation" (Cumberland 1750, 32). According to Cumberland, we can discover the truth of the laws of nature by examining natural causal regularities, and we can see that these are laws that oblige, by recognizing that they are established by divine authority. He accuses Hobbes of inconsistency, attempting to prove, for instance, the incoherence of Hobbes's claim that in the state of nature everybody has a right to anything they desire, and arguing, by contrast, that "reason points out the necessity of coming to a division of things" which the later translator renders, "right reason ... discovers the absolute Necessity there is for private Property" (Cumberland 1727, 81, 1750, 101).

It is not clear whether Macaulay knew Cumberland's work, and if she did so, she may well have known it through Tyrrell's adaptation, but it is evident that she shared a good deal of his outlook. The political system to which she looks forward, in which power and liberty will be equally distributed is one in which "the generous plan of universal happiness [is] adopted, and common good becomes the common care" (Macaulay 1763–1783, 5.20). In a recent article on the history of the reception of Locke's political philosophy, James Harris has argued that the contemporary tendency to read Locke's *Second Treatise* as a rebuttal of Hobbes's philosophy was not characteristic of the eighteenth-century reception of Locke, whose political tract was characteristically read as a refutation of Filmer (Harris 2020). But the works of Cumberland, Tyrrell, and the now forgotten Abraham Tucker, whose *The Light of Nature Pursued* is recommended by Macaulay, suggest that eighteenth-century defenders of limited monarchy or republicanism were well aware that social contract theorists, of a Lockean persuasion, needed to demonstrate that there is a law of nature that obliges, independently of political coercion, and that this moral law justifies the political reforms they desired (Macaulay 1790a, 135; Tucker 1768). In these works, there is either an explicit or implicit engagement with Hobbes, in so far as it is assumed to be necessary, in order to defeat his conclusions, to demonstrate the existence of a moral law that is independent of human convention. Tucker's long and tedious work, for instance, sets out to "try the strength of reason upon the subject of morality" noting that:

> many judicious persons, Mr. Locke for one, have pronounced it capable of demonstration equally with mathematics: but howmuchsoever morality may be demonstrable in its own nature the demonstration has hitherto been found impracticable, being prevented I conceive by one main obstacle Mr. Locke has pointed out, that is, because the ideas and terms belonging to it are more indistinct unsettled and variable than those of number and measure. (Tucker 1768, 1.xxxvii–xxxviii)

He hopes to remedy this situation by clarifying the abstract ideas that we are able to form on the basis of concrete experience, in order to accomplish a Lockean demonstration of the laws of morality.

Although I have not been able to demonstrate that Macaulay knew Cumberland's work, she would definitely have read Gilbert Burnet's brief condemnation of *Leviathan* in his *History of His Own Time*, for this is a work that was in her father's library and she quotes it in her own history (Burnet 1724; Green 2020, 20; Macaulay 1763–1783, 1.xiv). According to Burnet, Hobbes is a pantheist and materialist who "thought interest and fear were the chief principles of society" and who "put all morality in the following that which was our own private will or advantage" (Burnet 1724, 1.187–8). The Hobbes who claimed that "the original of all great and lasting societies consisted not in the mutual good will men had towards each other, but in the mutual fear they had of each other" is the Hobbes that Macaulay sets out to refute (EW II.6). It is out of this background that her work emerges.

30.2 Macaulay's *Loose Remarks*

Whereas Cumberland attacks Hobbes from all angles, Macaulay is content to point out a few inconsistencies and absurdities in his reasoning and to refute what is at the time the essence of the issue dividing Hobbes from reformist social contract theorists, that is, his attempt to demonstrate in *De cive* that an absolute monarchy is the best form of government. A comment in the introduction to Macaulay's *History of England from the accession of James I* implies that Hobbes's arguments had not been completely neglected by her contemporaries, for she mentions him as an authority appealed to by those wranglers, who failed to correctly understand the nature of liberty and the respective privileges of the monarch and the people (Macaulay 1763–1783, 1.xiv–xv). She thus represents him as still having some authority and so worth refuting, though it is difficult to discover which followers of Hobbes she had in mind.

First, Macaulay picks on Hobbes's account of human nature and the view that the only natural motive inducing humans to submit to the laws of society is fear of death or desire for self-preservation. He had claimed, against the contrary view that humans are social by nature, that since infants "know not what society is" they cannot enter into it and "that all men, because they are born in infancy, are born unapt for society" (Hobbes 1651, I.1, 7; EW II.2). She points out that this is like arguing that humans are not naturally bipedal, since they are not born walking. Humans are born with the capacity to learn to walk, and similarly are capable of developing reason and of appreciating the reasons there are for submitting to the laws of society. Hence, she claims, it is clear that humans are born fit for society, using against Hobbes his own demonstration of the reasonableness of accepting subjection to a power that can uphold the law. "Man," she says, "by being born with the necessary means, is born a creature apt for reason; and a creature apt for reason is a creature apt for society" (Macaulay 1767, 3). The capacity to engage in the kind of reasoning that recommends subjection to an equitable law, which protects life and property, marks us, according to Macaulay, as rational, social, creatures. Thus, she in effect turns Hobbes's own argument against him, for he recognizes that humans are born rational, in the sense of having the capacity to acquire reason, and he demonstrates that, as rational beings, we are motivated to promote peace and, towards the attainment of this end, to establish or contract with a sovereign power that can uphold the law.

Beyond this, she argues, his reasoning breaks down, for the idea that once the people have contracted with a sovereign to be governed, they "dissolve" and the sovereign becomes absolute is, she says, "a jumble." Taking "contract" as ordinarily understood, Macaulay argues that if one of the parties to a contract were to cease to exist, then the contract would be void. Strictly speaking, her reasoning here is defective, since a contract can easily be drawn up which commits a party to fulfil some obligation after the death of one or other contractor. But, in the case of the "social contract" the people who contract are assumed to be identical with the people whose peace and prosperity are to be promoted by the sovereign, and clearly if the people cease to exist once the contract is settled, there is no substance to the contract. In her response to Burke's *Reflections on the Revolution in France*, Macaulay implicitly returns to this argument. One might respond, after all, that the substance of the social contract is that the sovereign will henceforth provide the power necessary to uphold the law, including legal contracts, but the people who are protected by this law are not identical with the people who contract to give up the uncertain liberties of the state of nature, in exchange for the peace that is guaranteed by political subjection. Indeed, this is Hobbes's reasoning, for according to him, the people who contract with each other to set up a sovereign create a new political "person" that did not formerly exist (EW II.69). Although she recognizes this feature of his account, Macaulay does not engage with it but assumes that the people whose assent makes a government lawful are identical with the people then lawfully governed (Macaulay 1767, 6). So, she can counter this reasoning along the lines found in her response to Burke, where she says,

> if we say that *lawful* governments are formed on the authority of conventions, it will be asked, *who gave these conventions their authority*? If we grant that they derived their authority from the *assent of the people*, how came the people, it will be said, to exert such an authority at *one* period of society, and not at another? If we say it was *necessity* that recovered to the social man the full rights of his nature, it will be asked, *who is to be the judge* of this necessity? why *certainly* the people. (Macaulay 1790b, 94)

Following Locke, she concludes that the people always retain the right to rescind their contract with a particular sovereign, if the implicit terms of the social contract are abrogated by that sovereign, and, as Locke would say, since the sovereign is no longer constrained by law, the people and sovereign are returned to the state of nature (Locke 1988, II.7.94).

She continues her assault on Hobbes's view that sovereignty must be absolute by noting that, given the ordinary understanding of the executive and legislature it is perfectly possible to have an executive that is bound by law and not absolute (Macaulay 1767, 5–6). She then turns to his positive arguments for preferring a monarchy to a republic. She is particularly dismissive of his claim that monarchy is pre-eminent because "paternall government instituted by God himselfe in Creation, was *Monarchicall*" (Hobbes 1651, II.10.150; EW 2.129). For, she fails to see how the legitimacy of God's government of a world created by him can bestow legitimacy when people are governed by someone who had no share in their creation (Macaulay 1767, 12–13). Nor does she see how Hobbes can accuse those who resent rule by one man of also resisting government by one God, without his fallaciously placing man and God on a par. Many "who would not be in the power of a creature, as weak, and perhaps weaker than themselves" would be happy to be subjected to "the merciful unerring jurisdiction of God" (Macaulay 1767, 16–17). So, the analogy does not hold. To an extent, she may be thought to be unfair to Hobbes in bothering to respond to his "theological" reasons for preferring monarchy, since he passes over them, because they are not "based on solid reason" (Gunther-Canada 2006; Hobbes 1651, II.10, 151; EW II.129). She is on stronger ground in her response to his ineffectual attempts to argue that the injustices that have been committed by historical monarchs derived from the faults of those individuals, rather than from the nature of the institution. These are rejected as overlooking the fact that it is the institution that provides vicious individuals with the power to tyrannize over their subjects, and that well-constituted governments would be designed to prevent the exercise of such tyrannical power (Macaulay 1767, 22).

On the costs of democracy as against monarchy, Macaulay simply challenges Hobbes's facts. It is simply not true that the fact that there is only one sovereign means that there are few whose wants are to be satisfied. A monarch brings with him a "train of kindred, wives, concubines, and favorites." History shows that "the lusts of one man is sufficient to dissipate all the riches that the industry and frugality of a whole nation can collect" (Macaulay 1767, 18–19). By contrast, democracies reward their citizens "with honors of little cost, tho' peculiarly adapted to please and reward generous minds," such as crowns, statues, and other forms of accolade (Macaulay 1767, 20). Similarly, she simply disagrees with Hobbes's claim that monarchs promote more worthy people to power than do democracies, arguing that since the interests of the monarch are "to gratify his own lusts and private advantages" he will tend to employ "those villains, whose abilities are equal only to cunning, and proper only to the destruction of the commonweal" (Macaulay 1767, 21).

With regard to Hobbes's claim that "kings are only severe against those who either trouble them with reproachful words, or control their wills" so that anyone who wants to avoid such severity can simply lead a retired life, she wonders whether he is joking (Hobbes 1651, II.10, 154; EW II.133; Macaulay 1767, 24). For, she says, in this passage he exposes the difficulty that people generally face in giving advice to absolute monarchs, without being offensive, even when ignorance or stupidity makes the monarch incapable of judging well. Moreover, if retirement is the only remedy that will cure the danger that attaches to advising a monarch, the wise and prudent will avoid the danger, leaving the court open to "those desperate people, whose mad desire of raising their fortunes, or their necessities, incites them to run the hazard which attends" court stations (Macaulay 1767, 26).

To be fair to Hobbes, it should be noted that she does not consider his more astute criticisms of democratic assemblies, the difficulty there is in bringing a large group of people to agree on the best course of action, and the tendency of such groups to fall into factions. Macaulay may well have thought that she had sufficiently responded to these problems in the second part of her pamphlet, *A Short Sketch of a Democratical Form of Government, In a Letter to Signor Paoli* in which she attempts to describe a form of democratic government that places the most able and virtuous in positions of power, enhanced by mechanisms, such as rotation and an agrarian law, intended to prevent that accumulation of excess of power in private hands that might lead it astray from its end of producing legislation, as far as possible, in the interests of the people as a whole. Perhaps with Hobbes's complaints in mind, her design involves a relatively small Senate, elected from among those who have previously been representatives, the role of which is to design and debate legislation. Once the Senate has formulated laws, these are to be debated and voted on by the much larger house of representatives. Before being accepted or rejected, she suggests further, that the proposed laws should be published, so that the people can direct their representatives on how they would like them to vote. Thus, she attempts to achieve the benefits of both small, expert, group discussion, and broad popular consent.

Macaulay's *Loose Remarks* was positively reviewed in the contemporary press, and it is a mark of how low Hobbes's reputation had then sunk that one criticism that was raised was that she had bothered to refute him at all. The *Critical Review* was:

> unable, from perusing the works of Mr. Hobbes, to discern where that fund of knowledge lies, which has procured him so considerable a rank among modern philosophers. Those who are acquainted with his private history know him to have been vain and peevish, and so inconstant in his principles, that from a violent republican even to democracy, he became a monarchist even to tyranny. It is, however, justly doubted, whether this veering from one extreme to another did not proceed from venality more than inconstancy. (Anon 1767, 284–5)

The biography, which had been published in 1750, had related the charge that Hobbes had published *Leviathan* in order to curry favor with Oliver Cromwell and to secure his return to England, and it is certainly possible to read the work as providing a justification for Cromwell's dictatorship (Hobbes 1750, xvi). Burnet similarly had asserted that Hobbes had originally written his *Leviathan* "in favour of absolute monarchy, but turned it afterwards to gratify the republican party," by which he presumably meant Cromwell. Even the biography published with his collected works represents Hobbes as irascible and inclined to easily take offense, so the reviewer's belief in Hobbes's personal peevishness and political inconstancy appears to be typical of the accounts available at the time.

Unlike the eighteenth-century authors mentioned by Harris, Macaulay's attitude to the relationship between Hobbes's political philosophy and Locke's is modern. Comments in her history suggests that, like modern readers of the *Two Treatises*, she found the urge to refute Filmer, which was clearly important to Locke, to be something requiring an explanation for an audience no longer moved by monarchy's claims to divine right, for of Filmer's *Patriacha* (1680) she says:

> The whole work is a jumble of gross absurdity, false assertions, and false conclusions; and if it proves anything, it proves that every modern government is an usurpation: yet the mere attempt to ascertain a divine right to government, gave it some weight with the monarchical enthusiasts of these times, and on this reason was deemed worthy of the notice of Sidney and of Locke. (Macaulay 1763–1783, 7.475, note)

But, once the authority of government is agreed to derive from the consent of the people, not from divine right, Hobbes emerges as a potent enemy of the advocates of limited monarchy or republicanism, since while he concedes that civil government is grounded in contract, he attempts to build a defense of absolute monarchy on this ground.

At the same time, returning to Macaulay and her eighteenth-century precursors suggests that the role that Hobbes has come to play in the history of democratic republicanism, as it is currently represented, is distorted. The advocates of limited monarchy or republicanism during the eighteenth century did not base their political philosophy on Hobbes's account of human nature, but instead rejected his attempt to reduce morality to rational self-interest and denied that fear or the desire for self-preservation are the only natural human motives. Reformers, such as Macaulay, who believed that they lived in a period "enlightened with the unobstructed ray of rational learning," accepted that there is a law of nature, the truths of which are available to reason, and that this rational morality ought to constrain positive law and govern the actions of any legitimate sovereign (Macaulay 1763–1783, 4.431). Social contract theory had come to take on a character that was rather different to that found in Hobbes, by the time it was being put to use by Macaulay, to justify democratic republicanism.

One of the important inspirations for Macaulay's republicanism was John Milton, whose works were in her father's library. In his *Tenure of King's and Magistrates* (1649) he had asserted that,

> all men naturally were born free, being the image and resemblance of God himself, and were by privilege above all the creatures, born to command and not to obey: and that they lived so, till from the root of Adam's transgression, falling among themselves to do wrong and violence, and foreseeing that such courses must needs tend to the destruction of them all, they agreed by common league to bind each other from mutual injury, and jointly to defend themselves against any that gave disturbance or opposition to such agreement. Hence came cities, towns, and commonwealths. (Milton 1753, 1.344)

This was one of the works quoted by her, along with Locke's *Second Treatise*, in the passages of the fourth volume of her *History of England from the accession of James I* in which she justified the trial and execution of Charles I (Macaulay 1763–1783, 4.428–31). In one of her most memorable passages, she sums up the arguments she has extracted from Milton's *Tenure of Kings and Magistrates*, his *Defence of the People of England in Answer to Salmasius's Defence of the King*, Locke's *Second Treatise*, and Sidney's *Discourses on Government* as follows:

> The positions to be found in these arguments, that government is the ordinance of man; that, being the mere creature of human invention, it may be changed or altered according to the dictates of experience, and the better judgment of men; that it was instituted for the protection of the people, for the end of securing not overthrowing the rights of nature; that it is a trust either formally admitted or supposed; and that magistracy is consequently accountable; will meet with little contradiction in a country enlightened with the unobstructed ray of rational learning. (Macaulay 1763–1783, 4.428–31)

Since Charles I had "acted in opposition to the just ends for which government was instituted," the parliament had "by the right of self-preservation" legitimately taken steps to protect themselves from "the lawless power and enterprizes of the tyrant" (Macaulay 1763–1783, 4.433–4). For Macaulay, the significance of Hobbes is that he develops the social contract tradition, but perverts it, so that instead of supporting limited monarchy or democratic republicanism, he uses it to attempt to justify absolute monarchism. Thus, his version of the story demands refutation.

Since Macaulay's time, belief in God, in natural law, and in immutable moral truths, knowledge of which is available to reason, has been significantly eroded. These provided the background for her advocacy of inalienable natural rights, as they did for many radical reformers of her time. Once this grounding in rational religion is removed, the social contract theorist can no longer assume that humans are made in God's image, or that reason will reveal the natural moral law. Thus, it becomes tempting to read the "reason" to which Locke or Macaulay appeals as no different from the rational calculation of self-interest assumed by Hobbes. The religious grounds of social contract theory come to seem as insecure as the religious grounds of the divine right of kings. But, in fact, Hobbes's assumptions concerning human nature were directly opposed to those of the reformers, who believed that they had a moral mission to restrain the power of kings and preserve the liberties of the people. The weaknesses in the actual social contract theories that resulted in the democratic American and French revolutions would therefore seem to lie in quite other places than the theory of human nature assumed by Hobbes. This is overlooked, because he offers arguments more easily adapted to the preferences of a secular age, whatever his actual religious commitments, than do the actual republicans of the seventeenth century (Mortimer and Robertson 2012, 4).

At the same time, Macaulay's *ad hominem* attack on Hobbes also indicates how he can be assumed to provide a foundation for democratic social contract theory. She refuted his claim that humans are not social by nature by observing that he had accepted that, on the basis of mere reason, plus a desire for peace, humans can recognize the desirability of political subjection. So, one might conclude, reason alone is sufficient for sociability and the justification of equal government based on a social contract. If this conclusion could be established, one would have an appealingly secular explanation of the legitimacy and limits of political subjection. But Macaulay and her progressive friends did not really believe that the conclusion could be established on such slender grounds. They believed that reason, plus the fact that we are free moral agents made "in the image of God," implied sociability and justified equal government based on a social contract. It is doubtful whether the arguments of the religiously inspired, progressive, social contract theorists could survive the removal of their theologically grounded assumptions about human nature. Secular progressives had to hope that that they could survive, and Macaulay's *ad hominem* refutation of Hobbes's claim that we are not social by nature encourages that hope, helping to explain how Hobbes comes to be transformed into an assumed source for the development of support for liberal democracy.

30.3 Conclusion

Despite the impression that is often conveyed in textbooks and by theorists such as C.B. Macpherson and Carole Pateman, Hobbes's moral psychology was not a significant influence on the most vocal advocates of democratic republicanism during the eighteenth-century. Writers such as Catharine Macaulay, whose justification of the execution of Charles I spelled out the principles used by the Americans in their Declaration of Independence and reiterated in the French Declaration of the Rights of Man, followed Hobbes in grounding government in a social contract, but rejected his legal positivism and his 'possessive individualism' along with his absolutism. It was their belief in rational religion and a moral law whose principles were available to the "unobstructed ray of rational learning" that inspired them with the hope that democratic institutions would foster societies in which reasonable laws would promote the common good, which would become the common care. Whether this optimistic hope in the perfectibility of humanity, through better designed political institutions, could have been justified independently of their belief in a benevolent, omnipotent God remains an unanswered question, obscured by the tendency to minimize the differences between Hobbes's philosophy and that of Locke and his eighteenth-century followers.

Note

1 Only the first five volumes were published in French. For her correspondence see Green (2019).

References

Anon. 1767. "Review of *Loose Remarks on Certain Positions to Be Found in Mr Hobbes's Rudiments of Government.*" *The Critical Review or Annals of Literature* 23 (April): 284–8.

Beiser, Frederick C. 1996. *The Sovereignty of Reason. The Defense of Rationality in the Early English Enlightenment*. Princeton, NJ: Princeton University Press.

Burnet, Gilbert. 1724. *Bishop Burnet's History of His Own Time*, 2 vols. London: Thomas Ward.

Cumberland, Richard. 1727. *A Treatise of the Laws of Nature*, translated by John Maxwell. London: R. Phillips. Reprint, Garland Publishing, 1978.

Cumberland, Richard 1750. *A Philosophical Enquiry into the Laws of Nature*, translated by John Towers. Dublin: Samuel Powell.

Darwall, Stephen. 1995. *The British Moralists and the Internal 'Ought': 1640–1740*. Cambridge: Cambridge University Press.

Green, Karen. 2012. "When is a Contract Theorist Not a Contract Theorist?" In *Feminist Interpretations of Thomas Hobbes*, edited by Nancy Hirschmann and Joanne Wright, 169–89. State Park: Pennsylvania State University Press.

Green, Karen. 2018. "Catharine Macaulay's Enlightenment Faith and Radical Politics." *History of European Ideas* 44 (1): 35–44.

Green, Karen., ed. 2019. *The Correspondence of Catharine Macaulay*. New York: Oxford University Press.

Green, Karen. 2020. *Catharine Macaulay's Republican Enlightenment*. New York: Routledge.

Gunther-Canada, Wendy. 2006. "Catharine Macaulay on the Paradox of Paternal Authority in Hobbesian Politics." *Hypatia* 21 (2 Spring): 150–73.

Harris, James. 2020. "The Interpretation of Locke's *Two Treatises* in Britain, 1778–1956." *British Journal for the History of Philosophy* 28 (3): 483–500.

Hobbes, Thomas. 1651. *Philosophical Rudiments Concerning Government and Society*. London: R. Royston.

Hobbes, Thomas. 1750. *The Moral and Political Works of Thomas Hobbes of Malmesbury. Never before Collected Together*. London: n.p.

Hume, David. 1751. *An Enquiry Concerning the Principles of Morals*. London: A. Millar.

Hume, David. 1757. *The History of Great Britain, Vol. II, Containing the Commonwealth and the Reigns of Charles II and James II*. London: A. Millar.

Locke, John. 1954. *Essays on the Law of Nature*, edited by Wolfgang von Leyden. Oxford: Clarendon Press.

Locke, John. 1975. *An Essay Concerning Human Understanding*, edited by Peter H. Nidditch. Oxford: Clarendon Press.

Locke, John. 1988. *Two Treatises of Government*, edited by Peter Laslett. Cambridge: Cambridge University Press.

Macaulay, Catharine. 1763–1783. *The History of England from the Accession of James I. To that of the Brunswick Line*. 8 vols. London: Vols. 1–4, Printed for the author and sold by J. Nourse, J. Dodsley and W. Johnston: Vols 5–8 Edward and Charles Dilly.

Macaulay, Catharine. 1767. *Loose Remarks on Certain Positions to Be Found in Mr Hobbes's Philosophical Rudiments of Government and Society, with a Short Sketch of a Democratical Form of Government, in a Letter to Signor Paoli*. London: T. Davies, in Russell-Street, Covent Garden; Robinson and Roberts, in Pater-noster Row; and T. Cadell, in the Strand.

Macaulay, Catharine. 1783. *A Treatise on the Immutability of Moral Truth*. London: A. Hamilton.

Macaulay, Catharine. 1790a. *Letters on Education. With Observations on Religious and Metaphysical Subjects*. London: C. Dilly.

Macaulay, Catharine. 1790b. *Observations on the Reflections of the Right Hon. Edmund Burke, on the Revolution in France, in a Letter for the Right Hon. The Earl of Stanhope*. London: C. Dilly.

Macaulay, Catharine. 1791–1792. *Histoire D'angleterre; depuis l'avènement de Jacques I, jusqu'a la revolution*, translated by Gabriel Riquetti, Count de Mirabeau and Charles Philippe Toussaint Guiraudet. 5 vols. Paris: Gattey.

Macpherson, Crawford B. 1962. *The Political Theory of Possessive Individualism: Hobbes to Locke*. Oxford: Clarendon Press.

Milton, John. 1753. *The Works of John Milton, Historical, Political, Miscellaneous*. 2 vols. London: A. Millar.

Mortimer, Sarah and John Robertson, eds. 2012. *The Intellectual Consequences of Religious Heterodoxy, 1600–1750*. Leiden: Brill.

Pateman, Carole. 1991. "'God Hath Ordained to Man a Helper': Hobbes, Patriarchy and Conjugal Right." In *Feminist Interpretations and Political Theory*, edited by Carole Pateman and Mary Lyndon Shanley, 53–73. University Park: Pennsylvania University Press.

Price, Richard. 1758. *A Review of the Principal Questions and Difficulties in Morals*. London: A. Millar.

Taylor, Natalie Fueher. 2019. "The Social Contract Tradition." In *The Wollstonecraftian Mind*, edited by Sandrine Bergès, Eileen Hunt Botting, and Alan Coffee, 36–48. Abingdon: Routledge.

Tucker, Abraham. 1768. *The Light of Nature Pursued. By Edward Search*, Esq:. 5 vols. London: T. Jones.

Tyrrell, James. 1701. *A Brief Disquisition of the Law of Nature, According to the Principles and Method Laid down in the Reverend Dr. Cumberland's (Now Lord Bishop of Peterborough's) Latin Treatise on that Subject. As Also His Confutation of Mr. Hobbs's Principles, Put into Another Method*, 2nd edn. London: W. Rogers, R. Knaplock, A. Bell, and T. Cockeril.

Withey, Lynne E. 1976. "Catharine Macaulay and the Uses of History: Ancient Rights, Perfectionism, and Propaganda." *Journal of British Studies* 16 (1): 59–83.

Index

A Companion to Hobbes, First Edition. Edited by Marcus P. Adams.